SAT® 2013

PREMIER

Kaplan offers resources and options to help you prepare for the PSAT, SAT, ACT, AP exams, and other high-stakes exams. Go to www.kaptest.com or scan this code below with your phone (you will need to download a QR code reader) for free events and promotions.

snap.vu/m87n

essay

Scct 6+7

SAT®

PREMIER

2013 EDITION

The Staff of Kaplan Test Prep and Admissions

 PUBLISHING

New York

© 2012 Kaplan, Inc.

Published by Kaplan Publishing, a division of Kaplan, Inc.
395 Hudson Street
New York, NY 10014

Printed in the United States of America

10 9 8 7 6 5 4 3 2

ISBN-13: 978-1-60978-253-5

Table of Contents

HOW TO USE THIS BOOK

Welcome to *SAT Premier 2013*!

In this section, we'll walk you through everything you'll need to know to take advantage of the book, CD-ROM, and and online resources.

HERE'S A HANDY CHECKLIST TO GET YOUR STUDYING ON TRACK:

❏ **Register your online companion** for extra practice, Live Online classroom events, Fast Fact videos, and more.

❏ **Take the online diagnostic quiz** to figure out your strong and weak areas. You should also **take the full-length Diagnostic Test in the book,** which will help further guide your study.

❏ **Figure out which chapters you need to study the most** and review those chapters first. As needed, refer to the Fast Fact videos online.

❏ When you've learned all of Kaplan's proven score-raising strategies, you can **practice, practice, practice with our full-length tests in the book and online,** or on the CD-ROM.

▶ ABOUT SMARTPOINTS

To help you focus your test prep on the areas that will earn you the most points on test day, we ranked the most tested topics and crucial SAT skills using our exclusive SmartPoints bars system.

The more SmartPoint bars an item has (from one bar to five bars), the more important it likely will be on test day. As you go through this book, you'll see SmartPoints skills and topics discussed throughout.

Knowing the SAT inside and out will gain you points on *every section*. So, **Part One: Getting Ready for Test Day** covers basic information on the SAT and Kaplan's overall strategies for approaching the test. These are the fundamentals you need to be ready for the exam and to get a great score.

Part Two: Diagnostic Test is your first opportunity to take a full-length practice test. Take the Diagnostic Test and use your results to see how you would do if you took the test today without any additional preparation. Then, use the detailed answer explanations to understand what questions you missed and why. You should also use your score to figure out which chapters of the book you need to review most.

If you struggled with the Writing section, or you just need more review, turn to **Part Three: How to Attack the Writing Sections**, which covers the Writing section of the SAT in depth. You'll learn about the essay, the three multiple-choice question types, and several proven strategies that will help you earn a top score.

Part Four: How to Attack the Critical Reading Sections of this book covers the two Critical Reading question types: Sentence Completion and Reading Comprehension. You will also learn specific strategies to use for short passages, long passages, and paired passages. Chapter 10 gives you specific tips and strategies for improving your vocabulary—something that will help you earn important points on test day.

Part Five: How to Attack the Math Sections switches gears to math skills. The four chapters in this part of the book cover SAT math strategies as well as a review of both basic and advanced math concepts you will need to know for the exam. There's even a whole chapter on how to avoid the most common math "traps" found on the SAT.

When you are ready to apply everything you've learned in the review chapters, **Part Six: Practice Tests and Explanations** offers three additional full-length practice tests. Again, you should use the detailed answer explanations to understand what you missed and to learn more about the score-raising strategies that could help you answer similar questions on test day.

USING YOUR SAT ONLINE COMPANION

REGISTER YOUR ONLINE COMPANION

Register your online companion using these simple steps:

1. **Go to Kaptest.com/booksonline.**
2. **Follow the on-screen instructions. Please have a copy of your book available.**

GET A MOBILE VERSION OF THIS BOOK

Sign up for your online companion and learn how to get a mobile version of this book!

After you register for your online companion and set up a Kaplan ID and password, you will receive an email explaining how to get a mobile version of the *Kaplan SAT Premier*.

JOIN A LIVE ONLINE EVENT

Kaplan's SAT Live Online sessions are interactive, instructor-led SAT prep lessons that you can participate in from anywhere you can access the Internet.

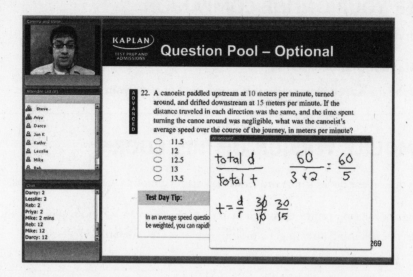

SAT Live Online sessions are held in a state-of-the-art virtual classroom—actual lessons in real time, just like a physical classroom experience. Interact with your teacher and other classmates using audio, instant chat, whiteboard, polling, and screen-sharing functionality. And just like courses at Kaplan centers, SAT Live Online sessions are led by experienced Kaplan instructors.

TO REGISTER FOR AN SAT LIVE ONLINE EVENT:

1. Once you've signed in to your student home page, open your Syllabus.
2. In the Syllabus window, go to the "Live Online Registration" menu option.
3. Click on the link. A separate window will appear with registration instructions.

There are three SAT Live Online events available. These events are scheduled to take place throughout 2012. Please check your online companion for dates and times! **Please note:** Registration begins one month before the session date. Be sure to sign up early, since spaces are reserved on a first-come, first-serve basis.

WATCH THE FAST FACT VIDEOS

In Fast Fact Videos, one of Kaplan's highly rated SAT tutors explains and reinforces the most important concepts from each chapter.

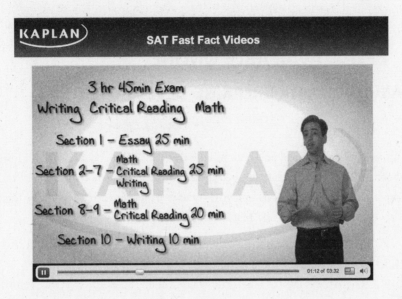

Fast Fact Videos can only be accessed through your online companion. Here's how:

1. Once you've signed into your student home page, open your Syllabus.

2. In the Syllabus window, go to the "Fast Fact Videos" menu option.

3. Click on the link for the video you'd like to see. A separate window will appear with your video.

BUT WAIT, THERE'S MORE...

If you want to study offline, use the CD-ROM included with this book to access more test information and five full-length Practice Tests.

Good Luck!

AVAILABLE ONLINE

FOR ANY TEST CHANGES OR LATE-BREAKING DEVELOPMENTS

kaptest.com/publishing

The material in this book is up-to-date at the time of publication. However, the College Board may have instituted changes in the test after this book was published. Be sure to carefully read the materials you receive when you register for the test. If there are any important late-breaking developments—or any changes or corrections to the Kaplan test preparation materials in this book—we will post that information online at kaptest.com/publishing.

FEEDBACK AND COMMENTS

kaplansurveys.com/books

We'd love to hear your comments and suggestions about this book. We invite you to fill out our online survey form at kaplansurveys.com/books. Your feedback is extremely helpful as we continue to develop high-quality resources to meet your needs.

For customer service, please contact us at booksupport@kaplan.com.

PARENTS' GUIDE TO SURVIVING THE SAT

PARENTS' GUIDE TO SURVIVING THE SAT

For many parents, the SAT was a long time ago, in a galaxy far, far away. In particular, it was a galaxy where you took the SAT once, got your score, and went to college. Prepping for the SAT probably involved sharpening your pencils the night before and brushing your teeth before leaving in the morning.

Today, the SAT is a bit more complicated, and the competition to get into a top college and get financial aid to cover the steep costs is tougher than ever! And what about all those other exams you may have heard about? Your child can now take the SAT, the PSAT, or SAT Subject Tests. Are they the same? Different? Does your son or daughter need to take all of them? What about the ACT? What does your son or daughter need to do in order to get into a good college?

These questions, as well as many others, probably fill your mind, your child's mind, and possibly your dinner table conversations and Internet searches as well! Fear not—Kaplan is here to help your family get through this important exam successfully!

Use this guide to learn everything you need to know about the SAT, discover ways you can help your child prepare for this important exam, and manage your family's SAT stress.

After reviewing this section, we recommend that you and your child visit the official College Board website at www.collegeboard.com for additional SAT details and information. It's a great way to get involved and stay informed!

FREQUENTLY ASKED QUESTIONS

Kaplan gets a lot of questions from parents about the SAT exam. The following FAQs should help you get up to speed on SAT basics:

Q: What is the SAT and why should my child take it?

A: The SAT is a standardized test administered by the College Board and taken by millions of high school students annually. It measures students' critical reading, math, and writing skills and is used by college admissions officers to determine their ability to do college-level work. Many colleges look at SAT scores in conjunction with grade point average (GPA) and extracurricular activities when deciding about admissions acceptance.

Q: What is the SAT exam like?

A: The SAT is a 3 hour and 45 minute test broken into three sections: Critical Reading, Math, and Writing. Most of the exam is composed of multiple-choice questions, although one-third of the Writing section score is based on the 25-minute essay students write in the first section of the exam.

Q: When should my child take the SAT exam?

A: Most students take the SAT as juniors or seniors, and many take the exam more than once.

Q: How is the SAT exam scored?

A: The highest score possible on the SAT is a 2400, computed from 800 in each section, Critical Reading, Math, and Writing.

Q: How can my child register for the SAT?

A: Your child can register online or by mail. Visit the official College Board website at www.collegeboard.com for complete registration information.

Q: How much does the SAT exam cost?

A: The basic test fee is $47. Families who cannot afford this fee can request a fee waiver from their school counselor.

Q: How is the SAT different from other college admissions exams?

A: The Preliminary SAT/National Merit Scholarship Qualifying Test (PSAT/NMSQT®) is also administered by the College Board in conjunction with the National Merit Scholarship Corporation. The PSAT can help your child prepare for the SAT and enter the competition for a National Merit Scholarship—but taking the PSAT is not a requirement for taking the SAT.

SAT Subject Tests are different from the SAT because they are subject-specific (Literature, U.S. History, French, etc.), whereas the SAT is a general-knowledge exam. Some colleges may require these exams, but they are not required for all schools. Check the admissions requirements of the schools your child is applying to.

The ACT is a general-knowledge exam similar in scope to the SAT. It also includes an essay component, English, Reading, and Math sections, but it includes a Science section as well. Many schools throughout the country accept either the SAT or the ACT. Because the tests are different, some students feel more comfortable taking one exam versus the other. It really is a matter of personal preference and college admissions requirements.

COMMON SAT MISCONCEPTIONS

There's a lot of inaccurate information floating around about the SAT. Let's clear up some common sources of confusion:

FALSE: ONLY SOME STUDENTS CAN GET A 2400.

Theoretically, every student who takes the SAT could get a 2400. Your child is not competing against his classmates and friends to get his score. The tests are scaled prior to test day. The scaled score is what colleges use to compare scores from different test administrations.

FALSE: THERE IS NO PENALTY FOR WRONG ANSWERS.

For each question a student answers correctly, the student gains 1 point. For each question a student misses on the test, the student loses $\frac{1}{4}$ of a point. If a student skips a question, no points are gained or lost.

FALSE: STUDENTS WHO RECEIVE ACCOMMODATIONS FOR A DISABILITY ARE PENALIZED.

Parents sometimes fear that applying for accommodations for disabilities will cause their child to be penalized—that their child's score reports will indicate the accommodation received, be it additional time, computer assistance, extended breaks, etc. If your child has a documented disability, contact your school's guidance counselor or visit www.collegeboard.com for more information.

FALSE: WHEN IT COMES TO COLLEGE ADMISSIONS, THE SAT IS EVERYTHING!

Yes, college admissions are becoming more and more competitive each year. But the SAT is just one component of your child's full application. Help your child—and yourself—by keeping the SAT in perspective. Your child's SAT score goals should align with his or her college choices. Know the target score range of the schools your child is applying to and set reasonable goals. Having a defined goal will help your child see what she is working toward, help her measure success along the way, and help her feel a strong sense of accomplishment when she reaches that goal. Remember: A 2400 is a great score, but NO school requires a 2400 for admission!

HELPING YOUR CHILD SUCCEED ON THE SAT

There are lots of SAT test-prep options available, from courses to self-study guides like this one. Your study choices should align with your child's needs and resources. Buying this book is a great option! By giving your child access to Kaplan's expert resources, you are helping her build an excellent foundation for SAT success. You can also assist your child by keeping the following things in mind:

HELP REDUCE TEST ANXIETY BY EMPATHIZING

Whether your child is the nonchalant "Mom, don't worry about it" type or the up-until-midnight crammer, your child is probably nervous about the SAT. It's an important exam, and if your child has already taken the PSAT, he could be worried about whether his SAT score will be better. Or maybe he's worried he won't be able to do as well as he did on the PSAT and won't get into his dream school? Perhaps you've bought this book because your child has already taken the SAT and wants to do better than the first time around. Maybe your child has never taken the PSAT or the SAT before, and the fear of the unknown is causing anxiety. Whatever the case, for most people, just saying "SAT" will send shivers down their spines, and for your child, the pressure is on. One of the biggest ways you can help is by empathizing.

You probably took the SAT, but even if you didn't, you can remember some time when you had to prepare for an important event—a test, a presentation at work, or a job interview. All of these events are daunting because, to some degree, they shape the course of our lives. You might not remember what you got on the SAT, but saying, "Oh, in 15 years, no one will care what you got on the SAT" WILL NOT HELP! This test matters to them right now, a lot. Recognize that, and make sure your child knows that *you know* how important this test is and that his anxiety isn't abnormal or strange.

Most of all, talk to him about this anxiety—gently! Know when it's the right time to approach your child and start a casual discussion. Try sharing a time when you were worried about a big life event over dinner. Then let your child open up on his terms and share his thoughts and feelings. Let him know you believe in succeeding at this together, and no matter what happens, life will continue after the SAT.

SET MEASURABLE GOALS AND INCREASE YOUR CHILD'S CONFIDENCE

A good first step is to determine some target schools. Offer to help your child with this, serving as a sounding board for her thoughts and offering helpful advice. Keep in mind that your goals and hers might be completely different. Even if you don't have a sense of where your child's SAT scores are right now, consider things like size, location, academic competitiveness, and academic majors. Having a realistic list of schools will help the unmotivated student see the point of studying for the SATs and will help the super-motivated student keep things in perspective.

By setting goals, you can reward steps along the way. If your daughter learned 25 new vocabulary words this week, reward her—an iTunes download or snack perhaps?—even if she hasn't shown a 20-point increase on her Practice Test yet. If your child continually sees how proud of her you are, she'll be more likely to be proud and confident herself on test day. Successes along the way will make test day feel much less like a "make or break" event and more like an "I'm going to conquer this test" opportunity!

LEAD BY EXAMPLE AND MANAGE YOUR OWN STRESS

If you want your child to stick to his study schedule, lead the way. Share some tricks that you use to help with time management, and most importantly, use them! If you say you're going to be home at 5:00 to drive him to hockey practice, be home at 5:00, not 5:30. If you say you're going to exercise three times per week, then exercise. We've all had that boss who tells you to respond to his emails within 24 hours, but who only responds to yours after three follow-up emails. You know what you think when he says, "Please respond within 24 hours to all emails." You think, *If you don't do it, then why should I?* Your kids think this, too.

Also, manage your own stress about the SAT by keeping these things in mind:

- With commitment and dedication, it will all work out. Your son's confidence may waver, he may have moments while preparing for the SAT where he feels as if he's fighting a losing battle, but stay positive and believe that in the future, it all works out.

- Your child gets to focus on her SAT score; you get to focus on praising your child for her effort and encouraging her to succeed in a healthy and positive way.

- Stay calm and supportive and your child will come to you for help.

- By choosing Kaplan, you have a lot of resources to guide you through this process.

LISTEN TO KAPLAN—THE SAT EXPERTS

You don't have to have all the answers for the SAT, but keep in mind that you and your child have a larger support network than you might realize. By choosing Kaplan you get the benefit of nearly 70 years of experience and the wisdom from Kaplan's SAT experts. We asked a veteran Kaplan Premier tutor for some SAT advice for parents. Here's what she had to say:

1. **Keep everything in perspective.** The SAT gets a lot of press nowadays, but you have to keep in mind that the SAT is simply a piece of your child's college application—not the whole story. Keeping the SAT in perspective will help you and your child keep your cool while preparing for test day.

2. **Don't get caught up on the "SAT treadmill."** I always encourage my students to set a realistic score goal that they will be satisfied with on test day. Sure, if they score higher than that, that's great, but you don't want them to be caught on the treadmill of "Oh, I only got

a 630 in Math; why didn't I get a 650 or a 670?" I always tell my students, "Know what your goal is and work toward it. And most of all: Be happy when you reach it and proud that you tried!"

3. **Utilize the accommodations the College Board provides.** If your child has a documented disability, your child will not be stigmatized for it, because the use of accommodations is not indicated on SAT score reports. Just make sure to start arranging for accommodations several months before your child will actually take the SAT.

4. **Don't expect a miracle on test day.** I sometimes have students who will take a Practice Test a week before test day and still be 80 or 100 points shy of their score goal. You can just imagine how disheartening this can be. Unless this is their last possible opportunity to take the test, review the option of taking a later test with your child. That way, your child can study more and wait until her Practice Test scores are solidly in score goal range. Remember, even with the SAT's new "Score Choice" option, you still send the scores from an ENTIRE test. In other words, you can't pick and choose the Math score from the October test, the Writing score from the December test, and the Critical Reading score from the March test. Know your options and make the most of them!

5. **Keep an optimistic eye on your child's future.** Remember, college is great. Your child just has to get through the SAT to get there. No matter what your child's SAT score is, stay positive and know that he will get into college and have a positive experience. Everyone I know loved college, but virtually no one I know loved the SAT. Just help your child choose a range of colleges, set a target score, and make a study plan—and be that positive motivating force until test day. Freshman move-in day will be here before you know it!

Best of luck and success!

Part One

GETTING READY FOR TEST DAY

CHAPTER 1: SAT BASICS

SAT REGISTRATION

There are a few different ways to register for the SAT exam. Check out the College Board website at www.collegeboard.com for complete information about registering for the SAT and for the most up-to-date information concerning changes in dates, fees, etc.

PERFECT SCORE TIP

" I made sure to schedule the SAT on a weekend where I didn't have much else going on. That way, I could focus on one thing: doing well on the SAT! "

REGISTER EARLY

Try to register early to secure the test center of your choice and to avoid late registration fees.

TEST DATES

Please visit the official College Board website at www.collegeboard.com for a complete list of test dates.

HOW TO REGISTER

- **To register by mail,** you'll need to get a Registration Bulletin from your high school guidance counselor and follow the instructions.

- **To register online,** you'll need to visit www.collegeboard.com. The website contains easy, step-by-step instructions for electronically submitting your registration. Read the instructions and requirements carefully.

- **Students with disabilities** can call (609) 771-7137 (TTY: Domestic 888-857-2477/International (609) 882-4118) for more information regarding special testing accommodations.

OTHER IMPORTANT REGISTRATION INFORMATION

- **The basic fee for the SAT is $47** in the United States. This price includes reports for you, your high school, and up to four colleges and scholarship programs. There are additional fees for late registration, standby testing, international processing, changing test centers or test dates, rush reporting, and for additional services and products.

- **Make sure to bring proper identification and your admission ticket with you to the test center.** Some acceptable forms of identification include photo IDs, such as a driver's license, a school identification card, or a valid passport. Unacceptable forms of identification include a Social Security card, credit card, or birth certificate.

TEST FORMAT

The SAT is 3 hours and 45 minutes long, and there are two 10-minute breaks. The exam is mostly multiple-choice, and it's divided into three Math, three Critical Reading, and three Writing sections. There is also an experimental section, but we will discuss that section later. The essay section is always first. Sections 2–7 can appear in *any order* on test day. Sections 8 and 9 are either Critical Reading or Math, and Section 1 is *always* Writing.

The SAT sections are broken down like this:

SECTION	LENGTH	CONTENT	TYPE
Critical Reading	25 minutes	Sentence Completion and Reading Comprehension	Multiple-choice questions
Critical Reading	25 minutes	Sentence Completion and Reading Comprehension	Multiple-choice questions
Critical Reading	20 minutes	Sentence Completion and Reading Comprehension	Multiple-choice questions
Math	25 minutes	High School Geometry and Algebra, Numbers and Operations, Statistics, Probability, and Data Analysis	Multiple-choice questions and student-produced responses
Math	25 minutes	High School Geometry and Algebra, Numbers and Operations, Statistics, Probability, and Data Analysis	Multiple-choice questions and student-produced responses
Math	20 minutes	High School Geometry and Algebra, Numbers and Operations, Statistics, Probability, and Data Analysis	Multiple-choice questions
Writing	25 minutes	Student-written Essay	Long-form essay
Writing	25 minutes	Identifying Sentence Errors, Improving, Sentences, Improving Paragraphs	Multiple-choice questions
Writing	10 minutes	Improving Sentences	Multiple-choice questions
Experimental	25 minutes	Math, Writing, or Critical Reading	(Anything is fair game)

EXPERIMENTAL SECTION

Every SAT has an experimental section. The experimental section is used by the test developers to try out new questions before including them in upcoming SATs.

DID YOU KNOW?

The experimental section DOES NOT COUNT in your score.

It can show up anywhere on the exam and will look just like a normal section. You shouldn't try to figure out which SAT section is experimental. You will fail to do so. Just treat all the sections as if they count toward your score.

The Diagnostic Test and the Practice Tests in this book do **not** include an experimental section. There are only nine sections in each. Because these tests do not include a 25-minute experimental section, you should only take 3 hours and 20 minutes to complete the tests in this book.

SAT COMPONENTS

Now it's time for brief summaries of each of the SAT's three components: Writing, Critical Reading, and Math.

THE WRITING COMPONENT

The SAT has three Writing sections: one essay section and two multiple-choice sections.

THE ESSAY

The essay directions ask you to write a persuasive essay answering the assigned question, which typically asks you to respond to a quotation. Here is an example of a quote and essay prompt that you might see on the test:

> "My future starts when I wake up every morning. . . . Every day I find something creative to do with my life."
>
> —Miles Davis

Assignment: Are there more advantages to planning for the future than living in the moment?

We know what kind of essay the SAT graders are looking for, and we'll tell you exactly how to write one in chapter 6.

MULTIPLE-CHOICE QUESTIONS

Multiple-choice questions test your ability to spot errors in grammar, sentence structure, and paragraph structure or organization. Here's an example of a sentence structure question:

Directions: Part of the sentence below is underlined; beneath it are five ways of phrasing the underlined material. Choice (A) repeats the original phrasing; the other four choices are different. If you think the original phrasing produces a better sentence than any of the alternatives, select choice (A); if not, select one of the other choices.

The lawyer advised her client to wear a suit, shave, <u>and stopping crying.</u>

(A) and stopping crying.
(B) and crying is stopped.
(C) also stopping crying.
(D) and they should stop crying.
(E) and stop crying.

Answer (E) is correct. Look for parallelism in verb usage: *wear*, *shave*, and *stop*.

We go into detail on the Writing component's multiple-choice questions in chapter 5.

THE CRITICAL READING COMPONENT

There are two kinds of questions in the Critical Reading component of the SAT. Both are multiple-choice.

PERFECT SCORE TIP

I planned the time I spent studying for the SAT so that it didn't interfere with my activities at all. The SAT doesn't have to take over your whole life!

SENTENCE COMPLETION QUESTIONS

These questions test your ability to determine how words or ideas work together to create meaning in a sentence. About half have one word missing from a sentence; the other half have two words missing. Both types test vocabulary and reasoning skills.

Here is a sample question:

Directions: The sentence that follows has two blanks, each blank indicating that something has been omitted. Beneath the sentence are five sets of words labeled A through E. Choose the word or set of words that, when inserted in the sentence, *best* fits the meaning of the sentence as a whole.

> The king's ------- decisions as a diplomat and administrator led to his legendary reputation as a just and ------- ruler.
>
> (A) quick . . . capricious
>
> (B) equitable . . . wise
>
> (C) immoral . . . perceptive
>
> (D generous . . . witty
>
> (E) clever . . . uneducated

The answer is choice (B). Focus on clue words *diplomat* and *just*.

Sentence Completion questions are arranged in order of difficulty. The first few questions in a set will be fairly easy. The middle few questions are harder, and the last few are the most difficult. Keep this in mind as you work through this section of the exam.

READING COMPREHENSION QUESTIONS

These questions test your ability to understand a piece of writing. Some passages are short (100–150 words), others are long (400–850 words), and at least one passage contains two related readings. Most Reading Comprehension questions test how well you understand the information in the passage, some ask you to draw conclusions, and some test your vocabulary or your ability to determine the meaning of words in context.

Here is a sample question:

According to lines 52–56, one difficulty of using a linear representation of time is that

(A) linear representations of time do not meet accepted scientific standards of accuracy

(B) prehistoric eras overlap each other, making linear representation deceptive

(C) the more accurate the scale, the more difficult the map is to copy and study

(D) there are too many events to represent on a single line

(E) our knowledge of pre-Cambrian time is insufficient to construct an accurate linear map

Reading Comprehension questions are **not** arranged by difficulty. Whenever you find yourself spending too much time on a question in these sections, you should skip it and return to it later. We recommend you circle it in your test booklet so you can find it later.

THE MATH COMPONENT

There are two kinds of Math questions on the SAT: Multiple-choice and Grid-in.

MULTIPLE-CHOICE QUESTIONS

These are straightforward multiple-choice questions with five answer choices.

Here is a sample question:

At a diner, Joe orders three strips of bacon and a cup of coffee and is charged $2.25. Stella orders two strips of bacon and a cup of coffee and is charged $1.70. What is the price of two strips of bacon?

(A) $0.55

(B) $0.60

(C) $1.10

(D) $1.30

(E) $1.80

Answer: (C).

> **EXPERT TUTOR TIP**
>
> " How does your mind work? Do what's most comfortable for you as a test taker. It will help you stay focused and lead to a higher score. "

GRID-IN QUESTIONS

Grid-in questions are not multiple-choice. Instead of picking an answer choice, you write your response in a grid like the one below.

Here is a sample Grid-in answer:

Both question types cover *the same* math concepts across the full range of difficulty. Either one can ask you a geometry, algebra, or statistics question. However, Grid-ins are more challenging because you don't have answers to choose from, as in the multiple-choice questions; you are totally on your own to come up with the correct answer.

You should answer all Grid-in questions because you've got nothing to lose; there is no penalty for an incorrect answer.

HOW MATH QUESTIONS ARE SCORED

A wrong multiple-choice answer loses you $\frac{1}{4}$ point. A wrong Grid-in loses you *nothing*.

ORDER OF DIFFICULTY

On the SAT, some sections will have their multiple-choice questions arranged in order of difficulty. Here's a breakdown:

	TEST SECTION	ARRANGED EASIEST TO HARDEST?
Math	Regular Math	Yes
	Grid-ins	Yes
Critical Reading	Sentence Completion	Yes
	Reading Comprehension	No
Writing	Essay	N/A
	Identifying Sentence Errors	No
	Improving Sentences	No
	Improving Paragraphs	No

As you work through a set that is organized by order of difficulty, *be aware of where you are in a set.* When working on the easy problems, you can generally trust your first impulse—the obvious answer is likely to be right. As you get to the end of the set, you need to be more suspicious of *obvious* answers, because the answer should not come easily. If it does, look at the problem again. It may be one of those distracters—a wrong answer choice meant to trick you.

EXPERT TUTOR TIP

" Don't rush through easier questions and make careless errors on your way to the harder ones. They're all worth the same points! "

SCORING

Here's a rundown of how the SAT is scored:

- You gain one point for each correct answer on the SAT and lose a fraction of a point ($\frac{1}{4}$ point, to be exact) for each wrong answer (except with Grid-ins, where you lose *nothing* for a wrong answer).

- You do NOT lose any points for questions you leave blank.

- The totals for the Critical Reading, Writing, and Math questions are added up to produce three raw scores. These raw scores equal the number you got right minus a fraction of the number you got wrong.

- These scores are converted into scaled scores, with 200 as the lowest score and 800 the highest.

EXPERT TUTOR TIP

" The wrong answer penalty exists to discourage *random* guessing. But if you can eliminate at least one answer choice you *know* is wrong, it's in your best interest to guess! "

SCORE BREAKDOWN

The three scaled scores are added together to produce your final score of 600–2400, as follows:

Scaled Scores:	Writing	Math	Critical Reading	Total
	200–800	200–800	200–800	600–2400

SAT GROUND RULES

These are SAT rules you can use to your advantage. Knowing these rules will keep you from asking questions and wasting precious time and from committing minor errors that result in serious penalties.

- You are NOT allowed to jump back and forth between sections.
- You are NOT allowed to return to earlier sections to change answers.
- You are NOT allowed to spend more than the allotted time on any section.
- You CAN move around within a section.
- You CAN flip through your section at the beginning to see what types of questions are coming up.

KEY POINTS YOU'VE LEARNED IN THIS CHAPTER

1. The SAT is made up of ten sections that will take 3 hours and 45 minutes; there are three sections each of Critical Reading, Math, and Writing, and one experimental section, which does **not** count toward your score.

2. Writing consists of one essay and three types of multiple-choice questions: Identifying Sentence Errors, Improving Sentences, and Improving Paragraphs; Critical Reading consists of two types of multiple-choice questions: Sentence Completion and Reading Comprehension; Math consists of two kinds of questions: multiple-choice questions and Grid-ins.

3. The Math sections and the Sentence Completion questions of the Critical Reading sections are arranged in order of difficulty. That means the first questions are the easiest and the last ones are the hardest. Knowing this will help you decide whether you can trust that the obvious answer is the correct one.

4. You gain one point for each right answer, lose a quarter $\left(\frac{1}{4}\right)$ of a point for each wrong answer, and neither gain nor lose points for answers you leave blank. The only exceptions are the Essay and the Math Grid-ins, where you don't lose points for incorrect answers.

CHAPTER 2: **SAT STRATEGIES**

KEY SAT STRATEGIES

Kaplan's exclusive strategies for scoring higher on the SAT are based on decades of proven test-prep experience. Use the following information to conquer the exam on test day:

KNOW THE DIRECTIONS BEFORE TEST DAY

One of the easiest things you can do to help your performance on the SAT is to understand the directions before taking the test. Because the directions are always exactly the same, knowing them in advance will help you save time.

We provide sample SAT directions throughout this book. Learn them as you go through it so you can just skim them during the test. Save your time on test day for the questions!

USE ORDER OF DIFFICULTY TO YOUR ADVANTAGE

Not all of the questions on the SAT are equally difficult. Some question types are ordered easiest to hardest.

As you work:

- Always be aware of where you are in the set.
- When working on the easy problems, you can generally trust your first impulse—the obvious answer is likely to be right.
- As you get to the end of the set, you need to become more suspicious. The answers probably *shouldn't* come easily. If they do, look at the problem again because the obvious answer is likely to be wrong.

PERFECT SCORE TIP

" I casually talked to my friends about the SAT. We swapped tips and it was great to pick up some new strategies and techniques from them. "

EXPERT TUTOR TIP

" Although there are lots of strategies and theories for how best to tackle the SAT, you should find a test pace and plan that works for *you*—and stick to it! "

- Watch out for the answer that *just looks right*. It may be a *distracter*—a wrong answer choice meant to entice you. (We'll go into detail on the most common kinds of distracters later.)

YOU DON'T HAVE TO ANSWER THE QUESTIONS IN ORDER

You are allowed to skip around within each section of the SAT. High scorers know this and use their test time wisely. They move through the test efficiently. They don't dwell on any one question, even a hard one, until they've tried every question at least once.

There's another benefit to coming back to hard ones later. On a second look, troublesome questions can turn out to be simple. By answering some easier questions first, you can come back to a harder question with fresh eyes, a fresh perspective, and more confidence.

DON'T GET STUCK

When you run into questions that look tough, circle them in your test booklet and skip them. Go back and try again after you have answered the easier ones. Remember, you don't get more points for answering hard questions. If you get two easy ones right in the time it would have taken you to get one hard one right, you just improved your score.

TAKE A GOOD GUESS

If you have come back to a tough question and still can't find the correct answer the second time around, consider a different approach. Begin eliminating choices that are absolutely wrong. If you can whittle the choices down to two, your chances of guessing the correct answer just increased from 20 percent to 50 percent.

ANSWER ALL GRID-INS

If you get an answer wrong on a Math Grid-in question, you lose nothing. So you should write in an answer for every Grid-in. The worst that can happen is that you get zero points for the questions you guessed on. If you get just one right, that's an extra ten points.

Avoid Answer Sheet Trouble

It sounds simple, but it's extremely important: Don't make mistakes filling out your answer grid. When time is short, it's easy to get confused going back and forth between your test book and your grid. To avoid mistakes on the answer grid, try some of these methods:

Circle the questions you skip

Perhaps the most common SAT disaster is filling in all of the right answers—in the wrong spots. Put a big circle in your test book around any question numbers you skip to help you locate these questions when you are ready to go back to them. Also, if you accidentally skip a box on the grid, you can always check your grid against your book to see where you went wrong.

Circle your answers in your test book

Circling your answers in the test book makes it easier to check your grid against your book. It also makes the next grid strategy possible.

Grid sets of answers at once

To save time and make sure you are marking your answers in the correct bubbles, transfer your answers after every five questions, or at the end of each reading passage, rather than after every question. That way, you won't keep breaking your concentration to mark the grid. You'll end up with more time and less chance to make a mistake on your answer sheet.

Wear a Watch to Keep Track of Time

Throughout the test, it is important to keep track of time. The test monitor will alert you at certain time intervals, usually at a halfway point and "five minutes left," but you might want to be more aware of how the time is passing:

- You don't want to have your answers in the test booklet and run out of time before you're able to transfer them to your answer grid.
- This is also true when you are gridding your answers in groups. Toward the end of each section, you should grid each answer one at a time.

Write Your Essay—Even If You're Short on Time

If you write a terrible essay, you still get two raw points, no matter how bad it is. (We go into essay scoring in detail in chapters 5 and 6.) If you freeze and skip the essay,

> **PERFECT SCORE TIP**
>
> " I didn't fill in my answer grid until I had answered all the questions on a page. It helped me stay focused and keep up my momentum. "

> **PERFECT SCORE TIP**
>
> " Try avoiding on-and-off studying. If I didn't study on a regular schedule, I frequently forgot some tricks and strategies and had to relearn them. "

EXPERT TUTOR TIP

" Wear a watch on test day. I've had students tell me that they couldn't see the room clock on test day and couldn't keep track of time. Don't let this happen to you! "

you get zero. So write *something*. The essay is worth one-third of your total 800-point Writing score. Even if you get the lowest possible score that you can get on your essay, that's 44 more points than zero!

DON'T GET DISTRACTED BY TRICK ANSWERS

On the SAT, there will always be distracters among the answer choices. Distracters are answer choices that look right but aren't, and they are easy to choose if you haven't read the question carefully. If you jump right into the answer choices without thinking first about exactly what you're looking for, you're much more likely to fall into one of these traps.

LOCATE EASIER QUESTIONS IF YOU'RE RUNNING OUT OF TIME

In sections that are not ordered from easy to hard, you can skip ahead when time runs short. For example, in a multiple-choice Writing section, you may be able to find questions you know you can answer correctly. Don't leave any of these unanswered.

READ QUESTIONS CAREFULLY

Look for keywords or symbols; rephrase them in simple words. *You won't be able to find the right answer if you don't know what you are looking for.*

USE BACKDOOR STRATEGIES

There are usually a number of ways to get to the right answer on an SAT question. Most of the questions on the SAT are multiple-choice. That means the answer is right in front of you—you just have to find it. This makes SAT questions open to several different ways of finding the answer.

EXPERT TUTOR TIP

" If you believe in yourself and study regularly for the SAT, be ready for a serious score improvement! "

If you can't figure out the answer in a straightforward way, try other techniques. We'll talk about specific Kaplan methods such as Backsolving and Picking Numbers in upcoming math chapters.

KAPLAN SMARTPOINTS

To help you focus your test prep on the areas that will earn you the most points on test day, we ranked the most tested topics and crucial SAT skills using our exclusive SmartPoints bars system.

The more SmartPoint bars an item has (from 1 bar to 5 bars), the more important it likely will be on test day. As you go through this book, you'll see SmartPoints skills and topics discussed throughout.

Use SmartPoints to prioritize your SAT studies. Customize your study plan according to your strengths and weaknesses, giving extra time to items with higher SmartPoints rankings. If you're short on time, focus your study on items with higher SmartPoints rankings first, and review items with lesser rankings as time allows.

KEY POINTS YOU'VE LEARNED IN THIS CHAPTER

1. Knowing the test directions, which sections are arranged in order of difficulty, and when to skip questions that seem hard will help you score higher on the SAT.

2. On the multiple-choice questions, take a guess if you've narrowed your answer choices down to two. Also, make sure you fill in the answer grid correctly, keep track of time, read the questions and answers carefully, and answer all the easy questions if you're running out of time.

3. Use SmartPoints to focus your studies on the most tested topics.

CHAPTER 3: STRATEGIES FOR TEST DAY SUCCESS

GET READY FOR TEST DAY

There's no need to panic or lose confidence as test day approaches. You've studied hard and Kaplan has provided you with all the tools you need to make your SAT experience a success. The following information will help you structure the crucial days right before, during, and after test day—to your best advantage.

ONE WEEK TO SAT GREATNESS

The week leading up to test day can be a stressful time for test takers. Students are often worried about how they're going to do on the exam and wonder what they should be doing to get ready.

Does this sound familiar? If so, then worry no more! Keep reading, and remember: Kaplan's got you covered!

SEVEN DAYS BEFORE THE TEST

Take a full-length Practice Test under timed conditions. Approach the test strategically, actively, and confidently. Use the techniques and strategies you've learned in this book:

- Circle and skip the questions you would omit on test day. You can go back later and try answering them, if there's time.

  Note: Analyze your omitting strategy now. This reduces the time you spend wondering about omitting on test day—streamlining these decisions leaves more time for answering the questions you do know.

> **PERFECT SCORE TIP**
>
> " Whenever I took a complete Practice Test, it was really important for me to simulate test conditions as much as possible. I really recommend you do so as well! "

- Use the Answer Sheet provided to practice your bubbling techniques. Accuracy is very important.
- Have a bottle of water, fruit, or an energy bar handy for your two timed breaks that usually occur after Sections 3 and 7.
- Wear a digital watch to help you keep track of the time.
- Read all the explanations of the questions you get wrong.
- Write down the types of questions you struggle with and go back to the relevant sections of the book to fine-tune these areas.

TWO DAYS BEFORE THE TEST

Flip through the answer explanations to examine your performance on specific questions with an eye to how you might get through each one faster and better on the test to come.

THE NIGHT BEFORE THE TEST

Our advice is to not do any studying on this day. Get together an SAT Kit containing the following items:

- A calculator with fresh batteries
- A watch
- A few No. 2 pencils (pencils with slightly dull points fill the ovals better)
- Erasers
- Photo ID card (e.g., passport, driver's license, or student ID)
- Your admission ticket from ETS
- A snack—on breaks, you'll probably get hungry

Know exactly where you're going, exactly how you're getting there, and exactly how long it takes to get there. It's probably a good idea to visit your test center sometime before the day of the test so that you know what to expect—what the rooms are like, how the desks are set up, and so on.

Relax the night before the test. Do some relaxation and visualization techniques. Read a magazine, take a long hot shower, or watch something on TV. Get a good night's sleep. Go to bed early, and leave yourself extra time in the morning.

> **PERFECT SCORE TIP**
>
> " I didn't bring extra batteries for my calculator on test day, which was a mistake. Even though I didn't need them, another student's calculator ran out of batteries. Don't be that student! "

THE MORNING OF THE TEST

First, wake up. After that:

- Eat breakfast. Make it something substantial but not anything too heavy or greasy.

- Don't drink a lot of coffee if you're not used to it. Bathroom breaks cut into your time, and too much caffeine may make you jittery.

- Dress in layers so that you can adjust to the temperature of the testing room.

- Read something. Warm up your brain with a newspaper or a magazine. You shouldn't let the SAT be the first thing you read that day.

- Be sure to get there early. Allow yourself extra time for traffic, mass transit delays, or detours.

DURING THE TEST

Don't be shaken. If you find your confidence slipping, remind yourself how well you've prepared. You know the structure of the test; you know the instructions; you've had practice with—and have learned strategies for—every question type.

If something goes really wrong, don't panic. If the test booklet is defective—two pages are stuck together or the ink has run—raise your hand, and tell the proctor you need a new book. If you accidentally misgrid your answer page or put the answers in the wrong section, raise your hand and tell the proctor. He or she might be able to arrange for you to regrid your test after it's over when it won't cost you any time.

Remember, don't think about which section is experimental. You never know for sure which section won't count. Besides, you can't work on any other section during that section's designated time slot.

AFTER THE TEST

Congratulate yourself!

Now, you might walk out of the SAT thinking that you blew it. This is a normal reaction. Lots of people—even the highest scorers—feel that way. You tend to remember the questions that stumped you, not the ones that you knew.

> **EXPERT TUTOR TIP**
>
> " Try your hardest on every section of the SAT—because you won't be able to tell which section is experimental. "

WORRIED ABOUT YOUR SCORE?

You can always call ETS within 24 hours to find out about canceling your score, but there's usually no good reason to do so. Remember, colleges typically accept your highest SAT score, and no test experience is going to be perfect.

If you were distracted by a weird smell or a particularly loud test proctor this time around, next time you may be even more distracted by construction noise, a cold, or a particularly hot room. Carefully consider your performance before canceling your score.

PERFECT SCORE TIP

❝ After I finished the SAT, the last thing I wanted to do was think about it. I went out to dinner with my family that night, and got on with my life! ❞

However, we're positive that you performed well and scored your best on the exam because you prepared with *SAT Premier 2013*. Be confident that you were prepared, and celebrate in the fact that the SAT is a distant memory.

If you want more help or just want to know more about the SAT, college admissions, or Kaplan prep courses for the SAT, give us a call at 800-KAP-TEST or visit us at www.kaptest.com. We're here to answer your questions and to help you in any way we can.

| Part Two |

DIAGNOSTIC TEST

SAT Diagnostic Test
Answer Sheet

Remove (or photocopy) the answer sheet and use it to complete the Diagnostic Test.
See the answer key following the test when finished.

Start with number 1 for each section. If a section has fewer questions than answer spaces, leave the extra spaces blank.

SECTION

1

Section 1 is the Writing section's essay component.

SECTION

2

1. Ⓐ Ⓑ Ⓒ Ⓓ Ⓔ	11. Ⓐ Ⓑ Ⓒ Ⓓ Ⓔ	21. Ⓐ Ⓑ Ⓒ Ⓓ Ⓔ	31. Ⓐ Ⓑ Ⓒ Ⓓ Ⓔ
2. Ⓐ Ⓑ Ⓒ Ⓓ Ⓔ	12. Ⓐ Ⓑ Ⓒ Ⓓ Ⓔ	22. Ⓐ Ⓑ Ⓒ Ⓓ Ⓔ	32. Ⓐ Ⓑ Ⓒ Ⓓ Ⓔ
3. Ⓐ Ⓑ Ⓒ Ⓓ Ⓔ	13. Ⓐ Ⓑ Ⓒ Ⓓ Ⓔ	23. Ⓐ Ⓑ Ⓒ Ⓓ Ⓔ	33. Ⓐ Ⓑ Ⓒ Ⓓ Ⓔ
4. Ⓐ Ⓑ Ⓒ Ⓓ Ⓔ	14. Ⓐ Ⓑ Ⓒ Ⓓ Ⓔ	24. Ⓐ Ⓑ Ⓒ Ⓓ Ⓔ	34. Ⓐ Ⓑ Ⓒ Ⓓ Ⓔ
5. Ⓐ Ⓑ Ⓒ Ⓓ Ⓔ	15. Ⓐ Ⓑ Ⓒ Ⓓ Ⓔ	25. Ⓐ Ⓑ Ⓒ Ⓓ Ⓔ	35. Ⓐ Ⓑ Ⓒ Ⓓ Ⓔ
6. Ⓐ Ⓑ Ⓒ Ⓓ Ⓔ	16. Ⓐ Ⓑ Ⓒ Ⓓ Ⓔ	26. Ⓐ Ⓑ Ⓒ Ⓓ Ⓔ	36. Ⓐ Ⓑ Ⓒ Ⓓ Ⓔ
7. Ⓐ Ⓑ Ⓒ Ⓓ Ⓔ	17. Ⓐ Ⓑ Ⓒ Ⓓ Ⓔ	27. Ⓐ Ⓑ Ⓒ Ⓓ Ⓔ	37. Ⓐ Ⓑ Ⓒ Ⓓ Ⓔ
8. Ⓐ Ⓑ Ⓒ Ⓓ Ⓔ	18. Ⓐ Ⓑ Ⓒ Ⓓ Ⓔ	28. Ⓐ Ⓑ Ⓒ Ⓓ Ⓔ	38. Ⓐ Ⓑ Ⓒ Ⓓ Ⓔ
9. Ⓐ Ⓑ Ⓒ Ⓓ Ⓔ	19. Ⓐ Ⓑ Ⓒ Ⓓ Ⓔ	29. Ⓐ Ⓑ Ⓒ Ⓓ Ⓔ	39. Ⓐ Ⓑ Ⓒ Ⓓ Ⓔ
10. Ⓐ Ⓑ Ⓒ Ⓓ Ⓔ	20. Ⓐ Ⓑ Ⓒ Ⓓ Ⓔ	30. Ⓐ Ⓑ Ⓒ Ⓓ Ⓔ	40. Ⓐ Ⓑ Ⓒ Ⓓ Ⓔ

☐ # right in Section 2

☐ # wrong in Section 2

SECTION

3

1. Ⓐ Ⓑ Ⓒ Ⓓ Ⓔ	11. Ⓐ Ⓑ Ⓒ Ⓓ Ⓔ	21. Ⓐ Ⓑ Ⓒ Ⓓ Ⓔ	31. Ⓐ Ⓑ Ⓒ Ⓓ Ⓔ
2. Ⓐ Ⓑ Ⓒ Ⓓ Ⓔ	12. Ⓐ Ⓑ Ⓒ Ⓓ Ⓔ	22. Ⓐ Ⓑ Ⓒ Ⓓ Ⓔ	32. Ⓐ Ⓑ Ⓒ Ⓓ Ⓔ
3. Ⓐ Ⓑ Ⓒ Ⓓ Ⓔ	13. Ⓐ Ⓑ Ⓒ Ⓓ Ⓔ	23. Ⓐ Ⓑ Ⓒ Ⓓ Ⓔ	33. Ⓐ Ⓑ Ⓒ Ⓓ Ⓔ
4. Ⓐ Ⓑ Ⓒ Ⓓ Ⓔ	14. Ⓐ Ⓑ Ⓒ Ⓓ Ⓔ	24. Ⓐ Ⓑ Ⓒ Ⓓ Ⓔ	34. Ⓐ Ⓑ Ⓒ Ⓓ Ⓔ
5. Ⓐ Ⓑ Ⓒ Ⓓ Ⓔ	15. Ⓐ Ⓑ Ⓒ Ⓓ Ⓔ	25. Ⓐ Ⓑ Ⓒ Ⓓ Ⓔ	35. Ⓐ Ⓑ Ⓒ Ⓓ Ⓔ
6. Ⓐ Ⓑ Ⓒ Ⓓ Ⓔ	16. Ⓐ Ⓑ Ⓒ Ⓓ Ⓔ	26. Ⓐ Ⓑ Ⓒ Ⓓ Ⓔ	36. Ⓐ Ⓑ Ⓒ Ⓓ Ⓔ
7. Ⓐ Ⓑ Ⓒ Ⓓ Ⓔ	17. Ⓐ Ⓑ Ⓒ Ⓓ Ⓔ	27. Ⓐ Ⓑ Ⓒ Ⓓ Ⓔ	37. Ⓐ Ⓑ Ⓒ Ⓓ Ⓔ
8. Ⓐ Ⓑ Ⓒ Ⓓ Ⓔ	18. Ⓐ Ⓑ Ⓒ Ⓓ Ⓔ	28. Ⓐ Ⓑ Ⓒ Ⓓ Ⓔ	38. Ⓐ Ⓑ Ⓒ Ⓓ Ⓔ
9. Ⓐ Ⓑ Ⓒ Ⓓ Ⓔ	19. Ⓐ Ⓑ Ⓒ Ⓓ Ⓔ	29. Ⓐ Ⓑ Ⓒ Ⓓ Ⓔ	39. Ⓐ Ⓑ Ⓒ Ⓓ Ⓔ
10. Ⓐ Ⓑ Ⓒ Ⓓ Ⓔ	20. Ⓐ Ⓑ Ⓒ Ⓓ Ⓔ	30. Ⓐ Ⓑ Ⓒ Ⓓ Ⓔ	40. Ⓐ Ⓑ Ⓒ Ⓓ Ⓔ

☐ # right in Section 3

☐ # wrong in Section 3

Remove (or photocopy) this answer sheet and use it to complete the Diagnostic Test.

Start with number 1 for each section. If a section has fewer questions than answer spaces, leave the extra spaces blank.

SECTION

4

1. Ⓐ Ⓑ Ⓒ Ⓓ Ⓔ	11. Ⓐ Ⓑ Ⓒ Ⓓ Ⓔ	21. Ⓐ Ⓑ Ⓒ Ⓓ Ⓔ	31. Ⓐ Ⓑ Ⓒ Ⓓ Ⓔ	
2. Ⓐ Ⓑ Ⓒ Ⓓ Ⓔ	12. Ⓐ Ⓑ Ⓒ Ⓓ Ⓔ	22. Ⓐ Ⓑ Ⓒ Ⓓ Ⓔ	32. Ⓐ Ⓑ Ⓒ Ⓓ Ⓔ	
3. Ⓐ Ⓑ Ⓒ Ⓓ Ⓔ	13. Ⓐ Ⓑ Ⓒ Ⓓ Ⓔ	23. Ⓐ Ⓑ Ⓒ Ⓓ Ⓔ	33. Ⓐ Ⓑ Ⓒ Ⓓ Ⓔ	
4. Ⓐ Ⓑ Ⓒ Ⓓ Ⓔ	14. Ⓐ Ⓑ Ⓒ Ⓓ Ⓔ	24. Ⓐ Ⓑ Ⓒ Ⓓ Ⓔ	34. Ⓐ Ⓑ Ⓒ Ⓓ Ⓔ	# right in Section 4
5. Ⓐ Ⓑ Ⓒ Ⓓ Ⓔ	15. Ⓐ Ⓑ Ⓒ Ⓓ Ⓔ	25. Ⓐ Ⓑ Ⓒ Ⓓ Ⓔ	35. Ⓐ Ⓑ Ⓒ Ⓓ Ⓔ	
6. Ⓐ Ⓑ Ⓒ Ⓓ Ⓔ	16. Ⓐ Ⓑ Ⓒ Ⓓ Ⓔ	26. Ⓐ Ⓑ Ⓒ Ⓓ Ⓔ	36. Ⓐ Ⓑ Ⓒ Ⓓ Ⓔ	
7. Ⓐ Ⓑ Ⓒ Ⓓ Ⓔ	17. Ⓐ Ⓑ Ⓒ Ⓓ Ⓔ	27. Ⓐ Ⓑ Ⓒ Ⓓ Ⓔ	37. Ⓐ Ⓑ Ⓒ Ⓓ Ⓔ	
8. Ⓐ Ⓑ Ⓒ Ⓓ Ⓔ	18. Ⓐ Ⓑ Ⓒ Ⓓ Ⓔ	28. Ⓐ Ⓑ Ⓒ Ⓓ Ⓔ	38. Ⓐ Ⓑ Ⓒ Ⓓ Ⓔ	# wrong in Section 4
9. Ⓐ Ⓑ Ⓒ Ⓓ Ⓔ	19. Ⓐ Ⓑ Ⓒ Ⓓ Ⓔ	29. Ⓐ Ⓑ Ⓒ Ⓓ Ⓔ	39. Ⓐ Ⓑ Ⓒ Ⓓ Ⓔ	
10. Ⓐ Ⓑ Ⓒ Ⓓ Ⓔ	20. Ⓐ Ⓑ Ⓒ Ⓓ Ⓔ	30. Ⓐ Ⓑ Ⓒ Ⓓ Ⓔ	40. Ⓐ Ⓑ Ⓒ Ⓓ Ⓔ	

SECTION

5

1. Ⓐ Ⓑ Ⓒ Ⓓ Ⓔ	11. Ⓐ Ⓑ Ⓒ Ⓓ Ⓔ	21. Ⓐ Ⓑ Ⓒ Ⓓ Ⓔ	31. Ⓐ Ⓑ Ⓒ Ⓓ Ⓔ	
2. Ⓐ Ⓑ Ⓒ Ⓓ Ⓔ	12. Ⓐ Ⓑ Ⓒ Ⓓ Ⓔ	22. Ⓐ Ⓑ Ⓒ Ⓓ Ⓔ	32. Ⓐ Ⓑ Ⓒ Ⓓ Ⓔ	
3. Ⓐ Ⓑ Ⓒ Ⓓ Ⓔ	13. Ⓐ Ⓑ Ⓒ Ⓓ Ⓔ	23. Ⓐ Ⓑ Ⓒ Ⓓ Ⓔ	33. Ⓐ Ⓑ Ⓒ Ⓓ Ⓔ	
4. Ⓐ Ⓑ Ⓒ Ⓓ Ⓔ	14. Ⓐ Ⓑ Ⓒ Ⓓ Ⓔ	24. Ⓐ Ⓑ Ⓒ Ⓓ Ⓔ	34. Ⓐ Ⓑ Ⓒ Ⓓ Ⓔ	# right in Section 5
5. Ⓐ Ⓑ Ⓒ Ⓓ Ⓔ	15. Ⓐ Ⓑ Ⓒ Ⓓ Ⓔ	25. Ⓐ Ⓑ Ⓒ Ⓓ Ⓔ	35. Ⓐ Ⓑ Ⓒ Ⓓ Ⓔ	
6. Ⓐ Ⓑ Ⓒ Ⓓ Ⓔ	16. Ⓐ Ⓑ Ⓒ Ⓓ Ⓔ	26. Ⓐ Ⓑ Ⓒ Ⓓ Ⓔ	36. Ⓐ Ⓑ Ⓒ Ⓓ Ⓔ	
7. Ⓐ Ⓑ Ⓒ Ⓓ Ⓔ	17. Ⓐ Ⓑ Ⓒ Ⓓ Ⓔ	27. Ⓐ Ⓑ Ⓒ Ⓓ Ⓔ	37. Ⓐ Ⓑ Ⓒ Ⓓ Ⓔ	
8. Ⓐ Ⓑ Ⓒ Ⓓ Ⓔ	18. Ⓐ Ⓑ Ⓒ Ⓓ Ⓔ	28. Ⓐ Ⓑ Ⓒ Ⓓ Ⓔ	38. Ⓐ Ⓑ Ⓒ Ⓓ Ⓔ	# wrong in Section 5
9. Ⓐ Ⓑ Ⓒ Ⓓ Ⓔ	19. Ⓐ Ⓑ Ⓒ Ⓓ Ⓔ	29. Ⓐ Ⓑ Ⓒ Ⓓ Ⓔ	39. Ⓐ Ⓑ Ⓒ Ⓓ Ⓔ	
10. Ⓐ Ⓑ Ⓒ Ⓓ Ⓔ	20. Ⓐ Ⓑ Ⓒ Ⓓ Ⓔ	30. Ⓐ Ⓑ Ⓒ Ⓓ Ⓔ	40. Ⓐ Ⓑ Ⓒ Ⓓ Ⓔ	

If section 5 of your test book contains math questions that are not multiple-choice, continue to item 9 below. Otherwise, continue to item 9 above.

9.   10.   11.   12.   13.

14.   15.   16.   17.   18.

Remove (or photocopy) this answer sheet and use it to complete the Diagnostic Test.

Start with number 1 for each section. If a section has fewer questions than answer spaces, leave the extra spaces blank.

SECTION 6

1. Ⓐ Ⓑ Ⓒ Ⓓ Ⓔ 11. Ⓐ Ⓑ Ⓒ Ⓓ Ⓔ 21. Ⓐ Ⓑ Ⓒ Ⓓ Ⓔ 31. Ⓐ Ⓑ Ⓒ Ⓓ Ⓔ
2. Ⓐ Ⓑ Ⓒ Ⓓ Ⓔ 12. Ⓐ Ⓑ Ⓒ Ⓓ Ⓔ 22. Ⓐ Ⓑ Ⓒ Ⓓ Ⓔ 32. Ⓐ Ⓑ Ⓒ Ⓓ Ⓔ
3. Ⓐ Ⓑ Ⓒ Ⓓ Ⓔ 13. Ⓐ Ⓑ Ⓒ Ⓓ Ⓔ 23. Ⓐ Ⓑ Ⓒ Ⓓ Ⓔ 33. Ⓐ Ⓑ Ⓒ Ⓓ Ⓔ
4. Ⓐ Ⓑ Ⓒ Ⓓ Ⓔ 14. Ⓐ Ⓑ Ⓒ Ⓓ Ⓔ 24. Ⓐ Ⓑ Ⓒ Ⓓ Ⓔ 34. Ⓐ Ⓑ Ⓒ Ⓓ Ⓔ
5. Ⓐ Ⓑ Ⓒ Ⓓ Ⓔ 15. Ⓐ Ⓑ Ⓒ Ⓓ Ⓔ 25. Ⓐ Ⓑ Ⓒ Ⓓ Ⓔ 35. Ⓐ Ⓑ Ⓒ Ⓓ Ⓔ
6. Ⓐ Ⓑ Ⓒ Ⓓ Ⓔ 16. Ⓐ Ⓑ Ⓒ Ⓓ Ⓔ 26. Ⓐ Ⓑ Ⓒ Ⓓ Ⓔ 36. Ⓐ Ⓑ Ⓒ Ⓓ Ⓔ
7. Ⓐ Ⓑ Ⓒ Ⓓ Ⓔ 17. Ⓐ Ⓑ Ⓒ Ⓓ Ⓔ 27. Ⓐ Ⓑ Ⓒ Ⓓ Ⓔ 37. Ⓐ Ⓑ Ⓒ Ⓓ Ⓔ
8. Ⓐ Ⓑ Ⓒ Ⓓ Ⓔ 18. Ⓐ Ⓑ Ⓒ Ⓓ Ⓔ 28. Ⓐ Ⓑ Ⓒ Ⓓ Ⓔ 38. Ⓐ Ⓑ Ⓒ Ⓓ Ⓔ
9. Ⓐ Ⓑ Ⓒ Ⓓ Ⓔ 19. Ⓐ Ⓑ Ⓒ Ⓓ Ⓔ 29. Ⓐ Ⓑ Ⓒ Ⓓ Ⓔ 39. Ⓐ Ⓑ Ⓒ Ⓓ Ⓔ
10. Ⓐ Ⓑ Ⓒ Ⓓ Ⓔ 20. Ⓐ Ⓑ Ⓒ Ⓓ Ⓔ 30. Ⓐ Ⓑ Ⓒ Ⓓ Ⓔ 40. Ⓐ Ⓑ Ⓒ Ⓓ Ⓔ

right in Section 6

wrong in Section 6

SECTION 7

1. Ⓐ Ⓑ Ⓒ Ⓓ Ⓔ 11. Ⓐ Ⓑ Ⓒ Ⓓ Ⓔ 21. Ⓐ Ⓑ Ⓒ Ⓓ Ⓔ 31. Ⓐ Ⓑ Ⓒ Ⓓ Ⓔ
2. Ⓐ Ⓑ Ⓒ Ⓓ Ⓔ 12. Ⓐ Ⓑ Ⓒ Ⓓ Ⓔ 22. Ⓐ Ⓑ Ⓒ Ⓓ Ⓔ 32. Ⓐ Ⓑ Ⓒ Ⓓ Ⓔ
3. Ⓐ Ⓑ Ⓒ Ⓓ Ⓔ 13. Ⓐ Ⓑ Ⓒ Ⓓ Ⓔ 23. Ⓐ Ⓑ Ⓒ Ⓓ Ⓔ 33. Ⓐ Ⓑ Ⓒ Ⓓ Ⓔ
4. Ⓐ Ⓑ Ⓒ Ⓓ Ⓔ 14. Ⓐ Ⓑ Ⓒ Ⓓ Ⓔ 24. Ⓐ Ⓑ Ⓒ Ⓓ Ⓔ 34. Ⓐ Ⓑ Ⓒ Ⓓ Ⓔ
5. Ⓐ Ⓑ Ⓒ Ⓓ Ⓔ 15. Ⓐ Ⓑ Ⓒ Ⓓ Ⓔ 25. Ⓐ Ⓑ Ⓒ Ⓓ Ⓔ 35. Ⓐ Ⓑ Ⓒ Ⓓ Ⓔ
6. Ⓐ Ⓑ Ⓒ Ⓓ Ⓔ 16. Ⓐ Ⓑ Ⓒ Ⓓ Ⓔ 26. Ⓐ Ⓑ Ⓒ Ⓓ Ⓔ 36. Ⓐ Ⓑ Ⓒ Ⓓ Ⓔ
7. Ⓐ Ⓑ Ⓒ Ⓓ Ⓔ 17. Ⓐ Ⓑ Ⓒ Ⓓ Ⓔ 27. Ⓐ Ⓑ Ⓒ Ⓓ Ⓔ 37. Ⓐ Ⓑ Ⓒ Ⓓ Ⓔ
8. Ⓐ Ⓑ Ⓒ Ⓓ Ⓔ 18. Ⓐ Ⓑ Ⓒ Ⓓ Ⓔ 28. Ⓐ Ⓑ Ⓒ Ⓓ Ⓔ 38. Ⓐ Ⓑ Ⓒ Ⓓ Ⓔ
9. Ⓐ Ⓑ Ⓒ Ⓓ Ⓔ 19. Ⓐ Ⓑ Ⓒ Ⓓ Ⓔ 29. Ⓐ Ⓑ Ⓒ Ⓓ Ⓔ 39. Ⓐ Ⓑ Ⓒ Ⓓ Ⓔ
10. Ⓐ Ⓑ Ⓒ Ⓓ Ⓔ 20. Ⓐ Ⓑ Ⓒ Ⓓ Ⓔ 30. Ⓐ Ⓑ Ⓒ Ⓓ Ⓔ 40. Ⓐ Ⓑ Ⓒ Ⓓ Ⓔ

right in Section 7

wrong in Section 7

SECTION 8

1. Ⓐ Ⓑ Ⓒ Ⓓ Ⓔ 11. Ⓐ Ⓑ Ⓒ Ⓓ Ⓔ 21. Ⓐ Ⓑ Ⓒ Ⓓ Ⓔ 31. Ⓐ Ⓑ Ⓒ Ⓓ Ⓔ
2. Ⓐ Ⓑ Ⓒ Ⓓ Ⓔ 12. Ⓐ Ⓑ Ⓒ Ⓓ Ⓔ 22. Ⓐ Ⓑ Ⓒ Ⓓ Ⓔ 32. Ⓐ Ⓑ Ⓒ Ⓓ Ⓔ
3. Ⓐ Ⓑ Ⓒ Ⓓ Ⓔ 13. Ⓐ Ⓑ Ⓒ Ⓓ Ⓔ 23. Ⓐ Ⓑ Ⓒ Ⓓ Ⓔ 33. Ⓐ Ⓑ Ⓒ Ⓓ Ⓔ
4. Ⓐ Ⓑ Ⓒ Ⓓ Ⓔ 14. Ⓐ Ⓑ Ⓒ Ⓓ Ⓔ 24. Ⓐ Ⓑ Ⓒ Ⓓ Ⓔ 34. Ⓐ Ⓑ Ⓒ Ⓓ Ⓔ
5. Ⓐ Ⓑ Ⓒ Ⓓ Ⓔ 15. Ⓐ Ⓑ Ⓒ Ⓓ Ⓔ 25. Ⓐ Ⓑ Ⓒ Ⓓ Ⓔ 35. Ⓐ Ⓑ Ⓒ Ⓓ Ⓔ
6. Ⓐ Ⓑ Ⓒ Ⓓ Ⓔ 16. Ⓐ Ⓑ Ⓒ Ⓓ Ⓔ 26. Ⓐ Ⓑ Ⓒ Ⓓ Ⓔ 36. Ⓐ Ⓑ Ⓒ Ⓓ Ⓔ
7. Ⓐ Ⓑ Ⓒ Ⓓ Ⓔ 17. Ⓐ Ⓑ Ⓒ Ⓓ Ⓔ 27. Ⓐ Ⓑ Ⓒ Ⓓ Ⓔ 37. Ⓐ Ⓑ Ⓒ Ⓓ Ⓔ
8. Ⓐ Ⓑ Ⓒ Ⓓ Ⓔ 18. Ⓐ Ⓑ Ⓒ Ⓓ Ⓔ 28. Ⓐ Ⓑ Ⓒ Ⓓ Ⓔ 38. Ⓐ Ⓑ Ⓒ Ⓓ Ⓔ
9. Ⓐ Ⓑ Ⓒ Ⓓ Ⓔ 19. Ⓐ Ⓑ Ⓒ Ⓓ Ⓔ 29. Ⓐ Ⓑ Ⓒ Ⓓ Ⓔ 39. Ⓐ Ⓑ Ⓒ Ⓓ Ⓔ
10. Ⓐ Ⓑ Ⓒ Ⓓ Ⓔ 20. Ⓐ Ⓑ Ⓒ Ⓓ Ⓔ 30. Ⓐ Ⓑ Ⓒ Ⓓ Ⓔ 40. Ⓐ Ⓑ Ⓒ Ⓓ Ⓔ

right in Section 8

wrong in Section 8

Remove (or photocopy) this answer sheet and use it to complete the Diagnostic Test.

Start with number 1 for each section. If a section has fewer questions than answer spaces, leave the extra spaces blank.

SECTION

9

1. Ⓐ Ⓑ Ⓒ Ⓓ Ⓔ	11. Ⓐ Ⓑ Ⓒ Ⓓ Ⓔ	21. Ⓐ Ⓑ Ⓒ Ⓓ Ⓔ	31. Ⓐ Ⓑ Ⓒ Ⓓ Ⓔ
2. Ⓐ Ⓑ Ⓒ Ⓓ Ⓔ	12. Ⓐ Ⓑ Ⓒ Ⓓ Ⓔ	22. Ⓐ Ⓑ Ⓒ Ⓓ Ⓔ	32. Ⓐ Ⓑ Ⓒ Ⓓ Ⓔ
3. Ⓐ Ⓑ Ⓒ Ⓓ Ⓔ	13. Ⓐ Ⓑ Ⓒ Ⓓ Ⓔ	23. Ⓐ Ⓑ Ⓒ Ⓓ Ⓔ	33. Ⓐ Ⓑ Ⓒ Ⓓ Ⓔ
4. Ⓐ Ⓑ Ⓒ Ⓓ Ⓔ	14. Ⓐ Ⓑ Ⓒ Ⓓ Ⓔ	24. Ⓐ Ⓑ Ⓒ Ⓓ Ⓔ	34. Ⓐ Ⓑ Ⓒ Ⓓ Ⓔ
5. Ⓐ Ⓑ Ⓒ Ⓓ Ⓔ	15. Ⓐ Ⓑ Ⓒ Ⓓ Ⓔ	25. Ⓐ Ⓑ Ⓒ Ⓓ Ⓔ	35. Ⓐ Ⓑ Ⓒ Ⓓ Ⓔ
6. Ⓐ Ⓑ Ⓒ Ⓓ Ⓔ	16. Ⓐ Ⓑ Ⓒ Ⓓ Ⓔ	26. Ⓐ Ⓑ Ⓒ Ⓓ Ⓔ	36. Ⓐ Ⓑ Ⓒ Ⓓ Ⓔ
7. Ⓐ Ⓑ Ⓒ Ⓓ Ⓔ	17. Ⓐ Ⓑ Ⓒ Ⓓ Ⓔ	27. Ⓐ Ⓑ Ⓒ Ⓓ Ⓔ	37. Ⓐ Ⓑ Ⓒ Ⓓ Ⓔ
8. Ⓐ Ⓑ Ⓒ Ⓓ Ⓔ	18. Ⓐ Ⓑ Ⓒ Ⓓ Ⓔ	28. Ⓐ Ⓑ Ⓒ Ⓓ Ⓔ	38. Ⓐ Ⓑ Ⓒ Ⓓ Ⓔ
9. Ⓐ Ⓑ Ⓒ Ⓓ Ⓔ	19. Ⓐ Ⓑ Ⓒ Ⓓ Ⓔ	29. Ⓐ Ⓑ Ⓒ Ⓓ Ⓔ	39. Ⓐ Ⓑ Ⓒ Ⓓ Ⓔ
10. Ⓐ Ⓑ Ⓒ Ⓓ Ⓔ	20. Ⓐ Ⓑ Ⓒ Ⓓ Ⓔ	30. Ⓐ Ⓑ Ⓒ Ⓓ Ⓔ	40. Ⓐ Ⓑ Ⓒ Ⓓ Ⓔ

right in
Section 9

wrong in
Section 9

CHAPTER 4: DIAGNOSTIC TEST

SECTION 1
Time—25 Minutes
ESSAY

The essay gives you an opportunity to show how effectively you can develop and express ideas. You should, therefore, take care to develop your point of view, present your ideas logically and clearly, and use language precisely.

Your essay must be written in your Answer Grid Booklet—you will receive no other paper on which to write. You will have enough space if you write on every line, avoid wide margins, and keep your handwriting to a reasonable size. Remember that people who are not familiar with your handwriting will read what you write. Try to write or print so that what you are writing is legible to those readers.

You have 25 minutes to write an essay on the topic assigned below.
DO NOT WRITE ON ANOTHER TOPIC. AN OFF-TOPIC ESSAY WILL RECEIVE A SCORE OF ZERO.

Think carefully about the issue presented in the following excerpt and the assignment below.

> "Everything comes if a man will only wait."
> —Benjamin Disraeli, *Tancred*
>
> "Destiny is not a matter of chance, it is a matter of choice; it is not a thing to be waited for, it is a thing to be achieved."
> —William Jennings Bryan, *Memoirs*

Assignment: Should we wait for good things to come, or is destiny not something we can wait for? Plan and write an essay in which you develop your point of view on this issue. Support your position with reasoning and examples taken from your reading, studies, experience, or observations.

DO NOT WRITE YOUR ESSAY IN YOUR TEST BOOK.
You will receive credit only for what you write in your Answer Grid Booklet.

IF YOU FINISH BEFORE TIME IS CALLED, YOU MAY CHECK YOUR WORK ON
THIS SECTION ONLY. DO NOT TURN TO ANY OTHER SECTION IN THE TEST.

SECTION 2

Time—25 Minutes

24 Questions

Directions: For each of the following questions, choose the best answer and darken the corresponding oval on the answer sheet.

Each sentence below has one or two blanks, each blank indicating that something has been omitted. Beneath the sentence are five words or sets of words labeled (A) through (E). Choose the word or set of words that, when inserted in the sentence, <u>best</u> fits the meaning of the sentence as a whole.

EXAMPLE:

Today's small, portable computers contrast markedly with the earliest electronic computers, which were -------.

(A) effective
(B) invented
(C) useful
(D) destructive
(E) enormous

1. Because Mark has a tendency to -------, he often fails to meet the deadlines established by his manager.

   (A) prevaricate
   (B) obstruct
   (C) dispel
   (D) pacify
   (E) procrastinate

2. Roman legions ------- the mountain ------- of Masada for three years before they were able to seize it.

   (A) dissembled . . . bastion
   (B) assailed . . . symbol
   (C) besieged . . . citadel
   (D) surmounted . . . dwelling
   (E) honed . . . stronghold

3. Unlike his calmer, more easygoing colleagues, the senator was -------, ready to quarrel at the slightest provocation.

   (A) whimsical
   (B) irascible
   (C) gregarious
   (D) ineffectual
   (E) benign

4. Although historians have long thought of Genghis Khan as a ------- potentate, new research has shown he was ------- by many of his subjects.

   (A) tyrannical . . . abhorred
   (B) despotic . . . revered
   (C) redundant . . . venerated
   (D) jocular . . . esteemed
   (E) peremptory . . . invoked

GO ON TO THE NEXT PAGE

5. Jill was ------- by her employees because she often ------- them for not working hard enough.

   (A) deified . . . goaded
   (B) loathed . . . berated
   (C) disregarded . . . eulogized
   (D) cherished . . . derided
   (E) execrated . . . lauded

6. Reconstructing the skeletons of extinct species like dinosaurs is ------- process that requires much patience and effort by paleontologists.

   (A) a nascent
   (B) an aberrant
   (C) a disheveled
   (D) a worthless
   (E) an exacting

7. Nearly ------- by disease and the destruction of their habitat, koalas are now found only in isolated parts of eucalyptus forests.

   (A) dispersed
   (B) compiled
   (C) decimated
   (D) infuriated
   (E) averted

8. Deep ideological ------- and internal power struggles ------- the government.

   (A) disputes . . . facilitated
   (B) similarities . . . protracted
   (C) distortions . . . accelerated
   (D) agreements . . . stymied
   (E) divisions . . . paralyzed

GO ON TO THE NEXT PAGE

Directions: The passages below are followed by questions based on their content; questions following a pair of related passages may also be based on the relationship between the paired passages. Answer the questions on the basis of what is <u>stated</u> or <u>implied</u> in the passages and in any introductory material that may be provided.

Questions 9–12 refer to the following passages.

Passage 1

Musicologists and linguists argue about the relationship between music and language. Prominent ethnomusicologist Bruno Nettl has concluded that like language, music is a
(5) "series of symbols." However, music has traditionally been used purely to express emotions, while language has also been used for more functional, prosaic tasks. This distinction was especially evident in the Romantic era of
(10) Western music, when many composers and critics felt that music could stand by itself to connote emotions without any extra-musical references.

Passage 2

The fundamental building blocks of both
(15) language and music are quite similar, as are the manners in which these components are combined to form a cohesive whole. In the same way that an entire piece of music can be divided into phrases, and further subdivided
(20) into specific notes, language can be subdivided into paragraphs, sentences, and words. A single note can have different meanings depending on the piece; a lone word can have different meanings depending on the context
(25) in the sentence. Words and notes are also similar in that they have little intrinsic meaning, but instead act as symbols to convey larger ideas.

9. The author of Passage 1 most likely cites the "Romantic era of Western music" (lines 9–10) in order to establish that

   (A) our modern perception of Romantic music is different from that held in the Romantic era
   (B) unlike language, Romantic music is not used functionally
   (C) composers of Romantic music always used music to express emotion
   (D) in the Romantic era it was commonly thought that music used without words could convey emotion
   (E) music of the Romantic era is compromised because it contains no extra-musical references

10. In line 12, the term "extra-musical" most nearly means

   (A) especially musical
   (B) nonmusical
   (C) more than musical
   (D) better than musical
   (E) classically musical

11. In both passages, the authors state that music and language

   (A) make use of symbols
   (B) are subdivided sections
   (C) are functional parts
   (D) are fundamentally distinct
   (E) convey emotion

GO ON TO THE NEXT PAGE

12. About which of the following statements
would the author of Passage 1 and the author
of Passage 2 most likely disagree?

(A) Music and language can both be subdivided into several parts.

(B) Although significantly similar, music and
language have several fundamentally distinct aspects.

(C) A group of notes used in a musical composition has the same meaning in a piece
by a different composer.

(D) Language is not an effective means to
express emotions.

(E) The meaning of a particular word is
solely dependent on context.

Questions 13–24 refer to the following passage.

*In the following passage, a 19th-century American
writer recalls his boyhood in a small town along the
Mississippi River.*

My father was a justice of the peace, and I
supposed he possessed the power of life and
death over all men and could hang anybody
that offended him. This was distinction enough
(5) for me as a general thing; but the desire to be
a steamboatman kept intruding, nevertheless.
I first wanted to be a cabin boy so that I could
come out with a white apron on and shake a
tablecloth over the side, where all my old com-
(10) rades could see me. Later I thought I would
rather be the deck hand who stood on the end
of the stage plank with a coil of rope in his
hand, because he was particularly conspicuous.
But these were only daydreams—too heav-
(15) enly to be contemplated as real possibilities. By
and by one of the boys went away. He was not
heard of for a long time. At last he turned up as
an apprentice engineer or "striker" on a steamboat. This thing shook the bottom out of all my
(20) Sunday-school teachings. That boy had been
notoriously worldly, and I had been just the
reverse—yet he was exalted to this eminence,
and I was left in obscurity and misery. There
was nothing generous about this fellow in his
(25) greatness. He would always manage to have a
rusty bolt to scrub while his boat was docked at
our town, and he would sit on the inside guard
and scrub it, where we could all see him and
envy him and loathe him.
(30)   He used all sorts of steamboat technicalities in
his talk, as if he were so used to them that he
forgot common people could not understand
them. He would speak of the "labboard" side
of a horse in an easy, natural way that would
(35) make you wish he was dead. And he was always
talking about "St. Looy" like an old citizen.

GO ON TO THE NEXT PAGE

Two or three of the boys had long been persons of consideration among us because they had been to St. Louis once and had a vague general
(40) knowledge of its wonders, but the day of their glory was over now. They lapsed into a humble silence and learned to disappear when the ruthless "cub" engineer approached. This fellow had money, too, and hair oil, and he wore a showy
(45) brass watch chain, a leather belt, and used no suspenders. No girl could withstand his charms. He "cut out" every boy in the village. When his boat blew up at last, it diffused a tranquil contentment among us such as we had not known
(50) for months. But when he came home the next week, alive, renowned, and appeared in church all battered up and bandaged, a shining hero, stared at and wondered over by everybody, it seemed to us that the partiality of Providence
(55) for an undeserving reptile had reached a point where it was open to criticism.

This creature's career could produce but one result, and it speedily followed. Boy after boy managed to get on the river. Four sons of the
(60) chief merchant, and two sons of the county judge became pilots, the grandest position of all. But some of us could not get on the river—at least our parents would not let us.

So by and by I ran away. I said I would
(65) never come home again till I was a pilot and could return in glory. But somehow I could not manage it. I went meekly aboard a few of the boats that lay packed together like sardines at the long St. Louis wharf and very humbly
(70) inquired for the pilots but got only a cold shoulder and short words from mates and clerks. I had to make the best of this sort of treatment for the time being, but I had comforting daydreams of a future when I should
(75) be a great and honored pilot, with plenty of money, and could kill some of these mates and clerks and pay for them.

13. The author makes the statement that "I supposed he . . . offended him" (lines 1–4) primarily to suggest the

(A) power held by a justice of the peace in a frontier town
(B) naive view that he held of his father's importance
(C) respect in which the townspeople held his father
(D) possibility of miscarriages of justice on the American frontier
(E) harsh environment in which he was brought up

14. As used in line 4, the word "distinction" most nearly means

(A) difference
(B) variation
(C) prestige
(D) desperation
(E) clarity

15. The author decides that he would rather become a deck hand than a cabin boy (lines 7–13) because

(A) the job offers higher wages
(B) he believes that the work is easier
(C) he wants to avoid seeing his older friends
(D) deck hands often go on to become pilots
(E) the job is more visible to passersby

GO ON TO THE NEXT PAGE

16. The author most likely mentions his "Sunday-school teachings" in line 20 in order to emphasize

    (A) the influence of his early education in later life

    (B) his sense of injustice at the engineer's success

    (C) his disillusionment with longstanding religious beliefs

    (D) his determination to become an engineer at all costs

    (E) the unscrupulous nature of the engineer's character

17. The author most likely concludes that the engineer is not "generous" (line 24) because he

    (A) has no respect for religious beliefs

    (B) refuses to share his wages with friends

    (C) flaunts his new position in public

    (D) takes pride in material possessions

    (E) ignores the disappointment of other people

18. The author probably mentions the use of "steamboat technicalities" (line 30) in order to emphasize the engineer's

    (A) expertise after a few months on the job

    (B) fascination for trivial information

    (C) ignorance on most other subjects

    (D) desire to appear sophisticated

    (E) inability to communicate effectively

19. The word "consideration" in line 38 most nearly means

    (A) generosity

    (B) deliberation

    (C) contemplation

    (D) unselfishness

    (E) reputation

20. According to the passage, the "glory" of having visited St. Louis (lines 39–41) was over because

    (A) the boys' knowledge of St. Louis was much less detailed than the engineer's

    (B) St. Louis had changed so much that the boys' stories were no longer accurate

    (C) the boys realized that traveling to St. Louis was not a mark of sophistication

    (D) the engineer's account revealed that the boys' stories were lies

    (E) travel to St. Louis had become too commonplace to be envied

21. The author describes the engineer's appearance (lines 43–46) primarily in order to

    (A) suggest one reason why many people found the engineer impressive

    (B) convey the way steamboatmen typically dressed

    (C) emphasize the inadequacy of his own wardrobe

    (D) contrast the engineer's behavior with his appearance

    (E) indicate his admiration for fashionable clothes

GO ON TO THE NEXT PAGE

22. In lines 50–56, the author's response to the engineer's survival is one of

   (A) thankfulness for what he believes is God's providence

   (B) astonishment at the engineer's miraculous escape

   (C) reflection on the occupational hazards of a steamboating career

   (D) outrage at his rival's undeserved good fortune

   (E) sympathy for the extent of the engineer's wounds

23. The major purpose of the passage is to

   (A) sketch the peaceful life of a frontier town

   (B) relate the events that led to a boy's first success in life

   (C) portray the unsophisticated youthful ambitions of a boy

   (D) describe the characteristics of a small-town boaster

   (E) give a humorous portrayal of a boy's conflicts with his parents

24. At the end of the passage, the author reflects on

   (A) his new ambition to become either a mate or a clerk

   (B) the wisdom of seeking a job in which advancement is easier

   (C) the prospect of abandoning a hopeless search for fame

   (D) the impossibility of returning home and asking his parents' pardon

   (E) his determination to keep striving for success in a glorious career

IF YOU FINISH BEFORE TIME IS CALLED, YOU MAY CHECK YOUR WORK ON THIS SECTION ONLY. DO NOT TURN TO ANY OTHER SECTION IN THE TEST.   STOP

SECTION 3

Time—25 Minutes
20 Questions

Directions: For this section, solve each problem and decide which is the best of the choices given. Fill in the corresponding oval on the answer sheet. You may use any available space for scratchwork.

Notes:

(1) Calculator use is permitted.

(2) All numbers used are real numbers.

(3) Figures are provided for some problems. All figures are drawn to scale and lie in a plane UNLESS otherwise indicated.

(4) Unless otherwise specified, the domain of any function f is assumed to be the set of all real numbers x for which $f(x)$ is a real number.

Information

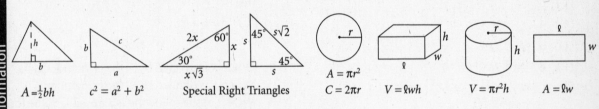

$A = \frac{1}{2}bh$ $\qquad$ $c^2 = a^2 + b^2$ $\qquad$ Special Right Triangles $\qquad$ $A = \pi r^2$ $\qquad$ $V = \ell wh$ $\qquad$ $V = \pi r^2 h$ $\qquad$ $A = \ell w$
$\qquad\qquad\qquad\qquad\qquad\qquad\qquad\qquad\qquad\qquad\qquad$ $C = 2\pi r$

The sum of the degree measures of the angles in a triangle is 180.
The number of degrees of arc in a circle is 360.
A straight angle has a degree measure of 180.

1. Which of the following must be equal to 30 percent of x?

    (A) $\dfrac{3x}{1,000}$

    (B) $\dfrac{3x}{100}$

    (C) $\dfrac{3x}{10}$

    (D) $3x$

    (E) $30x$

2. $(2 \times 10^4) + (5 \times 10^3) + (6 \times 10^2) + (4 \times 10^1) =$

    (A) 2,564

    (B) 20,564

    (C) 25,064

    (D) 25,604

    (E) 25,640

GO ON TO THE NEXT PAGE

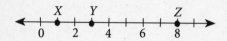

3. On the number line shown above, the length of YZ is how much greater than the length of XY?

   (A) 3
   (B) 4
   (C) 5
   (D) 6
   (E) 7

4. If $2^{x+1} = 16$, what is the value of x?

   (A) 2
   (B) 3
   (C) 4
   (D) 5
   (E) 6

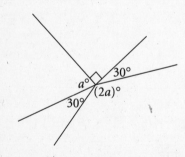

Note: Figure not drawn to scale.

5. In the figure above, what is the value of a?

   (A) 50
   (B) 55
   (C) 60
   (D) 65
   (E) 70

6. A machine labels 150 bottles in 20 minutes. At this rate, how many minutes does it take to label 60 bottles?

   (A) 2
   (B) 4
   (C) 6
   (D) 8
   (E) 10

7. If $x - 1$ is a multiple of 3, which of the following must be the next greater multiple of 3?

   (A) x
   (B) $x + 2$
   (C) $x + 3$
   (D) $3x$
   (E) $3x - 3$

8. When x is divided by 5, the remainder is 4. When x is divided by 9, the remainder is 0. Which of the following is a possible value for x?

   (A) 24
   (B) 45
   (C) 59
   (D) 109
   (E) 144

9. In triangle ABC, $AB = 6$, $BC = 12$, and $AC = x$. Which of the following cannot be a value of x?

   (A) 6
   (B) 7
   (C) 8
   (D) 9
   (E) 10

GO ON TO THE NEXT PAGE

10. The average of 20, 70, and x is 40. If the average of 20, 70, x, and y is 50, then $y =$

    (A)   30
    (B)   60
    (C)   70
    (D)   80
    (E)   100

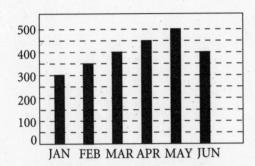

NUMBER OF BOOKS BORROWED
FROM MIDVILLE LIBRARY

11. According to the graph above, the number of books borrowed during the month of January was what fraction of the total number of books borrowed during the first six months of the year?

    (A) $\frac{1}{8}$

    (B) $\frac{1}{7}$

    (C) $\frac{1}{6}$

    (D) $\frac{3}{16}$

    (E) $\frac{5}{12}$

12. If 40 percent of r is equal to s, then which of the following is equal to 10 percent of r?

    (A) $4s$

    (B) $2s$

    (C) $\frac{s}{2}$

    (D) $\frac{s}{4}$

    (E) $\frac{s}{8}$

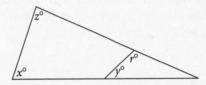

13. In the figure above, which of the following must be true?

    (A) $x + r = z + y$
    (B) $x + r = z - y$
    (C) $x - y = z + r$
    (D) $x - r = y - z$
    (E) $x + y = z + r$

14. If a *prifact* number is a nonprime integer such that each factor of the integer other than 1 and the integer itself is a prime number, which of the following is a *prifact* number?

    (A)   12
    (B)   18
    (C)   21
    (D)   24
    (E)   28

GO ON TO THE NEXT PAGE

15. If $3x + y = 14$, and x and y are positive integers, all of the following could be the value of $x + y$ EXCEPT

    (A) 4
    (B) 6
    (C) 8
    (D) 10
    (E) 12

16. A certain deck of cards contains r cards. After the cards are distributed evenly among s people, 8 cards are left over. In terms of r and s, how many cards did each person receive?

    (A) $\dfrac{s}{8 - r}$

    (B) $\dfrac{r - s}{8}$

    (C) $\dfrac{r - 8}{s}$

    (D) $s - 8r$

    (E) $rs - 8$

17. If d is an integer, which of the following CANNOT be an integer?

    (A) $\dfrac{d}{2}$

    (B) $\dfrac{\sqrt{d}}{2}$

    (C) $2d$

    (D) $d\sqrt{2}$

    (E) $d + 2$

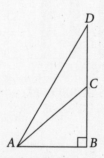

18. In the figure above, the area of triangle ABC is 6. If $BC = CD$, what is the area of triangle ACD?

    (A) 6
    (B) 8
    (C) 9
    (D) 10
    (E) 12

GO ON TO THE NEXT PAGE

19. What is the minimum number of rectangular tiles, each 12 centimeters by 18 centimeters, needed to completely cover five flat rectangular surfaces, each 60 centimeters by 180 centimeters?

(A) 50

(B) 100

(C) 150

(D) 200

(E) 250

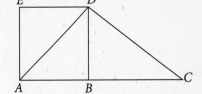

20. In the figure above, side AB of square $ABDE$ is extended to point C. If $BC = 8$ and $CD = 10$, what is the perimeter of triangle ACD?

(A) $18 + 6\sqrt{2}$

(B) $24 + 6\sqrt{2}$

(C) $26 + 6\sqrt{2}$

(D) 30

(E) 36

IF YOU FINISH BEFORE TIME IS CALLED, YOU MAY CHECK YOUR WORK ON THIS SECTION ONLY. DO NOT TURN TO ANY OTHER SECTION IN THE TEST.

STOP

SECTION 4

Time—25 Minutes
24 Questions

Directions: For each of the following questions, choose the best answer and darken the corresponding oval on the answer sheet.

Each sentence below has one or two blanks, each blank indicating that something has been omitted. Beneath the sentence are five words or sets of words labeled (A) through (E). Choose the word or set of words that, when inserted in the sentence, <u>best</u> fits the meaning of the sentence as a whole.

EXAMPLE:

Today's small, portable computers contrast markedly with the earliest electronic computers, which were -------.

(A) effective
(B) invented
(C) useful
(D) destructive
(E) enormous

1. The rain is so rare and the land is so ------- that few of the men who work there see much ------ in farming.

   (A) plentiful . . . hope
   (B) barren . . . difficulty
   (C) productive . . . profit
   (D) infertile . . . future
   (E) dry . . . danger

2. The principal declared that the students were not simply ignoring the rules, but openly ------- them.

   (A) accepting
   (B) redressing
   (C) reviewing
   (D) flouting
   (E) discussing

3. Some critics believe that the ------- of modern art came with dadaism, while others insist that the movement was a -------.

   (A) zenith . . . sham
   (B) pinnacle . . . triumph
   (C) decline . . . disaster
   (D) acceptance . . . success
   (E) originality . . . fiasco

4. She would never have believed that her article was so ------- were it not for the ------- of correspondence that followed its publication.

   (A) interesting . . . dearth
   (B) inflammatory . . . lack
   (C) controversial . . . spate
   (D) commonplace . . . influx
   (E) insignificant . . . volume

5. The writings of the philosopher Descartes are -------; many readers have difficulty following his complex, intricately woven arguments.

   (A) generic
   (B) trenchant
   (C) reflective
   (D) elongated
   (E) abstruse

GO ON TO THE NEXT PAGE

Directions: The passages below are followed by questions based on their content; questions following a pair of related passages may also be based on the relationship between the paired passages. Answer the questions on the basis of what is <u>stated</u> or <u>implied</u> in the passages and in any introductory material that may be provided.

Questions 6–7 refer to the following passage.

One of the hazards of swimming in the ocean is an unexpected encounter with a jellyfish. Contact with the poison in a jellyfish's tentacles can result in sharp, lingering pain, or
(5) even death if the person stung is highly allergic. While everyone, including the jellyfish, would like to avoid these encounters, they are not uncommon. This is hardly surprising considering that jellyfish live in every ocean in
(10) the world and have done so for more than 650 million years. The animals are likely so widespread because of their extreme adaptability— they are quite hardy and can withstand a wide range of temperatures and conditions in their
(15) environment.

6. The author uses the phrase "including the jellyfish" (lines 6–7) in order to

   (A) introduce a small note of humor to an otherwise serious discussion
   (B) encourage the reader's sympathy for the jellyfish
   (C) ridicule humans' fear of jellyfish
   (D) emphasize the danger that jellyfish pose for swimmers
   (E) contrast the jellyfish's reaction to the encounter to that of humans

7. According to the passage, encounters between humans and jellyfish in the ocean are relatively common because jellyfish

   (A) are more than 650 million years old
   (B) live in all the world's oceans
   (C) are extremely robust
   (D) have poisonous tentacles
   (E) can endure a range of temperatures

GO ON TO THE NEXT PAGE

Questions 8–9 refer to the following passage.

Connecting the northern frontier of
Pakistan with Afghanistan, the Khyber Pass
is one of the most noteworthy mountain
passes in the world. At its narrowest point in
(5) the north, the pass is walled on either side by
precipitous cliffs up to 300 meters in height,
while the pass itself is only 3 meters wide.
Because it is only 53 kilometers long, the pass
offers the best land route between India and
(10) Pakistan. This has led to a long and often violent history—conquering armies have used the
Khyber as an entry point for their invasions of
India, Pakistan, and Afghanistan. Today there
are two highways that snake their way through
(15) the Khyber Pass, one for motor traffic and
another for traditional caravans.

8. Which of the following topics is NOT
addressed by the passage?

(A) the origin of the pass

(B) the countries that border the pass

(C) the length of the pass

(D) the role of the pass in history

(E) the uses of the pass today

9. In line 14, the word "snake" most directly
emphasizes the

(A) function of the Khyber Pass as a means
to connect two points

(B) danger of crossing the Khyber Pass

(C) Khyber Pass as a direct route through the
Hindu Kush mountains

(D) relatively short length of the Khyber Pass

(E) winding quality of the Khyber Pass

GO ON TO THE NEXT PAGE

Questions 10–16 refer to the following passage.

In this excerpt, a Nobel Prize–winning scientist discusses ways of thinking about extremely long periods of time.

There is one fact about the origin of life which is reasonably certain. Whenever and wherever it happened, it started a very long time ago, so long ago that it is extremely difficult to form any
(5) realistic idea of such vast stretches of time. The shortness of human life necessarily limits the span of direct personal recollection.

Human culture has given us the illusion that our memories go further back than that.
(10) Before writing was invented, the experience of earlier generations, embodied in stories, myths, and moral precepts to guide behavior, was passed down verbally or, to a lesser extent, in pictures, carvings, and statues. Writing
(15) has made more precise and more extensive the transmission of such information and, in recent times, photography has sharpened our images of the immediate past. Even so, we have difficulty in contemplating steadily
(20) the march of history, from the beginnings of civilization to the present day, in such a way that we can truly experience the slow passage of time. Our minds are not built to deal comfortably with periods as long as hundreds or
(25) thousands of years.

Yet when we come to consider the origin of life, the time scales we must deal with make the whole span of human history seem but the blink of an eyelid. There is no simple way to
(30) adjust one's thinking to such vast stretches of time. The immensity of time passed is beyond our ready comprehension. One can only construct an impression of it from indirect and incomplete descriptions, just as a blind man
(35) laboriously builds up, by touch and sound, a picture of his immediate surroundings.

The customary way to provide a convenient framework for one's thoughts is to compare the age of the universe with the length of a
(40) single earthly day. Perhaps a better comparison, along the same lines, would be to equate the age of our earth with a single week. On such a scale the age of the universe, since the Big Bang, would be about two or three weeks. The oldest
(45) macroscopic fossils (those from the start of the Cambrian* Period) would have been alive just one day ago. Modern man would have appeared in the last 10 seconds and agriculture in the last one or two. Odysseus** would have lived only
(50) half a second before the present time.

Even this comparison hardly makes the longer time scale comprehensible to us. Another alternative is to draw a linear map of time, with the different events marked on
(55) it. The problem here is to make the line long enough to show our own experience on a reasonable scale, and yet short enough for convenient reproduction and examination. But perhaps the most vivid method is to compare time
(60) to the lines of print themselves. Let us make a 200-page book equal in length to the time from the start of the Cambrian to the present; that is, about 600 million years. Then each full page will represent roughly three million
(65) years, each line about ninety thousand years, and each letter or small space about fifteen hundred years. The origin of the earth would be about seven books ago and the origin of the universe (which has been dated only approxi-
(70) mately) ten or so books before that. Almost the whole of recorded human history would be covered by the last two or three letters of the book.

If you now turn back the pages of the book,
(75) slowly reading *one letter at a time*—remember, each letter is fifteen hundred years—then this may convey to you something of the immense

GO ON TO THE NEXT PAGE

stretches of time we shall have to consider. On this scale the span of your own life would be (80) less than the width of a comma.

Cambrian: the earliest period in the Paleozoic era, beginning about 600 million years ago.
**Odysseus*: the most famous Greek hero of antiquity; he is the hero of Homer's *The Odyssey*, which describes the aftermath of the Trojan War (ca. 1200 B.C.).

10. In line 13, the phrase "to a lesser extent" indicates that before the invention of writing, the wisdom of earlier generations was

(A) rejected by recent generations when portrayed in pictures, carvings, or statues
(B) passed down orally, or not at all
(C) transmitted more frequently by spoken word than by other means
(D) based on illusory memories that turned fact into fiction
(E) more strongly grounded in science than in the arts

11. The author most likely describes the impact of writing (lines 14–16) in order to

(A) illustrate the limitations of the human memory
(B) provide an example of how cultures transmit information
(C) indicate how primitive preliterate cultures were
(D) refute an opinion about the origin of human civilization
(E) explain the difference between historical facts and myth

12. The word "ready" in line 32 most nearly means

(A) set
(B) agreeable
(C) immediate
(D) apt
(E) willing

13. The analogy of the "blind man" (line 34) is presented primarily to show that

(A) humans are unable to comprehend long periods of time
(B) myths and legends fail to give an accurate picture of the past
(C) human history is only a fraction of the time since life began
(D) humans refuse to learn the lessons of the past
(E) long periods of time can only be understood indirectly

14. In lines 42–47, the references to the Big Bang and the Cambrian Period serve to

(A) illustrate that the age of the Earth can be understood using the time scale of a week
(B) suggest that agriculture was a relatively late development in human history
(C) argue that there are no existing fossils that predate the Cambrian period
(D) indicate that the Cambrian period lasted 600 million years
(E) argue that the customary framework for thinking about the age of the universe should be discarded permanently

GO ON TO THE NEXT PAGE ⟹

15. According to lines 53–58, one difficulty of using a linear representation of time is that

    (A) linear representations of time do not meet accepted scientific standards of accuracy

    (B) prehistoric eras overlap each other, making linear representation deceptive

    (C) a scale that allots enough space to show human experience clearly would make the map too long to copy and use conveniently

    (D) there are too many events to represent on a single line

    (E) our knowledge of pre-Cambrian time is insufficient to construct an accurate linear map

16. The author of this passage discusses several kinds of time scales primarily in order to illustrate the

    (A) difficulty of assigning precise dates to past events

    (B) variety of choices faced by scientists investigating the origin of life

    (C) evolution of efforts to comprehend the passage of history

    (D) immensity of time since life began on earth

    (E) development of the technology of communication

GO ON TO THE NEXT PAGE

Questions 17–24 refer to the following passage.

The following excerpt is from a speech delivered in 1873 by Susan B. Anthony, a leader in the women's rights movement of the 19th century.

Friends and fellow-citizens: I stand before you tonight under indictment for the alleged crime of having voted at the last Presidential election, without having a lawful right to vote.
(5) It shall be my work this evening to prove to you that in thus voting, I not only committed no crime, but, instead, simply exercised my citizen's rights, guaranteed to me and all United States citizens by the National Constitution,
(10) beyond the power of any State to deny.

The preamble of the Federal Constitution says: "We, the people of the United States, in order to form a more perfect union, establish justice, insure domestic tranquillity, provide
(15) for the common defense, promote the general welfare, and secure the blessings of liberty to ourselves and our posterity, do ordain and establish this Constitution for the United States of America."
(20) It was we, the people; not we, the white male citizens; nor yet we, the male citizens; but we, the whole people, who formed the Union. And we formed it, not to give the blessings of liberty, but to secure them; not to the half of our-
(25) selves and the half of our posterity, but to the whole people—women as well as men. And it is a downright mockery to talk to women of their enjoyment of the blessings of liberty while they are denied the use of the only
(30) means of securing them provided by this democratic-republican government—the ballot.

For any State to make sex a qualification that must ever result in the disfranchisement* of one entire half of the people is a violation of the
(35) supreme law of the land. By it the blessings of liberty are forever withheld from women and their female posterity. To them this government had no just powers derived from the consent of the governed. To them this government is not
(40) a democracy. It is not a republic. It is an odious aristocracy; a hateful oligarchy of sex; this oligarchy of sex, which makes father, brothers, husband, sons, the oligarchs over the mother and sisters, the wife and daughters of every
(45) household—which ordains all men sovereigns, all women subjects, carries dissension, discord and rebellion into every home of the nation. Webster, Worcester and Bouvier all define a citizen to be a person in the United States, entitled
(50) to vote and hold office.

The one question left to be settled now is: Are women persons? And I hardly believe any of our opponents will have the hardihood to say they are not. Being persons, then, women
(55) are citizens; and no State has a right to make any law, or to enforce any old law, that shall abridge their privileges or immunities. Hence, every discrimination against women in the constitutions and laws of the several States is
(60) today null and void, precisely as is every one against Negroes.

disfranchisement: to deprive of the right to vote

17. The author addresses her "fellow-citizens" (line 1) primarily in order to

(A) limit her intended audience to those who are citizens

(B) establish a spirit of good-natured cooperation

(C) irritate her audience, since they do not consider her a citizen

(D) introduce an important element of one of her main arguments

(E) make it clear that she intends to address only men

GO ON TO THE NEXT PAGE

18. In the first paragraph, Anthony states that her action in voting was

    (A) illegal, but morally justified

    (B) the result of her keen interest in national politics

    (C) legal, if the Constitution is interpreted correctly

    (D) an illustration of the need for a women's rights movement

    (E) illegal, but worthy of leniency

19. Which best captures the meaning of the word "promote" in line 15?

    (A) further

    (B) organize

    (C) publicize

    (D) commend

    (E) motivate

20. By saying "we, the people . . . the whole people, who formed the Union" (lines 20–22), Anthony means that

    (A) the founders of the nation conspired to deprive women of their rights

    (B) some male citizens are still being denied basic rights

    (C) the role of women in the founding of the nation is generally ignored

    (D) society is endangered when women are deprived of basic rights

    (E) all people deserve to enjoy the rights guaranteed by the Constitution

21. By "the half of our posterity" (line 25), Anthony means

    (A) the political legacy passed down from her era

    (B) future generations of male United States citizens

    (C) those who wish to enjoy the blessings of liberty

    (D) current and future opponents of the women's rights movement

    (E) future members of the democratic-republican government

22. In paragraph 4, lines 32–50, Anthony's argument rests mainly on the strategy of convincing her audience that

    (A) any state that denies women the vote undermines its status as a democracy

    (B) women deprived of the vote will eventually raise a violent rebellion

    (C) the nation will remain an aristocracy if the status of women does not change

    (D) women's rights issues should be debated in every home

    (E) even an aristocracy cannot survive without the consent of the governed

GO ON TO THE NEXT PAGE

23. The word "hardihood" in line 53 could best be replaced by

    (A) endurance
    (B) vitality
    (C) nerve
    (D) opportunity
    (E) stupidity

24. When Anthony warns that "no State . . . shall abridge their privileges" (lines 55–57), she means that

    (A) women should be allowed to live a life of privilege
    (B) women on trial cannot be forced to give up their immunity
    (C) every state should repeal its outdated laws
    (D) governments may not deprive citizens of their rights
    (E) the rights granted to women must be decided by the people, not the state

IF YOU FINISH BEFORE TIME IS CALLED, YOU MAY CHECK YOUR WORK ON THIS SECTION ONLY. DO NOT TURN TO ANY OTHER SECTION IN THE TEST.

STOP

SECTION 5

Time—25 Minutes
18 Questions

Directions: For this section, solve each problem and decide which is the best of the choices given. Fill in the corresponding oval on the answer sheet. You may use any available space for scratchwork.

Notes:

(1) Calculator use is permitted.

(2) All numbers used are real numbers.

(3) Figures are provided for some problems. All figures are drawn to scale and lie in a plane UNLESS otherwise indicated.

(4) Unless otherwise specified, the domain of any function f is assumed to be the set of all real numbers x for which $f(x)$ is a real number.

Information

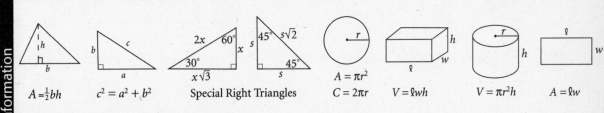

$A = \frac{1}{2}bh$ $c^2 = a^2 + b^2$ Special Right Triangles $A = \pi r^2$ $C = 2\pi r$ $V = \ell wh$ $V = \pi r^2 h$ $A = \ell w$

The sum of the degree measures of the angles in a triangle is 180.
The number of degrees of arc in a circle is 360.
A straight angle has a degree measure of 180.

1. If $100 + x = 100$, then $x =$

   (A) −100
   (B) −10
   (C) 0
   (D) 10
   (E) 100

2. Set X is the set of all odd numbers, and set Y is the set of all negative numbers. Which of the following represents the intersection of X and Y?

   (A) all odd numbers
   (B) all negative odd numbers
   (C) all negative numbers
   (D) all real numbers
   (E) all positive numbers

GO ON TO THE NEXT PAGE

3. If $x < y < 0$, which of the following is greater than $\frac{y}{x}$?

   (A) 0

   (B) $\frac{x}{y}$

   (C) $\frac{-x}{y}$

   (D) $\frac{-y}{x}$

   (E) $\frac{y}{2x}$

5. If $f(x) = \frac{(3x^2 - 9)}{(x + 1)}$, what is the value of $f(3)$?

   (A) $\frac{3}{2}$

   (B) 3

   (C) $\frac{9}{2}$

   (D) 6

   (E) 9

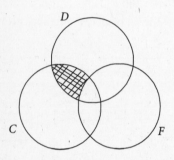

4. In the figure above, circular region D represents households with dogs, circular region C represents households with cats, and circular region F represents households with fish. What does the crosshatched region represent?

   (A) households with dogs, but no cats or fish

   (B) households with cats and fish, but no dogs

   (C) households with dogs, cats, and fish

   (D) households with dogs and cats, but no fish

   (E) households with dogs and fish, some of which may have cats

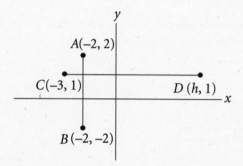

6. In the figure above, the length of CD is twice the length of AB. What is the value of h?

   (A) 2

   (B) 3

   (C) 4

   (D) 5

   (E) 6

GO ON TO THE NEXT PAGE

7. The percent decrease from 12 to 9 is equal to the percent decrease from 40 to what number?

   (A) 3
   (B) 10
   (C) 25
   (D) 30
   (E) 36

8. For a group of x people, Joe ordered 5 pizza pies, each of which was cut into 12 slices. Each person was originally supposed to have an equal number of slices. However, 4 people did not want any pizza, so when the pizza was distributed among the remaining people, each of them received 4 more slices. Which of the following equations could be used to find x?

   (A) $x^2 - 4x - 60 = 0$
   (B) $x^2 - 4x + 60 = 0$
   (C) $x^2 + 4x - 60 = 0$
   (D) $x^2 + 4x + 60 = 0$
   (E) $x^2 - 16x - 240 = 0$

GO ON TO THE NEXT PAGE

Directions: For student-produced response questions 9–18, use the grids at the bottom of the answer sheet page on which you have answered questions 1–8.

Each of the remaining ten questions requires you to solve the problem and enter your answer by marking the ovals in the special grid, as shown in the example below. You may use any available space for scratchwork.

Answer: 1.25 or $\frac{5}{4}$ or 5/4

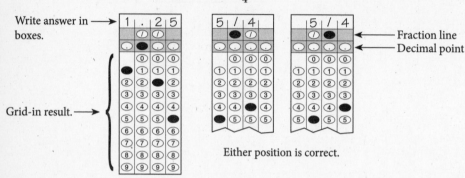

Either position is correct.

- It is recommended, though not required, that you write your answer in the boxes at the top of the columns. However, you will receive credit only for darkening the ovals correctly.

- Grid only one answer to a question, even though some problems have more than one correct answer.

- Darken no more than one oval in a column.

- No answers are negative.

- Mixed numbers cannot be gridded. For example: the number $1\frac{1}{4}$ must be gridded as 1.25 or 5/4.

(If ⌈1⌉1⌈/⌉4⌉ is gridded, it will be interpreted as $\frac{11}{4}$ not $1\frac{1}{4}$.)

- Decimal Accuracy: Decimal answers must be entered as accurately as possible. For example, if you obtain an answer such as 0.1666…, you should record the result as .166 or .167. **Less accurate values such as .16 or .17 are not acceptable.**

Acceptable ways to grid $\frac{1}{6}$ = .1666…

GO ON TO THE NEXT PAGE ▷

9. If $A = 2.54$ and $20B = A$, what is the value of B?

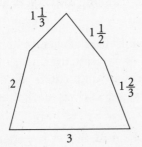

10. What is the perimeter of the figure shown above?

11. If $\dfrac{h}{3}$ and $\dfrac{h}{4}$ are integers, and if $75 < h < 100$, what is one possible value of h?

12. A retailer buys 16 shirts at $4.50 each, and she sells all 16 shirts for $6.75 each. If the retailer purchases more of these shirts at $4.50 each, what is the greatest number of these shirts that she can buy with the profit she made on the 16 shirts?

13. Lines ℓ and m intersect at a point to form four angles. If one of the angles formed is 15 times as large as an adjacent angle, what is the measure, in degrees, of the smaller angle?

14. If $x = -4$ when $x^2 + 2xr + r^2 = 0$, what is the value of r?

15. Let $n \text{✶} = n^2 - n$ for all positive numbers n. What is the value of $\dfrac{1}{4}\text{✶} - \dfrac{1}{2}\text{✶}$?

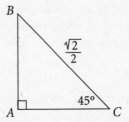

16. What is the area of $\triangle ABC$ shown above?

17. If x is a factor of 8,100 and if x is an odd integer, what is the greatest possible value of x?

18. In a certain class, $\dfrac{1}{2}$ of the male students and $\dfrac{2}{3}$ of the female students speak French. If there are $\dfrac{3}{4}$ as many girls as boys in the class, what fraction of the entire class speaks French?

IF YOU FINISH BEFORE TIME IS CALLED, YOU MAY CHECK YOUR WORK ON THIS SECTION ONLY. DO NOT TURN TO ANY OTHER SECTION IN THE TEST.

STOP

SECTION 6

Time—25 Minutes
35 Questions

Directions: For each question in this section, select the best answer from among the choices given and fill in the corresponding oval on the answer sheet.

The following sentences test correctness and effectiveness of expression. Part of each sentence or the entire sentence is underlined; beneath each sentence are five ways of phrasing the underlined material. Choice (A) repeats the original phrasing; the other four choices are different. If you think the original phrasing produces a better sentence than any of the alternatives, select choice (A); if not, select one of the other choices.

In making your selection, follow the requirements of standard written English; that is, pay attention to grammar, choice of words, sentence construction, and punctuation. Your selection should result in the most effective sentence—clear and precise, without awkwardness or ambiguity.

EXAMPLE:

Every apple in the baskets <u>are ripe and labeled according to the date it was picked</u>.

ANSWER:
Ⓐ ● Ⓒ Ⓓ Ⓔ

(A) are ripe and labeled according to the date it was picked
(B) is ripe and labeled according to the date it was picked
(C) are ripe and labeled according to the date they were picked
(D) is ripe and labeled according to the date they were picked
(E) are ripe and labeled as to the date it was picked

---

1. <u>Arranged as an event for funding a new wing for the art museum</u>, the museum's Board of Directors organized a fund-raiser for the construction of one.

    (A) Arranged as an event for funding a new wing for the art museum

    (B) Having been arranged as an event to fund a new wing for the art museum

    (C) A new wing for the art museum needed an event for funding

    (D) Although an event for funding a new wing for the art museum

    (E) Realizing that the art museum needed funding for a new wing

2. One of the most popular broadcasters on the evening news is a retired <u>politician; another one with nearly</u> as many fans is an executive recently retired from the film industry.

    (A) politician; another one with nearly

    (B) politician; near one with

    (C) politician, the one with nearly

    (D) politician, and also the one with near

    (E) politician; although the one with nearly

GO ON TO THE NEXT PAGE ⇨

3. Although the architects created a new earthquake-proof structural design, they <u>had refused to patent nor otherwise benefiting</u> from the design plans.

   (A) had refused to patent nor otherwise benefiting

   (B) had refused to patent or otherwise benefit

   (C) refused to patent or otherwise benefit

   (D) refuse to patent or otherwise benefit

   (E) refused to patent or otherwise benefiting

4. Oscar Wilde was <u>almost as brilliant a novelist as he was at writing plays</u>.

   (A) almost as brilliant a novelist as he was at writing plays

   (B) almost brilliant at writing novels and plays

   (C) almost equally brilliant, whether a novelist or a playwright

   (D) almost as brilliant a novelist as he was a playwright

   (E) a brilliant novelist, with almost as much brilliance as a playwright

5. Examining the sale offers in the catalogue, <u>the phrases</u> "while supplies last" and "get it while it's hot" are designed to encourage consumers to order the products immediately.

   (A) the phrases

   (B) the slogans

   (C) one sees that the phrases

   (D) although one saw the phrases

   (E) one may have noticed phrases

6. <u>In professional soccer, players kick the ball sharply and accurately; however, in other sports their technique is not quite so effective.</u>

   (A) In professional soccer, players kick the ball sharply and accurately; however, in other sports their technique is not quite so effective.

   (B) Most professional soccer players kick the ball sharply and accurately, however in other sports their technique is not quite so effective.

   (C) Although in other sports their technique is not quite so effective, most professional soccer players, however, kick the ball sharply and accurately.

   (D) Most professional soccer players which kick the ball sharply and accurately do not have such effective technique in other sports.

   (E) Most professional soccer players kick the ball sharply and accurately and in other sports their technique is not so effective.

7. The changing color of autumn leaves has a unique fascination for those people <u>which have an understanding of life cycles in them</u>.

   (A) which have an understanding of life cycles in them

   (B) who see the changes as part of the life cycles

   (C) which have seen life cycles in them

   (D) who understand that they have life cycles

   (E) who see about them the life cycles

GO ON TO THE NEXT PAGE

8. <u>The traffic rules were ignored by each of us,</u>
<u>failing to appreciate their role in ensuring</u>
<u>safety.</u>

   (A) The traffic rules were ignored by each
   of us, failing to appreciate their role in
   ensuring safety.

   (B) Each of us ignored the traffic rules
   because we failed to appreciate their role
   in ensuring safety.

   (C) Traffic rules, ignored by each of us, fail
   to appreciate their role in ensuring safety.

   (D) Failing to appreciate their role in ensuring safety, traffic rules were ignored by
   each of us.

   (E) Traffic rules ignored by each of us, failing to appreciate their role in ensuring
   safety.

9. The meaning of his words was even more
elusive in his own country than <u>either Europe</u>
<u>or Latin America.</u>

   (A) either Europe or Latin America
   (B) either Europe or in Latin America
   (C) either in Europe or Latin America
   (D) in either Europe or in Latin America
   (E) in either Europe or Latin America

10. It was primarily when I visited the seashore
that I felt nostalgic for my childhood home,
<u>growing up on a small island</u>.

   (A) growing up on a small island
   (B) as I had grown up on a small island
   (C) as on a small island I grow up
   (D) which is on a small island
   (E) on a small island growing up

11. By 1975, 12 percent of the households
with televisions were cable <u>subscribers and</u>
<u>established hundreds of cable stations</u>.

   (A) subscribers and established hundreds of
   cable stations

   (B) subscribers, and hundreds of cable stations had been established

   (C) subscribers, and there were established
   hundreds of cable stations

   (D) subscribers plus hundreds of cable stations established

   (E) subscribers and hundreds of cable
   stations

GO ON TO THE NEXT PAGE

Directions: The following sentences test your ability to recognize grammar and usage errors. Each sentence contains either a single error or no error at all. No sentence contains more than one error. The error, if there is one, is underlined and lettered. If the sentence contains an error, select the one underlined part that must be changed to make the sentence correct. If the sentence is correct, select choice (E). In choosing answers, follow the requirements of standard written English.

EXAMPLE:

<u>Whenever</u> one is driving late at night, <u>you</u> must take extra precautions <u>against</u>
  A   B   C

falling asleep <u>at the wheel</u>. <u>No error</u>
              D   E

(A) ● (C) (D) (E)

---

12. <u>As Picasso</u> matured as a painter, his <u>use of</u> shapes
    A   B

    <u>became</u> bolder, more abstract, and
    C

    <u>they can astonish people.</u> <u>No error</u>
                D   E

13. The chemical plant is already <u>such a</u> danger that
                            A

    <u>it became</u> imperative <u>to find other ways</u> of
      B   C

    developing effective pesticides <u>for</u> use in gardens.
                                   D

    <u>No error</u>
      E

14. John and Sue, <u>who were tired</u> after
               A

    <u>traveling</u>, brought <u>their</u> parents
      B   C

    <u>their</u> tickets to the show. <u>No error</u>
    D   E

15. The <u>lyric</u> novels of Virginia Woolf <u>which eerily</u>
       A   B

    <u>hint at</u> the despair <u>of her</u> later life. <u>No error</u>
    C   D   E

16. With <u>more than</u> 150 associated countries, the
         A

    United Nations owes <u>their</u> name <u>to a</u> worldwide
                      B   C

    membership <u>that oversees</u> international treaties
                    D

    and human rights. <u>No error</u>
                    E

17. <u>Walking along</u> the empty boardwalk, I <u>could hear</u>
        A   B

    the lapping of water against the docks as <u>well as</u>
                                       C

    the sound of Jake and Kelsey talking softly

    <u>as he approached</u>. <u>No error</u>
          D   E

18. <u>At the stoplight</u>, Hiam, <u>impatient</u> to be home on
      A   B

    that <u>rainy</u> night, drummed his fingers
         C

    <u>at the wheel</u>. <u>No error</u>
      D   E

GO ON TO THE NEXT PAGE ⟩

19. If you <u>surround</u> the roots of your new rose plant
         A

    with a <u>generously</u> mixture of mulch and
           B

    compost, you <u>will provide</u> the roots the space to
              C

    <u>grow</u> healthily. <u>No error</u>
     D   E

20. Of all <u>her many</u> skills, Kelly is <u>more</u> proud
          A   B

    <u>of her ability</u> to mediate <u>disputes</u>. <u>No error</u>
       C   D   E

21. We <u>had drove</u> no more than fifty yards <u>from our</u>
        A   B

    parking spot when it <u>became apparent</u> that Shelly
                 C

    <u>had left</u> her purse behind at the steakhouse.
     D

    <u>No error</u>
     E

22. <u>Most of</u> the small country stores in the United
      A

    States <u>are</u> in isolated, thinly populated areas where
        B

    there are <u>hardly no</u> supermarkets <u>within easy</u>
           C   D

    driving distance. <u>No error</u>
            E

23. <u>Working with</u> the ease and skill of a true
       A

    professional, Lehrmann quickly outlined a <u>sketch</u>
                             B

    of the young <u>but</u> experienced skater who was
            C

    <u>posing for</u> her. <u>No error</u>
      D   E

24. Many historians have <u>written about</u> the Roosevelt
                    A

    family, but <u>never before</u> <u>has</u> the characters of the
            B   C

    family members been <u>so skillfully</u> evaluated.
                    D

    <u>No error</u>
     E

25. <u>No matter</u> how <u>attentive</u> Mark applies himself to
      A   B

    his studies, he <u>never seems</u> to get the grades he
                 C

    <u>needs</u> to make the Dean's List. <u>No error</u>
     D   E

26. There has always been a <u>great deal of</u> antipathy
                    A

    between <u>Sarah and I</u> <u>because we</u> have opposing
            B   C

    opinions <u>about which</u> we are very outspoken.
            D

    <u>No error</u>
     E

27. The extraordinary breath control <u>used by</u> students
                           A

    of meditation to control stress and pain levels <u>is</u> a
                            B

    <u>benefit</u> to both <u>their</u> physical and mental well-
     C   D

    being. <u>No error</u>
          E

GO ON TO THE NEXT PAGE ▷

28. A scientist at the institute <u>indicated that</u> an
                                      A
<u>unusually high</u> percentage of <u>their</u> funding <u>comes</u>
       B   C   D
from money donated to it by private

philanthropists. <u>No error</u>
                     E

29. The candidate, John Kallan, is of an <u>undetermined</u>
                                              A
age, <u>and</u> he <u>uses</u> this ambiguity <u>to his benefit</u>.
       B   C   D
<u>No error</u>
   E

GO ON TO THE NEXT PAGE

Directions: The following passage is an early draft of an essay. Some parts of the passage need to be rewritten.

Read the passage and select the best answer for each question that follows. Some questions are about particular sentences or parts of sentences and ask you to improve sentence structure or word choice. Other questions ask you to consider organization and development. In choosing answers, follow the conventions of standard written English.

Questions 30–35 are based on the following passage.

(1) There is a duality in ballet that most people don't see. (2) Most often, it is seen only as beautifully graceful.

(3) First, ballet is tough physically. (4) Because the human body is not designed for ballet. (5) Dancers must perform steps that come from ballet's five fundamental positions in which dancers rotate their hips and legs unnaturally. (6) This makes dancers walk funny (you can always recognize dancers by the way they walk with their feet turning out instead of facing forward). (7) Unfortunately, it also often results in permanent injury.

(8) Ballet companies' financial struggles creating fierce competition between dancers for a place in a professional company. (9) Dancers often live below the poverty line, particularly as most companies pay by the dance season, which can last for as little as twenty weeks out of the year, instead of by year. (10) In general, most people who spend years training for their jobs stay in the same career until they retire at 65. (11) Not being the case with dancers, as ballet careers hardly ever extend beyond the mid-thirties, even though the dancers have trained since they were 5 years old. (12) Few retired dancers continue as ballet teachers or choreographers. (13) The vast majority find themselves unemployed in their mid-thirties.

30. Which of the following sentences is best inserted at the end of the first paragraph, after sentence 2?

(A) However, ballet is grueling, painful, and competitive.

(B) Yet few people really appreciate that fact.

(C) Missing, however, the extreme athleticism it requires.

(D) Many types of dance share this quality.

(E) Not every ballet dancer, however, dances for this reason.

31. Which of the following is the best way to revise the underlined portions of sentences 4 and 5 (reproduced below) in order to combine the sentences?

Because the human body is not designed for ballet. Dancers must perform steps that come from ballet's five fundamental positions in which dancers rotate their hips and legs unnaturally.

(A) for ballet, it is difficult for dancers to perform

(B) for ballet; dancers must perform

(C) for ballet, making it difficult for dancers to perform

(D) for ballet, their difficulty in performing

(E) for ballet; therefore, dancers must perform

GO ON TO THE NEXT PAGE

32. Which is the best sentence to insert before sentence 8 to begin the third paragraph?

   (A) Second, ballet is tough financially.

   (B) Secondly, ballet is competitive.

   (C) Furthermore, ballet dancers struggle financially.

   (D) In addition, ballet companies are difficult employers.

   (E) This is not the worst consequence, however.

33. In context, which is the best version of the underlined portion of sentence 8 (reproduced below)?

   Ballet companies' financial struggles creating fierce competition between dancers for a place in a professional company.

   (A) (As it is now)

   (B) compiling to create fiercely

   (C) created their fierce competition

   (D) create fierce competition

   (E) had created a fierce competition

34. In context, which is the best version of the underlined portion of sentence 11 (reproduced below)?

   Not being the case with dancers, as ballet careers hardly ever extend beyond the mid-thirties, even though the dancers have trained since they were 5 years old.

   (A) (As it is now)

   (B) Which is not true of

   (C) That model does not apply to

   (D) Or not so for

   (E) And so also for

35. Which of the following is the best way to combine sentences 12 and 13 (reproduced below)?

   Few retired dancers continue as ballet teachers or choreographers. The vast majority find themselves unemployed in their mid-thirties.

   (A) Although a few retired dancers continue as ballet teachers or choreographers, and the vast majority find themselves unemployed in their mid-thirties.

   (B) A few retired dancers continue as ballet teachers or choreographers, but the vast majority find themselves unemployed in their mid-thirties.

   (C) However, few retired dancers continued as ballet teachers or choreographers although the vast majority unemployed in their mid-thirties.

   (D) A few retired dancers continue as ballet teachers or choreographers, the vast majority find themselves unemployed in their mid-thirties.

   (E) Few retired dancers continued as ballet teachers or choreographers vastly the majority are found unemployed in their mid-thirties.

IF YOU FINISH BEFORE TIME IS CALLED, YOU MAY CHECK YOUR WORK ON THIS SECTION ONLY. DO NOT TURN TO ANY OTHER SECTION IN THE TEST.

 STOP

SECTION 7
Time—20 Minutes
19 Questions

Directions: For each of the following questions, choose the best answer and darken the corresponding oval on the answer sheet.

Each sentence below has one or two blanks, each blank indicating that something has been omitted. Beneath the sentence are five words or sets of words labeled (A) through (E). Choose the word or set of words that, when inserted in the sentence, best fits the meaning of the sentence as a whole.

EXAMPLE:

Today's small, portable computers contrast markedly with the earliest electronic computers, which were -------.

(A) effective
(B) invented
(C) useful
(D) destructive
(E) enormous

1. The prisoner was ------- even though he presented evidence clearly proving that he was nowhere near the scene of the crime.

   (A) abandoned
   (B) indicted
   (C) exculpated
   (D) exhumed
   (E) rescinded

2. Many biologists are critical of the film's ------- premise that dinosaurs might one day return.

   (A) scientific
   (B) onerous
   (C) speculative
   (D) unwitting
   (E) ambiguous

3. It is ------- that people so capable of treachery and brutality should also exhibit such a tremendous capacity for heroism.

   (A) unfortunate
   (B) explicable
   (C) paradoxical
   (D) distressing
   (E) appalling

4. To ------- the seasonal migration of caribou, engineers ------- the trans-Alaska pipeline in over 500 locations to allow large animals access through the pipeline corridor.

   (A) banish . . . buried
   (B) facilitate . . . elevated
   (C) admire . . . razed
   (D) prevent . . . erected
   (E) enable . . . delivered

GO ON TO THE NEXT PAGE

5. Most people today think of licorice as candy;
    however, the ------- properties of the licorice
    root were once used to treat coughs, digestive
    problems, and insomnia.

    (A) somnolent
    (B) basic
    (C) sweet
    (D) indelible
    (E) medicinal

6. To ------- free education for children
    with special needs, parents have had
    to ------- legislation guaranteeing services
    and programs targeted to those children.

    (A) ensure . . . demand
    (B) prevent . . . pass
    (C) assert . . . console
    (D) alleviate . . . request
    (E) provide . . . veto

GO ON TO THE NEXT PAGE

> **Directions:** The passages below are followed by questions based on their content; questions following a pair of related passages may also be based on the relationship between the paired passages. Answer the questions on the basis of what is <u>stated</u> or <u>implied</u> in the passages and in any introductory material that may be provided.

Questions 7–19 refer to the following passages.

The controversy over the authorship of Shakespeare's plays began in the 18th century and continues to this day. Here, the author of Passage 1 embraces the proposal that Francis Bacon actually wrote the plays, while the author of Passage 2 defends the traditional attribution to Shakespeare himself.

Passage 1

    Anyone with more than a superficial knowledge of Shakespeare's plays must necessarily entertain some doubt concerning their true authorship. Can scholars honestly accept the
(5) idea that such masterworks were written by a shadowy actor with limited formal education and a social position that can most charitably be called "humble"? Obviously, the author of the plays must have traveled widely, yet there is
(10) no record that Shakespeare ever left his native England. Even more obviously, the real author had to have intimate knowledge of life within royal courts and palaces, yet Shakespeare was a commoner, with little firsthand experi-
(15) ence of the aristocracy. No, common sense tells us that the plays must have been written by someone with substantial expertise in the law, the sciences, classics, foreign languages, and the fine arts—someone, in other words,
(20) like Shakespeare's eminent contemporary, Sir Francis Bacon.

    The first person to suggest that Bacon was the actual author of the plays was Reverend James Wilmot. Writing in 1785, Wilmot
(25) argued that someone of Shakespeare's educational background could hardly have produced works of such erudition and insight. But a figure like Bacon, a scientist and polymath* of

legendary stature, would certainly have known
(30) about, for instance, the circulation of the blood as alluded to in *Coriolanus*. And as an aristocrat, Bacon would have possessed the familiarity with court life required to produce *Love's Labour's Lost*.

(35)   Delia Bacon (no relation to Sir Francis) was next to make the case for Francis Bacon's authorship. In 1856, in collaboration with Nathaniel Hawthorne, she insisted that it was ridiculous to look for the creator of *Hamlet*
(40) among "that dirty, doggish group of players, who come into the scene [of the play *Hamlet*] summoned like a pack of hounds to his service." Ultimately, she concluded that the plays were actually composed by a committee consisting of
(45) Bacon, Edmund Spenser, Walter Raleigh, and several others.

    Still, some might wonder why Bacon, if indeed the plays were wholly or partly his work, would not put his own name on them.
(50) But consider the political climate of England in Elizabethan times. Given that it would have been politically and personally damaging for a man of Bacon's position to associate himself with such controversial plays, it is quite under-
(55) standable that Bacon would hire a lowly actor to take the credit—and the consequences.

    But perhaps the most convincing evidence of all comes from the postscript of a 1624 letter sent to Bacon by Sir Tobie Matthew. "The
(60) most prodigious wit that I ever knew . . . is your lordship's name," Matthew wrote, "though he be known by another." That name, of course, was William Shakespeare.

polymath—a person of wide and varied learning

GO ON TO THE NEXT PAGE ▷

Passage 2

Over the years, there have been an astonish-
(65) ing number of persons put forth as the "true
author" of Shakespeare's plays. Some critics
have even gone so far as to claim that only a
"committee" could have possessed the abundance of talent and energy necessary to produce
(70) Shakespeare's thirty-seven plays. Among the
individual figures most seriously promoted
as "the real Shakespeare" is Sir Francis Bacon.
Apparently, the fact that Bacon wrote most of
his own work in academic Latin does nothing to
(75) deter those who would crown him the premier
stylist in the English language.

Although the entire controversy reeks of
scholarly gamesplaying, the issue underlying
it is worth considering: how could an unedu-
(80) cated actor create such exquisite works? But
the answer to that is easy. Shakespeare's dramatic gifts had little to do with encyclopedic
knowledge, complex ideas, or a fluency with
great systems of thought. Rather, Shakespeare's
(85) genius was one of common sense and perceptive intuition—a genius that grows not out of
book-learning, but out of a deep understanding
of human nature and a keen grasp of basic emotions, passions, and jealousies.

(90)   One of the most common arguments
advanced by skeptics is that the degree of
familiarity with the law exhibited in a *Hamlet*
or a *Merchant of Venice* can only have been
achieved by a lawyer or other man of affairs.
(95) The grasp of law evidenced in these plays, however, is not a detailed knowledge of formal law,
but a more general understanding of so-called
"country law." Shakespeare was a landowner —
an extraordinary achievement in itself for an
(100) ill-paid Elizabethan actor—and so would have
been knowledgeable about legal matters related
to the buying, selling, and renting of real estate.
Evidence of such a common understanding of
land regulations can be found, for instance, in
(105) the gravedigging scene of *Hamlet*.

So no elaborate theories of intrigue and
secret identity are necessary to explain the
accomplishment of William Shakespeare.
Scholars who have made a career of ferreting
(110) out "alternative bards" may be reluctant to
admit it, but literary genius can flower in any
socioeconomic bracket. Shakespeare, in short,
was Shakespeare—an observation that one
would have thought was obvious to everyone.

7. In line 3, "entertain" most nearly means

    (A) amuse
    (B) harbor
    (C) occupy
    (D) cherish
    (E) engage

8. In Passage 1, the author draws attention to
   Shakespeare's social standing as a "commoner"
   (line 14) in order to cast doubt on the
   Elizabethan actor's

    (A) aptitude for writing poetically
    (B) knowledge of foreign places and habits
    (C) ability to support himself by playwriting
    (D) familiarity with life among persons of
        high rank
    (E) understanding of the problems of
        government

GO ON TO THE NEXT PAGE

9. *Coriolanus* and *Love's Labour's Lost* are mentioned in lines 31–34, as examples of works that

    (A) only Francis Bacon could have written
    (B) exhibit a deep understanding of human nature
    (C) resemble works written by Francis Bacon under his own name
    (D) portray a broad spectrum of Elizabethan society
    (E) reveal expertise more likely held by Bacon than Shakespeare

10. The quotation from Delia Bacon (lines 40–42) conveys a sense of

    (A) disdain for the disreputable vulgarity of Elizabethan actors
    (B) resentment at the way Shakespeare's characters were portrayed
    (C) regret that conditions for Elizabethan actors were not better
    (D) doubt that Shakespeare could actually have created such unsavory characters
    (E) disappointment at the incompetence of Elizabethan actors

11. The author of Passage 1 maintains that Bacon did not put his own name on the plays attributed to Shakespeare because he

    (A) regarded writing as an unsuitable occupation for an aristocrat
    (B) wished to protect himself from the effects of controversy
    (C) preferred being known as a scientist and politician rather than as a writer
    (D) did not want to associate himself with lowly actors
    (E) sought to avoid the attention that fame brings

12. In the first paragraph of Passage 2, the author calls into question Bacon's likely ability to

    (A) write in a language with which he was unfamiliar
    (B) make the transition between scientific writing and playwriting
    (C) write in the linguistic style used in the plays
    (D) cooperate with other members of a committee
    (E) single-handedly create 37 plays

13. The word "premier" in line 75 most nearly means

    (A) earliest
    (B) influential
    (C) inaugural
    (D) greatest
    (E) original

GO ON TO THE NEXT PAGE

14. In line 82, the word "encyclopedic" most nearly means

    (A) technical
    (B) comprehensive
    (C) abridged
    (D) disciplined
    (E) specialized

15. The author of Passage 2 cites Shakespeare's status as a landowner in order to

    (A) prove that Shakespeare was a success as a playwright
    (B) refute the claim that Shakespeare had little knowledge of aristocratic life
    (C) prove that Shakespeare didn't depend solely on acting for his living
    (D) dispute the notion that Shakespeare was a commoner
    (E) account for Shakespeare's apparent knowledge of the law

16. In Passage 2, lines 109–112, the author maintains that literary genius

    (A) is not dependent on a writer's external circumstances
    (B) must be based on an inborn comprehension of human nature
    (C) is enhanced by the suffering that poverty brings
    (D) frequently goes unrecognized among those of modest means and position
    (E) can be stifled by too much book-learning and academic training

17. The author of Passage 2 would probably respond to the speculation in paragraph 4 of Passage 1 by pointing out that

    (A) Shakespeare's plays would not have seemed particularly controversial to Elizabethan audiences
    (B) the extent and range of Bacon's learning have been generally exaggerated
    (C) such scenarios are farfetched and unnecessary if one correctly understands Shakespeare's genius
    (D) Bacon would not have had the knowledge of the lower classes required to produce the plays
    (E) the claim implies that Shakespeare was disreputable when in fact he was a respectable landowner

GO ON TO THE NEXT PAGE

18. The author of Passage 1 would probably respond to the skepticism expressed in Passage 2, lines 73–76, by making which of the following statements?

   (A) The similarities between English and Latin make it plausible that one person could write well in both languages.

   (B) Plays written in Latin would not have been likely to attract a wide audience in Elizabethan England.

   (C) The premier stylist in the English language is more likely to have been an eminent scholar than an uneducated actor.

   (D) Writing the plays in Latin would have shielded Bacon from much of the political damage he wanted to avoid.

   (E) The style of the plays is notable mostly for the clarity of thought behind the lines rather than their musicality or beauty.

19. In line 113, "observation" most nearly means

   (A) inspection
   (B) measurement
   (C) research
   (D) comment
   (E) memorandum

IF YOU FINISH BEFORE TIME IS CALLED, YOU MAY CHECK YOUR WORK ON THIS SECTION ONLY. DO NOT TURN TO ANY OTHER SECTION IN THE TEST.

STOP

SECTION 8

Time—20 Minutes

16 Questions

Directions: For this section, solve each problem and decide which is the best of the choices given. Fill in the corresponding oval on the answer sheet. You may use any available space for scratchwork.

Notes:

(1) Calculator use is permitted.

(2) All numbers used are real numbers.

(3) Figures are provided for some problems. All figures are drawn to scale and lie in a plane UNLESS otherwise indicated.

(4) Unless otherwise specified, the domain of any function f is assumed to be the set of all real numbers x for which $f(x)$ is a real number.

Information

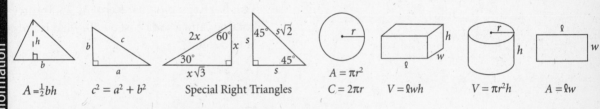

$A = \frac{1}{2}bh$ $c^2 = a^2 + b^2$ Special Right Triangles $A = \pi r^2$ $V = \ell wh$ $V = \pi r^2 h$ $A = \ell w$

$C = 2\pi r$

The sum of the degree measures of the angles in a triangle is 180.
The number of degrees of arc in a circle is 360.
A straight angle has a degree measure of 180.

---

1. If $p = -2$ and $q = 3$, then $p^3 q^2 + p^2 q =$

   (A) −84

   (B) −60

   (C)   36

   (D)   60

   (E)   84

Note: Figure not drawn to scale.

2. In the figure above, B is the midpoint of AC, and D is the midpoint of CE. If $AB = 5$ and $BD = 8$, what is the length of DE?

   (A) 3

   (B) 4

   (C) 5

   (D) 6

   (E) 8

GO ON TO THE NEXT PAGE

N	P
2	7
4	13
6	19
8	25

3. Which of the following equations describes the relationship of each pair of numbers (N, P) in the table above?

(A) $P = N + 5$

(B) $P = 2N + 3$

(C) $P = 2N + 5$

(D) $P = 3N + 1$

(E) $P = 3N - 1$

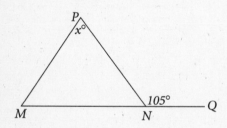

Note: Figure not drawn to scale.

4. In the figure above, MQ is a straight line. If PM = PN, what is the value of x?

(A) 30

(B) 45

(C) 60

(D) 75

(E) 90

5. Marty has exactly 5 blue pens, 6 black pens, and 4 red pens in his knapsack. If he pulls out one pen at random from his knapsack, what is the probability that the pen is either red or black?

(A) $\frac{1}{5}$

(B)

(C) $\frac{1}{2}$

(D) $\frac{2}{3}$

(E)

6. Two hot dogs and a soda cost $3.25. If three hot dogs and a soda cost $4.50, what is the cost of two sodas?

(A) $0.75

(B) $1.25

(C) $1.50

(D) $2.50

(E) $3.00

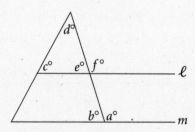

7. In the figure above, if $\ell \parallel m$, which of the following must be equal to a?

(A) $b + c$

(B) $b + e$

(C) $c + d$

(D) $d + e$

(E) $d + f$

GO ON TO THE NEXT PAGE

8. A certain phone call costs 75 cents for the first three minutes plus 15 cents for each additional minute. If the call lasted x minutes and x is an integer greater than 3, which of the following expresses the cost of the call, in dollars?

    (A) $0.75(3) + 0.15x$

    (B) $0.75(3) + 0.15(x + 3)$

    (C) $0.75 + 0.15(3 - x)$

    (D) $0.75 + 0.15(x - 3)$

    (E) $0.75 + 0.15x$

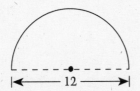

9. The figure above shows a piece of wire in the shape of a semicircle. If the piece of wire is bent to form a circle without any of the wire overlapping, what is the area of the circle?

    (A) 6π

    (B) 9π

    (C) 12π

    (D) 18π

    (E) 36π

10. If $a^2 - a = 72$, and b and n are integers such that $b^n = a$, which of the following CANNOT be a value for b?

    (A) -8

    (B) -2

    (C) 2

    (D) 3

    (E) 9

11. In the standard xy-coordinate plane, the midpoint of $\overline{XY}$ is (3, 4). If the coordinates of point X are (0, 2), what are the coordinates of point Y?

    (A) (3, 2)

    (B) (4, 3)

    (C) (6, 6)

    (D) (7, 6)

    (E) (8, 2)

12. If $4\sqrt{2x} - 2 = 16$, then $x =$

    (A) -4

    (B) -2

    (C) 8

    (D) $\dfrac{81}{8}$

    (E) $8\dfrac{1}{4}$

GO ON TO THE NEXT PAGE

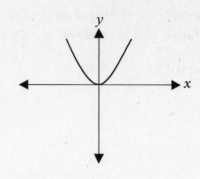

Note: Figure not drawn to scale.

13. If the above graph is $y = 3x^2$, which of the following is the graph of $y = -3x^2$?

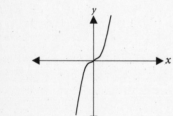

(A)

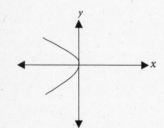

(B)

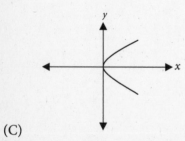

(C)

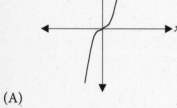

(D)

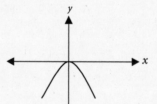

(E)

GO ON TO THE NEXT PAGE

14. What was the initial weight, in pounds, of a person who gained p pounds, then lost 8 pounds, and now weighs w pounds?

   (A) $w + p + 8$
   (B) $w + p - 8$
   (C) $w - p + 8$
   (D) $w - p - 8$
   (E) $p - w - 8$

16. The ratio of x to y to z is 3 to 6 to 8. If $y = 24$, what is the value of $x + z$?

   (A) 11
   (B) 33
   (C) 44
   (D) 66
   (E) 88

15. If a cube has a surface area of $36n^2$ square feet, what is its volume in cubic feet, in terms of n?

   (A) $n^3\sqrt{6}$
   (B) $6n^3\sqrt{6}$
   (C) $36n^3$
   (D) $36n^3\sqrt{6}$
   (E) $216n^3$

IF YOU FINISH BEFORE TIME IS CALLED, YOU MAY CHECK YOUR WORK ON THIS SECTION ONLY. DO NOT TURN TO ANY OTHER SECTION IN THE TEST.

STOP

SECTION 9

Time—10 Minutes

14 Questions

Directions: For each question in this section, select the best answer from among the choices given and fill in the corresponding oval on the answer sheet.

The following sentences test correctness and effectiveness of expression. Part of each sentence or the entire sentence is underlined; beneath each sentence are five ways of phrasing the underlined material. Choice (A) repeats the original phrasing; the other four choices are different. If you think the original phrasing produces a better sentence than any of the alternatives, select choice (A); if not, select one of the other choices.

In making your selection, follow the requirements of standard written English; that is, pay attention to grammar, choice of words, sentence construction, and punctuation. Your selection should result in the most effective sentence—clear and precise, without awkwardness or ambiguity.

EXAMPLE: ANSWER:

Every apple in the baskets <u>are ripe and labeled according to the date it was picked</u>.   (A) ● (C) (D) (E)

(A) are ripe and labeled according to the date it was picked
(B) is ripe and labeled according to the date it was picked
(C) are ripe and labeled according to the date they were picked
(D) is ripe and labeled according to the date they were picked
(E) are ripe and labeled as to the date it was picked

1. The dean stated that although the teacher shortage is partly due to low salaries, <u>they did not get resolved</u> when salaries increased.

    (A) they did not get resolved
    (B) there was no resolve
    (C) resolving there was not
    (D) they did not resolve
    (E) it did not get resolved

2. Animal behaviorists are researching how bats respond to abnormalities in their environments, detect light and sound, <u>and communicate with each other</u>.

    (A) and communicate with each other
    (B) and communicating with each other
    (C) and to communicate between each other
    (D) and how they communicate with each other
    (E) and communication amongst each other

GO ON TO THE NEXT PAGE

3. The first truly American art movement, formed in the early nineteenth century by a group of landscape painters, called the Hudson River School.

   (A) The first truly American art movement, formed in the early nineteenth century by a group of landscape painters, called the Hudson River School.

   (B) Formed in the early nineteenth century by a group of landscape painters was the first truly American art movement, called the Hudson River School.

   (C) Called the Hudson River School, it was formed in the early nineteenth century by a group of landscape painters, the first truly American art movement.

   (D) The first truly American art movement was formed in the early nineteenth century by a group of landscape painters called the Hudson River School.

   (E) By a group of landscape painters called the Hudson River School, the first truly American art movement was formed.

4. During the rainy season, a sloth's brown fur is usually covered with a coat of green algae, which helps the sloth blend with its surroundings.

   (A) algae, which helps
   (B) algae for the purpose of helping
   (C) algae; helps
   (D) algae being that it helps
   (E) algae, helping it does

5. Many researchers contend that driving while talking on a cellular phone poses essentially the same risks than if you drive while intoxicated.

   (A) than if you drive
   (B) than to drive
   (C) as if one drives
   (D) as driving
   (E) as it does when driving

6. Before 1988, the corporation's board of directors included 153 members, none of the members were women.

   (A) members, none of the members were women
   (B) members; and no women
   (C) members, none of whom were women
   (D) members, and of the members not one of them was a woman
   (E) members; none of them being women

7. The client was waiting for fifteen minutes when the receptionist suddenly looked up from her work, noticed him, and informed him that his appointment had been canceled.

   (A) The client was waiting for fifteen minutes when
   (B) The client, having waited for fifteen minutes, when
   (C) Already the client was waiting for fifteen minutes when
   (D) When the client waited for fifteen minutes,
   (E) The client had been waiting for fifteen minutes when

GO ON TO THE NEXT PAGE

8. Banquets are frequently thrown to honor
    guests in a Chinese <u>home, they often feature</u>
    shark fin as the main dish.

    (A) home, they often feature

    (B) home; often feature

    (C) home and often feature

    (D) home and they often feature

    (E) home, these often feature

9. <u>Many wealthy taxpayers pay</u> less than 10
    percent of their annual incomes to the
    government, some middle-income taxpayers
    pay a much larger percentage annually.

    (A) Many wealthy taxpayers pay

    (B) However, many wealthy taxpayers pay

    (C) With many wealthy taxpayers which pay

    (D) Many a wealthy taxpayer pays

    (E) Although many wealthy taxpayers pay

10. Mysteriously beautiful, the Nepalese shrine
    <u>inlaid with semiprecious stones</u> rare enough to
    honor the spiritual essence of the Buddha.

    (A) inlaid with semiprecious stones

    (B) inlaid with semiprecious stones which
    are

    (C) being inlaid with semiprecious stones
    that are

    (D) is inlaid with semiprecious stones

    (E) inlaid with semiprecious stones, these are

11. Most western European countries have
    decreased their consumption of fossil <u>fuels,
    a number of eastern European countries,
    however, have not done so.</u>

    (A) fuels, a number of eastern European
    countries, however, have not done so

    (B) fuels, however a number of eastern
    European countries have not done so

    (C) fuels, while on the other hand a number
    of eastern European countries have not
    done so

    (D) fuels; a number of eastern European
    countries, however, have not done so

    (E) fuels, a number, however, of eastern
    European countries have not done so

12. For reasons not fully understood, nearly all
    children on the island <u>gifted with musical
    ability</u> so strong they can master any
    instrument in hours.

    (A) gifted with musical ability

    (B) gifted with musical ability which is

    (C) are gifted with musical ability

    (D) being gifted with musical ability that is

    (E) are gifted with musical abilities, these are

GO ON TO THE NEXT PAGE

13. <u>That many people believe him to be</u> the most competent and well-informed of all the candidates currently listed on the ballot.

    (A) That many people believe him to be
    (B) Many people believe he is
    (C) Because many people believe him to be
    (D) That many people believe he is
    (E) That many people believe him

14. Although the superintendent's proposal received crucial support from the teachers, <u>but it was rejected by</u> the school board's widespread influence.

    (A) but it was rejected by
    (B) rejecting it because of
    (C) and what made its rejection possible
    (D) it was rejected because of
    (E) and it was rejected by

IF YOU FINISH BEFORE TIME IS CALLED, YOU MAY CHECK YOUR WORK ON THIS SECTION ONLY. DO NOT TURN TO ANY OTHER SECTION IN THE TEST.

STOP

Diagnostic Test: **Answer Key**

SECTION 1

Essay

SECTION 2

1. E
2. C
3. B
4. B
5. B
6. E
7. C
8. E
9. D
10. B
11. A
12. B
13. B
14. C
15. E
16. B
17. C
18. D
19. E
20. A
21. A
22. D
23. C
24. E

SECTION 3

1. C
2. E
3. A
4. B
5. E
6. D
7. B
8. E
9. A
10. D
11. A
12. D
13. D
14. C
15. A
16. C
17. D
18. A
19. E
20. B

SECTION 4

1. D
2. D
3. A
4. C
5. E
6. A
7. B
8. A
9. E
10. C

SECTION 5

1. C
2. B
3. B
4. D
5. C
6. D
7. D
8. A
9. .127
10. 9.5 or $\frac{19}{2}$
11. 84 or 96
12. 8
13. $\frac{45}{4}$ or 11.2 or 11.3
14. 4
15. $\frac{1}{16}$ or .062 or .063

11. B
12. C
13. E
14. A
15. C
16. D
17. D
18. C
19. A
20. E
21. B
22. A
23. C
24. D

16. $\frac{1}{8}$ or .125
17. 2,025
18. $\frac{4}{7}$ or .571

SECTION 6

1. E
2. A
3. C
4. D
5. C
6. A
7. B
8. B
9. E
10. B
11. B
12. D
13. B
14. D
15. B
16. B
17. D
18. D
19. B
20. B
21. A
22. C
23. E
24. C
25. B
26. B
27. E
28. C

29. A
30. A
31. A
32. A
33. D
34. C
35. B

SECTION 7

1. B
2. C
3. C
4. B
5. E
6. A
7. B
8. D
9. E
10. A
11. B
12. C
13. D
14. B
15. E
16. A
17. C
18. C
19. D

SECTION 8

1. B
2. A
3. D
4. A
5. D
6. C
7. C
8. D
9. B
10. C
11. C
12. D
13. E
14. C
15. B
16. C

SECTION 9

1. E
2. A
3. D
4. A
5. D
6. C
7. E
8. C
9. E
10. D
11. D
12. C
13. B
14. D

DIAGNOSTIC TEST: ASSESS YOUR STRENGTHS

Use the following tables to determine which question types you need to review most. If you had trouble with the essay, be sure to review Chapter 5: SAT Writing Basics and Chapter 6: The Essay.

Question Type	Section and Question	If you missed these questions, study these chapters ...
Sentence Completion	Section 2, 1–8 Section 4, 1–5 Section 7, 1–6	Chapter 8: SAT Critical Reading Basics Chapter 9: Sentence Completion Strategies Chapter 12: Vocabulary-Building Strategies
Reading Comprehension	Section 2, 9–24 Section 4, 6–24 Section 7, 7–19	Chapter 8: SAT Critical Reading Basics Chapter 10: Reading Comprehension Strategies—Short Passages Chapter 11: Reading Comprehension Strategies—Long Passages Chapter 12: Vocabulary-Building Strategies
Regular Math	Section 3, 1–20 Section 5, 1–8 Section 8, 1–16	Chapter 13: SAT Math Strategies Chapter 14: Basic Math Concepts Chapter 15: Advanced Math Concepts Chapter 16: How to Avoid SAT Math Traps
Grid-in Math	Section 5, 9–18	Chapter 13: SAT Math Strategies Chapter 14: Basic Math Concepts Chapter 15: Advanced Math Concepts Chapter 16: How to Avoid SAT Math Traps
Identifying Sentence Errors	Section 6, 12–29	Chapter 5: SAT Writing Basics Chapter 7: The Multiple-Choice Questions
Improving Sentences	Section 6, 1–11 Section 9, 1–14	Chapter 5: SAT Writing Basics Chapter 7: The Multiple-Choice Questions
Improving Paragraphs	Section 6, 30–35	Chapter 5: SAT Writing Basics Chapter 7: The Multiple-Choice Questions

Question Type	Number of Questions on Test	Number Correct
Sentence Completion	19	
Reading Comprehension	48	
Regular Math	44	
Grid-in Math	10	
Identifying Sentence Errors	18	
Improving Sentences	25	
Improving Paragraphs	6	

Don't forget to refer to the Compute Your Score section following the Practice Tests to get an idea of what your scaled score on the SAT might be.

ANSWERS AND EXPLANATIONS

SECTION 1

5 ESSAY

I believe that a person's destiny is the result of hard work, not luck. One example that convinces me of this is someone I admire a lot, Michelle Kwan. I've read a lot about her and I know she has to work hard to keep in shape, develop routines, and to face the pressure of competition. She has also suffered some injuries, but she hasn't let them stop her from reaching her goals. Since the middle of the 1990s Michelle has won titles at World, National, and Olympic figure skating events. She is the only woman to lose a world title and then regain it two times. Michelle is able to acomplish all these things because she sets goals for herself and then works toward them with discipline and determination.

Probably if you have seen Michelle skate you have noticed that she always wears the same necklace. Its a Chinese good luck symbol that her grandmother gave her. Michelle will never part from it. But she wears it because of her deep feelings for her grandmother, not for luck. Even though its a good luck symbol, I don't think Michelle acomplished her goals by being lucky. Her hard work is what got her all the fame and medals.

So, as I said at the beginning, I believe that a person's destiny is the result of hard work, not luck. Since I believe this and I can see how Michelle's hard work has led to her sucess, I try to work hard, too. I set goals for myself and then put in the work that I need to, without expecting that success will be easy, or a gift from fate. Right now my goal is to get good grades and get into a good college.

GRADER'S COMMENTS

All essays are evaluated on four basic criteria: Topic, Support, Organization, and Language. Though it is on the short side for a 5 essay, it sticks to the topic throughout. The author supports the thesis quite well by explaining how hard work has actually resulted in achieving the goals that Kwan set for herself—a completely relevant and responsive example. This strong follow-through on an argument the writer feels strongly about raises the essay above mere technical competence.

This essay is highly organized. Paragraph 2, which could seem at first like a digression, is actually support for the author's thesis. The language is pretty good, though not exceptional. The vocabulary is straightforward and not challenging. There are a few grammatical and spelling errors, but not enough to mar the overall effect: paragraph 1, sentence 3, is not parallel. *Accomplish* and *success* are misspelled. *Its* is misused for *it's* twice.

3 ESSAY

I agree that people need to work hard for their destiny and not rely on luck. When I think of people who have worked hard to get their destiny, I always think of Abraham Lincoln. He started out very poor in a log cabin in Kentucky, but he became President of the United States. He did this because he worked very hard instead of hoping good things would just happen to him.

Lincoln didn't go to school too much because his father wanted him to work on the farm. Resulting from this, Lincoln had to teach himself law by reading law books on his own. He worked hard among the people of Illinois to get into Congress. In 1860 Lincoln was elected as the 16th President of the United States. This was a result of his hard work.

Lincoln is a great example of the statement above that destiny or fate is not dependent on luck, but rather is the result of planning and effort.

GRADER'S COMMENTS

All essays are evaluated on four basic criteria: Topic, Support, Organization, and Language. This essay sticks to the topic throughout. However, the thesis is not very well supported. The author tends to repeat thoughts rather than develop them. He also does something that should be avoided—his final paragraph is almost entirely a repeat of a statement in the prompt. This adds nothing to the author's reasoning and uses too much of the very limited time to write. The author supports his thesis by explaining how Lincoln studied law and worked on his own. However, this example is not elaborated on with any detail.

This essay is well organized, with each paragraph covering a separate idea. The meaning is always clear, but the author's language is sometimes below standard. For example, in paragraph 2, sentence 2, "Resulting from this" is not idiomatic. There are no misspellings in the essay.

1 ESSAY

For me its true that people have to work hard to get their destiny. Roger Clemons is the greatest pitcher ever and he works very hard. Someday I would like to be like Roger Clemons. I want to pitch in the majors. I practise real hard to get to do this.

On my last game I almost had a perfect no-hitter. To bad, though, that the last hitter got a single. But my coach said I did real good anyway and we did win the game. The score was 5 to 4.

In conclusion, I want to say again that as far as the statement above, I beleive its true.

GRADER'S COMMENTS

All essays are evaluated on four basic criteria: Topic, Support, Organization, and Language. This author starts out with promise. He states his opinion and then offers an example to support his opinion. Unfortunately, he digresses to discuss his desire to succeed as a pitcher and his baseball record. The essay offers little support for the author's opinion. While this essay is fairly well organized, it's mostly off topic.

The author's language is unsophisticated and, in some cases, substandard. There are grammatical and spelling errors that break the flow of thought: "My coach said I did real good. . . ." *Its* is misused for *it's* twice. *Practice* and *believe* are misspelled. *To* is misused for *too*.

SECTION 2

1. E

The word *because* is a structural clue. It tells us that the blank is defined by the phrase after the comma, *fails to meet deadlines*. We can predict "put off" or "delay." (E), *procrastinate*, is a perfect match. *Prevaricate* means to lie. *Pacify* means to calm or soothe.

2. C

If it took Roman legions three years to seize Masada, we can predict that they spent a long time surrounding or isolating the mountain fortress or stronghold of Masada before they were finally able to take it. (C) is the best choice. (B), *assailed*, meaning attacked, would make sense in the first blank, and (E), *stronghold*, and (A), *bastion*, would fit the second blank, but the first words of (A), (B), and (E) don't make sense when plugged in.

3. B

If the senator was *unlike his calmer, more easygoing colleagues* and *ready to quarrel at the slightest provocation*, it's fair to infer that the senator was short-tempered or extremely irritable. The best choice is (B)—*irascible*.

4. B

You don't have to know that Genghis Khan was a violent dictator to get this question right. What's important to know is that the first word of the sentence, *although*, implies that the two blanks have to contain words that contrast each other. (B) is the best choice—although historians had thought that Genghis Khan was a *despotic* potentate, new research shows that many of his subjects nevertheless *revered* him. Although (A), *tyrannical*, is synonymous with *despotic*, (A)'s second-blank choice, *abhorred*, doesn't provide the predicted contrast. Choice (C), *venerated*, doesn't really contrast with *redundant*. And in (E), it doesn't make sense to say that Khan's subjects *invoked* him despite his *peremptory* reputation.

5. B

The clue *because* in the middle of the sentence tells us that the words in the blanks have the same charge. We could predict two positive words, such as "appreciated" and "forgave" or two negative words, such as "disliked" and "scolded." (B) matches the latter prediction. None of the other choices contain two words that are both positive or both negative. *Execrated* means hated extremely. *Lauded* means praised.

6. E

If a task *requires much patience and effort,* we can predict that the activity is painstaking or tough. (E) matches this prediction. *Nascent* means not fully formed. *Aberrant* means not being consistent with what is typical.

7. C

Disease and *destruction* are clues. We can predict "killed off" or "destroyed." *Decimated* means wiped out, so (C) is a great match.

8. E

Take the first blank first. The phrase *internal power struggles* provides a clue, as does *ideological.* Predict that the government has differences or conflicts. With this prediction for the first blank, we know that (B), (C), and (D) can't be correct. *Ideological divisions* would hamper or get in the way of government. (E), *paralyzed,* is a good match for this prediction.

MUSIC AND LANGUAGE PASSAGES

9. D

The author includes lines 8–13 as evidence that in the Romantic era, folks believed that music by itself could signify emotion, (D). There is no evidence in Passage 1 to support choice (A). While you know what the perception was during the Romantic era, the author doesn't mention the current perception, so you can't support this choice. Although the author states that language is used functionally as opposed to music, this claim is not made specifically for Romantic music in these lines, as in choice (B). (C) is too extreme—the author is not saying that Romantic music composers always used music to connote emotions. (E) expresses a negativity absent from the passage.

10. B

The prefix *extra* covers a lot of ground. Look at the context. The sentence is about music *standing by itself*, so *extra-musical references* must be information from nonmusical sources. (A) is the common meaning. Nothing in the context suggests the author would consider them better than music, (D), just different.

11. A

Both authors mention the symbolic nature of music and language, (A). In Passage 1, the author says, *Nettl has concluded that like language, music is a "series of symbols."* The author of Passage 2 says something similar in the last line of the passage. Only the author of Passage 2 compares both to subdivided sections, (B). Only the author of Passage 1 compares both to functional parts, (C). (D) is a contradiction. (E) fits Passage 2 pretty well, but Passage 1 never links emotions and language.

12. B

Remember that the correct answer here will be something that the authors disagree on, or something that is not mentioned at all in one of the passages. Author 1 would agree with (B), whereas author 2 would disagree. Author 2 would agree with (A) and (E), but you don't know how author 1 would feel; she might agree, or she might disagree. Author 2 would probably disagree with (C) since context is so important, but there's no telling what author 1 would think about the statement. (D) is too extreme—you don't know that author 1 would agree with this.

THE TWAIN PASSAGE

This excerpt from Mark Twain's *Life on the Mississippi* should be amusing and easy to read. All the humor comes from the same technique—using deadpan, matter-of-fact language to describe the exaggerated daydreams and jealousies of a boy's life. The central point here is the author's envy of the engineer, and many of the questions focus on this. The author starts with his own glamorous ideas about steamboating, then spends most of the passage on the show-off engineer. The passage finishes with the author's own failure to find work as a pilot. The slightly old-fashioned style isn't hard to follow, but several questions focus on the author's figurative use of words.

13. B

The keyword in the sentence is *supposed*. Of course, a justice of the peace doesn't possess unlimited power, but because of inexperience, the author *supposed* he did. (B) accurately uses *naive* (inexperienced, gullible) to characterize the author's misconception. Three of the wrong choices assume that the father really did have unlimited powers and explain this in different ways—frontier justice (A and D) and public support (C). (E) mistakenly views the boy's description of his father as an indication that the boy's childhood environment was harsh.

14. C

Distinction has several meanings, including those in (A), (B), (C), and (E). The key to its use here is context: In the previous sentence the author is talking about his naive ideas of his father's great power. *Prestige,* (C), suggesting high status and honor, fits this context; the other three don't. (D) is not a meaning of *distinction* at all.

15. E

This question asks about the literal meaning of the sentence, but inference and context help, too. The sentence explains that the author wanted the job because a deck hand was *conspicuous,* or easily seen. The previous sentence stresses standing *where all my old comrades could see me,* so you can deduce that the author wants to be seen and admired in what he imagines is a glamorous profession, (E). (A) and (B) invent advantages that are not mentioned and miss the humor by suggesting common sense economic motivations. (C) assumes that if the author could be seen by his *old comrades* in the first job, he must want not to be seen by them in a different job; but this is false, since he'd be *conspicuous* in the second job, too. (D) brings in an ambition—becoming a pilot—that the author doesn't develop until the end of the passage.

16. B

Again, context helps you to figure out the answer to the question. The *Sunday-school* reference is explained in the next sentence. The engineer had been *worldly*—which is what Sunday-school probably taught students not to be—and the author had been *just the reverse.* In other words, the author followed his Sunday-school teachings and the engineer didn't—yet the engineer gets the glory. The underlying idea is that this was unjust, choice (B). (A) is never mentioned. (C) takes the Sunday-school reference literally and misses the humorous tone. (D) invents an ambition that the author never mentions; his reaction is pure envy, not frustrated ambition. (E) misconstrues the reference to the engineer as *worldly*; it means he didn't take Sunday school seriously, not that he was *unscrupulous* (dishonest or crooked).

17. C

To get this question, you need to read the sentence that follows. The engineer was not generous because he sat about where *we all could see him and envy him.* The implication is that great people should be generous by not showing off or (C), *flaunting* their success. (A) refers to the Sunday-school comment, but that was about undeserved greatness, not lack of generosity. (B) and (D) interpret *generous* in the literal sense of not caring for money, but the author is using the word figuratively. (E) relates to the author's unfulfilled desire to work on a steamboat, but the engineer is not thinking about the author; he is just showing off.

18. D

The engineer does everything for the purpose of showing off. He talks the jargon of the trade to make himself look knowledgeable or (D), *sophisticated*. Reading between the lines, we realize he's not an expert, (A), and doesn't care about knowledge for its own sake, (B). His ignorance, (C), on other subjects is not mentioned; in fact, he has a working knowledge of St. Louis. (E) takes literally the phrase about how the engineer *forgot common people could not understand*. But the author says the engineer talked *as if* he forgot common people. In other words, he didn't fail to communicate; he chose not to, to impress others.

19. E

Choices (A), (B), (C), and (D) are all common meanings of *consideration,* but the context makes it clear that the figurative use in (E) is meant. The boys had *consideration* because they knew something about St. Louis, but their glory is over because the engineer knows much more. Prestige, respect, or *reputation,* (E), supplies the meaning that fits. Boys are not likely to have the qualities of *generosity, deliberation, contemplation,* or *unselfishness* as a result of knowing a little about St. Louis.

20. A

The context makes it clear that the engineer had, or at least seemed to have, much more familiarity with St. Louis than the other boys with their *vague knowledge*; their *glory* is ended because he can talk rings around them about St. Louis, (A). There's no indication that *St. Louis has changed,* (B), or that the boys had been lying—their knowledge was *vague*, not false, (D). Reading between the lines, it's clear that travel to St. Louis was still rare enough to seem enviable, (E). As for choice (C), the passage implies just the opposite.

21. A

With his *hair oil . . . showy brass watch chain, [and] leather belt*, the engineer was obviously out to impress, (A). The next sentence confirms that, telling us *no girl could withstand his charms*. The author never says the young man's dress is typical, as in choice (B). (C) and (E) are both wrong; the emphasis here is on the engineer's charms, not the author's wardrobe or fashion ideas. (D) won't work because the engineer's behavior is as showy and superficial as his clothes.

22. D

As often in these questions, wrong choices give flatfooted, literal interpretations where the author is being humorous. (A) misunderstands the reference to Providence—the author is criticizing Providence, not thanking it, because it has spared an *undeserving reptile*, the engineer. So the author feels resentment, or *outrage,* (D), because the engineer's good luck seems *undeserved.* Choice (B) sounds believable at first, but the passage doesn't emphasize the lucky escape—it focuses on people's sense that the engineer got better than he deserved. (C) and (E) are never mentioned.

23. C

The passage focuses on the author's ambition to work on a steamboat and his envy of the engineer. This makes (C) and (D) the strongest choices, so you need to decide between them. Looking at (D), the passage certainly emphasizes the engineer's *boastfulness,* but only within the framework of the author's dreams and ambitions (paragraphs 1 and 5) and the author's reactions to the engineer. So (C) describes the *whole* passage whereas (D) describes only the long central paragraphs. In a *major purpose/major focus* question, the answer that sums up the *whole* passage will be correct. The life of the town, (A), is barely suggested. (B) is wrong because the passage's events don't end in success—although in reality, Mark Twain did go on to become a pilot. The author's *conflict with his parents,* (E), is mentioned only briefly, toward the end of paragraph 4.

24. E

The last paragraph discusses the author's failed attempts to become a pilot and his daydreams that he will still become one, so (E) works best. Mates and clerks are mentioned as ignoring the author, but he never considers becoming either a mate or a clerk, (A), looking for some other job, (B), giving up his aim of being a pilot, (C), or asking for his parents' forgiveness, (D).

SECTION 3

 Picking Numbers

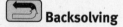 **Backsolving**

 **Eyeballing**

1. C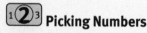

Use the formula Percent × Whole = Part.

30 percent is $\frac{30}{100}$, or $\frac{3}{10}$. So $\frac{3}{10} \times x =$ part, and choice (C) is correct.

2. E

$2 \times 10^4 = 20{,}000$. $5 \times 10^3 = 5{,}000$. $6 \times 10^2 = 600$. $4 \times 10^1 = 40$. So the sum is 25,640, choice (E).

3. A

Find the length of each segment, and then subtract the length of XY from the length of YZ. Y is at 3 on the number line and Z is at 8, so the length of YZ is $8 - 3 = 5$. X is at 1 on the number line and Y is at 3, so the length of XY is $3 - 1 = 2$. So the length of YZ is $5 - 2 = 3$ greater than the length of XY, choice (A).

4. B

To find the value of x, you need to change 16 into a power of 2: $16 = 2^4$. Therefore, $2^{x+1} = 2^4$. So $x + 1 = 4$, or $x = 3$, so choice (B) is correct.

5. E

The number of degrees around a point is 360. Therefore:

$$90 + 30 + 2a + 30 + a = 360$$
$$150 + 3a = 360$$
$$3a = 210$$
$$a = 70, \text{ choice (E).}$$

6. D

$$\frac{150 \text{ bottles}}{20 \text{ minutes}} = \frac{60 \text{ bottles}}{x \text{ minutes}}$$
$$150x = 1{,}200$$
$$x = 8, \text{ choice (D).}$$

7. B

To find the next multiple of 3, simply add 3 to the expression: $x - 1 + 3 = x + 2$, choice (B).

If this is unclear, pick a number for x. If $x = 4$, $4 - 1 = 3$; the next greatest multiple of 3 is 6. Plugging 4 for x into each answer choice, we find that only choice (B) gives us 6.

8. E

Since x leaves a remainder of 4 when divided by 5, it must end in either a 4 or a 9, so choice (B) can be eliminated. Since x leaves no remainder when divided by 9, it is evenly divisible by 9. Of the remaining choices, only 144 is divisible by 9, so choice (E) is correct.

9. A

The sum of the lengths of any two sides of a triangle must be greater than the length of the third side. So $AB + AC$ must be greater than BC; $6 + x > 12$. If $x = 6$, $6 + 6 = 12$ is not greater than 12, so x cannot equal 6. Thus, choice (A) is correct.

10. D

Number of Terms × Average = Sum of the Terms. For the first group, $3 \times 40 = 120$, so the sum of 20, 70, and x is 120. For the second group, $4 \times 50 = 200$, so $20 + 70 + x + y = 200$. Since the sum of the first three terms is 120, $120 + y = 200$, so choice (D) is correct, $y = 80$.

11. A

Looking at the graph, you can see that the number of books borrowed in January was 300. To find the total number of books borrowed during the first six months of the year, add the values of each bar: $300 + 350 + 400 + 450 + 500 + 400 = 2{,}400$ books. So the number of books borrowed in January is $\frac{300}{2{,}400}$ or $\frac{1}{8}$ of the total number of books borrowed during the first six months of the year, choice (A).

12. D ①②③

We're told that 40% of $r = s$. The value of 40% of r is 4 times the value of 10% of r, so 10% of $r = \frac{1}{4} \times s = \frac{s}{4}$.

An alternative method is to pick numbers. Since you're dealing with percents, let $r = 100$. 40% of $r = s$, so 40% of $100 = 40 = s$. You're asked which answer choice is equal to 10% of r; 10% of $100 = 10$. Now plug the value for s into the answer choices to see which ones give you 10:

(A) $4s = 4 \times 40 = 160$. Eliminate.

(B) $2s = 2 \times 40 = 80$. Eliminate.

(C) $\frac{s}{2} = \frac{40}{2} = 20$. Eliminate.

(D) $\frac{s}{4} = \frac{40}{4} = 10$. Works!

(E) $\frac{s}{8} = \frac{40}{8} = 5$. Eliminate.

Since (D) is the only choice that produces the desired result, it is the correct answer. But remember, when picking numbers you need to check all the answer choices; if more than one works, pick new numbers and plug them in until only one answer choice works.

13. D ①②③

The two overlapping triangles share a common angle, which we can label $p°$. Since the interior angles of any triangle add up to $180°$, we have two equations: $x + z + p = 180$ and $y + r + p = 180$. Subtracting p from both sides of each equation, we have $x + z = 180 - p$ and $y + r = 180 - p$. Since $x + z$ and $y + r$ both equal the same quantity, $x + z$ and $y + r$ must be equal to each other. Rearranging $x + z = y + r$, we get $x - r = y - z$, which matches choice (D).

14. C

Check the answer choices. If a number has even one factor (not including 1 and itself) that is not a prime number, eliminate that choice:

(A) 12: 4 is not prime. Eliminate.

(B) 18: 6 is not prime. Eliminate.

(C) 21: 3 and 7 are its only other factors, and both are prime. Correct!

(D) 24: 6 is not prime. Eliminate.

(E) 28: 4 is not prime. Eliminate.

Thus, choice (C) is correct.

15. A ①②③

Try different possible values for x and y, eliminating the incorrect answer choices. Since x is multiplied by 3, let's begin with the smallest positive integer value for x: 1. If $3(1) + y = 14$, then $y = 11$, and $x + y = 12$. So choice (E) is out.

If $3(2) + y = 14$, then $y = 8$, and $x + y = 10$, so choice (D) is out. If $3(3) + y = 14$, then $y = 5$, and $x + y = 8$, so choice (C) is also out. If you're really clever, you'll see at this point that answer choice (A) is impossible (which makes it the right choice). After all, the next smallest possible value of x is 4, and since x and y must both be positive integers, neither one can equal 0. (Zero is *not* positive—or negative.) So the sum of x and y must be greater than 4. (Sure enough, if $x = 4$, then $y = 2$, and $x + y = 6$, you can eliminate choice (B) as well.) Thus, choice (A) is correct.

16. C ①②③

When the r cards are distributed, there are 8 left over, so the number of cards distributed is $r - 8$. Divide the number of cards distributed by the number of people. Since there are s people, each person gets $\frac{r - 8}{s}$ cards. Thus, choice (C) is correct.

Another approach is to pick numbers. Let $r = 58$ and $s = 10$; if $58 - 8$ or 50 cards were distributed evenly among 10 people, each would receive 5 cards. Plug the values you picked for r and s into the answer choices to see which ones give you 5:

(A) $\dfrac{s}{8-r} = \dfrac{10}{8-58} = -\dfrac{1}{5}$. Eliminate.

(B) $\dfrac{r-s}{8} = \dfrac{58-10}{8} = 6$. Eliminate.

(C) $\dfrac{r-8}{s} = \dfrac{58-8}{10} = 5$. Works!

(D) $s - 8r = 10 - (8 \times 58) = -454$. Eliminate.

(E) $rs - 8 = (58 \times 10) - 8 = 572$. Eliminate.

Since (C) is the only answer choice that gives you 5, it is the correct answer. But be sure to check all the answer choices when picking numbers.

17. D ①②③

Check each answer choice to see which doesn't work:

(A) $\dfrac{d}{2}$: If d is an even integer, say 2, then $\dfrac{d}{2} = \dfrac{2}{2} = 1$ is an integer. Eliminate.

(B) $\dfrac{\sqrt{d}}{2}$: If d is a perfect square with an even square root, say $d = 4$, then $\dfrac{\sqrt{4}}{2} = \dfrac{2}{2} = 1$ is an integer.
Eliminate.

(C) $2d$: This will always produce an even integer; if $d = 3$, $2d = 2 \times 3 = 6$ is an integer. Eliminate.

(D) $d\sqrt{2}$ CANNOT produce an integer. An integer would result if $\sqrt{2}$ is multiplied by another multiple of $\sqrt{2}$, which is impossible because d must be an integer. So (D) is correct.

Let's check (E) just to make sure.

(E) $d + 2$: This will always produce an integer; if $d = 5$, $d + 2 = 5 + 2 = 7$ is an integer. Eliminate.

18. A 👁

The area of a triangle is $\dfrac{1}{2}$(base $\times$ height). Since the area of $\triangle ABC$ is 6, $\dfrac{1}{2}(AB \times BC) = 6$. If you consider CD as the base of $\triangle ACD$, you will notice that its height is represented by altitude AB. So the area of $\triangle ACD = \dfrac{1}{2}(CD \times AB)$. Since $CD = BC$, the area of $\triangle ACD$ can be expressed as $\dfrac{1}{2}(BC \times AB)$, which you know equals 6, or choice (A).

19. E

Each of the five surfaces is 60 by 180 centimeters, so tiles measuring 12 by 18 centimeters can be laid down in 5 rows of 10 to exactly cover one surface. There are 5 surfaces so $5 \times 5 \times 10 = 250$ tiles that are needed, choice (E).

20. B

The perimeter of triangle $ACD = AD + AB + BC + CD$. You are given the lengths of BC and CD, so you need to find the lengths of AD and AB. Angle DBC is a right angle because it is supplementary to angle DBA, one of the four right angles of square $ABDE$. Since right triangle DBC has sides of length 8 and 10, you should recognize it as a 6-8-10 right triangle (a multiple of the 3-4-5 right triangle) and realize that $BD = 6$. (If you didn't recognize this, you could have used the Pythagorean theorem to find the length of BD.) BD is also a side of the square, and since all sides of a square are equal, $AB = 6$.

So triangle DBA is an isosceles right triangle with sides in the ratio of $1:1:\sqrt{2}$. That means hypotenuse AD is equal to the length of a side times $\sqrt{2}$, so $AD = 6\sqrt{2}$. Now you can find the perimeter of triangle ACD: $6\sqrt{2} + 6 + 8 + 10 = 24 + 6\sqrt{2}$. Thus, choice (B) is correct.

SECTION 4

1. D

The use of the word *and* tells us that we're looking for a word to fill the first blank that is consistent with *scarcity of rain*—a word like "dry." We can, therefore, eliminate (A) and (C) at once. Since farming conditions are *bad*, our second blank should express the idea that there's no point in trying to work there. By that criterion, choices (B) and (E) can be eliminated. This leaves us with (D), *future*. (D)'s first word, *infertile*, also fits perfectly, so (D) is the correct answer.

2. D

The structural clue in this sentence is *not simply . . . but*, which suggests that the students were doing something even worse than ignoring the rules. The only word that fits here is *flouting*, choice (D).

3. A

The word *while* following the comma in the second part of the sentence tells us that there will be a contrast between what some critics believe about dadaism and what *others insist the movement was*. The best choice is (A)—*some critics believe that the* zenith of *modern art came with dadaism, while others insist the movement was a* sham. Choices (B), (C), (D), and (E) have single words that would make sense in one of the blanks, but none of the pairs except (A) expresses the contrast that is implied by the sentence.

4. C

In this question, you are asked to make a logical connection between two parts of a sentence. It is clear that the content of the journalist's article either had no impact, in which case there was little or no response from the public, or it attracted a great deal of attention and was followed by a lot of correspondence. (C) is the correct answer. The author would never have thought her article was *controversial* were it not for the *spate* of correspondence. The other answer choices are wrong because they sound contradictory when plugged into the sentence. For example, in choice (A), if the article were *interesting*, one would expect it to be followed by a lot of correspondence— not by a *dearth*, or lack of it. In choice (D), if the article were *commonplace* (ordinary), why would an *influx* of letters follow its publication?

5. E

If many readers have difficulty following Descartes's complex, intricately woven arguments, then it's likely that his writings are complicated, esoteric, or obscure. The best choice is (E), *abstruse*.

JELLYFISH PASSAGE

6. A

Since it's clear that a jellyfish couldn't have any feelings about its encounter with humans, the author is apparently using this image to make the reader smile, as in choice (A). (Even if you don't think it's funny, you should note that this is the author's intent.) The author doesn't ask us to feel sympathy for either the jellyfish or humans, (B), and doesn't discuss whether humans are afraid of jellyfish, (C). Although the author does discuss the danger of jellyfish, the quote in question doesn't accomplish that purpose. The passage never discusses how humans or jellyfish react to these encounters, (E).

7. B

The third and fourth sentences contain the key to answering this question. You learn there that the relatively common encounters are not surprising because jellyfish *live in every ocean in the world* (B). (A), (C), (D), and (E) are all details from the passage, but none of them help to explain why encounters are so common.

KHYBER PASS PASSAGE

8. A

For this question, eliminate everything that *does* appear, and you'll be left with the answer. The passage does mention (B) (*Pakistan and Afghanistan*), (C) (*53 kilometers*), (D) (*was used in several wars*), and (E) (*two roads pass through today*). The origin of the pass, (A), is never mentioned.

9. E

Function questions ask you to consider what a statement adds to the author's reasoning. To find the answer, consider what claim or argument the phrase relates to and what it adds to the author's argument. Here, the word *snake* implies a twisting, turning path, like a snake, (E). Although the Khyber Pass connects two points, (A), the word *snake* implies a winding path. Although crossing the Khyber Pass may be dangerous, (B), that doesn't follow from the word *snake*. (C) is the opposite of what you're looking for; the word implies that the pass is anything but direct. (D) comes from the wrong part of the passage. The short length of the Khyber Pass is mentioned earlier in the passage, but this is not why the author stated that the path *snakes*.

THE TIME PASSAGE

Next up is a fairly abstract science passage. This particular passage is perhaps a little bit harder than the ones you're going to encounter on the test—but don't be intimidated by the subject matter. Even if your passage is written by a Nobel Prize winner, it's going to contain ideas that you can relate to and probably some ideas that you've seen before. The topic of the passage is how difficult it is to comprehend long stretches of time. Paragraph 2 tells us that our minds aren't built to handle the idea of thousands of years passing. We have some conception of the past through the art, writing, and photography of previous generations, but the scale of longer time periods eludes us. Paragraphs 4 and 5 attempt to bridge this gap by providing a few everyday yardsticks; the time the human race has been around is compared to a few seconds in a week or a few letters in a book. Essentially, that's all you need to take from your first reading of the passage; you can come back to the details later.

10. C

Before writing existed, we're told, the wisdom of generations was passed down in two ways—verbally, and *to a lesser extent*, in pictures, carvings, and statues. This means that the wisdom of the past was transmitted less frequently by nonverbal means and thus *more frequently by the spoken word than by other means*, choice (C). Choices (A) and (B) *distort* this idea. Nowhere are we told that wisdom was rejected, and since spoken words *and* pictures were both used, it was obviously not an all or nothing proposition. (E) doesn't make much sense. How could there be an emphasis on science before writing existed? (D), finally, makes no sense at all—the author never says that all ancient wisdom was fiction.

11. B

This question asks about the purpose of a detail. The question asks why the author discusses the impact of writing. Looking at the lines around the line reference given, we see that writing has made the transmission of information about the past a lot more precise and extensive. Pictures and photography are also mentioned as ways in which the experience of the past has been passed down.

So choice (B) is correct here—writing is mentioned as an *example* of how cultures record knowledge about the past. (A) is a distortion—the author is showing us something about the past, not why we remember hardly anything. He never implies any criticism of preliterate cultures, so choice (C) is out, too. Choices (D) and (E) are wrong because the author never mentions them in the context referred to or in the whole passage.

12. C

This is another Vocabulary-in-Context question. The word *ready* can mean several things—choices (A), (C), (D), and (E) are all possible meanings. In this context, however, it most nearly means *immediate,* choice (C). In the sentence before the cited line, the author says *there is no simple way* to understand vast stretches of time. In the sentence following the cited line, the author compares the way we understand time to the way a blind man *laboriously* constructs a picture of his surroundings. This implies that our understanding of time is a difficult and time-consuming task, not something we can do *readily* or *immediately.*

13. E

This question is asking about the purpose behind part of the author's argument. Give the context a quick scan. Once again, the author's talking about how difficult it is to understand vast stretches of time. We're told that it's like a blind man building up a sensory picture of his surroundings. This is an *indirect* process, so choice (E) is right. Choice (C) is dealt with later in paragraph 4, so you can eliminate it right away. (A) is too sweeping; the author never says that human beings are *completely unable to comprehend time.* (B) and (D) have nothing to do with the passage.

14. A

Inference skills are required here. What is the author's underlying point in mentioning the Big Bang and the Cambrian Period? The author introduces this discussion in the cited passage by saying that *a week* provides a better yardstick for the age of the earth than a day. The Big Bang and the Cambrian Period are used as examples to support this point. So (A) is right—it's the point about the time scale that the author's trying to demonstrate. Choices (D) and (E) both distort the point in different ways. The author is not suggesting that the time scale of a day should be totally abandoned—just that the week is a better scale. The development of *agriculture,* (B), is another supporting example like the Big Bang and the Cambrian Period, but it's not the author's central point here. Finally, *fossils* have nothing to do with the question at hand, so (C) is easily eliminated.

15. C

This is a more straightforward comprehension question. When we go back to the lines referred to, we're told about the problem with linear maps: When you produce one that's big enough to show us on it, the map becomes too big to study and reproduce conveniently. (C) gets the right paraphrase here. Notice especially the match up in synonyms for *convenient reproduction* and *examination*. (A), (B), and (E) aren't supported here—there's nothing about *overlapping* periods, *scientific standards,* or ignorance about *pre-Cambrian times* in the passage. (D) doesn't address the problem. The question is about getting our human experience on the map.

16. D

What's the overall point the author is trying to prove? The big picture is that life started on Earth so long ago that it is difficult for us to comprehend. Everything that follows is meant to illustrate this point, including the time scales. Don't let the material confuse you. The point is (D)—*the immensity of time* since the origin of *life*. (C) is tricky because it's an aspect of the larger argument, but it's not the whole point. The other wrong choices mention issues that the author hardly touches on. In paragraphs 4–6, the author's *not* concerned with getting dates right, (A), the question of how life actually began, (B), or the development of communication, (E).

THE SUSAN B. ANTHONY PASSAGE

This humanities passage is from a speech by Susan B. Anthony, a 19th-century women's rights leader. Anthony admits at the outset that she was recently charged with the *crime* of voting. Her intention is to prove that her vote was no crime, but rather the exercise of her constitutional rights, which no state should be allowed to impinge upon. This generates the passage's big idea: that Anthony—and by extension all women—should be allowed to vote. You may have found Anthony's style a little dated or confusing. Don't worry; the questions will help you focus on specific details.

17. D

To answer this question, you have to consider the entire context of the speech. Anthony reasons that all citizens automatically have the right to the vote, so the word is a part of her principal argument, and her audience would recognize that as soon as the word was spoken. Thus, she introduces an important element of her argument, choice (D). Since she wants to persuade her audience on an issue of great importance to her, she wouldn't be starting out by trying to irritate or offend them as noted in choice (C). Choices (A), (B), and (E) don't reflect the context at all.

18. C

The important thing here is to see what exactly Anthony is saying. The question stem is keyed to the first paragraph. In the second sentence, she states that she *not only committed no crime, but . . . simply exercised my citizen's rights, guaranteed me . . . by the National Constitution.* The words *no crime* are the first important clue. You can immediately rule out (A) and (E) because Anthony does not believe the act was illegal. The second part of the line discusses the Constitution, so

(C) is clearly a restatement of her argument. (B) and (D) both make sense, but she does not state these points in the first paragraph. Therefore, they are wrong.

19. A

In Vocabulary-in-Context questions, the right answer is usually not the most common meaning of the given word. Be sure to reread the context. The most common meaning of *promote* is to move up to a higher position, rank, or job. This doesn't make sense, though, in the phrase *promote the general welfare. General welfare* means the good of all people, so (A), *further,* makes the most sense. (B), *organize,* and (C), *publicize,* both could apply to the general welfare but not as well as (A). They refer more to promotion as you would do with a concert or sports event. (D), *commend,* means *praise,* which seems silly in the context given, as does (E), *motivate.*

20. E

Anthony points out that no subgroup was excluded by the wording of the preamble of the Constitution. . . . *we formed it . . . to secure* [*the blessings of liberty*]; *not to the half of ourselves . . . but to . . . women as well as men.* Therefore, (E) is correct: *All people deserve to enjoy the rights of the Constitution.* Anthony never claims that the Founding Fathers plotted to deny women their rights as in (A). (B) is incorrect because the author's concern is women's rights and not rights of any other group. Although *some male citizens may still be denied basic rights,* (B) goes against the gist of what is being said. (C) is like (A) in that it's a claim Anthony never makes. Finally, though (D) is a point that Anthony does make, she doesn't make it until the next paragraph.

21. B

We're still looking at the same part of the passage. Look at the structure of the quoted sentence: *We didn't do it only for X, but for X and Y. Posterity* means *future generations,* which would include men and women. So the *X,* the *half of our posterity,* refers to the posterity of those who already enjoy the blessings of liberty. In other words, men. (B) is the right choice. (A) has nothing to do with what Anthony is discussing. Since the construction of the sentence makes it clear that the *half of our posterity* is not the whole of those who want to vote, (C) is out. There's no way of saying that one-half of the people are and will be opponents of women's rights, so (D) is wrong. (E) wrongly suggests that in the future, one-half of the country's population will be members of government.

22. A

Reread the keyed paragraph. Anthony is saying that a state that prohibits women from voting violates federal law—the Constitution. Therefore, it becomes *an odious aristocracy, a hateful oligarchy.* Neither of these things is a democracy. (A) is the correct answer. Anthony mentions rebellion, but she doesn't mean the kind of violent rebellion (B) talks about. (C) is wrong because of the word *remain.* The nation is not and never has been an aristocracy. (D) plays off the same sentence as (B) does, but instead of going too far, it doesn't go far enough. Anthony wants the laws against women voting repealed; she doesn't want them merely discussed. (E) is totally wrong because at no point is Anthony arguing that an aristocracy should be preserved.

23. C
You might readily associate *hardihood* with (A), *endurance,* and (B), *vitality,* but a quick check back in context shows you these aren't correct. Anthony says she doesn't believe her opponents would have the ---- to say women aren't *persons.* Saying such an offensive thing would take a lot of *nerve,* choice (C). It might also take a lot of *stupidity,* (E), but that's too strong a word, considering Anthony's diplomatic tone.

24. D
The stem sends you to the second to last sentence of the passage. *Abridge* means *deprive,* so Anthony is saying that no state can deprive citizens of their rights. (D) states exactly this. In (A), *privilege* means *luxury,* but voting is a basic right, not a luxury. (B) comes out of nowhere; there's no discussion of courts in this passage. (C) plays off Anthony's reference to *any old law.* She's not talking about *any* outdated laws in this passage; she means any law *that prohibits women from voting.* Anthony never addresses how the laws will be changed, but only that they must be changed, so (E) is out.

SECTION 5

1. C
Subtract 100 from both sides of the equation to find $x = 0$.

2. B
The intersection of X and Y is the set of elements common to X (odds) and to Y (negatives), thus all negative odd numbers.

3. B
If x and y are both negative numbers and x is less than y, then $\frac{y}{x}$ is a number greater than zero and less than one. For example, assume that $x = -2$ and $y = -1$. Then $\frac{y}{x} = \frac{1}{2}$. Since $\frac{y}{x}$ must be a positive number, we know that is it greater than zero, so (A) is incorrect. (C) and (D) are also incorrect, as they are negative and therefore smaller than the positive $\frac{y}{x}$. (E) would be exactly half of

$\frac{y}{x}$ and is therefore smaller and incorrect. The only remaining option is (B), which is larger than $\frac{y}{x}$. (Returning to our earlier example, $\frac{x}{y}$ would be 2, which is larger than $\frac{1}{2}$.)

4. D

The small region in the middle represents households with dogs, cats, and fish, (C). The crosshatched region includes all households with dogs and cats except those that also have fish, (D).

5. C

Like many questions about functions, this one looks complex but really just boils down to straightforward substitution. Plug in 3 wherever you see x:

$$f(x) = \frac{(3x^2 - 9)}{(x + 1)}$$

$$f(3) = \frac{(3(3)^2 - 9)}{(3 + 1)}$$

$$f(3) = \frac{(3(9) - 9)}{4}$$

$$f(3) = \frac{(27 - 9)}{4}$$

$$f(3) = \frac{18}{4}$$

$f(3) = \frac{9}{2}$. Choice (C) is correct.

6. D

First, we need to find the length of the line segment AB. It is a vertical line stretching from $(-2, 2)$ to $(-2, -2)$, so its length is $2 - (-2) = 4$. Line segment CD is twice this length, so it is $4 \times 2 = 8$ units long. CD stretches from $(-3, 1)$ to $(h, 1)$, so it is a horizontal line. If it is 8 units long, $h - (-3) = 8$. Subtract 3 from each side of this equation to get $h = 5$, choice (D).

7. D

Percent change is actual change over original amount. The change from 12 to 9 is 3. The amount being changed from is 12, so $\frac{3}{12}$, or 25% is the percent decrease. 25% of 40 is $40(.25) = 10$, so the percent decrease from 40 to $40 - 10 = 30$ is the same as the percent decrease from 12 to 9. Another way to solve this problem is to set up a proportion: $\frac{12}{9} = \frac{40}{x}$, where x is the number we are looking for. Cross-multiply to find $12x = 360$, then divide by 12 to find $x = 30$, choice (D).

8. A ①②③

There are $5 \times 12 = 60$ slices of pizza. If these are equally distributed among x people, each person gets $\frac{60}{x}$ slices of pizza. When the same number of slices are distributed among four fewer people, each person got $\frac{60}{x} + 4$ slices of pizza. You can also describe this number of slices as $\frac{60}{x-4}$. So you have an equation you can use to find x: $\frac{60}{x} + 4 = \frac{60}{x-4}$. This looks nothing like the answer choices, so you'll have to play with it a bit. Multiply both sides by x to get $60 + 4x = \frac{60x}{x-4}$, then multiply both sides by $x - 4$ to get $(x-4)(60 + 4x) = 60x$. Distribute and simplify to get $60x + 4x^2 - 240 - 16x = 60x$, $4x^2 - 16x - 240 = 0$, and $x^2 - 4x - 60 = 0$, choice (A).

9. .127

If $A = 2.54$ and $20B = A$, then $20B = 2.54$. So $B = \frac{2.54}{20}$ or .127.

10. 9.5 or $\frac{19}{2}$

The perimeter of the figure is equal to the sum of the lengths of its sides: $2 + 1\frac{1}{3} + 1\frac{1}{2} + 1\frac{2}{3} + 3 = 9\frac{1}{2}$, which is $\frac{19}{2}$ expressed as an improper fraction, or 9.5 expressed as a decimal.

11. 84 or 96

If $\frac{h}{3}$ and $\frac{h}{4}$ are both integers, then h must be a multiple of 3×4, or 12. Since it's given that h is between 75 and 100, h must be 84 or 96.

12. 8

The profit made by the retailer on the shirts is equal to the difference between the selling price and the cost for each shirt multiplied by the number of shirts: $(\$6.75 - \$4.50) \times 16 = \$2.25 \times 16 = \$36.00$ profit. To find the number of \$4.50 shirts that can be bought for \$36.00, you need to divide \$36.00 by \$4.50, and $\frac{36}{4.5} = 8$.

13. $\frac{45}{4}$ or 11.2 or 11.3

Draw a diagram and label it according to the given information:

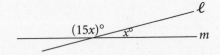

Let the smaller angle measure $x°$. Since the other angle formed is 15 times as large, label it $(15x)°$. Notice that these two angles are supplementary, that is, they add up to 180°. Therefore:

$$x + 15x = 180$$

$$16x = 180$$

$$x = \frac{45}{4}$$

So the smaller angle is $\frac{45}{4}$ degrees, which can also be gridded in decimal form as 11.2 or 11.3.

14. 4

Before you plug in −4 for x, you should factor the given equation:

$$x^2 + 2xr + r^2 = 0$$

$$(x + r)(x + r) = 0$$

$$(x + r)^2 = 0$$

Now plug in −4 for x to solve for r: $(−4 + r)^2 = 0$, $−4 + r = 0$, and $r = 4$.

15. $\frac{1}{16}$ or .062 or .063

Plug the values into the given definition:

$$\frac{1}{4} * = \left(\frac{1}{4}\right)^2 - \frac{1}{4}$$

$$= \frac{1}{16} - \frac{1}{4}$$

$$= \frac{1}{16} - \frac{4}{16}$$

$$= \frac{-3}{16}$$

$$\frac{1}{2} * = \left(\frac{1}{2}\right)^2 - \frac{1}{2}$$

$$= \frac{1}{4} - \frac{1}{2}$$

$$= \frac{1}{4} - \frac{2}{4}$$

$$= \frac{-1}{4}$$

So:

$$\frac{1}{4} * - \frac{1}{2} * = \frac{-3}{16} - \left(\frac{-1}{4}\right)$$

$$= \frac{-3}{16} - \left(-\frac{4}{16}\right)$$

$$= \frac{1}{16}$$

This can also be gridded as .062 or .063.

16. $\frac{1}{8}$ or .125

You should recognize that right $\triangle ABC$ is a 45-45-90 triangle, with side lengths in a ratio of $1:1:\sqrt{2}$. Therefore, the length of the two equal legs AB and AC is $\frac{1}{2}$.

To find the area of the triangle, plug in the values of the base and height (the lengths of the two equal legs) into the area formula:

Area of a triangle $= \frac{1}{2}$ (base $\times$ height)

$$= \frac{1}{2}\left(\frac{1}{2}\right)^2$$

$$= \frac{1}{2}\left(\frac{1}{4}\right)$$

$$= \frac{1}{8}, \text{ or } .125$$

17. 2,025

You're given that x is a factor of 8,100 and it's an odd integer. To find the greatest possible value of x, begin factoring 8,100 by using its smallest prime factor, 2, as one of the factors. Continue factoring out a 2 from the remaining factors until you find an odd one as shown below:

8,100

2   4,050

2   2,025

8,100

$2 \times 4,050$

$2 \times 2 \times 2,025$

Since 2,025 is odd, you can stop factoring; it is the greatest odd factor of 8,100.

18. $\frac{4}{7}$ or .571   ①②③

Translate the problem into math: Let b = number of boys; let g = number of girls. So $b + g$ = total number of students in the class.

$\frac{1}{2}$ of the boys speak French, so $\frac{1}{2}b$ = the number of boys who speak French.

$\frac{2}{3}$ of the girls speak French, so $\frac{2}{3}g$ = the number of girls who speak French.

Therefore, $\frac{1}{2}b + \frac{2}{3}g$ = total French speakers.

So the fraction of the class that speaks French

$$= \frac{\frac{1}{2}b + \frac{2}{3}g}{b + g}.$$

Since there are $\frac{3}{4}$ as many girls as boys in the class, $g = \frac{3}{4}b$. Plug in $\frac{3}{4}b$ for g into the fraction above.

So the fraction of the class that speaks French:

$$= \frac{\frac{1}{2}b + \frac{2}{3}\left(\frac{3}{4}b\right)}{b + \frac{3}{4}b}$$

$$= \frac{\frac{1}{2}b + \frac{1}{2}b}{\frac{7}{4}b}$$

$$= \frac{b}{\frac{7}{4}b}$$

$$= \frac{4}{7} \text{ or } .571$$

SECTION 6

1. E

The introductory phrase doesn't modify the correct noun. The fund-raiser is *arranged as an event*, not the Board of Directors. Also, the words *for funding* repeat information provided in the main clause. You need an introductory phrase that modifies the correct noun—the museum's Board of Directors. Only (E) does that. (B) and (D) don't correct the modification problem. (C) creates a run-on with a comma splice.

2. A

Don't forget that about 20 percent of Sentence Correction questions are correct as written. This sentence correctly uses a semicolon to connect two independent clauses, but (B) changes the meaning. (C) is a run-on sentence with a comma splice. (D) is a complete sentence because it adds the conjunction *and*, but it is wordy and incorrectly changes *nearly* to *near*. (E) should use a comma because it adds *although*, which subordinates the second clause.

3. C

Pay close attention to the sequence of events. The architects first made the design plans, then refused to copyright or benefit from them. The action *refused to patent* happened after, not before, the plans had been made, requiring the simple past tense. (C) and (E) make that change, but only (C) makes *patent* and *benefit* parallel. (B) keeps the past perfect tense. (D) uses the present tense, even though the entire sentence is in the past.

4. D

The comparison between Wilde's novel writing and play writing must be logical. (C), (D), and (E) correctly compare *novelist* and *playwright*. However, only (D) retains the original meaning. (C) doesn't show that Wilde is a more brilliant playwright than novelist. (E) reverses the meaning, making him a more brilliant novelist than playwright. (B) changes the meaning as well, making Wilde *almost brilliant*.

5. C

The introductory phrase doesn't modify the correct noun. You need a subject that can logically examine *the sale offers*. (C), (D), and (E) provide that subject (*one*). Only (C) uses the present tense. (D) and (E) switch to the past tense. (D) also illogically uses the contrasting transition word *although*; (E) incorrectly uses the tentative *may have noticed*. (B) doesn't address the modification problem.

6. A

This sentence is correct as written. (B) is incorrect because *however*, when used as a conjunction between two independent clauses, must be preceded by a semicolon. (C) is redundant, using two conjunctions *although* and *however*. (D) uses the relative pronoun *which* instead of *who* to refer to people. (E) loses the contrast between the two clauses (indicated by *however* in the original sentence).

7. B

The sentence incorrectly uses the pronoun *which* to refer to people and includes the wordy intervening phrase *which have an understanding of*. (B) correctly changes *which* to *who* and makes the sentence more concise. (D) and (E) also use *who* but (D) introduces the ambiguous pronoun *they*, which could refer to the people or the leaves, and (E) is awkwardly worded. (C) doesn't correct the original pronoun problem.

8. B

This sentence is confusing because it uses the passive voice. Be sure you understand the logic of the sentence: the traffic rules are the *they* and their role was not appreciated. (B) puts all these ideas into clear order by using the active voice and the transition word *because* instead of relying on a modifier. (C) distorts the meaning of the sentence. (D) creates a misplaced modifier problem—the traffic rules fail to appreciate their role. (E) is a fragment, with no verb in an independent clause.

9. E

There are two pairs of parallel structures: *even more elusive in . . . than in* and *either . . . or*. In the original sentence, the first pair is not parallel. (D) and (E) correctly add *in* to make the phrases *in his own country* and *in Europe or Latin America* parallel, but (D) introduces a new error by repeating *in*. (B) and (C) do not correct the parallelism problem.

10. B

My old home is not *growing up*. There is a misplaced modifier. (B) and (C) correct the modification problem by adding the transition word *as*, but only (B) doesn't introduce new errors. (C) incorrectly uses the present tense *grow up*. (D) loses the idea that the author grew up on the island. (E) doesn't correct the modification problem.

11. B

The sentence doesn't make sense because neither *households* nor *subscribers* is a logical subject for the verb *established*.

12. D

The pronoun *they* doesn't clearly refer to anything, and *they can astonish people* is not parallel to *bolder* and *more abstract*. (D) should be changed to *astonishing*. The phrases *as Picasso* in (A) and *use of* in (B) are idiomatically correct. The verb *became* in (C) is correctly in the past tense.

13. B

The sentence contains an error because it begins in present tense, but then changes to past tense. The chemical plant *is* a danger, at the present moment. *It became imperative* is past tense, which does not fit with the rest of the sentence. It should be changed to *it has become imperative*.

Note that you could also simply substitute *is* to form *it is imperative. Such a* in (A) is standard written English, as is *to find other ways* in (C). *For* in (D) is the correct preposition for *garden.*

14. D

This sentence contains an ambiguous pronoun. *Their* could refer to either *John and Sue* or to *parents.* On the SAT, any pronoun that doesn't have a clear antecedent is considered an error. Were the tickets John and Sue's, or were they their parents'? (A) describes *John and Sue* correctly. (B) is the correct use of the verb. (C) refers to *John and Sue* and is used correctly.

15. B

This is a sentence fragment; we need a verb. The phrase *which eerily hint at* in (B) and (C) should read *eerily hint at*, creating a complete sentence; thus, (B) contains the error. The adjective *lyric* in (A) agrees with the noun *novels.* (D)'s phrase *of her* is idiomatically correct.

16. B

The pronoun *their* refers to the United Nations. Because the United Nations is a singular proper noun, the correct pronoun is *its.* (B) is incorrect. (A) correctly uses the comparative form and *than* is idiomatically correct. (C) is the correct preposition with *owes.* (D) correctly uses *that* and the present tense.

17. D

Each pronoun in a sentence should agree in number with the word or words to which it refers. (A) is an appropriate modifier for the subject *I.* (B) is an appropriate verb tense. (C) is a correct idiom. (D) is the right answer. In this phrase, the pronoun refers to *Jake and Kelsey.* Therefore, it should be the plural *they,* as in *as they approached.*

18. D

Be sure that each word means precisely what the writer intended to say. (A) is an appropriate phrase modifying the subject *Hiam.* (B) is an adjective, also appropriately modifying *Hiam.* (C) is another adjective, here correctly modifying the noun *night.* (D) uses the wrong preposition for the intended meaning; the writers meant *on* or *against.*

19. B

Adverbs and adjectives can be easily mixed up. Check the sentence again to be sure there is no confusion. (A) uses the correct verb tense, and the verb agrees with the subject *you.* (B) shows an adverb used in place of an adjective *generous.* Therefore, (B) is the right answer. (C) shows a correct verb tense, and (D) shows an idiom used correctly to mean *flourish.*

20. B

When you see a comparative word like *more* underlined on the SAT, always check whether three or more things are being compared. *More* is correct only when the comparison is limited to two things. Because this sentence refers to *all* (more than two) of Kelly's skills, the superlative form *most* must be used instead of the comparative form *more*.

21. A

Irregular verbs do not follow the usual pattern in their past tense forms. Check the sentence carefully to be sure that the verbs are written correctly. (A) uses an incorrect past participle of the verb *drive*. The correct form is *driven*. (B) uses the correct preposition *from*. (C) is the correct verb tense and idiomatic expression. (D) uses the appropriate tense for another action that was completed before the action in the prior clause.

22. C

As you read the sentence, you pause at *hardly no*, (C). *Hardly* is a negative, and when it's paired with *no*, a double negative results. The subject (A) and the verb (B) agree. (D) is idiomatically correct.

23. E

Don't hyper-correct the sentences. All the elements in these sentences are correct.

24. C

(A) is the correct verb tense. (B) and (D) are idiomatically correct. (C) is incorrect because the subject is *the characters*, which is plural. *Has* should be *have*.

25. B

Remember that adverbs modify verbs and adjectives modify nouns, adverbs, and other adjectives. *Attentive* is an adjective, but it is modifying the verb *applies*, so it has to be changed to the adverb *attentively.*

26. B

Know when to use nouns in the subjective case and the objective case. Any noun or pronoun that is part of a prepositional phrase must be in the objective case. Here the prepositional phrase is between *Sarah and I,* (B). This is incorrect because *I* is a subjective case noun. To correct this sentence, you need to change *I* to *me*.

27. E

Don't be distracted by phrases and clauses that come between a subject and its verb. The verb *used* and the preposition *by* in (A) are used correctly. The subject *control* and its verb *is* in (B) agree. *Benefit* in (C), which means aid or advantage is correctly used in this sentence. The pronoun *their*, (D), agrees with its antecedent, *students*.

28. C

Let the parts of the sentence not underlined help you identify the errors that are underlined. The pronoun *it* is used at the end of the sentence to refer to *the institute*, but the other pronoun that refers to *the institute*, in (C), is *their*. You need to make the pronouns consistent and correct. *The institute* is a collective noun, which means it's made up of many people, but is treated in a sentence as a single entity, so any pronouns that refer to it should be singular. *Their* should be *its*.

29. A

This sentence confuses *undetermined* (which means not decided), (A), with *indeterminate*. You can see that this makes no sense. The word needed is *indeterminate*, which means you can't tell his age by looking at him. Notice how this meaning works well with the rest of the sentence—he takes advantage of the ambiguity or uncertainty about his age. The conjunction *and*, which indicates additional, related information, is correctly used in (B). In (C), the present tense is correct since it expresses something that the candidate does regularly. (D) is the correct preposition in this context.

30. A

The passage begins by stating that ballet has a *duality*, and the second sentence introduces the most common view of ballet. What follows should be a sentence that identifies the contrast suggested by the first sentence: the idea that ballet is *grueling, painful, and competitive*, as expressed in (A). This also gives a more clear transition to paragraphs 2 and 3, which talk about the difficulties of dancing. Although it starts appropriately with a contrast word, (B) goes off track; it even seems to contradict sentence 2. (C) is a fragment; it can't be correct even though it seems to follow the right line of reasoning. (D) and (E), like (B), go off the logical track. These would be digressions in this passage, which focuses only on the qualities of ballet.

31. A

To combine these two sentences, we must first determine their relationship. It is a causal relationship—because of the first clause (the human body is not designed for ballet), it is difficult for dancers to do the second clause (perform ballet steps). (A) correctly establishes this relationship and creates a complete sentence. (B) and (E) incorrectly use a semicolon to connect a dependent and an independent clause. (C) combines the sentences into one big fragment by adding the gerund *making*. (D) is also a fragment and introduces another error—*their* is an ambiguous pronoun.

32. A

To determine what sentence should begin paragraph 3, we must understand the passage's organization. Paragraph 1 introduces the topic. Paragraph 2 describes the first negative aspect of ballet (physical injury). Paragraph 3 describes the second negative aspect (financial problems). (A) both indicates that paragraph 3 is the second aspect and that the paragraph relates to financial problems. The sentence is also identical in construction to the first sentence of paragraph 2. (B) changes *second* to *secondly* and mentions only a part of paragraph 3, not the entire subject. (C) and (D) use transition words that do not indicate that this is the second portion of the passage. (E) incorrectly indicates that the financial consequences are worse than the physical—the author never makes such a comparison.

33. D

As it is now, the sentence is a fragment; we need a subject and verb in an independent clause. (D) replaces the gerund *creating* with the present tense *create*. This works in context because the rest of the paragraph is in present tense. (B) simply substitutes the gerund *compiling* for the gerund *creating*. The sentence is still a fragment. (C) and (E) are incorrectly in the past tense; (C) uses the word *their*, which would mean that the financial struggles were competitive instead of the dancers; and (E) changes the meaning to one competition.

34. C

Look at the context of sentence 11—how does it relate to sentence 10? Sentence 11 contrasts dancers' experience with that of *most people*. (C) expresses this contrast and uses a complete sentence. All of the other answer choices create fragments.

35. B

What is the relationship of this pair of sentences to what came before? We've been told in sentences 10 and 11 that people in most occupations retire at 65, but that isn't true of dancing. Now we're told a few dancers continue in related careers, but most are simply unemployed. Sentence 12 continues what preceded it, but contrasts with sentence 13. (B) captures this best. (A) confuses the contrast between these two sentences by offering transition words suggesting both contrast (*although*) and continuity (*and*). (C) offers too many contrast words and needlessly changes tense. (D) is a run-on sentence. (E) also changes tense and distorts some of the meaning.

SECTION 7

1. B

The phrase *even though* indicates contrast. So, *even though* the prisoner *proved that he was nowhere near the scene of the crime,* he was *indicted,* (B), or formally charged with committing the crime. None of the other answers fit. *Exculpated,* (C), means to be cleared from allegations of guilt or fault. *Exhumed,* (D), means unearthed. *Rescinded,* (E), means to put an end to.

2. C

A *premise* is a proposition that is used as the basis for an argument—or a story. If scientists are critical of the premise for a movie, we can infer that they are because they consider it to be unscientific, without basis in fact, or *speculative.* (C) is therefore the correct answer. (A) is wrong because if the premise, or underlying argument, were *scientific,* then it would hardly be open to criticism by scientists. (B) is wrong because there's no reason to think that the theme of the return of the dinosaurs is unexpressed in the movie.

3. C

In this sentence, we find a description of two contradictory characteristics that exist in the same group of people. On the one hand, they are brutal; on the other, they are heroic. Such an occurrence is termed a *paradox* and, therefore, (C), *paradoxical,* is the correct answer. Choices (A), (D), and (E) are wrong; it is *unfortunate, distressing,* and *appalling* that they are brutal—but not that they are heroic.

4. B

The second part of the sentence tells you that the engineers did something that allowed the movement of animals around the pipeline. You can, therefore, predict that this action would help the seasonal migration of caribou. This prediction eliminates choices (A) and (D) for the first blank. (B) and (E) both fit the first blank nicely. When you try the second blank, (B) describes how the pipeline could be designed to accommodate the passage of animals. (C) does not fit either blank. Be sure not to misread *razed* (meaning demolished, leveled to the ground) as *raised.*

5. E

The word *however* signals a contrast between *licorice as candy* and its use in earlier times when licorice root was used to treat a variety of medical problems. A good prediction for the blank would be "medical" or "healing." (E) matches the prediction. (A) is too narrow because licorice root treated conditions other than insomnia. (C) describes candy but not medicine. (B) and (D) do not match the prediction. Be sure not to misread *indelible* as *inedible,* which means unfit to be eaten.

6. A

In this sentence, parents are doing something to legislation that guarantees programs and services. The first part of the sentence tells you that education is one of those services. You're looking for a word that means to "make sure" or to "guarantee" in the first blank. (A) and (E) work for the first blank. Now look at the second blank. (A) works well. (E) would deny education to the children and can, therefore, be eliminated. *To ensure free education for children with special needs, parents have had to demand legislation guaranteeing services and programs targeted to those children.* (A) works for both blanks.

THE SHAKESPEARE PASSAGES

These paired passages present two opposing arguments on a single subject, *Who Really Wrote Shakespeare's Plays?* The author of the first passage maintains that Francis Bacon actually wrote the plays, basing that conclusion on the assertion that Shakespeare didn't have the education and social experience necessary to create such sophisticated plays. The author of the second passage takes issue with that, claiming that Shakespeare's genius grew out of a deep understanding of human nature rather than any wide learning or arcane knowledge.

7. B

Here we're asked the definition of the word *entertain* in line 3, where it is used in the phrase *entertain some doubt*. Well, when you entertain doubt, or entertain an idea, you are holding it in your head. You are *harboring* it, in the sense of *to harbor* as "to be host to." So choice (B) is correct. The other choices are all acceptable dictionary definitions of the verb *entertain*, but none fits the context as well as choice (B) does. (A) is a common synonym for *entertain*, but how does one amuse doubt? (C) and (E) are closer, but they don't fit the sentence either. One's *mind* is occupied or engaged, but the doubt itself is not occupied or engaged. Meanwhile, (D) adds a sense of valuing the entertained thing, as if it were something desirable.

8. D

The author claims that the person who actually wrote the plays must have had *intimate knowledge of life within royal courts and palaces*, but that Shakespeare was just a commoner, without that kind of *firsthand experience* of the aristocracy. He wants to cast doubt on Shakespeare's *familiarity with the life of [aristocrats]*, or choice (D). Shakespeare's ability to write *poetically*, (A), and his *ability to support himself* as a playwright, (C), never come up in Passage 1. The *knowledge of foreign places* mentioned in (B) does come up, but being a commoner is not necessarily related to Shakespeare's apparent lack of travel. Choice (E) is incorrect because the issue is his knowledge of all aspects of aristocratic life.

9. E

Two Shakespearian plays—*Coriolanus* and *Love's Labour's Lost*—are mentioned in lines 31–34 in connection with the allegedly specialized knowledge they contain. They support the point that the educated aristocrat Bacon was a more likely author than was the undereducated commoner Shakespeare. (E) answers the question best. Choice (A) is a clever wrong choice, but it's too extreme. The author's not trying to prove that *only* Bacon could have written these plays, just that Bacon was far more likely than Shakespeare to have written them. The *deep understanding of human nature* mentioned in (B) is something brought up in Passage 2, not Passage 1. The author is not comparing the two plays to *works written by Bacon,* as (C) claims. And (D) is wrong since nothing about society is mentioned with regard to *Coriolanus*. Also, it's not the *broad spectrum of Elizabethan society* the author alludes to with regard to *Love's Labour's Lost,* but rather the knowledge of just the upper range of society.

10. A

It's clear that Bacon looks down on actors, of which Shakespeare was one, regarding them with the *disdain* expressed in correct choice (A). Delia Bacon is not *resentful* at how the *characters are portrayed,* choice (B), since she's talking about the real-life actors. Given her opinion of actors, she certainly doesn't *regret that their conditions weren't better,* choice (C). (D) is closer, but it's a distortion. She never doubts that anyone could *create such characters;* she doubts that the author of the plays could *be like* such a character. Finally, in (E), there's no evidence in the quote that Bacon thinks the actors are inept at their art, just that they are vulgar and lowly persons.

11. B

This question sends you back to paragraph 4 of Passage 1, where Francis Bacon's preference for anonymity is explained. The author claims that, because the plays were controversial, Bacon felt that associating himself with them would have been politically and personally damaging. So, *he wished to protect himself from the effects of controversy,* choice (B). (A) is wrong because Bacon did publish a lot of writing under his own name. (C) is plausible, but it's not the reason given in paragraph 4 or anywhere else in the first passage. (D) tries to confuse us by introducing the subject of *lowly actors* from the preceding paragraph, and (E) is a fabrication since we know that Bacon was already famous from his other writings.

12. C

This question takes us to the first paragraph of Passage 2, where the emphasis is on language ability. The author doubts that Bacon, a writer primarily of academic Latin, would have had the ability to produce the exalted English in which the plays were written. That makes (C) the best answer. (A) is a distortion. Just because Bacon wrote most of his own work in another language doesn't mean that he was *unfamiliar* with English. (B)'s emphasis on the difficult switch from *scientific writing* to *writing plays* is close, but language rather than the type of writing is the focus. There's no reason to surmise that the author doubts Bacon's ability to *cooperate* on a *committee,* choice (D). Finally, (E) is wrong because there is no evidence in the first paragraph that the author has doubts about Bacon's ability to produce that amount of work.

13. D

This question asks about *premier* as it is used in the phrase *premier stylist in the English language.* The author definitely wants to indicate the sublime language of the plays here, so *premier* is being used in the sense of "the first rank," or as (D) has it, *greatest.* (A), (C), and (E) all play on the sense of premier as *first in sequence* (inaugural, by the way, means marking the commencement or beginning), but the author is not referring here to *when* Shakespeare wrote. He's writing about how *well* Shakespeare wrote. On the other hand, (B), *influential,* misses on two counts—first, it's not a definition of *premier* in any context, and second, the issue of influence on other writers is not brought up here.

14. B

This question concerns the adjective *encyclopedic* in Passage 2, line 82, where it's used to modify the noun *knowledge.* The author says that Shakespeare's genius was one of common sense and perceptive intuition, not encyclopedic knowledge, which is related to great book learning. So the knowledge described as *encyclopedic* is wide-ranging and in-depth—*comprehensive,* in other words, choice (B). (A), *technical,* doesn't mean wide-ranging. (C) won't work since *abridged* (meaning condensed) cannot describe the kind of exhaustive knowledge the author is describing here. While it may take discipline to gain encyclopedic knowledge, *encyclopedic* itself cannot be defined as *disciplined,* so cut (D). Finally, (E), *specialized,* isn't quite right, since it implies a narrowness of focus.

15. E

The reference to Shakespeare's status as a landowner comes in the third paragraph of Passage 2, where it is brought up to show that Shakespeare would have been *knowledgeable about legal matters related to . . . real estate.* That makes (E) the best answer, *legal matters* being equivalent to *the law.* (A) is tempting, since the author does say that owning land was quite an accomplishment for a playwright, but it has nothing to do with his knowledge of the law. (B) is off, since owning land doesn't make one automatically friendly with the highborn set. (C) is wrong, because Shakespeare's financial state is just a side issue; it's not the point of bringing up Shakespeare's landowning status. And (D) doesn't fit, since no one doubts that Shakespeare was a commoner.

16. A

This question directs us to Passage 2, lines 111–112, where the author claims that *literary genius can flower in any socioeconomic bracket*. That implies that genius has little to do with a person's social and financial position—or, as correct choice (A) has it, genius doesn't depend *on a writer's external circumstances*. (B) fails by bringing in the notion of *comprehension of human nature* from elsewhere in the passage. (C) is a common cliché, but there's no evidence here that the author felt that Shakespeare's genius was *enhanced by poverty*. In fact, this author implies that Shakespeare wasn't even all that poor. (D) may be a true statement, but recognition of genius isn't really under discussion here; it's the simple existence of genius. (E) is a distortion; the author claims that at least one kind of genius does not *stem* from *book-learning and academic training*, but that doesn't mean that those things would *stifle literary genius*.

17. C

Go back to the fourth paragraph of Passage 1, where our first author claims that Bacon may have *hired a lowly actor* like Shakespeare to put his name to the plays and take the heat of controversy. How would our second author respond to this claim? The second author, remember, writes in the concluding paragraph of Passage 2 that *no elaborate theories of intrigue and secret identity are necessary to explain the accomplishment of William Shakespeare*. Surely author 2 would regard the *scenario* described in Passage 1 as just this kind of *unnecessary* theory, so (C) is the best guess for how author 2 would react. As for choice (A), author 2 may or may not agree that the plays were *controversial* in their time, so (A) won't work. (B) gets the thrust of author 2's argument wrong. Author 2 denigrates the notion that Bacon wrote the plays *not* by arguing that Bacon wasn't a great scholar, but by arguing that it didn't require a great scholar to write the plays. (D) tries to turn author 1's argument on its head, but author 2 shows no hint of doing anything of the kind. (E) brings up the notion of Shakespeare's social *respectability*, which really isn't of much concern to author 2.

18. C

What would be author 1's reaction to author 2's skepticism that Bacon, the author of Latin treatises, could be the *premier stylist in the English language*? Well, author 1's repeated assertions of Bacon's scholarly genius and Shakespeare's lack of education are both reflected in choice (C), which makes it a good bet as the correct answer. (A)'s mention of the *similarities between Latin and English* is enough to kill this choice, since author 1 mentions no such similarities in the passage. (B) is a true statement, perhaps, but it doesn't really address the issue. (D) is fairly nonsensical, since it would weaken author 1's entire theory about why Bacon hired Shakespeare. Finally, (E) makes a good point, but again, there is no hint of this sentiment in author 1's statements.

19. D

Always check back to the passage to figure out the meaning of a Vocabulary-in-Context word. Here, the word *observation* refers to the statement that *Shakespeare, in short, was Shakespeare*—a jokey comment on the author's part. Choices (A), (B), (C), and (E) do not fit the context of an informal remark, so (D) is correct here.

SECTION 8

1. B

Plug in –2 for p and 3 for q: $p^3q^2 + p^2q = (-2)^33^2 + (-2)^23 = (-8)(9) + 4(3)$, or $(-72) + 12 = -60$. (Note that a negative number raised to an even power becomes positive, but raised to an odd power stays negative.) Thus, choice (B) is correct.

2. A

Keep track of the lengths you know on the diagram. B is the midpoint of AC, so $AB = BC$. Since $AB = 5$, $BC = 5$. $BD = 8$, so $BC + CD = 8$. $BC = 5$, so $5 + CD = 8$, $CD = 3$. D is the midpoint of CE, so $CD = DE = 3$, choice (A).

3. D ₁②₃

Try each answer choice until you find one that works for all of the pairs of numbers.

Choice (A), $P = N + 5$, works for 2 and 7, but not for 4 and 13. Eliminate.

Choice (B), $P = 2N + 3$, also works for 2 and 7, but not for 4 and 13. Eliminate.

Choice (C), $P = 2N + 5$, doesn't work for 2 and 7. Eliminate.

Choice (D), $P = 3N + 1$, works for all four pairs of numbers, so that's the answer. Works!

4. A

$\angle PNM$ is supplementary to $\angle PNQ$, so $\angle PNM + 105° = 180°$, and $\angle PNM = 75°$. Since $PM = PN$, triangle MPN is an isosceles and $\angle PMN = \angle PNM = 75°$. The interior angles of a triangle sum to 180°, so $75 + 75 + x = 180$, and $x = 30$. Thus, choice (A) is correct.

5. D

Probability is defined as the number of desired events divided by the total number of possible events. There are $5 + 6 + 4 = 15$ pens in the knapsack. If he pulls out 1 pen, there are 15 different pens he might pick, or 15 possible outcomes. The desired outcome is that the pen be either red or black. The group of acceptable pens consists of $4 + 6$, or 10 pens. So the probability that one of these pens will be picked is 10 of 15, or $\frac{10}{15}$, which we can reduce to $\frac{2}{3}$, choice (D).

6. C

Pick variables for the two items and translate the given information into algebraic equations. Let h = the price of a hot dog and s = the price of a soda. The first statement is translated as $2h + s =$ $3.25 and the second as $3h + s =$ $4.50. If you subtract the first equation from the second, the s is eliminated so you can solve for h:

$$3h + s = \$4.50$$

$$-(2h + s = \$3.25)$$

$$h = \$1.25$$

Plug in this value for h into the first equation to solve for s:

$$2(\$1.25) + s = \$3.25$$

$$\$2.50 + s = \$3.25$$

$$s = \$0.75$$

So two sodas would cost $2 \times \$0.75 = \$1.50$, choice (C).

7. C ①②③

$a = f$, since all the obtuse angles formed when two parallel lines are cut by a transversal are equal. f is an exterior angle of the small triangle containing angles c, d, and e, so it is equal to the sum of the two nonadjacent interior angles, c and d. Since $a = f$ and $f = c + d$, $a = c + d$, answer choice (C).

8. D ①②③

The first 3 minutes of the phone call cost 75 cents or 0.75 dollars. If the entire call lasted x minutes, the rest of the call lasted $x - 3$ minutes. Each minute after the first 3 cost 15 cents or $0.15, so the rest of the call cost $0.15(x - 3)$. Thus, the cost of the entire call is $0.75 + 0.15(x - 3)$ dollars.

If this isn't clear, pick numbers. Let $x = 5$. The first 3 minutes cost $0.75 and the additional $5 - 3$ $= 2$ minutes are $0.15 each. So the entire call costs $\$0.75 + 2(\$0.15) = \$1.05$. Plug 5 for x into all the answer choices to see which ones give you 1.05:

(A) $0.75(3) + 0.15x = 2.25 + 0.15(5) = 2.25 + 0.75 = 3.00$. Eliminate.

(B) $0.75(3) + 0.15(x + 3) = 2.25 + 0.15(5 + 3) = 2.25 + 1.20 = 3.45$. Eliminate.

(C) $0.75 + 0.15(3 - x) = 0.75 + 0.15(3 - 5) = 0.75 - 0.30 = 0.45$. Eliminate.

(D) $0.75 + 0.15(x - 3) = 0.75 + 0.15(5 - 3) = 0.75 + 0.30 = 1.05$. Works!

(E) $0.75 + 0.15(5) = 0.75 + 0.75 = 1.50$. Eliminate.

The only choice that yields the desired result is (D), so it must be correct.

9. B

Before you can find the area of the circle, you need to find the length of the wire. The wire is in the shape of a semicircle with diameter 12. Since circumference $= \pi d$, the length of a semicircle is half of that, $\frac{\pi d}{2}$. So the length of the wire is $\frac{\pi(12)}{2}$, or 6π. When this wire is bent to form a circle, the circumference of this circle will equal 6π. So the length of the circle's diameter must equal 6, and the radius must be 3. Now you can find the area of the circle:

Area $= \pi r^2$

$= \pi(3)^2$

$= 9\pi$, choice (B).

10. C

If $a^2 - a = 72$, then $a^2 - a - 72 = 0$. Factoring this quadratic equation: $(a - 9)(a + 8) = 0$, so $a - 9 = 0$ or $a + 8 = 0$, and $a = 9$ or $a = -8$. b to the nth power equals a, so b must be a root of either 9 or –8. Look through the answer choices to find the choice that is not a root of either 9 or –8:

(A) $(-8)^1 = -8$, so this can be a value for b. Eliminate.

(B) $(-2)^3 = -8$, so this can be a value for b. Eliminate.

(C) $2^3 = 8$, not –8, so this *cannot* be a value for b. Works!

(D) $3^2 = 9$, so this can be a value for b. Eliminate.

(E) $9^1 = 9$, so this can be a value for b. Eliminate.

So (C) is the only answer choice that cannot be a value for b.

11. C

The most efficient way to answer this question is to use the midpoint formula: the midpoint of points (x_1, y_1) and (x_2, y_2) is $\left(\dfrac{x_1 + x_2}{2}, \dfrac{y_1 + y_2}{2} \right)$. You'll use the formula more skillfully if, rather than merely memorize it, you think about what it means—namely, that the midpoint of two points is merely the average of their x- and y-coordinates:

$$\left(\frac{(0 + x_2)}{2} = 3, \frac{(2 + y_2)}{2} = 4 \right)$$

$(x_2 = 6, y_2 = 6)$.

Thus, choice (C) is correct.

12. D

$$4\sqrt{2x} - 2 = 16$$

$$4\sqrt{2x} = 18$$

$$\sqrt{2x} = \frac{18}{4}$$

$$\left(\sqrt{2x} \right)^2 = \left(\frac{18}{4} \right)^2$$

$$2x = \frac{18^2}{4^2}$$

$$x = \frac{18 \times 18}{4 \times 4 \times 2} = \frac{9 \times 9}{2 \times 2 \times 2} = \frac{81}{8}, \text{ choice (D)}.$$

13. E

If you can't visualize a graph, plug in points and graph it yourself. If doing so is helpful, use your calculator.

Plug in 2 for x:

$$y = -3x^2$$

$$y = -3(2)^2$$

$$y = -3(4)$$

$$y = -12$$

This eliminates (A) and (B).

Plug in −2 for x:

$$y = -3x^2$$

$$y = -3(-2)^2$$

$$y = -3(4)$$

$$y = -12$$

This eliminates (C) and (D), leaving only (E).

14. C ①②③

Think backward. If the person now weighs w pounds, then his or her weight before losing 8 pounds was 8 pounds more than w, or $w + 8$. The person's weight before gaining p pounds was $w + 8 - p$, which can also be written as $w - p + 8$, choice (C).

15. B ①②③

The surface area of a cube is $6e^2$, where e = the length of an edge of the cube. Since the surface area is $36n^2$:

$$6e^2 = 36n^2$$

$$e^2 = 6n^2$$

$$e = n\sqrt{6}$$

The volume of a cube is e^3. To solve for the volume in terms of n, plug in the value for an edge that you just found: Volume = $e^3 = (n\sqrt{6})^3 = 6n^3\sqrt{6}$, answer choice (B).

16. C

Since the ratio of x to y to z is 3:6:8, if $y = 24$ or 4×6, x and z must also be multiplied by 4 for the ratio to hold. So $x = 4 \times 3 = 12$ and $z = 4 \times 8 = 32$, and $x + z = 44$, choice (C).

SECTION 9

1. E

The pronoun in the sentence must correspond with *teacher shortage* (not *salaries*). Therefore, the pronoun should be *it*. (E) is the only answer choice with this pronoun.

2. A

Items in a series must have the same structure, which is the case for the original sentence, (A). (B), (C), (D), and (E) break the parallelism.

3. D

(A) is a run-on, so it cannot be correct. (B), (C), and (E) are awkward and confusing. (D) has the cleanest structure and is the best answer choice.

4. A

(C) does not use a semicolon correctly. (B), (D), and (E) all unnecessarily add extra words. Be suspicious of answer choices that make the sentence more complex. (A) is correct because it is clear and concise.

5. D

Idiomatically, *the same* should be followed by the preposition *as*, not *than*. There is also a problem of parallelism here; the two things being compared should be in the same grammatical form. Since *talking* is a gerund, the thing it's being compared to should also be a gerund: *driving*.

6. C

This run-on sentence is best corrected by (C), which is grammatically correct and doesn't include extra verbiage. (B) and (E) use the semicolon improperly, and (D) is wordy.

7. E

The sentence is unclear because it doesn't use the correct sequence of tenses. Since the client had already been waiting for 15 minutes *before* the moment when the receptionist looked up, the first verb must be in the past perfect: *had been waiting*, choice (E).

8. C

This run-on sentence is a comma splice, which can be corrected by exchanging the comma for a semicolon. (B) does this, but (B) also removes *they* and with it the second independent clause. (C) is the only choice with correct sentence structure.

9. E

Because the second part of the sentence is an independent clause, the underlined portion must be altered to create a dependent clause. (C) and (E) do this, but (E) is clearer and better constructed.

10. D

(D) is the only answer choice that creates a complete sentence. Also, the words *rare enough to honor the spiritual essence of the Buddha* is descriptive of *stones*. Therefore, (D) makes sense.

11. D

The two independent clauses in this sentence must be separated by either a semicolon or a coordinating conjunction. (D) uses the semicolon correctly, so it is correct.

12. C

The original sentence does not contain a verb. (C) and (E) insert *are* to create a working verb structure. However, (E) incorrectly creates a dependent clause with *these are*.

13. B

The word *that* at the beginning of (A), (D), and (E) makes the sentence incomplete. The *because* in (C) creates the same problem. (B) is the answer because it contains both a subject, *many people*, and a verb, *believe*.

14. D

(A) is incorrect because the word *but* repeats the idea expressed by *although*. (B) and (C) are incorrect because they leave the sentence without an independent clause. (D) is correct because it provides the necessary independent clause. (E) is incorrect because it uses *and* incorrectly.

Part Three

HOW TO ATTACK THE WRITING SECTIONS

CHAPTER 5: SAT WRITING BASICS

SMARTPOINTS COVERED IN THIS CHAPTER

ESSAY

WHAT TO EXPECT ON TEST DAY

There are three Writing sections on the SAT, one essay and two multiple-choice sets. You will have 25 minutes to complete the essay. The multiple-choice sets will have a total of 49 questions. One set will be 25 minutes long, and the other will be 10 minutes long.

The essay will be the first section of the test and will count for approximately one-third of your 800-point Writing score. Your essay and multiple-choice section scores will be combined into a single scaled score that reflects the weight given to each section. This new scaled score will then be converted into a final score ranging from 200–800 points.

 ## THE ESSAY

For the essay portion of the test, your task is to write a short, persuasive essay on an assigned topic.

The keywords here are *persuasive*, *specific*, and *relevant*. Your essay must convince the grader of your point of view using concrete and pertinent examples. If any of these elements are missing, or if you repeat statements without adding new insight or new information, your score will suffer.

PERFECT SCORE TIP

" Whenever an essay asked me to take a position on an issue, I made sure to take a position very clearly and stick with it. "

You are required to write about the topic you are given, but you don't need any specific knowledge to complete the SAT essay, and you do have a lot of freedom in what you actually write. Because the topic will be very broad in scope, you can write about what you know and what you are interested in.

ESSAY SCORING

Your essays will be scored holistically by two readers. *Holistically* means your essay gets a single score—a number—that indicates its overall quality. This number takes into account a variety of essay characteristics, including organization and development of ideas, sentence structure, vocabulary, and grammar and usage. Thus, a highly persuasive and eloquent essay that has several run-ons or other minor errors could still earn a top score because of its overall effectiveness and impact.

HOW WILL MY ESSAY BE SCORED?

Each reader will assign your essay a score ranging from a high of 6 to a low of 1. These two scores are added together to get a total score ranging from a high of 12 to a low of 2. The essay score accounts for approximately one-third of your final Writing section score.

The following chart shows the main criteria that the graders use to score your essay:

THE ESSAY SCORING CHART

SCORE	COMPETENCE	SUPPORT AND ORGANIZATION	LANGUAGE
6	Understanding: clear **Focus:** clear **Critical thinking skills:** insightful	**Examples:** developed, specific, relevant **Paragraphs:** organized **Logic:** strong **Transitions:** clear	**Language use:** good **Vocabulary:** varied, appropriate **Sentence structure:** varied, effective **Errors:** few, if any, small
5	Understanding: reasonably clear **Focus:** clear **Critical thinking skills:** strong	**Examples:** generally specific and relevant, developed **Paragraphs:** generally organized **Logic:** strong **Transitions:** effective	**Language use:** competent **Vocabulary:** appropriate, sometimes varied **Sentence structure:** somewhat varied, effective **Errors:** few, small

4	**Understanding:** some **Focus:** generally good **Critical thinking skills:** competent	**Examples:** adequate with adequate development **Paragraphs:** generally clearly organized **Logic:** generally good **Transitions:** used sporadically	**Language use:** adequate **Vocabulary:** somewhat appropriate, sometimes varied **Sentence structure:** somewhat varied **Errors:** some, may be distracting
3	**Understanding:** some **Focus:** inconsistent **Critical thinking skills:** developing	**Examples:** may be irrelevant and/or inadequate with inconsistent development **Paragraphs:** limited organization **Logic:** inconsistent **Transitions:** limited	**Language use:** limited **Vocabulary:** developing, but inconsistent **Sentence structure:** lacks variety **Errors:** numerous, may affect readability, clarity
2	**Understanding:** vague or limited **Focus:** poor **Critical thinking skills:** weak	**Examples:** may be irrelevant and/or inadequate with very limited development **Paragraphs:** poorly organized **Logic:** not presented well **Transitions:** weak	**Language use:** little facility **Vocabulary:** limited, may be incorrect **Sentence structure:** frequent problems **Errors:** many, sometimes affect readability, clarity
1	**Understanding:** little or none **Focus:** fails to do so **Critical thinking skills:** lacking	**Examples:** limited or nonexistent with poor development **Paragraphs:** poorly organized **Logic:** not presented well **Transitions:** not used well	**Language use:** no facility **Vocabulary:** little or no mastery **Sentence structure:** seriously flawed **Errors:** many, often affect readability, clarity

Chapter 4 will show you Kaplan's strategies for writing a top-scoring essay.

MULTIPLE-CHOICE QUESTIONS

The multiple-choice portion of the Writing section consists of 49 questions, 35 in the 25-minute section and 14 in the second 10-minute section. They are divided into three types:

1. 18 Identifying Sentence Errors questions
2. 25 Improving Sentences questions
3. 6 Improving Paragraphs questions

The Identifying Sentence Errors and Improving Sentences questions are based on single, unrelated sentences on a variety of topics. The Improving Paragraphs questions are based on a brief passage. The sentences and passages upon which the questions are based will usually (but not always) contain one or more grammar, usage, or organizational errors. Your task is to spot (and sometimes fix) the mistakes in as many of the multiple-choice questions as you can in 25 minutes and 10 minutes, respectively.

HOW MULTIPLE-CHOICE QUESTIONS ARE SCORED

- If you get a multiple-choice question right, you earn 1 point. If you get a multiple-choice question wrong, you lose $\frac{1}{4}$ of a point. If you omit a multiple-choice question, you neither gain nor lose any points.

- Your raw score for the multiple-choice questions is converted into a scaled score ranging from 200–800.

- This scaled score will account for approximately two-thirds of your total Writing score.

KEY POINTS YOU'VE LEARNED IN THIS CHAPTER

1. The Writing sections consist of one essay and two multiple-choice tests.

2. You will have 25 minutes to write the essay, which is always the first section of the test. Two people will read your essay, each person rating it from 1 to 6, with 6 being the highest.

3. You will have two sections of multiple-choice questions, one 25 minutes long and one 10 minutes long. There will be 18 Identifying Sentence Errors questions, 25 Improving Sentences questions, and 6 Improving Paragraphs questions, for a total of 49 questions.

CHAPTER 6: THE ESSAY

ESSAY

WHAT TO EXPECT ON TEST DAY

There are three important elements to master in order to succeed on the essay—content, length, and neatness.

The SAT essay is a *persuasive* essay that you write in response to a particular question, also called a *prompt*. The essay is the first section you tackle on the test, and many students are glad to get it out of the way.

CONTENT

You will be given a quote, or a pair of quotes, and a prompt that is related to the content of the quote. It is the prompt that will guide your essay topic; the quote is there just to get your creative juices flowing. The graders will be looking for whether your subject matter is relevant to the prompt, whether your stance is insightful, and whether your essay is persuasive. It is very important that you take a firm stance in your essay and stick to it.

Essays are graded by high school teachers and college professors. They'll be impressed by an essay that goes beyond your personal experience to make interesting and meaningful connections.

> **PERFECT SCORE TIP**
>
> " I found that I didn't need to be overly creative to get a good score on the essay. Simply following Kaplan's rough format is enough to get you a good score. "

WRITING A PERSUASIVE ESSAY

If you remember nothing else, remember that your essay needs to be *persuasive*. You are trying to persuade your reader to see something from your point of view, and the bulk of your essay should be used to explain *why* you have taken your chosen stance.

Also, if the topic allows, it's a good idea to include specific examples related to current events, history, and literature in your essay. You don't have to draw from these three areas, but you *do* have to use specific examples.

EXPERT TUTOR TIP

Remember, your job is to answer the essay question, not just analyze the quote's meaning. If you forget this, you will lose points.

Please also note that grammar and punctuation are a part of a successful essay. However, errors in grammar and punctuation aren't the most important factor affecting your score. Naturally, you want as few errors as possible, but you can still achieve a high score with some mistakes, so don't stress yourself out worrying about grammar and punctuation if they are not your strongest skills. Strong organization, transitions, and specific examples relevant to your topic can overcome minor weaknesses in the use of language.

EXAMPLE BANK #1: BRAINSTORM ON PAPER

Step 1: Take several sheets of blank or lined paper and write a favorite topic in the center of each page. Be sure your topic isn't too narrow or too broad. (WWII—too broad; my dog—too narrow)

Step 2: Draw a few lines, similar to bicycle wheel spokes, extending from the word(s). At the end of the lines, write subtopics. From the subtopics, you can draw more lines for sub-subtopics.

Step 3: Repeat steps 1 and 2 at least *nine more times*. More is better here.

So, if your main topic for a page is "Getting into College," you might write the names of some colleges you are interested in, the SAT, getting organized, college trips, and more.

Note: All the words you write on these pages are examples that would work for any essay, as long as they are relevant to the topic you are asked to discuss.

EXAMPLE BANK #2: ANSWER QUESTIONS AND PROMPTS ON INDEX CARDS

Answering the following five questions should help you get started building your example bank (feel free to make up more questions). Use one card for each.

1. What book changed your mind about something and why?

2. What non-school subject do you know the most about and why?

3. List three people—whether real or fictional, living or dead, famous or personal friends/family—whom you respect and admire. Why did you choose them?

4. Think of an event that changed your life. What happened? Where? When? How and why did it happen? What happened after that that demonstrates its importance?

5. What major historical event is the one you know most about? Why did you learn about it? Does it have any significance for your own life?

DEVELOP AN EXTENSIVE EXAMPLE BANK

You should have a ready stable of examples, ones that can easily be trotted out to answer whatever essay you get on test day. By assembling a wide variety of specific examples relating to a wide variety of topics, you'll be ready to tackle any prompt.

Along with being concrete and relevant, the best examples are those that are interesting to the person who is writing the essay. This will allow your passion to shine through to the reader. For example, if you know only about music, concentrate on that. If you love movies, that works, too. Nothing is off limits (except obscenities).

The previous boxed examples show two ways to create an Example Bank. Either one is equally effective. Just pick the one that appeals to you and be thorough in your efforts.

LENGTH

It's true that the content and quality of your essay are two important aspects of achieving a high score, but there is also a certain expectation from the essay graders concerning the length of a well-written essay. Specifically, your essay should range between 300–400 words if you want to receive a 5 or 6.

If your essay is too short, no matter how well written, it could mean the difference between a low 3 or 4 and a 5 or 6, a difference that would have a considerable impact on your overall Writing score. That is not to say that a wordy essay will grab the top score or that you should spend time counting each word. Just keep in mind that your essay should at least be *long enough* to put you in the running for a good score.

Another aspect of length is the space in which you will write your essay. You will only receive two pages with 45 lines, and you must use a pencil.

DON'T FORGET

When you begin to write your essay, try to remember the following:

- A high-scoring essay will be approximately 300–400 well-written words.
- Small, yet legible, handwriting will conserve space.

EXPERT TUTOR TIP

" Keep in mind that essay graders particularly remember the first and last things they see in your work, so start strong and finish the same way. And write legibly! "

NEATNESS

Your essay must be readable. If you edit what you've written, do it neatly. If you add a word, change a phrase, or cross out a sentence, do it carefully. It may sound silly, but neatness matters. You can't earn a good score if the graders can't read what you've written.

The graders have tons of essays to read and grade in a short amount of time. That means they don't have much time to spend reading your essay (about a minute, on average), and they aren't going to read an essay three or four times in order to decipher illegible handwriting.

A NOTE ON HANDWRITING SIZE

How large or small you write will affect the length of your essay. You get two pages on which to write—no more. Just filling up the lines with large letters and not focusing on writing a well-developed argument will not earn you more points. Practice using smaller handwriting before the test so you don't run out of space and waste time rewriting on test day.

You're not expected to produce a perfect piece of writing. The graders know that you only have 25 minutes to think about, write, and proofread your work. What they expect is an organized and readable piece of writing that makes an argument supported by real examples. The rest of this chapter will show you how to accomplish this task.

HOW TO WRITE A HIGH-SCORING SAT ESSAY

The directions for the essay are as follows:

The essay gives you an opportunity to show how effectively you can develop and express ideas. You should, therefore, take care to develop your point of view, present your ideas logically and clearly, and use language precisely.

Your essay must be written in your Answer Grid Booklet—you will receive no other paper on which to write. You will have enough space if you write on every line, avoid wide margins, and keep your handwriting to a reasonable size. Remember that people who are not familiar with your handwriting will read what you write. Try to write or print so that what you are writing is legible to those readers.

You have 25 minutes to write an essay on the topic assigned below.
DO NOT WRITE ON ANOTHER TOPIC. AN OFF-TOPIC ESSAY WILL RECEIVE A SCORE OF ZERO.

Think carefully about the issue presented in the following excerpt and the assignment below.

> "When I played pro football, I never set out to hurt anybody deliberately . . . unless it was, you know, important, like a league game or something."
>
> –Dick Butkus

Assignment: Have professional sports influenced the values of American society? Plan and write an essay in which you develop your point of view on this issue. Support your position with reasoning and examples taken from your reading, studies, experience, or observations.

DO NOT WRITE YOUR ESSAY IN YOUR TEST BOOK.
You will receive credit only for what you write in your Answer Grid Booklet.

PERFECT SCORE TIP

When choosing examples, I found it better to choose from a variety of sources (one from history, one from personal experience, and one from a book). That way, my essays were more interesting.

KAPLAN'S TARGET STRATEGY FOR ESSAY WRITING

We have developed a system that we think will make writing the essay much easier—Kaplan's 4 Ps Strategy.

Prompt—read and understand it.

Plan—collect and organize your ideas and examples.

Produce—write your essay.

Proofread—check for consistency and errors.

PERFECT SCORE TIP

" Kaplan's essay strategy gives you enough time to write a great essay, but you definitely have to write fast! Keeping track of time helped me avoid rushing at the end. "

You have 25 minutes to write your essay. Here is a minute-by-minute rundown of Kaplan's 4 Ps Strategy:

MINUTES 1–2: PROMPT—READ AND UNDERSTAND IT

Take one minute to read the quote and think about the prompt (you'll be surprised how long a minute is). Begin to think about your stance and possible examples that pop into your head. Start to jot some notes as ideas come to you.

DON'T QUOTE THE QUOTE!

It is *not* desirable to refer to the quotation, or to quote it, in your essay. Use it as inspiration and come up with your own examples—that is what the graders are looking for. The quotation should be used only as a last resort.

Let's say that you get the following quote and assignment:

> "A man walking down a crowded street noticed a dog lying by the side of the road that looked like it might be injured; but since everyone else just passed by, the man was satisfied to assume that the dog was fine. The next day he learned that the dog had been hit by a car and lay injured for two hours before a concerned man stopped and took it to the vet. The animal recovered, but the man never forgave himself for leaving it for someone else to help."
>
> —Narawhal Bherundi, *Autobiography*

Assignment: What is your view on individual responsibility in a situation in which many people could have reacted?

Then the assignment asks you to take a specific example from your personal experience, from current events, or from history, literature, or any other discipline and develop it to support your argument. You may refer to the quotation if you want to, but you're not required to.

CAN'T CHOOSE A SIDE?

If you can't decide which stance to take, draw a large "T" on the page and label the sides *Pro* and *Con*. Then write each supporting example under the side it belongs on. The side with the most wins.

The most important aspect of this step is to fully understand what you need to write about and how you will develop your essay based on that.

MINUTES 3–5: PLAN—COLLECT AND ORGANIZE YOUR IDEAS AND EXAMPLES

You have already started to do this in Minute 1. Now your job is to zero in on getting organized as you continue to brainstorm examples and decide your position on the issue. Before the test, practice using your first five minutes effectively; they are the keys to a successful essay!

GATHER YOUR EXAMPLES FIRST

Because it doesn't matter which stance you take, choose the one for which you have the more concrete and relevant examples. Now is the moment when all your work on the Example Bank comes in handy. If you have done your job, you should have at least two, if not three, good supporting examples to write about.

NO EXAMPLES?

Pick keywords—*responsibility* and *reacted* in this chapter's prompt—then ask yourself:

- **Who hasn't taken responsibility, but should have?** (Witnessing a cheating incident at school, observing a bully in action)

- **Who reacts well?** (Firemen, parents)

If need be, you can create a concrete example or two from these ideas. Just be sure the examples you make up are plausible.

EVALUATE YOUR EXAMPLES

Take the time to be sure that the examples relate to the topic. Ask yourself the following questions:

- Are your examples specific or vague? For example, which of the following is a more specific example?

  When you see an elderly lady struggling with her groceries, you should offer to help carry them.

  Last month, I was sitting around with my friends when we saw my neighbor, who is 85 and recently had hip surgery, struggling with his grocery bags. I excused myself and went over to help him.

The second example is more specific than the first. Unlike the first example, the second detailed an incident in which the writer was with other people who also could have taken the initiative to help someone in need, but he or she was the one who actually did.

- Are your examples relevant to the topic?

  No one was paying attention to the new girl, so the teacher told me to sit with her at lunch.

  I saw that the new girl had been sitting by herself at lunch all week, so I asked her to join our table.

The second example is more relevant to the topic. The essay asked you to talk about individual responsibility. In the first example, the teacher was the one to tell the student to take responsibility for reaching out to the new girl. That is not an example of an individual taking charge on his or her own when he or she sees that no one else has. In the second example, the writer took it upon himself or herself to invite the girl over when no one else had.

If any examples don't measure up, be ruthless and toss them out. If you have the luxury of more than three, choose the ones that are the most varied and interesting.

FINE-TUNE YOUR STANCE AND WRITE YOUR THESIS SENTENCE

Once you have your examples lined up, you can work on a statement that expresses your stance. It is the heart of your first paragraph.

COMPARE AND CONTRAST YOUR EXAMPLES

When you were evaluating your examples, you were to think about how they related to the topic. Now, you'll need to think about this again. Make a few notes about each example in relation to the others you have on your list. Then make a few notes on how each example relates *back to the topic*.

These notes become the transitions between paragraphs that will round out and add interest—*and prevent you from repeating yourself.*

CREATE A BRIEF OUTLINE FOR YOUR FIVE-PARAGRAPH ESSAY

Ideally, SAT essays have five paragraphs:

- An introduction with your thesis statement or stance

- A paragraph for each of three examples

- A conclusion

If you have only one example, you will have three paragraphs; a two-example essay should have four paragraphs.

Here's one possible outline for the Bherundi prompt in this chapter:

SAMPLE ESSAY OUTLINE

Paragraph 1: Introduction—People have a responsibility to help others, especially when others have ignored those in need. (Should help, power of individual and groups of individuals)

Paragraph 2: Example #1—Saw bully pick on a kid in school/felt badly/was the only person to report it to the teacher. *Transition:* Anybody can/should fix a small injustice.

Paragraph 3: Example #2—Mother Teresa started own charity order/helped outcasts, those who no one else would help. *Transition:* A very dedicated person can make a huge difference.

Paragraph 4: Example #3—Doctors Without Borders/doctors who could make a lot of money at home go to dangerous places and help others/no one else there would help. *Transition:* Group of individuals can be dedicated to a larger cause, can be effective.

Paragraph 5: Conclusion—It is easy to ignore the needs of others, but people have the responsibility to react/respond to need. Small to large efforts are important; a group of organized people is very powerful.

Note: To save time, your outline will be briefer, using abbreviations and shorthand notes that you understand.

MINUTES 6–23: PRODUCE—WRITE YOUR ESSAY

The writing step of your essay should take about 18 minutes. That's plenty of time to write solid paragraphs using your outline and notes.

HAVE A PLAN

> When you have a good written plan, writing the essay is just a matter of turning your notes into full, descriptive sentences.

To write your strongest essay, follow your outline. You spent five minutes considering the prompt and planning your essay, so stick to it! Don't panic and write from the opposing point of view. However, if you come up with the perfect example halfway through your essay, replace it in your outline, see how it works, then continue. But *try* not to erase and rewrite any big chunks of text. You don't have time. (That's why starting out with a written plan is so crucial!)

You also need to write clearly, write concisely, write complete sentences, and use proper grammar. But you have only 18 minutes. So write fast. Here is a quickly written essay (a draft version, you might say) about responsibility:

An individual can have a major effect on another individual or situation. In the example above, an individual save a dog's life. A group of people ignored the situation but an individual man actually did something. He stepped out of the mob mentality. Everyone else conformed to each other and walked by. This man stopped and saved the dog.

However, the primary man in the example did not do so. He conformed and walked by. He shirked his responsibility. This is like that one time my sister needed help and didn't get it. On her way home from college, she had car trouble and was stranded on the side of the road at night. Many cars passed by but no one stopped to see if they could give her a hand. After waiting for forever, she ended up having to walk to the nearest gas station two miles away, which is not safe for a young girl to do by herself. Here, no individual took responsibility to help her, and this refusal of responsibility could have led to more severe consequences.

On a lighter but related note, I had personal experience with individual responsibility. At the beginning of last year, I was walking to first period science class when I noticed a confused, nervous girl standing in the hallway. She looked like she was about to cry as everyone rushed past her. She was obviously lost, but no one who knew the way took responsibility to help her. I felt badly so approached her and asked if I could help. It turned out that she had just moved from another part of the country and knew no one at my high school. She couldn't find her science class, which turned out to be my science

---

EXPERT TUTOR TIP

" Don't be afraid to use *I/me/mine*, especially if you're writing about a personal experience. Using *one* can make your essay sound formal or stilted. "

class, and was too shy to ask for help. I walked with her to science class, made a new friend, and took the responsibility to help someone.

At the end of the day, everyone has the responsibility not to conform in a situation in which many people can react. Each person should be the individual who takes action and helps. No one should assume that someone else will take responsibility, because maybe no one will.

MINUTES 24–25: PROOFREAD—CHECK FOR CONSISTENCY AND ERRORS

This step takes two minutes. It involves quickly reading over your essay and improving its readability. Ideally, all you'll need to do is fix minor grammatical or spelling errors, change a few words here and there, and maybe add a sentence or two for clarity's sake.

If you spend the bulk of the 25 minutes thinking about, planning, and writing the essay, the proofreading step should entail nothing more than putting the finishing touches on an already strong essay.

Here is our edited essay with changes underlined:

An individual can have a major effect on another individual or situation. In the example above, an individual saved a dog's life. A group of people ignored the situation, but an individual man actually did something. He stepped out of the mob mentality. Everyone else conformed to each other and walked by. This man stopped and saved the dog.

However, the man in the example did not do so. He conformed and walked by. He shirked his responsibility. This relates to a situation that my sister experienced. On her way home from college, she had car trouble and was stranded on the side of the road at night. Many cars passed by, but no one stopped to see if they could give her a hand. After waiting for over an hour, she ended up having to walk to the nearest gas station two miles away, which is not safe for a young girl to do by herself. Here, no individual took responsibility to help her, and this refusal of responsibility could have led to more severe consequences.

On a lighter but related note, I had a personal experience with individual responsibility. At the beginning of last year, I was walking to first period science class when I noticed a confused, nervous girl standing in the hallway. She looked like she was about to cry as everyone rushed past her. She was obviously lost, but no one who knew the way took responsibility to help her. I felt badly for her, so I approached her and asked if I could help. It turned out that she had just moved from another part of the country and knew no one at my high school. She couldn't find her science class, which turned out to be my science class, and was too shy to ask for help. I walked with her to science class, made a new friend, and took the responsibility to help someone.

At the end of the day, everyone has the responsibility not to conform in a situation in which many people can react. Each person should be the individual who takes action and helps. No one should assume that someone else will take responsibility, because maybe no one will.

Okay, now it's your turn. Let's go through each of the steps.

PRACTICE PLANNING PROMPTS

Below are ten sample statements. Look at your watch (a digital one, if possible, or use a digital kitchen timer). Spend exactly five minutes understanding the prompt and planning essays for each one as described above. Working without quotes is harder, but it helps you think more independently. See how you do.

ESSAY PROMPT ONE

Do you have to be brave to do something courageous?

ESSAY PROMPT TWO

Mark Twain once said, "Don't part with your illusions. When they are gone you may still exist but you have ceased to live." What are your thoughts on whether it matters if a person stops setting dreams and goals for himself or herself?

ESSAY PROMPT THREE

Some schools have begun allowing students in biology classes to use computer programs that simulate animal dissections instead of physically cutting up the animals. Which method do you think schools should use?

ESSAY PROMPT FOUR

Is financial status the most important factor governing an individual's quality of life?

ESSAY PROMPT FIVE

In an address to the joint session of Congress in 2009, President Barack Obama said, "In a global economy where the most valuable skill you can sell is your knowledge, a good education is no longer just a pathway to opportunity; it is a prerequisite." Do you believe that knowledge from a good education is necessary in order to succeed?

ESSAY PROMPT SIX

Does the media have too much influence on the young adult population?

ESSAY PROMPT SEVEN

Should high school students be allowed to take college classes?

ESSAY PROMPT EIGHT

In the interest of security in air travel, some airports have begun using full-body scanners to screen passengers in addition to metal detectors. Do you believe that is a necessary precaution, or do you believe it might be an invasion of privacy?

ESSAY PROMPT NINE

Before posting photos or videos on the Internet, such as on social networking sites, should you seek permission from people in those photos or videos?

ESSAY PROMPT TEN

Thomas Edison once said, "Genius is one percent inspiration and ninety-nine percent perspiration." What is your view of Edison's belief? Do you agree with that definition of *genius*?

ESSAY PLANNING PRACTICE

Read the essay directions below and try to outline an essay based on the prompt. In your outline, you will want to try to include the stance you're taking, the evidence that supports your stance, and how this information will be arranged.

The essay gives you an opportunity to show how effectively you can develop and express ideas. You should, therefore, take care to develop your point of view, present your ideas logically and clearly, and use language precisely.

Your essay must be written in your Answer Grid Booklet—you will receive no other paper on which to write. You will have enough space if you write on every line, avoid wide margins, and keep your handwriting to a reasonable size. Remember that people who are not familiar with your handwriting will read what you write. Try to write or print so that what you are writing is legible to those readers.

You have 25 minutes to write an essay on the topic assigned below.

DO NOT WRITE ON ANOTHER TOPIC. AN OFF-TOPIC ESSAY WILL RECEIVE A SCORE OF ZERO.

Think carefully about the issue presented in the following excerpt and the assignment below.

> "A man walking down a crowded street noticed a dog lying by the side of the road that looked like it might be injured; but since everyone else just passed by, the man was satisfied to assume that the dog was fine. The next day he learned that the dog had been hit by a car and lay injured for two hours before a concerned man stopped and took it to the vet. The animal recovered, but the man never forgave himself for leaving it for someone else to help."
>
> —Narawhal Bherundi, *Autobiography*

Assignment: What is your view on individual responsibility in a situation in which many people could have reacted? Plan and write an essay in which you develop your point of view on this issue. Support your position with reasoning and examples taken from your reading, studies, experience, or observations.

DO NOT WRITE YOUR ESSAY IN YOUR TEST BOOK.
You will receive credit only for what you write in your Answer Grid Booklet.

Plan your paragraphs on a separate sheet of paper. Remember that on the SAT you will plan your essay by using space on the test booklet, and your essay MUST be written on the lined pages of your answer sheet.

I. Introduction

A. General argument: A person should take responsibility, as a member of a community, in a group situation to help those in need.

B. Examples:

1. Given example of man and injured dog.

2. My mom's experience in the grocery store.

II. Body

A. Given example of man and injured dog.

1. Man assumes that others would help if it was really needed.

2. Ignores his instinct to help and conforms to others' actions.

3. Feels guilty for not acting.

B. My mom's experience in the grocery store.

1. People assumed she was crazy and weird.

2. Others didn't help because no one else was.

3. Not helping could have been matter of life or death.

III. Conclusion

A. It's easy to just walk by and do what everyone else does.

B. As a part of a community, everyone is responsible for the well-being of others.

CREATE A GOOD ESSAY OUTLINE

A good outline will help you write a better essay and save time. Always take the time to prepare a solid written plan.

PRODUCING PRACTICE

This in-depth outline may lead to a more complete and organized essay. It is also a little different from the first way we went about answering this question. This proves our point—there is not *one way* to write these essays. You have to use *your* knowledge and *your* experiences.

Now that you're done with your outline, you're ready to start writing. Start your practice with the essay topic that you just outlined. Write your essay on separate sheets of paper.

PROOFREADING PRACTICE

When you are done, take two minutes to proofread for spelling, grammar, and any other glaring errors. Some things to look for are comma splices, run-on sentences, misspelled or skipped words, ideas that are not sufficiently developed, vague references to the elements in the essay (e.g., *this* is a good example, *that* is important because, etc.), and making sure you have taken a clear stance and have explained that stance persuasively.

HOW YOUR ESSAY IS GRADED

To help you get a sense of how your essay might be graded, we have included a sample high-scoring essay. Evaluate your essay according to the following criteria to get a sense of how well you've done:

- My essay has a clear stance on the given issue.
- I provided specific support using examples and evidence.
- I have logical organization.
- I have used appropriate transitions between ideas.
- I have used variety in my sentence structure and vocabulary.
- My sentences are clear and have an even tone.

Now let's look at a Grade 5 essay:

GRADE 5 ESSAY (STRONG)

A person should take responsibility in a group situation. A group is made up of individuals, after all. People hide too much behind others' actions and don't think for themselves. Rather than hiding, they should be proactive.

The first man in the example had a responsibility, as did everyone on the sidewalk, to help the dog. He saw the dog, the potential bad situation, and instead of following his instinct to check out the problem, he decided to walk by because no one else was helping. He consciously decides to walk by, assuming that if the dog were really that hurt, someone else would take care of it. It doesn't occur to him that everyone is thinking the same thing and doing nothing. He feels badly because he knows he was persuaded by the actions of others and ignored his responsibility toward another living creature.

Something similar happened to my mother in a grocery store. There was a puddle of something in one of the aisles, and she slipped, fell to the ground, and hit her head. Unfortunately, no one saw what happened, so when people came around the corner and saw her lying on the floor, they just kept going past thinking that she was crazy or weird. Others came down the aisle, too, but did nothing because they saw that the people in front of them did nothing. She remained dizzy and injured on the floor until her husband came down the aisle and found her on the ground. It is sad that no one took the responsibility to help an injured woman. Someone should have called for help or at least asked her if she was OK, especially because it could have been a matter of life or death.

It's very easy to just walk by, to do what everyone else in the group does. Everyone could just look the other way and not listen to the pleas for help. But that is not how a community is run, and as humans who share this planet, we are entitled to act as a community, and that entails having a responsibility to help.

ESSAY PRACTICE

This is your chance to put the 4 Ps to work. Give yourself 25 minutes to go through this target strategy:

      Prompt—read and understand it.

      Plan—collect and organize your ideas and examples.

      Produce—write your essay.

      Proofread—check for consistency and errors.

After you finish, read the three sample essays—a strong essay, a mediocre essay, and a weak essay—and the sample grader comments. Use these essays and comments to judge the quality of your own essays.

The essay gives you an opportunity to show how effectively you can develop and express ideas. You should, therefore, take care to develop your point of view, present your ideas logically and clearly, and use language precisely.

Your essay must be written in your Answer Grid Booklet—you will receive no other paper on which to write. You will have enough space if you write on every line, avoid wide margins, and keep your handwriting to a reasonable size. Remember that people who are not familiar with your handwriting will read what you write. Try to write or print so that what you are writing is legible to those readers.

You have 25 minutes to write an essay on the topic assigned below.
DO NOT WRITE ON ANOTHER TOPIC. AN OFF-TOPIC ESSAY WILL RECEIVE A SCORE OF ZERO.

Think carefully about the issue presented in the following excerpt and the assignment below.

> "Don't flatter yourself that friendship authorizes you to say disagreeable things to your intimates. The nearer you come into relation with a person, the more necessary do tact and courtesy become. Except in cases of necessity, which are rare, leave your friend to learn unpleasant things from his enemies; they are ready enough to tell them."
>
> —Oliver Wendell Holmes, *The Autocrat of the Breakfast-Table*
>
> "A good friend can tell you what is the matter with you in a minute. He may not seem such a good friend after telling."
>
> —Arthur Brisbane, *The Book of Today*

Assignment: Should friends be honest with each other, even if a truthful comment could be hurtful? Plan and write an essay in which you develop your point of view on this issue. Support your position with reasoning and examples taken from your reading, studies, experience, or observations.

DO NOT WRITE YOUR ESSAY IN YOUR TEST BOOK.
You will receive credit only for what you write in your Answer Grid Booklet.

Organize your paragraphs and write your essay on separate sheets of paper.

SAMPLE ESSAYS

Grade 6 Essay

One of the defining qualities of a good friendship is that both friends can be completely honest with each other. This does not mean that the two friends don't consider each others feelings or blurt out comments without thinking, but it does mean that each person can rely on the other to tell the truth, even if the truth can sometimes be awkward or hurtful.

My sister and I have always been close friends, even when we were younger. When my sister was in junior high school and I was in elementary school, she decided to get her hair permed because all of her friends were doing the same

EXPERT TUTOR TIP

This essay does something really important: it frames the issue in the introduction. The writer clearly defines the scope of her argument in her intro paragraph.

thing. Unfortunately, the treatment didn't work well on her hair and she ended up with a big, frizzy clump of curls that stuck out on the sides. Most of her friends didn't have the courage to tell her that it didn't look good. Instead, they just made fun of her behind her back. So it was up to me to tell her the truth. I was a bit scared to confront my older sister, because I knew that she would be upset. But I also knew that she would be more upset if no one dared to be honest with her. A few years earlier, we were in the opposite roles, and she had gently but firmly advised me against a choice that I later realized would have been embarrassing for me when I started school.

Although my sister was hurt when I told her that the perm didn't look good, she was more hurt to learn that some of her other friends had thought the same thing but hadn't said anything to her. She was angry with me at first for making a negative comment, but in the end she was glad I had told her so that she could go back to the hair stylist to fix the problem. Since my sister was very concerned about her appearance and personal style at that time in her life, she appreciated my honesty because it helped her get through a tough situation and our friendship grew stronger as a result of this experience.

In the years since this incident, my sister and I have both continued to be honest and upfront with each other, and we value this aspect of our relationship. After all, friendly honesty is far better than hostile honesty, so being a good friend involves telling the truth, no matter what the circumstances. Honesty truly is an essential component of a good friendship.

(388 words)

Grader's Comments: The author begins this essay with a clear statement based on the prompt, showing that she has clearly understood the topic. The remainder of the essay presents and develops an example to support her opinion. The example provided is relevant to multiple aspects of the prompt—the importance of honesty in friendship as well as the possibility that being honest can be difficult in certain situations.

The essay is well organized, with a clear narrative flow framed by a cohesive introduction and conclusion. The structure of the essay reflects that the author took time to plan before writing and carefully followed her plan as she composed her essay. Although the vocabulary used in the essay is not very sophisticated, the author's ideas are communicated effectively. Finally, there are few grammatical or spelling errors—*others* instead of *other's* in the first paragraph—and a couple of sentences lacking commas in the second and third paragraphs. This author clearly managed her time effectively so that she could proofread her essay.

GRADE 4 ESSAY

Being honest is part of being a *good* friend. However, their are times when you shouldn't be completely honest because what you say might hurt your friend's feelings.

For example, imagine that your best friend tells you his parents are getting divorced. He is obviously upset by this even though you know his parents haven't been getting along well because he constantly complained about their fights and even joked about hoping they'd get a divorce so he wouldn't have to listen to them anymore. In this situation, reminding your friend of his earlier comments or pointing out that his parents will be happier apart isn't the right thing to do because at a time like this you're friend doesn't need you to tell him the harsh truth, he needs you to by sympathetic and supportive. It's pretty likely that he'll hear all about the negative things from other people or even from his parents, so your job as his best friend is to try not to say or do anything unpleasant.

Another example could be if you're friend has bought something that she's really excited about. You might not agree that she's made a good choice or you might not like what she bought, but you don't need to spoil her enthusiasm by making a negative comment. Again, this is a time when you should keep quiet about your own opinion so that your friend can be happy.

There are certain situations when it's okay not to tell the complete truth to your friends. You should never lie to your friends, but an important part of being a good friend is knowing when to be totally honest and when to keep silent because a truthful comment could do more harm than good.

(292 words)

Grader's Comments: The author introduces his essay with a clear statement of his opinion, showing that he has understood the prompt. His two examples provide decent support for the topic, but the second example is vague and not well developed. The author would have a stronger essay if he expanded upon the prompt and provided additional details for the first example rather than trying to include a weak second example. Having a clear plan could help to accomplish this change in structure.

The essay is fairly well organized, with several keywords *(However, For example, Another example, Again)* that add structure to the author's argument. The weakest parts of this essay are some simplistic language and awkward sentences: in the second paragraph, the second sentence is long and wordy, and the third sentence is a run-on sentence and is very difficult to follow, so the author's meaning almost gets obscured by the effort it takes to decipher his thoughts. There are also a few usage/spelling errors: *their* instead of *there* in the first paragraph; *you're* instead of *your* in the second and third paragraphs. The author needs to be more deliberate when writing the essay and needs to proofread to catch these spelling errors and prevent run-on sentences or awkward sentence structure.

GRADE 2 ESSAY

No matter what, friends should tell each other the truth. That's the whole point of having friends, so you have some people around you that you can trust and talk to and that you know will tell you everything.

Friends can tell you negative things in a kind way so you can here the truth even if its not so good. Enemies tell you the same negative things in a mean way because their trying to hurt you. But friends can accomplish this in a nicer way.

Its important to know and learn the truth even if its about yourself or its something you don't want to face. You need honest friends to tell you the truth, because they do it out of love not hate like enemies.

(128 words)

Grader's Comments: This author starts strongly with a clear statement of her opinion, which is directly related to the topic of the prompt. However, the author continues with a series of generalizations, none of which are specific examples to support her opinion. She needs to spend more time planning her essay to make sure that she's got at least one strong example to support her argument.

This essay does not follow an organized structure, and it lacks good transitions and keywords. To improve this part of her writing, the author should make an outline during her planning stage and should focus on using several keywords while she writes, which will give her essay a stronger and clearer structure.

The author's language is simplistic and repetitive. The essay contains several grammatical and spelling errors: *that* twice instead of *whom/who* when referring to *people* in the first paragraph; *here* and *their* are misused for *hear* and *they're* in the second paragraph; *its* is misused numerous times for *it's* in the second and third paragraphs. The author should study the SAT grammar materials to improve this aspect of her writing and should also be sure to proofread to avoid careless errors.

EXPERT TUTOR TIP

" What's the biggest problem with this essay? No support! This writer goes on and on telling us her opinion but never supports it with any examples. "

KEY POINTS YOU'VE LEARNED IN THIS CHAPTER

1. Memorize Kaplan's 4 Ps strategy:
   - Prompt (read and understand it)

   - Plan (collect and organize your ideas and examples)

   - Produce (write your essay)

   - Proofread (check for consistency and errors)

2. You will be given a quote, or a pair of quotes, and a prompt that is related to the content of the quote. That prompt will guide your essay topic.

3. You should aim to write 300–400 words to get a score of 5 or 6.

4. Neatness counts.

CHAPTER 7: THE MULTIPLE-CHOICE QUESTIONS

SMARTPOINTS COVERED IN THIS CHAPTER

SUBJECT-VERB AGREEMENT

VERB TENSE

PRONOUNS

IDIOMS

DICTION

COMPARISONS

PARALLELISM

RUN-ONS AND FRAGMENTS

MISPLACED MODIFIERS

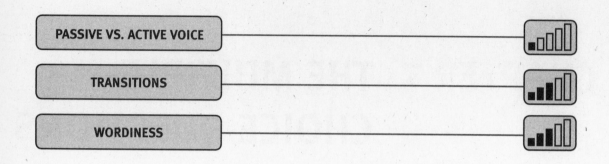

PASSIVE VS. ACTIVE VOICE

TRANSITIONS

WORDINESS

WHAT TO EXPECT ON TEST DAY

The Writing section's multiple-choice questions are like a mini-SAT all to themselves. The Writing section uses three different types of multiple-choice questions to test three different writing skills, but each question type works basically the same way: You need to determine what mistake (if any) has been made in the sentences or paragraphs in question. For two of the three types, you will also need to determine the best way to correct those mistakes. Throughout this chapter, we'll show you the kinds of writing mistakes the SAT wants you to catch and how you can catch them.

Note: This is a long chapter. It might be helpful to treat it like three short chapters, one for each multiple-choice question type:

1. Identifying Sentence Errors
2. Improving Sentences
3. Improving Paragraphs

Tackle just one question type in a single study session.

IDENTIFYING SENTENCE ERRORS QUESTIONS

The word *usage* means the customary or standard way in which words are used. The Identifying Sentence Errors questions on the SAT cover four main areas of written English:

1. Basic grammar
2. Sentence structure
3. Idiomatic expressions
4. Choice of words (diction)

That sounds like a lot of ground to cover, but as you'll see, most Identifying Sentence Errors questions test only a few key grammar and usage concepts. We'll show you the kind of grammar the SAT usually tests and help you become an expert on the SAT's spot-the-mistake questions.

Remember, the Writing section measures your ability to recognize acceptable and unacceptable uses of *written* English. Standard *written* English is a bit more formal than the average person's spoken English, and it is what professors will expect you to use on college papers. That's why it is being tested on the SAT.

THREE STEPS TO TEST DAY SUCCESS

KAPLAN'S TARGET STRATEGY FOR IDENTIFYING SENTENCE ERRORS

To tackle Identifying Sentence Errors questions, Kaplan's test experts have devised a Target Strategy that will guide you in answering these types of questions. The three steps are as follows:

Step 1: Read the sentence, and listen for an error.

Step 2: Identify the error.

Step 3: If you cannot identify an error, eliminate the choices that don't contain errors. Choose from the remaining answer choices.

Try this out on the following example. Start by reading it to yourself.

<u>Although</u> the number of firms declaring
　　A

bankruptcy <u>keep</u> growing, the mayor <u>claims that</u> the
　　　　　　　B　　　　　　　　　　　　C

city <u>is thriving</u>. <u>No error</u>
　　　　D　　　　　E

Did you hear the error? If so, your work is done. Fill in the appropriate oval, and move on. If you didn't hear the error on the first reading, go back, read each underlined part, and start eliminating underlined parts that are right.

> **PERFECT SCORE TIP**
>
> " Kaplan's strategy to read each sentence aloud definitely worked (but remember to be quiet!). More often than not, I could hear the mistake the first time. "

> **EXPERT TUTOR TIP**
>
> " Work systematically through the underlined segments for these question types. Familiarize yourself with common types of errors, and keep a sharp eye out for them. "

The word *although* seems fine in this context. The word *keep* is a plural verb, but its subject is *the number*, which is singular. That seems to be an error. The phrase *claims that* sounds all right; it has a singular verb for a singular subject, *mayor*. Similarly, *is thriving* sounds all right, and it, too, provides a singular verb for the singular subject *city*. Choice (B) contains the mistake, so (B) is the correct answer.

This is a classic example of subject-verb agreement, which is a common error tested in the Writing section. You'll learn more about the most common errors in the following pages, which offer a quick reference to the most frequently made and tested grammatical mistakes. It's much easier to spot errors when you know what to look for.

NO ERROR

Keep in mind that not all the Identifying Sentence Errors questions on the Writing section contain errors. Some will be choice (E), or No error. These are often the hardest to pick because you must be confident that there's nothing wrong with the sentence. Knowing the most common errors used on the test—and therefore knowing that those aren't in a given sentence—will make you more confident in choosing (E).

PERFECT SCORE TIP

"At first, I worried about the number of (E) answers I had as I went through the section—and that was very stressful. I found it better not to worry about them until the end, when I went back over each question that I thought had no error."

HOW TO AVOID COMMON ERRORS

Although the SAT Writing questions will test your knowledge of grammar and usage, you won't have to recite any rules on the exam. In fact, you don't have to know all the rules *per se*; you just have to be able to recognize when something is *not* correct. So instead of trying to review all of the rules, we'll show you the top 16 errors you need to watch out for on the SAT. Once you are used to seeing these Identifying Sentence Errors in practice, you'll have an easier time spotting them on test day.

REMEMBER!

Being familiar with the most commonly tested errors will help you tackle Identifying Sentence Errors questions.

SUBJECT-VERB AGREEMENT

- **Rule: Singular** subjects call for **singular** verbs. **Plural** subjects call for **plural** verbs.

COMMON ERROR 1: WHEN THE SUBJECT FOLLOWS THE VERB

In this situation, it is hard to find the subject of the verb because it comes later in the sentence. "There is" is a common sentence construction of this sentence error. For example:

> Despite an intensive campaign to encourage conservation, there is many Americans who have not accepted recycling as a way of life.

This sentence demonstrates a common subject-verb agreement error found on the Writing section. It generally occurs once or twice on each test. Words such has *there* or *here* cannot be subjects of sentences. The subject of the sentence is not *there*. The subject is *Americans*, which is plural. Therefore, the singular verb is incorrect; *is* should be replaced by the plural verb *are*.

Here's another example in which the subject follows the verb:

> High above the Hudson River rises the gleaming skyscrapers of Manhattan.

The sentence is tricky because a prepositional phrase with a singular noun, *Hudson River*, comes before the verb *rises*. Because the object of a preposition cannot be the subject of a sentence, a noun even later in the sentence, skyscrapers, is the subject. Think about it. What's doing the rising? Not the river, the *skyscrapers*. The subject is plural, and so the verb should be *rise*.

> ### EXPERT TUTOR TIP
>
> " Don't waste time trying to figure out how many "No error" questions there are in your section. Consider each question alone, and don't worry about the pattern your answer choices are making on the grid. It *is* possible that the same letter could indicate the correct answer for three questions in a row. "

WHAT'S A PREPOSITION?

It is a word that (usually) tells where something is: *above* the door, *over* the hill, *under* a tree, and more. The SAT uses very small ones most often: *in, at, on, of,* and *to.*

COMMON ERROR 2: WHEN THE SUBJECT AND VERB ARE SEPARATED

The SAT has another way to complicate a subject-verb agreement. The test maker inserts some additional information about the subject before the verb appears.

Consider the following sentence:

> The local congressman, a reliable representative of both community and statewide interests, are among the most respected persons in the public sector.

What is the subject of this sentence? You see several nouns before the verb: *congressman, representative, community,* and *interests.* So which is it? *Congressman.* If you thought any of the others was the subject, here's what to do: Take a pencil and put parentheses around the phrase set off by the commas. This phrase is "oh-by-the-way" descriptive information. You can do without it and still have a complete sentence. Therefore, it doesn't contain the subject.

Another tip-off is the presence of a small preposition, such as *of, in, to,* and *at.* Look at the following sentence:

> The collection of paintings entitled "Clammy Clam Clams" are one of the most widely traveled exhibits in recent years.

Again, there are nouns to consider before the verb: *collection, paintings,* and *Clammy Clam Clams.* Find the subject? It is *collection.* If you thought it was *paintings,* you overlooked the little preposition *of. Paintings* is the object of that little preposition and isn't eligible for the job. The subject is singular and the verb should be *is,* not *are.*

The SAT writers like this type of question because the intervening modifying phrases or clauses can cause you to lose track of the subject. These phrases simply modify the subject they follow, without changing its number. Don't be fooled by the placement of these intervening phrases.

ALWAYS FIND THE SUBJECT

When you see an underlined verb, automatically look for its subject. Draw parentheses around any prepositional phrases and modifiers that stand between subject and verb. Do this routinely to build speed, confidence, and accuracy in your answering process.

Rule: Only the conjunction *and* can form a plural verb. The word pairs *neither . . . nor* and *either . . . or* take singular verbs, if each side of the pair is singular.

COMMON ERROR 3: WHEN THE SUBJECT SEEMS PLURAL (BUT ISN'T)

Sometimes the sentence includes what seems to be, but in fact is not, a plural subject. Here's an example:

> Neither ambient techno nor trance were a part of mainstream listening habits in the United States ten years ago.

This sentence is tough because it has two singular subjects (*ambient techno* and *trance*), but with *neither* and *nor* in the mix, they don't add up to a plural subject. The verb should be *was*.

Note: If the nouns in a *neither ... nor* or *either ... or* sentence are plural on their own, then the verb should be plural. The SAT doesn't usually test this, though.

VERB TENSE

Make it a habit to examine all verbs in every sentence and remember the following rules:

- **Rule:** Tenses must be as simple as possible (most often, present, past, and future) and make sense in context.
- **Rule:** Verbs must be complete, with *to be* predicate helpers (*am thinking*).
- **Rule:** If a sentence has more than one complete verb in it, be consistent. Don't change tenses unless it makes sense to do so.

COMMON ERROR 4: WRONG TENSES

Here's a sentence with a verb in the wrong tense:

> Over the last half-century, the building of passenger airliners had grown into a multibillion-dollar industry.

In a one-verb sentence like this one, time-descriptive phrases help you determine what the time frame of a sentence is. The action being described is a process that began during the last half-century and that is continuing to the present day. Any action starting in the past and continuing today is expressed by a verb in the present perfect tense. The present perfect form of this verb is *has grown*. Using the verb *had* makes it seem that passenger airliners aren't being made anymore. That can't be! The key is to pay attention to the time cues in the sentence. With practice, you'll be able to spot errors like this with confidence.

Another type of sentence might have two verbs and an unnecessary or confusing shift in tense. Here's an example:

> Many superb tennis players turn professional at an alarmingly early age, but because of their lack of physical stamina, suffered early in their careers.

When there are two verbs in a sentence, first study the time relation between the verbs, and determine whether it is logical as presented. In this sentence, the verb in the first clause of this sentence is *turn*, a present tense verb. The action is not occurring at any specified occasion but in the general present. The verb *suffered* is in the simple past, but it should remain in the general present, even though the phrase *early in their careers* may suggest a past time. On the SAT, when a sentence contains an underlined verb, make sure it is used logically in context. Check to see whether the underlined verb makes sense in relation to any non-underlined verb or any time-related phrases that may appear in the sentence.

COMMON ERROR 5: INCORRECT USE OF PAST PARTICIPLES AND INCOMPLETE VERBS

A typical error tested on the Writing section is confusion between the simple past tense and the past participle forms of a verb. The error is to put the past participle form where the simple past tense should be. Consider the following sentence:

> Several passersby seen the bank robber leaving the scene of the crime.

The verb form *seen* is the past participle and should be used only with a helping verb, such as *have* or *be*. This sentence requires the simple past form *saw*.

 PRONOUNS

Like verbs, all pronouns in a Writing multiple-choice sentence should be examined carefully. Let's review some types of pronouns:

- Personal pronouns stand for persons or things (*I, she, they, him, it, my, theirs,* etc.).

- Demonstrative pronouns identify or point to nouns (*that, this, those, these, such,* etc.).

- Relative pronouns are used to join clauses to create complex sentences and to give additional information about the main clause (*that, who, whom, whose, where, when,* etc.).

- Indefinite pronouns function as nouns and do not stand for any specific nouns (*all, each, every, somebody, everybody, none,* etc.).

Remember the following rules:

- A pronoun must agree in number and gender with the noun it replaces (called an *antecedent*).
- A pronoun must be in the proper case (*subjective, objective, possessive*).
- The antecedent must be clear. If a pronoun could refer to more than one thing or person, or if there is no antecedent, you have found an SAT error.

COMMON ERROR 6: PRONOUN IN THE WRONG NUMBER

You'll be tested on your ability to tell whether a noun and the pronoun that refers to that noun agree in number. A singular pronoun should be used to refer to a singular noun; a plural pronoun should be used with a plural noun. In the following examples, the pronoun and the noun to which it refers do not agree in number:

> The typical college student has difficulty adjusting to academic standards much higher than those of their school.

The pronoun *their* should refer to a plural noun, but in this sentence, it refers back to *student*, a singular noun. Therefore, the pronoun should be the singular form *his* or *hers*, and not the plural form *their*. Look for the same kind of mistake in the next sentence:

> Most infants, even unusually quiet ones, will cry with greater intensity when it begins teething.

In this sentence, the subject is *infants*, a plural noun. But the pronoun that refers back to this plural noun is *it*, a singular form. The correct form of the pronoun is *they*, referring back to the plural subject. Be sure that a pronoun agrees in number with its antecedent (the noun or other pronoun that it refers to).

COMMON ERROR 7: WRONG CASE

Errors involving pronoun case tend to appear on the SAT. Remember that the proper case is determined by how the pronoun functions in the sentence.

- **Subjective pronouns:** *I, you, he, she, it, we, they*
- **Objective pronouns:** *me, you, him, her, it, us, them*
- **Possessive pronouns:** *my, your, his, her, its, our, their*

Here's an example:

> For my sister and I, the trip to Paris was the fulfillment of a life-
> long wish we had scarcely dared to express.

Take out the words *my sister and*, and the error of pronoun case becomes obvious—you wouldn't say *for I*. Because this pronoun is the object of the preposition *for*, it should be in the objective case: for my sister and *me*.

COMMON ERROR 8: PRONOUN SHIFT

Pronoun shift is a switch in pronoun person or number within a given sentence. Here's an example:

> One cannot sleep soundly if you exercise vigorously before retiring to bed.

The subject in the first clause is *one*, and the subject in the second clause is *you*. These two pronouns refer to the same performer of two actions, so they should be consistent in person and number. The sentence should not shift to the second person *you* form.

Look for another kind of pronoun shift in this next sentence:

> If someone loses his way in the airport, they can ask any employee for directions.

The subject is *someone* in the first clause, but *they* in the second clause. Clearly, both pronouns refer to the same agent; the performer of both actions, losing and asking, is the same. This switch in number from singular to plural is not grammatical. In creating such a sentence, SAT writers play on a common logical confusion. In English, singular words like *one*, *someone*, and *a person* can represent people in general. So can plural words like *people* or *they*. Be on the lookout when general statements use pronouns and consider whether these pronouns are consistent.

> **DON'T FORGET**
>
> You may see a question about the pronoun *one* on the SAT; be sure this pronoun and all other pronouns are used consistently. Don't mix *one* and *you* in the same sentence.

COMMON ERROR 9: PRONOUN WITH AMBIGUOUS REFERENCE

There are two ways the Writing section might test your ability to recognize an ambiguous pronoun reference. First, a sentence may be given in which it is impossible to determine what noun the pronoun refers to. Take a look at this example:

> The United States entered into warmer relations
> with China after its compliance with recent weap-
> ons agreements.

To which country does the pronoun *its* refer? Grammatically and logically, either country could be the antecedent of the pronoun. With the limited information provided by this sentence alone, you simply can't determine which country the pronoun stands in for. The reference is ambiguous, or unclear.

Pronoun reference can also be ambiguous if the pronoun's antecedent is not explicitly stated in the sentence:

> After the derailment last month, they are inspecting
> trains for safety more often than ever before.

The question to ask about this sentence is *who* is *they*? There is no group of people identified in this sentence to whom the pronoun could refer. You can logically infer that *they* refers to agents of a railroad safety commission, but because these inspectors are not explicitly mentioned in the sentence, the personal pronoun usage here is ambiguous. Be sure to locate the antecedent of any pronoun in Identifying Sentence Errors sentences. If an SAT sentence doesn't contain a noun that an underlined pronoun can clearly and logically refer to, the underlined pronoun is considered an error.

IDIOMS

An idiom, also called an *idiomatic expression*, is a term that refers to a wide range of commonly accepted combinations of words. Your language "ear" will be very helpful. While there is no definitive list to memorize, some general rules are helpful:

- **Rule:** Listen for the wrong verb combination (infinitive vs. gerund).
- **Rule:** Watch for an odd sounding preposition after a verb.

COMMON ERROR 10: CONFUSION OF INFINITIVE AND GERUND

Some questions test your sense of idiomatic use of English. *Idiomatic use* means combinations of words that sound right or words that sound right in particular contexts.

For example, there is generally at least one Identifying Sentence Errors question in which the infinitive is used where a gerund would be appropriate, or vice versa, as in the following example:

> Team officials heralded Cap Day as an attempt at
> attracting a larger turnout of fans.

This sentence is not idiomatic. There's no grammar rule that explains why it's wrong to say *an attempt at attracting*. But if you have a good sense of idiom, your ear tells you it should be *an attempt to attract*. This sentence confuses the *-ing* gerund form with the *to + verb infinitive* form. Here's another sentence:

> Surveillance cameras are frequently placed in con-
> venience stores to prevent customers to shoplift.

After *prevent* you don't use the infinitive but rather the word *from* plus the gerund. The sentence should end *to prevent customers from shoplifting*.

Why? There's no real grammatical reason. That's just the way we say and write it in English. You have to trust yourself on these. Although there are some general patterns, there are no hard and fast rules that determine when to use an infinitive or gerund. Moreover, there are so many possible combinations that there's no way to list all that could possibly appear on the Writing section. But don't worry. You don't need to see every possible combination in advance. Just remember to prick up your ears whenever an infinitive or gerund is underlined on the test.

COMMON ERROR 11: WRONG PREPOSITION AFTER VERB

The Writing section also tests your recognition of prepositions that idiomatically combine with certain verbs. Here's a sentence that uses the wrong preposition:

> City Council members frequently meet until the early
> morning hours in order to work in their stalemates.

It's not always wrong to write *work in*. You might speak about the field one *works in* or the place one *works in*. But this combination does not correspond to the meaning of this sentence. The writer means to say *work through* or *work out*—that is, overcome—the stalemates.

Here's another sentence with the wrong preposition:

> The rapper's new CD was frowned at by many par-
> ents because of its violent lyrics.

That's just not the way we say it in English. The preferred verb-preposition combination is *frowned upon*. That's the idiomatic expression. Once again, you'll have to trust your ear. Just remember to pay attention and think for a moment when you see an underlined preposition after a verb.

EXPERT TUTOR TIP

" Watch out for some commonly tested "wrong words": *affect/effect*, *raise/rise*, and *accept/except*. "

DICTION

Diction means word choice. The right word is dictated by accepted use or meaning. On the SAT, diction questions may test *sit* vs. *set*, *lie* vs. *lay*, and *rise* vs. *raise*, as well as expressions of quantity and frequently confused words. Here are rules to help you with diction issues tested in the SAT multiple-choice Writing sections:

- **Confused Verb Rule:** *Sit, lie,* and *rise,* the "I" verbs, have no objects. *Set, lay,* and *raise,* the no "I" verbs, are action verbs with objects.

- **Quantity Rule:** Use amount words *when referring to an uncountable noun*. Use number words to refer to a countable one.

- **Similar Sounding Words Rule:** Be on the lookout for frequently confused words. They sound very similar but don't mean the same thing.

Illustrations of each rule appear below.

COMMON ERROR 12: WRONG WORD IN CONTEXT

Some verbs are often used interchangeably and incorrectly, especially in spoken English. The correct use should be as follows:

Verbs without objects:	**Verbs with objects:**
I sit down.	I set the table.
I lie down.	I lay the book on the table.
The sun rises.	I raise my hand.

Here are two sentences that misuse these verbs:

> **Wrong:** I am working so hard that my grade point average raises every semester.

> **Right:** I am working so hard that my grade point average rises every semester.

> A grade point average *rises* (no object).

> **Wrong:** I set with my neighbors on the front porch until dark.

> **Right:** I sat with my neighbors on the front porch until dark.

> *With my neighbors* is a prepositional phrase, so the verb should be *sat*, which is the past tense of *sit*. *Sit* does not take an object.

Quantity issues: How much coffee have you had? How much sugar did you put in your tea? It depends whether you can count the units or not. You can't count coffee, but you can count the cups. The same is true for *sugar, sand, information, time*, and more.

- *Many cups* of coffee, but *much coffee*
- *A few teaspoons* of sugar, but *too little sugar*

Frequently confused words: The list here shows words that the SAT is likely to test.

- *Imply*: to suggest; *implicate*: to accuse or charge (with a crime)
- *Accept*: receive willingly (verb); *except*: not including (preposition)
- *Affect*: create a result (verb); *effect*: the result (noun)

The examples above are among the most common. So on the test you might see: I *excepted* his invitation to the prom. Be on the lookout for these "hidden" errors.

 ## COMPARISONS

There are three questions to think about here:

1. What's being compared?
2. Do items being compared use parallel (similar) phrasing?
3. How many items are being compared?

Remember the following rules for comparison issues:

- **Rule:** Compare similar things and use similar wording.
- **Rule:** Use comparative (*better*) for comparing two things; use superlative (*best*) for comparing more than two.

COMMON ERROR 13: FAULTY COMPARISON

Most faulty comparisons occur when two things of different types are compared. A comparison can be faulty either logically or grammatically. Look for the comparison error in the following sentence:

> Though Elie Wiesel is a Nobel Peace Prize winner and the author of several respected novels, his name is still less well known than last year's Heisman Trophy winner.

In every sentence, you should first identify what things or actions are being compared. In this sentence, Elie Wiesel's *name* is compared to last year's Heisman Trophy *winner*. This comparison is faulty because a person's name is compared to another person. If the first item were *Elie Wiesel*, then the comparison would be valid.

Try to identify the comparison error in the next sentence:

> To lash back at one's adversaries is a less coura-
> geous course than attempting to bring about recon-
> ciliation with them.

The comparison in this sentence is logically correct in that two actions are compared. But the problem lies in the grammatical form of the words compared. An infinitive verb, *to lash*, expresses the first action, but a gerund, *attempting*, expresses the second action. These verb forms should match to make the comparison parallel. If *lashing* replaced *to lash*, the comparison would be grammatically parallel and logically valid. Check all comparisons for logic and grammatical consistency.

EASY-TO-OVERLOOK ISSUES

Hidden in the Identifying Sentence Errors questions are three other errors to be aware of. Because they are usually small errors (and may only have a missing letter or an extra small word inserted), it pays to know what they are. We'll look at them one at a time.

BE CAREFUL!

Be wary of vague subject references such as *its*, *their*, *they*, and *those*. If you can't tell what the pronoun refers to, something is missing from the sentence.

 ## PARALLELISM

COMMON ERROR 14: NUMBER AGREEMENT PROBLEMS

The Writing section also tests number agreement between a noun and a phrase or word describing it. For instance, a noun may be plural while a phrase describing the noun belongs with a singular noun. That sounds complicated, but fortunately, you don't need to be able to explain the grammar involved; you just need to be able to spot this type of mistake. Here's an example:

> The advertisement in the newspaper requested that
> only persons with a high school diploma apply for
> the position.

Nouns in a sentence must have logical number relations. The noun in question, the subject of the second clause of this sentence, is *persons*, a plural noun. However, the noun *diploma* is singular. Because the phrase *with a high school diploma* is singular, it

PERFECT SCORE TIP

" Number agreement problems were the hardest ones for me to catch. Following Kaplan's rules and paying attention to the nouns in each sentence were the best ways for me to tackle these questions. "

suggests that *persons* share one diploma, when in fact each person has his own diploma. The phrase should read *with high school diplomas.*

Here's an example of number disagreement in which a singular noun is coupled with a plural subject:

> Mary's rose gardens are considered by many to be the symbol of beauty in the neighborhood.

Again, identify the subject of the sentence, *gardens.* The noun that corresponds to the subject is *symbol,* a singular noun. There is no agreement in number between *gardens* and *symbol.* Each individual garden is a symbol; many gardens would not be a single symbol. The plural form, *symbols,* makes this sentence grammatically correct. Make sure that the nouns in a sentence agree in number.

COMMON ERROR 15: MISUSE OF ADJECTIVE OR ADVERB

Remember the following rules regarding the misuse of adjectives and adverbs:

- **Rule:** An adjective can describe only a noun or pronoun.

- **Rule:** An adverb modifies a verb, an adjective, or another adverb and answers the question *How?*

These questions test your ability to recognize misuses of one-word modifiers. Now ask yourself what the word *decent* is intended to modify as you look at the sentence below:

> The applicants for low-interest loans hoped to buy **decent** built houses for their families.

The word *decent* is an adjective. However, this modifier describes an adjective, explaining how the houses were built. A word that modifies an adjective like *built* is an adverb. So the word needed in this sentence is the adverb *decently.* Notice also that this adverb ends in *-ly,* the most common adverbial ending.

Now take a look at the second sentence:

> The critics who reviewed Dave Eggers's first two novels liked the second one best.

The word *best* is a superlative modifier. Superlative adverbs and adjectives (adverbs and adjectives ending in *-est,* such as *biggest, loudest, fastest,* etc.) should express comparisons between three or more things or actions. Comparative adverbs and adjectives end in *-er* (*bigger, louder, faster,* etc.) and express comparisons between two things or actions. This sentence compares critics' responses to only two novels by Dave Eggers. Thus, instead of the superlative *best,* this sentence needs the comparative modifier *better.*

Remember that some adjectives and adverbs, usually those of two or more syllables, form the comparative with *more* instead of the *-er* ending and form the superlative with *most* instead of the *-est* ending.

Trust your ear to distinguish adjectives from adverbs in Writing section Identifying Sentence Errors questions, but do *listen* carefully. Pay close attention when you decide whether a sentence needs a comparative or superlative modifier.

COMMON ERROR 16: DOUBLE NEGATIVE

When dealing with double negatives, remember the following rule:

- **Rule:** Don't use two negatives in a sentence unless the intention is to have one cancel out the other.

On the Identifying Sentence Errors portion of the SAT, a double negative is wrong. Double negatives can be correct in certain circumstances, but they won't be in the Writing sections. Notice the two negative words in this sentence:

> James easily passed the biology exam without hardly studying his lab notes.

Without is a negative, as is any word that indicates absence or lack. *Hardly* is also considered a negative word. Therefore, it should **not** be used with another negative word, such as *no, not,* or *none.*

Now look at the next sentence:

> In the history of the major leagues, barely no one has maintained higher than a .400 batting average for an entire season.

Clearly, *no one* is a negative, but so is *barely.* Just like *hardly, barely* is considered negative. In Identifying Sentence Errors questions, be on the lookout for sentences that contain one of three negative words that may not seem obviously negative: *hardly, barely,* and *scarcely.*

PRACTICE IDENTIFYING SENTENCE ERRORS

Let's practice what you've learned.

Directions: The following sentences test your ability to recognize grammar and usage errors. Each sentence contains either a single error or no error at all. No sentence contains more than one error. The error, if there is one, is underlined and lettered. If the sentence contains an error, select the one underlined part that must be changed to make the sentence correct. If the sentence is correct, select choice (E).

1. Because the government <u>was</u> bankrupt, many
   A

   of the soldiers <u>which</u> were sent <u>to quell</u> the
   B   C

   riots had <u>not been</u> paid in months. <u>No error</u>
   D   E

2. Although farmers complained that the

   company's new product was expensive,

   malodorous, and <u>dangerous to handle</u>,
   A

   <u>there was</u> few who <u>would dispute</u> its
   B   C

   effectiveness <u>as</u> an insecticide. <u>No error</u>
   D   E

3. In the wake <u>of</u> recent thefts, the town's
   A

   wealthier residents <u>have installed</u> gates,
   B

   alarm systems, and even video surveillance

   equipment in their neighborhoods, hoping

   <u>that it will</u> prevent <u>further burglaries</u>. <u>No error</u>
   C   D   E

4. <u>To repair</u> the damage <u>that</u> time and the
   A   B

   elements <u>had wrought</u> on the ancient fresco,
   C

   the restorer used a simple mixture <u>from</u>
   D

   plaster, pigment, and a little water. <u>No error</u>
   E

5. <u>That</u> J. L. Solomon's first novel <u>was selected for</u>
   A   B

   several major literary prizes <u>was surprising</u> to
   C

   no one who had read his <u>previous</u> collections
   D

   of short stories, poems, and essays. <u>No error</u>
   E

6. <u>Though</u> Patricia's résumé was <u>not nearly as</u>
   A   B

   long and impressive as <u>the other applicant</u>,
   C

   her personal charisma was <u>so great that</u>
   D

   Mr. Alvarez hired her on the spot. <u>No error</u>
   E

7. If only the factory owners had conducted
   A   B

   regular safety inspections of their equipment,
                              C

   the horrible accident of 1969 may have been
                                      D

   averted. No error
            E

8. The symphony had not hardly begun when a
                    A   B

   group of schoolchildren, who had been forced
                                   C

   to attend, began irritating the rest of the

   audience by talking loudly and kicking the
            D

   seats. No error
         E

9. Fast-food chains are among the most ubiquitous
                        A

   restaurants in our town; they welcome everyone
                              B

   with no distinction between you and me, teachers
              C   D

   and students, or parents and kids. No error
                                     E

10. High Fidelity, a successful book and film, became
                                               A

    known as a cult classic because of its sharp wit
    B

    and by presenting a quirky main character,
        C

    Rob, as a common man. No error
         D   E

ANSWERS AND EXPLANATIONS

1. B

SMARTPOINT CATEGORY: PRONOUNS

The relative pronoun *which* refers to the soldiers, but *which* cannot be used to refer to people, only to things. The sentence should use the relative pronoun *who* instead.

2. B

SMARTPOINT CATEGORY: SUBJECT-VERB AGREEMENT

In the second half of the sentence, the verb *was* does not agree with the subject. As you've learned, *there* is not the subject of the sentence; *few* is the subject. *Few* is a plural noun, so the sentence should read *there were few*.

3. C

SMARTPOINT CATEGORY: PRONOUNS

If you look for the antecedent of the pronoun *it* here, you won't find it—this is a case of an ambiguous pronoun reference.

4. D

SMARTPOINT CATEGORY: IDIOMS

This is an example of an idiom error. The correct preposition should be *a mixture of*, not *a mixture from*.

5. E

SMARTPOINT CATEGORY: FINDING NO ERROR

The sentence contains no error, although the phrasing may have sounded strange to your ear. In (A), *that* may sound odd as a beginning of a sentence, but it is grammatically correct. (B) and (C) are correct as singular verbs with proper idiomatic uses of the prepositions *for* and *to*. (D) is correct as an adjective.

6. C

SMARTPOINT CATEGORY: COMPARISONS

The way this sentence is written, *Patricia's résumé* is being compared to the *other applicant*, which is not logical. *Patricia's résumé* should be compared to the *other applicant's résumé*. On the SAT, compare people to people and things to things. Don't mix people and things in a comparison.

7. D

SMARTPOINT CATEGORY: VERB TENSE

The sentence may sound correct, but take a closer look. It is clear that the accident was *not* averted, so the sentence is describing a situation that happened in the past. When you know that something *did* happen (but most likely would have been avoided had things been different), *might* is the correct word to use. *May have* suggests that you are not sure whether a thing happened or not; for example, "I will try calling Dr. Miller's office, but she may have left already."

8. A

SMARTPOINT CATEGORY: DICTION

Remember that *hardly* is a negative; it denotes a scarcity of something. Using *hardly* with *not* creates a double negative.

9. E

SMARTPOINT CATEGORY: FINDING NO ERROR

(A) correctly uses *among* and *most* in a comparison of more than two items. (It's safe to assume that the town has more than one restaurant.) (B) uses the appropriate plural pronoun with the antecedent *fast-food chains*. (C) correctly uses *between* to compare two items. (Each compound object of this preposition is separate. Remember, only the conjunction *and* can form a compound; *or* cannot.) (D) correctly uses the objective pronoun form.

10. C

SMARTPOINT CATEGORY: PARALLELISM

Its sharp wit and *by presenting* should have parallel structures, so (C) is incorrect. *High Fidelity* is already a classic, so (A) is correct in the past tense. (B) properly uses an adjective to modify *High Fidelity*, and (D) is appropriate idiomatic usage.

IMPROVING SENTENCES QUESTIONS

Just like Identifying Sentence Errors questions, most Improving Sentences questions relate to a small number of grammatical issues. Here's the main difference between the two question types: while the errors in the Identifying Sentence Errors questions consist of single words or short phrases, the errors in the Improving Sentences questions generally involve the structure of the whole sentence.

THREE STEPS TO TEST DAY SUCCESS

KAPLAN'S TARGET STRATEGY FOR IMPROVING SENTENCES

Step 1: Read the sentence carefully, and listen for an error.

Step 2: Identify the error or errors.

Step 3: Eliminate the choices that don't address the error, and choose the most correct, concise, and relevant answer.

Let's use the method on the following example:

The Emancipation Edict freed the Russian serfs <u>in 1861; that being four years</u> before the Thirteenth Amendment abolished slavery in the United States.

(A) in 1861; that being four years

(B) in 1861 and is four years

(C) in 1861 and this amounts to four years

(D) in 1861, being four years

(E) in 1861, four years

> **EXPERT TUTOR TIP**
>
> " When trying to choose between two choices for Improving Sentences questions, look at the shortest answer choice first. Shorter is usually better. "

STEP 1: READ THE SENTENCE CAREFULLY, AND LISTEN FOR AN ERROR

The stem sentence (sentence part in question) in the example doesn't sound right. The semicolon might be wrong.

STEP 2: IDENTIFY THE ERROR OR ERRORS

The semicolon and phrase *that being* sound like the wrong way of joining the two parts of the sentence.

Joining the two sentence fragments with a simple comma would probably work. (Plus, as you'll learn later, answer choices that contain the word *being* are usually wrong.) Plug in your choice to be sure it sounds best.

STEP 3: ELIMINATE THE CHOICES THAT DON'T ADDRESS THE ERROR, AND CHOOSE THE MOST CORRECT, CONCISE, AND RELEVANT ANSWER

Scan the choices. All of them begin with *in 1861* and end with *four years*, so you have to look at what comes in between to see which forms the best link. You should see that *and is* in (B), *and this* in (C), and *being* in (D) are not better alternatives to *that being* in (A).

(E) is the best way to rewrite the underlined portion of the sentence. The phrase following the comma is used to modify *1861*. (E) is the correct answer because it is both concise and grammatically correct.

Remember, not every sentence contains an error. Choice (A) is correct about one-fifth of the time. In any event, because you should begin by reading the original sentence carefully, you should never waste time reading choice (A).

HOW TO AVOID COMMON MISTAKES

As you work through the Improving Sentences section, *read each sentence carefully*. We can't say that often enough. The error, if there is one, will often be obvious to you in the first reading.

If it isn't, remember that only a limited range of grammar rules is tested. Once your ear has become attuned to the Improving Sentences section's most common error types, you'll have an easier time spotting them on test day.

Remember the following rules:

- **Rule:** An independent clause has a subject and a complete verb and can stand alone as a sentence.
- **Rule:** A dependent, or subordinate, clause has a subject and a complete verb but needs an independent clause to become a sentence.
- **Rule:** To combine two independent clauses correctly, you must do one of three things:
  1. Insert a semicolon
  2. Make one clause dependent/subordinate

> **PERFECT SCORE TIP**
>
> " Sometimes I would pick an answer choice that fixed the error in the original sentence but introduced a new error. Reading the revised sentence was an absolute necessity for me to avoid these mistakes. "

3. Use one of the following conjunctions with a comma: **F**or, **A**nd, **N**or, **B**ut, **O**r, **Y**et, **S**o (FANBOYS)

Here are five classic Improving Sentences mistakes:

 ## COMMON MISTAKE 1: RUN-ON SENTENCES

The Improving Sentences questions on the Writing section always include run-on sentences. In a typical run-on sentence, two independent clauses, each of which could stand alone as a complete sentence, are erroneously joined together, either with no punctuation or, most often, with just a comma.

Here's an example:

> Even the town's most apathetic citizens rallied behind the cause, this support resulted in the passage of the law.

Both clauses in this sentence are independent; each could stand alone as a sentence. So it's incorrect to join them with a comma. There are several ways to correct run-on sentences. One way is to change the comma to a semicolon, so you would see the following:

> Even the town's most apathetic citizens rallied behind the cause; this support resulted in the passage of the law.

Another common way to fix a run-on is to keep the comma and add a FANBOYS conjunction (see list). This type of change can affect the meaning of the sentence, so be careful here—you don't want to change the meaning of the sentence. You might see the following:

> Even the town's most apathetic citizens rallied behind the cause, and this support resulted in the passage of the law.

Yet another way to fix a run-on sentence is to make one of the independent clauses dependent. To correct the original sentence in this way, you could see the following answer choice:

> Because even the town's most apathetic citizens rallied behind the cause, this support resulted in the passage of the law.

Adding *because* to the first clause makes it a dependent or subordinate clause. Now the comma is fine. Be sure, as stated previously, that the "fix" does not change the meaning of the sentence.

SUSPICIOUS COMMAS

When you see a long sentence with just a comma in the middle, suspect a run-on sentence. Then look to see which answer choice the test makers have chosen as a fix.

COMMON MISTAKE 2: SENTENCE FRAGMENTS

The Improving Sentences section usually includes one or two sentence fragments. Sentence fragments come in many forms, but they all share the same problem: They cannot stand alone because they have no independent clauses.

What looks like a sentence on the Writing section may actually be merely a fragment. Take a look at the following example:

> While many office managers are growing more
> and more dependent on facsimile machines, others
> resisting this technological breakthrough.

This just sounds wrong, doesn't it? Here's why. This is a sentence fragment because it has no independent clause. The first clause begins with the subordinating conjunction *while*, and the phrase following the comma contains the incomplete verb form *resisting*. Plus, a sentence must always have at least one clause that could stand alone, and here neither of the clauses can do that. The easiest way to repair this sentence is to insert the helping verb *are*:

> While many office managers are growing more and
> more dependent on facsimile machines, others are
> resisting this technological breakthrough.

Here's another sentence fragment:

> In the summertime, the kindergarten class that plays
> on the rope swing beneath the crooked oak tree.

Once again, the clause cannot stand alone. Here we have a fragment not because something is missing, but because something is included that makes the clause

PERFECT SCORE TIP

" I caught most of the sentence fragment errors when I read the sentences out loud. Even if I didn't know exactly what was wrong, I usually noticed that something didn't sound right. "

dependent. The word *that* makes everything after the comma a dependent clause. Simply remove the word *that*, and look at what you get:

> In the summertime, the kindergarten class plays on the rope swing beneath the crooked oak tree.

Now you have a grammatically complete sentence that is shorter than the fragment.

 ## COMMON MISTAKE 3: MISPLACED MODIFIERS AND PASSIVE VOICE

A modifier is a word or group of words that gives the reader more information about a noun or verb in the sentence.

KEY POINT

To be grammatically correct, the modifier must be positioned so that it is clear which word is being modified.

The best place to put a modifier is as close as possible to the word it modifies. Here is an example of a misplaced modifier like those you may see on the Writing section:

> Flying for the first time, the roar of the jet engines intimidated the small child, and he grew frightened as the plane roared down the runway.

The modifying phrase is found at the beginning of the sentence: *Flying for the first time*. A modifying phrase that begins a sentence should relate to the sentence's subject. Usually, a comma sets off this kind of introductory modifier, and the subject is the first noun that follows the comma.

Logically, in this example, you know that it is the child who is flying for the first time. But because of the grammatical structure of the sentence (the placement of the modifier), the sentence actually states that it is the *roar* that is flying for the first time. Of course, this doesn't make sense: roars don't fly for the first time (or the second time or the third time). The sentence needs to be revised so that the modifier is as close as possible to the noun it modifies:

> Flying for the first time, the small child was intimidated by the roar of the jet engines and grew frightened as the plane roared down the runway.

Here's another example of a sentence with a misplaced modifying phrase:

> An advertisement was withdrawn by the producer of the local news program that the city's minority communities considered offensive.

Grammatically, the phrase *that was considered offensive by the city's minority communities* refers to *the local news program*, because this is the nearest noun. Is that what the writer means? Is it the local news program or the advertisement that was offensive to the minority communities? Think about the logic of this sentence. What exactly is it that was considered offensive—the program or the advertisement? As the sentence is written, the phrase *that the city's minority communities considered offensive* seems to modify the noun *program*, because that's the noun the phrase is closest to. However, since *the advertisement was withdrawn*, it makes more sense to think that it was the *advertisement*—not the *program*—that was *considered offensive*. Here's a revision that makes that logic clear.

> An advertisement that the city's minority community considered offensive was withdrawn by the producer of the local news program.

Note: There is no one way to fix a modifier that's in the wrong place. You can add a subject and verb to the modifying phrase and create a dependent clause, or rearrange the words. Look at the following examples:

- **Wrong:** Being a good athlete, the team was glad to have Maria on the team.
- **Right:** Because she was a good athlete, the team was glad to have Maria on the team.
- **Right:** Because she was a good athlete, Maria was welcomed *by* the team. (Note passive voice here—weaker than the first right answer, but correct all the same.)

The first revision transforms the modifying phrase *Being a good athlete* into a dependent clause with a subject *she* and the verb *was*. The second turns *Maria* into the subject and makes the verb construction passive, *was welcomed by*.

 PASSIVE VS. ACTIVE VOICE

Avoid, if possible, sentences with passive voice verbs. What are these?

- **Passive verbs** are weak and wordy, and focus on who/what receives the action.
- **Active verbs** are stronger and use fewer words. Active voice emphasizes the action.

Consider the following examples:

- **Passive:** The panic button was pushed *by* me.
- **Active:** I pushed the panic button.

If you see *by*, think passive voice. When you can, choose sentences with the active voice.

How do you tell whether the passive voice constitutes an error on the SAT? Keep this guideline in mind: if the answer choices include an active-voice phrasing that contains no other errors, choose it instead of a passive-voice phrasing. Be sure to check for the presence of a modifier error like the one previously discussed. Sometimes it's actually necessary to use the passive voice to avoid having a modifying phrase in the wrong place. Remember, the passive is not always incorrect. If a perfectly correct active-voice phrasing is among the answer choices, though, the active voice will be the correct answer.

Now that you know about active and passive voice, let's come back to the sentence in which we corrected the modifier placement. The sentence we wound up with was passive.

> An advertisement that the city's minority communities considered offensive was withdrawn by the producer of the local news program.

Notice that the phrase *by the producer* is a clue that this sentence is in the passive voice. Here's how we could improve the sentence by stating it in the active voice.

> The producer of the local news program withdrew an advertisement that the city's minority communities considered offensive.

 ## Common Mistake 4: Faulty Parallelism

Certain sets of words in a sentence, or the general design of a sentence, often require a parallel construction—that is, the words or phrases must share the same grammatical structure. If they don't, the sentence will be off balance.

KEY POINT

> Sentences with two or more similar elements must be worded similarly. Lists or series of items, comparisons, and connective pairs are examples that require similar wording.

Use parallel structure with connective phrases, such as *neither . . . nor, either . . . or, not only . . . but also*, and lists.

For example:

- I looked for the dog *under the sofa, in the garage*, and *in the backyard*.
- I *asked* my mother for a snack, *went* to my room, and *started* to study.

Remember the following rules:

- **Rule:** A conjunction is a connective word joining two clauses or phrases.
- **Rule:** Two independent clauses in a sentence must be connected logically.
- **Rule:** Phrases and clauses in a sentence must be connected logically.

For example, compare these two sentences:

> My hobbies include swimming, gardening, and to read science fiction.

> My hobbies include swimming, gardening, and reading science fiction.

In the first sentence, two of the hobbies use the *-ing* gerund form, but the third uses a different structure—the infinitive. The sentence is not parallel. In the second version, all three hobbies correctly use the same *-ing* form, creating a balanced sentence.

PARALLEL STRUCTURE

> Use parallel structure with connective phrases such as *neither . . . nor* in comparisons and in lists.

Two kinds of parallel construction errors appear repeatedly on the Writing section. The first occurs in sentences with pairs of connective words that require parallelism. These connective words include those in the following list:

> neither . . . nor
>
> either . . . or
>
> both . . . and
>
> the better . . . the better
>
> the more . . . the more (or less)
>
> not only . . . but also

In the sentence below, look at that first pair of words, *neither . . . nor*, and the phrases that follow both words:

> Nineteenth-century nihilists were concerned with neither the origins of philosophical thought nor how societal laws developed.

PERFECT SCORE TIP

" Taking the first item in a list and then comparing it to the others was an easy way for me to catch parallel structure problems. "

The phrases following the words *neither* and *nor* must be parallel in grammatical structure. That is, if a noun phrase (*the origins of philosophical thought*) follows *neither*, then a noun phrase must follow *nor* too. But here *nor* is followed by *how societal laws developed*—a dependent clause. The two parts of the sentence are not grammatically parallel.

In this example, the dependent clause must be rewritten as a noun phrase (*nor the development of societal laws*) to make the sentence parallel. With both connective words followed by a noun and a prepositional phrase, the sentence now has proper parallel construction.

 ## COMMON MISTAKE 5: FAULTY TRANSITIONS IN CLAUSES AND PHRASES

These errors occur when sentence clauses are joined incorrectly. The FANBOYS appeared on page 182. They are back because they can be incorrect in context. The SAT may insert a *but* into a sentence that should have an *and* instead. You'll need to be on the lookout for these situations.

Besides the FANBOYS conjunctions, other transition phrases may connect dependent clauses to their independent neighbors. You must be alert to a poor connection in these cases as well.

Here are some of the most common connectors:

- **Similarity:** *like, as, as if, as though, just as, as well as*
- **Continuation:** *plus, in addition*
- **Cause and effect:** *because, since, due to, as a result of, as a consequence*
- **Contrast:** *while, though, although, nevertheless, rather than, despite*
- **Emphasis:** *in fact, indeed*

KEY POINT

> Don't forget the FANBOYS conjunctions that connect two independent clauses. Don't pick one that doesn't make sense in context (for example, *and* instead of *but*).

Using illogical transitions creates two types of errors: faulty coordination and faulty subordination.

Coordination between two clauses is faulty if it doesn't express the logical relation between the clauses. Often, this error involves a misused conjunction. A conjunction is a connective word joining two clauses or phrases in one sentence. These are the most common conjunctions:

and

but

because

however

for

or

Identify the conjunction in the following sentence. Why does it fail to connect the clauses logically?

> Ben Franklin was a respected and talented states-
> man, and he was most famous for his discovery of
> electricity.

To identify and correct the faulty coordination, determine what the relationship between the sentence's two clauses really is. Does the conjunction *and* best express the relationship between the two facts the writer states about Ben Franklin? *And* normally expresses a consistency between two equally emphasized facts. However, the fact that Franklin is best known for his discovery of electricity is presented in contrast to the fact that he was a talented statesman. Thus, the use of *and* is an error in coordination.

A better way to connect these two contrasting ideas would be to use the conjunction *but*, which indicates some contrast between the two clauses. In this sentence, *but* points to a common expectation. An individual usually distinguishes herself or himself in one field of accomplishment—in politics or in science—but not in both. So Franklin's distinction in two diverse fields seems to contradict common expectations and calls for a *but*.

Faulty subordination is most often found on the Writing section in a group of words that contains two or more subordinate, or dependent, clauses but no independent clause. There are several connective words that, when introducing a sentence or clause, always indicate that the phrase that follows is dependent, or subordinate. They are as follows:

since

because

so that

if

> **EXPERT TUTOR TIP**
>
> " Most often these types of questions are testing *contrast* vs. *continuation/conclusion*. If you see one of these phrases or clauses underlined, ask yourself: Is this contrast or continuation? Do I need to make it the other? "

> **PERFECT SCORE TIP**
>
> " Kaplan's method of taking out the conjunction made it easier to see what the relationship between two clauses was. It was really easy to pick the best conjunction after doing that! "

Whenever a dependent clause begins a sentence, an independent clause must follow somewhere in the sentence. Look at the group of words below and identify the faulty subordination:

> Since the small electronics industry is one of the world's fastest growing sectors, because demand for the computer chip continues to be high.

Since indicates that the first clause in the group of words is subordinate and needs to be followed by an independent clause. But *because* in the second clause indicates that the second clause is also subordinate. The sentence is faulty because there is no independent clause to make the group of words grammatically complete. Result: two sentence fragments. The second connective word *because* should be eliminated to make the group of words a complete and logical sentence. With this revision, the *since* clause expresses a cause, and the independent clause expresses an effect or result.

 ## WORDINESS: IT'S EVERYWHERE

One of the most important concepts in the Improving Sentences (and Improving Paragraphs) section is wordiness. You'll find this style problem everywhere you look: in the questions themselves and in many wrong answers. As such, wordiness isn't a stand-alone error. It's an invasive weed that wends its way through these two parts of the multiple-choice section and into Improving Paragraphs, too.

KEY POINT

> A sentence that uses more words than necessary to make its point may not contain any *grammatical* errors, but it does contain a *style* error: wordiness.

For example, can you find three areas that can be trimmed in the following sentence?

> At this point in time, we are meeting for the purpose of deciding if we have the ability to choose a charity.

At this point in time = now
for the purpose of deciding = to decide
have the ability to = can

In this concise version, 4 words replace 14 in the above example. On the SAT you may find sentences that *take into consideration*, instead of *consider*, or discuss an *annual* parade that takes place *every year*.

Take care as you go through the multiple-choice questions to avoid all redundancies (e.g., the *parade* example) and excessive wordiness, such as the following example. As you read it, note how much easier it is to understand the concise version.

WORDY:

I am of the opinion that the aforementioned managers should be advised that they will be evaluated with regard to the utilization of responsive organizational software for the purpose of devising a responsive network of customers.

CONCISE:

We should tell the managers that we will evaluate their use of flexible computerized databases to develop a customers' network.

EXPERT TUTOR TIP

"Don't assume that wordy, hard to understand sentences are correct because they sound "smarter." Proofread multiple-choice questions for wordiness just like you would proofread your essay for wordiness."

PRACTICE IMPROVING SENTENCES

Let's practice what you've learned.

Directions: The following sentences test correctness and effectiveness of expression. Part of each sentence or the entire sentence is underlined; beneath each sentence are five ways of phrasing the underlined material. Choice (A) repeats the original phrasing; the other four choices are different. If you think the original phrasing produces a better sentence than any of the alternatives, select choice (A); if not, select one of the other choices.

1. Memorial Day celebrates <u>the country's veterans, but we decided to place flags</u> on soldiers' graves in the cemetery.

   (A) the country's veterans, but we decided to place flags

   (B) the country's veterans, because we decided to place flag

   (C) the country's veterans, and they place flags

   (D) the country's veterans, so we decided to place flags

   (E) the country's veterans and places flags

2. <u>Having overslept, the class left on the overnight college visit without Sean.</u>

   (A) Having overslept, the class left on the overnight college visit without Sean.

   (B) The class left on the overnight college visit without Sean, who overslept.

   (C) The class, having overslept, left on the overnight college visit without Sean.

   (D) Having overslept, Sean's class left on the overnight college visit without him.

   (E) Sean's class left on the overnight college visit without him, who overslept.

3. To combat late-night mischief, the city was <u>planning to either install street cameras or enforcing a curfew for teens.</u>

   (A) planning to either install street cameras or enforcing a curfew for teens

   (B) planning installing street cameras or enforcing a curfew for teens

   (C) planning to install street cameras and enforce a curfew for teens

   (D) installing street cameras and enforcing a curfew for teens

   (E) planning to either install street cameras or enforce a curfew for teens

4. The computer science professor <u>always had the latest gadgets, he still preferred</u> real books to electronic ones.

   (A) always had the latest gadgets, he still preferred

   (B) always had the latest gadgets, but he still preferred

   (C) always had the latest gadgets because he still preferred

   (D) always had the latest gadgets, including

   (E) always preferred the latest gadgets, including

5. <u>Buckling himself into the seat, Jason, who often suffered from severe motion sickness,</u> wondered whether riding the monstrous roller coaster was a good idea.

   (A) Buckling himself into the seat, Jason, who often suffered from severe motion sickness

   (B) Jason, buckling himself into the seat, who often suffered from severe motion sickness

   (C) Jason, who often suffered from motion sickness, buckled himself into the seat

   (D) Jason buckled himself into the seat and often suffered from severe motion sickness

   (E) Buckling himself into the seat, Jason suffered from severe motion sickness and

6. <u>The senior citizens who come together on
Sunday afternoons to gossip, knit, and show
off their latest projects.</u>

   (A) The senior citizens who come together
   on Sunday afternoons to gossip, knit,
   and show off their latest projects.

   (B) The senior citizens come together on
   Sunday afternoons to gossip, knit, and
   show off their latest projects.

   (C) The senior citizens who come together
   on Sunday afternoons gossiping,
   knitting, and showing off their latest
   projects.

   (D) The senior citizens coming together on
   Sunday afternoons to gossip, knit, and
   show off their latest projects.

   (E) Coming together on Sunday afternoons
   to gossip, knit, and show off their latest
   projects are the senior citizens.

7. <u>The dinner was made by Vanessa, who saw
that her mom</u> had had a long day at work.

   (A) The dinner was made by Vanessa, who
   saw that her mom

   (B) Vanessa, who saw her mom, made
   dinner after she

   (C) Vanessa made dinner after she saw that
   her mom

   (D) The dinner was made by Vanessa, seeing
   that her mom

   (E) The dinner was made by her mom, who
   saw that Vanessa

8. Because of its length, <u>Tara's cat has the ability
to stand on its hind legs</u> and turn the knob to
open the door.

   (A) Tara's cat has the ability to stand on its
   hind legs

   (B) Tara's cat can stand on its hind legs

   (C) Tara's cat can stand on her hind legs

   (D) Tara has a cat that has the ability to
   stand on its hind kegs

   (E) Tara's cat is able to stand on its hind legs

9. <u>Because they can detect scents, bloodhounds
are often used</u> to sniff out the trails of
escaped convicts and missing children.

   (A) Because they can detect scents,
   bloodhounds are often used

   (B) Because bloodhounds are often used to
   detect scents, they are used

   (C) Detecting scents, bloodhounds are often
   used

   (D) Bloodhounds, detecting scents, have the
   ability

   (E) Bloodhounds detect scents and have the
   ability

10. The girls will be spending the summer
<u>volunteering as lifeguards, going to the mall,
and as babysitters of their neighbors' kids</u>.

   (A) volunteering as lifeguards, going to
   the mall, and as babysitters of their
   neighbors' kids

   (B) at the pool, at the mall, and at their
   neighbors' houses

   (C) and volunteering as lifeguards, going to
   the mall, and babysitting their neighbors'
   kids

   (D) volunteering as lifeguards, going to the
   mall, and babysitting their neighbors'
   kids

   (E) as volunteer lifeguards, as mall patrons,
   and as babysitters of their neighbors'
   kids

ANSWERS AND EXPLANATIONS

1. D

SMARTPOINT CATEGORY: TRANSITIONS .ıılll

The two independent clauses in this sentence are improperly connected. The second half of the sentence describes people placing flags on soldiers' graves because of the holiday that celebrates veterans. *But* signals a contrast, which doesn't describe the relationship between the clauses. That rules out (A). Instead, a connector for a cause-and-effect relationship is needed here. (B) uses *because*, which is a cause-and-effect connector, but the sentence doesn't make sense. (C) and (E) also do not make sense. (D) is your best answer.

2. B

SMARTPOINT CATEGORY: MISPLACED MODIFIERS .ıllll

This sentence contains a misplaced modifier. *Having overslept* appears to modify *the class*. The class didn't oversleep; Sean did. That rules out (A), (C), and (D). In (E), the sentence is worded awkwardly. (B) is your best answer.

3. E

SMARTPOINT CATEGORY: PARALLELISM .ıılll

The connective words *either . . . or* often appear on the SAT, and they give a clue that you should check to make sure the phrases they connect are parallel. Here, one phrase uses the *-ing* gerund form, while the other does not, ruling out (A). (B) is grammatically incorrect. (C) and (D) are grammatically correct, but are missing *either . . . or*. The word *and* changes the meaning of the original sentence. (E) is your best answer.

4. B

SMARTPOINT CATEGORY: RUN-ON .ıllll

The key to this sentence is realizing that it contains two independent clauses that are connected by a mere comma. This run-on sentence requires a connector to make it correct. First, figure out the relationship between the clauses. You should see that the clauses present a contrast: The professor likes gadgets, except when it comes to books. (B) is the only answer that fits.

5. A

This sentence is long, but it's correct. *Buckling himself into the seat* correctly modifies *Jason*, and *who often suffered from severe motion sickness* is set off correctly in commas. (B) is incorrect because *who often suffered from severe motion sickness* cannot logically modify *the seat*. (C) and (D) are missing a conjunction that would connect the end of the answer choice with the rest of the sentence. (E) changes the meaning of the sentence and doesn't make sense because it sounds as if Jason suffered from motion sickness when he buckled himself into the seat.

6. B

SMARTPOINT CATEGORY: FRAGMENT

As you read this sentence, you should see that it is missing a proper verb to make it a complete sentence. (C) and (D) have the same problem. (E) is unnecessarily wordy and awkward. (B) is your best answer.

7. C

SMARTPOINT CATEGORY: ACTIVE VS. PASSIVE VOICE

As is, the sentence is not grammatically incorrect, but it can be worded better. *The dinner was made by Vanessa* is in passive voice. A better way to write this sentence is to put it in active voice. (B) changes the meaning of the sentence and makes it unclear *who* had had a long day at work. (D) and (E) are not only passive, but they also change the meaning of the original sentence. Your best answer is (C). On the SAT, two choices may be *grammatically* correct. If so, check to see if one uses active voice and the other uses passive voice. If that is the only difference, the active-voice sentence is the right answer.

8. B

SMARTPOINT CATEGORY: WORDINESS

As is, this sentence is not grammatically incorrect, but it can be worded better. As you know from the chapter, *has the ability to* is a wordy way of saying "can." (D) makes the sentence even more wordy. (E) shortens *has the ability to* but is still unnecessarily wordy. (C) changes the original sentence in that you don't know whether the cat is a her or a him. In addition, this answer choice can be read to say that the cat stands on Tara's hind legs. (B) is your best answer.

9. A

This sentence is correct. *Because they can detect scents* refers to *bloodhounds*. (B) makes the sentence redundant and wordy. (C) and (D) both use the gerund *detecting scents*, which makes the sentences awkward. (E) removes the cause-and-effect aspect of the sentence.

10. D

SMARTPOINT CATEGORY: PARALLELISM

The key to this sentence is realizing that it contains a series of items that are not parallel. You have *volunteering, going,* and *as babysitters*. You're looking for the answer choice that has *babysitting*, which is (D). (E) is another way of wording the sentence, but it is unnecessarily wordy. (B) oversimplifies the sentence and removes what the girls will be doing at these places. (C) makes the sentence unclear because it doesn't explain how the girls will be *spending*.

IMPROVING PARAGRAPHS QUESTIONS

As the title implies, these questions (a total of six on the test) follow a single, short essay. You don't need to worry much about the content to answer the questions correctly:

- About three will be standard grammar and style questions similar to the ones presented in the previous Improving Sentences section.

- The other three will test your understanding of the overall paragraph(s). Here, context is critical and you'll need to know the gist of the passage:

  - What is the best transition sentence to start a new paragraph?

  - What is the best way to combine two poorly worded sentences or fragments?

You'll see the following question types:

- Content-related Wording questions

- Sentence Revision questions

- Combining Sentences questions

- Paragraph Transition questions

THREE STEPS TO TEST DAY SUCCESS

KAPLAN'S TARGET STRATEGY FOR IMPROVING PARAGRAPHS

Kaplan's Target Strategy works for all kinds of Improving Paragraphs questions.

Step 1: Read the passage, and listen for any possible errors.

Step 2: Read the question. If necessary, reread the relevant portion, and identify the error.

Step 3: Eliminate the choices that don't address the error, and choose the most correct, concise, and relevant answer.

Let's use the method on the following example:

(1) Until recently, I was convinced that I had no musical ability whatsoever. (2) In grade school, I could hardly keep my voice in tune with other singers around me. (3) I thought that I would never play a musical instrument or become a rock star. (4) I really enjoyed music, just no one thought I had any talent at all.

(5) When I entered junior high I took music classes with our teacher, Mr. Daniels. (6) At first he seemed really stern and strict. (7) He gave us a lot of warnings that even though he

had a reputation of being harsh around school, the reality was ten times worse. (8) But after a couple of weeks, he started encouraging us to get into musical ensembles. (9) At first I was disinterested, thinking that I would be ridiculed as to my contribution. (10) Mr. Daniels kept insisted that everyone had to play some kind of instrument, so I chose his handbell choir. (11) Other kids thought handbells were stupid, but I liked the sound they made—it was so much purer than the electric guitar. (12) Mr. Daniels coached us regular after school. (13) Not only did the group actually start to sound good, but also I discovered that I had some rhythmic talents that no one had suspected. (14) Maybe I will be a rock star yet! (15) The whole experience showed me that with encouragement and a sense of adventure you can overcome your limitations. (16) As our former First Lady Eleanor Roosevelt once said, sometimes "you must do that which you think you cannot do."

> **EXPERT TUTOR TIP**
>
> " If you're looking to save some time, read the passage quickly and jump right to the questions, which often repeat the key piece you need. "

STEP 1: READ THE PASSAGE, AND LISTEN FOR ANY POSSIBLE ERRORS

Read the entire essay quickly. Get a sense of the essay's overall purpose, as well as the main idea of each paragraph. This will come in handy when you're asked to answer questions that relate to the essay as a whole.

After a quick read, you should understand that this essay is about a student who has recently discovered that he has musical talent, which he realized after encouragement from a teacher, Mr. Daniels. You may have spotted some areas that could use revising.

STEP 2: READ THE QUESTION; IF NECESSARY, REREAD THE RELEVANT PORTION, AND IDENTIFY THE ERROR

Let's take a look at some questions. Read the question closely. Make sure that you understand exactly what you're asked to do. Questions that require you to revise or combine sentences will supply you with the sentence numbers.

Which of the following versions of sentence 4 (reproduced below) is best?

I really enjoyed music, just no one thought I had any talent at all.

(A) (As it is now)
(B) Even though I really enjoyed music, just no one thought I had any talent at all.
(C) I really enjoyed music, and therefore no one thought I had any talent at all.
(D) Although I really enjoyed music, no one thought I had any talent at all.
(E) The music was enjoyable to me, however no one thought I had any talent at all.

This question is asking you to choose the best way to revise the sentence. Go back and reread that sentence in the original text. *Also reread the sentences before and after the target sentence.* This will provide you with the context (the surrounding ideas or information) for the sentence. Context helps you choose the best answer from the choices.

The word *just* creates a run-on sentence here that needs fixing. To combine both clauses in a logical manner, you need to remove *just* and add conjunctions that express the idea of *contrast—in spite of* the author's enjoyment of music, everyone thought he or she had no talent.

STEP 3: ELIMINATE THE CHOICES THAT DON'T ADDRESS THE ERROR, AND CHOOSE THE MOST CORRECT, CONCISE, AND RELEVANT ANSWER

(B) is wrong because it still includes *just*. (C) is not logical—why would people conclude the author was talentless if he or she enjoyed music? (E)'s *however* is the wrong conjunction—it expresses contrast, but it doesn't link the two phrases to fix the run-on. (D) is the best answer.

Let's take a look at the other type of question you'll find in this section—questions about the entire essay. These types of questions generally won't refer to specific sentences. Read the question closely. Make sure you understand exactly what you're asked to do.

> Which of the following sentences, if added after sentence 4, would best link the first paragraph with the rest of the essay?
>
> (A) As a result, I learned that other people's opinions are irrelevant.
> (B) However, I soon met an inspiring person who disproved this assumption.
> (C) This was why no one thought I would become a rock star.
> (D) Nevertheless, I knew all along that I possessed a form of musical genius.
> (E) I have held these beliefs about my musical ability for many years.

This question is asking you for the best transition sentence. A good setup for paragraph 2 would be a sentence that leads into the author's discovery that he or she had musical ability and introduces Mr. Daniels.

(A) is illogical because Mr. Daniels's opinion soon persuades the author to try playing music. (C) and (E) are non sequiturs—they don't lead into paragraph 2 in any way. (D) is too extreme and a bit premature—the author doesn't discover his or her talent until the middle of paragraph 2. (B) is the best answer.

> **EXPERT TUTOR TIP**
>
> " Keep in mind that errors often have multiple possible corrections. Don't be so intent upon finding the correction that you predicted that you miss another valid correction. "

PRACTICE IMPROVING PARAGRAPHS

Let's practice what you've learned.

Directions: The following passage is an early draft of an essay. Some parts of the passage need to be rewritten.

Read the passage, and select the best answer for each question that follows. Some questions ask you to improve sentence structure or word choice in particular sentences or parts of sentences. Other questions ask you to consider organization and development. In choosing answers, follow the conventions of standard written English.

(1) I disagree with the editor's view that after-school sports programs should be cut in our city government's search for ways to reduce spending. (2) The editor argues that extracurricular sports play a less important role than academic studies, distracting students from the opportunity to increase their knowledge after school is out. (3) However, I myself believe that playing sports enhances students' academic performance. (4) Why is sports so effective in this regard? (5) The main reason is that an athletic endeavor teaches people to excel. (6) It gives students the chance to strive for greatness. (7) It shows them that it takes courage and discipline to succeed in competition with others. (8) Top athletes such as Michael Jordan become role models for young people everywhere, inspiring them with his brilliant individual performances. (9) In addition to these personal attributes, playing in team sports show young people how to interact with each other, achieving shared goals. (10) Such principles have a direct impact on how students perform in their academic studies. (11) I know that being selected for the school lacrosse team taught me many valuable lessons about working with others. (12) Not only that, friendships that I have made there were carried into the rest of my school life. (13) In summary, I would urge the editor to strongly reconsider his stance on extracurricular sports. (14) There are doubtless other ways of city government saving the money they require.

1. Which of the following is the best way to revise the underlined portion of sentence 3 (reproduced below)?

   However, I myself believe that playing sports enhances students' academic performance.

   (A) However, I myself believe that playing sports should enhance
   (B) Playing sports, however, I believe enhances
   (C) However, I personally believe that playing sports enhances
   (D) I believe, however, that playing sports enhances
   (E) However, I myself believe that to play sports is to enhance

2. In the context of the second paragraph, which of the following is the best version of the underlined portion of sentence 8 (reproduced below)?

   Top athletes such as Michael Jordan become role models for young people everywhere, inspiring them with his brilliant individual performances.

   (A) (As it is now)
   (B) inspiring him with their
   (C) inspiring them with their
   (D) to inspire them with his
   (E) inspiring him with his

3. Which of the following is the best way to revise the underlined portion of sentence 12 (reproduced below)?

   Not only that, friendships that I have made there were carried into the rest of my school life.

   (A) And,
   (B) Moreover,
   (C) Nevertheless,
   (D) Sequentially,
   (E) Finally,

4. Which of the following is the best way to revise and combine sentences 6 and 7 (reproduced below)?

   It gives students the chance to strive for greatness. It shows them that it takes courage and discipline to succeed in competition with others.

   (A) Although it gives students the chance to strive for greatness, it also shows them that it takes courage and discipline to succeed in competition with others.
   (B) While it gives students the chance to strive for greatness, also showing them that it takes courage and discipline to succeed in competition with others.
   (C) It gives students the chance to strive for greatness, showing them that it takes courage and discipline to succeed in competition with others.
   (D) Because it gives students the chance to strive for greatness, they are shown that it takes courage and discipline to succeed in competition with others.
   (E) It gives students the chance to strive for greatness and show them that it takes courage and discipline to succeed in competition with others.

5. How can the author best improve sentence 14 (reproduced below)?

   There are doubtless other ways of city government saving the money they require.

   (A) By making an analogy to historical events
   (B) By taking alternative points of view into account
   (C) By including a personal anecdote about her participation in team sports
   (D) By speculating about the motivations of those advocating cuts
   (E) By providing examples of other areas in which spending could be reduced

6. Which sentence would be most appropriate to follow sentence 11 (reproduced below)?

   I know that being selected for the school lacrosse team taught me many valuable lessons about working with others.

   (A) For example, in working with my classmates on a group project, it's harder to get a good grade if we don't all cooperate on it.
   (B) For example, all my hard work has allowed me to become the captain of the team, and I am just a junior.
   (C) In addition, I enjoy playing the sport and getting to prove myself as an aggressive player on and off the field.
   (D) In addition, being on the team allows me to get out of chemistry class every now and then when the team has to leave early for a game far away.
   (E) For example, I have learned which players I shouldn't pass the ball to because they are terrible players.

ANSWERS AND EXPLANATIONS

1. D

SMARTPOINT CATEGORY: WORDINESS 📶

The key to this problem is realizing that *I myself* is redundant; if the author has already used *I*, there is no need to add *myself* to clarify. Choices (A) and (E) still include *myself*. (C) substitutes another redundancy—the word *personally*. (B) is unnecessarily convoluted. (D) provides the best fix here—notice that it's also the shortest, most straightforward answer.

2. C

SMARTPOINT CATEGORY: PRONOUNS 📶

The key to this sentence is spotting a pronoun reference problem; the subject in the sentence is *top athletes*, not *Michael Jordan*—he's only introduced as an example of a top athlete. So the underlined pronouns should be *them* (to agree with *young people*) and *their* (to agree with *top athletes*) as in choice (C).

3. B

SMARTPOINT CATEGORY: TRANSITIONS 📶

To fix this ambiguous introductory phrase, look for a conjunction that expresses the idea of listing an *additional benefit* of participation in team sports. (A) is not an idiomatic conjunction with which to begin a sentence. (C) creates an unnecessary contrast. In (D), *Sequentially* means "in order," not *consequently*. (E), *Finally*, is wrong because this sentence describes the second item in a list of two. (B), *Moreover*, is the best answer.

4. C

SMARTPOINT CATEGORY: TRANSITIONS 📶

The context here suggests a strong link between the two sentences—the idea is that sports provide students with the chance to strive for greatness by showing them it takes courage. (A) introduces an illogical contrast. (B) creates a sentence fragment. (D) uses the passive voice unnecessarily. In (E), the verb *show* doesn't agree with the subject *it*. (C) is the best answer.

5. E

SMARTPOINT CATEGORY: TRANSITIONS

Sentence 14 provides a weak ending to the passage because it refers to *other ways of the city government saving money,* without suggesting what these might be. (A) would be an odd solution—historical events haven't been mentioned thus far in the passage. (B) would weaken the essay just at the point at which the author needs to strengthen it. (C) would be repetitive—the author has already included a personal anecdote. Finally, (D) would simply offer a digression at this point. So the best improvement to sentence 14 would be (E), to provide examples of alternative areas for cuts.

6. A

SMARTPOINT CATEGORY: TRANSITIONS

You are looking for a sentence that is related to sentence 11. The five answer choices all start with either *For example* or *In addition,* so you are looking for a sentence that will either show a way being on the team has taught the author to work with others or expand on sports' influence academically. (B) starts out with *For example,* and you can rule that out as the answer because it doesn't discuss teamwork. (C) and (D) are wrong because they do not focus on working well with others. (E) is wrong because it's not about teamwork. (A) is your best answer.

PRACTICE

Use everything you have learned about Identifying Sentence Errors questions, Improving Sentences questions, and Improving Paragraphs questions to answer the questions in the practice set that follows. All of the questions are similar to the ones that will be on the SAT.

For the questions you get wrong, reread the part of this chapter that covers the specific question type. Make sure you understand all the strategies from this chapter.

Questions 1–18

Directions: The following sentences test your ability to recognize grammar and usage errors. Each sentence contains either a single error or no error at all. No sentence contains more than one error. The error, if there is one, is underlined and lettered. If the sentence contains an error, select the one underlined part that must be changed to make the sentence correct. If the sentence is correct, select choice (E).

1. Although <u>they had been</u> political rivals on
              A

   <u>more than one</u> occasion, John Quincy Adams
      B

   <u>remained</u> one of Thomas Jefferson's closest
     C

   friends until <u>his</u> death. <u>No error</u>
            D   E

2. Even <u>those who</u> profess <u>to care</u> about "green"
        A   B

   issues often fail to consider <u>how</u> their daily
                     C

   choices <u>effect</u> the environment. <u>No error</u>
          D   E

3. Ants, <u>which</u> have inhabited the earth for at
        A

   least 100 million years, <u>are without doubt</u> the
                     B

   <u>more successful</u> of all the social insects of the
    C

   Hymenoptera, an order <u>that also</u> includes
                  D

   wasps and bees. <u>No error</u>
              E

4. The volunteers, <u>upon discovering</u> that
            A

   <u>a large number</u> of the village children <u>were</u>
      B   C

   infected by parasites <u>from</u> unclean drinking
                    D

   water, decided to make the well-digging

   project their highest priority. <u>No error</u>
                          E

5. Opponents of the act <u>argued that</u> the
                        A

   legislation <u>was not only</u> vaguely formulated
                  B

   and unconstitutional, but also impossible

   <u>to enforce</u> in an international <u>and virtually</u>
        C   D

   unregulated arena. <u>No error</u>
                          E

6. One reason that a growing number of people

   <u>have no</u> family doctor <u>may be that</u> fewer and
      A   B

   fewer medical students <u>are choosing to train</u> as
                              C

   <u>a general practitioner</u>. <u>No error</u>
         D   E

7. Citizens <u>protesting</u> the planned demolition of
               A

   the historic YMCA building claim <u>that without</u>
                                        B

   the YMCA, many young people in the town

   <u>would of</u> grown up <u>with no</u> access to sports
      C   D

   facilities and no place for after-school

   recreation. <u>No error</u>
                   E

8. When questioned, <u>a surprising</u> number of
                       A

   fifth-graders said that telling the truth—even

   <u>if it</u> meant <u>being</u> punished—was preferable
      B   C

   <u>than living</u> with a lie. <u>No error</u>
      D   E

9. <u>Under</u> the proposed law, which many <u>deem</u>
      A   B

   too harsh, any motorist <u>convicted of</u> drunk
                              C

   driving would spend thirty days in prison and

   lose <u>their license</u> for five years. <u>No error</u>
           D   E

10. When <u>it became apparent</u> to Clive that not one
              A

    of the remaining jurors <u>were going to</u> believe
                                B

    his <u>client's</u> alibi, he began to reconsider the
           C

    district attorney's <u>offer of a</u> plea bargain.
                            D

    <u>No error</u>
       E

11. The gods of Greek mythology, who

    <u>were neither</u> omniscient nor <u>particularly</u>
       A   B

    ethical, amused themselves <u>by taking on</u>
                                   C

    disguises and <u>meddling</u> in the affairs of
                      D

    mortals. <u>No error</u>
                 E

12. Like other gourmet restaurants, M. Dubois
    $\underline{}$
              A

    creates magnificent meals in which he likes
                           $\underline{}$ $\underline{}$
                               B   C

    to use only the finest ingredients. No error
    $\underline{}$ $\underline{}$
     D   E

13. Often believed to be dangerous and dirty places
          $\underline{}$ $\underline{}$
                A   B

    where tourists were always mugged, New York
                    $\underline{}$
                      C

    City has been reforming its image radically with
         $\underline{}$
              D

    dropping crime rates over the past few years.

    No error
    $\underline{}$
     E

14. To understand the current Russian government,
    $\underline{}$
         A

    we have to be highly aware of the theory and
    $\underline{}$ $\underline{}$
         B   C

    history of communism, whether or not one

    agrees with its tenets. No error
    $\underline{}$ $\underline{}$
         D   E

15. Bill had hoped to go to the baseball game
         $\underline{}$
              A

    that night, but as the afternoon wore on, he
    $\underline{}$
      B

    realized he would have to work late to meet his
                  $\underline{}$ $\underline{}$
                       C   D

    deadline. No error
             $\underline{}$
              E

16. The process of learning new languages require a
                 $\underline{}$ $\underline{}$
                      A   B

    commitment to memorization and

    pronunciation practice, even if progress
                          $\underline{}$
                            C

    seems slow. No error
    $\underline{}$ $\underline{}$
         D   E

17. Widely divergent opinions could be heard from
    $\underline{}$ $\underline{}$
         A   B

    the audience as the planning commission

    unveiled their proposal for a remodeled
             $\underline{}$ $\underline{}$
              C   D

    city square. No error
               $\underline{}$
                E

18. The advisory board cautioned employees that
                    $\underline{}$
                       A

    the existing program of health benefits were
        $\underline{}$ $\underline{}$ $\underline{}$
          B   C   D

    likely to be eliminated. No error
                          $\underline{}$
                           E

Questions 19–43

Directions: The following sentences test correctness and effectiveness of expression. Part of each sentence or the entire sentence is underlined; beneath each sentence are five ways of phrasing the underlined material. Choice (A) repeats the original phrasing; the other four choices are different. If you think the original phrasing produces a better sentence than any of the alternatives, select choice (A); if not, select one of the other choices.

19. <u>The runners coming this far, they</u> decided to push through the very strenuous final miles of the marathon.

    (A) The runners coming this far, they
    (B) Although they came this far, the runners
    (C) Having come this far, the runners
    (D) To come this far, the runners
    (E) The runners came this far; so that they

20. <u>Our English teacher handed out the worksheet, and we started filling in the answers quickly, and we continued to do so until the bell rang.</u>

    (A) Our English teacher handed out the worksheet, and we started filling in the answers quickly, and we continued to do so until the bell rang.
    (B) Upon starting to fill in the answers quickly after we were given the worksheet by our English teacher, we continued to do so until the bell rang.
    (C) Following our English teacher's giving us the worksheet, we started filling in the answers quickly and continued doing just that until the bell rang.
    (D) After our English teacher gave us the worksheet, we filled in the answers quickly until the bell rang.
    (E) We filled in the answers quickly until the bell rang when the worksheet had been given to us by our English teacher.

21. Some of the classes taught in American <u>classrooms are interpretations of lessons used worldwide, particularly those in European history.</u>

    (A) classrooms are interpretations of lessons used worldwide, particularly those in European history
    (B) classrooms, there are interpretations of lessons used worldwide, particularly European history
    (C) classrooms, and in particular European history, is an interpretation of lessons used worldwide
    (D) classrooms, particularly in European history, are interpretations of lessons used worldwide
    (E) classrooms being interpretations, European history in particular, of those used worldwide

22. <u>Olga Korbut, a Soviet gymnast, whose fame as an athlete</u> on the Olympic stage almost equals that of Nadia Comaneci.

    (A) Olga Korbut, a Soviet gymnast, whose fame as an athlete
    (B) Olga Korbut, who was a Soviet gymnast and whose fame as an athlete
    (C) A Soviet with fame as an Olympic athlete, Olga Korbut
    (D) Olga Korbut was a Soviet gymnast whose fame as an athlete
    (E) A Soviet, Olga Korbut who was a gymnast and whose fame

23. Many parents believe that extreme sports are too <u>dangerous, consequently, some of those parents do not allow</u> their children to bungee jump.

    (A) dangerous, consequently, some of those parents do not allow
    (B) dangerous, therefore, some of those parents do not allow
    (C) dangerous; consequently, some do not allow
    (D) dangerous, some people do not allow
    (E) dangerous, and therefore not allowing

24. <u>Although its being fictional in form</u>, the new book on America raises many historical questions.

    (A) Although its being fictional in form
    (B) Despite its fictional form
    (C) Whereas it was fictional in form
    (D) Its form being fictional
    (E) Even though fictional form was there

25. The novels of Louisa May Alcott are sought out by each new generation of readers <u>considering that her books blend both wild youthfulness and a rational side</u>.

    (A) considering that her books blend both wild youthfulness and a rational side
    (B) considering that her books blend both wild youthfulness and rationality
    (C) because her books blend wild youthfulness and rationality
    (D) because her books will blend not only wild youthfulness but also a rational side
    (E) being that her books will blend both wild youthfulness and rationality

26. Joann, the newest student at Leon Blum High School, has been portrayed as <u>the brightest student and also the most unruly of them</u>.

    (A) the brightest student and also the most unruly of them
    (B) not only the brightest student, but also more unruly than any
    (C) the brightest student at the same time as she is the most unruly student
    (D) at once the brightest and also the most unruly of them
    (E) the brightest and yet the most unruly of students

27. Anaelle's parents explained that she was promoted to head journalist <u>for the reason that her articles were mindful always for both sides of the issues</u>.

    (A) for the reason that her articles were mindful always for both sides of the issues
    (B) since her articles for issues were always mindful of both sides
    (C) because her mindfulness of both sides of the issues was always in her articles
    (D) for the fact being that her articles were always mindful about both sides of the issues
    (E) because her articles were always mindful of both sides of the issues

28. Of all the countries in the UN Security Council, <u>the representative of China was the only one to speak</u> to the General Assembly today.

    (A) the representative of China was the only one to speak
    (B) making the representative from China the only one to speak
    (C) China's representative only spoke
    (D) China's governor spoke only
    (E) China was the only one whose representative spoke

29. Patients with Alzheimer's disease typically exhibit symptoms such as confusion, memory loss, <u>and their language skills are impaired</u>.

    (A) and their language skills are impaired
    (B) and it also impairs their language skills
    (C) and impaired language skills
    (D) besides their language skills being impaired
    (E) in addition to their language skills being impaired

30. <u>Upon entering the jail, the prisoners' personal belongings are surrendered to the guards.</u>

    (A) Upon entering the jail, the prisoners' personal belongings are surrendered to the guards.
    (B) Upon entering the jail, the prisoners surrender their personal belongings to the guards.
    (C) The prisoners' personal belongings having been surrendered to the guards upon entering the jail.
    (D) Upon entering the jail, the guards are to whom the prisoners surrender their personal belongings.
    (E) Upon entering the jail, the prisoners will have been surrendering their personal belongings to the guards.

31. <u>The albatross has a broad wingspan, it is graceful in the air but ungainly on dry land.</u>

    (A) The albatross has a broad wingspan, it is graceful in the air but ungainly on dry land.
    (B) The albatross, with its broad wingspan, is graceful in the air but ungainly on dry land.
    (C) Having a broad wingspan, the albatross is graceful in the air, however it is ungainly on dry land.
    (D) The albatross, which has a broad wingspan, graceful in the air but ungainly on dry land.
    (E) The albatross, although having a broad wingspan, is graceful in the air but ungainly on dry land.

32. King John of England is remembered not so much for his administrative successes <u>but for failing in military engagements</u>.

    (A) but for failing in military engagements
    (B) but more for the fact that he failed in military engagements
    (C) than he was for having failed militarily
    (D) the reason being that he failed in military engagements
    (E) as for his military failures

33. According to older fishermen, cod and haddock were once plentiful in the North Sea, but years of overfishing and pollution have <u>had a negative overall impact on the fish stocks</u>.

    (A) had a negative overall impact on the fish stocks
    (B) impacted the fish stocks negatively
    (C) the result that the fish stocks are diminished
    (D) depleted the fish stocks
    (E) been depleting the fish stocks overall

34. <u>During the winter months, several feet of
    snow cover the narrow mountain pass, which
    is the only route to the monastery.</u>

    (A) During the winter months, several feet
        of snow cover the narrow mountain
        pass, which is the only route to the
        monastery.
    (B) The only route to the monastery, several
        feet of snow cover the narrow mountain
        pass during the winter months.
    (C) Several feet of snow cover the narrow
        mountain pass during the winter
        months which is the only route to the
        monastery.
    (D) Several feet of snow cover the narrow
        mountain pass, which is the only route
        to the monastery during the winter
        months.
    (E) During the winter months, covering the
        narrow mountain pass which is the only
        route to the monastery is snow.

35. The Townshend Acts, a piece of British
    legislation enacted on June 29, 1767, <u>were
    intended for the raising of revenue, to tighten
    customs enforcement, and assert</u> imperial
    authority in America.

    (A) were intended for the raising of revenue,
        to tighten customs enforcement, and
        assert
    (B) were intended to raise revenue, tighten
        customs enforcement, and assert
    (C) were with the intention of raising
        revenue, tightening customs
        enforcement, and assert
    (D) had for their intention the raising
        of revenue, tightening of customs
        enforcement, and asserting
    (E) were intended to raise revenue, also to
        tighten customs enforcement and assert

36. The border crossing proved more unpleasant
    than the two American reporters had
    <u>expected, having their cameras seized</u> and
    their tape recorders smashed by belligerent
    soldiers.

    (A) expected, having their cameras seized
    (B) expected, their cameras being seized
    (C) expected: their cameras were seized
    (D) expected; when their cameras were
        seized
    (E) expected and so their cameras had been
        seized

37. <u>Without the warming effects of the Gulf
    Stream, England's climate would resemble
    that of Greenland.</u>

    (A) Without the warming effects of the
        Gulf Stream, England's climate would
        resemble that of Greenland.
    (B) Had the Gulf Stream not such warming
        effects, England's climate would
        resemble Greenland.
    (C) Without the warming effects of the
        Gulf Stream, England's climate were
        resembling Greenland's.
    (D) If not for the warming effects of the
        Gulf Stream, therefore England's climate
        would have resembled that of Greenland.
    (E) If the Gulf Stream would not have had
        its warming effects, England's climate
        would resemble that of Greenland.

38. Perhaps best known for his portrayal of T. E. Lawrence in the film *Lawrence of Arabia*, <u>Peter O'Toole's distinguished acting career spans nearly five decades.</u>

   (A) Peter O'Toole's distinguished acting career spans nearly five decades

   (B) Peter O'Toole has a distinguished acting career spanning nearly five decades

   (C) Peter O'Toole spans nearly five decades in his distinguished acting career

   (D) Peter O'Toole's distinguished acting career will have spanned nearly five decades

   (E) nearly five decades have been spanned by Peter O'Toole's distinguished acting career

39. In their haste to complete the new stadium before the Olympic games, the contractors disregarded safety <u>codes, thereby they endangered the lives of thousands of spectators.</u>

   (A) codes, thereby they endangered the lives of thousands of spectators

   (B) codes they have endangered the lives of thousands of spectators

   (C) codes and thus endangered the lives of thousands of spectators

   (D) codes; thus the lives of thousands of spectators endangered

   (E) codes, they endangered the lives of thousands of spectators as a result

40. When Dr. Park presented an abridged version of his paper at the conference, <u>several tantalizing theories about the origins of life on Earth were introduced, but these were not fully developed by him.</u>

   (A) several tantalizing theories about the origins of life on Earth were introduced, but these were not fully developed by him

   (B) he introduced several tantalizing theories about the origins of life on Earth, but they had not been fully developed

   (C) several tantalizing theories about the origins of life were introduced by him and not fully developed

   (D) several tantalizing theories about the origins of life on Earth were introduced, but he did not fully develop these

   (E) he introduced, but did not fully develop, several tantalizing theories about the origins of life on Earth

41. <u>Climbing into the car, Sean's backpack, packed</u> so tightly that it was bursting at the seams, broke open, spilling his belongings onto the road.

   (A) Climbing into the car, Sean's backpack, packed

   (B) Sean's backpack, climbing into the car and packed

   (C) As Sean climbed into the car, his backpack, packed

   (D) Climbing into the car, Sean's packed backpack

   (E) Climbing into the car, Sean packed his backpack

42. The family arrived at the airport four hours early <u>in spite of the fact that there were</u> warnings of delays broadcast on all the news stations.

    (A) in spite of the fact that there were
    (B) there were, in spite of the fact that
    (C) but there were
    (D) in spite of the fact that
    (E) even though there were

43. In preparation for the dance, Jenny <u>will be picking up her dress from the cleaners, buying a pair of shoes, and have dinner with her parents.</u>

    (A) will be picking up her dress from the cleaners, buying a pair of shoes, and have dinner with her parents.
    (B) will be picking up her dress from the cleaners, buying a pair of shoes, and having dinner with her parents.
    (C) will be picking up her dress from the cleaners, buy a pair of shoes, and have dinner with her parents.
    (D) will be pick up her dress from the cleaners, buying a pair of shoes, and having dinner with her parents.
    (E) will be pick up her dress from the cleaners, buy a pair of shoes, and having dinner with her parents.

Questions 44–49

<u>Directions:</u> The following passage is an early draft of an essay. Some parts of the passage need to be rewritten. Read the passage, and select the best answer for each question that follows. Some questions ask you to improve sentence structure or word choice in particular sentences or parts of sentences. Other questions ask you to consider organization and development. In choosing answers, follow the conventions of standard written English.

(1) Despite his early death at 35, Austrian composer Wolfgang Amadeus Mozart is one of the most famous musicians in history for three reasons. (2) He was extraordinarily talented, he was exposed to music at an early age, and his love of it. (3) Mozart's talent showed early. (4) At age seven, he was already writing sonatas for the harpsichord. (5) He could improvise music at the keyboard and played any piece of music in any style—even when blindfolded!

(6) Mozart was always encouraged and even driven by his father. (7) Leopold Mozart was a composer, and Wolfgang learned to play and read music when he was a small child. (8) To establish his son early and build a path for his future career, he lost no time showing him off to audiences. (9) He arranged for six-year-old Wolfgang to play in the palaces of most of the major European cities. (10) Leopold Mozart determining that his gifted son should reap the rewards his talent deserved.

(11) And Mozart loved music. (12) As a child, Leopold was often surprised with tunes his son had written. (13) Some of these little pieces were so technically challenging that although Wolfgang could play them easily, his father's adult friends and colleagues could not play them at all! (14) He once wrote that composing music was such a delight to him that he could not describe it in words.

44. In context, what is the best way to revise and combine sentences 1 and 2 (reproduced below)?

Despite his early death at 35, Austrian composer Wolfgang Amadeus Mozart is one of the most famous musicians in history for three reasons. He was extraordinarily talented, he was exposed to music at an early age, and his love of it.

(A) Despite his early death at 35, Austrian composer Wolfgang Amadeus Mozart is one of the most famous musicians in history for three reasons: he was extraordinarily talented, he was exposed to music at an early age, and he loved it.

(B) Despite his early death at 35, Austrian composer Wolfgang Amadeus Mozart is one of the most famous musicians in history for three reasons, this is because he was extraordinarily talented, he was exposed to music at an early age, and his love of it.

(C) Despite his early death at 35 years of age, Austrian composer Wolfgang Amadeus Mozart is one of the most famous musicians in history for the following three reasons: he was extraordinarily talented, he was exposed to music at an early age, and he loved it.

(D) Despite his death at 35, which was early, Austrian composer Wolfgang Amadeus Mozart is one of the most famous musicians in history for three reasons: that he was extraordinarily talented, that he was exposed to music at an early age, and that he had a love of it.

(E) Despite his early death at 35, Austrian composer Wolfgang Amadeus Mozart is one of the most famous musicians in history for three reasons: he was extraordinarily talented, he was exposed to music at an early age, and his love of it.

45. In context, which revision is needed in sentence 5?

(A) No revision is needed.
(B) Replace "He" with "Mozart."
(C) Replace "could improvise" with "could have improvised."
(D) Replace "played" with "play."
(E) Eliminate the phrase "in any style."

46. In context, which is the best version of sentence 8 (reproduced below)?

To establish his son early and build a path for his future career, he lost no time showing him off to audiences.

(A) (As it is now)
(B) To establish his son early and build a path for his future career, Leopold Mozart lost no time showing him off to audiences.
(C) To establish Wolfgang early and build a path for his future career, he lost no time showing him off to audiences.
(D) To establish his son early and build a path for his future career, he lost no time showing Wolfgang off to audiences.
(E) To establish his son early and build a path for his future career, Mozart lost no time showing him off to audiences.

47. In context, what revision is necessary in sentence 10?

(A) No revision is necessary.
(B) Change "determining" to "determines."
(C) Change "determining" to "determined."
(D) Change "determining" to "having determined."
(E) Change "should reap" to "should be reaping."

48. In context, what is the best version of sentence 12 (reproduced below)?

    As a child, Leopold was often surprised with tunes his son had written.

    (A) As a child, the tunes his son had written often surprised Leopold.

    (B) As a child, his son often surprised Leopold with tunes he had written.

    (C) As a child, surprising Leopold with tunes he had written was his son.

    (D) Leopold was often surprised with tunes that, as a child, his son had written.

    (E) Tunes written by his son as a child often surprised Leopold.

49. Sentence 14 would make the most sense if placed after

    (A) sentence 2
    (B) sentence 6
    (C) sentence 11
    (D) sentence 12
    (E) sentence 13

ANSWERS AND EXPLANATIONS

IDENTIFYING SENTENCE ERRORS QUESTIONS

1. D

SMARTPOINT CATEGORY: PRONOUNS

In this sentence, it is not clear whether *his* refers to Adams or to Jefferson; hence, this sentence contains a vague pronoun reference.

2. D

SMARTPOINT CATEGORY: DICTION

Affect and *effect* are commonly confused words. Here, *affect* (meaning to influence or to have an effect on) would be the correct word, not *effect*.

3. C

SMARTPOINT CATEGORY: COMPARISONS

In this sentence, ants are being compared to all the other social insects in the *Hymenoptera* order. Because this order includes far more than two insect species, the superlative *most successful* should be used instead of the comparative *more successful*.

4. E

SMARTPOINT CATEGORY: FINDING NO ERROR

The sentence contains no error. (A) is a correct use of a verb gerund, (B) and (D) are idiomatically correct, and (C) is correct because the word *number* when used in the phrase *a number* takes a plural verb.

5. E

SMARTPOINT CATEGORY: FINDING NO ERROR

The sentence contains no error. In (A), the use of the verb is correct. In (B), the verb agrees with its subject, *legislation*. (C) is a correct idiomatic use of the infinitive *to enforce*. (D) correctly uses the adverb *virtually* to modify the adverb *unregulated*.

6. D

SMARTPOINT CATEGORY: PARALLELISM

The sentence contains a number agreement error. Because *students* is a plural noun, the second part of the sentence should also be plural: *as general practitioners.*

7. C

SMARTPOINT CATEGORY: DICTION

This sentence contains a nonidiomatic preposition after verb: *Would of* is not standard written English, and it makes no sense. The sentence should read *would have grown up.*

8. D

SMARTPOINT CATEGORY: IDIOMS

The correct idiom here is *preferable to,* not *preferable than.*

9. D

SMARTPOINT CATEGORY: PRONOUNS

The pronoun *their* is plural and does not agree in number with its singular antecedent, *motorist.* The sentence should read *his or her license.*

10. B

SMARTPOINT CATEGORY: SUBJECT-VERB

The subject *one* takes a singular verb: *not one* of the jurors *was* going to believe the alibi.

11. E

SMARTPOINT CATEGORY: FINDING NO ERROR

The sentence contains no error. (A) has a plural verb to match *gods,* and *neither* must accompany the *nor* later in the sentence. (B) is a correct use of the adverb *particularly* to modify the adjective *critical.* (C) and (D) are parallel and correctly use verb gerunds.

12. A

SMARTPOINT CATEGORY: COMPARISONS ▪▫▫▫

Here, *M. Dubois* is being compared to *other gourmet restaurants*. To form a correct comparison, (A) should read *Like chefs in other gourmet restaurants*. (B) uses the correct pronoun form as the object of the preposition. In (C), *he* is the proper pronoun to refer to M. Dubois, and the verb agrees with its singular subject. (D) makes appropriate use of the infinitive verb form.

13. B

SMARTPOINT CATEGORY: PARALLELISM ▪▪▪▫

Dangerous and dirty places in (B) refers to the singular subject in the second clause, *New York City*. Therefore, *places* should also be singular. (A) is correct usage of both the past tense and the infinitive in context. (C) agrees with its plural subject *tourists*. (D) is the appropriate verb tense, because the action is in the recent past and is still occurring (*over the past few years* indicates this).

14. B

SMARTPOINT CATEGORY: PRONOUNS ▪▪▪▫

The singular pronoun *one* is used near the end of the sentence. Since it is not underlined, it cannot be changed. Therefore, the underlined pronoun *we* must be changed because it is inconsistent; the error is in (B). (A) is appropriate use of the infinitive. (C) properly uses an adverb to modify an adjective. (D) uses the appropriate preposition in context.

15. E

SMARTPOINT CATEGORY: FINDING NO ERROR

The sentence contains no errors. (A) is a correct use of the past perfect to express one past action (*Bill had hoped*) that preceded another (*he realized*). (B) is correct idiomatic usage. (C) is an appropriate verb phrase in context. (D) is proper use of the infinitive.

16. B

SMARTPOINT CATEGORY: SUBJECT-VERB ▪▪▪▫

Even though *languages* is closer to the verb *require*, its subject is actually the singular *process*; the error is in (B). (A) and (C) are correct idiomatic usage. (D) correctly uses a present tense verb and properly uses the adjective *slow* to modify the noun *progress*.

17. C

SMARTPOINT CATEGORY: PRONOUNS ▮▮▯▯

Although a commission is made up of a number of people, the noun itself is singular, so (C) should be *its*. (A) appropriately uses an adverb to modify the adjective *divergent* and an adjective to modify the noun *opinions*. (B) is an appropriate verb phrase in context. (D) uses the idiomatically correct preposition and an adjective to describe *city square*.

18. D

SMARTPOINT CATEGORY: SUBJECT-VERB ▮▮▯▯

Although *benefits* is the closest noun to the verb *were*, the subject of the verb is actually the singular *program*, so (D) should be *was*. (A) uses an appropriate verb tense in context. (B) appropriately modifies the noun *program*. (C) correctly uses an adjective to modify a noun.

IMPROVING SENTENCES QUESTIONS

19. C

SMARTPOINT CATEGORY: RUN-ONS AND FRAGMENTS ▮▮▯▯

As written, the sentence is not properly structured. (C) corrects the problem. (B) and (D) use transitions that are inappropriate in context. (E) misuses the semicolon splice.

20. D

SMARTPOINT CATEGORY: WORDINESS ▮▮▯▯

As written, this sentence is unnecessarily wordy, and the conjunction *and* merely strings the ideas together, without relating them in any way. (D) corrects both errors. (B) is awkward and introduces the passive voice unnecessarily. (C) is even wordier than the original sentence. (E) is awkward and still too wordy.

21. D

SMARTPOINT CATEGORY: MODIFIERS ▮▮▯▯

As the sentence is written, it is unclear what noun *particularly those in European history* is intended to modify. (D) corrects this error without adding any other ones. (B) is grammatically incorrect. The singular verb *is* in (C) does not agree with its subject *Some*, which is grammatically plural. (E) creates a sentence fragment.

22. D

SMARTPOINT CATEGORY: RUN-ONS AND FRAGMENTS

As written, this sentence is a fragment. (D) adds a predicate verb without introducing any additional errors. (B) and (E) do not address the error. (C) is incorrect grammatical structure.

23. C

SMARTPOINT CATEGORY: RUN-ONS AND FRAGMENTS

As written, this is a run-on sentence. Both clauses are independent, so a comma cannot join them. (C) corrects this error by using a semicolon splice. (B) and (D) do not address the error. (E) leaves the meaning of the second clause incomplete.

24. B

SMARTPOINT CATEGORY: WORDINESS

The underlined selection here is awkward and wordy. (B) expresses the same idea more clearly and concisely. (C) introduces an inconsistent verb tense. (D) does not express the correct relationship between the clauses. (E) is awkward and unnecessarily wordy.

25. C

SMARTPOINT CATEGORY: TRANSITIONS

The transition words *considering that* do not accurately express the cause-and-effect relationship between the clauses. Both (C) and (D) correct this error with the *because*. However, (D) and (E) use a verb tense that is incorrect in context; *will blend* indicates a future action, but Louisa May Alcott's books were written in the past. (B) does not address the error.

26. E

SMARTPOINT CATEGORY: PARALLELISM

The preposition *as* here has a compound object; (E) is the only choice that puts *brightest and . . . most unruly* in parallel form. (B), (C), and (D) do not address the error.

27. E

SMARTPOINT CATEGORY: WORDINESS

As written, this sentence is overly wordy. Additionally, *mindful . . . for* is idiomatically incorrect; in English, we are *mindful of*. (E) corrects both errors. In (B), *for* is the incorrect preposition in context. (C) and (D) are even wordier than the original sentence, and *for the fact being* in (D) is incorrect grammatical structure.

28. E

SMARTPOINT CATEGORY: MODIFIERS

As written, this sentence calls *the representative of China* one of *the countries on the UN Security Council*. Although it's slightly longer than some of the other choices, only (E) is correct in context. (B), (C), and (D) do not address the error.

29. C

SMARTPOINT CATEGORY: PARALLELISM

For the sake of parallelism, all three things in this list must be in the same grammatical form. *Confusion* and *memory loss* are both nouns, so (C), *impaired language skills*, is the best choice to complete the sentence.

30. B

SMARTPOINT CATEGORY: MODIFIERS

Upon entering the jail is an introductory phrase that describes the prisoners (they are the ones entering the jail). As the sentence is worded, it sounds as though the prisoners' personal belongings are entering the jail. (B) and (E) are the only two choices that place *the prisoners* right next to the phrase that describes them. (E) uses an incorrect tense, so (B) is the best choice.

31. B

SMARTPOINT CATEGORY: RUN-ONS AND FRAGMENTS

Choice (B) is the best way to rephrase this run-on sentence; it expresses, in an economical and graceful way, the logical connection between these two pieces of information about the albatross.

32. E

SMARTPOINT CATEGORY: IDIOMS

So much should be followed by the preposition *as*. (E) completes the comparison and conforms to the rules of parallelism; *administrative successes* (an adjective-noun pair) is balanced by *military failures*.

33. D

SMARTPOINT CATEGORY: WORDINESS

The underlined portion of the sentence is wordy and awkward. (D) is a concise and correct rephrasing (note that it is also the shortest answer choice).

34. A

SMARTPOINT CATEGORY: CORRECT AS WRITTEN

The sentence contains no error. (B), (C), and (E) are all awkward or grammatically incorrect. (D) may at first seem correct, but it is incorrect because it changes the meaning of the original sentence. The original sentence indicates that there is a single route to the monastery at all times. (D) suggests that only during the winter is there a single route to the monastery.

35. B

SMARTPOINT CATEGORY: PARALLELISM

The three items in this list should be in parallel grammatical form. The best way to correct the error is to rephrase all three as infinitive verbs as in (B). (Note, again, that the correct answer is also the shortest and most concise.)

36. C

SMARTPOINT CATEGORY: RUN-ONS AND FRAGMENTS

The second half of the sentence is an explanation of the first half, and a colon best expresses this logical connection. (A), (B), and (D) all introduce sentence fragments, and (E) uses the wrong verb tense and incorrectly presents the camera seizure as a consequence (not an explanation) of the first half of the sentence.

37. A

SMARTPOINT CATEGORY: CORRECT AS WRITTEN

The sentence is correct as written. The introductory phrases in (B) and (E) are awkward. (C) uses the wrong verb tense. (D) has an awkward introductory phrase and an incorrect verb tense, and it is wordy.

38. B

SMARTPOINT CATEGORY: MODIFIERS ⬛

The sentence contains a misplaced modifier: it sounds as though O'Toole's *career* is known for his portrayal of T. E. Lawrence. The introductory phrase describes *Peter O'Toole* (the man, not his career); hence, *Peter O'Toole* should come directly after it. Only choices (B) and (C) begin correctly, and (C) is poorly worded.

39. C

SMARTPOINT CATEGORY: RUN-ONS AND FRAGMENTS ⬛

The best way to repair this run-on sentence while preserving the logical relationship between the two halves of the sentence is with choice (C), which correctly presents the second half of the sentence as a consequence of the first. (A), (B), and (E) are all run-ons, and (D) makes *spectators* the subject of *endangered*.

40. E

SMARTPOINT CATEGORY: WORDINESS ⬛

The underlined portion of this sentence is passive, wordy, and awkward. A good rephrasing will begin with *he* and will be in the active voice. (B) and (E) are possibilities, but (B) is still somewhat awkward and uses the wrong tense for *had . . . been . . . developed*. (E) is clear and concise.

41. C

SMARTPOINT CATEGORY: MODIFIERS ⬛

This sentence contains a misplaced modifier. *Sean's backpack* didn't climb into the car; Sean did. So you can eliminate the answer choices that contain this error, (A), (B), and (D). In (E), *Climbing into the car* correctly modifies *Sean*, but the meaning of the sentence has changed. Sean didn't pack his backpack as he climbed into the car. (C) is the correct answer.

42. E

SMARTPOINT CATEGORY: WORDINESS ⬛

In spite of the fact that is a wordy way of saying *even though*. That rules out (A), (B), and (D). (C) is incorrect because *but* changes the meaning of the sentence. (E) is the correct answer.

43. B

SMARTPOINT CATEGORY: PARALLELISM 📶

The error in this sentence has to do with parallelism. Jenny will be doing three things before the dance: *picking up her dress from the cleaners, buying a pair of shoes, and having dinner with her parents.* Each of the items in this series has to start with an *-ing* word: *picking, buying,* and *having.* (A), (C), (D), and (E) don't do this; only (B) does this.

IMPROVING PARAGRAPHS QUESTIONS

44. A

SMARTPOINT CATEGORY: PARALLELISM 📶

There are two problems here. The sentences are choppy as written, and the items in the second sentence's list are not parallel. (A) does the best job of combining the sentences and corrects the parallelism error. (B) creates a run-on sentence: two independent clauses combined with a comma splice. (C) and (D) address the errors but unnecessarily add additional words and phrases, making the sentence wordier than it needs to be. (E) correctly combines the sentences but fails to address the parallelism problem.

45. D

SMARTPOINT CATEGORY: PARALLELISM 📶

The conjunction *and* requires that the two verbs in the compound predicate be in parallel form, which they are not here (*He could improvise . . . and played . . .*). (D) makes the two verbs parallel. (B) is unnecessary—the pronoun *He* clearly refers to Mozart. (C) introduces an inconsistent verb tense. (E) alters the meaning of the sentence.

46. B

SMARTPOINT CATEGORY: PRONOUNS 📶

This sentence uses the pronouns *his, he,* and *him.* Sometimes the pronoun refers to the elder Mozart, sometimes it refers to Wolfgang, so the reader is likely to lose track of which person is being referred to. (B) is best because none of the pronouns is ambiguous. (C) and (D) still leave some pronoun usage unclear. (E) is confusing because *Mozart* could refer to either father or son.

47. C

SMARTPOINT CATEGORY: RUN-ONS AND FRAGMENTS

As written, this sentence is actually a fragment. (Remember, the *-ing* verb form can never be a predicate verb.) Changing *determining* to *determined* corrects the problem. (B) and (E) introduce verb tenses that are inappropriate in context. (D) does not correct the error. (C) corrects the problem.

48. B

SMARTPOINT CATEGORY: MODIFIERS

Leopold was not a child when he was surprised by his son's tunes; his son was. (B) corrects the error without introducing any additional errors. In (A), the phrase *As a child* is modifying *tunes*. (C) and (E) introduce the passive voice unnecessarily. (D) is awkwardly worded.

49. C

SMARTPOINT CATEGORY: READING COMPREHENSION

The best choice here is (C), because the pronoun *he* in sentence 14 refers to *Mozart*, and the ideas make sense in sequence. (A) might seem tempting because sentence 14 appears to flow well from sentence 2. However, sentence 14 does not lead into sentence 3. (B) is incorrect because sentence 6 refers to Mozart and his father, so the pronoun *he* in sentence 14 would be unclear if sentence 14 were to follow sentence 6. (D) is wrong because sentences 12 and 13 deal with the same specific detail and should not be separated. (E) is incorrect because the pronoun reference would be unclear, and the ideas in sentence 14 do not follow as logically from sentence 13 as they do from sentence 11.

KEY POINTS YOU'VE LEARNED IN THIS CHAPTER

1. Kaplan's strategy for identifying sentence errors:

   - **Step 1:** Read the sentence, and listen and for an error.

   - **Step 2:** Identify the error.

   - **Step 3:** If you cannot identify an error, eliminate the choices that don't contain errors. Choose from the remaining answer choices.

2. Common errors tested in Identifying Sentence Errors questions (subject-verb agreement, verb tense, pronoun use, idioms, diction, comparison, parallelism, adjectives and adverbs, and double negatives).

3. Kaplan's strategy for improving sentences:

   - **Step 1:** Read the sentence carefully, and listen for an error.

   - **Step 2:** Identify the error or errors.

   - **Step 3:** Eliminate the choices that don't address the error, and choose the most correct, concise, and relevant answer.

4. Common errors tested in improving sentences questions (run-on sentences, sentence fragments, misplaced modifiers, active and passive voice, parallelism, faulty transitions, and wordiness).

5. Kaplan's strategy for improving paragraphs

   - **Step 1:** Read the passage, and listen for any possible errors.

   - **Step 2:** Read the question. If necessary, reread the relevant portion, and identify the error.

   - **Step 3:** Eliminate the choices that don't address the error, and choose the most correct, concise, and relevant answer.

6. Common question types for improving paragraphs (content-related wording, sentence revision, combining sentences, and paragraph transition).

Part Four

HOW TO ATTACK THE CRITICAL READING SECTIONS

CHAPTER 8: SAT CRITICAL READING BASICS

SMARTPOINTS COVERED IN THIS CHAPTER

| DEFINITION |
| CONTRAST |
| CAUSE AND EFFECT |
| DETAILS |
| FUNCTION |
| INFERENCE |
| GLOBAL |
| VOCABULARY-IN-CONTEXT |

WHAT TO EXPECT ON TEST DAY

There are three Critical Reading sections on the SAT, as shown in the table below:

LENGTH	CONTENT	TYPE
25 minutes	Sentence Completion and Reading Comprehension (short and long)	Multiple-choice
25 minutes	Sentence Completion and Reading Comprehension (short and long)	Multiple-choice
20 minutes	Sentence Completion and Reading Comprehension (long only)	Multiple-choice

The Critical Reading component of the SAT is designed to test three basic skills:

1. **Vocabulary**—both the breadth of your vocabulary and your ability to determine meaning from context
2. **Reasoning skills**—including your ability to determine the relationship between words and ideas
3. **Reading skills**—how well you understand what you read (main idea, tone, etc.)

The Critical Reading section of the SAT includes two types of questions:

1. Sentence Completion
2. Reading Comprehension

To do well on SAT Critical Reading, you need to be systematic in your approach to each question type. We'll describe each type in more detail in a moment.

QUICK SCORING TIP

Sentence Completion questions are the faster question type because there is no passage to read—just a sentence with one or two blanks that you need to fill in. You can earn points faster on these questions than on Reading Comprehension questions, which require you to read one or more paragraphs.

You might want to do the Sentence Completion questions first and the Reading Comprehension questions based on the shorter passages right after that. Why? It takes less time to read a short passage than it does to read a long one, so the short passage points can be accumulated faster. By working on the long passage questions last, you won't run the risk of getting bogged down on the longer passages and leaving yourself only a few minutes for the short passages and Sentence Completion questions.

Now that you know what order to work through each Critical Reading section, let's take a brief look at the question types. (We go into detail in the chapters that follow.)

SENTENCE COMPLETION QUESTIONS

The Sentence Completion sections test your vocabulary—both the extent of your word knowledge and your ability to determine meaning from the context of a particular sentence. These sentences are the quickest ones to answer in the section. You have to read only one sentence and plug in the right answer.

Sentence Completions fall into three main categories:

 1. Definition/Similar Meaning

 2. Contrast

 3. Cause and Effect/Makes Sense in Context

The Sentence Completion question sets are arranged in order of difficulty. The first few questions in a set might be fairly straightforward and manageable. The middle few questions will be a little harder, and the last few questions should be the most difficult. Keep this in mind as you work.

Sentence Completion questions look like this:

> Although this small and selective publishing house is famous for its ------ standards, several of its recent novels have appealed to the general population.
>
> (A) proletarian
> (B) naturalistic
> (C) discriminating
> (D) imitative
> (E) precarious

> **PERFECT SCORE TIP**
>
> " Getting the Sentence Completion questions out of the way early really reduced my stress and let me focus on the passage-based questions for the rest of the time. "

To answer this type of question, you must choose the word that best completes the sentence. In chapter 7, we give you specific strategies for tackling this question type. In case you're curious, the answer for this question is (C), *discriminating*.

READING COMPREHENSION QUESTIONS

As we mentioned, there are two kinds of Reading Comprehension passages: short and long. Short passages are approximately 100–150 words long. They are typically followed by 2 questions. Long passages are approximately 400–850 words long and are typically followed by 8–13 questions.

The passages and questions are predictable. The topics are drawn from the following:

- Humanities
- Social sciences
- Natural sciences
- Fiction

The questions ask about the overall tone and content of a passage, the details used, and the author's overall meaning. You will also have one or more *paired-passage* question sets consisting of two related excerpts. Some of the associated questions will ask you to compare and contrast the two passages.

DON'T FORGET!

Reading Comprehension questions are not arranged by difficulty. That means easy, medium, and hard questions can appear in any order. Any time you find yourself spending too much time on a question, skip it and return to it later.

Reading Comprehension questions are covered in detail in chapters 8 and 9.

SHORT PASSAGES STRATEGY

Short passages have about 100–150 words and are followed by 1 or 2 questions. Long passages have 500–800 words and are followed by 5–13 questions.

These questions test how well you understand and can identify the following:

- **Details** in the passage
- The **Function** or role of certain words, details, and paragraphs in the passage
- Small **Inference** statements that can be made from the passage
- The **Global** or main idea/purpose of the passage
- **Vocabulary-in-Context**

Because a short passage has only a few lines to read, you can keep the one or two question stems in mind as you read. Predicting an answer while you read will save time in the section.

Remember to read the question stem (not the answers) first and underline words and phrases you are likely to see in the passage. They often use the same, or similar, words in the stems and in the body of the passage. These flags will speed you up as you gather points.

KEY POINTS YOU'VE LEARNED IN THIS CHAPTER

1. The Critical Reading sections test vocabulary, reasoning skills, and reading skills, and have two types of questions: Sentence Completions and Reading Comprehension.

2. You will have two 25-minute sections and one 20-minute section.

3. There will be 19 Sentence Completion questions and 48 Reading Comprehension questions.

4. Sentence Completion questions are arranged in order of increasing difficulty.

5. The Reading Comprehension questions are based on short passages (100–150 words) and long passages (400–850 words).

CHAPTER 9: SENTENCE COMPLETION STRATEGIES

SMARTPOINTS COVERED IN THIS CHAPTER

DEFINITION	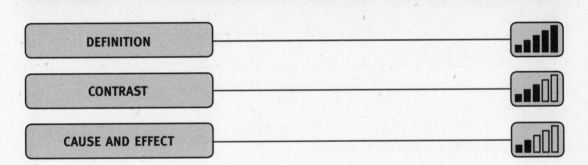
CONTRAST	
CAUSE AND EFFECT	

WHAT TO EXPECT ON TEST DAY

Sentence Completion questions are probably the Critical Reading section's most student-friendly question type. Unlike the Reading Comprehension questions that make up the bulk of the Critical Reading section, Sentence Completion questions require you to pay attention to just one sentence at a time.

ONE-BLANK SENTENCE COMPLETIONS

The word you are looking for to fill the blank will have one of three types of relationships to the sentence as a whole:

 1. **Definition** (similar meaning to a keyword in the sentence)

 2. **Contrast** (a contrasting word to a keyword in the sentence)

 3. **Cause and Effect** (makes sense in the context of the sentence)

TWO-BLANK SENTENCE COMPLETIONS

In two-blank sentence completions, the relationships between the words will *relate to each other* in three ways:

 1. **Definition**

 2. **Contrast**

 3. **Cause and Effect** (both make sense in the context of the sentence)

Note: Both words must fit in the sentence. If one word fits and the other doesn't, the answer is wrong.

FOUR STEPS TO TEST DAY SUCCESS

KAPLAN'S TARGET STRATEGY FOR SENTENCE COMPLETION QUESTIONS

Here's Kaplan's powerful Target Strategy for tackling Sentence Completion questions:
- **Step 1:** Read the sentence for clue words.
- **Step 2:** Predict the answer.
- **Step 3:** Select the best match.
- **Step 4:** Plug your answer choice back into the sentence.

> **PERFECT SCORE TIP**
>
> " I found that predicting the answers to Sentence Completion questions was helpful. I usually found a synonym in the answer choices, and occasionally I would even predict the correct answer. "

Let's unleash the powers of Kaplan's Target Strategy for Sentence Completion questions on a sample question:

The king's ------- decisions as a diplomat and administrator led to his legendary reputation as a just and ------- ruler.

(A) quick . . . capricious

(B) equitable . . . wise

(C) immoral . . . perceptive

(D) generous . . . witty

(E) clever . . . uneducated

STEP 1: READ THE SENTENCE FOR CLUE WORDS

Read the sentence. Now think about the sentence for five seconds. Take special note of the clue words. A clue word like *but* tells you to expect a contrast in the next part of the sentence; a clue word like *moreover* tells you that what follows is a continuation of the same idea. Clue words such as *and, but, such as, however,* and *although* tell you how the parts of the sentence will relate to each other.

The clues here are the phrase *led to* and the word *just.* You know that the kind of decisions the king made *led to* his having a reputation as a just and ------- ruler. So whatever goes in both blanks must be consistent with *just.*

AND & BUT

And is a clue for a definition. *But* is a keyword for contrast. Keep your eyes out for these.

STEP 2: PREDICT THE ANSWER

Decide what sort of word should fill the blank or blanks. Do this before looking at the answer choices. You don't have to guess the *exact* word; a rough idea of the *kind* of word you'll need will do. It's often enough to simply predict whether the missing word is positive or negative. But often you will be able to go farther. For example, you may be able to predict whether you need a pair of synonyms to fill in the blanks or two words that contrast.

Here, the word *and* means that the second blank must be similar to *just.* Now the key is to know what *just* means. (It means *fair.*) If you didn't know for sure what *just* means, you could also rely on the word *diplomat,* which is also a positive word (one who keeps peaceful relations between countries). Between these two context words, you'd be able to predict that the king was a careful or good ruler. Now write a + sign in each blank.

A NOTE ON TWO-BLANK QUESTIONS

Another approach for two-blank Sentence Completion questions is to take them one blank at a time. Choose the easier blank, cross out any choices that clearly don't fit, and finish by checking ONLY the remaining choices for the other blank.

STEP 3: SELECT THE BEST MATCH

Compare your prediction to each answer choice. Read every answer choice before deciding which answer best completes the sentence.

For this sentence, check each answer to see which pair has two positive words—and are synonyms—as descriptive words for the king.

Choice (A): *Quick* and *capricious* are not necessarily positive, and they are not similar in meaning (*capricious* means erratic or fickle).

Choice (B): *Equitable* means fair. *Equitable* and *wise* are similar, and they're both positive. This is the best choice so far, but check the rest.

Choice (C): *Immoral* is a negative word, so eliminate this choice right away.

Choice (D): *Generous* and *witty* are positive, but they are not similar and don't make sense in the sentence.

Choice (E): *Uneducated* is negative, so eliminate this choice.

Don't stop until you have checked out all five answers. The best choice may well be the last one!

STEP 4: PLUG YOUR ANSWER CHOICE INTO THE SENTENCE

Put your answer choice in the blank (or blanks). Only one choice should really make sense. If you've gone through the four steps and more than one choice still looks possible, eliminate the choice(s) that you can, guess from the remaining choices, and move on. If all of the choices look great or all of the choices look terrible, circle the question and come back to it when you've finished the section.

The king's equitable decisions as a diplomat and administrator led to his legendary reputation as a just and wise ruler. Choice (B) is the correct answer.

ONE BLANK AT A TIME

Many times the second blank is easier to fill than the first, especially when the first comes early in the sentence. Lean heavily on the second blank prediction and eliminate the ones that don't fit. Chances are, you'll be down to two choices. Now look at the first-blank choices and go from there.

TECHNIQUES FOR TACKLING THE HARDEST QUESTIONS

Sentence Completion questions will go from easiest to hardest, though some sections will start with medium-difficulty questions. The higher the question number, the harder the question, so the last few Sentence Completion questions in a set will be the most difficult.

IF YOU GET STUCK

If you find yourself getting stuck, we have a few techniques to pull you through:
- Avoid tricky wrong answers.
- Decode tricky sentences.
- Work around tough vocabulary.
- If all else fails, guess strategically.

AVOID TRICKY WRONG ANSWERS

Toward the end of a set, watch out for tricky answer choices. Avoid the following:

- Opposites of the correct answer
- Words that sound right just because they're hard
- Two-blankers in which one word fits but the other doesn't

Sometimes a sentence may seem to mean one thing, but a word or two turns it into the opposite meaning.

Take a look at the following example:

Granted, Janyce is extremely -------; still, it is difficult to imagine her as a professional comedian.

(A) dull
(B) garrulous
(C) effusive
(D) conservative
(E) witty

Read this sentence carefully or you may get tricked. If you read too quickly, you might think, "If Janyce is hard to imagine as a comedian, she's probably extremely dull or conservative. So I'll pick either (A) or (D)." But the sentence is saying something else.

Remember to pick up the clues:

- One key here is the clue word *granted*, which is another way of saying, "Sure, Janice is extremely_____."
- The words *still* and *difficult* might also throw you off.

> **PERFECT SCORE TIP**
>
> " Stay calm and don't get thrown off or flustered while answering Sentence Completion questions. That way, you won't miss important sentence clues. "

- Taken all together, the clues means that she is *funny*, but not really a stand-up comedian.

Choice (E) is correct. If you read this sentence quickly, you might have thought she was extremely *dull*, (A).

HELPFUL WORD TOOLS

Remember the following:

- **Word charge:** This is the positive, negative, or neutral feeling of words.
- **Foreign language:** English words are sometimes similar.
- **Word roots:** The meaning of Latin and Greek roots connect large families of words in English.
- **Similar words:** These are often related (example: *antique* and *antiquarian*: *old*).

For more on these word tools, see chapter 10.

DECODE TRICKY SENTENCES

Some sentences are difficult because they seem to lack the context you need to determine the correct answer. Let's look again at a previously used example:

Although this small and selective publishing house is famous for its -------
standards, several of its recent novels have appealed to the general public.

(A) proletarian
(B) naturalistic
(C) discriminating
(D) imitative
(E) precarious

In this sentence, the parts of the sentence surrounding the blank seem a little vague, and the word choices are advanced adjectives. What sort of publishing house is it? The answer here is not clear right off the bat. But what if you were stumped and had no idea which word to pick or what the meaning of all of the words were? Sometimes the only thing to do in this situation is to plug in the answer choices and make the best guess based on which word you think gives the most information. Here, we are looking for a word that describes standards that would keep them from publishing books that appeal to the general public.

Choice (A): *Proletarian* standards? Hmmm . . . doesn't seem appropriate. *Proletarian* means characteristic of the average citizen or working class, so in fact, it's the opposite of what we need.

Choice (B): *Naturalistic* standards? Not great. It doesn't seem to contrast with the idea of popular appeal.

Choice (C): *Discriminating* standards? Seems to fit. If the publishing house is discriminating, it is very selective and would probably not publish books just because they are popular with the general public.

Choice (D): *Imitative* standards? Sounds weird and doesn't really make sense.

Choice (E): *Precarious* standards? Nope. Again, it doesn't make sense in the context of the sentence, whatever kind of publisher it is.

Choice (C) sounds best and is correct. Although the small publishing house has *discriminating*, or picky, standards, several of its recent novels appeal to a general audience.

PERFECT SCORE TIP

If I couldn't predict an answer accurately, and rereading didn't help, I immediately plugged in the answer choices—trial and error takes time but works.

TIME MANAGEMENT

Sentence Completions are easy to come back to at the end of a 25-minute section. Reading passages, especially the long ones, are not. Plan your timing with this in mind.

Now try a medium-difficulty sentence with two blanks, in the following order in conjunction with Kaplan's Target Strategy:

These latest employment statistics from the present administration are so loosely documented, carelessly explained, and potentially misleading that even the most loyal senators will ------- the ------- of the presidential appointees who produced them.

(A) perceive . . . intelligence
(B) understand . . . tenacity
(C) recognize . . . incompetence
(D) praise . . . rigor
(E) denounce . . . loyalty

It's not so easy to see what goes in the first blank, so try the second blank. You need a word to describe presidential appointees who produced the *loosely documented, carelessly explained,* and *misleading* statistics. Based on these keywords, we know that the second blank must be negative. The only second-word answer choice that's definitely negative is (C), *incompetence*, or inability to perform a task. Now try *recognize* in the first blank. It fits, too. (C) must be correct. See how much time you save? This step safely eliminates all choices except the correct answer.

WORK AROUND TOUGH VOCABULARY

Fortunately, you can often figure out enough context to get the correct answer, even if you don't know all of the vocabulary words in the sentence. That's because test developers often provide other clues to help you figure out the intended meaning. Look at the following sentence as an example:

Despite her ------- of public speaking experience, the student council member was surprisingly cogent, and expressed the concerns of her classmates persuasively.

(A) hope
(B) depth
(C) method
(D) lack
(E) union

If you don't know what *cogent* means, work around it. From the sentence, especially the clue word *and*, you know that *cogent* goes with *expressed the concerns of her classmates persuasively*. So you don't have to worry about what *cogent* means. All you need to know is that the student council member was persuasive despite a ------- of speaking experience. *Surprisingly* is another clue. It suggests that the student was not expected to express herself so effectively because she did not have much public speaking experience. Further, two of the answer choices don't really make sense if you insert them in the blank—a *method* or *union* of speaking experience? Can't be.

Only (D), *lack*, fits the context. *Despite her lack of public speaking experience, the student council member expressed the concerns of her classmates persuasively.* (By the way, *cogent* means convincing, believable, roughly the same as *expressing concern persuasively*.)

IF ALL ELSE FAILS, GUESS STRATEGICALLY

If you're really stumped, don't be afraid to guess. Eliminate all answer choices that can't possibly be right, and guess from the remaining choices. If you have eliminated at least one or two choices, the chance to gain points outweighs the possibility of losing points for incorrect answers.

With Kaplan's strategies, you will nearly always be able to eliminate one or two incorrect answers. If you truly cannot rule out any choices, you will do well to omit the question. Random—that is, blind—guessing isn't advisable on the SAT. Any time you can confidently eliminate at least one answer, you're making a "strategic" guess. A blind guess isn't likely to improve your score, but a strategic guess is.

Now take a deep breath before you go on to practice the strategies you've learned on this Sentence Completion problem set.

PRACTICE

Select the lettered word or set of words that best completes the sentence.

1. The stranger was actually smaller than I had thought; his stature was ------- by the alarm he caused as he loomed up suddenly in the dark alley.

   (A) worsened
   (B) magnified
   (C) disparaged
   (D) disfigured
   (E) admonished

2. Although the risk of a major accident remained -------, the public's concern about such an accident gradually -------.

   (A) steady . . . waned
   (B) acute . . . persisted
   (C) unclear . . . shifted
   (D) obvious . . . endured
   (E) pressing . . . remained

3. Prior to the American entrance into World War I, President Woodrow Wilson strove to maintain the ------- of the United States, warning both sides against encroachments on American interests.

   (A) involvement
   (B) belligerence
   (C) versatility
   (D) magnanimity
   (E) neutrality

4. The graceful curves of the colonial-era buildings that dominated the old part of the city contrasted sharply with the modern, ------- subway stations and made the latter appear glaringly out of place.

   (A) festive
   (B) grimy
   (C) angular
   (D) gigantic
   (E) efficient

5. The discovery of the Dead Sea Scrolls in the 1940s quickly ------- the popular imagination, but the precise significance of the scrolls is still ------- by scholars.

   (A) impressed . . . understood
   (B) alarmed . . . obscured
   (C) troubled . . . perceived
   (D) sparked . . . disputed
   (E) eluded . . . debated

6. In Kafka's characteristically surreal story "The Hunger Artist," the main character "entertains" the public by starving himself until he is too ------- to survive.

   (A) glutted
   (B) lachrymose
   (C) emaciated
   (D) superfluous
   (E) satiated

7. Recent editions of the Chinese classic *Tao Te Ching*, based on manuscripts more authoritative than those hitherto available, have rendered previous editions -------.

(A) incomprehensible
(B) interminable
(C) inaccessible
(D) obsolete
(E) illegible

8. Despite their outward resemblance, the brothers could not be more ------- temperamentally; while one is quiet and circumspect, the other is brash and -------.

(A) inimical . . . timid
(B) passionate . . . superficial
(C) dissimilar . . . audacious
(D) different . . . forgiving
(E) alike . . . respectful

9. Her scholarly rigor and capacity for ------- enabled her to undertake research projects that less ------- people would have found too difficult and tedious.

(A) fanaticism . . . slothful
(B) comprehension . . . indolent
(C) analysis . . . careless
(D) negligence . . . dedicated
(E) concentration . . . disciplined

10. It was difficult to tell what the auditor was thinking, as his expression was -------.

(A) palpable
(B) salient
(C) titular
(D) impassive
(E) bilious

11. Because he was confined to the rim of the excavation site, the archeologist found it difficult to surmise exactly what the ------- chamber might hold.

(A) potable
(B) fulsome
(C) insensate
(D) beatific
(E) subterranean

12. Casey's creative writing teacher praised his story but said it was somewhat ------- and suggested that he ------- it a bit.

(A) adept . . . declaim
(B) gauche . . . filibuster
(C) verbose . . . pare
(D) contiguous . . . diffuse
(E) abortive . . . abscond

13. Dr. Fowler's compact disc collection clearly revealed his ------- for early jazz recordings.

(A) penchant
(B) tenet
(C) confluence
(D) phalanx
(E) hegemony

14. If all world leaders were to ------- violent solutions to problems, there would soon be a ------- of war.

(A) emulate . . . tutelage
(B) condole . . . paean
(C) eschew . . . cessation
(D) becloud . . . demagogue
(E) mitigate . . . recidivism

15. The austere life of a medieval monk required sleeping in ------- cell.

    (A) a variegated

    (B) a specious

    (C) a spartan

    (D) an inchoate

    (E) an intransigent

16. The corrupt judge's ------- insistence on his honesty was belied by his ------- unfair rulings.

    (A) colloquial . . . amorphously

    (B) disingenuous . . . blatantly

    (C) macabre . . . morosely

    (D) saturnine . . . stringently

    (E) opprobrious . . . truculently

17. The chess-playing computer Big Blue is ------- opponent, as it never makes a careless mistake.

    (A) an illusory

    (B) a formidable

    (C) a circuitous

    (D) a novel

    (E) a temporal

18. The leader of the minority party met with members of the business ------- to devise an economic reform package.

    (A) caucus

    (B) aerie

    (C) milieu

    (D) rostrum

    (E) interregnum

19. Because of her -------, the cat burglar was finally caught, when she showed a neighbor her ------- of stolen jewels.

    (A) hubris . . . cache

    (B) pseudonym . . . fodder

    (C) yen . . . vernacular

    (D) calumny . . . onus

    (E) kismet . . . platitude

20. One who betrays the trust of a close-knit group is likely to be shunned by his former compatriots, as when, for example, a whistle-blower becomes ------- within the organization.

    (A) an exponent

    (B) a pariah

    (C) a sybarite

    (D) a potentate

    (E) a paragon

21. Gerald felt his history assignment was not well defined; in fact, he found it rather -------.

    (A) prosaic

    (B) importunate

    (C) epochal

    (D) nebulous

    (E) febrile

22. Just as a criminal could ------- honesty in order to dupe a victim, likewise a superhero might fake ------- in order to trick a villain.

    (A) burnish . . . histrionics

    (B) ingratiate . . . aplomb

    (C) feign . . . duplicity

    (D) aver . . . sinecure

    (E) thwart . . . convergence

23. By choosing to live in a relatively impoverished country, Mr. Jones enjoyed a ------- lifestyle, despite having a rather ------- income by European standards.

   (A) replete . . . squalid
   (B) lavish . . . paltry
   (C) licentious . . . obstinate
   (D) cumulative . . . complacent
   (E) winsome . . . tortuous

24. Later, it was hard for Maia to say which had been more frightening: the tyrant's ------- stare or his ------- words.

   (A) mawkish . . . wry
   (B) gamely . . . imperious
   (C) tenuous . . . sanctimonious
   (D) incarnadine . . . implacable
   (E) malevolent . . . virulent

ANSWERS AND EXPLANATIONS

1. B

SMARTPOINT CATEGORY: CONTRAST

The clue here is the phrase *was actually smaller than I had thought.* The missing word has to mean "made larger" or "made to seem larger." Choice (B), *magnified,* is the answer. (C), *disparaged,* means belittled. (E), *admonished,* means scolded. (A) and (D) do not make sense in the context. The stranger's stature cannot be *worsened* because it was never suggested that it was bad in the first place. (D), *disfigured,* doesn't make sense as a description of *stature.*

2. A

SMARTPOINT CATEGORY: CONTRAST

The word *although* indicates contrast. The contrast is between the *risk* and the *public's concern.* Choice (A) is the only one that presents a clear contrast: the risk didn't decrease, but the public's concern did.

3. E

SMARTPOINT CATEGORY: DEFINITION

The phrase *warning both sides against encroachments on American interests* indicates that Wilson was attempting to prevent each side from taking an action that would force the United States to get involved in the war. Choice (E), *neutrality,* gets this point across. (A), *involvement,* suggests the opposite of the correct answer. (B), *belligerence,* is the quality of being warlike; (C), *versatility,* means being able to handle a variety of different situations; (D), *magnanimity,* is generosity.

4. C

SMARTPOINT CATEGORY: CONTRAST

You're specifically told that there's a contrast between the buildings and the subway stations. The phrase *graceful curves* is a clue. Predict something that means the opposite, such as "not gracefully curving." This prediction matches (C), *angular,* which means jagged or angled.

5. D

SMARTPOINT CATEGORY: CONTRAST

The word *but* indicates contrast. If it's hard to predict for a Sentence Completion question, try plugging in the choices. (D) makes the most sense with the word *imagination* and completes the contrast: the public became quickly excited about the issue, but agreement among experts as to the significance of the scrolls has been slower in coming. None of the other choices provides a clear contrast of ideas. In addition, *still* suggests a lack of understanding, so (A) and (C) cannot be correct.

6. C

SMARTPOINT CATEGORY: CAUSE AND EFFECT

The missing word describes people who starve themselves and become malnourished. Choice (C), *emaciated*, which means extremely thin, is the only choice that really fits. (A) and (E) are the exact opposites of what's needed, and (B), *lachrymose*, means tearful. (D), *superfluous*, means unnecessary.

7. D

SMARTPOINT CATEGORY: CONTRAST

If new editions of this book are based on *more authoritative*, or more accurate, manuscripts, previous editions would be rendered out-of-date, or *obsolete*, (D)—scholars wouldn't use the old editions because the new ones are markedly superior. However, the new edition wouldn't render the old edition (A), *incomprehensible*, (B), *interminable*, (C), *inaccessible*, or (E), *illegible*.

8. C

SMARTPOINT CATEGORY: CONTRAST

The clue word *despite* indicates that the brothers must have different temperaments—making (C), *dissimilar*, and (D), *different*, both possibilities. The second word has to contrast with *quiet and circumspect* and be similar in tone to *brash*; *audacious*, or bold, is the only choice that makes sense, so (C) is correct.

9. E

SMARTPOINT CATEGORY: CONTRAST

It's easier to start with the second blank. You need a word that goes with *rigor* and contrasts with finding things *difficult and tedious*. (A), *slothful*, and (B), *indolent*, both mean lazy, so they're the opposite of what you need. Only (D), *dedicated*, and (E), *disciplined*, fit. Eliminate the other choices and try (D) and (E) in the first blank. The correct choice will be a quality held by a dedicated, rigorous scholar, so (E), *concentration*, is the answer. (D), *negligence*, is the opposite of what you're looking for.

10. D

SMARTPOINT CATEGORY: DEFINITION

The key to this question is the word *as*, which signals a definition. You must look for a word that tells you why *it was difficult to tell what the auditor was thinking*. (D), *impassive*, means expressionless, revealing nothing. (A), *palpable*, means obvious or easily perceived. (B), *salient*, means prominent. Choice (C), *titular*, refers to having a title, often in name only. (E), *bilious*, means sickly or ill-humored, both with a connotation of too much bile.

11. E

SMARTPOINT CATEGORY: CAUSE AND EFFECT

The logical relationship within this sentence is cause and effect, signaled by the word *because*. The archeologist cannot determine what the chamber holds because he is *confined to the rim of the excavation site*. On the rim of a hole, one could not see what is "underground," the meaning of (E), *subterranean*, (*sub*, below, and *terranean* from *terre*, meaning earth). (A), *potable*, means fit to drink. (B), *fulsome,* means abundant, often with a connotation of insincerity, as in the phrase *fulsome praise*. (C), *insensate*, means unconscious or lacking awareness. (D), *beatific,* means showing joy and calmness.

12. C

SMARTPOINT CATEGORY: CONTRAST

The second part of the sentence, after *but*, contrasts with the first part, in which Casey's teacher praises his story. Therefore, you are looking for a word for the first blank that denotes a flaw in the writing. The keyword for the second blank is *suggested*. That means you are looking for a second word that will correct the flaw noted in the first blank. *Verbose* means wordy, while to *pare* is to trim or cut, in this case words; thus, (C) is correct. (A) is incorrect, as *adept* is a positive word meaning skilled. To *declaim* is to recite or speak, usually vehemently. In (B), *gauche* means lacking in social polish, though it's an adjective appropriate to a human, not to writing. To *filibuster* is to delay through speechmaking. (D), *contiguous* and *diffuse* are in the relationship of possible flaw and remedy, but *contiguous* means touching or adjacent without a break, while *diffuse* means to spread out; so the choices don't fit the sentence. (E)'s choices, *abortive* and *abscond*, mean fruitless or imperfectly developed (*abortive*) and to flee and hide oneself (*abscond*), which are extreme choices for a bit of good, though somewhat flawed, writing.

13. A

SMARTPOINT CATEGORY: CAUSE AND EFFECT

The word *revealed* is the key to this question. It directs you to look for the word that connects *Dr. Fowler's compact disc collection* to *early jazz recordings*. (A), *penchant,* means a definite liking. (B), *tenet*, refers to a belief of doctrine or principle. Choice (C), *confluence*, means a gathering or flowing together, either literally or figuratively. (D), *phalanx*, is a close-knit group of people, often used in reference to troops or guards. (E), *hegemony*, refers to the dominance of one nation over others.

14. C

SMARTPOINT CATEGORY: CAUSE AND EFFECT

The logical relationship in this sentence is cause and effect, an *if . . . then* relationship, although in this case, the *then* is implied. To *eschew* is to forego or avoid. *Cessation* refers to stopping or ceasing. Avoiding violence, the sentence says, would stop war. Thus, (C) is correct. (A) is incorrect because to *emulate* is to strive to equal or surpass through imitation, while *tutelage* is instruction or guardianship, from the same root as *tutor*. The words in (B), *condole* and *paean*, are incorrect because *condole* means to feel or express sympathy for another, while *paean* means joyful praise, as a hymn. In (D), *becloud* and *demagogue* mean to obscure or cover, as with clouds (becloud), and a popular leader who appeals to the emotions of the people (demagogue). At first, (E) seems as though it could be correct: to *mitigate* is to alleviate or moderate; but *recidivism* is a relapse into previous bad behaviors, often applied to repeat criminals, and so it does not fit the sense of the sentence.

15. C

SMARTPOINT CATEGORY: DEFINITION

The verb *required* is the key to this sentence. The *austere life* of a monk *required sleeping in* what kind of cell? Choice (C), *spartan*, from the Greek city of Sparta, means simple or frugal, in other words, austere. (A), *variegated*, means characterized by variety, especially of color. (B), *specious*, refers to something that is false, though it has the appearance of truth. (D), *inchoate*, means in an early, imperfect state of development. (E), *intransigent*, means extreme and uncompromising.

16. B

SMARTPOINT CATEGORY: CONTRAST

The correct answer can be determined by the context of the sentence. *Corrupt* is a keyword, as are *honesty* and *belied* (shown to be false, and thus a relationship of contrast), so look for words that relate to honesty or corruption. In choice (B), *disingenuous* means not straightforward; *blatantly* means obviously offensive, without any effort to conceal. In other words, the judge misrepresented his honesty but his obviously unfair rulings showed his representation to be false. In (A), *colloquial* means conversation-like in its informality, and *amorphously* means shapeless or lacking form. In (C), *macabre* means gruesomely horrifying or reminiscent of death, and *morosely* means in a sullen or melancholy manner. In (D), *saturnine* means tending to be bitter or sardonic in manner, while *stringently* means rigorous or severe. In (E), *opprobrious* means either scornful and abusive, or disgraceful and shameful, so it could possibly fit in the first blank. *Truculently*, however, means bitterly or violently opposed and does not fit the sentence.

17. B

SMARTPOINT CATEGORY: DEFINITION

This sentence includes a logical restatement in its structure, signaled by the word *as*. Ask yourself what kind of opponent never makes a careless mistake. (B), *formidable,* means difficult to defeat, thus inspiring awe and dread. (A), *illusory,* means deceptive, as in the word *illusion.* (C), *circuitous,* means roundabout, as in *circuit.* (D), *novel,* means new and different, when it's not referring to a literary form. (E), *temporal,* means limited by time, as is the material world.

18. A

SMARTPOINT CATEGORY: DEFINITION

This question must be answered by looking at context. First, note the words that are clues, such as *minority party*, *members*, and *business*, as well as *economic reform package*. You are looking for a term that is used in politics to apply to a group with members. (A), *caucus,* means a group with a special focus within a larger group or party. (B), *aerie,* is a nest or a house built on a high place. (C), *milieu,* is an environment or setting. (D), *rostrum,* is an elevated platform for public speaking. (E), *interregnum,* refers to the interruption of the usual functions of government.

19. A

SMARTPOINT CATEGORY: CAUSE AND EFFECT

This sentence contains a cause-and-effect relationship, signaled by the word *because.* The second part of the sentence sheds more light on the chain of cause and effect. In choice (A), *hubris* is another word for excessive pride. It was the cat burglar's pride that led her to show her neighbor her *cache,* her concealed store, of jewels. In (B), *pseudonym* means alias or assumed name: *fodder* is food or raw material. In (C), *yen* means desire, and *vernacular* means everyday, informal language. In (D), *calumny* and *onus* mean slander or false statements and burden or blame, respectively. In (E), *kismet* and *platitude* mean fate or fortune and cliché statement, respectively.

20. B

SMARTPOINT CATEGORY: DEFINITION

Good clues in this sentence are the phrases *likely to be shunned* and *for example.* Together, they tell us that the word we're looking for means one who is shunned. This prediction is a great match for *pariah.* (B), *pariah,* is a social outcast, one who is shunned by a community. (A), *exponent,* in the nonmathematical sense, is one who advocates or speaks for. (C), *sybarite,* refers to a person devoted to pleasure. (D), *potentate,* means one who exercises extensive power. (E), *paragon,* refers to a model of excellence, even perfection.

21. D

SMARTPOINT CATEGORY: DEFINITION

The sentence requires a definition. The logical form of this sentence directs you to look for a restatement of the phrase *not well defined*. (D), *nebulous*, means vague, that is, not well defined. (A), *prosaic*, from the same root as the word *prose*, means straightforward, lacking in imagination. (B), *importunate*, means urgent and persistent in requesting. (C), *epochal*, means significant or momentous. (E), *febrile*, means feverish, either literally or figuratively.

22. C

SMARTPOINT CATEGORY: DEFINITION

The relationship signaled in this sentence by *just as* and *likewise* is one of comparison. The comparison is inverted by the choice of the two subjects, the criminal and the superhero. The words *dupe* and *trick* are synonyms that help you see the comparison. When inserted into the blanks, (C)'s words *feign* and *duplicity* work by aligning with their counterparts *fake* (feign) and *honesty* (duplicity). Though *fake* and *feign* are synonyms, *honesty* and *duplicity* (deception) are antonyms, which makes sense because a criminal and a superhero would be faking, or feigning, opposite traits. In (A), *burnish* means to make smooth or glossy by rubbing, and *histrionics* is exaggerated emotional behavior. *Ingratiate* in (B) means to seek the good graces of another, and *aplomb* is self-confidence or assurance. (D), *aver*, is to declare or affirm, and a *sinecure* is a job that requires little or no effort to secure or maintain. In (E), to *thwart* is to frustrate or prevent the realization of plans, and *convergence* means meeting or coming together from different directions.

23. B

SMARTPOINT CATEGORY: CONTRAST

The logical relationship in this sentence is one of contrast, signaled by the word *despite*. You want to make sure that the first word, an adjective describing *lifestyle*, contrasts with the adjective that describes *income*. Then you also want to look at the introductory clause that tells you Mr. Jones has chosen to live in an *impoverished country* and ask yourself why someone would make that choice in relation to lifestyle and income. In choice (B), the word *lavish* means abundant, even extravagant, while *paltry* means lacking in worth or trivial, which makes this the correct choice. In (A), *replete* means abundantly supplied, and *squalid* means dirty and wretched, as from poverty. These words fit the general sense of the sentence, but *squalid* is used to describe an environment, not an income level. In (C), *licentious* means lacking restraint, especially in sexual connotations, and *obstinate* means stubborn. In (D), *cumulative* means enlarged by successive additions, and *complacent* means unconcerned due to self-satisfaction. In (E), *winsome* means charming, often in a childish way, and *tortuous* means devious and not straightforward, either literally or figuratively.

24. E

SMARTPOINT CATEGORY: DEFINITION

In this sentence, the colon indicates an elaboration on the word *frightening*. The word *tyrant* reinforces this concept, so you are looking for words that could express frightening qualities of a tyrant's stare and words. In choice (E), *malevolent* means exhibiting ill will, and *virulent* means hostile, harmful, or poisonous. The other answer choices can be eliminated, as they do not have the same connotations. In (A), *mawkish* means sickeningly sentimental, and *wry* means dryly humorous. In (B), *gamely* means bravely, and *imperious* means arrogantly overbearing. In (C), *tenuous* means having little substance, literally or figuratively, and *sanctimonious* means feigning righteousness. In (D), *incarnadine* means flesh or blood colored, and *implacable* means impossible to appease or satisfy.

KEY POINTS YOU'VE LEARNED IN THIS CHAPTER

1. Sentence Completion questions test definition, contrast, and cause and effect.

2. Memorize Kaplan's strategy for Sentence Completions:

   - **Step 1:** Read the sentence for clue words.

   - **Step 2:** Predict the answer.

   - **Step 3:** Select the best match.

   - **Step 4:** Plug your answer choice back into the sentence.

3. Learn Kaplan's techniques for tackling hard questions (decode tricky sentences, work around tough vocabulary, and if all else fails—guess strategically).

CHAPTER 10: READING COMPREHENSION STRATEGIES— SHORT PASSAGES

SMARTPOINTS COVERED IN THIS CHAPTER

DETAIL

GLOBAL

VOCABULARY-IN-CONTEXT

FUNCTION

INFERENCE

WHAT TO EXPECT ON TEST DAY

The Reading Comprehension questions are based on two types of passages—short passages and long passages. We'll cover the short passages in this chapter and then look at the longer passages in chapter 9. The question types that go with short passages are actually the same as the question types associated with long passages. Therefore, what you learn in this chapter will also help you tackle the longer passages.

As we have mentioned, the topics you will see will be drawn from the humanities, social sciences, natural sciences, and fiction. In order to do well on these, you must read actively and analyze information. You will not, however, need to have any previous knowledge about a topic to answer the questions. Everything you need to know will be right there in front of you.

SHORT PASSAGE QUESTION TYPES

The Reading Comprehension section has five basic types of questions that follow both short and long passages.

The three more straightforward, and usually easier, questions are:

1. Detail (What?) questions
2. Global (Big Picture) questions
3. Vocabulary-in-Context questions

The two often more challenging types ask you either to understand the author's intent or to identify conclusions drawn from the passage. They are:

4. Function (Why?) questions
5. Inference questions

Let's look at these in order of difficulty, starting with the easiest.

 ## DETAIL QUESTIONS

These *What?* questions ask about specific facts or details in the passage and often provide you with a line reference or at least indicate the paragraph where the detail is located.

Detail questions test:

- Whether you understand significant information that's stated in the passage
- Your ability to locate information within a text
- Your ability to differentiate between main ideas and specific details

BE SMART!

> Detail questions are usually easier to answer than other questions. Keep this in mind if you're short on time.

Sometimes the answer to a question will be stated directly in the line or lines that are referenced. Other times, you might need to read a few sentences before or after the referenced line(s) to find the correct answer. When in doubt, use the context (surrounding sentences) to confirm the right choice.

Detail questions may be worded as:

- According to the passage . . .
- In lines 12–16, what does the author say about . . .
- How does the author describe . . .

 ## GLOBAL QUESTIONS

Global questions test how well you understand the passage as a whole. They ask about:

- The main point or purpose of a passage or an individual paragraph
- The author's overall attitude or tone
- The logic underlying the author's argument
- How ideas relate to each other in a passage

If you are stumped on a Global question, even after reading the passage, do the Detail questions first. They can often help you understand the big picture (and even some of the other, harder questions).

Global questions may be worded as:

- The passage is primarily concerned with . . .
- What is the author's attitude toward . . .
- What is the main idea of the passage?

 VOCABULARY-IN-CONTEXT QUESTIONS

Vocabulary-in-Context questions ask about the meaning of a single word. These questions do not test your ability to define hard words like *archipelago* and *garrulous*. Instead, they test your ability to infer the meaning of a word from context.

Words tested in SAT Vocab-in-Context questions are usually fairly common words with more than one definition. But that's the trick! Many of the answer choices will be definitions of the tested word, but only one will work in context. Vocabulary-in-Context questions always have a line reference, and you should always use it!

Sometimes one of the answer choices will jump out at you. It will be the most common meaning of the word in question—but it's RARELY right. You can think of this as the *obvious* choice. Say *curious* is the word being tested. The obvious choice is *inquisitive*. But curious also means *odd*, and that's more likely to be the answer.

Using context to find the answer will prevent you from falling for this kind of trap. But you can also use these obvious choices to your advantage. If you get stuck on a Vocabulary-in-Context question, you can eliminate the obvious choice and guess from the remaining answers.

Vocabulary-in-Context questions may be worded as:

- As used in line 8, _____ most nearly means . . .
- The term _____ most likely refers to . . .

KAPLAN'S STRATEGY FOR VOCABULARY-IN-CONTEXT QUESTIONS

Step 1: Reread the sentence containing the word and the sentences nearby.

Step 2: Treat it as you would a Sentence Completion question. Predict.

FUNCTION QUESTIONS

These *Why?* questions are a little tricky because they require you to take an extra step *beyond* the *What?* of the passage. To answer these questions effectively, you must put yourself in the author's place.

A Function question will ask you:

- Why include this detail?
- Why include this word?
- Why include this sentence?
- Why include this quote?
- Why include this paragraph?

Your job is to look back in the passage using the line references or other hints the question stem gives you. There you will discover clues to the answer. Most often, you have to read *around* any lines the question stem gives.

Keep these points about Function questions in mind:

- Function questions are easy to spot because they have distinctive phrasing. You'll see the following phrases in the question stem: *serves to, in order to, is meant to, is used to,* or *functions as.*
- Be careful as you go through the answers. Sometimes you'll see an answer that is really a Detail/What answer, and a perfectly good answer—for a different question.

Function questions may be worded as:

- The "_____" mentioned in lines 4–5 serves primarily to . . .
- The author uses the description of "_____" in lines 5–7 mainly to . . .
- The second paragraph primarily serves to . . .
- The author cites "_____" in lines 8–9 in order to . . .

 INFERENCE QUESTIONS

To *infer* is to draw a conclusion based on reasoning or evidence. For example, if you wake up in the morning and there's three feet of fresh snow on the ground, you can infer that school will be canceled.

Often, writers will use suggestion or inference rather than state ideas directly. But they will also leave you plenty of clues so you can figure out just what they are trying to convey. Inference clues include word choice (diction), tone, and specific details. For example, say a passage states that a particular idea *was perceived as revolutionary*. You might infer from the use of the word *perceived* that the author believes the idea was not truly revolutionary but only *perceived* (or seen) that way.

Thus, Inference questions test your ability to use the information in the passage to come to a logical conclusion. The key to Inference questions is to stick to the evidence in the text. Most Inference questions have pretty strong clues, so avoid any answer choices that seem far-fetched. The right answer to an Inference question is strongly grounded in the passage.

DON'T FORGET!

Make sure you read Inference questions carefully. Some answer choices may be true, but if they can't be inferred from the passage, then they can't be the correct answer.

Inference questions ask you to read between the lines. The correct answer will be a small step from what is directly said in the passage. Inference questions are easy to spot because they have distinctive phrasing.

You'll see one of the following phrases in the question stem:

- *Suggests, implies, infers, would regard as, most directly supports the conclusion that*

Inference questions may be worded as:

- It can be inferred from the passage that . . .
- The phrase "_____" implies that . . .
- The description of _____ primarily suggests that . . .

FOUR STEPS TO TEST DAY SUCCESS

You'll find the following strategies helpful when answering Reading Comprehension questions. You must be able to identify the type of question being asked, do research, make predictions, and identify trick answers.

The SAT is an open-book test, and focusing on details is a waste of time, especially on long passages. Instead, concentrate only on the main focus of each paragraph.

The key is to know where to read closely *once you have begun to answer the questions*. Begin by reading the entire passage quickly, knowing that you are going to come back in search of answers—and points.

KAPLAN'S TARGET STRATEGY FOR READING COMPREHENSION QUESTIONS

Serious skimming is a vital component of Kaplan's Target Strategy for attacking Reading Comprehension questions. Once you have seriously skimmed the passage, here's how to attack the questions:

Step 1: Read the question stem.

Step 2: Locate the material you need.

Step 3: Predict the answer.

Step 4: Select the best answer choice.

Try Kaplan's Target Strategy on the passage and question that follow:

Question 1 refers to the following passage:

Recently, at my grandmother's eightieth birthday party, my family looked at old photographs. In one of them, I saw a scared little boy holding tightly to his mother's skirt, and I scarcely recognized myself. My foremost memory of that
(5) time is simply being cold—the mild Vietnamese winters that I had known couldn't prepare me for the bitter winds of the American Midwest. The cold seemed emblematic of everything I hated about my new country—we had no friends, no extended family, and we all lived together in a
(10) two-room apartment. My mother, ever shrewd, remarked that selling heat in such a cold place would surely bring fortune, and she was right. My parents now own a successful heating supply company.

1. The author's attitude toward the "scared little boy" mentioned in line 3, indicates that the author

(A) is unsure that the photograph is actually of his family

(B) believes that the boy is likely overly dependent on his mother

(C) feels that he has changed considerably since childhood

(D) regards his mother's strategy to sell heating supplies as clever

(E) regrets his family's move to the United States

> **EXPERT TUTOR TIP**
>
> " Be cautious about choosing extreme answer choices that include *all*, *nothing*, *always*, or *never*. Only choose that answer choice if the passage explicitly supports it. "

STEP 1: READ THE QUESTION STEM

This is the time and place to read very carefully. Make sure you understand exactly what the question is asking.

Keep the following in mind:

- Look for the following flag words and phrases: *in order to, implies, because,* etc.
- Are you looking for a main idea or specific information?
- Are you trying to determine the author's attitude or *why* someone did something?

In this case, the question is straightforward: What does the author think about the little boy? You need to make an inference about the author's attitude.

BOTTOM LINE

Remember to read the question stems *before* you read short passages. Underline the words that you'll likely see while reading the passage. This short, preliminary step will save you time and help you find the right answers.

STEP 2: LOCATE THE MATERIAL YOU NEED

If you are given a line reference, read the material surrounding the line mentioned. It will clarify exactly what the question is asking and provide you with the context you need to answer the question correctly.

If you're not given a line reference, scan the text to find the lines that relate to the question, and quickly reread those few sentences. Keep the main point of the passage in mind.

For the question here, you're given a line reference, so be sure to go back to that line. But don't read just that specific line—read the line or two before and after it as well. When you do, you see that the author says that he scarcely recognizes himself. From this, you know that the boy in the picture is the author when he was younger.

STEP 3: PREDICT THE ANSWER

Don't spend time making up a precise answer. You need only a general sense of what you're after so you can recognize the correct answer quickly when you read the choices.

Why would the author of this passage say that he scarcely recognizes himself? The implication is that the author (now grown) is so different from that frightened little

> **EXPERT TUTOR TIP**
>
> " Remember to select the answer that best matches your prediction. Don't get swayed by a wrong answer that is too extreme or out of the scope of the passage. "

boy that it's hard to believe they're the same person. So look for an answer choice that matches this prediction.

STEP 4: SELECT THE BEST ANSWER CHOICE

Scan the choices, looking for one that fits your prediction. If you don't find an ideal answer, quickly eliminate wrong choices by checking in the passage. Rule out choices that are too extreme or go against common sense. Get rid of answers that sound reasonable but don't make sense in the context of the passage or the question. Don't pick far-fetched inferences, and make sure there is evidence for your inference in the passage. Remember, the answers to SAT Inference questions tend to be strongly implied in the passage.

Let's take a look at the answer choices:

Choice (A): This is too literal—the author is speaking figuratively when he says he scarcely recognizes the boy.

Choice (B): This choice goes too far in making an inference. Although the boy is sticking close to his mother in the picture, there's no evidence that the author thinks this is a bad thing.

Choice (C): This is a great match for your prediction and is the correct answer.

Choice (D): This might be a true statement, but it comes later in the passage. It has nothing to do with the author's attitude toward the boy in the picture.

Choice (E): Like (B), this choice is too great a leap and can't safely be inferred from the information in the passage.

WRONG ANSWER TRAPS

It is as important to read the answers as it is the question stems in the Reading Comprehension section. The test makers often set traps throughout the section. Don't worry—once you know where trouble lies, you won't be fooled!

These are the most common wrong answer traps:

- **Out of Scope:** The answer lies outside the passage topic or is only vaguely connected to it.
- **Extreme:** If it's strong, it's wrong. Beware of answer choices with words such as *all, only, never, always, most, least,* or *unique.*
- **Opposite:** Small syllables (*unusual* vs. *usual*) or a small word, such as *not,* change everything.

> **EXPERT TUTOR TIP**
>
> " Predict an answer before looking at the choices; otherwise, you'll see several choices that sound plausible, and you'll lose time determining the best one. "

> **PERFECT SCORE TIP**
>
> " Knowing why the incorrect answer choices were wrong really let me understand the traps that come up frequently, which helped raise my score. "

- **Distortion:** An answer starts out promising but turns into a wrong answer with the addition of a single word or two.
- **Misused Detail:** This is an answer that is true, but refers to a different section of the text.

PRACTICE

Now try Kaplan's Target Strategy on the remaining questions for the passages. Answers begin on page 162. We also show you there how to apply the Target Strategy to questions 1–4.

Questions 1–2 refer to the following passage.

Recently, at my grandmother's eightieth birthday party, my family looked at old photographs. In one of them, I saw a scared little boy holding tightly to his mother's skirt, and I scarcely recognized myself. My foremost memory of that
(5) time is simply being cold—the mild Vietnamese winters that I had known couldn't prepare me for the bitter winds of the American Midwest. The cold seemed emblematic of everything I hated about my new country—we had no friends, no extended family, and we all lived together in a
(10) two-room apartment. My mother, ever shrewd, remarked that selling heat in such a cold place would surely bring fortune, and she was right. My parents now own a successful heating supply company.

1. In line 5, the author mentions "the mild Vietnamese winters" in order to

    (A) explain his grandmother's childhood in Vietnam

    (B) recall his past growing up in Vietnam

    (C) detail the weather conditions in his home country

    (D) describe how much he despises the cold

    (E) provide contrast to how cold the author felt in the new country

PERFECT SCORE TIP

" Approaching really tough questions calmly was crucial. It was easier to determine word charges, guess meanings to words, and find sentence clues when I was confident and collected! "

2. Lines 10–13 ("My mother . . . heating supply company") suggest that the author's mother regarded the cold of the American Midwest as

(A) more drastic than the cold of Vietnam

(B) an opportunity for economic success

(C) an obstacle to familial happiness

(D) symbolic of other challenges and problems

(E) unimportant to the family's future

Questions 3–4 refer to the following passage.

Many mammals instinctively raise their fur when they are cold—a reaction produced by tiny muscles just under the skin which surround hair follicles. When the muscles contract, the hairs stand up, creating an increased air space
(5) under the fur. The air space provides more effective insulation for the mammal's body, thus allowing it to retain more heat for longer periods of time. Some animals also raise their fur when they are challenged by predators or even other members of their own species. The raised fur makes
(10) the animal appear slightly bigger, and, ideally, more powerful. Interestingly, though devoid of fur, humans still retain this instinct. So, the next time a horror movie gives you "goosebumps," remember that your skin is following a deep-seated mammalian impulse now rendered obsolete.

3. The "increased air space under the fur" mentioned in lines 4–5 serves primarily to

(A) combat cold

(B) intimidate other animals

(C) render goosebumps obsolete

(D) cool overheated predators

(E) make mammals more powerful

4. Based on the passage, the author would most likely describe "goosebumps" in humans as

(A) an unnecessary and unexplained phenomenon

(B) a harmful but necessary measure

(C) an amusing but dangerous feature

(D) a useless but interesting remnant

(E) a powerful but infrequent occurrence

Questions 5–6 refer to the following passage.

Elizabeth Barrett Browning, a feminist writer of the Victorian Era, used her poetry and prose to take on a wide range of issues facing her society, including "the woman question." In her long poem *Aurora Leigh*, she explores this
(5) question as she portrays both the growth of the artist and the growth of the woman within. Aurora Leigh is not a traditional Victorian woman—she is well educated and self-sufficient. In the poem, Browning argues that the limitations placed on women in contrast to the freedom men
(10) enjoy should incite women to rise up and effect a change in their circumstances. Browning's writing, including *Aurora Leigh*, helped to pave the way for major social change in women's lives.

5. It can be inferred from the passage that the author believes the traditional Victorian woman

    (A) wrote poetry
    (B) was portrayed accurately in *Aurora Leigh*
    (C) fought for social change
    (D) was not well educated
    (E) had a public role in society

6. As used in line 10, "effect" most nearly means

    (A) imitate
    (B) result
    (C) cause
    (D) disturb
    (E) prevent

Questions 7–8 refer to the following passage.

Each passing evening brings more frustration. Tonight I spent an hour in front of the typewriter staring at the silent keys, listening to the girl upstairs play the piano and sing. I'd never noticed her ability before; she is remarkable. It
(5) seems everything she plays is of her own spontaneous creation, an absolute movement of feeling. Her music is a painting, the lines so intense and colorful that it manages to exist above the realm of the material, impressing a desolate image of the pianist upon my mind. But even the
(10) beauty of this pure work of art failed to inspire me, and after she stopped I was again without refuge.

7. In lines 2–3 the phrase "silent keys" implies that the narrator

   (A) can't play the piano
   (B) is suffering from writer's block
   (C) is tone deaf
   (D) is searching for clues
   (E) is annoyed by the girl upstairs

8. The narrator uses the description of the girl's playing in lines 4–6 ("It seems . . . feeling") mainly to

   (A) contrast it with his inability to write
   (B) illustrate her talents as a musician
   (C) compare it with painting
   (D) criticize her lack of skill
   (E) indicate his inferiority as an artist

Questions 9–10 refer to the following passage.

Bear Mountain State Park opened in 1916 and rapidly
became a popular weekend destination for many New
Yorkers looking for an escape from the city grind. The
ensuing unnaturally high volume of visitors to the area
(5) caused an upsurge in traffic, and it was soon apparent that
the ferry services used to cross the Hudson were insufficient. In 1922, the New York State Legislature introduced a
bill that authorized a group of private investors led by
Mary Harriman to build a bridge across the river. The
(10) group, known as the Bear Mountain Hudson Bridge
Company, was allotted thirty years to construct and maintain the bridge, after which the span would be handed over
to New York State.

9. In context, "volume" (line 4) most closely means

   (A) loudness
   (B) pollution
   (C) resentment
   (D) capacity
   (E) quantity

10. According to the passage, which is true about the
    bridge?

    I. It was originally constructed by New York State.
    II. It opened to the public in 1916.
    III. It was necessitated by inadequate ferry services.

    (A) Statement II
    (B) Statement III
    (C) Statements I and II
    (D) Statements I and III
    (E) Statements II and III

Questions 11–12 refer to the following passage.

Like the writers of the Beat Generation almost a half-century before, many of the original grunge musicians who helped give birth to a movement were horrified at the final result of their efforts. Grunge music and culture were
(5) spawned in Seattle in the late 1980s as an underground revolt against the shallow values of the time. But with Nirvana's 1991 release of *Nevermind,* and the successive popularity of other Seattle bands like Pearl Jam and Soundgarden, the once-countercultural grunge movement
(10) skyrocketed into popular consciousness. Many aspects of the culture that were originally forms of rebellion, such as the hairstyles and fashions worn by grunge musicians, found their way into the most mainstream of places.

11. In lines 1–2, the author invokes the Beat Generation in order to

(A) detail an earlier movement in music

(B) introduce the topic by illustrating a similarity

(C) imply the insignificance of grunge

(D) recall an important time in American cultural history

(E) emphasize grunge's influence upon today's music

12. As used in line 3, "movement" most closely means

(A) an organized attempt at change

(B) a specific manner of moving

(C) the changing of location or position

(D) a rhythmic progression or tempo

(E) a mainstream belief

Questions 13–14 refer to the following passage.

Bovine spongiform encephalopathy (BSE) is a fatal, transmissible, neurological disorder found in cattle that slowly attacks a cow's brain cells, forming what resemble sponge-like holes in its brain. As the disease progresses, the

(5) cow begins to behave abnormally, hence BSE's more common name, "Mad Cow Disease." On December 23, 2003, the first case of BSE in the U.S. was detected in a cow from Washington State. The ensuing national hysteria was largely unfounded; years earlier, in response to the

(10) previous epidemics abroad, the USFDA had implemented preventative measures to contain an outbreak of the disease before it could spread. These measures were in place for a good reason: there is a causal link between eating BSE-infected meat and the development of a fatal human

(15) brain disorder known as new variant Creutzfeldt-Jakob Disease (nvCJD).

13. Lines 1–6 mostly serve to

    (A) explain the origin of the term "Mad Cow Disease"

    (B) introduce background information on BSE

    (C) warn of BSE's transmissibility to humans

    (D) dissuade people from eating meat

    (E) provide an in-depth description of BSE's different stages

14. The author suggests that the "national hysteria" (line 8) was

    (A) totally justified

    (B) necessary for USFDA policy change

    (C) rooted in misinformation about BSE's harmfulness

    (D) completely inexcusable

    (E) understandable, but unnecessary

Questions 15–16 refer to the following passage.

Ann's footsteps crunching upon the fallen leaves are
amplified by the pre-dusk serenity that is quickly setting
upon the forest. The path before her is quickly dissolving
into the growing shadows, yet the fear that would normally
(5) be creeping into her chest is absent. Somewhere secretly
inside she finds the prospect of disappearing into the
woods exhilarating. Liberated, all her daily burdens would
go as the daylight goes, into the empty night, spattered
with benevolent stars. But as the trail opens onto her back-
(10) yard, Ann is surprised to find herself breaking into
a trot, eager to return to the familiar warmth of her home.

15. Ann's absence of fear (lines 4–5) suggests that she

    (A) is brave in the face of danger

    (B) doesn't realize she is lost

    (C) is an apathetic person

    (D) longs for a change in her life

    (E) never feels fear

16. In line 8, "the empty night" is symbolic of

    (A) everyday life

    (B) a lack of responsibility

    (C) being lost

    (D) loneliness

    (E) death

ANSWERS AND EXPLANATIONS

1. E
SMARTPOINTS CATEGORY: FUNCTION

Here's how you could answer this question using Kaplan's Target Strategy:

STEP 1: READ THE QUESTION STEM

The phrase *in order to* tells you this is a Function question. Why did the author mention "the mild Vietnamese winters"?

STEP 2: LOCATE THE MATERIAL YOU NEED

After reading lines 6–9, you should see that the author is comparing "the mild Vietnamese winters" with "the bitter winds of the American Midwest." That helps you form a prediction of what the answer is.

STEP 3: PREDICT THE ANSWER

The author is seeking to contrast winters in Vietnam with winters in the American Midwest.

STEP 4: SELECT THE BEST ANSWER CHOICE

(E) says what you've predicted, so it's the answer. (C) is true, but it is only part of the reason why he mentions the winters. And (A), (B), and (D) are not mentioned in the passage.

2. B
SMARTPOINTS CATEGORY: INFERENCE

Here's how you could answer this question using Kaplan's Target Strategy:

STEP 1: READ THE QUESTION STEM

The word *suggest* indicates that this is an Inference question. What do those lines imply about the mother's view of the cold in the Midwest?

STEP 2: LOCATE THE MATERIAL YOU NEED

After reading lines 10–13, you should see that the mother helped the family profit from the cold by selling heat. That helps you form a prediction of what the answer is.

STEP 3: PREDICT THE ANSWER

The mother saw the cold in the Midwest as an opportunity to make money.

STEP 4: SELECT THE BEST ANSWER CHOICE

(B) says what you've predicted, so it's the answer. Although (A) is certainly true of the passage, it is not specifically referred to in the lines cited. There was no mention of the cold being an obstacle, so that rules out (C). And the author doesn't say the cold was unimportant to the family, ruling out (E), or symbolic of other challenges, ruling out (D).

3. A

SMARTPOINTS CATEGORY: FUNCTION

Here's how you could answer this question using Kaplan's Target Strategy:

STEP 1: READ THE QUESTION STEM

Because the question has the words *serves primarily to*, you know it is a Function question.

STEP 2: LOCATE THE MATERIAL YOU NEED

When you read around the lines given (meaning lines 3–7), you see that the air space *provides more effective insulation for the mammal's body*. This leads directly to a good prediction, and Step 3.

STEP 3: PREDICT THE ANSWER

It looks like the increased air space helps keep the animal warm.

STEP 4: SELECT THE BEST ANSWER CHOICE

Choice (B) can be tempting because raised fur also intimidates other animals. However, that point is made later in the passage and is a Misused Detail. Your prediction is about combating cold. You are left with (A) as your choice. It is the only one that fits. Note that if you had not followed the Four-Step Method, you could have been easily sidetracked by (B) or (E).

4. D

SMARTPOINTS CATEGORY: INFERENCE

The phrase *would most likely describe* in question 4 flags this as an Inference question. Here's how you might answer it with Kaplan's Target Strategy:

STEP 1: READ THE QUESTION STEM

The question seems simple enough: What does the author think about goosebumps?

STEP 2: LOCATE THE MATERIAL YOU NEED

This question doesn't cite the lines where *goosebumps* are discussed, but because you underlined the keyword *goosebumps* in the question stem before reading the passage, you know where to look. In addition, you know to read around the lines given, so you probably would begin rereading at line 9.

STEP 3: PREDICT THE ANSWER

You might say something like, "Goosebumps are left over from when people had fur."

STEP 4: SELECT THE BEST ANSWER CHOICE

(D) looks very good. Note that the word *interesting* in the answer echoes *Interestingly* in the passage—another clue that it is the right answer.

5. D

SMARTPOINTS CATEGORY: INFERENCE

The answer to this question can be found in lines 6–8. The author writes, *Aurora Leigh is not a traditional Victorian woman—she is well educated and self-sufficient.* This statement sets up the contrast between Aurora, who is well educated, and the traditional Victorian woman, who is not well educated, answer choice (D).

6. C

SMARTPOINTS CATEGORY: VOCABULARY-IN-CONTEXT

The word *effect* is both a noun and a verb, so you must look at its use in the sentence to determine its part of speech and meaning. The word is used in the phrase *to rise up and effect a change.* If you are unclear of the meaning, try inserting answer choices (A) through (E) in the sentence to see if they make sense: to *imitate* a change, to *result* a change, to *cause* a change, to *disturb* a change, to *prevent* a change. Although you may have been tempted to choose (B), *result*, thinking that effect is a noun, the only answer choice that makes sense in the context of the sentence is choice (C), *cause.*

7. B

SMARTPOINTS CATEGORY: INFERENCE

The word *implies* shows that this is an Inference question. The *silent keys* referred to in the passage are the keys of a typewriter, and the fact that they are described as *silent* implies that they are not in use. Using what the author offered you in the first sentence about his mounting frustration, you are looking for the choice that best reflects what conclusions can be drawn from this phrase. (A) is a distortion; the silent keys are those of a typewriter, not a piano. The author never mentions whether he can play the piano. (C) is the opposite of what you're looking for. The author's detailed description of the music upstairs proves that he is obviously not *tone deaf*. (D) is out of scope. The narrator may be searching for clues to break his writer's block, but this implication makes no sense within the scope of the paragraph. (E) is also opposite. The girl's playing does not annoy the narrator; in fact, in the paragraph's final sentence, he admits that he found *refuge* in it. (B) is the best answer.

8. A

SMARTPOINTS CATEGORY: FUNCTION 📶

This is a Function question. The narrator's description of the piano player has one overarching function in the paragraph—the ease with which she plays the piano offers a stark contrast to the narrator's writer's block, thus highlighting his frustration. (B) and (C) are distortions. Although the description does serve to *illustrate her talents*, (B), its true function in the paragraph is to emphasize the author's frustration with his own writer's block. Also, the author compares the piano player's music to a painting, (C), in the sentence that follows the one in question. (D) is the opposite of what you're looking for. The narrator describes the girl's playing as *remarkable*. (E) is out of scope; nowhere in the passage does the author offer a critique of his own skills—he simply tells of his frustration at not being able to employ them. (A) is a solid match with your prediction.

9. E

SMARTPOINTS CATEGORY: VOCABULARY-IN-CONTEXT 📶

To predict, look at the context: *A high _____ of visitors caused an upsurge in traffic*. A large "number" of visitors would cause an increase in traffic, so "number" is a great prediction. It's a perfect match for (E). (A) is a distortion; this synonym of volume might have been a product of *the upsurge in traffic*, but it is unlikely to have been the cause of it. (B) and (C) are both out of scope. *Pollution* is an effect of traffic, but this makes no sense in context, and *resentment* is never alluded to in the passage. (D) is also a distortion. Although exceeding the *capacity* for cars in an area is the cause of traffic, this definition of *volume* does not work in terms of the sentence's structure.

10. B

SMARTPOINTS CATEGORY: DETAIL 📶

Don't let the Roman numeral statements affect your approach; this is a simple Detail question whose answer is specifically based in the facts of the passage. Verify or rule out each given statement, and find the answer choice that corresponds with the statement or statements that you validated. (A) is a distortion. Bear Mountain State Park opened in 1916. The bridge opened later, but the date is not mentioned. You can thus eliminate (C) and (E) as well. (D) is also a distortion. Statement III is true, but I is false: New York State did not build the bridge, *it introduced a bill that authorized a group of private investors* to build it. (B) is the best answer.

11. B

SMARTPOINTS CATEGORY: FUNCTION

The phrase in the question stem *in order to* lets you know that this is a Function question. The author uses the similar experiences of the Beat writers and grunge musicians to establish the main idea of the passage. Look for the choice that best illustrates this statement, which is (B). (A) is a distortion. The first sentence clearly establishes that the Beats were writers, not musicians. (C) is out of scope. The author never implies that the grunge movement was insignificant. By invoking the Beats, the author is recalling *an important time in American cultural history*, (D), but this is not the purpose for the author's doing so. (E) is also out of scope. The author only mentions *grunge's influence* upon mainstream culture of the early 1990s.

12. A

SMARTPOINTS CATEGORY: VOCABULARY-IN-CONTEXT

In line 4, the author describes the movements of the Beat writers and grunge musicians as *efforts*, and then in line 6 characterizes the grunge movement as a *revolt*. Look for the choice that contains the best definition of what both of these words could imply. (B) is out of scope. This alternate definition of *movement* makes no sense in the context of the passage. (C) is also out of scope. Again, this definition makes no sense in context. (D) is a distortion. The definition of *movement* used in the passage refers to the efforts of musicians, not a *rhythmic progression or tempo* in music. (E) is the opposite of what you're looking for. A movement is usually an organized effort by an individual or group to change a *mainstream belief.* (A) is the best choice.

13. B

SMARTPOINTS CATEGORY: FUNCTION

The phrase *serves to* lets you know that this is a Function question. The author uses the first paragraph to brief the reader on the basic facts about BSE, and then uses the second paragraph to explore the subject a bit further. You are looking for the choice that best fits the first paragraph's role in fulfilling the author's purpose. (A) is a distortion. This is only a supporting detail of the first paragraph—you are looking for the paragraph's overall purpose in the passage. (C) and (E) are also distortions; the transmissibility of BSE to humans, (C), is not established until the second paragraph, and the quick summary of BSE's stages hardly amounts to *in-depth description*, (E). (D) is out of scope. Although this first paragraph certainly may dissuade some from eating meat, that is not the intended function of the paragraph or the passage. (B) is an excellent match for your prediction.

14. E

SMARTPOINTS CATEGORIES: INFERENCE
GLOBAL

The word *suggests* tells you that this is an Inference question. You are looking for a phrase that best captures the author's point of view about the nation's reaction to BSE. The answer to this question lies in one important detail of the passage: the use of the word *largely* (line 8). The author describes the *national hysteria* as *largely unfounded* because, while the USFDA was well prepared for such a scenario, the dire consequences of the disease should not be overlooked. (A) is the opposite of what the answer is. By definition, the word *hysteria* implies going a bit overboard in terms of response or emotion. (B) and (C) are distortions; the details of the passage clearly state that the USFDA had effected BSE policy change, (B), long before the first case in the country. (C) is incorrect because, although BSE is harmful, the passage doesn't state that misinformation about it spread. (D) is too extreme; BSE is a fatal, transmissible disease. (E) is the best choice.

15. D

SMARTPOINTS CATEGORY: INFERENCE

The word *suggests* alerts you that this is an Inference question. The passage states that rather than fear, Ann secretly feels exhilarated by the *prospect of disappearing into the woods* because she would be *liberated* from *all her daily burdens*. You are looking for the choice that best conveys what these statements suggest about Ann. (A) is a distortion; the passage states that *normally*, Ann would be scared by the prospect of being lost in the woods at night. (B) is also a distortion. Ann is not lost; the passage deals only with the prospect of her losing her way in the woods. (C) is the opposite of the correct answer. The fact that Ann could find something *exhilarating* (line 7) proves that she is not *apathetic*. (E) is an extreme. The passage does state that Ann *normally* would feel fear.

16. B

SMARTPOINTS CATEGORY: VOCABULARY-IN-CONTEXT

Ann wants her burdens, like the *daylight* (line 8), to disappear into the night. Using this comparison, the answer is the choice that best expresses what the empty night represents with respect to her *daily burdens*. (A) is the opposite of the best answer; in the passage, *the empty night* is symbolic of what Ann hopes would replace her *everyday life*. (C) and (D) are distortions. Don't be fooled by (C); *being lost* could be a literal representation of the empty night, but you're looking for the symbolic meaning. Although *empty night* may invoke images of *loneliness*, (D), the author never suggests that Ann is lonely. (E) is also opposite of the correct choice. The passage deals with themes of life, not *death*. (B) is a solid choice.

KEY POINTS YOU'VE LEARNED IN THIS CHAPTER

1. There are five types of questions associated with short reading passages: Detail, Global, Vocabulary-in-Context, Function, and Inference.

2. Memorize Kaplan's strategy for Reading Comprehension questions:

   - **Step 1:** Read the question stem.

   - **Step 2:** Locate the material you need.

   - **Step 3:** Predict the answer.

   - **Step 4:** Select the best answer choice.

3. Watch out for common wrong answer traps (answer choices that are out of scope, extreme, or opposite, or have distortions or misused details).

CHAPTER 11: READING COMPREHENSION STRATEGIES— LONG PASSAGES

SMARTPOINTS COVERED IN THIS CHAPTER

| DETAIL |
| FUNCTION |
| INFERENCE |
| GLOBAL |
| VOCABULARY-IN-CONTEXT |
| COMPARISONS |

WHAT TO EXPECT ON TEST DAY

You will use the same strategy to tackle long passages as you do short passages—Kaplan's Target Strategy for Reading Comprehension questions. Topics for short passages are taken from similar areas as long passages: humanities, social sciences, natural sciences, and fiction.

What's the difference? With longer passages, you need to work harder to stay focused and organized. Here's how.

LONG PASSAGE STRATEGIES

There are a few things to keep in mind when you read the long passages. Consider these as strategies that will help you master the section:

QUESTION ORDER

Although Reading Comprehension questions are not arranged by degree of difficulty, they do follow a specific order for longer passages. In general, the questions correspond to the passage, so the first few questions ask about the beginning of the passage, the middle questions about the middle, and the last few questions about the end. The last couple of questions are likely to be Big Picture questions that ask you about the overall main idea of the passage.

INTRODUCTION

Each long passage is preceded by a brief introduction that tells you what the passage is about. This is an important part of the question set and should not be skipped. The introduction helps you focus your reading by preparing you for the kind of information and ideas to come.

LEARN TO READ ACTIVELY

A key skill to master for the Reading Comprehension passages is active reading. What does this mean? It means you take an active role as you read. You ask yourself questions as you read:

- Why did the author write this?
- What is the purpose of this paragraph?
- Why include this detail?

Contrast this style of reading with the casual way you read a magazine. When you read casually, you don't take special care; you know it doesn't really matter what you understand. On the SAT Critical Reading section, however, you need to be on your toes. It will pay to remember the following two rules:

THE 3 Ws OF ACTIVE READING: WHY, WHAT, WHO

1. *Why* is more important than *what*.
2. Keep straight *who* said *what*.

As you read a passage, you'll want to look for the author's motivation and keep track of the various opinions and points of view. The author's view is likely to be different from those of any of the people the author mentions in the paragraphs. And the opinions of the characters in the text may well differ from each other. Why? These are some of the concerns to keep an eye out for.

MAP THE PASSAGE

Longer passages cover several aspects of a topic. For example, the first paragraph might introduce the subject, the second paragraph might present one viewpoint, and the third paragraph might argue for a different viewpoint. Within each of these paragraphs, there are several details that help the author carry out his or her purpose.

Because there is a lot to keep track of, you need to mark up long passages as follows:

- **Write** the simplest notes possible in the margin—abbreviations work well, but be sure you understand them.

- **Note** the purpose of each paragraph—such as *backgrd, opin, pro, con*, etc.

- **Bracket or circle** key points (keep underlining to a minimum).

- **Mark** places where opinion and point of view are expressed—the chance of seeing questions on these points is nearly 100 percent.

- **Pay attention** to all contrasting elements—one person thinks one thing, while another thinks another. *Keep these, along with what the author thinks, straight.*

These notes are your *passage map*. The passage map helps you find the part of the passage that contains the information you need. The process of creating your passage map also forces you to read actively. This is especially helpful in the SAT's second and third hour when your energy is flagging. Because you are constantly

EXPERT TUTOR TIP

" Writing down the main idea of each paragraph is the most valuable part of mapping the passage, yet it is the part that most students skip. Don't skip it! "

trying to identify the author's viewpoint and the purpose of each sentence and paragraph, you will be working hard to understand what's happening in the passage. This translates into points on the test.

PASSAGE MAPS

A good passage map:

- Contains short words or phrases
- Uses clear marks like brackets and circled words
- Concentrates on viewpoints and opinions
- Notes opinions other than the author's
- Avoids too-specific details

Note: Keep underlining to an absolute minimum. Some students go into "autopen" mode and underline everything, thinking they are going to remember what the passage is about. But when the time comes to look for answers, everything—and nothing—stands out in the text.

ABCs OF ACTIVE READING

An easy mnemonic to keep in mind when reading actively:

A = Abbreviate margin notes

B = Bracket key sentences

C = Circle keywords and phrases

READING RATE

How you mark a passage often depends on how fast or slowly you read:

- Some students read quickly and have time to make fairly detailed notes.
- Others read more slowly and have to keep their notes to a minimum.

Do you know what kind of reader you are and how fast you can go without losing all understanding? It pays to figure out what works well for you and practice it.

Note: The time allowance for each Reading section in the test means that you need to read long passages in two or three minutes, at most. But you *don't* get points for reading, just for answering questions correctly.

What's the bottom line? The better you are at Active Reading, the more time you'll have for point-gathering.

PASSAGE MAP PRACTICE

Write a passage map of this sample SAT passage using the guidelines we just provided.

What a marvelous and celestial creature was Leonardo da Vinci. As a scientist and engineer, his gifts were unparalleled. But his accomplishments in these capacities were hindered by the fact that he was, before all else, an artist. As one con-
(5) versant with the perfection of art, and knowing the futility of trying to bring such perfection to the realm of practical application, Leonardo tended toward variability and inconstancy in his endeavors. His practice of moving compulsively from one project to the next, never bringing any of them to
(10) completion, stood in the way of his making any truly useful technical advances.

When Leonardo was asked to create a memorial for one of his patrons, he designed a bronze horse of such vast proportions that it proved utterly impractical—even impossible—to
(15) produce. Some historians maintain that Leonardo never had any intention of finishing this work in the first place. But it is more likely that he simply became so intoxicated by his grand artistic conception that he lost sight of the fact that the monument actually had to be cast.
(20) Similarly, when Leonardo was commissioned to paint the *Last Supper*, he left the head of Christ unfinished, feeling incapable of investing it with a sufficiently divine demeanor. Yet, as a work of art rather than science or engineering, it is still worthy of our greatest veneration, for Leonardo succeed-
(25) ed brilliantly in capturing the acute anxiety of the Apostles at the most dramatic moment of the Passion narrative.

PERFECT SCORE TIP

"It's incredibly important to read actively. Whenever I broke my concentration, I couldn't remember anything and wasted time having to reread the passage."

EXPERT TUTOR TIP

" The author usually gives the reader the main idea of each paragraph in his topic sentences. Pay close attention to these when creating your passage map. "

Such mental restlessness, however, proved more problematic when applied to scientific matters. When he turned his mind to the natural world, Leonardo would
(30) begin by inquiring into the properties of herbs and end up observing the motions of the heavens. In his technical studies and scientific experiments, he would generate an endless stream of models and drawings, designing complex and unbuildable machines to raise great weights, bore
(35) through mountains, or even empty harbors.

It is this enormous intellectual fertility that has suggested to many that Leonardo can and should be regarded as one of the originators of modern science. But Leonardo was not himself a true scientist. "Science" is not the hun-
(40) dred-odd principles or *pensieri* that have been pulled out of his *Codici*. Science is comprehensive and methodical thought.

Granted, Leonardo always became fascinated by the intricacies of specific technical challenges. He possessed
(45) the artist's interest in detail, which explains his compulsion with observation and problem solving. But such things alone do not constitute science, which requires the working out of a systematic body of knowledge—something Leonardo displayed little interest in doing.

Before you turn the page to see how we marked up this passage, remember that there is no *one* way to mark up a passage. You should develop your own style within the guidelines we have set up.

Now take a look at our passage map notes on the next page. Did you highlight similar parts of the passage? Did you concentrate on the author's views? Look carefully at your markup. How would you summarize the author's main idea?

What a marvelous and celestial creature was Leonardo da Vinci. As a scientist and engineer, his gifts were unparalleled. But his accomplishments in these capacities were hindered by the fact that he was, before all else, an artist. As

(5) one conversant with the perfection of art, and knowing the futility of trying to bring such perfection to the realm of practical application, Leonardo tended toward variability and inconstancy in his endeavors. His practice of moving compulsively from one project to the next, never bringing

(10) any of them to completion, stood in the way of his making any truly useful technical advances.

When Leonardo was asked to create a memorial for one of his patrons, he designed a bronze horse of such vast proportions that it proved utterly impractical—even

(15) impossible—to produce. Some historians maintain that Leonardo never had any intention of finishing this work in the first place. But it is more likely that he simply became so intoxicated by his grand artistic conception that he lost sight of the fact that the monument actually had to be cast.

(20) Similarly, when Leonardo was commissioned to paint the *Last Supper*, he left the head of Christ unfinished, feeling incapable of investing it with a sufficiently divine demeanor. Yet, as a work of art rather than science or engineering, it is still worthy of our greatest veneration, for Leonardo

(25) succeeded brilliantly in capturing the acute anxiety of the Apostles at the most dramatic moment of the Passion narrative.

Such mental restlessness, however, proved more problematic when applied to scientific matters. When he turned

(30) his mind to the natural world, Leonardo would begin by inquiring into the properties of herbs and end up observing the motions of the heavens. In his technical studies and scientific experiments, he would generate an endless stream of models and drawings, designing complex and unbuild-

(35) able machines to raise great weights, bore through mountains, or even empty harbors.

It is this enormous intellectual fertility that has suggested to many that Leonardo can and should be regarded as one of the originators of modern science. But Leonardo

(40) was not himself a true scientist. "Science" is not the hundred-odd principles or *pensieri* that have been pulled out of his *Codici*. Science is comprehensive and methodical thought. Granted, Leonardo always became fascinated by the intricacies of specific technical challenges. He possessed

(45) the artist's interest in detail, which explains his compulsion with observation and problem solving. But such things

---

Margin annotations:

OP– L is great

MainPoint—L is genius, but never stuck w/1 thing long enuf 2B a "scientist"

OP – L underachieved

Ex #1 – horse

alt. opinion

OP – L is a genius but impractical

Ex #2 – last Sup

MainPoint L gets caught up in idea, forgets actual work

OP – switching from art to science here

Ex #1 – Natural

Ex #2 – technical

MainPoint: L's short attention span bad for science

alt. opinion

OP

back?

MainPoint—L is genius & compulsive problem-solver, but no scientist

---

PERFECT SCORE TIP

" Mapping really helped me get through some of the more difficult passages. Underlining key sentences and writing down the topic of each paragraph helped me understand what the passage was actually saying. "

KEY

Op = opinion
Ex = example
L = Leonardo

alone do not constitute science, which requires the working out of a
systematic body of knowledge—something Leonardo displayed little——— *L not good at*
interest in doing.

Now let's take a look at some sample questions based on the passage you just marked up. See how
your passage map may have helped you answer these two questions:

1. Which of the following does NOT describe how the author views Leonardo da Vinci?

    (A) He knew much about both art and science.

    (B) It was difficult for him to complete projects because he had such a short attention
         span.

    (C) His art designs were brilliant, but they were also often impractical to carry out.

    (D) He was compulsive when it came to problem solving.

    (E) He was a brilliant scientist who always lived up to technical challenges.

At first glance, this question might seem overwhelming. But you've saved yourself a lot of time by
mapping the passage. From the map that we've done for you, you know that (A) is not the answer
because the author spends half the passage talking about Leonardo's knowledge of art and the other
half describing his knowledge of science. (B) is also wrong; see the notes around lines 5 and 35.
They all point to Leonardo's short attention span. (C) is described in the horse memorial project,
around line 13. (D) is described in the notes around lines 25 and 45. That leaves (E). You can come
to the conclusion that (E) is the answer just by reading the notes in the passage map. The author
did not think Leonardo was *a true scientist* (line 40) and instead believed that his compulsiveness
stood in the way of his making any truly useful technical advances (lines 10–11).

2. The author cites "the natural world" (line 30) in order to

    (A) detail Leonardo's love of herbs

    (B) explain Leonardo's great contributions to science

    (C) describe Leonardo's inability to achieve what he'd set out to do in the first place

    (D) contrast Leonardo's accomplishments in art with his failures in science

    (E) support the author's argument that Leonardo should not have entered his scientific
         endeavors

Because you've drawn attention to *natural world* by circling it while doing the passage map, it
already sticks out. Now, remember to use Kaplan's strategy for Reading Comprehension questions.
Go back and reread the sentence *natural world* appears in. It seems the author is talking about
Leonardo's tendency to start out doing one thing and end up doing another thing. It's an example
of his short attention span, as noted by the passage map. And that's answer choice (C). Even

though the author mentions herbs, he never says that Leonardo loved herbs, ruling out (A). You know (B) is wrong because the author believes that Leonardo's short attention span was actually bad for science. And (D) and (E) are incorrect because the author never really talks about whether Leonardo should have dabbled in science.

PAIRED PASSAGES

The SAT will include at least one long paired passage and one short paired passage. Paired passages are two separate passages that relate to the same topic. Questions following paired passages are generally ordered the same way. The first few questions relate to the first passage, the next few to the second passage, and the final questions ask about the passages as a pair.

Don't let the paired passages intimidate you—they're not twice as hard as the single-passage reading selections. In fact, students often find the paired passages the most interesting selections on the test.

> **EXPERT TUTOR TIP**
>
> " A challenging part of paired passages is keeping straight *who* says *what*. Kaplan's method makes this much easier because you consider each passage individually. "

KAPLAN'S TARGET STRATEGY FOR PAIRED PASSAGES

Follow the Reading Comprehension strategies given and use the following systematic approach for paired passages:

- **Step 1:** Read Passage 1 and answer the questions about it.
- **Step 2:** Read Passage 2 and answer the questions about it.
- **Step 3:** Answer the questions asking about both passages.

Because you have to keep track of two different viewpoints with paired passages, it's especially important to read actively and create a map for each passage.

Ask yourself as you read the *first* passage:

- What is the author's main point?

When you read the *second* passage, ask yourself:

- How is this different from or similar to the first passage?

Let's take a look at a sample set of short paired passages and questions:

> **PERFECT SCORE TIP**
>
> " It definitely helped to do the questions that related to both passages last. After answering the other questions, I understood the purposes and themes of each really well. "

PAIRED PASSAGES PRACTICE QUESTIONS

Questions 1–4 refer to the following passages.

Passage 1

In 1984, great fanfare and optimism accompanied the funding of an ecosystem research project called "Biosphere 2." The project's mission was to create an airlock-sealed habitat that
(5) could support a human crew for several years without contact with or resources from the outside world. Less than a decade later, however, enthusiasm for the project had almost entirely eroded after serious questions were raised about
(10) adherence to that mission. Media scrutiny began with reports that the mission's managers had quietly supplied the crew with goods from the outside, and this scrutiny intensified when these same administrators denied having
(15) tampered with the project. As an unfortunate result, doubts regarding the integrity of all the scientific data generated by the project began to surface.

Passage 2

Consistently propped up by the press since
(20) its inception, Biosphere 2 came to be regarded during the late 1980s as an indicator of the possibility of human habitation in space. Even as many scientists worked to quench such lofty goals, the press was dubbing Biosphere 2 the
(25) most exciting scientific project undertaken since the moon landing. Then, as the project's first crew emerged from a supposed two-year isolation to be greeted by a swirl of negative attention and controversy, the publications that had
(30) trumpeted the project quickly reversed direction. Frustrated with their conception's failures, the project's financiers fired their management team and, in a reversal of their own, lashed out at the same press they had once courted.

1. The word "quietly" as it is used in line 12 most nearly means

   (A) gingerly
   (B) easily
   (C) meekly
   (D) secretly
   (E) carelessly

2. In the second sentence of Passage 2 (lines 22–26), the author implies that

   (A) the media's expectations for the project were probably unrealistic
   (B) many scientists thought that aeronautical projects should not have ambitious goals
   (C) some scientists found the Biosphere 2 project more exciting than the moon landing
   (D) the project's management team should have heeded the advice of scientists
   (E) few could have predicted how controversial the project would become

3. Both authors agree that the Biosphere 2 project

   (A) failed to produce any useful data
   (B) became more scientifically valuable over time
   (C) neglected to supply the crew properly
   (D) was comparable to the moon landing
   (E) resulted in disappointment

4. The two passages differ in their approaches to the topic of the Biosphere 2 project in that

   (A) Passage 1 emphasizes both the successes and failures of the project, while Passage 2 focuses primarily on the project's disappointments

   (B) Passage 1 indicates that the goal of the project was to create a self-sufficient habitat, while Passage 2 states that the project was only intended to explore space habitation

   (C) Passage 1 is supportive of the financiers, while Passage 2 is critical of the financiers' anger with the media

   (D) Passage 1 focuses on how excitement for the project declined, while Passage 2 focuses largely on the media's relationship to the project

   (E) Passage 1 concludes that the management team ruined the project, while Passage 2 indicates that the media caused its failure

Answers and Explanations

1. D

SMARTPOINTS CATEGORY: VOCABULARY-IN-CONTEXT

Because the cited line describes an act that caused people to question the project's adherence to its mission of self-sufficiency, you can infer that the managers would probably have tried to be secretive about any supplies they were providing to the crew. Look for a choice that reflects the undercover or illicit nature of the activity. Doing something (A), *gingerly*, means doing it in a cautious, tentative way. While this comes close to capturing the meaning of the cited word, it does not express the idea that the managers' actions were not intended to be seen or discovered. The context of the passage does not indicate how easy it was for the managers to supply the crew with outside goods, thus (B) is incorrect. While a quiet person might be meek or submissive, (C), *meekly*, does not fit the context. Though you might infer that the managers were careless because they got caught, (E) is not a meaning of the cited word. (D) nicely matches your prediction.

2. A

SMARTPOINTS CATEGORY: INFERENCE

The phrase *implies that* signals an Inference question. The sentence tells you that many scientists were trying to suppress or extinguish the *lofty goals* or overly high expectations for the project, suggesting that the scientists thought such goals were unrealistic. Since it was the press that was *dubbing* the project as so exciting, this indicates that the unrealistic expectations were put forth or perpetuated by the media, choice (A). (B) is out of scope; the passage only discusses the Biosphere 2 project, not projects dealing with aircraft or flight. (C) is a distortion; the passage only suggests that the *press* believed the project was *as* exciting as the moon landing, not that scientists found it more exciting. The author makes no recommendations regarding what the management team should or should not have done, (D), and the passage does not mention whether the management team consulted scientists. While (E) may be accurate given all the hype about the project, the cited sentence does not support this statement.

3. E

SMARTPOINTS CATEGORIES: GLOBAL
COMPARISONS

When tackling Comparison questions, think only of one passage at a time. Choose whichever passage you understand best and scan the answers with that one in mind. You should be able to eliminate one to four answers this way. Then analyze the remaining answer(s) thinking only of the other passage. Generally, Passage 1 states that it began with *great fanfare and optimism* that later became *almost entirely eroded*, and Passage 2 notes that the project was initially seen as *exciting* but eventually caused frustration. Both passages, then, discuss how high expectations were let down. (A) is too extreme; both passages suggest that the project failed to achieve its main goal, but they do not rule out the possibility that some useful data was produced. (B) is out of scope; neither passage explores changes over time in the scientific value of the project. (C) misinterprets a statement in Passage 1 about managers sneaking outside supplies to the crew. (D) is also out of scope; Passage 1 does not mention the moon landing. (E) is the best answer choice.

4. D

SMARTPOINTS CATEGORIES: GLOBAL
COMPARISONS

As with all Comparison questions, think of only one passage at a time. The pattern of the answers is Passage 1 says . . ., while Passage 2 says . . . . Go down the answers with either passage in mind, eliminating as you can; then repeat with the other one in mind.

Passage 1 focuses on how and why enthusiasm for the project declined, while Passage 2 focuses on the media's role in portraying the project. You are looking for a choice that captures this difference. (A) is out of scope; neither passage emphasizes successes of the project. (B) is a distortion; Passage 2 does not state that exploring space habitation was the project's only goal. (C) is also a distortion; Passage 1 does not express an opinion of the financiers, and Passage 2 describes but does not evaluate the financiers' anger with the media. (E) is too extreme; both characterizations are too strong given the rather objective tone of the passages. Thus, (D) is the best answer.

TIMING STRATEGIES FOR THE CRITICAL READING SECTION

What's the best way to use your time in the Critical Reading sections?

Leave as much time as possible for reading and answering the long passage questions. These take more time than either the short reading or the Sentence Completions.

Here is a possible plan for a 25-minute section:

- Spend only two or three minutes on the Sentence Completions.

- Save a minute or two at the end to come back to the harder Sentence Completion questions.

- Short passages should take no more than five minutes, less if possible.

- Two long passages (paired or not) usually follow; you'll want *at least* 15 minutes for reading and answering the questions, more if possible.

Note: The shorter 20-minute section has 19 questions and often has no short passages, so you'll be able to adapt the above timing strategy to fit.

Also, remember to skip around within the section if you need to. You can tackle the passages in any order you like within the same section. So if you can see from the introductions that one passage will be much easier for you than the others, work through that one first. But don't skip around after you've already read most or all of a passage. You've already invested your time reading, so try all the questions that go with it before you move to another text.

PRACTICE

Test your reading skills on the following sample long passage, keeping our tips in mind. Remember to read actively and construct a passage map. Then use the Kaplan's Target Strategy to answer the questions that follow. Answers and explanations start on page 303.

Questions 1–8 refer to the following passage.

In this essay, the author writes about her childhood on a Caribbean island that was an English colony for many years.

When I saw England for the first time, I was
a child in school sitting at a desk. The England
I was looking at was laid out on a map gently,
beautifully, delicately, a very special jewel; it lay
(5) on a bed of sky blue, its yellow form mysterious,
because though it looked like a leg of mutton*,
it could not really look like anything so familiar as a leg of mutton because it was England.
England was a special jewel all right, and only
(10) special people got to wear it. The people who
got to wear England were English people. They
wore it well and they wore it everywhere: in jun-
gles, in deserts, on plains, in places where they
were not welcome, in places they should not
(15) have been. When my teacher had pinned this
map up on the blackboard, she said, "This is
England"—and she said it with authority, seriousness, and adoration, and we all sat up. We
understood then—we were meant to under-
(20) stand then—that England was to be our
source of myth and the source from which we
got our sense of reality, our sense of what was
meaningful, our sense of what was meaningless—
and much about our own lives and much
(25) about the very idea of us headed that last list.
At the time I was a child sitting at my desk
seeing England for the first time, I was already
very familiar with the greatness of it. Each
morning before I left for school, I ate a break-
(30) fast of half a grapefruit, a bowl of oat porridge,
bread and butter and a slice of cheese, and
a cup of cocoa. The can of cocoa was often
left on the table in front of me. It had written
on it the name of the company, the year the
(35) company was established, and the words "Made
in England." Those words, "Made in England,"

were written on the box the oats came in too.
The shoes I wore were made in England; so
were my socks and cotton undergarments and
(40) the satin ribbons I wore tied at the end of two
plaits of my hair. My father, who might have
sat next to me at breakfast, was a carpenter
and cabinet maker. The shoes he wore to work
would have been made in England, as were
(45) his khaki shirt and trousers, his underpants
and undershirt, his socks and brown felt hat.
Felt was not the proper material from which
a hat that was expected to provide shade from
the hot sun should be made, but my father
(50) must have seen and admired a picture of an
Englishman wearing such a hat in England. As
we sat at breakfast a car might go by. The car,
a Hillman or a Zephyr, was made in England.
The very conception of the meal itself, breakfast,
(55) and its substantial quality and quantity was an
idea from England; we somehow knew that
in England they began the day with this meal
called breakfast and a proper breakfast was a big
breakfast.
(60) At the time I saw this map—seeing England
for the first time—I did not say to myself, "Ah,
so that's what it looks like," because there was
no longing in me to put a shape to those three
words that ran through every part of my life,
(65) no matter how small; for me to have had such a
longing would have meant that I lived in a certain atmosphere, an atmosphere in which those
three words were felt as a burden. But I did not
live in such an atmosphere. My father's brown
(70) felt hat would develop a hole in its crown, the
lining would separate from the hat itself, and six
weeks before he thought that he could not be
seen wearing it—he was a very vain man—he
would order another hat from England. And
(75) my mother taught me to eat my food in the
English way: the knife in the right hand, the fork
in the left, my elbows held still close to my side.

When I had finally mastered it, I overheard her
saying to a friend, "Did you see how nicely she
(80) can eat?" But I knew then that I enjoyed my
food more when I ate it with my bare hands,
and I continued to do so when she wasn't looking. And when my teacher showed us the map,
she asked us to study it carefully, because no test
(85) we would ever take would be complete without
this statement: "Draw a map of England."

I did not know then that the statement "Draw
a map of England" was something far worse than
a declaration of war. I did not know then that
(90) this statement was part of a process that would
result in my erasure, not my physical erasure,
but my erasure all the same. I did not know
then that this statement was meant to make
me feel in awe and small whenever I heard
(95) the word "England": awe at its existence, small
because I was not from it. I did not know very
much of anything then—certainly not what a
blessing it was that I was unable to draw a map
of England correctly.

mutton: the flesh of a sheep

1. According to the author, England could not
really look "like a leg of mutton" (line 6)
because

   (A) maps generally don't give an accurate
   impression of what a place looks like

   (B) England was too grand and exotic a
   place for such a mundane image

   (C) England was an island not very different
   in appearance from her own island

   (D) the usual metaphor used to describe
   England was a precious jewel

   (E) mutton was one of the few foods
   familiar to her that did not come from
   England

2. The author's reference to felt as "not the proper
material" (line 47) for her father's hat chiefly
serves to emphasize her point about the

   (A) extremity of the local weather

   (B) arrogance of island laborers

   (C) informality of dress on the island

   (D) weakness of local industries

   (E) predominance of English culture

3. The word "conception" as used in line 54
means

   (A) beginning

   (B) image

   (C) origination

   (D) notion

   (E) plan

4. The word "substantial" in line 55 means

   (A) important

   (B) abundant

   (C) firm

   (D) down-to-earth

   (E) materialistic

5. The author implies that a longing to "put a
shape to those three words" (lines 63–64)
would have indicated

   (A) a resentment of England's predominance

   (B) an unhealthy desire to become English

   (C) an inability to understand England's
   authority

   (D) an excessive curiosity about England

   (E) an unfamiliarity with English customs

6. The author cites the anecdotes about her father and mother in lines 69–80 primarily to convey their

   (A) love for their children
   (B) belief in strict discipline
   (C) distaste for anything foreign
   (D) reverence for England
   (E) overemphasis on formal manners

7. For the author, the requirement to "Draw a map of England" (lines 86–89) represented an attempt to

   (A) force students to put their studies to practical use
   (B) glorify one culture at the expense of another
   (C) promote an understanding of world affairs
   (D) encourage students to value their own heritage
   (E) impart outmoded and inappropriate knowledge

8. The word "erasure" (line 92) as used by the author most nearly means

   (A) total annihilation
   (B) physical disappearance
   (C) sense of insignificance
   (D) enforced censorship
   (E) loss of freedom

Questions 9–15 refer to the following passage.

The following passage is adapted from a biology textbook.

Blood, a connective tissue, is a sticky fluid that has multiple functions. It transports oxygen, nutrients, and other solutes to cells; carries away metabolic wastes and secretions; and
(5) helps stabilize internal pH. Plasma, red blood cells, white blood cells, and platelets are its components.

Plasma, which is mostly water, functions as a transport medium for blood cells and
(10) platelets. It also serves as a solvent for ions and molecules, including hundreds of different kinds of plasma proteins. Some of the plasma proteins transport lipids and fat-soluble vitamins through the body. Others have roles in
(15) blood clotting or in defense against pathogens. Collectively, the concentration of plasma proteins affects the blood's fluid volume, for it influences the movement of water between blood and interstitial fluid.
(20) Erythrocytes, or red blood cells, are biconcave disks, like doughnuts with a squashed-in center instead of a hole. They transport the oxygen used in aerobic respiration and carry away some carbon dioxide wastes. When oxygen
(25) diffuses into blood, it binds with hemoglobin, the iron-containing pigment that gives red blood cells their color.

Mature red blood cells no longer have their nucleus, nor do they require it. They have
(30) enough hemoglobin, enzymes, and other proteins to function for about 120 days. At any time, phagocytes are engulfing the oldest red blood cells or the ones already dead, but ongoing replacements keep the cell count fairly stable.
(35) Leukocytes, or white blood cells, arise from stem cells in bone marrow. They function in daily housekeeping and defense. Many patrol tissues, where they target or engulf damaged or dead cells and anything chemically recognized
(40) as foreign to the body. Many others are massed together in the lymph nodes and spleen. There

they divide to produce armies of cells that battle specific viruses, bacteria, and other invaders.

White blood cells differ in size, nuclear
(45) shape, and staining traits. There are five categories: neutrophils, eosinophils, basophils, monocytes, and lymphocytes. The neutrophils and monocytes are search-and-destroy cells. The monocytes follow chemical trails to
(50) inflamed tissues where they develop into macrophages that can engulf invaders and debris. Two classes of lymphocytes, B cells and T cells, make highly specific defense responses.

Some stem cells in bone marrow give rise
(55) to giant cells called megakaryocytes. These shed fragments of cytoplasm enclosed in a bit of plasma membrane. The membrane-bound fragments are platelets, which initiate blood clotting. Each platelet only lasts five to nine
(60) days, but hundreds of thousands are always circulating in blood.

9. The passage is primarily concerned with

   (A) blood function
   (B) plasma and platelets
   (C) blood components
   (D) blood
   (E) the circulatory system

10. According to the passage, plasma is

    (A) a biconcave disk
    (B) composed of ions and molecules
    (C) interstitial fluid
    (D) mostly water
    (E) hemoglobin

11. In lines 20–27, the author does all of the following EXCEPT

    (A) describe a biological process
    (B) use a comparison to illustrate a point
    (C) describe the average lifespan of a cell
    (D) refer to color to make the information more accessible
    (E) explain a technical term in more familiar language

12. According to the passage, what gives blood its red color?

    (A) hemoglobin
    (B) oxygen
    (C) iron
    (D) the nucleus
    (E) hemoglobin, enzymes, and other proteins

13. The author's use of the words "defense" and "patrol" (line 37) and "armies" and "battle" (line 42) implies that

    (A) white blood cells serve as protection against invaders
    (B) white blood cells differ in size, shape, and traits
    (C) white blood cells are violent
    (D) B and T cells are highly specific
    (E) phagocytes attack old red blood cells

14. In line 50, "inflamed" most nearly means

    (A) on fire
    (B) under attack
    (C) engulfed
    (D) irritated
    (E) healthy

15. As described in the passage, megakaryocytes are

    (A) components of plasma
    (B) large cells that shed cytoplasm
    (C) types of neutrophils
    (D) cells that initiate blood clotting
    (E) platelets that last five to nine days

Questions 16–22 refer to the following passage.

This passage is adapted from an essay on twentieth-century American culture.

A renaissance is a rebirth. The Harlem Renaissance of the 1920s was a time when African-American art and literature flourished. Blacks migrating from the South brought with
(5) them a key element to the thriving Harlem area: jazz. The rhythms of this music set the stage for a new kind of literature and a new kind of art. But the vitality was not only exhibited in the fine arts; it was also present
(10) in the politics of the era. Inevitably, it changed African-Americans and America through the power of its legacy.

Inspired by the freedom that jazz construction provided, poet Langston Hughes began
(15) writing riffs that contained the elements of jazz and blues but maintained the structure of poetry. However, it was the language in his writing that was truly revolutionary. Instead of the highly stylized, theatrical black voice used
(20) at the time, Hughes wrote in the everyday language he heard around him. It was the language of musicians, workers, and servants, and it became a poetic revolution.

Likewise, African-American art was revitalized.
(25) The works of Aaron Douglas could be seen throughout New York City. He was a prolific muralist and graphic illustrator. His subjects were rendered in the art deco style that was popular at the time. His murals depicted jazz
(30) musicians and singers posing heroically above the cityscape. No major literary work from the Harlem Renaissance was published without his design gracing its cover. Other notable artists, like Archibald Motley Jr. and Malvin Gray Johnson,
(35) gave African-American subjects dignity and grace that were considered radical in the America of 1920.

At the same time, African-American scholars, like W.E.B. Du Bois, urging racial pride,
(40) were publishing magazines. Activist Marcus Garvey campaigned against the coloniza-

tion of Africa and started an organization called the Universal Negro Improvement Association to further the goal of racial pride.
(45) This was a reformation; an intellectual rebellion shouting out that the black voice in America would be heard.

And heard it was, not just in America but around the world. Paris, considered the cul-
(50) tural capital of the world, was quick to assimilate the sounds, textures and words that were coming out of Harlem. The sound of Duke Ellington and the songs of Bessie Smith swung from the Cotton Club in Harlem to the night-
(55) clubs of Paris. The world was taking notice of the artists, activists, and writers of Harlem. This meant that the world was also taking note of black Americans, their struggles and their achievements.

(60) 1920s Harlem, with its intellectuals and artists, its activists and musicians, inspired generations. Its influence can be seen in the novels of Toni Morrison, the music of Wynton Marsalis, the films of Spike Lee and, perhaps most impor-
(65) tantly, the politics of Malcolm X and Martin Luther King, Jr. Inspired by the art and politics of the time, African-Americans redefined themselves and the world had to take notice.

16. Why were the intellectuals and artists of 1920s Harlem considered to be part of a renaissance?

(A) They studied the revival of art and learning from the 14th, 15th, and 16th centuries in Europe.

(B) They underwent a religious transformation.

(C) Their work is the basis of all African-American art and politics today.

(D) Their works are still considered masterpieces today.

(E) Their collective works of art and thought were instrumental in changing the perception of African-Americans.

17. What impact did the migration of blacks from the South have on the Harlem Renaissance?

   (A) More black people in New York City allowed Harlem to flourish.

   (B) Southern thought and art were superior to that found in the north.

   (C) African-Americans from the South brought their musical sensibilities, which influenced the writings, art, and thought of the 1920s.

   (D) Southern African-Americans were not interested in music so more time could be spent on writing, painting, and politics.

   (E) Duke Ellington played in Paris, thus allowing African-American music to gain acceptance.

18. Which of the following best describes the difference between the language of Langston Hughes and the "highly stylized, theatrical black voice" (line 19) that was common at the time?

   (A) Hughes avoided the Shakespearean English that was preferred by his contemporaries.

   (B) Hughes wrote in the language of ordinary people instead of the artificial voice used by other poets.

   (C) While Southern dialects were an important influence on Hughes, other poets used primarily Northern dialects.

   (D) Hughes employed several literary devices that had been rejected by other poets of his time.

   (E) Hughes embraced a more affected style than the one preferred by other writers of his time.

19. The primary purpose of the passage is to

   (A) describe the origins and influence of a particular group of artists

   (B) refute a myth about a political figure

   (C) criticize the viewpoint of a prominent theorist

   (D) trace the history of a controversial topic

   (E) illustrate the unbreakable link between art and politics

20. In lines 35–36, the author uses the phrase "dignity and grace" to suggest that

   (A) previous depictions of African-American subjects were largely based on stereotypical biases present at the turn of the century

   (B) all African-American artwork prior to the Harlem Renaissance was unflattering

   (C) African-American artists were working with inferior supplies and were unable to create artwork that reflected their subjects in a respectful manner

   (D) Art Deco, by virtue of the stylistic approach, lent an air of nobility and culture to the subject matter

   (E) the artistic atmosphere created by the Harlem Renaissance resulted in a more dignified and tasteful depiction of African-Americans

21. As used in line 45, "reformation" most nearly means

   (A) the act of reshaping an object

   (B) an act of civil disobedience to further a cause

   (C) a decision made by a group of people to investigate a community need

   (D) a vote taken directly to the people to decide an issue

   (E) a transformation that corrects and improves a current condition

22. In lines 52–53, the author refers to "the sound of Duke Ellington and the songs of Bessie Smith" in order to

   (A) show that audiences in Harlem were more receptive than those in Paris to the music inspired by the Harlem Renaissance

   (B) indicate that Duke Ellington and Bessie Smith were the most well-known musicians of their time

   (C) identify some of the music that was likely to have influenced Malcolm X and Martin Luther King, Jr.

   (D) illustrate that the music inspired by the Harlem Renaissance was known outside of the United States

   (E) argue that the musical styles of Duke Ellington and Bessie Smith had much in common

Questions 23–29 refer to the following passage.

The following passage is about a form of expression called conceptual art.

Conceptual "art" is a relatively recent artistic movement that began in the 1960s. After abstract impressionism and minimalism, artists were left at a dead end as far as finding new
(5) inroads into abstraction; there was nowhere left to go with traditional artistic media. Those who wished to further pursue abstraction to its absurd end became conceptual artists.
Conceptual artists were heavily influenced by
(10) the French dadaist/surrealist artist Marcel Duchamp, who maintained that the most important part of a work of art is its idea, rather than its physical expression. A 1970s bumper sticker capitalized on this idea and made fun
(15) of it: "If you like conceptual art, think about honking."
Conceptual art, for the most part, completely left behind a physical representation and relied only on the concept of the work that might (or
(20) might not) result. For example, Sol LeWitt created a *Wall Drawing* series that was composed only of a set of instructions for creating the drawings—that is to say, a blueprint for the eventual work. No physical representation of the
(25) ideas ever resulted. On a slightly different track, the contemporary conceptual artist Adib Fricke deals with language; his company The Word Company produces and distributes "words that do not yet exist" (*protonyms*). Similarly, per-
(30) formance art was a natural outgrowth of the idea of conceptual art, and visual one-time events became popular in the 1960s. They were often documented by pictures or narrative statements, but the actual work could not be preserved;
(35) only its idea could be.
This type of "art" stretches the limits of credibility; the bumper sticker referenced previously shows the slanted light in which many view conceptual art. Abstract art blurs the
(40) boundaries between "art" and "not art" nearly

to unrecognizability, but conceptual art obliterates this distinction completely. It is thus a way to avoid having to undertake the effort and exhibit the skill necessary to produce a lasting
(45) physical work of art. The author Leo Tolstoy created intricate plot outlines on the walls of the room in which he wrote. If he had left only the outlines and had never made them into books, would he still receive the same acclaim he now
(50) receives for works such as *War and Peace*?

23. The author puts the word "art" in quotation marks in order to

(A) show that he plans to define the term "art"

(B) suggest that he doesn't believe conceptual art is truly art

(C) indicate that the meaning of the word "art" changed in the 1960s

(D) convey his high opinion of conceptual art

(E) persuade the reader that art is important

24. In line 11, the word "maintained" most nearly means

(A) repaired

(B) asserted

(C) kept up

(D) argued

(E) disputed

25. An appropriate title for this passage might be

(A) "Conceptual Art: An Important Advance"

(B) "Marcel Duchamp: Life and Times"

(C) "Bumper Stickers and Art"

(D) "Conceptual Art: A Negative Opinion"

(E) "All Art Is Absurd"

26. According to the author, a *protonym* is

(A) a word that does not yet exist

(B) a subatomic particle

(C) one of a pair of words that sound alike

(D) a prototypical sound

(E) a type of visual art

27. According to the passage, all of the following statements are true EXCEPT

(A) Adib Fricke uses language as a medium for conceptual art

(B) Leo Tolstoy's outlines are an example of conceptual art

(C) a work of conceptual art can exist with no physical representation

(D) the author believes that the creation of conceptual art does not require discipline and dedication

(E) conceptual art is an extension of abstract art

28. The author of this passage would probably view a work of art that consisted only of a description of how to create a sculpture (rather than of an actual sculpture) with

(A) sadness

(B) architectural curiosity

(C) anger

(D) joy

(E) disdain

29. This passage mainly serves to

(A) provide a history of conceptual art

(B) describe Leo Tolstoy's literary methods

(C) convince the reader that conceptual art is of little value

(D) introduce the work of Adib Fricke

(E) compare and contrast conceptual and abstract art

Questions 30–42 are based on the following passages.

The following adaptations from recent scholarly articles offer different perspectives on the harsh conditions faced by nineteenth century female factory workers in the urban centers of the United States. Both passages reflect the oppressive working environment created by the Waltham-Lowell system of organization in textile factories.

Passage 1

The Waltham-Lowell system, a business philoso-phy and manufacturing strategy, was named for its creator and the Massachusetts town in which it was first implemented in 1815. As a manu-
(5) facturing system, it combined the various stages of the textile manufacturing process under one roof, while as a business system, it detailed a set of comprehensive rules and regulations for work-ers. To implement the Waltham-Lowell system,
(10) factory owners preferred to employ female work-ers—often called factory girls—because women would work for lower wages and were then con-sidered easier to control than men.

Many of the system's regulations, including a
(15) requirement that the women live in company-owned boarding houses, had been created prima-rily to assure families that their daughters would not be corrupted by factory life. Ironically, how-ever, many of the women employed were actually
(20) forced to leave their families' homes, even when those families lived within easy commuting dis-tance of the factories, and even when the women were married. Needless to say, living away from home and among strangers was a stressful and
(25) disorienting experience for many.

The extremely poor living conditions of the boarding houses created further problems. Most factory houses were overcrowded, dirty, and infested with vermin. These conditions, combined
(30) with shared beds and poor ventilation, allowed diseases to spread and caused health problems for many of the workers. However, it's important for modern researchers to note that American facto-ries were not alone in maintaining boarding
(35) houses for workers. In fact, conditions in company-run American boarding houses were actually uniformly superior to those in Europe, where conditions were even more cramped and the ethics of the owners more base.

(40) While these living conditions were regret-table, some economists have advanced that the managers of the textile factories had little choice. The American textile market of the last century was extremely competitive, since the supply of
(45) textiles created by the nation's numerous domes-tic factories far exceeded consumer demand. Furthermore, foreign competitors, including English and Indian factories, began selling excess textile products in America at the beginning of the
(50) 1800s. Compounding the problem, foreign textile factories could often afford to sell their products in the American market for less than domestic manufacturers, because foreign factories set their wages far below what Americans found tolerable.
(55) American factories were thus constantly facing the risk of bankruptcy, and many managers felt that taking measures to preserve the health, comfort, and safety of their factory workers would have been financial suicide.

Passage 2

(60) Widely utilized in the mid-nineteenth century, the Waltham-Lowell system encompassed a set of atrocious working rules that created a dismal environment for workers in textile factories. Many factory practices had ill effects on the health
(65) of workers, the majority of whom were young women. Loud machines running all day long in a small space affected the hearing of the workers, while poor ventilation filled the air with cotton lint and toxins from the whale-oil lamps used to
(70) light the factories.

Problems were not limited to purely environ-mental factors. Workers also lived in constant fear of the factories' agents—supervisors who would punish them severely for any time spent not
(75) working. In fact, agents could fire workers almost at whim because of the seemingly endless supply of labor willing to replace the young women on the factory floor. The workers were usually not permitted to speak while operating the machines
(80) because the agents feared that talking would distract the women from their work and slow production. Not surprisingly, breaks were also infrequent, or absent altogether—even bathroom breaks were strongly discouraged. Ironically given these condi-
(85) tions, workers were expected to be neatly dressed in clean clothes at all times in case someone of

note came to visit the mill. As a result, much of
what little free time the young women had was
spent washing or mending clothes.

(90)   Some aspects of the Waltham-Lowell system
were not only degrading but downright dangerous. The factory management's obsession with
keeping workers at their tasks extended to keeping
all factory doors locked during working hours.

(95) As a result, emergency evacuations were difficult
or impossible. In 1911, a fire broke out in New
York City's Triangle Shirtwaist Factory, and many
workers died. Though one might hope that such a
tragedy would have finally brought about changes,

(100) the factory owners were actually acquitted of
criminal charges, and required to pay damages
of only seventy-five dollars to each of 23 victims'
families that sued. Sadly, the practice of locking
factory doors remained common for several years.

(105)   Though some charge that the Waltham-Lowell
system was a result of economic necessity, we
must realize that the factory managers who implemented this system made deliberate decisions to
increase profits at the expense of their workers,

(110) and that these workers—even those who fell ill or
died—were treated by factory managers as objects
to be replaced. Owners should instead have
replaced the reprehensible Waltham-Lowell system with another: that of common decency, to be

(115) respected above the baser "ideals" of nineteenth-
century capitalism.

30. The attitude of the author of Passage 1 toward
the factory workers who endured harsh
conditions is best described as

(A) reserved sympathy

(B) complete disinterest

(C) ironic contempt

(D) spirited befuddlement

(E) unreserved appreciation

31. The word "base" as used in line 39 most nearly
means

(A) elevated

(B) immoral

(C) absent

(D) harmful

(E) foundational

32. According to Passage 1, the primary reason
that factories required factory workers to live
in boarding houses was to

(A) placate the fears of the workers' families

(B) ensure that the girls were not corrupted
by city life

(C) prevent disease among factory girls

(D) restrict the social activities of female factory workers

(E) separate girls from their families

33. "Advanced" as used in line 41 most closely
means

(A) proceeded

(B) argued

(C) denied

(D) progressed

(E) concealed

34. Which of the following, if true, would most weaken the assertion in Passage 1 about the necessity of subjecting factory girls to unsafe conditions?

    (A) Textile factories in France were financially successful even though they refused to make factory girls endure harsh conditions.

    (B) The Waltham-Lowell system actually produced a smaller increase in profit than did the competing Bennington system.

    (C) The estimated costs of increasing worker safety and health in the nineteenth century to acceptable levels would have been more than the total profits of factories in that era.

    (D) Many twentieth-century factories treated factory workers with care and dignity and still had higher profits than nineteenth-century factories.

    (E) An early nineteenth-century workers' rights activist approached all American and foreign factories with a plan to improve working conditions while maintaining profits, but this plan was rejected by all factories.

35. In lines 71–89 of Passage 2, the description of the conditions imposed by factory agents serves to

    (A) argue that American factory conditions were superior to those in Europe

    (B) illustrate the role of factory agents in creating the poor working conditions discussed

    (C) argue that such conditions were immoral by modern standards

    (D) explain why factory agents were responsible for the 1911 fire

    (E) illustrate the economic necessity of the harsh conditions

36. In the context of Passage 2, the reference to the Triangle Shirtwaist Factory fire in lines 96–104 serves to

    (A) illustrate the prevalence of fires in factories that used the Waltham-Lowell system

    (B) elicit unwarranted sympathy for the victims of a tragic factory accident

    (C) demonstrate the dangerous conditions created by the uncaring attitude of factory owners toward their workers

    (D) exemplify the extent to which factories tried to protect the safety of female workers

    (E) illustrate the negligent behavior common among factory workers in New York City

37. According to Passage 2, the "tragedy" mentioned in line 99

    (A) claimed 23 victims

    (B) led to imprisonment for those responsible

    (C) remained common for several years

    (D) resulted from the whale-oil lamps used to light the factories

    (E) failed to bring about immediate reform in working conditions

38. Which of the following most accurately describes the organization of the final paragraph of Passage 2?

    (A) Evidence is questioned but ultimately accepted, leading to the main conclusion.

    (B) An assertion is made and then supported with statistical evidence.

    (C) A view is mentioned, then argued against.

    (D) A widely held view is dismissed, and a new view is defended with historical evidence.

    (E) Past circumstances are described in both moral and economic terms, resulting in a contradiction.

39. The passages differ in their evaluations of factory owners in that Passage 1 claims that

   (A) market conditions partially excuse the poor work environment created by factory owners

   (B) factory owners compensated society for their reprehensible actions in the factory through philanthropic work

   (C) the use of the Waltham-Lowell system enabled American factories to compete with European and Indian factories

   (D) factory regulations caused many health problems for workers

   (E) the Waltham-Lowell system was superior to previous factory organization schemes

40. Which of the following is an aspect of the Waltham-Lowell System emphasized in Passage 2, but not in Passage 1?

   (A) The difficult conditions in factory boarding houses

   (B) The role of agents in factory life

   (C) Health hazards faced by factory girls

   (D) The demands of the families of factory girls

   (E) The role of safety supervisors on the factory floor

41. Both passages mention which of the following aspects of nineteenth-century factory life?

   (A) The extensive demands of factory agents

   (B) The health problems caused by factory life under the Waltham-Lowell system

   (C) The demand that workers dress neatly

   (D) The superiority of working conditions in factories outside of New York State

   (E) The generosity of factory owners toward workers

42. The author of Passage 1 would most likely agree with which of the following statements about the "economic necessity" (line 106) cited by the author of Passage 2?

   (A) Such necessity cannot excuse the inhumane treatment of factory workers.

   (B) The results of the necessity were likely more drastic in the United States than overseas.

   (C) This economic necessity resulted from the pressures created by the demands of the families of factory workers.

   (D) The necessity forced unfortunate compromises that could not easily be avoided.

   (E) These conditions were solely a result of pressure from European and Indian competitors.

ANSWERS AND EXPLANATIONS

1. B

SMARTPOINTS CATEGORY: DETAIL .ıll

Here's how you might use your passage map and Kaplan's Target Strategy to answer question 1:

STEP 1: READ THE QUESTION STEM

The word *because* shows that this is a Detail question. There's no mystery about what the question is asking: Why couldn't England really look like a leg of mutton? (Notice that *mutton* is defined at the end of the passage—you aren't expected to know the meaning of unfamiliar terms.)

STEP 2: LOCATE THE MATERIAL YOU NEED

Here's where active reading and your passage map come into play. In the margin by the first paragraph, you might have written "England = impt." You might also have bracketed *England was to be our source of myth and the source from which we got our sense of reality*. All that information around the cited lines helps you make a prediction.

STEP 3: PREDICT THE ANSWER

A good prediction might be, "England was too special to look like a familiar leg of mutton."

STEP 4: SELECT THE BEST ANSWER CHOICE

Choice (B) comes close to the ideal—it might have jumped out. But if you weren't sure, you could have quickly eliminated the other choices. Thinking of the main idea would have helped you eliminate (A) and (C)—ideas that are not discussed in the passage. England was precious—like a jewel—but the author doesn't imply that England was usually compared to a *jewel*, (D), and you never learn where mutton *comes from*, (E). Choice (B) is the only one that works here. By reading the material surrounding the line reference and putting an answer into your own words, you should have been able to choose (B) with confidence.

2. E

SMARTPOINTS CATEGORY: FUNCTION .ıll

The phrase *serves to* indicates a Function question. Reading around lines 43–46 tells you that the things her father wore could have been made in England and that her father must have admired a picture of an Englishman wearing a felt hat (lines 50–51). This supports choice (E). Choices (B) and (C) might be tempting (if you had not done the research). The same is true for choice (A), which references the weather. (D) is off the point of the passage.

3. D

SMARTPOINTS CATEGORY: VOCABULARY-IN-CONTEXT

Use context clues to predict. *The very _____ of the meal itself . . . was an idea from England.* Here, a word from the context, *idea*, serves as a great prediction. (D), *notion*, is a good match. None of the other choices fit the context.

4. B

SMARTPOINTS CATEGORY: VOCABULARY-IN-CONTEXT

This Vocabulary-in-Context question is unusual in that an earlier part of the passage, rather than the sentence where the word appears, helps you to predict. We know that whatever *substantial* means, it describes the breakfast. Look back to where the breakfast is described in lines 30–32: *half a grapefruit, a bowl of oat porridge, bread and butter and a slice of cheese, and a cup of cocoa.* In other words, there was "a lot of" food in this breakfast. This prediction is a good match for (B), *abundant*.

5. B

SMARTPOINTS CATEGORY: INFERENCE

The word *implies* tells you this is an Inference question. You are only told to look in paragraph 3, so you'll need to rely on a margin note that the narrator had negative thoughts about England (*au = neg about being Eng*) and bracketed or circled words *there was no longing in me, I did not live in such an atmosphere,* and *I enjoyed my food more when I ate with my bare hands.* These all indicate you are looking for a negative attitude toward England. While (A), (C), (D), and (E) all have some negative meaning, only (B) captures the author's attitude toward *Made in England* that she first discusses in paragraph 2.

6. D

SMARTPOINTS CATEGORY: FUNCTION

Throughout the passage, the author is commenting on her parents' love for England and its traditions. The anecdotes refer to their behavior relating to English custom, so the author is conveying her parents' (D), *reverence* for *England*.

7. B

SMARTPOINTS CATEGORY: INFERENCE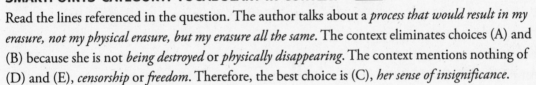

Read the last paragraph to predict. The author suggests that she (later) concluded that the teacher's direction to *draw a map of England* was *far worse than a declaration of war.* She elaborates on this, saying that being told to draw the map *was part of a process that would result in my erasure* and would make her *feel in awe and small.* While it can be tough to make an exact prediction, keeping these lines in mind will help you eliminate incorrect answers. (B) is the only choice that's consistent with the last paragraph. (A), (C), and (E) are out of scope, and (D) is an opposite.

8. C

SMARTPOINTS CATEGORY: VOCABULARY-IN-CONTEXT

Read the lines referenced in the question. The author talks about a *process that would result in my erasure, not my physical erasure, but my erasure all the same.* The context eliminates choices (A) and (B) because she is not *being destroyed* or *physically disappearing.* The context mentions nothing of (D) and (E), *censorship* or *freedom.* Therefore, the best choice is (C), *her sense of insignificance.*

9. C

SMARTPOINTS CATEGORY: GLOBAL

Carefully read the opening paragraph and notice that the topic becomes more detailed as the paragraph progresses. The topics mentioned are blood, blood attributes, blood function, and blood components. (A) is a misused detail; although the *function* of blood is discussed, the passage focuses on the components of blood and the attributes of those components. (C), although similar, is a better answer. (B), *plasma and platelets,* are discussed, but they are not the main concern of the entire passage. (D) and (E) are both out of scope. The passage is concerned with (D), *blood,* but focuses on a more detailed topic, and although blood is a component of (E), *the circulatory system,* this is never mentioned in the passage. (C) is the best choice.

10. D

SMARTPOINTS CATEGORY: DETAIL

Line 8 states that plasma is *mostly water.* (A) is a misused detail; red blood cells, not plasma, are biconcave disks. (B) is a distortion; plasma serves as a solvent for ions and molecules, but the passage does not state that it is composed of them. (C) and (E) are both too extreme; plasma interacts with the movement of water between blood and (C), *interstitial fluid,* but is not itself *interstitial fluid.* Likewise, the passage does not say that plasma is (E), *hemoglobin,* which is mentioned in the next paragraph pertaining to red blood cells. (D) is the only answer supported in the passage.

11. C

SMARTPOINTS CATEGORY: VOCABULARY-IN-CONTEXT

The best way to handle a question phrased with "EXCEPT" is to refer to the passage and eliminate choices you find there. You can rule out (A) because lines 22–24 describe the process through which oxygen is used by the body. Eliminate (B) because line 21 (*like doughnuts*) makes a comparison that helps the reader imagine what erythrocytes look like. It might be tempting to eliminate (C), but it is actually the correct answer. Lines 30–31 state that mature red blood cells *function for about 120 days*. However, this is a misused detail, because the question stem asks specifically about what the author does in lines 20–27. Always read the question carefully! (D) can be eliminated because the author does refer to the color *red* twice in lines 20–27. Eliminate (E) based on the first sentence, where the author provides the phrase *or red blood cells* to explain what erythrocytes are.

12. C

SMARTPOINTS CATEGORY: DETAIL

Notice that many elements are responsible for eventually coloring blood red. Oxygen must bind with hemoglobin, and the (C), *iron*, in hemoglobin is mentioned as giving *red blood cells their color*, making choice (A) a distortion of what is stated in the passage. (B) is also a distortion; *oxygen* binds with hemoglobin and plays a part in coloring red blood cells, but the passage provides more details than that. (D) is too extreme; mature red blood cells no longer have their nucleus, and the nucleus does not color them. (E), *hemoglobin, enzymes, and other proteins*, help in red blood cell function, but this fact is not detailed enough to describe what makes blood cells red.

13. A

SMARTPOINTS CATEGORY: INFERENCE

As always, the word *implies* denotes an Inference question. Writers use metaphor to better illustrate their argument. Consider what patrols and armies do, and picture what that role would be within the blood system and body. (B) is a misused detail; these are attributes of white blood cells, but the author's metaphors do not apply to them. (C) is too extreme because although white blood cells may be considered violent by the invader's standpoint, the passage implies that they must be provoked before acting. Indeed, (D), *B and T cells are highly specific*, combative cells, but this is too detailed an answer given the broad range of the question. (E) is a distortion; phagocytes engulf old red blood cells, and these metaphors do not pertain to red blood cells but rather white blood cells. (A) is the best choice.

14. B

SMARTPOINTS CATEGORY: VOCABULARY-IN-CONTEXT

The sentence states that macrophages *engulf invaders and debris* at the site of *inflamed tissues*. It can therefore be inferred that *inflamed* describes the state of being attacked, or choice (B). (A) is out of scope; although *flame* can be found in *inflamed*, this answer solely relies on the assumptions of the reader and not the context of the sentence. (C) and (D) are distortions; macrophages engulf the invaders, which are responsible for inflaming the tissue, and (D), *irritated*, is often synonymous with *inflamed*. However, the reader should extricate the meaning of *inflamed* from the context of the sentence, which points out that inflammation is the result of invaders and debris. (E) is too extreme; an inflamed tissue is clearly not healthy but is one in need of rescue.

15. B

SMARTPOINTS CATEGORY: DETAIL

The first paragraph names platelets as a blood component that will be discussed. Carefully read the paragraph on platelet production, and find the role megakaryocytes play in their development. (A) is a misused detail; megakaryocytes work with *plasma* to produce platelets. (C) and (D) are distortions. (E) is opposite of the correct answer; megakaryocytes are responsible for the development of platelets, and their life span is not mentioned in the passage. (B) is the best choice.

16. E

SMARTPOINTS CATEGORY: GLOBAL

To answer this question, you need to understand the passage as a whole, and thus it is a Global question. A renaissance indicates a dramatic and lasting change. How did the intellectuals and artists of the 1920s make dramatic or lasting changes? (A) and (B) are out of scope; the author never talks about the (A), European Renaissance, or a (B), religious transformation. (C) is too extreme; the author does not say that all contemporary African-American artists and politicians were influenced by the Harlem Renaissance. (D) is a distortion; the artists and intellectuals of 1920s Harlem certainly created some masterpieces, but this would not constitute a renaissance. (E) speaks of a lasting change that would characterize a *rebirth,* or *renaissance*, and thus is the correct answer.

17. C

SMARTPOINTS CATEGORY: DETAIL

The first two paragraphs of this passage describe the musical influence inherent in the roots of the Harlem Renaissance. Where did these musical styles originate? (A) is a distortion; it could be inferred that there were more black people living in New York, but this does not explain the flourishing of arts and ideas that characterized the Harlem Renaissance. (B) is out of scope; there is nothing in the passage that would indicate that Southern thought and art was superior. (D) is opposite of what the correct answer should be. The first paragraph states that African-Americans from the South brought jazz to the North, which clearly influenced the works of the Harlem writers, artists, and intellectuals. (E) is a misused detail; Duke Ellington is mentioned in the passage, but this is unrelated to the question being asked. (C) most closely reflects the author's intention.

18. B

SMARTPOINTS CATEGORY: DETAIL

This question asks you to contrast two styles. Which answer best shows a contrast? (A) is out of scope; there is no mention of Shakespeare in this passage. (C) is a distortion; it could be inferred that Southern dialects were present in the Harlem of 1920, but there is nothing in the passage to indicate that Hughes was influenced by them or that the elite found the dialects unimportant. (D) is also out of scope; there is no mention of similes or metaphors in the passage. (E) is opposite; a voice that is *highly stylized and theatrical* would be more affected than the voice of ordinary people used by Hughes. (B) best contrasts two different styles: the voice of ordinary people versus the accepted artificial voice.

19. A

SMARTPOINTS CATEGORIES: GLOBAL

The correct answer to a Global question is one that encompasses the passage as a whole. It does not focus too narrowly on a detail in the passage or bring in ideas that aren't present in the passage. (A) meets both requirements. (B) is incorrect because the author never *refutes* anything. (C) doesn't work because no *theorist* is mentioned. (D) is tempting because the passage does *trace a history*, but it is not the history of a *controversial* topic. (E) is extreme; the author never suggests there is *an unbreakable* connection between *art and politics*.

20. E

SMARTPOINTS CATEGORY: INFERENCE

The author talks about Langston Hughes's poetry as revolutionary because it used the language of the people he encountered instead of the stylized voice common at the time. You can't make any assumptions about other art forms based on this passage. (A) is out of scope; while this may be true, it is not addressed in the passage. There is no indication in the passage that African-American art was (B), *unflattering*. (C) is also out of scope; there is no mention in the passage about what kind of art supplies were used by the artists of the time. (D), *Art Deco*, is mentioned as a style used by one of the artists. It does not indicate that all Art Deco works were, by virtue of the style, imbued with an air of dignity and grace. (E) best fits the overall mood of the Harlem Renaissance that allowed for a more realistic depiction of the African-American life of the 1920s.

21. E

SMARTPOINTS CATEGORIES: VOCABULARY-IN-CONTEXT

Even though this question is long and out of the usual Vocabulary-in-Context *most nearly means* mold, it is still a Vocabulary-in-Context question. *Reformation* has been used to describe any movement that alters the status quo and moves a group toward a specified goal. Which of the definitions best fits with the historical use of the word? While *reform* can mean to (A), reshape something, this definition does not make sense in the context of the passage. There is no indication of (B), *civil disobedience*, being a part of the Harlem Renaissance, so this answer cannot be correct. (C) does not make sense in the context of the sentence or passage. Community need does not come into play here. (D) is the definition of a referendum, not a reformation. (E) is the best fit in the context of the sentence. It is used to show that social reform was necessary to bring about change and better the current conditions.

22. D

SMARTPOINTS CATEGORY: FUNCTION

To predict for a Function question, pay attention to context. In this case, the sentence immediately before the cited lines is helpful: *Paris . . . was quick to assimilate the sounds, textures, and words that were coming out of Harlem.* Predict that the author wants to show that works of the Harlem Renaissance artists were appreciated in Europe. This matches well with (D). (A), (B), and (E) go too far beyond what's stated in the passage. (C) is a distortion.

23. B

SMARTPOINTS CATEGORY: FUNCTION

When a Function question asks the author's purpose in using quotation marks, you can be certain that it is highlighting the fact that the author is using a term in a way that's different from the way it's normally used. Knowing this, you can eliminate all choices except (B) and (C). Consider those more closely. The author does refer to *the 1960s* in the third paragraph, but never says that *the meaning of the word "art" changed during* that decade. Therefore, (B) is the correct answer.

24. B

SMARTPOINTS CATEGORY: VOCABULARY-IN-CONTEXT

Several wrong answer choices reflect a more common meaning of *maintain*. Eliminate these, and try the others in the sentence, paying close attention to the surrounding context. The correct answer is (B), *asserted*. *Maintain* most often means repair or keep up, but as always, don't reactively select the first answer choice that looks as if it might be correct. Choices (D) and (E) make sense in the sentence, but not with its surrounding context (no dispute or argument is involved).

25. D

SMARTPOINTS CATEGORY: GLOBAL
INFERENCE

Skim the passage, and try to understand how the author seems to feel about the topic. Is there an answer choice that reflects your impression? (A) is opposite; the author clearly does not believe that conceptual art is important and, in fact, calls it *absurd*. (B) is a misused detail; Marcel Duchamp is mentioned in the passage but only as a supporting detail. It would therefore be inappropriate to title the passage accordingly. (C) is also a misused detail; one bumper sticker is referenced in the passage, but again, this is only a supporting detail and not worthy of inspiring a title for the passage. (E) is too extreme; the word *all* should alert you that this may be an extreme answer choice, but in addition, the passage does not attempt to describe *all art* or make any value judgments about it. The passage is written to explain what conceptual art is and why the author dislikes it. The last paragraph, in particular, makes it very clear that the author holds a negative opinion of this type of art, which makes (D) correct.

26. A

SMARTPOINTS CATEGORY: DETAIL

This is not a Vocabulary-in-Context question because it directly asks you what a word means. However, it doesn't give you a line reference to go to, so you'll have to rely on skimming the passage to find the word, or better yet, find the word you circled as you were reading. This word is defined immediately before it appears. The correct answer, (A), is based on lines 28–29: *words that do not yet exist.*

27. B

SMARTPOINTS CATEGORY: DETAIL

The EXCEPT question is a time-consuming one, because you have to systematically eliminate the four that are true before you can pick the one you are looking for. If time is short, save this one for the end of the passage group of questions. Answering this question requires you to make several inferences and then exclude each answer choice that can be supported by the passage. (A) is supported by lines 26–27, *the contemporary conceptual artist Adib Fricke deals with language.* (C) is supported by lines 17–20, *Conceptual art, for the most part, completely left behind a physical representation. . . .* (D) is supported by lines 42–45, *It is thus a way to avoid having to undertake the effort and exhibit the skill necessary to produce a lasting physical work of art.* (E) is supported by lines 6–8, *Those who wished to further pursue abstraction to its absurd end became conceptual artists.* Tolstoy's outlines are actually given as an example that is NOT conceptual art, and thus choice (B) is the correct answer.

28. E

SMARTPOINTS CATEGORY: INFERENCE

The author . . . would view is a clause that indicates an Inference question about the author's opinion of conceptual art. To answer this question, you must first use your inference skills to determine how the author feels about this type of art. The correct answer is (E), *disdain.* This inference can be made on the basis of the author's example about Leo Tolstoy; the rhetorical question in the last sentence, as well as the clearly stated opinion about this type of art, show that the author's main feeling toward conceptual art is disdain.

29. C

SMARTPOINTS CATEGORIES: FUNCTION
GLOBAL

This question combines understanding the passage as a whole (Global) and knowing the author's intent (Function), as shown by the phrase *serves to*. The author has a strongly negative opinion on the topic of the passage, as discussed in question 28.

The author has a strong opinion on the topic of the passage. What is it? (A) is a distortion; the middle paragraphs do describe the history of conceptual art, but this is not the main point of the passage. (B) is a misused detail; Tolstoy's literary methods are described in order to support the author's opinion about conceptual art; however, this is not the main subject or goal of the passage. From the first line of the passage (in which *art* is placed in quotation marks to cue the reader that the author has a disparaging opinion of the subject matter) to the last paragraph (in which the author states outright that conceptual art is *a way to avoid having to undertake the effort and exhibit the skill necessary to produce a lasting physical work of art*, lines 42–45, the author attempts to convince the reader that conceptual art is undeserving of attention as a real art form. (D) is also a misused detail; Adib Fricke's work with The Word Company is treated in the passage as a way to clarify what conceptual art consists of. Still, this is a supporting detail and is not the main point of the passage. (E) is out of scope; abstract art is mentioned, but it is neither compared nor contrasted with conceptual art. Thus, (C) is the correct choice.

30. A

SMARTPOINTS CATEGORY: INFERENCE

In questions about the author's attitude, beware of extreme answer choices. The answer is often quite moderate.

From the description of boarding-house life in the third paragraph, you know that the author feels sorry for the women. But the last paragraph suggests that the author also feels the conditions were perhaps necessary in order for the factories to be economically successful. Look for something that sums up these mixed feelings.

31. B

SMARTPOINTS CATEGORY: VOCABULARY-IN-CONTEXT
Treat a challenging Vocabulary-in-Context like a Sentence Completion problem.

In the sentence in question, the author says that European boarding houses were worse than their American counterparts. So even if you've never seen the word *base* used in this way, you know that it must be negative since it applies to the European boarding-house owners. Look for a negative word that could describe ethics, and keep in mind other meanings for the word *base*, like the base of a mountain.

In choice (A), in this context, this word indicates that something is highly moral, the opposite of what you're looking for. In choice (B), *immoral* ethics sounds good. Choice (C) is a tempting meaning, but *absent* doesn't seem to match any of the other, more familiar meanings of *base*. Choice (D) is tempting, but it's the actions that were *harmful*, not the ethics that motivated the actions. Choice (E) matches *base*, but doesn't fit in the sentence.

32. A

SMARTPOINTS CATEGORY: DETAIL

According to Passage 1 tells you that this will ask about a specific detail. Don't try to answer from memory. This detail appears in the second paragraph. Check out lines 16–18: *Primarily to assure families that their daughters would not be corrupted by factory life.*

Choice (A) is a good match. Choice (B) is distortion; the passage discusses *factory* life, not *city* life. Choice (C) is a misused detail; the boarding houses spread—rather than prevented—disease. Choice (D) is out of scope; the social activities of the workers are never discussed. Choice (E) is distortion; this was indeed an effect, as shown in the second sentence of the second paragraph, but it's not the reason that factory owners instituted the policy.

33. B

SMARTPOINTS CATEGORY: VOCABULARY-IN-CONTEXT

The correct answer in a Vocabulary-in-Context question won't just work in a particular sentence—it will also make the sentence work in the entire passage.

Since *the economists advanced* an idea, *advanced* must be something that you can do with an idea. The final paragraph presents this idea, and the author seems to regard the idea as reasonable, so look for something that says the economists stated the idea.

Choice (A) is the typical meaning of *advanced*—but it doesn't fit here. When you read choice (B), it makes perfect sense. In choice (C), the word makes sense in the sentence, but then the sentence doesn't work with the rest of the paragraph. The author wouldn't talk about a group *denying* an idea that hasn't been stated yet. In choice (D), can you *progress* an idea? That doesn't make much sense. Choice (E), like (C), sounds okay in the sentence, but that sentence then doesn't make sense in the paragraph as a whole.

34. E

SMARTPOINTS CATEGORY: INFERENCE

For Reasoning questions, summarize the author's argument in your own words before looking at the answer choices. The author thinks that factory owners had no choice because they would have lost money and gone out of business if they had instituted better working conditions. Look for an answer choice that would weaken this argument.

Choice (A) is out of scope; tempting, but no. Conditions in France don't necessarily have anything to do with conditions in America. Maybe it's easier to run a factory in France for some reason that just doesn't apply in America. Choice (B) is out of scope; maybe this Bennington system is even crueler to workers. We don't know anything about this Bennington system, so this fact doesn't weaken the argument. Choice (C) is an opposite; this doesn't weaken the argument—it strengthens it. It just proves that it would have been a poor business strategy to improve working conditions. Choice (D) is out of scope; maybe twentieth-century factories had technologies or other advantages not available to nineteenth-century factories. Since the situations are not the same, the improved twentieth-century conditions don't weaken the argument that poor conditions were necessary in the nineteenth century. Choice (E) fits. If factory owners had a way to improve conditions without lowering profits, then this weakens the author's argument that poor conditions were necessary.

35. B

SMARTPOINTS CATEGORY: FUNCTION

In paired passages, it's extremely important to keep the authors straight. Don't fall for choices that mix up the authors' points of view.

What part does this paragraph play in the passage as a whole? The author feels that the system created poor working conditions, and the second paragraph explains the part of agents in this process.

Choice (A) is a misused detail; this comes from the author of Passage 1, not Passage 2. Choice (B) matches your prediction. Choice (C) is a misused detail; the author speaks of the immorality of the system in the final, but not in the second, paragraph. Choice (D) is a misused detail; the fire isn't mentioned until the third paragraph. Choice (E) is a misused detail; again, this comes from Passage 1, not Passage 2.

36. C

SMARTPOINTS CATEGORY: FUNCTION

Read each answer choice carefully, and don't get caught in a trap: for example, (E) is incorrect because of a single word. The third paragraph, which describes the fire, says that *the Waltham-Lowell system … [was] downright dangerous.* So look for something that says the factory owners created dangerous conditions.

Choice (A) is out of scope; the author only mentions a single fire and doesn't suggest that such events happened often. Choice (B) is distortion; the author feels the accident was a tragedy, so sympathy wouldn't be *unwarranted.* Choice (C) matches your prediction. Choice (D) is an opposite; the author feels that factory owners didn't do enough to protect workers. Choice (E) is distortion; it's the factory owners, not the workers, who were negligent.

37. E

SMARTPOINTS CATEGORY: DETAIL

On Detail questions, watch out for answer choices that bring in irrelevant information from other parts of the passage. Reread the sentence in which the word appears. The author notes that one would hope that the tragedy would bring about change, but that nothing much happened to the factory owners and that factories continued to lock their doors for several years.

Choice (A) is distortion; the passage mentions 23 families, not 23 victims. There might have been victims whose families did not sue. Choice (B) is an opposite; the next-to-last sentence in the third paragraph states that the owners were acquitted of criminal charges, so they *didn't* go to jail. Choice (C) is distortion; the practice of locking doors remained common, but we don't know that tragedies of this sort remained common, since we don't know if fires continued to happen frequently. Choice (D) is a misused detail; the whale-oil lamps in the first paragraph created pollution, not fires. Choice (E) matches the last two sentences of the paragraph.

38. C

SMARTPOINTS CATEGORY: INFERENCE

If you're asked about the structure of a paragraph, go back and quickly reread each sentence to figure out what's going on. Author 2 mentions the view also held by author 1—that factory owners had to create poor working conditions in order to make money and stay in business. Author 2 then goes on to disagree and proposes that a system *of common decency* should have been used instead.

In choice (A), no evidence is introduced in the final paragraph. In choice (B), no statistical evidence is introduced in the final paragraph. Choice (C) matches your prediction. In choice (D), we don't know how widely held any of the views discussed are, and no historical evidence is presented in the final paragraph. In choice (E), the author doesn't say that there is a contradiction. To the author, the choice is clear: the factory owners were in the wrong.

39. A

SMARTPOINTS CATEGORIES: INFERENCE

COMPARISONS

With paired passages, you will almost always see a question that asks you to pinpoint an issue or issues on which the two authors disagree.

Both authors agree that the working conditions were bad, but they disagree in their final paragraphs. Author 1 states that the conditions were necessary in order for factories to stay in business, while author 2 states that the conditions were unacceptable and that another system should have been implemented.

In choice (A), here, the phrase *market conditions* means the economic situation, so this matches your prediction. Choice (B) is out of scope; neither author mentions philanthropy. Choice (C) is an opposite; both authors seem to agree that the system made American textile mills more competitive. Choice (D) is an opposite; the authors agree that health problems arose from the system. Choice (E) is out of scope; neither author mentions previous systems.

40. B

SMARTPOINTS CATEGORIES: INFERENCE

COMPARISONS

When asked about the differences between two authors, watch out for opposite answer choices.

Both passages talk about poor conditions, but Passage 1 deals more with boarding houses, while Passage 2 deals with working conditions in the factories.

Choice (A) is an opposite; boarding houses are discussed in Passage 1, not Passage 2. Choice (B) is correct; this appears in the second paragraph of Passage 2, but never appears in Passage 1. Choice (C) is an opposite; this is discussed by both authors. Choice (D) is an opposite; this appears in Passage 1, but not Passage 2. Choice (E) is out of scope; safety supervisors are not mentioned in either paragraph.

41. B

SMARTPOINTS CATEGORIES: DETAIL .:ıll

COMPARISONS .ıll

Remember to consult your outline if you need to find a detail quickly.

There are too many possibilities here to make a prediction, so get your outline of the passages ready and eliminate anything that doesn't appear in both passages.

Choice (A) is an opposite; this is mentioned in Passage 2, but not Passage 1. In choice (B), the final paragraph of Passage 2 and the third paragraph of Passage 1 both mention that health problems were caused by factory conditions. Choice (C) is an opposite; this is mentioned in Passage 1, but not Passage 2. Choice (D) is out of scope; this is not mentioned in either passage. Choice (E) is an opposite; both authors stress that factory owners were anything but generous.

42. D

SMARTPOINTS CATEGORIES: INFERENCE .ıll

COMPARISONS .ıll

Paired passage Inference questions hinge directly on your ability to keep straight the viewpoints of the two authors. Author 2 is using the phrase *economic necessity* with some irony. She doesn't believe that these conditions were really necessary. Author 1, however, feels that economic conditions did in fact force the factory owners to create poor working conditions. Since the question asks about author 1, this is the viewpoint you are looking for.

Choice (A) is an opposite; this choice presents the viewpoint of the wrong author. Choice (B) is an opposite; actually, Passage 1 states that conditions in boarding houses in the United States were better than those overseas. Choice (C) is a misused detail; the boarding houses were seen as a response to workers' families, but the economic conditions had a different cause (overseas competition). Choice (D) is a good match. Choice (E) is extreme; this choice is tempting, but *solely* is a bit too strong. We don't know that overseas competition is definitely the *only* cause.

KEY POINTS YOU'VE LEARNED IN THIS CHAPTER

1. The same five question types that go with short passages are also used with long passages: Detail, Global, Vocabulary-in-Context, Function, and Inference.

2. Apply Kaplan's Strategy for Reading Comprehension questions to long passages as you did with short passages.

3. Other techniques useful for answering questions on long passages:

   - These questions are usually arranged in an order to match where the answers appear in the passage.

   - Read the introduction to the passage or passages.

   - Learn active reading. Keep in mind: *Why* did the author write this? *What* is the purpose of this paragraph? *Why* include this detail?

   - Map the passage with the ABCs of Active Reading: Abbreviate margin notes. Bracket key sentences. Circle keywords and phrases.

4. Kaplan's Target Strategy for Paired Passages questions:

   - **Step 1:** Read Passage 1 and answer the questions about it.

   - **Step 2:** Read Passage 2 and answer the questions about it.

   - **Step 3:** Answer the questions asking about both passages.

CHAPTER 12: VOCABULARY-BUILDING STRATEGIES

SMARTPOINTS COVERED IN THIS CHAPTER

DEFINITION	

VOCABULARY-IN-CONTEXT	

WHAT TO EXPECT ON TEST DAY

A good score on the Critical Reading component depends upon, in part, your ability to work with unfamiliar words. You will probably need to work with words you don't know to answer both the Sentence Completion and Reading Comprehension questions.

- What are the types of words I'm going to see on the SAT?
- What strategies will help me learn the right vocabulary words?
- What skills will help me succeed with the tough SAT vocabulary words?

MASTERING SAT VOCABULARY

There are two types of hard SAT words:

1. Unfamiliar words
2. Familiar words with secondary meanings

Some words are hard because you haven't seen them before. The words *scintilla* and *circumlocution*, for instance, are probably not part of your everyday vocabulary. But they might pop up on your SAT.

Easy words, such as *recognize* or *appreciation*, can also trip you up on the test because they have secondary meanings that you aren't used to. Reading Comprehension, in particular, will throw you familiar words with unfamiliar meanings.

THREE STEPS TO TEST DAY SUCCESS

KAPLAN'S TARGET STRATEGY FOR LEARNING VOCABULARY

A great vocabulary can't be built overnight, but it can be improved in a relatively short period of time with a minimum amount of pain.

Here's our three-step plan for building your vocabulary for the SAT:

- **Step 1:** Learn words strategically.
- **Step 2:** Learn word roots, prefixes, suffixes, and word families.
- **Step 3:** Personalize your vocabulary study.

STEP 1: LEARN WORDS STRATEGICALLY

The best words to learn are words that have appeared often on the SAT. The test makers are formulaic in test creation, so the test is consistent from one administration to the next; thus, words that have appeared frequently are likely bets to show up again.

STEP 2: LEARN WORD ROOTS, PREFIXES, SUFFIXES, AND WORD FAMILIES

Sometimes, recognizing root words, prefixes, or suffixes will provide enough clues for you to determine whether an answer choice is correct. Below are some of the more commonly used root words, prefixes, and suffixes and their meanings. Knowing as many as possible will help you when you encounter words you don't know because, chances are, words with similar root words, prefixes, or suffixes will have similar meanings, too.

ROOT WORDS	MEANING	EXAMPLES
a-, an-	not, without	apathy, amoral, anesthetic
alter	other	alternative, alter ego
aud	sound	audiology, auditorium, audible
bene-	good	benevolent, benefit, benefactor
ced	yield, go	proceed, intercede, recede
-cide	killing	patricide, infanticide, suicide
cred	believe	credibility, credulous, credo
culp	guilt	culpable, culprit
dys-	ill, bad	dysentery, dysfunctional
-ia, -y	state, act	democracy, anarchy, amnesia
il-	not	illegal, illegible, illicit
-ism	the belief in	terrorism, pacifism, communism
-ite	one connected with	meteorite, cosmopolite
mag	large	magnate, magnify
mon	warn	premonition, admonition
mono-	one, single	monogamy, monotheism, monarchy
ob-	against	object, obstruct
pan-	all, every	panorama, pandemic, pantheism
path	feel, suffer	empathy, sympathy, pathology, telepathy
proto-	first	prototype, protoplasm
se-	away from	seduce, secede
soph	wisdom, knowledge	sophisticated, sophomore, philosophy
trans-	across	transatlantic, transient, transport
ver	truth	veracity, verify, verity

Word families may also be of some use. A word family is a group of words that shares a similar meaning. For example, *loquacious, verbose,* and *garrulous* all mean *wordy, talkative. Taciturn, laconic, terse, concise,* and *pithy* all mean *not talkative, not wordy.* Instead of learning just one of these words, learn them all together—you get eight words for the price of just two definitions.

STEP 3: PERSONALIZE YOUR VOCABULARY STUDY

- There isn't just one *right* way to study vocabulary. Figure out a study method that works best for you and stick to it.

PERFECT SCORE TIP

" Knowing prefixes and roots really helped me determine the meanings of challenging words. "

- Use flash cards. Write down new words or word groups and run through them whenever you have a few spare minutes. Put one new word or word group on one side of a 3" × 5" index card and a short definition on the back.

- Make a vocabulary notebook. List words in one column and their meanings in another. Test yourself. Cover up the meanings, and see what words you can define from memory. Make a sample sentence using each word in context.

- Think of hooks that lodge a new word in your mind. Create visual images of words. For example, to remember the verb form of *flag*, you can picture a flag drooping or losing energy as the wind dies down.

- Use rhymes and other devices that help you remember the words. For example, you might remember that a *verbose* person uses a lot of verbs.

It doesn't matter which techniques you use, as long as you learn words steadily and methodically. Doing so over several months with regular reviews is ideal.

WORD ASSOCIATION

Associating words together really can help sharpen your vocabulary skills. Take the word *gregarious*:

- If you think of your friend Greg as a sociable sort, then you'll long remember the meaning of the word *gregarious*.

- Now add the word root: If you know that the root *greg* means *crowd*, you'll be able to remember the following:

  - *Segregate* means to separate a *crowd*.
  - *Integrate* means to *crowd* together.
  - *Aggregate* means a *crowd* of different elements.

Now you have four new words firmly stuck in your head!

DECODING STRANGE WORDS ON THE TEST

Trying to learn every word that could possibly appear on the SAT is like trying to memorize the license plate number of every car on the road. There are just too many to commit to memory.

No matter how much time you spend with flash cards or word lists, you're bound to face some mystery words on your SAT. Just as you can use your basic multiplication skills to find the product of even the largest numbers, you can use what you know about words to focus on likely meanings of tough vocabulary words.

REMEMBER WHERE YOU'VE HEARD THE WORD BEFORE

If you can recall a phrase in which the word appears, that may be enough to eliminate some answer choices or even zero in on the right answer. Look at the following example:

Between the two villages was a ---- through which passage was difficult and hazardous.

(A) precipice
(B) beachhead
(C) quagmire
(D) market
(E) prairie

To answer this question, you need to know whether or not to eliminate the word *quagmire*. You may remember *quagmire* from news reports referring to "a foreign policy *quagmire*" or "a *quagmire* of financial indebtedness." If you can remember how *quagmire* was used, you'll have a rough idea of what it means, and you'll see it fits. You may also be reminded of the word *mire*, as in "We got *mired* in the small details and never got to the larger issue." Sounds something like stuck, right? You don't need an exact definition. A *quagmire* is a situation that's difficult to get out of, so (C) is correct. Literally, a *quagmire* is a bog or swamp.

DECIDE WHETHER THE WORD HAS A POSITIVE OR NEGATIVE CHARGE

Simply knowing whether the words are positive or negative will help you eliminate possible answers. Knowing root words, prefixes, and suffixes comes in handy here. For example, *pro-*, *bene-*, and *magn-* are positive—*proponent, beneficial,* and *magnificent.* But *de-, mal-,* and *mis-* are negative—*deficient, malnutrition,* and *misappropriate.* Sometimes, words can even *sound* positive or negative. For example, look at the word *cantankerous.* Say it to yourself. Can you guess whether it's positive or negative? Often words that sound harsh (such as *irk*) have a negative meaning, whereas smooth-sounding words (such as *benevolent*) tend to have positive meanings. If *cantankerous* sounded negative to you, you were right. It means *ill-tempered, disagreeable,* or *difficult to handle.*

Not all words sound positive or negative; some sound neutral. But if you can define the charge, you can probably eliminate some answer choices on that basis alone. Here's an example:

PERFECT SCORE TIP

" For answering two-blank Sentence Completions with really tough vocab, I used compare/contrast clues to eliminate incorrect answer choices. "

He seemed at first to be honest and loyal, but before long it was necessary to ---- him for his ---- behavior.

(A) admonish . . . steadfast

(B) extol . . . conniving

(C) reprimand . . . scrupulous

(D) exalt . . . insidious

(E) castigate . . . perfidious

All you need to know to answer this question is that negative words are needed in both blanks. Then you can scan the answer choices for one that contains two clearly negative words. Even if you don't know what all the words mean, you can use your sense of positive or negative charge to eliminate answers. Choice (E) is right. *Castigate* means to punish or scold harshly, and *perfidious* means treacherous.

USE YOUR FOREIGN LANGUAGE SKILLS

Are you fluent in a foreign language? Or perhaps you're studying one in school? Have you come upon words such as *alchemy, debonair, sycophant,* and *portico* in your foreign language studies? The English language has integrated some words from other languages, and that borrowing might help you. In addition, many of the roots you'll encounter in SAT words come from Latin. Spanish, French, and Italian also come from Latin and have retained much of it in their modern forms. English is also a cousin to German and Greek. That means that if you don't recognize a word, try to remember if you know a similar word in another language. Look at the word *carnal.* Unfamiliar? What about *carne,* as in *chili con carne? Carn* means meat or flesh, which leads you straight to the meaning of *carnal*—pertaining to the flesh.

> **PERFECT SCORE TIP**
>
> " If I didn't feel totally confident in an answer, I would make a note to review it at the end if there was time, instead of wasting time dwelling on it. "

You could decode *carnivorous* (meat-eating) in the same way. You can almost always figure out something about strange words on the test. Chances are that few words on the SAT will be totally new to you, even if your recollection is more subliminal than vivid.

WHEN ALL ELSE FAILS—GUESS

If you feel totally at a loss in determining the exact meaning of the word, eliminate choices that are clearly wrong and make an educated guess from the remaining choices. A wrong answer won't hurt you much, but a right answer can help you a lot.

KEY POINTS YOU'VE LEARNED IN THIS CHAPTER

1. Follow Kaplan's Target Strategy to build your vocabulary (learn words strategically; learn word roots, prefixes, and word families; and personalize your vocabulary study).

2. Remember Kaplan's techniques for decoding unfamiliar words (recall where you've heard the word before, decide whether the word is positive or negative, use your foreign language skills, and make an educated guess after eliminating some choices).

Part Five

HOW TO ATTACK THE MATH SECTIONS

CHAPTER 13: SAT MATH STRATEGIES

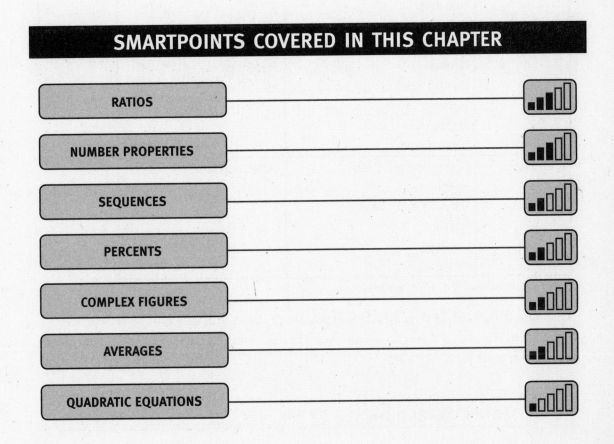

SMARTPOINTS COVERED IN THIS CHAPTER

RATIOS

NUMBER PROPERTIES

SEQUENCES

PERCENTS

COMPLEX FIGURES

AVERAGES

QUADRATIC EQUATIONS

WHAT TO EXPECT ON TEST DAY

There are three Math sections on the SAT. They can appear anywhere during the test, except section 1, in any order. They are:

LENGTH	CONTENT	TYPE
25 minutes	High school geometry Algebra Numbers and operations Statistics Probability Data analysis	Multiple-choice Student-produced responses*
25 minutes	High school geometry Algebra Numbers and operations Statistics Probability Data analysis	Multiple-choice Student-produced responses*
20 minutes	High school geometry Algebra Numbers and operations Statistics Probability Data analysis	Multiple-choice

*Grid-ins will appear in one of the two 25-minute sections.

Questions in the Math sections are arranged to gradually increase in difficulty. Be aware of the difficulty level as you go through a question set. The harder the question seems, the more traps you will have to avoid.

MATH COVERED ON THE SAT

The tested math concepts on the SAT are as follows:

- Numbers and operations
- Algebra I, II, and functions
- Geometry
- Statistics, probability, and data analysis

FOUR STEPS TO TEST DAY SUCCESS

On the more basic questions, you may find that you know the answers right away and are able to work through them quickly. However, when working through the harder problems, a few extra seconds spent looking for traps, thinking about your approach, and deciding whether to work on the problem immediately or to come back to it later is very important and will help you accrue more points.

KAPLAN'S TARGET STRATEGY FOR THE MATH COMPONENT

Kaplan's Target Strategy is a good system for tackling *all* SAT Math problems:

- **Step 1:** Estimate the question's difficulty.
- **Step 2:** Read the question.
- **Step 3:** Skip or do.
- **Step 4:** Look for the fastest approach.

We will now show you how our Target Strategy works as we use it to answer this sample SAT question:

At a diner, Joe orders three strips of bacon and a cup of coffee and is charged $2.25. Stella orders two strips of bacon and a cup of coffee and is charged $1.70. What is the price of two strips of bacon?

(A) $0.55
(B) $0.60
(C) $1.10
(D) $1.30
(E) $1.80

STEP 1: ESTIMATE THE QUESTION'S DIFFICULTY

SAT Math questions are arranged in order of difficulty. Keep this in mind as you work through a set. In a Math set, the first few questions are basic, the middle few are moderately difficult, and the last few are hard. The question above is a moderately difficult word problem.

On difficult questions, watch out for math traps (see chapter 14). Hard questions are often written to be misleading, containing one or two answers that will seem to be right at first glance. Be careful of these easy answers for hard questions. They are there specifically to trick you. Make sure you always know what's being asked.

> **EXPERT TUTOR TIP**
>
> Remember Kaplan's Target Strategy for Math: **estimate, read, skip** (or not), and **look**. It may help to create a catchy phrase to help you remember.

> **PERFECT SCORE TIP**
>
> When I read a Math question, I always circled "trap" words or ones that might cause me to make a mistake. That way, I could proceed with caution!

STEP 2: READ THE QUESTION

If you try to start solving the problem before reading the question all the way through, you may end up doing unnecessary work. The question above looks straightforward, but read through it carefully, and you will see a slight twist.

You're asked to find the cost of two strips of bacon, not one. Many people will find the price of a single bacon strip and forget to double it. Don't make this mistake.

STEP 3: SKIP OR DO

If a problem renders you clueless, circle it in your test booklet and move on. Spend your time on the problems you can solve; if there's still time at the end of the section, come back to the ones you had trouble with then. It is better to get two points from two less challenging problems than spend the same amount of time on one tricky question you are unsure of.

STEP 4: LOOK FOR THE FASTEST APPROACH

On an easy question, all the information you need to solve the problem may be provided in the question stem or in a diagram. Harder questions often hide the information that will help you solve the problem.

For instance, for a question like the one on the previous page that would appear in the middle of the question set, you would want to be suspicious of easy answers and cautious in your approach to it. If you get the answer too easily, you may have missed something. (In this case, you're asked to find the price of two strips of bacon, not one.)

> **PERFECT SCORE TIP**
>
> " When I was practicing for the SAT, I noticed that familiarity with a question type helped me solve it much faster. Practice makes perfect! "

LOOK FOR SHORTCUTS!

Sometimes the obvious way of doing a problem is the long way. If the method you choose involves lots of calculating, look for another route. There's usually a shortcut you can use that won't involve tons of arithmetic.

Again, in the sample question, the cost of bacon and coffee could be translated into two distinct equations using the variables b and c. You could find c in terms of b, and then plug this into the other equation. But if you think carefully, you'll see there's a quicker way:

The difference in price between three bacon strips and a cup of coffee and two bacon strips and a cup of coffee is the price of one bacon strip. So one bacon strip costs $2.25 – $1.70 = $0.55.

(Remember, you have to find the price of two strips of bacon: $2 \times \$0.55 = \$1.10$.)

Now that we know how to determine whether to attempt a problem, we are going to cover the two categories of problems: multiple-choice and Grid-ins. Let's look at the specifics for each type of problem.

MULTIPLE-CHOICE QUESTIONS

The multiple-choice question setup in the Math section is the same as in the other two sections. You will be given five answers from which to choose the best one. Thus, certain techniques will help you eliminate answer choices and make the problems more manageable. We will go over those techniques later in this chapter.

DIRECTIONS

Read these directions through carefully. By test day, you will want to know these directions by heart so you won't waste precious time trying to decipher their meaning.

> **PERFECT SCORE TIP**
>
> " Really knowing math formulas was incredibly helpful. They came up a lot, so I saved tons of time by not having to flip back to the directions all the time. "

Directions: For this section, solve each problem and decide which is the best of the choices given. Fill in the corresponding oval on the answer sheet. You may use any available space for scratchwork.

Notes:

(1) Calculator use is permitted.

(2) All numbers used are real numbers.

(3) Figures are provided for some problems. All figures are drawn to scale and lie in a plane UNLESS otherwise indicated.

(4) Unless otherwise specified, the domain of any function f is assumed to be the set of all real numbers x for which $f(x)$ is a real number.

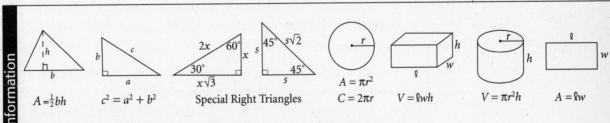

$A = \frac{1}{2}bh$ $c^2 = a^2 + b^2$ Special Right Triangles $A = \pi r^2$ $C = 2\pi r$ $V = \ell w h$ $V = \pi r^2 h$ $A = \ell w$

The sum of the degree measures of the angles in a triangle is 180.
The number of degrees of arc in a circle is 360.
A straight angle has a degree measure of 180.

TWO EFFECTIVE TECHNIQUES FOR MULTIPLE-CHOICE QUESTIONS

Kaplan's Target Strategy for the Math component will help you save time and avoid mistakes on the SAT. But sometimes you won't know how to do the math needed to find the answer or doing so would simply be too time-consuming. Luckily, there are several methods for working through Math problems.

There are two techniques, in particular, that can be useful when you don't know where to start: picking numbers and backsolving.

PICKING NUMBERS

Sometimes you get stuck on a Math question just because it's too general or abstract. A good solution to this problem is to substitute particular numbers for the equation variables.

WHEN TO PICK NUMBERS

The picking numbers strategy works especially well with **even/odd questions**.

If a is an odd integer and b is an even integer, which of the following must be odd?

(A) $2a + b$

(B) $a + 2b$

(C) ab

(D) a^2b

(E) ab^2

Rather than trying to wrap your brain around abstract variables, simply pick numbers for a and b. When you are adding, subtracting, or multiplying even and odd numbers, you can generally assume that what happens with one pair of numbers generally happens with similar pairs of numbers.

Let's say, for the time being, that $a = 3$ and $b = 2$. Plug those values into the answer choices, and there's a good chance that only one choice will be odd:

(A) $2a + b = 2(3) + 2 = 8$

(B) $a + 2b = 3 + 2(2) = 7$

(C) $ab = (3)(2) = 6$

(D) $a^2b = (3^2)(2) = 18$

(E) $ab^2 = (3)(2^2) = 12$

Choice (B) is the only odd answer for $a = 3$ and $b = 2$; thus, it is fair to assume that it must be the only odd answer choice, no matter what odd numbers you plug in for a and b. The answer is (B).

ANOTHER TIME TO PICK NUMBERS

Percent problems are great for picking numbers. If you see answers with percent signs in them, choose 100 and get started.

Look at the following example:

From 1985 to 1990, the berry production of bush x increased by 20 percent. From 1990 to 1995, the berry production increased by 30 percent. What was the percent increase in the berry production on the bush over the entire ten-year period from 1985–1995?

(A) 10%

(B) 25%

(C) 50%

(D) 56%

(E) 60%

Rather than attempting to solve this problem in the abstract, choose a number for the berry production in 1985 and see what happens. There's no need to pick a realistic number. You're better off picking a number that's easy to work with. In percent problems, the number that's easiest to work with is almost always 100.

Now that we have our number, let's plug it into the problem:

- The number of berries on the bush in 1985 was 100. What would the 1990 berry production be?

- Twenty percent more than 100 is 120.

- Now, if 1990's berry production was 120, what would the number of berries in 1995 be?

- What's 30 percent more than 120?

- Be careful. Don't just add 30 to 120. You need to find 30 percent of 120 and add that number on.

- Thirty percent of 120 is $(.30)(120) = 36$.

PERFECT SCORE TIP

" Picking numbers was something that I got better at the more I practiced. I tried to determine the number that would make each problem as simple as possible. "

- Add 36 to 120, and you get 156 berries in 1995.

- What percent greater is 156 than 100? That's easy—that's why we picked 100 to start with.

- It's a 56 percent increase. The answer is (D).

YET ANOTHER TIME TO PICK NUMBERS

A third problem ideal for picking numbers is when the answer choices to a word problem are **algebraic expressions,** or variables.

Consider the following example:

If n sunglass lenses cost p dollars, then how many dollars would q sunglass lenses cost?

(A) $\dfrac{nq}{q}$

(B) $\dfrac{nq}{p}$

(C) $\dfrac{pq}{n}$

(D) $\dfrac{n}{pq}$

(E) $\dfrac{p}{nq}$

The hard thing about this question is it uses variables instead of numbers. So make it real. Pick numbers for the variables. Pick numbers that are easy to work with. Let's say that $n = 2$, $p = 4$, and $q = 3$.

The question then becomes: "If two sunglass lenses cost \$4, how many dollars would three sunglass lenses cost?" That's easy—\$6. When $n = 2$, $p = 4$, and $q = 3$, the correct answer should equal 6. Plug those values into the answer choices and see which ones yield 6:

(A) $\dfrac{np}{q} = \dfrac{(2)(4)}{3} = \dfrac{8}{3} = 2\dfrac{2}{3}$

(B) $\dfrac{nq}{p} = \dfrac{(2)(3)}{4} = \dfrac{6}{4} = \dfrac{3}{2} = 1\dfrac{1}{2}$

(C) $\dfrac{pq}{n} = \dfrac{(4)(3)}{2} = \dfrac{12}{2} = 6$

(D) $\dfrac{n}{pq} = \dfrac{2}{(4)(3)} = \dfrac{2}{12} = \dfrac{1}{6}$

(E) $\dfrac{p}{nq} = \dfrac{4}{(2)(3)} = \dfrac{4}{6} = \dfrac{2}{3}$

Choice (C) is the only one that yields 6, so it must be the correct answer.

When picking numbers for an abstract word problem like this one, try all five answer choices. Sometimes more than one choice will yield the correct result. When that happens, pick another set of numbers to eliminate the coincidences. *Avoid picking 0 and 1.* These often give several *possibly correct* answers.

BACKSOLVING

Sometimes it is not possible simply to pick numbers and solve the problem. In these cases, the answer choices become your tools, and you can work backward to find the right choice. We call this backsolving, which essentially means plugging the choices back into the question until you find the one that fits.

Backsolving works best when:

- The question is a complex word problem, and the answer choices are numbers
- The alternative is setting up multiple algebraic equations

Backsolving is not ideal:

- If the answer choices include variables
- On algebra questions or word problems that have ugly answer choices, such as radicals and fractions (plugging them in takes too much time)

A NOTE ON . . . WHY BACKSOLVING WORKS

The answer choices on the SAT are arranged in order, either descending or ascending, from (A) to (E). Choosing choice (C) first will guide your next step in solving the problem. For example, if plugging choice (C) into the equation gives you too small of a value, then either (A) and (B) or (D) and (E) can be eliminated, depending on which values are smaller than (C).

COMPLEX QUESTION, SIMPLE ANSWER CHOICES

Sometimes backsolving is faster than setting up an equation. For example:

A music club draws 27 patrons. If there are 7 more musicians than singers in the club, how many patrons are musicians?

(A) 8
(B) 10
(C) 14
(D) 17
(E) 20

EXPERT TUTOR TIP

" Backsolving can save time and energy, especially when you can avoid remembering and setting up equations. "

The five answer choices represent the possible number of musicians in the club, so try them in the question stem. The choice that gives a total of 27 patrons, with 7 more musicians than singers, will be the correct answer.

When backsolving, start with answer choice (C). For example, plugging in (C) gives you 14 musicians in the club. Because there are 7 more musicians than singers, there are 7 singers in the club. But $14 + 7 < 27$. The sum is too small, so there must be more than 14 musicians; thus, you can eliminate answer choices (A), (B), and (C) just like that.

Either (D) or (E) will be correct. Plugging in (D) gives you 17 musicians in the club; $17 - 7$ equals 10 singers, and $17 + 10 = 27$ patrons total. Answer choice (D) is correct.

Backsolving can also be useful if the problem has multiple equations relating the same variables:

If $a + b + c = 110$, $a = 4b$, and $3a = 2c$, then $b =$

(A) 6
(B) 8
(C) 9
(D) 10
(E) 14

You're looking for b, so plug in the answer choices for b in the question and see what happens. The choice that gives us 110 for the sum $a + b + c$ must be correct.

Start with the midrange number, 9, choice (C).

If $b = 9$, then $a = 4 \times 9 = 36$.

$2c = 3a = 3 \times 36 = 108$

$c = 54$

$a + b + c = 36 + 9 + 54 = 99$

Because this is a smaller sum than 110, the correct value for b must be larger. Therefore, eliminate answer choices (A), (B), and (C). Now, plug in either (D) or (E), and see which answer works.

GUESSING UNDER THE GUN

If you are short on time and have two answers left, choose a number that makes the most sense after your backsolving work.

Short on time? Try guessing between (D) and (E). But guess intelligently. Because (C) wasn't that far off the correct answer, you want to choose a number just slightly bigger than 9. That's choice (D).

USING PICKING NUMBERS AND BACKSOLVING

Because picking numbers and backsolving are such great techniques, and problems you can solve with them are so common, we have identified every problem from the Practice Tests that can be solved using them. If you look in the Answers and Explanations section of the four Practice Tests at the end of this book, you will notice a ①②③ or a ⟲ next to some of the answer explanations. These symbols mean that the problem can be solved with one of these two techniques. Since we explain how to use these techniques in this chapter, the book will often use the traditional method for solving the problem in the explanations. This doesn't mean those ways are better than backsolving or picking numbers. In general, whenever you can use one of these two techniques, you should. The techniques help you save time, eliminate common errors, and make harder problems much easier. Remember, there are multiple ways to solve a lot of the problems on the test, and picking numbers and backsolving are two fantastic and easy ones.

STRATEGIES FOR GUESSING ON MULTIPLE-CHOICE QUESTIONS

You *can* and *should* make *educated* guesses on the Math section of the SAT. If you can eliminate one or more wrong answer choices, it increases your odds of guessing correctly. This increases your score, which is a good thing. We'll show you how.

To make an educated guess, you need to eliminate answer choices that you know are wrong and guess from what's left. The more answer choices you can eliminate, the better chance you have of guessing the correct answer from what's left over. You do this by:

1. Eliminating unreasonable answer choices

2. Eliminating the obvious answers on hard questions

3. Eyeballing lengths, angles, and areas on geometry problems

> **EXPERT TUTOR TIP**
>
> " Only guess if you can follow one of Kaplan's strategies for educated guesses. Avoid guessing randomly. "

ELIMINATING UNREASONABLE ANSWER CHOICES

Before you guess, think about the problem, and decide which answers don't make sense:

> The ratio of celebrities to agents in a certain room is 13:11. If there are 429 celebrities in the room, how many agents are there?
>
> (A) 143
> (B) 363
> (C) 433
> (D) 507
> (E) 792

The ratio of celebrities to agents is 13:11, so there are more celebrities than not. Because there are 429 celebrities, there must be fewer than 429 agents. You can eliminate choices (C), (D), and (E). The answer must be either (A) or (B), so guess. The correct answer is (B).

ELIMINATING THE OBVIOUS ON HARD QUESTIONS

On the hard questions late in a set, obvious answers are usually wrong. So eliminate them when you guess.

This strategy does not hold true for easier questions that may appear at the beginning of the Math set, when the obvious answer could be right.

In the following difficult problem, found late in a question set, which obvious answer would you eliminate?

> A number x is increased by 30 percent, and then the result is decreased by 20 percent. What is the final result of these changes?
>
> (A) x is increased by 10 percent.
> (B) x is increased by 6 percent.
> (C) x is increased by 4 percent.
> (D x is decreased by 5 percent.
> (E) x is decreased by 10 percent.

If you picked (A) as the obvious choice to eliminate, you'd be right. Most people would combine the decrease of 20 percent with the increase of 30 percent, getting a net increase of 10 percent. That's the easy, obvious answer, but not the correct answer. If you must guess, avoid (A). The correct answer is (C).

> **PERFECT SCORE TIP**
>
> 66 When eliminating trap answer choices, think about why the choice was wrong. This often helped me work through the problem. 99

EYEBALLING LENGTHS, ANGLES, AND AREAS ON GEOMETRY PROBLEMS

Use diagrams that accompany geometry problems to help you eliminate wrong answer choices.

First, double-check for specific instructions involving whether or not the diagram is drawn to scale. Diagrams are always drawn to scale unless there's a note like this: Note: Figure not drawn to scale. If it's not drawn to scale, you cannot use this strategy. If it is, estimate quantities or eyeball the diagram, then eliminate answer choices that are way too large or too small.

Length—When a geometry question asks for a length, use the given lengths to estimate the unknown length. Measure off the given length by making a nick in your pencil with your thumbnail. Then hold the pencil against the unknown length on the diagram to see how the lengths compare. Try it.

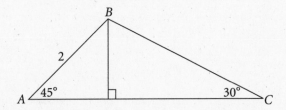

In the figure, what is the length of BC?

(A) $\sqrt{2}$

(B) 2

(C) $2\sqrt{2}$

(D) 4

(E) $4\sqrt{2}$

- AB is 2, so measure off this length on your pencil.

- Compare BC with this length.

- BC appears almost twice as long as AB, so BC is approximately 4.

- Because $\sqrt{2}$ is approximately 1.4, and BC is clearly longer than AB, choices (A) and (B) are too small.

- Choice (E) is greater than 4, so eliminate that.

- Now guess between (C) and (D). The correct answer is (C).

> **EXPERT TUTOR TIP**
>
> " Remember, unless it specifies in the problem, figures are always drawn to scale. "

Angles—You can also eyeball angles. To eyeball an angle, compare the angle with a familiar angle, such as a straight angle (180 degrees), a right angle (90 degrees), or half a right angle (45 degrees). The corner of a piece of paper is a right angle, so use that to see if an angle is greater or less than 90 degrees.

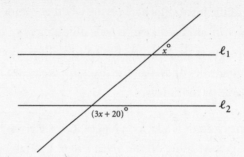

In the figure above, if $l_1 \parallel l_2$, what is the value of x?

(A) 40

(B) 50

(C) 80

(D) 100

(E) 130

- You see that x is less than 90 degrees, so eliminate choices (D) and (E).

- Because x appears to be much less than 90 degrees, eliminate choice (C).

- Now pick between (A) and (B). In fact, the correct answer is (A).

Areas—Eyeballing an area is similar to eyeballing a length. You compare an unknown area in a diagram to an area that you do know.

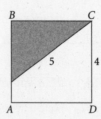

In square $ABCD$, what is the area of the shaded region?

(A) 4

(B) 6

(C) 8

(D) 9

(E) 10

Because *ABCD* is a square, it has the area 4^2, or 16. The shaded area is less than one-half the size of the square, so its area must be less than 8. Eliminate answer choices (C), (D), and (E). The correct answer is (B).

That wraps up the multiple-choice questions. Let's now move on to the other category of questions on the SAT, the Grid-in.

USING EYEBALLING ON THE TEST

Much like picking numbers and backsolving, eyeballing is a technique that can be used on many different problems in a single test. All of the problems in the four Practice Tests that can be solved by eyeballing have been identified with the 👁 symbol in the Answers and Explanations sections. Keep an eye out for this symbol as you check your answers, as it will help you learn when it is best to use this technique.

That wraps up the multiple-choice questions. Let's now move on to the other category of questions on the SAT, the Grid-in.

GRID-IN QUESTIONS

The Grid-in section on the SAT is more like the math tests you're used to taking at school. Rather than choosing your answer from five choices provided by the test makers, you have to work through the problem and write whatever answer you came up with in grid boxes on the answer sheet. Some Grid-in questions only have one correct answer, whereas others have several correct answers. *There is no penalty for wrong answers on the Grid-in section.*

DIRECTIONS

Each Grid-in question provides four boxes and a column of ovals, or bubbles, to write your answer in. The elements of your answer, that is, the digits, decimal points, or fraction signs, should be written in a separate box for each part. The corresponding bubbles underneath should be shaded in to match the box at the top of the column. There are limitations to what you may grid and what will not be counted.

> **PERFECT SCORE TIP**
>
> " Looking at the type of answer choice helps narrow down guesses for Grid-ins. If the question asks for a decimal or a fraction, don't put an integer in. "

> **EXPERT TUTOR TIP**
>
> " Think of Grid-in questions as a safe space to show off the math skills you've learned. And there aren't any pesky answer choices to confuse you! "

Each of the remaining ten questions requires you to solve the problem and enter your answer by marking the ovals in the special grid, as shown in the example below. You may use any available space for scratchwork.

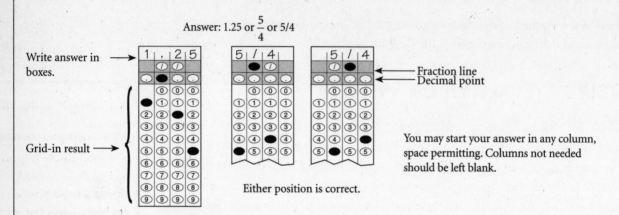

Answer: 1.25 or $\frac{5}{4}$ or 5/4

Write answer in boxes.

Grid-in result →

Fraction line
Decimal point

Either position is correct.

You may start your answer in any column, space permitting. Columns not needed should be left blank.

- It is recommended, though not required, that you write your answer in the boxes at the top of the columns. However, you will receive credit only for darkening the ovals correctly.

- Grid only one answer to a question, even though some problems have more than one correct answer.

- Darken no more than one oval in a column.

- No answers are negative.

- Mixed numbers cannot be gridded. For example: the number $1\frac{1}{4}$ must be gridded as 1.25 or 5/4.

(If ⊡ 1 ⊡ 1 ⊡ / ⊡ 4 is gridded, it will be interpreted as $\frac{11}{4}$, not $1\frac{1}{4}$.)

- Decimal Accuracy: Decimal answers must be entered as accurately as possible. For example, if you obtain an answer such as 0.1666..., you should record the result as .166 or .167. Less accurate values such as .16 or .17 are not acceptable.

Acceptable ways to grid $\frac{1}{6} = .1666...$

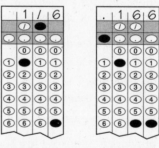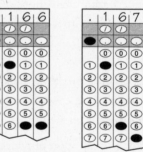

A NOTE ON GRID-INS AND MIXED NUMBERS

To grid a mixed number, you must first convert it to an improper fraction or decimal and then grid that new value. For example, $2\frac{1}{2}$ will be read as $\frac{21}{2}$ if gridded as a mixed number. Thus, gridding it as $\frac{5}{2}$ or 2.5 will ensure that your answer will be correct.

You **cannot** grid:

- Negative answers

- Answers with variables (x, y, w, etc.)

- Answers greater than 9,999

- Answers with commas (write 1000, not 1,000)

- Mixed numbers (such as $2\frac{1}{2}$)

GRID-IN STRATEGIES

The Grid-in section is special. Grid-in questions are not multiple-choice, and there is no penalty for wrong answers. You have to solve the equation in the question yourself and fill in your answer on a special grid.

WRITE YOUR ANSWERS IN THE NUMBER BOXES

This doesn't get you points by itself, but you will make fewer mistakes if you write your answers in the number boxes. You may think that gridding directly will save time, but writing first then gridding helps guarantee accuracy, which means more points.

ALWAYS START YOUR ANSWER IN THE FIRST COLUMN BOX

Of course, you can start in any column you choose, but if you go in order, you will avoid any confusion. If you always start with the first column, even if your answer has only one or two figures, your answers will always fit. However, there is no oval for 0 in the first column, so you will need to grid an answer with 0 in any other column.

GRID SMARTLY!

If your answer is .7, don't grid 0.7!

PERFECT SCORE TIP

Knowing my strengths improved my time management. I like algebra, so I tended to do all the algebra problems the first time I went through a section.

IN A FRACTIONAL ANSWER, GRID (/) IN THE CORRECT COLUMN

The sign (/) separates the numerator from the denominator. It appears only in columns two and three. A fractional answer with four digits—like $\frac{31}{42}$—won't fit and will need to be converted.

PLACE DECIMAL POINTS CAREFULLY

A few pointers:

- For a decimal less than 1, such as .127, enter the decimal point in the first column.

- Only grid in a zero before the decimal point if it is part of the answer, as in 20.5—don't put one there (if your answer is, say, .5) just to make your answer look more accurate. Don't begin an answer with a zero in the first column.

- Never grid a decimal point in the last column.

HOW TO HANDLE LONG OR REPEATING DECIMALS

Grid the first three digits only, and plug in the decimal point where it belongs. Say three answers are .45454545, 82.452312, and 1.428743:

- Grid .454, 82.4, and 1.42, respectively.

- You could round 1.428743 up to the nearest hundredth (1.43), but it's not required, and you could make a mistake.

- Note that rounding to an even shorter answer —1.4—would be incorrect.

MORE THAN ONE RIGHT ANSWER? CHOOSE ONE AND ENTER IT

Say you're asked for a two-digit integer that is a multiple of 2, 3, and 5. You might answer 30, 60, or 90. Whichever you grid would be right.

SOME GRID-INS HAVE A RANGE OF POSSIBLE ANSWERS

Suppose you're asked to grid a value of m where $1 - 2m < m$ and $5m - 2 < m$. Solving for m in the first inequality, you find that $\frac{1}{3} < m$. Solving for m in the second inequality, you find that $m < \frac{1}{2}$. So $\frac{1}{3} < m < \frac{1}{2}$. Grid in any value between $\frac{1}{3}$ and $\frac{1}{2}$. (Gridding in $\frac{1}{3}$ or $\frac{1}{2}$ would be wrong.) When the answer is a range of values, it's often easier to work with decimals: $.333 < m < .5$. This way, you can quickly grid .4 (or .35 or .45, etc.) as your answer.

GUESSING ON GRID-IN QUESTIONS

There are a lot of guessing techniques in the multiple-choice section of this chapter. Unfortunately, most of those techniques do not apply to Grid-ins—how could you eliminate obvious choices when there aren't any? However, there is one nice thing about guessing on Grid-ins: there is no penalty for it. This means you should **never** leave a Grid-in question blank, even if you just randomly write a number in.

FINDING THE RANGE ON GRID-INS

The main technique you can use for guessing on Grid-ins is to find the range of the question. This means you should figure out approximately what value the question is looking for. Is the question talking about fractions, or hundreds, or integers? Here is an example of a question where finding the range can help you to guess:

> How many integers between the values of 13 and 19,
> inclusive, have an even number of prime factors?

This could be a difficult question if you are not familiar with prime factorization. Even with the knowledge of how to solve the problem it still requires a lot of steps, and there are many opportunities to make errors. Instead, think about what the question is asking for—it wants some number of integers between 13 and 19. Well, there are seven numbers between these two values, and our answer has to be a whole number, so just guess a value between 0 and 7. Doing a little analysis can help to very quickly determine the range of possible answers, which makes guessing a lot easier.

USING YOUR CALCULATOR (OR NOT)

You've read about all of our techniques for finding the answers to Math questions using just your pencil and your mind. However, there are times when you can get some extra help and make life a little easier.

You are allowed to use a calculator on the SAT. However, that doesn't mean that you should always use your calculator on the SAT. Yes, you can do computations faster, but you may be tempted to waste time using a calculator on questions that shouldn't involve lengthy computation.

Remember, you never need a calculator to solve an SAT problem. If you ever find yourself doing extensive calculations—elaborate division or long, drawn-out multiplication—stop. You probably missed a shortcut.

SHOULD I JUST LEAVE MY CALCULATOR AT HOME?

No. Bring it. By zeroing in on the parts of problems that need calculation, you can increase your score and save yourself time on the SAT by using your calculator.

WHAT KIND OF CALCULATOR SHOULD I BRING?

One that you're comfortable with. If you don't have a calculator now, buy one right away, and practice using it between now and test day. You can use just about any small calculator; however, there are a few restrictions you must abide by.

You may not bring:

- Calculators that print out your calculations
- Handheld minicomputers or laptop computers
- Any calculators with a typewriter keypad
- Calculators with an angled readout screen
- Calculators that require a wall outlet
- Calculators that make noise

WHEN SHOULD I USE MY CALCULATOR?

Calculators help the most on Grid-ins. Because Grid-ins don't give you answer choices to choose from, it's especially important to be positive about your results, and calculators can help you check your work and avoid careless errors.

Remember, a calculator can be useful when used selectively and strategically. Not all parts of a problem will necessarily be easier with a calculator.

Consider this problem:

> If 4 grams of peanuts can make 32 Peanut Joy candy bars, how many Peanut Joy candy bars could be produced from 86 grams of peanuts?

This word problem has two steps. Step one is to set up the following proportion:

4 g of peanuts = 32 bars

A little algebraic engineering tells you that:

1 g of peanuts = 8 bars

Here's where you whip out that calculator. This problem has now been reduced down to pure calculation:

$86 \times 8 = 688$

WHEN SHOULD I AVOID MY CALCULATOR?

You may be tempted to use your calculator on every problem, but many questions will be easier without it. Look at this example:

If $x \neq \dfrac{1}{3}$ and $\dfrac{51}{3x-1} = \dfrac{51}{29}$, then what is the value of x?

One way of answering this question would be to cross-multiply and then isolate x:

$$(51)(29) = (3x - 1)(51)$$
$$1{,}479 = 153x - 51$$
$$1{,}530 = 153x$$
$$\frac{1{,}530}{153} = x$$
$$10 = x$$

Notice how much more quickly you'll arrive at the answer if, rather than reflexively reaching for your calculator, you invest a few moments in thinking about the question—specifically what you're given and what you're asked for. Notice that after you cross-multiplied the equation above, you were left with $(51)(29) = (3x - 1)(51)$. Simply cancel out 51 from both sides. You are now left with the following equation:

$$3x - 1 = 29$$
$$3x = 30$$
$$x = 10$$

TWO COMMON CALCULATOR MISTAKES

Be aware of the two following common calculator mistakes. Learning how to avoid them now will help you keep from losing points on test day.

EXPERT TUTOR TIP

" Don't rely too much on your calculator—you might not find the answer you need. Use it only to save time. "

PERFECT SCORE TIP

" If I couldn't think of a reason why using a calculator would make a problem easier or quicker to solve, I didn't use it. "

COMMON CALCULATOR MISTAKE #1: CALCULATING BEFORE YOU THINK

On the Grid-in problem below, how should (and shouldn't) you use your calculator?

> The sum of all the integers from 1 to 44, inclusive, is subtracted from the sum of all the integers from 7 to 50, inclusive. What is the result?

THE WRONG APPROACH:

1. Grab calculator.
2. Punch in all the numbers.
3. Put down answer and hope you didn't hit any wrong buttons.

You might be tempted to punch in all the numbers from 1 to 44, find their sum, do the same for the numbers 7 through 50, and then subtract the first sum from the second. But doing that means punching 252 keys. The odds are you'll hit the wrong key somewhere and get the wrong answer. Even if you don't, punching in all those numbers takes too much time.

THE KAPLAN APPROACH:

1. Think first.
2. Decide on the best way to solve the problem.
3. Only then, use your calculator.

The right approach is to *think first*. The amount of computation involved in directly solving this tells you that there must be an easier way. You'll see this if you realize that both sums contain the same number of consecutive integers. Each integer in the first sum has a corresponding integer 6 digits greater than it in the second sum:

$$
\begin{array}{cc}
1 & 7 \\
+2 & +8 \\
+3 & +9 \\
\ldots & \\
\ldots & \\
\ldots & \\
+42 & +48 \\
+43 & +49 \\
+44 & +50 \\
= & = \\
\end{array}
$$

As you'll see in the Math Traps chapter, the way to find the number of integers in a consecutive series is to subtract the smallest from the largest and add:

1 (44 − 1 = 43; 43 + 1 = 44 or 50 − 7 = 43; 43 + 1 = 44).

So there are 44 pairs of integers that are 6 apart.

Therefore, the total difference between the two sums will be the difference between each pair of integers times the number of pairs. Now take out your calculator, punch $6 \times 44 =$, and get the correct answer of 264 with little or no time wasted.

COMMON CALCULATOR MISTAKE #2: FORGETTING THE ORDER OF OPERATIONS

Even when you use your calculator, you can't just enter numbers in the order they appear on the page—you have to follow the order of operations. This is a very simple error, but it can cost you lots of points. The order of operations is PEMDAS, which stands for:

Parentheses first, then deal with

Exponents, then

Multiplication and

Division (from left to right), and finally

Addition and

Subtraction (from left to right)

For example, say you want to find the value of the expression $\frac{x^2+1}{x+3}$ when $x = 7$.

If you just punched in $7 \times 7 + 1 \div 7 + 3 =$, you would get the wrong answer.

The correct way to work it out is:

$$(7^2 + 1) \div (7 + 3) = (7 \times 7 + 1) \div (7 + 3) = (49 + 1) \div 10 = 50 \div 10 = 5$$

Combining a calculator with an understanding of when and how to use it can help you boost your score.

> **PERFECT SCORE TIP**
>
> " If my calculations involved parentheses in any way, I would always make sure that they were correct before pressing "Enter." I avoided a lot of errors this way! "

PUNCH WISELY!

Don't just grab your calculator, punch in all the numbers, and put down an answer. You'll have to hope you didn't hit any wrong keys. If you have time, always check your answers.

PRACTICE

REGULAR MATH

1. A certain pump can drain a full 375-gallon tank in 15 minutes. At this rate, how many more minutes would it take to drain a full 600-gallon tank?

   (A) 9
   (B) 15
   (C) 18
   (D) 24
   (E) 25

2. A gardener plants flowers in the following order: carnations, daffodils, larkspurs, tiger lilies, and zinnias. If the gardener planted 47 flowers, what kind of flower did he plant last?

   (A) carnation
   (B) daffodil
   (C) larkspur
   (D) tiger lily
   (E) zinnia

3. How many different positive two-digit integers are there such that the tens' digit is greater than 5 and the units' digit is odd?

   (A) 10
   (B) 12
   (C) 15
   (D) 20
   (E) 25

4. If a and b are positive integers, what is a percent of b percent of 200?

   (A) $\dfrac{ab}{100}$
   (B) $\dfrac{ab}{50}$
   (C) ab
   (D) $50ab$
   (E) $100ab$

5. A 7.5-L mixture of water and molasses is 60 percent molasses. If 1.5 L of water is added, approximately what percent of the new mixture is molasses?

   (A) 40%
   (B) 50%
   (C) 63%
   (D) 64%
   (E) 68%

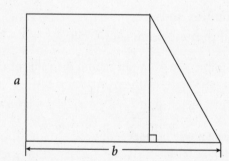

6. The figure above is formed from a square and a right triangle. What is its area?

   (A) $\dfrac{a(a+b)}{2}$
   (B) $\dfrac{a^2+b^2}{2}$
   (C) $\dfrac{a(b-a)}{2}$
   (D) a^2+b^2
   (E) $a^2+\dfrac{ab}{2}$

7. If Jason read x pages on Wednesday, twice as many pages on Thursday as on Wednesday, and 3 pages more on Friday then on Thursday, what was Jason's average number of pages read over those three days?

   (A) $x + 3$

   (B) $x + 1$

   (C) $3x + 3$

   (D) $\frac{5}{3}x + 1$

   (E) $5x + 3$

8. A certain number, first added to 4, then multiplied by 3, and finally subtracted from 100, is 13. What is the number?

   (A) 21

   (B) 22

   (C) 23

   (D) 24

   (E) 25

9. If $3x = 2y$, $x + 1 = z$, and $3y - 2z = 8$, what is the value of x?

   (A) 4

   (B) 5

   (C) 6

   (D) 7

   (E) 8

10. If a and b are even numbers and c is an odd number, which of the following must be an odd number?

   (A) $3(a - bc)$

   (B) $2ab + cb$

   (C) $\dfrac{4c}{a + b}$

   (D) $3(a + b + c)$

   (E) $5abc$

GRID-INS

11. If the three-digit number 11Q is a prime number, what digit is represented by Q?

12. The sum of five consecutive odd integers is 425. What is the greatest of these integers?

13. A triangle has one side of length 3 and another of length 7. If the length of the third side is a solution to the equation $x^2 - 2x = 63$, what is the length of the third side?

14. A dress in a store costs x dollars. After a sale, the dress is reduced by 20%. Then, when it still isn't sold, it is reduced by another 20%. The new cost is what percentage of the original price of the dress?

15. What does the expression $\left(\dfrac{5x}{4}\right)\left(\dfrac{4x}{5}\right)\left(\dfrac{10}{x^2}\right) + \left(\dfrac{1}{5}\right)\left(\dfrac{2}{3}\right)\left(\dfrac{5}{2}\right)$ simplify to?

16. How many integers are there from −21.33 to 8.99?

ANSWERS AND EXPLANATIONS

1. A
SMARTPOINTS CATEGORY: RATIOS

You are given that the pump drains 375 gallons in 15 minutes and asked for the number of additional minutes it would take to drain a 600-gallon tank. Because we are dealing with the *additional* minutes, we're really just looking for the amount of time that it'd take to drain 600 − 375 = 225 gallons. 225 gallons is less than 375, so it should take less than 15 minutes. The only choice *less than 15* is (A).

2. B
SMARTPOINTS CATEGORY: SEQUENCES

You're looking for the 47th flower in a repeating pattern. Because there are five different flowers in the pattern, the last flower in the pattern corresponds to a multiple of 5. So the 5th, 10th,... and 45th flowers will be zinnias. But there will also be two *remainders*, and so the 46th will be the first flower in the pattern and the 47th will be the second flower, which is (B), daffodil.

3. D
SMARTPOINTS CATEGORY: NUMBER PROPERTIES

We want two-digit numbers with a tens' digit greater than 5 and a units' digit that's odd, so we're looking for odd two-digit numbers greater than 60. From 60 to 99, there are 99 − 60 + 1 = 39 + 1 = 40 numbers. Half of these are even and half are odd, so the answer is 40 ÷ 2 = 20, choice (D).

4. B
SMARTPOINTS CATEGORY: PERCENTS

Multiple percents with variables *look* scary but they're really not that bad if you remember to pick numbers. In even the scariest, most abstract math problem on the SAT, there will always be at least one concrete spot for you to work from. In this problem, that's the number 200. Working backwards in that sentence, we're looking for b percent of 200, then a percent of the result. So pick 100 for b and 50 for a. Now the problem becomes: "What's 50 percent of 100 percent of 200?" Well, 100 percent of 200 is 200 and 50 percent of that is half of 200, or 100, so the correct choice needs to evaluate to 100 when $a = 50$ and $b = 100$. Right away, you may have noticed that (C), (D), and (E) would be way too large. Both (A) and (B) involve 50 × 100 in the numerator. (A) divides that by 100, leaving you with 50, while (B) divides it by 50, leaving you with 100, so (B) is correct.

5. B

SMARTPOINTS CATEGORY: PERCENTS

First find the amount of molasses in the original mixture. There are 7.5 L of the mixture, of which 60% is molasses, so there are $\frac{60}{100} \times 7.5 = 4.5$ L of molasses. An additional 1.5 L of water is added, so now the mixture is $7.5 + 1.5 = 9$ L, of which 4.5 L is molasses. Percent $= \frac{\text{Part}}{\text{Whole}} \times 100\%$, so in this case, $\frac{4.5}{9} \times 100\% = .5 \times 100\% = 50\%$.

If you were low on time and needed to guess, you may have noticed that we're *diluting* a mixture that was originally 60% molasses, so the resulting mixture must be less than 60% molasses. That allows you to eliminate (C), (D), and (E) right off the bat. Choice (B) is correct.

6. A

SMARTPOINTS CATEGORY: COMPLEX FIGURES

With all those variables in the answer choices, this problem is perfect for picking numbers. First, relabel the diagram as follows:

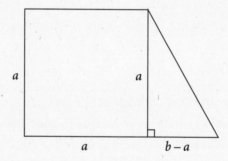

Let's pick some numbers for a and b. Because b is clearly greater than a, try $a = 3$ and $b = 5$. The area of a square is the square of its side, so the area of this square is $3^2 = 9$. The area of a right triangle is $\frac{1}{2} \times$ base $\times$ height, so the area of this triangle is $\frac{1}{2} \times 2 \times 3 = 3$. So the combined area when $a = 3$ and $b = 5$ is $9 + 3 = 12$.

Now plug those values into each of the choices and see which one returns a value of 12:

(A) $\frac{a(a+b)}{2} = \frac{3(3+5)}{2} = \frac{3(8)}{2} = \frac{24}{2} = 12$

(B) $\frac{a^2+b^2}{2} = \frac{3^2+5^2}{2} = \frac{9+25}{2} = \frac{34}{2} = 17$. Eliminate.

(C) $\frac{a(b-a)}{2} = \frac{3(5-3)}{2} = \frac{3(2)}{2} = 6$. Eliminate.

(D) $a^2 + b^2 = 3^2 + 5^2 = 9 + 25 = 34$. Eliminate.

(E) $a^2 + \frac{ab}{2} = 3^2 + \frac{3(5)}{2} = 9 + \frac{15}{2} = \frac{18}{2} + \frac{15}{2} = \frac{33}{2} = 16\frac{1}{2}$. Eliminate.

Only (A) works, so it must be correct.

7. D

SMARTPOINTS CATEGORY: AVERAGES

Quickly identify that this problem can be solved by picking numbers (hint: there are variables in the answer choice).

There are no constraints on x, so pick $x = 4$ and rewrite the problem with that value:

If Jason read 4 pages on Wednesday, twice as many pages on Thursday as on Wednesday, and 3 pages more on Friday than on Thursday, what was Jason's average number of pages read over those 3 days?

So, Jason read 4 pages on Wednesday, $4 \times 2 = 8$ pages on Thursday, and $8 + 3 = 11$ pages on Friday. The total number of pages he read was 23, and the average is $\dfrac{23}{3}$.

(A) $x + 3 = 4 + 3 = 7$. Eliminate.

(B) $x + 1 = 4 + 1 = 5$. Eliminate.

(C) $3x + 3 = 3(4) + 3 = 15$. Eliminate.

(D) $\dfrac{5}{3}x + 1 = \dfrac{5}{3}(4) + 1 = \dfrac{20}{3} + \dfrac{3}{3} = \dfrac{23}{3}$. Works.

(E) $5x + 3 = 5(4) + 3 = 23$. Eliminate.

Only (D) works, so it must be correct. Note: Picking $x = 3$ would have resulted in both (A) and (D) working. It is always a good idea to avoid picking numbers that already occur in the problem.

8. E

SMARTPOINTS CATEGORY: NUMBER PROPERTIES

Since the question asks to determine what number works in the problem, backsolving is a good approach. Starting with 23:

$3(23 + 4) = 3(27) = 81$ and $100 - 81 = 19$

Our value is too large, so eliminate (D) and (E). But wait! Notice that the value we plug in eventually gets subtracted from 100, so using larger numbers will actually result in smaller values. Therefore, eliminate (A) and (B).

Trying 25:

$3(25 + 4) = 3(29) = 87$ and $100 - 87 = 13$

This is the difference we wanted, so (E) must be the answer.

While it happens seldom, there are times when backsolving with a larger number results in a smaller answer. You should always try to determine if this is the case when eliminating.

9. A

SMARTPOINT CATEGORIES: QUADRATIC EQUATIONS

We have three equations and three variables, so x could be found by substituting and solving for variables. However, this problem can also be solved with backsolving.

Starting with (C):

$3(6) = 2y$, so $y = 9$

$6 + 1 = z$, so $z = 7$

$3(9) = 2(7) = 27 - 14 = 13$. This is too large, so eliminate (D) and (E).

Trying (A):

$3(4) = 2y$, so $y = 6$

$4 + 1 = z$, so $z = 5$

$3(6) - 2(5)$, $18 - 10 = 8$

Backsolving with 4 results in 8, so (A) is the answer.

10. D

SMARTPOINTS CATEGORIES: NUMBER PROPERTIES

The question is about even and odd numbers, so let's pick numbers:

$a = 4, b = 6, c = 5$

(A) $3(a - bc) = 3(4 - 6(5)) = 3(4 - 30) = 3(-26) = -78$. Eliminate.

(B) $2ab + cb = 2(4)(6) - (6)(5) = 48 - 30 = 18$. Eliminate.

(C) $\dfrac{4c}{a+b} = \dfrac{4(5)}{4+6} = \dfrac{20}{10} = 2$. Eliminate.

(D) $3(a + b + c) = 3(4 + 6 + 5) = 3(15) = 45$

(E) $5abc = 5(4)(6)(5) = 600$. Eliminate.

(D) is the only one that works, so it must be the answer.

11. 3

SMARTPOINTS CATEGORY: NUMBER PROPERTIES 🔋

This problem may be a Grid-in, but you *can* actually backsolve it. Begin by narrowing down your list of possible values for Q to backsolve from. Q is a digit, so it must be one of the integers from 0 through 9. Because a prime number is a number that cannot be divisible by anything other than 1 and itself, eliminate digits that would make the number violate this property. We can begin by eliminating all the even digits, as they would produce numbers divisible by 2. Eliminate 1 and 7, as they would produce numbers divisible by 3 (a number is divisible by 3 if the sum of its digits is a multiple of 3). Eliminate 5, as that produces a number divisible by 5. You are now left with 3 and 9, and the only divisibility under 10 that we haven't checked is 7.

Dividing 113 and 119 by 7 reveals that $119 = 7 \times 17$, so the answer is 3.

12. 89

SMARTPOINTS CATEGORY: AVERAGES 🔋

The middle integer of an odd number of consecutive integers will be equal to their average. Five consecutive odd integers sum to 425, so the middle integer is $425 \div 5 = 85$. This is the third integer in the set, so the fourth integer is $85 + 2 = 87$, and the fifth (and greatest) integer is $87 + 2 = 89$, the correct answer.

13. 9

SMARTPOINTS CATEGORY: QUADRATIC EQUATIONS 🔋

The Triangle Inequality Theorem states that any side of a triangle is always shorter than the sum and longer than the difference of the other two sides. The two given sides are 3 and 7, so the third side must be shorter than $3 + 7 = 10$ and longer than $7 - 3 = 4$. SAT quadratic solutions tend to be integers, so we're really dealing with the integers 5, 6, 7, 8, or 9 as possible "choices."

That allows us to backsolve for the answer. Begin with 7, the middle value:

$$x^2 - 2x = 63$$

$$7^2 - 2(7) = 63$$

$$49 - 14 = 63$$

$$35 \neq 63$$

So 7 is much too small. Eliminate 5, 6, and 7. Let's try 9:

$$x^2 - 2x = 63$$

$$9^2 - 2(9) = 63$$

$$81 - 18 = 63$$

$$63 = 63$$

That works, so the answer is 9.

14. 64

SMARTPOINTS CATEGORIES: PERCENTS

Begin by picking a value for x. Since this is a percentage problem, 100 is the best choice. $20\%(100) = .2(100) = 20$, so after the first discount the dress is $100 - 20 = 80$ dollars. Now, the second discount:

$20\%(80) = .2(80) = 16$, so after the second discount the dress is $80 - 16 = 64$.

$\frac{64}{100} = 64\%$, so the second price is 64% of the original cost.

15. $\frac{31}{3}$, or 10.3

SMARTPOINTS CATEGORIES: NUMBER PROPERTIES

Multiplying the numerators and dividing by the denominators in each part of this expression results in

$$\frac{200x}{20x^2} + \frac{10}{30} = 10 + \frac{1}{3}$$

Notice though that you can't put in $10\frac{1}{3}$ as an answer, since it is a mixed number. Either convert to an improper fraction, $\frac{31}{3}$, or a decimal, $10.333 = 10.3$.

16. 30

SMARTPOINTS CATEGORIES: NUMBER PROPERTIES

The integers contained in the range start at −21 and end at 8, so just count up all the integers between these values.

−21 to −1 is 21 numbers, 0 is 1 number, 1 to 8 is 8 numbers.

$21 + 1 + 8 = 30$, so there are 30 integers.

KEY POINTS YOU'VE LEARNED IN THIS CHAPTER

1. SAT Math Facts:

   - Math questions are arranged by order of difficulty.

   - There are two types of questions on the test: multiple-choice and Grid-ins.

   - Don't automatically reach for the calculator to solve an equation. Often, there is an easier path to the answer.

   - All figures are drawn to scale unless otherwise indicated.

2. Multiple-Choice Questions:

   - You lose $\frac{1}{4}$ point for each incorrect multiple-choice answer.

3. Grid-in Questions:

   - You don't lose any points for incorrect Grid-in answers.

   - You have to calculate and write out (carefully) your own answers for them.

   - Mixed numbers must be converted to improper fractions or decimals for Grid-ins.

4. Kaplan's Target Strategy for Math:

   1. Estimate the question's difficulty.

   2. Read the question.

   3. Skip or do.

   4. Look for the fastest approach.

5. Problem-Solving Strategies:

   - Picking numbers is a good strategy for abstract questions.

   - Backsolving works well for complex word problems or questions requiring numerous algebraic equations.

6. Educated Guessing Strategies:

   - Eliminate unreasonable answer choices.

   - Eliminate the obvious answers on hard questions.

   - Eyeball lengths, angles, and areas.

   - Find the range on Grid-in questions.

CHAPTER 14: BASIC MATH CONCEPTS

SMARTPOINTS COVERED IN THIS CHAPTER

EQUATIONS

FUNCTIONS

TRIANGLES

RATIOS

RATES

DIVISIBILITY

AVERAGES

PERCENTS

COMPLEX FIGURES

PERMUTATIONS AND COMBINATIONS

WHAT TO EXPECT ON TEST DAY

The SAT Math section has always tested certain topics of basic math. When you are confident that you understand these basic math concepts, the SAT Math section gets a whole lot easier.

THE TEN MOST TESTED BASIC MATH CONCEPTS

This chapter reviews these basic math concepts and explains how the SAT tests them. We also teach you our techniques for solving these problems and how these techniques will work with both types of SAT Math questions: regular math and Grid-ins.

EQUATIONS

Equation problems can involve things as simple as $3 + 4 = 7$ or as complex as $15x^5z + 23yz^3 \div 13x^4y = 4$. Sometimes the SAT will even ask for the value of a variable derived from a set of equations, known as simultaneous equations.

To get a numerical value for each variable in a simultaneous equation, you need as many different equations as there are variables. So, if you have two variables, you need two distinct equations. Let's look at the following example:

If $p + 2q = 14$ and $3p + q = 12$, then $p =$

(Note: This is a Grid-in, so there are no answer choices.)

You could tackle this problem by solving for one variable in terms of the other and then plugging this expression into the other equation. But the simultaneous equations that appear on the SAT can usually be handled in an easier way.

Combine the equations, by adding or subtracting them, to cancel out all but one of the variables. You can't eliminate p or q by adding or subtracting the equations in their present forms. But if you multiply the second equation by 2, you'll have this equation:

$$2(3p + q) = 2(12)$$
$$6p + 2q = 24$$

With this new equation, subtracting one equation from the other is easier because the q's will cancel out, so you can solve for p:

$$6p + 2q = 24$$
$$-[p + 2q = 14]$$
$$5p + 0 = 10$$

If $5p = 10$, $p = 2$. On the answer sheet, you would grid in the answer 2.

Let's look at another example of a good equations problem:

If $m - n = 5$ and $2m + 4n = 16$, then $m + n =$

(A) 1

(B) 6

(C) 7

(D) 10

(E) 15

This problem could be solved the way we solved the previous example, eliminating one of the variables and then solving for the second. However, notice that the value you are looking for is $m + n$. Very often, problems like this have a shortcut to find the answer.

Let's see what happens if we simply add these two equations together:

$$
\begin{array}{r}
m - n = 5 \\
+[2m + 4n = 16] \\
\hline
3m + 3n = 21
\end{array}
$$

$3m + 3n$ is a multiple of $m + n$, so if we divide both sides by 3 we get $m + n = 7$, so (C) is the answer. This is a much faster way than finding both variables, but it takes practice to notice how you should combine the equations.

DIFFERENT IS NOT DISTINCT

Two equations are considered distinct *only* if one cannot simplify into the other.

$A + B = 4$ and $2A + 2B = 8$ may look *different*, but they aren't *distinct*.

FUNCTIONS

A common type of Function question on the SAT is one that uses symbols. You should be quite familiar with the arithmetic symbols $+$, $-$, $\times$, and $\div$. Finding the value of $10 + 2$, $18 - 4$, 4×9, or $96 \div 16$ is easy. However, on the SAT, you may come across bizarre symbols. You may even be asked to find the value of $10 \star 2$, $5 \ast 7$, $10 \bullet 6$, or $65 \heartsuit 2$.

BE READY FOR STRANGE SYMBOLS

The SAT puts strange symbols in questions to confuse or unnerve you. Don't let it succeed. The question stem always tells you what the strange symbol means. Although this type of question may look difficult, it is really an exercise in plugging in numbers.

Look at the following example:

If $a \star b = \sqrt{a+b}$ for all nonnegative numbers, what is the value of $10 \star 6$?

(A) 0
(B) 2
(C) 4
(D) 8
(E) 16

To solve, just plug in 10 for a and 6 for b into the expression $\sqrt{a+b}$. That equals $\sqrt{10+6}$, or $\sqrt{16} = 4$, choice (C). Don't get confused by the symbol; just plug in the numbers, and you'll be fine.

Let's look at another example of a strange symbol problem:

$x \star y = \dfrac{(x-y)}{x}$, where $x \neq 0$. If $9 \star 4 = 15 \star k$, then $k =$

(A) 3
(B) 6
(C) $\dfrac{20}{3}$
(D) $\dfrac{25}{3}$
(E) 9

This problem contains two strange symbol relationships, and a variable. Even though it looks much harder, remember, all you have to do is plug in the values:

$$\frac{(9-4)}{9} = \frac{(15-k)}{15}$$

Now there is an equation with a single variable. Let's cross multiply and solve for k:

$$15(5) = 9(15 - k)$$

$$75 = 135 - 9k$$

$$-60 = -9k$$

$$\frac{-60}{-9} = k$$

$$\frac{20}{3} = k$$

So we get answer choice (C). (Note: This problem could be solved problem with backsolving, though make sure to be careful with all those fractions.)

TRIANGLES

Look for the special triangles in geometry problems. Special triangles contain a lot of information. For instance, if you know the length of one side of a 30-60-90 triangle, you can easily work out the lengths of the others. Special triangles allow you to transfer one piece of information around the whole figure.

> ## KNOW THE TRIANGLES
>
> The SAT instructions list the properties of many triangles in the test book for easy referral. However, if you know them by heart, you'll save a lot of time on test day.

The following are the special triangles you should look for on the SAT. You don't have to memorize the ratios (they're listed in the instructions), but you'll need to be able to recognize them when you see them.

EQUILATERAL TRIANGLES

All interior angles are 60 degrees, and all sides have equal length.

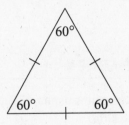

ISOSCELES TRIANGLES

Two sides have equal length, and the angles facing these sides are equal.

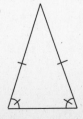

> **PERFECT SCORE TIP**
>
> " I almost always found special triangles in more complicated geometry figures. Knowing their properties usually eliminated all calculations I would have otherwise needed. "

RIGHT TRIANGLES

These contain a 90-degree angle. The sides are related by the Pythagorean theorem: $a^2 + b^2 = c^2$, where a and b are the legs and c is the hypotenuse.

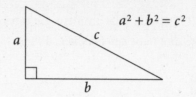

THE *SPECIAL* RIGHT TRIANGLES

Many triangle problems contain *special* right triangles in which the side lengths always come in predefined ratios. If you recognize them, you won't have to use the Pythagorean theorem to find the value of a missing side length.

THE 3-4-5 RIGHT TRIANGLE

(Be on the lookout for multiples of 3-4-5 as well.)

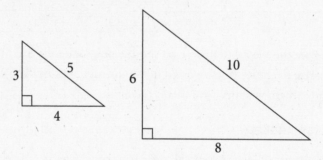

TRIANGLE INEQUALITY THEOREM

When you add the lengths of any two sides of any triangle, the result must be *greater* than the length of the third side.

THE ISOSCELES RIGHT TRIANGLE

(Note the side ratio: 1 to 1 to $\sqrt{2}$.)

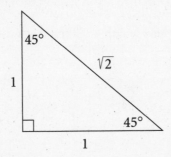

THE 30-60-90 RIGHT TRIANGLE

(Note the side ratio: 1 to $\sqrt{3}$ to 2, and which side is opposite which angle.)

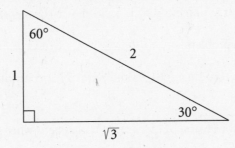

Now that we've gone through all the special triangles, try this problem:

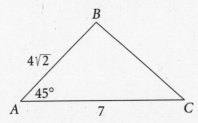

Note: Figure not drawn to scale.

In the triangle above, what is the length of side *BC*?

(A) 4
(B) 5
(C) $4\sqrt{2}$
(D) 6
(E) $5\sqrt{2}$

PERFECT SCORE TIP

" When it didn't seem like there was enough information to solve a problem, I always made sure to check for special triangles. More often than not, I found one, which was usually the key to solving the problem. "

You can drop a vertical line from *B* to line *AC*. This divides the triangle into two right triangles. That means you know two of the angles in the triangle on the left: 90° and 45°. The third angle must also be 45°, so this is an isosceles right triangle, with sides in the ratio of 1 to 1 to $\sqrt{2}$.

The hypotenuse here is $4\sqrt{2}$, so both legs have length 4. Filling this in, you have the following:

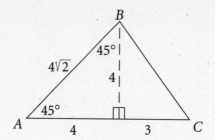

Now you can see that the legs of the smaller triangle on the right must be 4 and 3, making this a 3-4-5 right triangle, and the length of hypotenuse *BC* is 5. So choice (B) is correct.

Here's another example of a triangle problem:

In the coordinate plane, point *R* has coordinates (0, 0) and point *S* has coordinates (9, 12). What is the distance from *R* to *S*?

This problem might at first seem out of place, but let's see what happens when we draw a diagram:

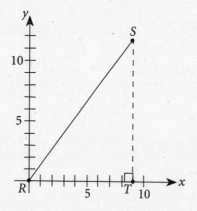

Because *S* has a *y*-coordinate of 12, it's 12 units above the *x*-axis, so the length of *ST* must be 12. Also, because *T* is the same number of units to the right of the *y*-axis as *S*, given by the *x*-coordinate of 9, the distance from the origin to *T* must be 9. So we have a right triangle with legs of 9 and 12. You should recognize this as a multiple of the 3-4-5 triangle. $9 = 3 \times 3$; $12 = 3 \times 4$; so the hypotenuse *RS* must be 3×5, or 15.

RATIOS

SAT test makers often write ratio questions in a way that tricks you into setting up the wrong ratio. For instance, try to work through the question below:

> Out of every 50 CDs produced in a certain factory, 20 are scratched. What is the ratio of unscratched CDs produced to scratched CDs produced?

(A) 2:5
(B) 3:5
(C) 2:3
(D) 3:2
(E) 5:2

You need to find the parts and the whole in this problem. In this case, the total number of CDs is the whole, and the numbers of unscratched CDs and scratched CDs, respectively, are the parts that make up this whole. You're given a part-to-whole ratio (the ratio of scratched CDs to all CDs) and asked to find a part-to-part ratio (the ratio of unscratched CDs to scratched CDs).

If 20 CDs of every 50 are scratched, the remaining 30 CDs must be okay. So the part-to-part ratio of good-to-scratched CDs is 30:20, or 3:2, choice (D). If you hadn't identified the part and the whole first, it would have been easy to become confused and compare a part to the whole, like the ratios in answer choices (A), (B), and (E).

Part:part ratio problems give you the whole number and one part number. Using simple math, you can usually figure out the quantity of the other part of the whole.

This approach also works for ratio questions where you need to find actual quantities. Here's an example:

> Of every 5 CDs produced in a certain factory, 2 are scratched. If 2,200 CDs were produced, how many were scratched?

(Note: This is a Grid-in, so there are no answer choices.)

Here you need to find a quantity: the number of defective CDs. If you're looking for the actual quantities in a ratio, set up and solve a proportion. You're given a part-to-whole ratio (the ratio of scratched CDs to all CDs) and the total number of CDs produced. You can find the answer by setting up and solving a proportion:

PERFECT SCORE TIP

❝ When solving ratio problems, I always circled what the question was asking and made sure to find all the parts and the whole so I didn't make any silly mistakes. ❞

EXPERT TUTOR TIP

❝ For *part* and *whole* questions, make sure you know if the question is asking you to compare *part* to *whole* or *part* to *part*. ❞

$$\frac{\text{Number of scratched CDs}}{\text{Total number of CDs}} = \frac{2}{5} = \frac{x}{2,200}$$

x = number of scratched CDs

$5x = 4,400$ (by cross-multiplying $\frac{2}{5} = \frac{x}{2,200}$)

$x = 880$ (by dividing both sides by 5)

Here's one last kind of ratio problem:

The ratio of right-handed pitchers to left-handed pitchers in a certain baseball league is 11:7. What fractional part of the pitchers in the league is left-handed?

(A) $\frac{6}{7}$

(B) $\frac{6}{11}$

(C) $\frac{7}{11}$

(D) $\frac{7}{18}$

(E) $\frac{11}{18}$

Once again, you need to find the parts and the whole in this problem. The parts are known, but not the whole. To calculate the whole, remember it is just the sum of the parts:

11 right-handed pitchers + 7 left-handed pitchers = 18 total pitchers

So there are 18 pitchers total as the whole. Now set up the ratio:

$\frac{\text{left-handed}}{\text{total}} = \frac{7}{18}$, or answer choice (D).

RATIOS

Remember that ratios compare only relative size; they don't tell you the actual quantities involved. Distinguish clearly between the parts and the whole in ratio problems.

RATES

A rate is a ratio that compares quantities represented by different units. In the following problem, the units are dollars and the number of headphones. **Pick numbers for the variables** to find the context of the relationship:

If 8 headphones cost a dollars, b headphones would cost how many dollars?

(A) $8ab$

(B) $\dfrac{8a}{b}$

(C) $\dfrac{8}{ab}$

(D) $\dfrac{a}{8b}$

(E) $\dfrac{ab}{8}$

This rate problem at first seems difficult because of the variables. It's hard to get a clear picture of what the relationship is between the units. You need to pick numbers for the variables to find the context of that relationship.

Pick numbers for a and b that will be easy for you to work with in the problem.

Let $a = 16$. Then 8 headphones will cost \$16. So the cost per headphone at this rate is $\dfrac{\$16}{8 \text{ headphones}} = \$2$ per headphone. Let $b = 5$. Therefore, the cost of 5 headphones at this rate will be 5 headphones $\times$ \$2 per headphone = \$10.

Now plug in $a = 16$ and $b = 5$ into the answer choices to see which one gives you a value of 10:

(A) $8 \times 16 \times 5 = 640$. Eliminate.

(B) $\dfrac{8 \times 16}{5} = \dfrac{128}{5}$. Eliminate.

(C) $\dfrac{8}{16 \times 5} = \dfrac{1}{10}$. Eliminate.

(D) $\dfrac{16}{8 \times 5} = \dfrac{2}{5}$. Eliminate.

(E) $\dfrac{16 \times 5}{8} = 10$

Because (E) is the only one that gives the correct value, it is the correct answer.

PERFECT SCORE TIP

" Picking numbers is a great way to tackle rate questions. Knowing when to plug in numbers and which ones to use was an unbelievable time-saver! "

DEALING WITH VARIABLES

> Don't let a problem with lots of variables throw you off. If a problem has
> variables and plenty of them, picking numbers *will* work!

Now let's look at another rate problem, this time with no variables:

> If Seymour drove 125 miles in 2.5 hours at a constant speed, how many miles did he travel
> in the first 24 minutes?
>
> (A) 15
> (B) 18
> (C) 20
> (D) 24
> (E) 30

Notice that we are working with three different units here: miles, hours, and minutes. We need to
convert our hours to minutes and then set up our rate:

2.5 hours is 2 hours and 30 minutes, for a total of 150 minutes. So:

$$\frac{125 \text{ miles}}{150 \text{ minutes}} = \frac{x \text{ miles}}{24 \text{ minutes}}$$

First, since our units line up, we can cross all of them out:

$$\frac{125}{150} = \frac{x}{24}$$

Second, while we could multiply the 24 over to the left side, we should notice that our fraction on
the left side can be simplified:

$$\frac{125}{150} = \frac{5}{6}$$

This will make our calculations much easier (and therefore we will be much less likely to make a
calculations error):

$$\frac{5}{6} = \frac{x}{24}$$
$$\frac{120}{6} = x$$
$$20 = x$$

USING THE RIGHT UNITS

> Don't forget to use the same units on both sides of the equation when working
> with rates. It is very hard to compare feet per second to miles per hour.

DIVISIBILITY

Questions that test divisibility will often ask about a **remainder**.

Remainder questions can be easier than they seem. Many students believe that the key to solving a remainder question is to find the value of a variable, which takes up a lot of time and causes confusion. However, that type of problem solving is usually not necessary. For example, look at the following remainder problem:

When n is divided by 7, the remainder is 4. What is the remainder when $2n$ is divided by 7?

(A) 0
(B) 1
(C) 2
(D) 3
(E) 4

This question doesn't depend on knowing the value of n. In fact, n has an infinite number of possible values.

The easy way to solve this kind of problem is to pick a number for n. Because the remainder when n is divided by 7 is 4, pick any multiple of 7 and add 4. The easiest multiple to work with is 7. So 7 + 4 = 11. Plug in 11 for n and see what happens:

What is the remainder when $2n$ is divided by 7?

. . . the remainder when 2(11) is divided by 7?

. . . the remainder when 22 is divided by 7?

$\frac{22}{7} = 3$, remainder 1

The remainder is 1 when $n = 11$. So the answer is (B). The remainder will also be 1 when $n = 18$, 25, or 46.

Here is another good example of a remainders problem:

A bracelet is made of colored beads in the repeated sequence red, orange, yellow, green, blue, indigo, and violet. If the first bead in the bracelet is red and the last is yellow, then the total number of beads in the bracelet could be

(A) 48
(B) 49
(C) 50
(D) 51
(E) 52

This sequence contains seven terms, the seven colors. We can represent them as letters to make organizing this problem easier:

R, O, Y, G, B, I, V

So we know V will be every seventh bead. That means the 7th, 14th, 28th, 35th, etc. Another way of saying this is that all the multiples of 7 will always be V. Now, it is important to notice that Y comes three after V. This means that if a bracelet ends in yellow it will have a number of beads equal to a multiple of 7 plus 3. Of all the answer choices, (E) is the only number 3 larger than a multiple of 7.

AVERAGES

Instead of giving you a list of values to plug into the average formula $\frac{\text{Sum of Terms}}{\text{Number of Terms}}$, SAT average questions often put a spin on the problem.

The following problem tells you the average of a group of terms and asks you to find the value of a missing term.

Work with the sum to get the answer:

The average weight of five amplifiers in a guitar shop is 32 pounds. If four of the amplifiers weigh 25, 27, 19, and 35 pounds, what is the weight of the fifth amplifier?

(A) 28 pounds

(B) 32 pounds

(C) 49 pounds

(D) 54 pounds

(E) 69 pounds

This problem tells you the average of a group of terms and asks you to find the value of a missing term. To get the answer, you need to work with the sum. Let the variable x = the weight of the fifth amplifier. Plug this into the average formula:

$$\text{Average} = \frac{\text{Sum of Terms}}{\text{Number of Terms}}$$

$$32 = \frac{25 + 27 + 19 + 35 + x}{5}$$

$$32 \times 5 = 25 + 27 + 19 + 35 + x$$

PERFECT SCORE TIP

" For questions with averages, I found that writing out all the terms and expressions to evaluate reduced the number of calculator mistakes I made. "

The average weight of the amplifiers times the number of amplifiers equals the total weight of the amplifiers. The new formula is:

$$\text{Average} \times \text{Number of Terms} = \text{Sum of Terms}$$

Remember this version of the average formula so you can find the total sum whenever you know the average of a group of terms and the number of terms. Now you can solve for the weight of the fifth amplifier as follows:

$$32 \times 5 = 25 + 27 + 19 + 35 + x$$

$$160 = 106 + x$$

$$54 = x$$

The weight of the fifth amplifier is 54 pounds, choice (D).

You now know how to find a missing value if you have the average. Now let's look at a slightly different averages problem:

Bart needs to buy five gifts with $80. If two of the gifts cost a total of $35, what is the average (arithmetic mean) amount Bart can spend on each of the remaining three gifts?

(A) $10
(B) $15
(C) $16
(D) $17
(E) $45

The key to this problem is translating it into an equation.

$80 = $35 + (the cost of the other 3 gifts)

Therefore, the cost of the other 3 gifts totals $45. You don't know what the individual gifts costs, but you don't need to. To find the average, all you have to do is divide the total, $45, by the number of gifts, 3.

$\dfrac{\$45}{3} = \$15$, so the average of the 3 gifts is $15 dollars.

BACKSOLVING FOR AVERAGES

If you forget how to set up an average problem, try backsolving the choices. This can help you earn some crucial extra points on test day.

PERCENTS

In percent problems, you're usually given two pieces of information and asked to solve for a third value, as in the following question:

Last year Aunt Edna's annual salary was $20,000. This year's raise brings her to an annual salary of $25,000. If she gets a raise of the same percentage every year, what will her salary be next year?

(A) $27,500

(B) $30,000

(C) $31,250

(D) $32,500

(E) $35,000

PERCENT FORMULAS

When you see a percent problem, remember the following formulas:

If you are solving for a percent: $\dfrac{\text{Part}}{\text{Whole}} = \text{Percent}$

If you need to solve for a part: $\text{Percent} \times \text{Whole} = \text{Part}$

This problem asks for Aunt Edna's projected salary for next year—that is, her current salary plus her next raise. You know last year's salary ($20,000), and you know this year's salary ($25,000), so you can find the difference between the two salaries: $25,000 − $20,000 = $5,000 = her raise.

Now your next step is to find the percent this raise represents by using the formula $\text{Percent} = \dfrac{\text{Part}}{\text{Whole}}$. Because Aunt Edna's raise was calculated on last year's salary, divide by $20,000. Be sure you know which *whole* to plug in. Here, you're looking for a percentage of $20,000, not of $25,000.

$$\text{Percent} = \frac{\$5,000}{\$20,000} = \frac{1}{4}, \text{ or } 25\%$$

You know Aunt Edna will get the same percent raise next year, so solve for the part. Use the formula $\text{Percent} \times \text{Whole} = \text{Part}$. Make sure you change the percent to either a fraction or a decimal before beginning calculations.

Her raise next year will be $25\% \times \$25,000 = \dfrac{1}{4} \times 25,000 = \$6,250$. Add that amount to this year's salary and you have her projected salary: $25,000 + $6,250 = $31,250, or answer (C).

Let's try another percents question, this one focusing on compound percents:

What is 25 percent of 25 percent of 72?

Problems like this can be easy, as long as we are careful not to make simple mistakes. 25 percent $= \frac{25}{100} = \frac{1}{4}$, so substituting in this value we see the problem just becomes

$$\frac{1}{4} \times \frac{1}{4} \times 72.$$

Multiply left to right and get $\frac{72}{16} = \frac{9}{2} = 4.5$. Note that you had to simplify the fraction, since $\frac{72}{16}$ would not fit in the Grid-in box.

WHICH WHOLE NUMBER?

Be sure you know which whole number to plug in when using a percent formula. Using the wrong whole number will give you a wrong answer.

COMPLEX FIGURES

In a problem that combines figures into more complex ones, you have to look for the relationship between the figures. Look for pieces the figures have in common. For instance, if two figures share a side, information about that side will probably be the key.

PERFECT SCORE TIP

" For problems with multiple figures, I'd determine what information was necessary to answer the question and think about how to use the multiple figures to find out what I needed. "

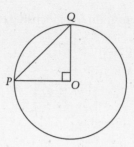

In the figure, if the area of the circle with center O is 9π, what is the area of triangle POQ?

(A) 4.5

(B) 6

(C) 9

(D) 3.5π

(E) 4.5π

In this case, the figures don't share a side, but the triangle's legs are important features of the circle—they are radii. You can see that $PO = OQ =$ the radius of circle O. The area of the circle is 9π. The area of a circle is πr^2, where $r =$ the radius. So $9\pi = \pi r^2$, $9 = r^2$, and the radius $= 3$.

The formula for the area of a triangle is $\mathbf{a} = \dfrac{1}{2}(\mathbf{base} \times \mathbf{height})$.

Therefore, the area of $\triangle POQ$ is $\dfrac{1}{2}(\text{leg}_1 \times \text{leg}_2) = \dfrac{1}{2}(3 \times 3) = \dfrac{9}{2} = 4.5$, answer choice (A).

But what if, instead of a number of familiar shapes, you are given something like this?

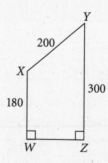

What is the perimeter of quadrilateral $WXYZ$?

(A) 680

(B) 760

(C) 840

(D) 920

(E) 1,000

Try breaking the unfamiliar shape into familiar ones. Once you do this, you can use the same techniques that you would for multiple figures.

Perimeter is the sum of the lengths of the sides of a figure, so you need to find the length of WZ.

Drawing a perpendicular line from point X to side YZ will divide the figure into a right triangle and a rectangle. Call the point of intersection A.

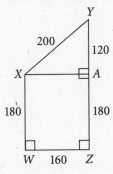

Opposite sides of a rectangle have equal length, so $WZ = XA$ and $WX = ZA$.

WX is labeled as 180, so $ZA = 180$.

Because YZ measures 300, AY is $300 - 180 = 120$.

In right triangle XYA, hypotenuse $XY = 200$, and leg $AY = 120$; you should recognize this as a multiple of a 3-4-5 right triangle.

The hypotenuse is 5×40, one leg is 3×40, so XA must be 4×40, or 160. (If you didn't recognize this special right triangle, you could have used the Pythagorean theorem to find the length of XA.)

Because $WZ = XA = 160$, the perimeter of the figure is $180 + 200 + 300 + 160 = 840$, answer choice (C).

> **PERFECT SCORE TIP**
>
> " Try looking for familiar figures in strange shapes. I would focus on the easiest ones—rectangles, squares, and right triangles—which made problems much easier! "

TRIANGLES, RECTANGLES, AND CIRCLES

Unfamiliar geometric figures on the SAT can always be broken down into familiar shapes. If a complex figure has you stumped, look for triangles, rectangles, or circles.

PERMUTATIONS AND COMBINATIONS

Combination problems ask you to find the different possibilities that can occur in a given situation. The order of events is NOT important.

Permutation problems ask for the number of possible arrangements among a given set of entities. The order of events IS important:

> If Alice, Betty, and Carlos sit in three adjacent empty seats in a movie house, how many different seating arrangements are possible?
>
> (A) 3
> (B) 4
> (C) 5
> (D) 6
> (E) 8

To solve this question, you need to find the number of possibilities by listing them in a quick but systematic way. Let the first letter of each name stand for that person. First, find all the combinations with Alice in the first seat as follows:

ABC

ACB

Use the same system, putting Betty in the first seat, and then Carlos. You get the following combinations:

BAC

BCA

CAB

CBA

At this point, we've exhausted every possibility. There are six possible arrangements, so (D) is the correct answer.

CONSIDER THE POSSIBILITIES

Some problems set up conditions that limit the possibilities somewhat. Some may ask for the number of distinct possibilities, meaning that if the same combination shows up twice in different forms, you should count it only once.

Consider the following problem:

Set I: {2, 3, 4, 5}

Set II: {1, 2, 3}

If x is a number generated by multiplying a number from Set I by a number from Set II, how many possible values of x are greater than 5?

(A) 3

(B) 4

(C) 5

(D) 6

(E) 7

Again, list the possibilities in a systematic way, pairing off each number in the first set with each number in the second set, so every combination is included. The following list is a good example of how this strategy works:

$2 \times 1 = 2$	$4 \times 1 = 4$
$2 \times 2 = 4$	$4 \times 2 = 8$
$2 \times 3 = 6$	$4 \times 3 = 12$
$3 \times 1 = 3$	$5 \times 1 = 5$
$3 \times 2 = 6$	$5 \times 2 = 10$
$3 \times 3 = 9$	$5 \times 3 = 15$

STAY ORGANIZED

Always write down the possibilities as you organize them so you can count them accurately and so you don't count the same combination twice.

How many of these values are greater than 5? Going down the list: 6, 6, 9, 8, 12, 10, and 15. Although there are seven answers for x that are greater than 5, two of them are the same. There are six different values of x greater than 5, not seven. The answer is (D).

Here, it would have been very easy to quickly take 7 as the correct answer and miss the last step. Be sure you carefully consider every possibility before moving on. We will teach you how to recognize and avoid traps like this one in chapter 14.

PRACTICE

We have labeled the following questions by the math concept they test. If you get stumped, go back to the appropriate part of this chapter and refresh your memory on how to solve that kind of problem. There is no time limit for this practice set.

SIMULTANEOUS EQUATIONS

1. If $x + y = 8$ and $y - x = -2$, then $y =$

   (A) -2
   (B) 3
   (C) 5
   (D) 8
   (E) 10

2. If $4a + 3b = 19$ and $a + 2b = 6$, then $a + b =$

FUNCTIONS

3. If $x \neq 0$, let $\neg x$ be defined by $\neg x = x - \frac{1}{x}$. What is the value of $\neg 2 - \neg \frac{1}{2}$?

SYMBOLS

4. If $r \heartsuit s = r(r - s)$ for all integers r and s, then $4 \heartsuit (3 \heartsuit 5)$ equals

   (A) -8
   (B) -2
   (C) 2
   (D) 20
   (E) 40

TRIANGLES

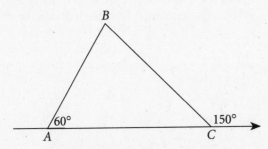

Note: Figure not drawn to scale.

5. In triangle *ABC* above, if *AB* = 4, then *AC* =

    (A) 6
    (B) 7
    (C) 8
    (D) 9
    (E) 10

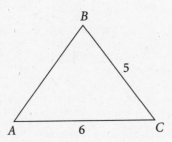

6. If the perimeter of triangle *ABC* above is 16,
    what is its area?

    (A) 8
    (B) 9
    (C) 10
    (D) 12
    (E) 15

RATIOS

7. In a group of 24 people who are either
    homeowners or renters, the ratio of
    homeowners to renters is 5:3. How many
    homeowners are in the group?

    (A) 8
    (B) 9
    (C) 12
    (D) 14
    (E) 15

8. Magazine *A* has a total of 28 pages, 16 of
    which are advertisements and 12 of which are
    articles. Magazine *B* has a total of 35 pages, all
    of them either advertisements or articles. If the
    ratio of the number of pages of advertisements
    to the number of pages of articles is the same
    for both magazines, then Magazine *B* has how
    many more pages of advertisements than
    Magazine *A* ?

    (A) 2
    (B) 3
    (C) 4
    (D) 5
    (E) 6

RATES

9. If David paints at the rate of h houses per day, how many houses does he paint in d days, in terms of h and d?

    (A) $\dfrac{h}{d}$

    (B) hd

    (C) $h + \dfrac{d}{2}$

    (D) $h - d$

    (E) $\dfrac{d}{h}$

10. Bill has to type a paper that is p pages long, with each page containing w words. If Bill types an average of x words per minute, how many hours will it take him to finish the paper?

    (A) $60wpx$

    (B) $\dfrac{wx}{60p}$

    (C) $\dfrac{60wp}{x}$

    (D) $\dfrac{wpx}{60}$

    (E) $\dfrac{wp}{60x}$

DIVISIBILITY

11. When z is divided by 8, the remainder is 5. What is the remainder when $4z$ is divided by 8?

    (A) 1
    (B) 3
    (C) 4
    (D) 5
    (E) 7

REMAINDERS

12. When n is divided by 12, the remainder is 0. What is the remainder when $2n$ is divided by 6?

AVERAGES

13. The average (arithmetic mean) of six numbers is 16. If five of the numbers are 15, 37, 16, 9, and 23, what is the sixth number?

    (A) −20
    (B) −4
    (C) 0
    (D) 6
    (E) 16

14. The average (arithmetic mean) of five numbers is 8. If the average of two of these numbers is −6, what is the sum of the other three numbers?

    (A) 28
    (B) 34
    (C) 46
    (D) 52
    (E) 60

PERCENTS

15. Eighty-five percent of the members of a student organization are registered to attend a certain field trip. If 16 of the members who registered were unable to attend, resulting in only 65 percent of the members making the trip, how many members are in the organization?

16. If a sweater sells for $48 after a 25 percent markdown, what was its original price?

    (A) $56
    (B) $60
    (C) $64
    (D) $68
    (E) $72

COMPLEX FIGURES

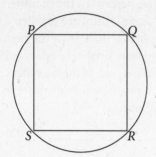

17. In the figure above, square *PQRS* is inscribed in a circle. If the area of square *PQRS* is 4, what is the radius of the circle?

    (A) 1
    (B) $\sqrt{2}$
    (C) 2
    (D) $2\sqrt{2}$
    (E) $4\sqrt{2}$

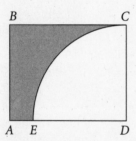

Note: Figure not drawn to scale.

18. In the figure above, the quarter circle with center *D* has a radius of 4, and rectangle *ABCD* has a perimeter of 20. What is the perimeter of the shaded region?

    (A) $20 - 8\pi$
    (B) $10 + 2\pi$
    (C) $12 + 2\pi$
    (D) $12 + 4\pi$
    (E) $4 + 8\pi$

PERMUTATIONS AND COMBINATIONS

19. Five people attend a meeting. If each person shakes hands once with every other person at the meeting, what is the total number of handshakes that take place?

20. Three people stop for lunch at a hot dog stand. If each person orders one item and there are three items to choose from, how many different combinations of food could be purchased? (Assume that order doesn't matter; e.g., a hot dog and two sodas are considered the same as two sodas and a hot dog.)

    (A) 6
    (B) 9
    (C) 10
    (D) 18
    (E) 27

ANSWERS AND EXPLANATIONS

1. B
SMARTPOINTS CATEGORY: EQUATIONS

When you add the two equations, the x's cancel out and you find that $2y = 6$, so $y = 3$, choice (B).

2. 5
SMARTPOINTS CATEGORY: EQUATIONS

Adding the two equations, you find that $5a + 5b = 25$. Dividing by 5 shows that $a + b = 5$.

3. 3
SMARTPOINTS CATEGORY: FUNCTIONS

Identify the value of $\neg 2$ and then of $\neg\frac{1}{2}$, and then subtract the second value from the first:

$$\neg 2 = 2 - \frac{1}{2} = 1\frac{1}{2} = \frac{3}{2}$$

$$\neg\frac{1}{2} = \frac{1}{2} - \frac{1}{\frac{1}{2}} = \frac{1}{2} - 2 = -1\frac{1}{2} = -\frac{3}{2}$$

$$\neg 2 - \neg\frac{1}{2} = \frac{3}{2} - \left(-\frac{3}{2}\right) = \frac{3}{2} + \frac{3}{2} = \frac{6}{2} = 3$$

4. E
SMARTPOINTS CATEGORY: FUNCTIONS

Start in the parentheses and work out: $(3 \heartsuit 5) = 3(3 - 5) = 3(-2) = -6$; $4 \heartsuit (-6) = 4[4 - (-6)] = 4(10) = 40$. Choice (E) is correct.

5. C
SMARTPOINTS CATEGORY: TRIANGLES

Angle BCA is supplementary to the angle marked 150°, so angle $BCA = 180° - 150° = 30°$. Because the sum of interior angles of a triangle is 180°, angle A + angle B + angle $BCA = 180°$, so angle $B = 180° - 60° - 30° = 90°$. So triangle ABC is a 30-60-90 right triangle, and its sides are in the ratio $1:\sqrt{3}:2$. The side opposite the 30°, AB, which we know has length 4, must be half the length of the hypotenuse, AC. Therefore, $AC = 8$, and that's answer choice (C).

6. D

SMARTPOINTS CATEGORY: TRIANGLES

To find the area, you need to know the base and height. If the perimeter is 16, then $AB + BC + AC = 16$; that is, $AB = 16 - 5 - 6 = 5$. Because $AB = BC$, this is an isosceles triangle. If you drop a line from vertex B to AC, it will divide the base in half. This divides the triangle into two smaller right triangles:

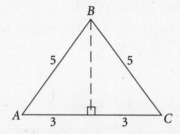

These right triangles each have one leg of 3 and a hypotenuse of 5; therefore, they are 3-4-5 right triangles. The missing leg (which is also the height of triangle ABC) must have a length of 4. We now know that the base of ABC is 6 and the height is 4, so the area is $\frac{1}{2} \times 6 \times 4$, or 12, answer choice (D).

7. E

SMARTPOINTS CATEGORY: RATIOS

The parts are the number of homeowners (5) and the number of renters (3). The whole is the total (homeowners + renters):

$$\frac{\text{Part}}{\text{Whole}} = \frac{\text{Homeowners}}{\text{Homeowners} + \text{Renters}} = \frac{5}{5+3} = \frac{5}{8}$$

Because there are 24 people in the group, $\frac{5}{8} = \frac{x}{24}$, making $x = 15$, answer choice (E).

8. C

SMARTPOINTS CATEGORY: RATIOS

The $\frac{\text{Part}}{\text{Whole}}$ ratio of advertisements (16) to total pages (28) in Magazine A is $\frac{16}{28}$, or $\frac{4}{7}$. Magazine B has the same ratio, so if there are 35 pages in Magazine B, $\frac{4}{7} \times 35$—or 20 pages—are advertisements. Therefore, there are 4 more pages of advertisements in Magazine B than in Magazine A.

9. B

SMARTPOINTS CATEGORY: RATES

Pick numbers for h and d. Let $h = 2$ and $d = 3$; that is, suppose he paints two houses per day and he paints for three days, so in three days he can paint six houses. You multiply the rate (h) by the number of days (d). The only answer choice that equals 6 when $h = 2$ and $d = 3$ is choice (B).

10. E

SMARTPOINTS CATEGORY: RATES

Pick numbers for p, w, and x that work well in the problem. Let $p = 3$ and let $w = 100$. So there are three pages with 100 words per page, or 300 words total. Say he types 5 words a minute, so $x = 5$. Therefore, he types 5×60, or 300 words an hour. It takes him one hour to type the paper. The only answer choice that equals 1 when $p = 3$, $w = 100$, and $x = 5$ is choice (E).

11. C

SMARTPOINTS CATEGORY: DIVISIBILITY

Let $z = 13$, as 13 divided by 8 produces a remainder of 5. Plug in $4z = 4(13) = 52$, which leaves a remainder of 4 when divided by 8. Thus, choice (C) is correct.

12. 0

SMARTPOINTS CATEGORY: DIVISIBILITY

If there's no remainder when n is divided by 12, then n is a multiple of 12, as is $2n$. Anything that's a multiple of 12 is a multiple of factors of 12, so $2n$ is a multiple of 6. Thus, the remainder is 0 when $2n$ is divided by 6. Picking numbers highlights this. Say n is 24. $2n$ is 48, and there's a remainder of 0 when 48 is divided by 6.

13. B

SMARTPOINTS CATEGORY: AVERAGES

Average × Number of Terms = Sum of Terms:

$$16 \times 6 = 15 + 37 + 16 + 9 + 23 + x$$
$$96 = 100 + x$$
$$-4 = x$$

Choice (B) is correct.

14. D

SMARTPOINTS CATEGORY: AVERAGES

Average × Number of Terms = Sum of Terms. The sum of all five numbers is 8 × 5 = 40. The sum of two of these numbers is (–6) × 2 = –12. So the difference of these two sums, 40 – (–12) = 52, is the sum of the other numbers. Answer choice (D) is correct.

15. 80

SMARTPOINTS CATEGORY: PERCENTS

You need to solve for the whole, so identify the part and the percent. If 85 percent planned to attend and only 65 percent did, 20 percent failed to attend, and you know that 16 students failed to attend. So:

$$\text{Percent} \times \text{Whole} = \text{Part}$$

$$\frac{20}{100} \times \text{Whole} = 16$$

$$\text{Whole} = 16 \times \frac{100}{20}$$

$$\text{Whole} = 80$$

16. C

SMARTPOINTS CATEGORY: PERCENTS

We want to solve for the original price, the whole. The percent markdown is 25 percent, so $48 is 75 percent of the whole:

$$\text{Percent} \times \text{Whole} = \text{Part}$$

$$75 \text{ percent} \times \text{original price} = \$48$$

$$\text{original price} = \frac{\$48}{0.75} = \$64, \text{ choice (C)}.$$

17. B

SMARTPOINTS CATEGORY: COMPLEX FIGURES

Draw in diagonal *QS*, and you will notice that it is also a diameter of the circle:

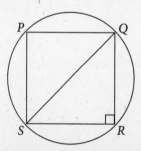

Because the area of the square is 4, its sides must each be 2. Think of the diagonal as dividing the square into two isosceles right triangles. Therefore, the diagonal $= 2\sqrt{2}$ = the diameter; the radius is half this amount, or $\sqrt{2}$. Thus, choice (B) is correct.

18. C

SMARTPOINTS CATEGORY: COMPLEX FIGURES

The perimeter of the shaded region is $BC + AB + AE +$ arc EC. The quarter circle has its center at D, and point C lies on the circle, so side DC is a radius of the circle and equals 4:

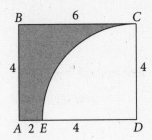

Opposite sides of a rectangle are equal, so AB is also 4.

The perimeter of the rectangle is 20, and because the two short sides account for 8, the two longer sides must account for 12, making BC and AD each 6. To find AE, subtract the length of ED, another radius of length 4, from the length of AD, which is 6; $AE = 2$.

Because arc EC is a quarter circle, the length of the arc EC is $\frac{1}{4}$ of the circumference of a whole circle with radius 4: $\frac{1}{4} \times 2\pi r = \frac{1}{4} \times 8\pi = 2\pi$. So the perimeter of the shaded region is $6 + 4 + 2 + 2\pi = 12 + 2\pi$. Thus, choice (C) is correct.

19. 10

SMARTPOINTS CATEGORY: PERMUTATIONS AND COMBINATIONS

Be careful not to count each handshake twice. Call the five people A, B, C, D, and E. We can pair them off like this:

A with B, C, D, and E (four handshakes)

B with C, D, and E (three more—note that we leave out A because the handshake between A and B is already counted)

C with D and E (two more)

D with E (one more)

The total is $4 + 3 + 2 + 1$, or 10 handshakes.

20. C

SMARTPOINTS CATEGORY: PERMUTATIONS AND COMBINATIONS

To find the number, let's call the three items they can purchase A, B, and C. The possibilities are as follows:

All three order the same thing: AAA, BBB, CCC

Two order the same thing: AAB, AAC, BBA, BBC, CCA, CCB

All three order something different: ABC

There are ten different ways the three items could be ordered.

KEY POINTS YOU'VE LEARNED IN THIS CHAPTER

THE TEN MOST TESTED BASIC MATH CONCEPTS AND METHODS FOR SOLVING EACH:

1. **Divisibility**—Pick a number for the variable.

2. **Averages**—Use the average formula, and work with the sum.

3. **Ratios**—Identify the parts and the whole.

4. **Rates**—Pick numbers for the variables to make the relationship between units clear.

5. **Percents**—Make sure you know which whole to plug in.

6. **Permutations and Combinations**—Be systematic and organized when listing possible combinations.

7. **Equations**—Combine equations by adding or subtracting them to cancel out all but one variable.

8. **Functions**—Use the symbols as a map of where to plug in numbers.

9. **Triangles**—Know the predefined ratios for special triangles.

10. **Complex Figures**—Find the parts that the different figures have in common.

CHAPTER 15: ADVANCED MATH CONCEPTS

SMARTPOINTS COVERED IN THIS CHAPTER

EQUATIONS

NUMBER PROPERTIES

FUNCTIONS

TRIANGLES

RATIOS

DATA ANALYSIS

NONLINEAR GRAPHS

SEQUENCES

EXPONENTS

CIRCLES

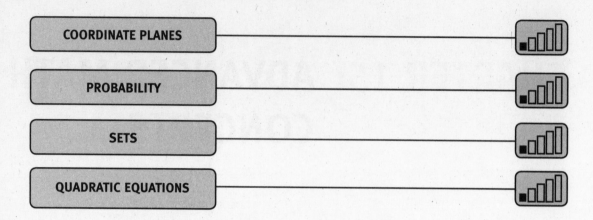

WHAT TO EXPECT ON TEST DAY

In this chapter, we review the advanced math concepts tested on the SAT. This list is extensive and may seem overwhelming. But remember, your goal should not be to memorize each concept and method, but rather to familiarize yourself with the review of each concept so you will know what to expect on test day.

THE 20 MOST TESTED ADVANCED MATH CONCEPTS

The SAT covers the following advanced math topics:

1. Radical equations
2. Rational equations and inequalities
3. Manipulation with integer and rational exponents
4. Absolute value
5. Function notation and evaluation
6. Concepts of domain and range
7. Functions as models
8. Linear functions—equations and graphs
9. Quadratic functions—equations and graphs
10. Qualitative behavior of nonlinear graphs and functions
11. Transformations and their effects on graphs of functions
12. Coordinate geometry
13. Properties of tangent lines
14. Sequences

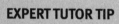

EXPERT TUTOR TIP

"" If math isn't your thing, don't worry. The ideas in this chapter should help you know what's coming, so you're not surprised on test day! ""

15. Sets

16. Direct and inverse variation

17. Data interpretation

18. Geometric notation

19. Trigonometry

20. Probability

As in chapter 12, the techniques we give for solving these problems will work with both types of SAT Math questions: regular math and Grid-in questions.

 EQUATIONS

The SAT contains many types of equations, with **radical equations** being one of the more popular advanced concepts.

Radical equations have at least one variable under a radical sign. Like rational equations, they follow the same rules as other kinds of algebraic equations, so solve them accordingly.

The last step is what makes them unique: often, you must square both sides of the equation.

Look at the following example:

If $4 - \sqrt{n} = -1$, what is the value of n?

(A) 3

(B) 5

(C) 9

(D) 25

(E) 81

Apply the same algebraic steps here as you would in any other question involving an equation, isolating the variable step-by-step. Just remember to square both sides of the equation as your last step. (Notice that (B) is a trap for test takers who forget to do so. We will cover math traps in more detail in the next chapter.)

$$4 - \sqrt{n} = -1$$
$$5 = \sqrt{n}$$
$$(5)^2 = (\sqrt{n})^2$$
$$25 = n$$

Answer choice (D) is correct.

QUADRATIC EQUATIONS

Quadratic equations on the SAT can involve two advanced concepts: **rational equations** and **quadratic functions**. A rational equation is one that contains at least one fraction in which the numerator and denominator are polynomials. Rational equations follow the same rules as simpler looking equations, and they are just as susceptible to Kaplan strategies, such as picking numbers, as the following illustration shows:

For all values of x not equal to -2 or 3, $\dfrac{x^4 - 5x^3 - 2x^2 + 24x}{x^2 - x - 6}$ is equal to

(A) $x^2 - 4x$

(B) $x^2 - 5x - 2$

(C) $x + 24$

(D) x

(E) $x - 4$

Say $x = 2$:

PICKING NUMBERS FOR ADVANCED EQUATIONS

Picking numbers works just as well for advanced equations as it does for easier ones. Use this strategy to your advantage!

$$\frac{2^4 - 5(2^3) - 2(2^2) + 24(2)}{2^2 - 2 - 6} = \frac{16 - 5(8) - 2(4) + 24(2)}{4 - 2 - 6} = \frac{16 - 40 - 8 + 48}{-4} = \frac{16}{-4} = -4$$

Now find the choice that has a value of -4 when $x = 2$. Only (A) works:

$2^2 - 4(2) = 4 - 8 = -4$, so (A) is the correct answer.

 ## EXPONENTS

Not every exponent on the SAT is a positive integer. Numbers can be raised to a fractional or negative exponent. Although such numbers follow their own special rules, they adhere to the same general rules of exponents with which you've probably worked before. Look at the following example:

If $x = \dfrac{1}{4}$, $x^{-4} =$

(A) $\dfrac{-1}{256}$

(B) $\dfrac{-1}{16}$

(C) 4

(D) 16

(E) 256

A NOTE ON EXPONENTIAL EQUIVALENTS

$$x^{-a} = \frac{1}{x^a}$$

$$x^{\frac{p}{q}} = \sqrt[q]{x^p}$$

To find the value of a number raised to a negative power, simply rewrite the number, without the negative sign in front of the exponent, as the bottom of a fraction with 1 as the numerator of the fraction: $3^{-2} = \dfrac{1}{3^2} = \dfrac{1}{9}$.

In this case:

$$x^{-4} = \frac{1}{x^4} = \frac{1}{\left(\frac{1}{4}\right)^4} = \frac{1}{\left(\frac{1}{256}\right)} = 256, \text{ or answer choice (E)}.$$

 ## Number Properties

The SAT will test your knowledge on a wide variety of concepts that relate to number properties. One advanced concept that you'll see on test day is absolute value. The absolute value of a number is the distance between that number and zero on the number line.

ABSOLUTE VALUES—ALWAYS POSITIVE

Because absolute value is a distance, it is *always* positive.

The absolute value of 7 is 7; this is expressed as $|7| = 7$. Similarly, the absolute value of -7 is 7: $|-7| = 7$. Every positive number is the absolute value of two numbers: itself and its negative counterpart. The following diagram helps to illustrate this point:

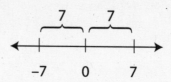

As you'll see in the following example, the SAT sometimes connects the concept of absolute value to the concept of inequalities:

If $|r + 7| < 2$, which of the following statements are true?

  I. $r < -9$

  II. $r < -5$

  III. $r > -9$

(A) I only

(B) II only

(C) III only

(D) I and II only

(E) II and III only

You can solve this problem algebraically, as shown below, or you can think about what the inequality would look like on a number line. You can express $|r + 7| < 2$ *as the difference between r and* -7 *is less than* 2 and determine that r must be between -5 and -9:

$$r + 7 < 2 \text{ and } -r - 7 < 2$$
$$r < -5 \text{ and } -r < 9$$
$$r < -5 \text{ and } r > -9$$

The correct answer here is (E).

 FUNCTIONS

A few questions on test day will probably focus on functions and use standard function notation such as $f(x)$. Evaluating a function sounds fancy, but it mostly involves substitution of numbers for variables—a skill you should already be familiar with.

FUNCTION NOTATION AND EVALUATION

Function Notation and Evaluation questions usually appear on the test, so know how to handle them:

- **Function notation** is the standard way to write numbers down in relation to the operations needed. The order follows the mnemonic **PEMDAS**.

- **Evaluation** involves substitution of numbers for variables, a skill you should already be familiar with.

For example, to evaluate the function $f(x) = 5x + 1$ for $f(3)$, replace x with 3 and simplify: $f(3) = 5(3) + 1 = 15 + 1 = 16$.

The example below presents a slightly more complex variation: a composition of functions. $h(g(a))$ requires you to first evaluate $g(a)$, and then apply h to the result.

If $g(a) = (a + 4)^2$ and $h(b) = 2b - 7$, then what is the value of $h(g(2))$?

(A) 1
(B) 36
(C) 45
(D) 65
(E) 79

Follow the order of operations:

$$g(2) = (2 + 4)^2 = 6^2 = 36$$
$$h(36) = 2(36) - 7 = 72 - 7 = 65$$

The correct answer is choice (D).

DOMAIN AND RANGE

- The **domain** of a function is the set of values for which the function is defined. For example, the domain of $f(x) = \dfrac{1}{1 - x^2}$ is all values of x except 1 and -1, because for those values, the denominator has a value of 0 and the fraction is therefore undefined.

- The **range** of a function is the set of outputs or results of the function. For example, the range of $f(x) = x^2$ is all numbers greater than or equal to zero because x^2 cannot be negative. Try the following sample question:

PERFECT SCORE TIP

" The trickiest domain and range questions for me were the ones that dealt with radicals and absolute values. I plugged in numbers or graphed the functions on my calculator to make sure that I had the correct domain and range. "

If $f(a) = a^2 + 7$ for all real values of a, which of the following is a possible value of $f(a)$?

(A) -2

(B) 0

(C) $\sqrt{5}$

(D) $\sqrt{7}$

(E) $100\sqrt{3}$

If a is a real number, then a^2 must be positive or equal to zero. Think about how this limits the range of $f(a)$: If $a = 0$, then $f(a) = 7$. All other values result in a higher value of $f(a)$. Only (E) is greater than 7 and is the correct answer.

FUNCTIONS AS MODELS

The SAT might challenge your ability to relate functional relationships to real-life situations.

For example, consider the question below, in which you're asked to interpret data about the relationship between the selling price of a car and the number of cars that sell at that price.

A NOTE ON FUNCTIONS

The **domain** of a function is the set of values for which the function is defined. The **range** of a function is the set of possible values of the function.

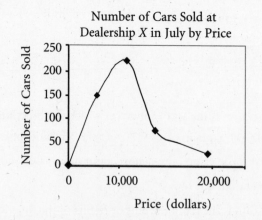

Number of Cars Sold at
Dealership X in July by Price

The above graph represents the number of cars sold at Dealership X in July. If the dealer wants to sell the maximum number of cars possible in August, at what price should he set the cars, based on his sales in July?

(A) $5,000

(B) $10,000

(C) $15,000

(D) $20,000

(E) $22,500

READ GRAPHS CAREFULLY

Make sure to read your graphs carefully, knowing what each axis represents. If you are not careful, you may choose the incorrect answer that is meant as a trap.

Use the graph of July to figure out which price point sold the most cars. The peak value is $10,000, which sold 225 cars. Based on this information, the dealer should price cars at $10,000 in August and hope to sell the maximum number of cars that he can in that month. Answer choice (B) is correct.

LINEAR FUNCTIONS—EQUATIONS AND GRAPHS

You'll most likely see a question or two on the SAT involving equations and graphs of linear functions.

A **linear function** is simply an equation whose graph is a straight line. The following question is an example of what could appear on the SAT:

Which of the following equations describes a line perpendicular to the line $y = 7x + 49$?

(A) $y = -7x - 49$

(B) $y = -\dfrac{1}{7}x + 10$

(C) $y = \dfrac{1}{7}x + 7$

(D) $y = 7x - 49$

(E) $y = 7x + 14$

If two lines are perpendicular, then the slope of one is the negative reciprocal of the slope of the other.

> **PERFECT SCORE TIP**
>
> " Make sure to look at what quadratic equation questions are actually asking. If you don't need to factor or expand the equation, don't waste your time. "

These lines are written in the form $y = mx + b$, where m is the slope and b is the y-intercept, or the value of y when $x = 0$.

In this case, the negative reciprocal of 7 is $-\dfrac{1}{7}$. The only equation with this slope is (B), the correct answer.

SLOPES: PERPENDICULAR AND PARALLEL LINES

- The slopes of **perpendicular** lines are **negative** reciprocals.
- The slopes of **parallel** lines are **equal**.

QUADRATIC FUNCTIONS—EQUATIONS AND GRAPHS

Quadratic functions are closely related to linear functions. A quadratic function is one that takes the form $f(x) = ax^2 + bx + c$. Rather than take the form of a straight line as, you'll recall, a linear function does, the graph of a quadratic function is a parabola.

As the following question illustrates, a quadratic function question could be similar to a quadratic equations question:

If $x^2 - 7x + 12 = 0$, what is the sum of the two possible values of x?

(A) −4
(B) −1
(C) 3
(D) 4
(E) 7

Factor:

$$x^2 - 7x + 12 = 0$$
$$(x - 4)(x - 3) = 0$$
$$x = 4 \text{ or } x = 3$$
$$4 + 3 = 7$$

PERFECT SCORE TIP

" When dealing with graphs, use the fact that you can write in your test booklet to your advantage. It can help you uncover key info like the number of intersections between two functions or the maximum value on a graph. "

You should have come up with (E) as the correct answer.

NONLINEAR GRAPHS

The SAT will likely ask you to show an understanding of a general or particular property of a complex graph, such as the one in the example problem below:

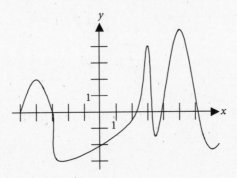

The figure shows the graph of $f(x)$. At how many values of x does $f(x)$ equal 4?

(A) 0

(B) 1

(C) 2

(D) 3

(E) 4

The value of $f(x)$ is measured on the y-axis. Find 4 on the y-axis, and then see how many points on the graph have a y-value of 4. The points are approximately (3, 4), (4.7, 4), and (5.4, 4). So your answer here is 3, or choice (D).

TRANSFORMATIONS

A **transformation** is an alteration in a function. An SAT question such as the following might present a graph and ask you to identify a specific transformation:

COMMON TRANSFORMATIONS ON THE SAT

- $f(x) + n$ shifts the graph of $f(x)$ n units **up.**
- $f(x) - n$ shifts the graph of $f(x)$ n units **down.**
- $f(x + n)$ shifts the graph of $f(x)$ n units **left.**
- $f(x - n)$ shifts the graph of $f(x)$ n units **right.**

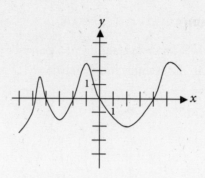

The figure above shows the graph of the function $r(x)$. Which of the following figures shows the graph of the function $r(x-2)$?

(A)

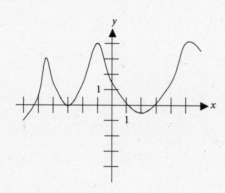

(B)

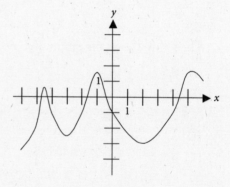

(C)

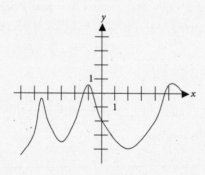

(D)

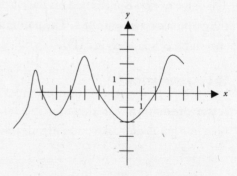

(E)

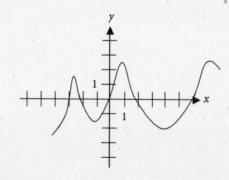

The graph of $r(x-2)$ will look like the graph of $r(x)$ shifted two units to the right. You can check this by plugging in a few points. For example, $r(-1) = 2.5$, so $r(1-2)$ should equal 2.5. This is only true of answer (E).

COORDINATE PLANES

Coordinate geometry questions on the SAT tend to focus on the properties of straight lines.

The equation of a straight line is $y = mx + b$, where y and x are the infinite number of coordinated (x, y) pairs that fall on the line. Variable b is the y-intercept, or the value of y when $x = 0$.

Variable m is the slope of the line and is expressed $\frac{\Delta Y}{\Delta X}$, or $\frac{y_2 - y_1}{x_2 - x_1}$.

> **PERFECT SCORE TIP**
>
> " Knowing midpoint and slope equations was really useful. Being able to plug in numbers quickly for coordinate geometry problems was a huge time saver! "

SLOPE

The slope or steepness of a line is the change in y-values in relation to the change in corresponding x-values.

- **Positive slopes** tilt upward to the **right.**
- **Negative slopes** tilt downward to the **right.**
- **Horizontal lines** have a slope of **zero.**
- **Vertical lines** have an **undefined slope.**
- **Parallel lines** have **equal slopes.**
- **Perpendicular lines** have **negative reciprocal slopes.**

As the question below illustrates, the SAT may also ask you to identify the midpoint of a line segment or the distance between two points:

If point P is at $(8, 10)$ and point Q is at $(0, 4)$, what is the midpoint of PQ?

(A) $(0, 10)$

(B) $(4, 2)$

(C) $(4, 5)$

(D) $(4, 7)$

(E) $(9, 2)$

FINDING THE MIDPOINT

The midpoint of a line segment with endpoints (x_1, y_1) and (x_2, y_2) is really just the average of its *x*-values and *y*-values.

To find it, plug the two sets of points into the following expression:

$$\left(\frac{x_1 + x_2}{2}, \frac{y_1 + y_2}{2} \right)$$

Now plug in the numbers from the question:

$$x = \frac{8 + 0}{2} = \frac{8}{2} = 4$$

$$y = \frac{10 + 4}{2} = \frac{14}{2} = 7$$

The midpoint is (4, 7), or choice (D).

PERFECT SCORE TIP

66 Knowing that the radius to the point of contact is perpendicular to the tangent line was something I used consistently on the SAT—it really came in handy! 99

 CIRCLES

Properties of circles are tested fairly often on the SAT. On some of the tougher questions, you will be expected to know how to deal with **tangent lines.**

When a line is tangent to a circle, it is perpendicular to the radius that it intersects. Look at the following example:

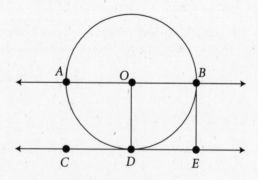

In the figure above, $\overline{AB}$ is a diameter of the circle, and $\overline{CE}$ is tangent to the circle at point D. $\overline{AB}$ is parallel to $\overline{CE}$. If the area of quadrilateral $OBED$ is 16 cm², what is the area of the circle whose center is at O?

(A) 4 cm²

(B) 4π cm²

(C) 8π cm²

(D) 16π cm²

(E) 256 cm²

A circle in a problem often means you'll need the radius at some point. To figure out how to get that from the area of quadrilateral $OBED$, you'll need the rest of the information in the question stem.

It may be helpful to add a few angles to the figure—for instance, because $\overline{CE}$ is tangent to the circle at point D, it is perpendicular to the radius of the circle at that point.

The information given in the first two sentences of the question stem tells you that $\overline{OD}$ is perpendicular to $\overline{CE}$ and therefore also to $\overline{AB}$.

$\overline{OD}$ and $\overline{OB}$ are both radii of the circle, so quadrilateral $OBED$ is a square.

The area of $OBED$ is 16, so each side has a length of 4.

This is also the radius of the circle. $4^2\pi = 16\pi$ is the area of the circle, so you should have chosen answer (D).

 ## SEQUENCES

Problems that test sequences are fairly common on the SAT. These problems normally can be broken down into two categories: arithmetic growth and geometric growth. Don't let the names scare you—both of these types of sequences have specific rules that dictate how they behave.

> **PERFECT SCORE TIP**
>
> ❝ For sequence questions, always double-check the formula with the problem to make sure that you're counting the terms correctly. ❞

ARITHMETIC SEQUENCES

A sequence in which consecutive terms have a fixed difference between them, expressed by the formula $a_n = a_1 + (n-1)d$, where a_n is the nth term, a_1 is the first, and d is the difference.

Most arithmetic sequence problems will involve this equation. Let's look at a quick example:

If the first term of an arithmetic sequence is 3, and the third term is 7, what is the fifth term?

(A) 9
(B) 10
(C) 11
(D) 12
(E) 13

Problems like this can be hard to keep organized if you forget to use the equation we just introduced. Plugging in the initial values we were given:

$7 = 3 + (3-1)d$, so $4 = 2d$ or $d = 2$.

Now that we have d, we can plug it back into our equation and solve for the fifth term:

$a_5 = 3 + (5-1)2$, or $a_5 = 11$

Our answer is 11, or choice (C).

Some arithmetic sequence problems can be solved without using the equation. Often you can figure out the difference in your head, and then just count until you reach the desired term. While this might *seem* faster, it is much more prone to error and will not help you with the more difficult sequence problems. Learning the arithmetic sequence equation will let you solve this problem type every time.

The other type of sequence problem that occurs on the SAT is a geometric sequence.

GEOMETRIC SEQUENCES

A geometric sequence of numbers is simply one in which a constant ratio exists between consecutive terms.

Questions about geometric sequences are likely to hinge on this formula:

If r is the ratio between consecutive terms, a_1 is the first term, and a_n is the nth term, then $a_n = a_1 r^{n-1}$.

RATIOS AND CONSECUTIVE TERMS

Remember that if r is the ratio between consecutive terms, a_1 is the first term, and a_n is the nth term, then $a_n = a_1 r^{n-1}$. Most questions concerning geometric sequences will involve this formula.

Now take a look at how the SAT might ask a question about geometric sequences:

If the first term in a geometric sequence is 4, and the fifth term is 64, what is the eighth term?

(A) 512

(B) 864

(C) 1,245

(D) 13,404

(E) 22,682

First, use the formula to solve for r:

$$64 = 4r^4$$
$$16 = r^4$$
$$r = 2$$

Now, using $r = 2$, solve for a_8:

$$a_8 = 4(2)^7$$
$$a_8 = 512$$

The correct answer is (A).

 SETS

Most questions about geometric sequences are likely to appear in the middle or end of an SAT Math section because such questions tend to be hard for most students. Sets, on the other hand, are slightly easier and are more likely to show up in the beginning or middle of a section.

TERMS AND CONDITIONS

Knowing the definitions of the terms used is the key to solving problems involving sets:

- **Elements** or **members** are the things in a set.

- A **union** of sets, sometimes expressed with the symbol $\cup$, is the set of elements that are in *either* or *both* of the different sets you start with. The *union set* is what you get when you merge sets.

  - For example, if Set A = {1, 2} and Set B = {3, 4}, then A $\cup$ B = {1, 2, 3, 4}.

- The **intersection** of sets, sometimes expressed with the symbol $\cap$, is the set of elements *common* to the sets you start with.

  - For example, if Set A = {1, 2, 3} and Set B = {3, 4, 5}, then A $\cap$ B = {3}.

Try to work through the following example:

If Set R contains 6 distinct numbers and Set S contains 5 distinct letters, how many elements are in the union of the two sets?

(A) 1
(B) 5
(C) 6
(D) 8
(E) 11

In this question, because Set R and Set S contain different kinds of elements, no element is in both sets. So the union set of S and R—$S \cup R$—contains everything in each: $6 + 5 = 11$. The correct answer is (E).

UNION AND INTERSECTION

Think of the **union** of sets as what you get when you merge the sets.

Think of the **intersection** of sets as the overlap of the sets.

 RATIOS

On the SAT, some of the most advanced ratio concepts tested involve *direct* and *inverse variation*.

In **direct variation**, $y = kx$, where k is a nonzero constant. In direct variation, the variable y changes directly as x does:

- If a unit of Currency A is worth 2 units of Currency B, then $A = 2B$.
- If the number of units of B were to double, the number of units of A would double, and so on for halving, tripling, etc.

In **inverse variation**, $xy = k$, where x and y are variables and k is a constant:

- A famous inverse relationship is *rate × time = distance*. Imagine having to cover a distance of 24 miles. If you were to travel at 12 miles per hour, you'd need 2 hours. But if you were to cut your rate in half, you would have to double your time.

The following is an example of direct variation:

> If the length of a sea turtle is directly proportional to its age, and a 2-year-old sea turtle is 3 inches long, how many feet long is an 80-year-old sea turtle?

   (A) 10

   (B) 12

   (C) 100

   (D) 120

   (E) 144

Relate the length of the turtle to its age. Use the equation to find the length of an 80-year-old sea turtle in inches; then convert from inches to feet. Because length is directly proportional to age, you can represent their relationship as $l = ka$, where l is length, a is age, and k is a constant:

$$3 = k(2)$$
$$1.5 = k$$
$$l = 1.5(80) = 120 \text{ inches} = 10 \text{ feet}$$

(A) is the correct answer.

 ## DATA ANALYSIS

Some SAT questions focus on the test taker's ability to interpret, evaluate, and draw conclusions from data presented in matrices or, like those below, in scatterplots:

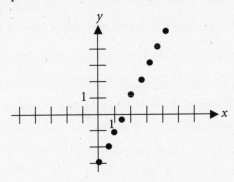

Which of the following equations best fits these points?

   (A) $y = 3x + 2$

   (B) $y = 3x - 2$

   (C) $y = 2x + 3$

   (D) $y = 2x - 3$

   (E) $y = x - 3$

PERFECT SCORE TIP

" I sketched graphs when I had to determine a linear equation or interpret scatterplots. It was the fastest approach, because I could find the y-intercept and approximate the slope as well! "

Try to figure out what sort of line would fit these points.

- What should the slope be?
- What should the *y*-intercept be? Remember that the standard equation for a line is in the form $y = mx + b$, where *m* is the slope and *b* is the *y*-intercept.

If you think visually, you might want to try sketching the line described by each answer choice to see which one fits the closest to the points on the graph.

If you're more comfortable working with numbers, you could try plugging a few points from the graph into each possible equation to see which one works.

The *y*-intercept of this graph is at –3.

The slope is around 2 because the graph is raised about 2 units for every 1 unit it moves along the *x*-axis.

The correct answer to this question is (D).

 TRIANGLES

Triangles are quite common on the SAT and acing these problems requires knowledge of two advanced concepts—**geometric notation** and **Pythagorean triplets.**

You should expect SAT geometry questions to use the symbols ↔, —, and ≅.

↔ signifies a line. $\overleftrightarrow{XY}$ is the line that passes through points *X* and *Y*.

— signifies a line segment: $\overline{XY}$ is the line segment whose endpoints are *X* and *Y*.

≅ symbolizes congruence. If two triangles are congruent, they coincide exactly when superimposed. You may want to think of two congruent figures as identical twins. Look at the following example:

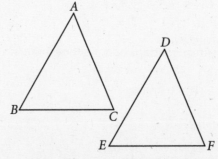

Note: Figure not drawn to scale.

$\angle CAB \cong \angle FDE$ and $\angle ABC \cong \angle DEF$. Which of the
following must be true?

  I. $\triangle ABC \cong \triangle DEF$

  II. Triangles *ABC* and *DEF* are similar.

  III. $\overline{AB} = \overline{DE}$

(A) II only

(B) III only

(C) I and III

(D) II and III

(E) I, II, and III

When a figure is not drawn to scale, it is most likely drawn in a misleading way. The figure above certainly looks as though *ABC* and *DEF* are identical and that all their parts are congruent, but you can't assume that based on the information in the problem.

WATCH THE SCALE

Even though a figure on the SAT may seem to be a certain size, if the text says "Figure not drawn to scale," one part of the drawing could be much smaller or larger than the other. Be careful.

You may want to draw your own diagrams to think about some of the different possibilities. All we know about these triangles is that they have two pairs of corresponding angles that are congruent. Therefore, the third angle of each triangle must also be congruent.

This tells us that the triangles are similar because their angles are the same. However, we know nothing about the lengths of the sides—one triangle could be much smaller than the other; thus, choice (A) is the correct answer.

KNOW TRIANGLE RELATIONSHIPS

Now more than ever, the SAT will reward test takers who recall the special relationships in 45-45-90 and 30-60-90 right triangles:

THE ISOSCELES RIGHT TRIANGLE
(Note the side ratio—$1:1:\sqrt{2}$.)

PERFECT SCORE TIP

Memorizing special right triangles is definitely worth the effort. They come up frequently in geometry problems, so don't waste time working out all the sides and angles for every question.

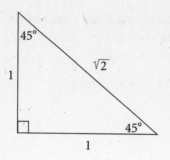

THE 30-60-90 RIGHT TRIANGLE
(Note the side ratio—$1:\sqrt{3}:2$, and which side is opposite which angle.)

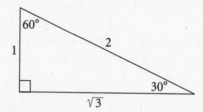

Try the following question:

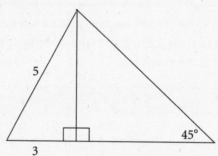

What is the total area of the figure above?

To find the area of a triangle, you need its height and the length of its base. Think about the information presented in the figure. What other data can you derive from it? The triangle on the left is a special triangle with side lengths of 3, 4, and 5. (You could also find the missing side using the Pythagorean theorem.) The triangle on the right is a 45-45-90 triangle, so its base must also equal 4. The total area of the figure is then $\frac{1}{2}(3+4)(4) = 14$.

PROBABILITY

Probability problems involve determining the chance that something might happen. A common way for the SAT to make these problems seem tougher is to throw geometry into the mix.

Geometric probability questions are those geometry questions that contain a final step in which you're asked to calculate a probability. At this final stage, use the formula Probability = $\dfrac{\text{Desired Outcome}}{\text{Possible Outcomes}}$. Try this formula on the following question:

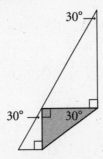

What is the probability that a point selected at random from the interior of the figure will fall within the shaded region?

(A) $\dfrac{\sqrt{3}}{13}$

(B) $\dfrac{3}{13}$

(C) $\dfrac{6}{13}$

(D) $\dfrac{1}{3}$

(E) $\dfrac{1}{2}$

The probability that a randomly selected point will fall into the shaded region is equal to the area of the shaded region divided by the area of the entire figure.

The figure is made up of three 30-60-90 triangles, so you can calculate the ratio of the lengths of the bases and heights of the various triangles and then find their areas.

This will be easier if you pick a number to be the length of the base of the smallest triangle.

The lengths of the sides of a 30-60-90 triangle are in the ratio $x{:}x\sqrt{3}{:}2x$.

If the length of the smallest triangle is 1, its height is $\sqrt{3}$. This is also the length of the base of the middle triangle.

The height of the middle triangle is $\sqrt{3} \times \sqrt{3} = 3$, which is also the length of the base of the largest triangle.

The height of the largest triangle is $3\sqrt{3}$.

$$\text{Area of smallest triangle: } \frac{1}{2}(1)(\sqrt{3}) = \frac{\sqrt{3}}{2}$$

$$\text{Area of middle triangle: } \frac{1}{2}(\sqrt{3})(3) = \frac{3\sqrt{3}}{2}$$

$$\text{Area of largest triangle: } \frac{1}{2}(3)(3\sqrt{3}) = \frac{9\sqrt{3}}{2}$$

Probability that a point will lie in the shaded region: $\dfrac{\frac{3\sqrt{3}}{2}}{\frac{\sqrt{3}}{2}+\frac{3\sqrt{3}}{2}+\frac{9\sqrt{3}}{2}} = \dfrac{\frac{3\sqrt{3}}{2}}{\frac{13\sqrt{3}}{2}} = \dfrac{3}{13}$

Use the techniques and knowledge you just gained to work through the practice set. Be sure to go over the concepts that you struggled with.

PRACTICE

We have labeled the following questions by the math concept they test. If you get stumped, go back to the appropriate part of this chapter and refresh your memory on how to solve that kind of problem.

QUADRATIC EQUATIONS

1. If $\dfrac{x^3-4x}{x^3-5x^2+6x}=0$, and $x \neq 0, 2,$ or 3, what is the value of x?

   (A) -3
   (B) -2
   (C) 0
   (D) 1
   (E) 4

EQUATIONS

2. If $\sqrt{x+2y}-2=15$, what is the value of y in terms of x?

   (A) $\dfrac{289-x}{2}$

   (B) $289-x$

   (C) $\dfrac{17-x}{2}$

   (D) $17-x$

   (E) 289

EXPONENTS

3. What is the value of $4^{\frac{1}{2}}+4^{\frac{3}{2}}$?

   (A) 4
   (B) 8
   (C) 10
   (D) 16
   (E) 64

NUMBER PROPERTIES

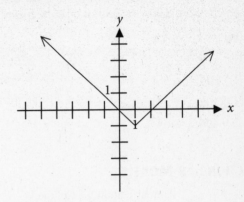

4. Which of the following equations best represents the graph?

   (A) $y=|x|$
   (B) $y=|x|-1$
   (C) $y=|x-1|$
   (D) $y=|x-1|-1$
   (E) $y=|x-2|$

FUNCTIONS

5. If $f(x)=\dfrac{(x^2-9)}{(x+3)}$, what is the value of $f(-4)$?

   (A) -7

   (B) $-\dfrac{1}{4}$

   (C) 0

   (D) $\dfrac{1}{4}$

   (E) 7

DOMAIN AND RANGE

6. If $g(x) = 2 - \sqrt{x-7}$, and $g(x)$ is a real number, which of the following cannot be the value of x?

   (A)   4

   (B)   7

   (C) 11

   (D) 102

   (E) 496

FUNCTIONS AS MODELS

Annual Tuition for College Y
(2000–2003)

[chart: Price (dollars) vs Year, points rising from about 9,000 in 2000 to about 18,000 in 2003]

7. The graph represents the annual tuition for college Y from 2000–2003. Based on the graph, what was most likely the tuition for college Y in 1999?

   (A) $6,000

   (B) $9,000

   (C) $15,000

   (D) $18,000

   (E) $21,000

FUNCTIONS

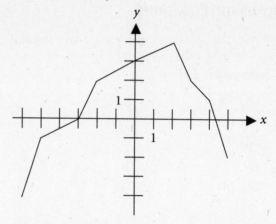

8. The graph shows the function $g(x)$. What is the value of $g(0)$?

   (A) −1

   (B) $-\dfrac{1}{2}$

   (C)   0

   (D)   1

   (E)   3

QUADRATIC EQUATIONS

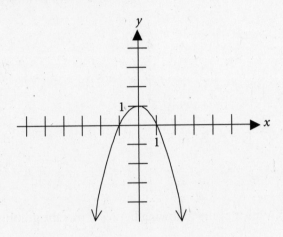

9. Which of the following equations best describes the curve?

(A) $y = x^2 + 4$

(B) $y = x^2 - 1$

(C) $y = -x^2 + 4$

(D) $y = -x^2 + 1$

(E) $y = -x^2 - 1$

Nonlinear Graphs

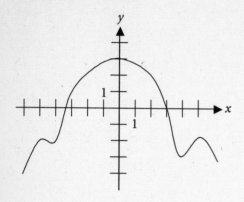

10. The figure above shows the graph of the function $h(x)$. Which of the following figures shows the graph of the function $h(x+1)$?

(A)
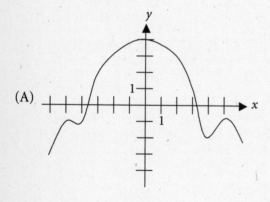

(C)
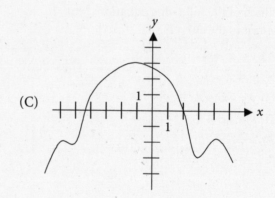

(B)
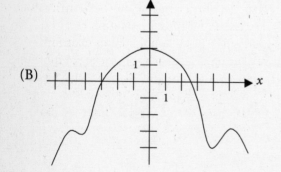

(D)
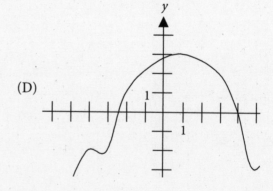

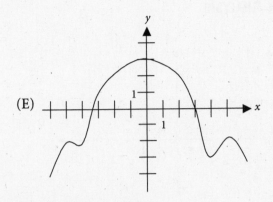

(E)

NONLINEAR GRAPHS

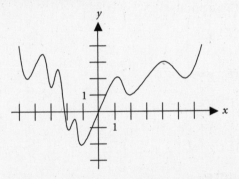

11. The figure above shows the graph of $g(x)$. What is the largest value of $g(x)$ shown in this figure?

    (A) −2
    (B)   2
    (C)   4
    (D)   6
    (E)   6.5

COORDINATE PLANES

12. If point R is $(2, 4)$ and point S is $(7, 7)$, what is the length of $\overline{RS}$?

    (A) 2
    (B) $\sqrt{7}$
    (C) $\sqrt{34}$
    (D) 9
    (E) $\sqrt{202}$

CIRCLES

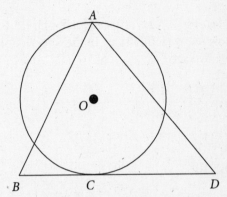

Note: Figure not drawn to scale.

13. In the figure, $\overline{BD}$ is 8 units long and tangent to the circle at point C. $\overline{AC}$ is a diameter of the circle. If the circumference of the circle is 6π, what is the area of $\triangle ABD$?

    (A) 9
    (B) 12
    (C) 24
    (D) 9π
    (E) 10π

SEQUENCES

14. A scientist is running an experiment with two species of bacteria that grow exponentially. If species A doubles in population every two days, species B doubles in population every five days, and each species began the experiment with a population of 50 bacteria, what will the difference be between the populations of the two species after ten days?

    (A)   200
    (B)   800
    (C) 1,200
    (D) 1,400
    (E) 1,500

SETS

15. If Set $A = \{2, 3, 5, 7, 10\}$ and Set $B = \{3, 4, 5, 6, 7\}$, how many elements are in the intersection of the two sets?

    (A) 2
    (B) 3
    (C) 5
    (D) 7
    (E) 10

RATIOS

16. The rate at which a certain balloon travels is inversely proportional to the amount of weight attached to it. If the balloon travels at 10 inches per second when there is a 2-gram weight attached to it, approximately how much weight must be attached to the balloon for it to travel 18 inches per second?

    (A) 0.4 grams
    (B) 1.0 gram
    (C) 1.1 grams
    (D) 3.6 grams
    (E) 10.0 grams

DATA ANALYSIS

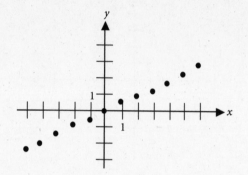

17. Which of the following equations best fits these points?

    (A) $y = \dfrac{1}{2}x$

    (B) $y = \dfrac{1}{2}x + 4$

    (C) $y = x$

    (D) $y = 2x - 4$

    (E) $y = 2x$

TRIANGLES

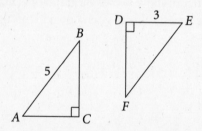

18. In the figure above, $\triangle ABC \cong \triangle EFD$. What is the area of $\triangle ABC$?

    (A) 6
    (B) 7.5
    (C) $6\sqrt{2}$
    (D) $6\sqrt{3}$
    (E) 12

PROBLEMS IN WHICH TRIGONOMETRY CAN BE USED AS AN ALTERNATIVE METHOD OF SOLUTION

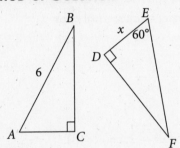

19. In the figure, $\triangle ABC \cong \triangle EFD$. What is the value of x?

   (A) 3
   (B) 4
   (C) 5
   (D) 6
   (E) 7

PROBABILITY

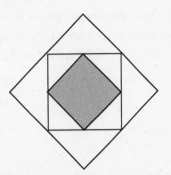

20. The figure above shows a square inscribed in a square inscribed in another square. What is the probability that a point selected at random from the interior of the largest figure will fall within the shaded region?

   (A) $\dfrac{1}{5}$

   (B) $\dfrac{1}{4}$

   (C) $\dfrac{1}{3}$

   (D) $\dfrac{4}{9}$

   (E) $\dfrac{1}{2}$

ANSWERS AND EXPLANATIONS

1. B

SMARTPOINTS CATEGORY: QUADRATIC EQUATIONS

In general, try to simplify problems with complex rational equations like this by factoring the numerator and denominator to see whether any parts cancel out. In this case, you need only to focus on the numerator. You know the fraction has a value of zero, so the numerator must equal zero:

$$x^3 - 4x = 0$$
$$x(x^2 - 4) = 0$$
$$x(x - 2)(x + 2) = 0$$
$$x = 0, 2, \text{ or } -2$$

The question stem states that $x \neq 0$ or 2, so the answer must be $x = -2$, choice (B).

2. A

SMARTPOINTS CATEGORY: EQUATIONS

Since y is part of the expression in the square root, you must start by isolating the square root and then squaring both sides of the equation:

$$\sqrt{x + 2y} - 2 = 15$$
$$\sqrt{x + 2y} = 17$$
$$(\sqrt{x + 2y})^2 = 17^2$$
$$x + 2y = 289$$
$$2y = 289 - x$$
$$y = \frac{289 - x}{2}$$

The correct answer is (A). This is an example designed to illustrate that squaring both sides is not always the last step.

3. C

SMARTPOINTS CATEGORY: EXPONENTS

If x is a positive real number and a is a nonzero integer, then $x^{\frac{1}{a}} = \sqrt[a]{n}$. So $4^{\frac{1}{2}} = \sqrt[2]{4} = 2$. If p and q are integers, then $x^{\frac{p}{q}} = \sqrt[q]{x^p}$. So $4^{\frac{3}{2}} = \sqrt[2]{4^3} = \sqrt{64} = 8$. Therefore, $2 + 8 = 10$, and answer choice (C) is correct.

4. D

SMARTPOINTS CATEGORY: NUMBER PROPERTIES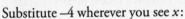

If you're not sure what these transformations of the graph look like, try plugging in a few points from the graph into each equation to see which one is correct.

The point $(1, -1)$ immediately eliminates (A), (C), and (E) because the absolute value of a quantity cannot be negative.

(B) evaluates to $-1 = |1| - 1$, which is a false statement.

This leaves (D), the correct answer: $|1 - 1| - 1 = 0 - 1 = -1$.

5. A

SMARTPOINTS CATEGORY: FUNCTIONS (NOTATION AND EVALUATION)

Substitute -4 wherever you see x:

$$f(x) = \frac{(x^2 - 9)}{(x + 3)}$$

$$f(-4) = \frac{[(-4)^2 - 9]}{(-4 + 3)}$$

$$f(-4) = \frac{(16 - 9)}{(-1)}$$

$$f(-4) = \frac{7}{-1}$$

$$f(-4) = -7, \text{ choice (A).}$$

6. A

SMARTPOINTS CATEGORY: FUNCTIONS (CONCEPTS OF DOMAIN AND RANGE)

If $g(x)$ is a real number, then $\sqrt{x - 7}$ must be a real number. Therefore, $x - 7$ must be zero or a positive number: $x - 7 \geq 0$, and so $x \geq 7$. Any number less than 7, such as choice (A), is outside the domain of the function, which is why it is the correct answer.

7. A

SMARTPOINTS CATEGORY: FUNCTIONS (FUNCTIONS AS MODELS)

Making inferences from a linear graph can be difficult, but remember that you can write in your test booklet. Use a straight surface or your free hand to extend the line on the graph. By looking at the graph, we can see that each year the tuition of college Y increases. In 2000, tuition was $9,000. So we know that in 1999 it should be less than that. The only option is choice (A).

8. E

SMARTPOINTS CATEGORY: FUNCTIONS (LINEAR) ▪▪▫▫

One question on test day might require you to evaluate the graph of a linear function, perhaps by indicating the value of y for a given value of x. This question essentially asks you to identify which value of y corresponds to an x-value of 0. Locate $x = 0$; then locate the corresponding y-value. In this case, that value is 3, or (E).

9. D

SMARTPOINTS CATEGORY: FUNCTIONS (QUADRATIC) ▪▪▫▫

If you encounter a question about the graph of a quadratic function, it's likely to ask you merely to evaluate a particular point on the graph or, as this question asked, to describe the graph as a whole.

Plug in some points from the graph into each equation to see which ones fit. Good points to test on this graph include (0, 1) and (1, 0). Tested in choice (D):

$$1 = -(0^2) + 1$$
$$0 = -(1^2) + 1$$

Both points work with $y = -x^2 + 1$, choice (D), so it is correct.

10. C

SMARTPOINTS CATEGORY: NONLINEAR GRAPHS ▪▫▫▫

The graph of $h(x + 1)$ is the graph of $h(x)$ shifted one unit to the left. If you're not sure what that would look like, try comparing a few points from each graph:

$$h(3) = h(2 + 1) = 0$$
$$h(0) = h(-1 + 1) = 3$$

11. C

SMARTPOINTS CATEGORY: NONLINEAR GRAPHS ▪▫▫▫

The value of $g(x)$ is the y-value of the graph. Don't worry about how much of the x-axis is shown; it isn't relevant. The largest value of $g(x)$ shown in the figure is 4, at the points (−5, 4) and (6.5, 4), so (C) is the correct answer.

12. C

SMARTPOINTS CATEGORY: COORDINATE PLANES

The distance between two points (x_1, y_1) and (x_2, y_2) can be found by using the distance formula:

$\sqrt{(x_2 - x_1)^2 + (y_2 - y_1)^2}$. Plug in the numbers from the question:

$$\sqrt{(7-2)^2 + (7-4)^2} = \sqrt{5^2 + 3^2} = \sqrt{25+9} = \sqrt{34}$$

The correct answer is choice (C).

13. C

SMARTPOINTS CATEGORY: CIRCLES

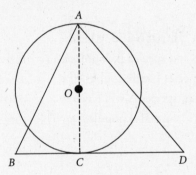

Note: Figure not drawn to scale.

When you see a figure that is not drawn to scale, you can often assume that it has been drawn to be deliberately misleading. Be careful not to assume anything from the apparent positions or lengths of any parts of the figure. Rely instead on the information in the question stem. You may wish to draw your own figure to incorporate that information. This figure includes a circle. Anytime you see a circle, you're going to want its radius at some point. How is the radius of the circle related to the triangle?

Using the circumference formula and the known circumference of the circle:

$$6\pi = 2\pi r$$
$$r = 3$$

The diagram that follows has been corrected to include the information in the question stem. Note that because $\overline{BD}$ is tangent to the circle at point C, it is perpendicular to $\overline{OC}$. Because $\overline{AC}$ is a diameter of the circle, it must pass through the center of the circle.

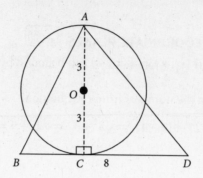

The area of a triangle is one half the length of the base times the height. The height of this triangle is $\overline{AC}$: $3 + 3 = 6$. The area is $\frac{1}{2}(8)(6) = 24$, choice (C).

14. D

SMARTPOINTS CATEGORY: SEQUENCES

Species A doubles every 2 days and species B doubles every 5 days, so in 10 days, species A will double $10 \div 2 = 5$ times and species B will double $10 \div 5 = 2$ times. After 10 days from an initial population of 50 in each species, species A will have $50 \times 2^5 = 50 \times 32 = 1{,}600$ population, while species B will have $50 \times 2^2 = 50 \times 4 = 200$ population. Their difference is $1{,}600 - 200 = 1{,}400$, or choice (D).

15. B

SMARTPOINTS CATEGORY: SETS

Focus on the overlap of the sets, which share three numbers: 3, 5, and 7. The correct answer is 3, choice (B).

16. C

SMARTPOINTS CATEGORY: RATIOS

To find the exact amount of weight required, set up a relationship between the height of the balloon and the weight attached to it. Because these quantities vary inversely, you can express that relationship as $h = \dfrac{k}{w}$, where h is the rate of travel of the balloon, w is the weight attached to it, and k is a constant. First, use the given values of h and w to find k, and then use the equation to find the amount of weight required to make the balloon travel at 18 inches per second:

$$10 = \frac{k}{2}$$

$$k = 20$$

$$18 = \frac{20}{w}$$

$w = \dfrac{20}{18} = \dfrac{10}{9} = 1.\overline{11}$, which is approximately 1.1, choice (C).

17. A

SMARTPOINTS CATEGORY: DATA ANALYSIS

Try to figure out what sort of line would fit these points. What should the slope be? What should the y-intercept be? A line through these points would cross the y-axis at or near 0. Its slope is positive but less than 1. Choice (A) fulfills both these criteria. You might want to check your answer by plugging in a few points from the graph into the equation to make sure they work.

18. A

SMARTPOINTS CATEGORY: TRIANGLES (GEOMETRIC NOTATION)

Because the two triangles are congruent, you can combine the information given about each triangle. That is, because $DE = 3$, CA also equals 3.

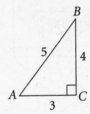

These are 3-4-5 right triangles, so their height is 4.

The area of the triangle is $\frac{1}{2}(3)(4) = 6$, so choice (A) is correct.

19. A

SMARTPOINTS CATEGORY: TRIANGLES

If two triangles are congruent, they are identical. Each angle or length in one triangle is equal to the corresponding angle or length in the other triangle. Combine the information in the two triangles to get the following triangle:

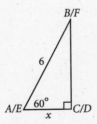

This is a 30-60-90 special triangle, so $x = \frac{1}{2}(6) = 3$, choice (A).

20. B

SMARTPOINTS CATEGORY: PROBABILITY

There are several different ways to approach this problem, but they all require some knowledge of triangles. The most important thing to notice about the figure is that all the triangles in it are 45-45-90 triangles. This allows you to either calculate the ratios between their sides or break them up further as shown below.

Adding two lines to this figure makes it much easier to work with:

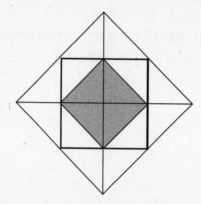

Note that every triangle in this new figure is identical. At this point, you can count the number of shaded triangles and divide by the total number of triangles.

$\frac{4}{16} = \frac{1}{4}$, choice (B).

KEY POINTS YOU'VE LEARNED IN THIS CHAPTER

THE 20 MOST TESTED ADVANCED MATH CONCEPTS AND METHODS FOR SOLVING EACH:

1. **Equations (Radical Equations)**—Remember that $\sqrt{3}$ refers only to the positive root of a number. If $\sqrt{25} = x$, then $x = 5$. But if $x^2 = 25$, then $x = \pm 5$.

2. **Quadratic Equations (Rational Equations)**—When an expression looks especially complex, try to simplify it by factoring.

3. **Exponents**—$x^{-a} = \dfrac{1}{x^a}$ and $x^{\frac{p}{q}} = \sqrt[q]{x^p}$

4. **Number Properties**—**Absolute value** is the distance of a number from zero on the number line.

5. **Functions (Notation and Evaluation)**—Substitute numbers for the variables.

6. **Functions (Domain and Range)**—The **domain** of a function is the set of values for which the function is defined. The **range** of a function is the set of possible values of the function.

7. **Functions (Functions as Models)**—Know the relationship and value of each part of a graph or chart.

8. **Functions (Linear Functions)**—Equations and Graphs—Parallel lines have equal slopes. Perpendicular lines have negative reciprocal slopes.

9. **Quadratic Functions**—Take the shape of a parabola and the form $f(x) = ax^2 + bx + c$. Solve them like you would a quadratic equation.

10. **Nonlinear Graphs (Graphs and Functions)**—Know the values for the x-axis and y-axis.

11. **Nonlinear Graphs (Transformations)**—A transformation is merely an adjustment to a function equation. Treat them similarly.

12. **Coordinate Planes**—The midpoint of two points is simply the average of the x-values and the average of the y-values.

13. **Circles (Properties of Tangent Lines)**—The radius of a circle is perpendicular to a tangent line at the point of contact.

14. **Sequences**—If r is the ratio between consecutive terms, a_1 is the first term, and a_n is the nth term, then $a_n = a_1 r^{n-1}$.

15. **Sets**—The union of sets is what you get when you merge the sets. The intersection of sets is the overlap of the sets.

16. **Ratios—Direct variation** is $y = kx$, where y changes as x does. **Inverse variation** is $xy = k$, where x and y change differently based on their relationship in the equation.

17. **Data Analysis**—Sketch the shape given in the equation, and try plugging in some data points into that equation.

18. **Triangles (Geometric Notation)**—If two figures are similar, they have the same shape. If two figures are congruent, they're identical. Any two 45-45-90 triangles are similar, even though one might be much larger than the other. Only if they are identical in size as well as proportion are they congruent.

19. **Triangles (Pythagorean Triplets)**—Know the special relationships between 45-45-90 and 30-60-90 right triangles.

20. **Probability (Geometric Probability)**—Probability $= \dfrac{\text{Desired Outcome}}{\text{Possible Outcomes}}$.

CHAPTER 16: HOW TO AVOID SAT MATH TRAPS

SMARTPOINTS COVERED IN THIS CHAPTER

RATIOS	
NUMBER PROPERTIES	
RATES	
PERCENTS	
GEOMETRIC VISUALIZATION	
AVERAGES	

WHAT TO EXPECT ON TEST DAY

As we've mentioned several times, Math sets are arranged in order of difficulty, with the easiest problems coming first and the hardest problems coming last. Knowing this leads you, the test taker, to treat question #3 differently from question #14. This is where SAT math traps come into play.

THE 10 MOST COMMON MATH TRAPS AND HOW TO AVOID THEM

If you arrive at an answer choice to a hard Math problem without too much effort, be suspicious; that answer is probably a math trap. Learning how to recognize and avoid common SAT math traps will help you be more successful on the Math sections.

There are ten common math traps on the SAT. We'll show you the trap, the wrong answer the trap wants you to choose, how to avoid that answer, and how to solve the problem quickly and correctly.

TRAP 1: PERCENT INCREASE/DECREASE

The Trap: When a quantity is increased or decreased by a percentage more than once, you can't simply add and subtract the percentages to get the answer.

In this kind of percentage problem, the first change is a percentage of the starting amount, but the second change is a percentage of the new amount:

> Sammy purchased a new car in 2000. Three years later, he sold it to a dealer for 40 percent less than he paid for it in 2000. The dealer then added 20 percent onto the price he paid and resold it to another customer. The price the final customer paid for the car was what percent of the original price Sammy paid in 2000?
>
> (A) 40%
> (B) 60%
> (C) 72%
> (D) 80%
> (E) 88%

THE WRONG ANSWER

The increase/decrease percentage problems usually appear at the end of a section and invariably contain a trap. Most students will figure that taking away 40 percent and then adding 20 percent will give them an overall loss of 20 percent, and they'll pick choice (D), 80 percent, as the correct answer. Those students will be wrong.

AVOIDING THE TRAP

Don't blindly add and subtract percentages. They can only be added and subtracted when they are of the same amount. Also, multiple percent changes on the SAT will *never* result in the straight sum or difference of those changes.

$$50\% - 50\% \neq 0\%$$

FINDING THE RIGHT ANSWER

We know:

- The *40 percent less* that Sammy got for the car is 40 percent of his original price.

- The *20 percent* the dealer adds on is 20 percent of what the dealer paid, which is a much smaller amount.

- Adding 20 percent of that smaller amount is *not* the same thing as adding back 20 percent of the original price.

SOLVING THE PROBLEM FAST

Pick the number 100 to start with. In theory, you could pick any number, but because the question asks for the percent of change, 100 is the best number to work with.

Now you are ready to follow these steps:

Step 1: What is 40 percent of the $100 Sammy paid for the car? $40

Step 2: What did *Sammy* sell the car for? Luckily, each percent equals $1. Thus, 100 − 40 = 60; Sammy sold the car for $60 (also the price the dealer paid).

Step 3: What did the *dealer* sell the car for? Figure what 20 percent of 60 is ($60 × .20 = $12).

Note: This is different from 20 percent of $100, which would be $20.

Step 4: Because 60 + 12 = $72, the dealer received $72.

Step 5: Finally, what percent of the starting price ($100) is $72? It's 72 percent, so the correct answer is choice (C).

PERFECT SCORE TIP

" On percentage problems, I frequently used my calculator (even though I wrote out all my work!) to plug in the numbers and percents and come up with my final answer. "

TRAP 2: WEIGHTED AVERAGES

The Trap: You cannot combine averages of different quantities by taking the average of those original averages.

In an averages problem, if one value occurs more frequently than others, it is *weighted* more. Remember, the average formula calls for the sum of all the terms divided by the total number of terms. Look at the following example:

> In a class of 27 plumbers, the average (arithmetic mean) score of the male plumbers on the final exam was 83. If the average score of the 15 female plumbers in the class was 92, what was the average of the whole class?
>
> (A) 86.2
> (B) 87.0
> (C) 87.5
> (D) 88.0
> (E) 88.2

THE WRONG ANSWER

Some students will rush in and simply average 83 and 92 to come up with 87.5 as the class average. Those students will be wrong.

AVOIDING THE TRAP

Don't just take the average of the averages; work with the sums.

FINDING THE RIGHT ANSWER

To find the combined average:

> **Step 1:** To find each sum, multiply each average by the number of terms (plumbers) it represents. So calculate (female plumbers × average) or (15 × 92) + (male plumbers × average) or (12 × 83).
>
> **Step 2:** Divide that number by the total number of plumbers, or 27.

Presenting this as a formula, you would have:

$$\text{Total class average} = \frac{\text{Sum of females' scores} + \text{Sum of males' scores}}{\text{Total number of students}}$$

$$= \frac{(\text{\# of females} \times \text{average score of females}) + (\text{\# of males} \times \text{average score of males})}{\text{Total number of students}}$$

$$= \frac{15(92) + 12(83)}{27} = \frac{1,380 + 996}{27} = 88$$

So the class average is 88, answer choice (D).

Note: Notice how using a calculator helps in this problem.

TRAP 3: RATIO:RATIO:RATIO

The Trap: Parts of different ratios don't always refer to the same whole.

In the classic ratio trap, two different ratios each share a common part that is represented by two different numbers. However, the two ratios do not refer to the same whole, so they are not in proportion to each other.

To solve this type of problem, restate both ratios so that the numbers representing the common part (in this case *dimes*) are the same. Then all the parts will be in proportion and can be compared to each other. Look at the following example:

> Mammo's coin collection consists of quarters, dimes, and nickels. If the ratio of the number of quarters to the number of dimes is 5:2, and the ratio of the number of dimes to the number of nickels is 3:4, what is the ratio of the number of quarters to the number of nickels?
>
> (A) 5:4
> (B) 7:5
> (C) 10:6
> (D) 12:7
> (E) 15:8

THE WRONG ANSWER

If you chose 5:4 as the correct answer, you fell for the classic ratio trap.

AVOIDING THE TRAP

Restate ratios so that the same number refers to the same quantity. Make sure the common quantity in both ratios has the same number in both.

PERFECT SCORE TIP

"The easiest way for me to avoid trap answers was to turn ratios into actual numbers *and* jot them down."

FINDING THE RIGHT ANSWER

To find the ratio of quarters to nickels, restate both ratios so that the number of dimes is the same in both. You are given two ratios:

quarters to dimes = 5:2   dimes to nickels = 3:4

Step 1. Determine the number of dimes in the first ratio, or 2.

Step 2. Determine the number of dimes in the second ratio, or 3.

Step 3. To restate the ratios, find the least common multiple of 2 and 3, or 6.

Step 4. Restate the ratios with the number of dimes as 6:
Quarters to dimes using 6 is $(5 \times 3):(3 \times 2)$, or 15:6 (the same as 5:2).
Dimes to nickels using 6 is $(3 \times 2):(4 \times 2)$, or 6:8 (the same as 3:4).

Step 5. See that the ratio of quarters to dimes to nickels is 15:6:8.

The ratios are still in their original proportions, but now they can be compared easily because the same number in both represents dimes.

The ratio of quarters to nickels is 15:8, which is answer choice (E).

TRAP 4: "LEAST" AND "GREATEST"

The Trap: In questions that ask for the *least*, *minimum*, or *smallest* something, the choice offering the smallest number is rarely right.

In questions that ask for the *greatest*, *maximum*, or *largest* something, the choice offering the largest number is very rarely right. Look at the following example:

What is the least positive integer that is divisible by both 2 and 5 and leaves a remainder of 3 when divided by 11?

(A) 30
(B) 32
(C) 33
(D) 70
(E) 80

THE WRONG ANSWER

(A) is the choice not to go for here.

AVOIDING THE TRAP

> Consider the constraints and requirements that the nature of the question has placed upon the possible answer. Don't leap to conclusions. In fact, if you ever need to guess on questions asking about the least number, the one place not to go is to the smallest choice and vice versa for questions asking about the largest number.

FINDING THE RIGHT ANSWER

Use an elimination process to find the answer:

Step 1. Eliminate all answers that aren't divisible by both 2 and 5—here, choices (B) and (C).

Step 2. Subtract 3 from all the other number choices. Only choice (E), which yields 77, is divisible by 11.

TRAP 5: TRICKY WORDING IN PERCENT QUESTIONS

There is a big difference between *of, less than*, and *greater than* in the ordering of percent problems. They each mean different things.

Consider the following example:

What number is $33\frac{1}{3}$% less than 9?

THE WRONG ANSWER

Three.

To avoid confusion on test day:

- Think **multiply** when you see *of*.
- Think **add** when you see *greater than*.
- Think **subtract** when you see *less than*.

FINDING THE RIGHT ANSWER

$33\frac{1}{3}$% less than 9 means $9 - \left(\frac{1}{3}\right)(9) = 9 - 3 = 6$.

> **PERFECT SCORE TIP**
>
> " Whenever there's more than one piece of information given in problems dealing with "least" and "greatest" numbers, try using each piece individually to eliminate as many answer choices as possible. "

TRAP 6: RATIO VERSUS QUANTITY

The Trap: You cannot simply add to or subtract from the parts of a ratio at will. Test takers unfamiliar with this rule would probably add 1 to 3 and to 4, coming up incorrectly with the ratio of 4:5. Look at the example:

> The ratio of two quantities is 3:4. If each of the quantities is increased by 1, what is the ratio of these two new quantities?
>
> (A) 9:16
> (B) 2:3
> (C) 3:4
> (D) 4:5
> (E) It cannot be determined from the information given.

> **PERFECT SCORE TIP**
>
> " Plugging in for ratio/quantity questions is sometimes the best way to solve a problem, but be wary of any trap answers that can trick students who don't know the difference between ratio and quantity. "

THE WRONG ANSWER

(D) is a trap.

AVOIDING THE TRAP

Avoid this trap by remembering the rule that you can multiply or divide a ratio or part of a ratio, but you cannot add to or subtract from a ratio or part of a ratio.

FINDING THE RIGHT ANSWER

For students on the lookout for violations of the rule we've been discussing, this question means quick points.

Once you realize that the ratio of the new quantities depends on the actual original quantities—not simply their ratio—you'll quickly recognize that the answer cannot be determined from the information provided. The correct answer is (E).

THE RATIO RULE

You can multiply or divide a ratio or part of a ratio:

- If the number of apples to oranges is 2 : 4 and you double the oranges, then the new ratio is 2 : 8.

- If instead you halve the number of oranges, then the new ratio is 2 : 2, or an equal number of each.

- However, you cannot add a fixed quantity to or remove one from a ratio without knowing the original quantity.

TRAP 7: NOT ALL NUMBERS ARE POSITIVE INTEGERS

The Trap: Not all numbers are positive integers. Don't forget there are negative numbers and fractions as well. This is important because negative numbers and fractions between 0 and 1 behave very differently from positive integers. Look at the following example:

If $n \neq 0$, then which of the following must be true?

   I. $n^2 > n$

  II. $2n > n$

 III. $n + 1 > n$

(A) I only

(B) II only

(C) III only

(D) I and III only

(E) I, II, and III

PERFECT SCORE TIP

❝ When solving questions that are open-ended as to which number to choose, try many different types—positive and negative integers and fractions and zero. ❞

THE WRONG ANSWER

In the example above, if you considered only positive integers greater than 1 for the value of n, you would assume that all three statements were true. However, that is not the case.

AVOIDING THE TRAP

When picking numbers for variables, consider fractions and negative numbers.

FINDING THE RIGHT ANSWER

Here, you are looking for *exceptions* to a statement, so look for instances when something might NOT be true.

Consider fractions and negative numbers in testing "must be true" questions:

- **Statement I:** You might assume that squaring a number will result in a larger number. But always? What happens if you square a *fraction between 0 and 1*? In fact, the result is quite different: $\frac{1}{2^2} = \frac{1}{4}$ and $(\frac{1}{10})^2 = \frac{1}{100}$. Thus, you can eliminate choices (A), (D), and (E).

- **Statement II:** You might assume that multiplying a number by 2 will result in a larger number. Again, be careful. What happens if you multiply a *negative number* by 2? Your result is smaller than the original number. For example, $-3 \times 2 = -6$. Eliminate (B).

- **Statement III:** This is the only possibility left, so answer choice (C) is correct. But let's look at why: Adding 1 to any number gives you a larger number as a result in any situation. For example, $5 + 1 = 6$, $\frac{1}{2} + 1 = 1\frac{1}{2}$, and $-7 + 1 = -6$.

Therefore, only Statement III must be true, so choice (C) is correct. If you didn't consider fractions or negative numbers, you would have fallen into the trap and answered the question incorrectly.

TRAP 8: HIDDEN INSTRUCTIONS

The Trap: A small clue, easily overlooked, can mean the difference between a right and wrong answer, as in the below example:

> At a certain restaurant, the hourly wage for a waiter is 20 percent more than the hourly wage for a dishwasher, and the hourly wage for a dishwasher is half as much as the hourly wage for a cook's assistant. If a cook's assistant earns $8.50 per hour, how much less than a cook's assistant does a waiter earn each hour?
>
> (A) $2.55
> (B) $3.40
> (C) $4.25
> (D) $5.10
> (E) $5.95

> **EXPERT TUTOR TIP**
>
> " Don't overlook small but very significant words on the SAT. Ignoring key question details can wreck your chances of finding the right answer. "

THE WRONG ANSWER

To solve this problem, you must find the hourly wage of the waiter. The cook's assistant earns $8.50 per hour. The dishwasher earns half of this—$4.25 per hour. The waiter earns 20 percent more than the dishwasher—$4.25 × 1.2 = $5.10. So the waiter earns $5.10 per hour, and your automatic reaction might be to fill in answer choice (D). But (D) is the wrong answer.

AVOIDING THE TRAP

Make sure you answer the question that's being asked. Watch out for hidden instructions.

FINDING THE RIGHT ANSWER

You have figured out that the waiter earns $5.10 per hour, and the cook's assistant earns $8.50 per hour.

To find out how much less the waiter earns than the cook's assistant, subtract the waiter's hourly wage from the cook's assistant's hourly wage. The correct answer is (B).

SPEED UP BY SLOWING DOWN

As you approach the end of a section and the clock begins to tick away, it can be extremely tempting to rush and start reading faster.

Don't make that mistake!

Reading faster will not only cause you to miss important words, it will also force you to reread things a second or third time, which wastes time rather than saving it.

Read it right by reading once—and carefully.

TRAP 9: AVERAGE RATES

The Trap: To get an average speed, you can't just average the rates.

A car traveled from *A* to *B* at an average speed of 40 mph and then immediately traveled back from *B* to *A* at an average speed of 60 mph. What was the car's average speed for the round-trip in miles per hour?

(A) 45

(B) 48

(C) 50

(D) 52

(E) 54

THE WRONG ANSWER

Do you see which answer choice looks too good to be true? The temptation is simply to add 40 and 60 and divide by two. The answer is *obviously* 50, or choice (C). But 50 is wrong.

AVOIDING THE TRAP

You can solve almost any average rate problem with this general formula:

$$\text{Average Rate} = \frac{\text{Total Distance}}{\text{Total Time}}$$

Use the given information to figure out the total distance and the total time.

FINDING THE RIGHT ANSWER

Pick a number for the total distance, if the total distance is not provided.

Step 1. Pick a number that's easy to work with. A good number to pick here would be 240 for the total distance because you can figure in your head the times for two 120-mile legs at 40 mph and 60 mph.

Step 2. Now plug *total distance = 240 miles* and *total time = 5 hours* into the general formula:

$$\text{Average Rate} = \frac{\text{Total Distance}}{\text{Total Time}} = \frac{240 \text{ miles}}{5 \text{ hours}} = 48 \text{ hours}$$

Thus, the correct answer is choice (B).

> **PERFECT SCORE TIP**
>
> " Picking numbers worked well for me when I came across average rate questions. I always approached them in a consistent and methodical way. "

TRAP 10: COUNTING NUMBERS

The Trap: Subtracting the first and last integers in a range will give you the difference of the two numbers. It won't give you the number of integers in that range. Look at the following example:

> The tickets for a certain raffle are consecutively numbered. If Louis sold the tickets numbered from 75 to 148 inclusive, how many raffle tickets did he sell?
>
> (A) 71
> (B) 72
> (C) 73
> (D) 74
> (E) 75

> **PERFECT SCORE TIP**
>
> " Look at your answer to avoid silly math mistakes. If it's clearly too big or too small, check your work or redo the problem. "

THE WRONG ANSWER

If you subtract 75 from 148 and get 73 as the answer, you are wrong.

AVOIDING THE TRAP

Don't rush through a problem such as this. Take the time to see if either *inclusive* or *exclusive* is specified in the wording. These words are the key to finding the right answer.

FINDING THE RIGHT ANSWER

- To count the number of integers in a range *inclusive*, subtract then add 1.

- If you forget the rule, pick two small numbers that are close together, such as 1 and 4. Obviously, there are four integers from 1 to 4, inclusive. If you had subtracted 1 from 4, your remainder would have been 3.

- The word *inclusive* tells you to include the first and last numbers given. In this problem, subtract 75 from 148. The result is 73. Adding 1 to this difference gives you 74, or choice (D).

PRACTICE

Directions: Identify the trap in each problem (and solve the problem correctly). Answers are found on page 454.

1. If x is 300 percent of 25 and y is 25 percent more than 40, then x is what percent of y? (Disregard the % sign when you grid your answer.)

2. In the figure above, what is the maximum number of nonoverlapping regions into which the shaded area can be divided using exactly two straight lines?

(A) 3

(B) 4

(C) 5

(D) 6

(E) 7

3. A certain school event was open only to juniors and seniors. Half the number of juniors who had planned to attend actually attended. Double the number of seniors who had planned to attend actually attended. If the ratio of the number of juniors who had planned to attend to the number of seniors who had planned to attend was 4 to 5, then juniors were what fraction of attendees?

(A) $\dfrac{1}{6}$

(B) $\dfrac{1}{5}$

(C) $\dfrac{4}{19}$

(D) $\dfrac{4}{15}$

(E) It cannot be determined from the information given.

4. If $p - q = 4$ and r is the number of integers less than p and greater than q, then which of the following could be true?

I. $r = 3$

II. $r = 4$

III. $r = 5$

(A) I only

(B) II only

(C) III only

(D) I and II

(E) I, II, and III

5. Pump 1 can drain a 400-gallon water tank in 1.2 hours. Pump 2 can drain the same tank in 1.8 hours. How many minutes longer than pump 1 would it take pump 2 to drain a 100-gallon tank?

   (A) 0.15
   (B) 1.2
   (C) 6
   (D) 9
   (E) 18

6. Volumes 12 through 30 of a certain encyclopedia are located on the bottom shelf of a bookcase. If the volumes of the encyclopedia are numbered consecutively, how many volumes of the encyclopedia are on the bottom shelf?

   (A) 17
   (B) 18
   (C) 19
   (D) 29
   (E) 30

7. A reservoir is at full capacity at the beginning of summer. By the first day of fall, the level in the reservoir is 30 percent below full capacity. Then during the fall, a period of heavy rains increases the level by 30 percent. After the rains, the reservoir is at what percent of its full capacity?

   (A) 60%
   (B) 85%
   (C) 91%
   (D) 95%
   (E) 100%

8. Two classes, one with 50 students and the other with 30, take the same exam. The combined average of both classes is 84.5. If the larger class averages 80, what is the average of the smaller class?

   (A) 87.2
   (B) 89.0
   (C) 92.0
   (D) 93.3
   (E) 94.5

9. In a pet shop, the ratio of puppies to kittens is 7:6, and the ratio of kittens to guinea pigs is 5:3. What is the ratio of puppies to guinea pigs?

   (A) 7:3
   (B) 6:5
   (C) 13:8
   (D) 21:11
   (E) 35:18

10. A typist typed the first n pages of a book, where $n > 0$, at an average rate of 12 pages per hour, and typed the remaining n pages at an average rate of 20 pages per hour. What was the typist's average rate in pages per hour for the entire book?

   (A) 14
   (B) 15
   (C) 16
   (D) 17
   (E) 18

11. Michael mows lawns for his summer job. He only averages 3 lawns a week for the first 8 weeks, but then averages 6 lawns a week for the last 4 weeks. What is the average number of lawns he mowed per week during the entire summer.

12. A salesman sold jackets for three days straight at his store. He sold $54 worth of jackets on Monday, $31 worth of jackets on Tuesday, and $17 less on Wednesday than on Monday. How much less did he sell on Tuesday than on Wednesday?

(A) $ 6
(B) $17
(C) $23
(D) $37
(E) $48

13. x is $33\frac{1}{3}\%$ less than y and $33\frac{1}{3}\%$ greater than z. What percentage of z is y?

(A) $33\frac{1}{3}\%$
(B) 40%
(C) 50%
(D) $66\frac{2}{3}\%$
(E) 75%

14. The farmers market has oranges, apples, and bananas. If the ratio of bananas to oranges is 5:4, and the ratio of bananas to apples is 4:3, what is the ratio of oranges to apples?

(A) 5:3
(B) 4:3
(C) 10:9
(D) 16:15
(E) 12:11

15. How many multiples of 5 are there from −20 to 20, inclusive?

(A) 4
(B) 5
(C) 8
(D) 9
(E) 10

16. A shop assistant increases the price of a sweater by 20%, increases it by another 25%, and then finally decreases it by 50%. If the sweater originally cost $100, what is the final price of the sweater?

(A) $60
(B) $75
(C) $80
(D) $95
(E) $105

17. What is the greatest value of x so that $3x + 7 < 21$?

(A) 3
(B) 4
(C) 5
(D) 6
(E) 7

18. The ratio of boys to girls in the school play is 2:5. Three new boys join the group, for a total of 9 boys. What is the new ratio of boys to girls?

   (A) 2:3
   (B) 3:4
   (C) 3:5
   (D) 4:5
   (E) 5:5

19. If $a > b$ and $a \neq b$, which of the following must be true?

   (A) $a + b > 0$
   (B) $ab > 0$
   (C) $3a + 2b > 0$
   (D) $\dfrac{a}{b} > 0$
   (E) $a - b > 0$

20. Jim averaged 30 miles per hour for the first 4 hours of his trip, then averaged 42 miles per hour for the next 2 hours. What was Jim's average speed for the entire trip?

ANSWERS AND EXPLANATIONS

DID YOU FALL FOR THE TRAPS?

Each wrong answer represents one trap you need to work on. Go back and reread the section on that trap. Then look at the practice set's problem again. Do you see the trap now?

1. 150
SMARTPOINTS CATEGORY: PERCENTS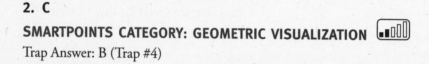
Trap Answer: 37.5 (Trap #5)

2. C
SMARTPOINTS CATEGORY: GEOMETRIC VISUALIZATION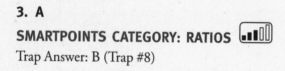
Trap Answer: B (Trap #4)

3. A
SMARTPOINTS CATEGORY: RATIOS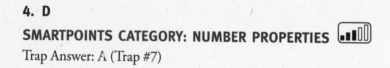
Trap Answer: B (Trap #8)

4. D
SMARTPOINTS CATEGORY: NUMBER PROPERTIES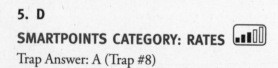
Trap Answer: A (Trap #7)

5. D
SMARTPOINTS CATEGORY: RATES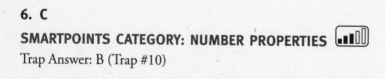
Trap Answer: A (Trap #8)

6. C
SMARTPOINTS CATEGORY: NUMBER PROPERTIES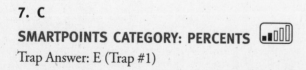
Trap Answer: B (Trap #10)

7. C
SMARTPOINTS CATEGORY: PERCENTS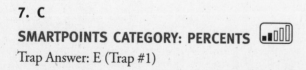
Trap Answer: E (Trap #1)

8. C

SMARTPOINTS CATEGORY: AVERAGES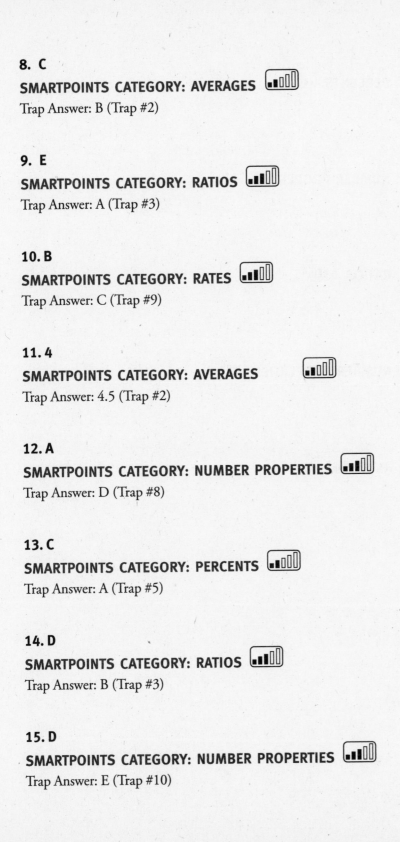

Trap Answer: B (Trap #2)

9. E

SMARTPOINTS CATEGORY: RATIOS

Trap Answer: A (Trap #3)

10. B

SMARTPOINTS CATEGORY: RATES

Trap Answer: C (Trap #9)

11. 4

SMARTPOINTS CATEGORY: AVERAGES

Trap Answer: 4.5 (Trap #2)

12. A

SMARTPOINTS CATEGORY: NUMBER PROPERTIES

Trap Answer: D (Trap #8)

13. C

SMARTPOINTS CATEGORY: PERCENTS

Trap Answer: A (Trap #5)

14. D

SMARTPOINTS CATEGORY: RATIOS

Trap Answer: B (Trap #3)

15. D

SMARTPOINTS CATEGORY: NUMBER PROPERTIES

Trap Answer: E (Trap #10)

16. B

SMARTPOINTS CATEGORY: PERCENTS

Trap Answer: D (Trap #1)

17. B

SMARTPOINTS CATEGORY: NUMBER PROPERTIES

Trap Answer: A (Trap #4)

18. C

SMARTPOINTS CATEGORY: RATIOS

Trap Answer: E (Trap #6)

19. E

SMARTPOINTS CATEGORY: NUMBER PROPERTIES

Trap Answer: A (Trap #7)

20. 34

SMARTPOINTS CATEGORY: RATES

Trap Answer: 36 (Trap #9)

KEY POINTS YOU'VE LEARNED IN THIS CHAPTER

THE MOST COMMON MATH TRAPS:

- Trap 1: Percent Increase/Decrease

- Trap 2: Weighted Averages

- Trap 3: Ratio:Ratio:Ratio

- Trap 4: "Least" and "Greatest"

- Trap 5: Tricky Wording in Percent Questions

- Trap 6: Ratio versus Quantity

- Trap 7: Not All Numbers Are Positive Integers

- Trap 8: Hidden Instructions

- Trap 9: Average Rates

- Trap 10: Counting Numbers

Part Six

PRACTICE TESTS AND EXPLANATIONS

Before taking the following Practice Tests, find a quiet room where you can work uninterrupted for 3 hours and 20 minutes. Make sure you have a comfortable desk, a calculator, and several No. 2 pencils. Use the answer sheets on the following pages to record your answers. (You can tear them out or photocopy them.)

Once you start each Practice Test, do not stop until you have finished. Remember, you may review any questions within a section, but you may not go back or forward a section.

When you have finished taking each Practice Test, you can go on to the section that follows Practice Test Three to calculate your scores.

Good luck!

SAT Practice Test One
Answer Sheet

**Remove (or photocopy) the answer sheet and use it to complete the Practice Test.
See the answer key following the test when finished.**

Start with number 1 for each section. If a section has fewer questions than answer spaces, leave the extra spaces blank.

SECTION

1

Section 1 is the Writing section's essay component.

SECTION

2

1. Ⓐ Ⓑ Ⓒ Ⓓ Ⓔ	11. Ⓐ Ⓑ Ⓒ Ⓓ Ⓔ	21. Ⓐ Ⓑ Ⓒ Ⓓ Ⓔ	31. Ⓐ Ⓑ Ⓒ Ⓓ Ⓔ
2. Ⓐ Ⓑ Ⓒ Ⓓ Ⓔ	12. Ⓐ Ⓑ Ⓒ Ⓓ Ⓔ	22. Ⓐ Ⓑ Ⓒ Ⓓ Ⓔ	32. Ⓐ Ⓑ Ⓒ Ⓓ Ⓔ
3. Ⓐ Ⓑ Ⓒ Ⓓ Ⓔ	13. Ⓐ Ⓑ Ⓒ Ⓓ Ⓔ	23. Ⓐ Ⓑ Ⓒ Ⓓ Ⓔ	33. Ⓐ Ⓑ Ⓒ Ⓓ Ⓔ
4. Ⓐ Ⓑ Ⓒ Ⓓ Ⓔ	14. Ⓐ Ⓑ Ⓒ Ⓓ Ⓔ	24. Ⓐ Ⓑ Ⓒ Ⓓ Ⓔ	34. Ⓐ Ⓑ Ⓒ Ⓓ Ⓔ
5. Ⓐ Ⓑ Ⓒ Ⓓ Ⓔ	15. Ⓐ Ⓑ Ⓒ Ⓓ Ⓔ	25. Ⓐ Ⓑ Ⓒ Ⓓ Ⓔ	35. Ⓐ Ⓑ Ⓒ Ⓓ Ⓔ
6. Ⓐ Ⓑ Ⓒ Ⓓ Ⓔ	16. Ⓐ Ⓑ Ⓒ Ⓓ Ⓔ	26. Ⓐ Ⓑ Ⓒ Ⓓ Ⓔ	36. Ⓐ Ⓑ Ⓒ Ⓓ Ⓔ
7. Ⓐ Ⓑ Ⓒ Ⓓ Ⓔ	17. Ⓐ Ⓑ Ⓒ Ⓓ Ⓔ	27. Ⓐ Ⓑ Ⓒ Ⓓ Ⓔ	37. Ⓐ Ⓑ Ⓒ Ⓓ Ⓔ
8. Ⓐ Ⓑ Ⓒ Ⓓ Ⓔ	18. Ⓐ Ⓑ Ⓒ Ⓓ Ⓔ	28. Ⓐ Ⓑ Ⓒ Ⓓ Ⓔ	38. Ⓐ Ⓑ Ⓒ Ⓓ Ⓔ
9. Ⓐ Ⓑ Ⓒ Ⓓ Ⓔ	19. Ⓐ Ⓑ Ⓒ Ⓓ Ⓔ	29. Ⓐ Ⓑ Ⓒ Ⓓ Ⓔ	39. Ⓐ Ⓑ Ⓒ Ⓓ Ⓔ
10. Ⓐ Ⓑ Ⓒ Ⓓ Ⓔ	20. Ⓐ Ⓑ Ⓒ Ⓓ Ⓔ	30. Ⓐ Ⓑ Ⓒ Ⓓ Ⓔ	40. Ⓐ Ⓑ Ⓒ Ⓓ Ⓔ

☐ # right in Section 2

☐ # wrong in Section 2

SECTION

3

1. Ⓐ Ⓑ Ⓒ Ⓓ Ⓔ	11. Ⓐ Ⓑ Ⓒ Ⓓ Ⓔ	21. Ⓐ Ⓑ Ⓒ Ⓓ Ⓔ	31. Ⓐ Ⓑ Ⓒ Ⓓ Ⓔ
2. Ⓐ Ⓑ Ⓒ Ⓓ Ⓔ	12. Ⓐ Ⓑ Ⓒ Ⓓ Ⓔ	22. Ⓐ Ⓑ Ⓒ Ⓓ Ⓔ	32. Ⓐ Ⓑ Ⓒ Ⓓ Ⓔ
3. Ⓐ Ⓑ Ⓒ Ⓓ Ⓔ	13. Ⓐ Ⓑ Ⓒ Ⓓ Ⓔ	23. Ⓐ Ⓑ Ⓒ Ⓓ Ⓔ	33. Ⓐ Ⓑ Ⓒ Ⓓ Ⓔ
4. Ⓐ Ⓑ Ⓒ Ⓓ Ⓔ	14. Ⓐ Ⓑ Ⓒ Ⓓ Ⓔ	24. Ⓐ Ⓑ Ⓒ Ⓓ Ⓔ	34. Ⓐ Ⓑ Ⓒ Ⓓ Ⓔ
5. Ⓐ Ⓑ Ⓒ Ⓓ Ⓔ	15. Ⓐ Ⓑ Ⓒ Ⓓ Ⓔ	25. Ⓐ Ⓑ Ⓒ Ⓓ Ⓔ	35. Ⓐ Ⓑ Ⓒ Ⓓ Ⓔ
6. Ⓐ Ⓑ Ⓒ Ⓓ Ⓔ	16. Ⓐ Ⓑ Ⓒ Ⓓ Ⓔ	26. Ⓐ Ⓑ Ⓒ Ⓓ Ⓔ	36. Ⓐ Ⓑ Ⓒ Ⓓ Ⓔ
7. Ⓐ Ⓑ Ⓒ Ⓓ Ⓔ	17. Ⓐ Ⓑ Ⓒ Ⓓ Ⓔ	27. Ⓐ Ⓑ Ⓒ Ⓓ Ⓔ	37. Ⓐ Ⓑ Ⓒ Ⓓ Ⓔ
8. Ⓐ Ⓑ Ⓒ Ⓓ Ⓔ	18. Ⓐ Ⓑ Ⓒ Ⓓ Ⓔ	28. Ⓐ Ⓑ Ⓒ Ⓓ Ⓔ	38. Ⓐ Ⓑ Ⓒ Ⓓ Ⓔ
9. Ⓐ Ⓑ Ⓒ Ⓓ Ⓔ	19. Ⓐ Ⓑ Ⓒ Ⓓ Ⓔ	29. Ⓐ Ⓑ Ⓒ Ⓓ Ⓔ	39. Ⓐ Ⓑ Ⓒ Ⓓ Ⓔ
10. Ⓐ Ⓑ Ⓒ Ⓓ Ⓔ	20. Ⓐ Ⓑ Ⓒ Ⓓ Ⓔ	30. Ⓐ Ⓑ Ⓒ Ⓓ Ⓔ	40. Ⓐ Ⓑ Ⓒ Ⓓ Ⓔ

☐ # right in Section 3

☐ # wrong in Section 3

Remove (or photocopy) this answer sheet and use it to complete the Practice Test.

Start with number 1 for each section. If a section has fewer questions than answer spaces, leave the extra spaces blank.

SECTION 4

1. Ⓐ Ⓑ Ⓒ Ⓓ Ⓔ   11. Ⓐ Ⓑ Ⓒ Ⓓ Ⓔ   21. Ⓐ Ⓑ Ⓒ Ⓓ Ⓔ   31. Ⓐ Ⓑ Ⓒ Ⓓ Ⓔ
2. Ⓐ Ⓑ Ⓒ Ⓓ Ⓔ   12. Ⓐ Ⓑ Ⓒ Ⓓ Ⓔ   22. Ⓐ Ⓑ Ⓒ Ⓓ Ⓔ   32. Ⓐ Ⓑ Ⓒ Ⓓ Ⓔ
3. Ⓐ Ⓑ Ⓒ Ⓓ Ⓔ   13. Ⓐ Ⓑ Ⓒ Ⓓ Ⓔ   23. Ⓐ Ⓑ Ⓒ Ⓓ Ⓔ   33. Ⓐ Ⓑ Ⓒ Ⓓ Ⓔ
4. Ⓐ Ⓑ Ⓒ Ⓓ Ⓔ   14. Ⓐ Ⓑ Ⓒ Ⓓ Ⓔ   24. Ⓐ Ⓑ Ⓒ Ⓓ Ⓔ   34. Ⓐ Ⓑ Ⓒ Ⓓ Ⓔ
5. Ⓐ Ⓑ Ⓒ Ⓓ Ⓔ   15. Ⓐ Ⓑ Ⓒ Ⓓ Ⓔ   25. Ⓐ Ⓑ Ⓒ Ⓓ Ⓔ   35. Ⓐ Ⓑ Ⓒ Ⓓ Ⓔ
6. Ⓐ Ⓑ Ⓒ Ⓓ Ⓔ   16. Ⓐ Ⓑ Ⓒ Ⓓ Ⓔ   26. Ⓐ Ⓑ Ⓒ Ⓓ Ⓔ   36. Ⓐ Ⓑ Ⓒ Ⓓ Ⓔ
7. Ⓐ Ⓑ Ⓒ Ⓓ Ⓔ   17. Ⓐ Ⓑ Ⓒ Ⓓ Ⓔ   27. Ⓐ Ⓑ Ⓒ Ⓓ Ⓔ   37. Ⓐ Ⓑ Ⓒ Ⓓ Ⓔ
8. Ⓐ Ⓑ Ⓒ Ⓓ Ⓔ   18. Ⓐ Ⓑ Ⓒ Ⓓ Ⓔ   28. Ⓐ Ⓑ Ⓒ Ⓓ Ⓔ   38. Ⓐ Ⓑ Ⓒ Ⓓ Ⓔ
9. Ⓐ Ⓑ Ⓒ Ⓓ Ⓔ   19. Ⓐ Ⓑ Ⓒ Ⓓ Ⓔ   29. Ⓐ Ⓑ Ⓒ Ⓓ Ⓔ   39. Ⓐ Ⓑ Ⓒ Ⓓ Ⓔ
10. Ⓐ Ⓑ Ⓒ Ⓓ Ⓔ   20. Ⓐ Ⓑ Ⓒ Ⓓ Ⓔ   30. Ⓐ Ⓑ Ⓒ Ⓓ Ⓔ   40. Ⓐ Ⓑ Ⓒ Ⓓ Ⓔ

☐ # right in Section 4

☐ # wrong in Section 4

If section 4 of your test book contains math questions that are not multiple-choice, continue to item 9 below. Otherwise, continue to item 9 above.

9.   10.   11.   12.   13.

14.   15.   16.   17.   18.

Remove (or photocopy) this answer sheet and use it to complete the Practice Test.

Start with number 1 for each section. If a section has fewer questions than answer spaces, leave the extra spaces blank.

SECTION
5

1. Ⓐ Ⓑ Ⓒ Ⓓ Ⓔ	11. Ⓐ Ⓑ Ⓒ Ⓓ Ⓔ	21. Ⓐ Ⓑ Ⓒ Ⓓ Ⓔ	31. Ⓐ Ⓑ Ⓒ Ⓓ Ⓔ
2. Ⓐ Ⓑ Ⓒ Ⓓ Ⓔ	12. Ⓐ Ⓑ Ⓒ Ⓓ Ⓔ	22. Ⓐ Ⓑ Ⓒ Ⓓ Ⓔ	32. Ⓐ Ⓑ Ⓒ Ⓓ Ⓔ
3. Ⓐ Ⓑ Ⓒ Ⓓ Ⓔ	13. Ⓐ Ⓑ Ⓒ Ⓓ Ⓔ	23. Ⓐ Ⓑ Ⓒ Ⓓ Ⓔ	33. Ⓐ Ⓑ Ⓒ Ⓓ Ⓔ
4. Ⓐ Ⓑ Ⓒ Ⓓ Ⓔ	14. Ⓐ Ⓑ Ⓒ Ⓓ Ⓔ	24. Ⓐ Ⓑ Ⓒ Ⓓ Ⓔ	34. Ⓐ Ⓑ Ⓒ Ⓓ Ⓔ
5. Ⓐ Ⓑ Ⓒ Ⓓ Ⓔ	15. Ⓐ Ⓑ Ⓒ Ⓓ Ⓔ	25. Ⓐ Ⓑ Ⓒ Ⓓ Ⓔ	35. Ⓐ Ⓑ Ⓒ Ⓓ Ⓔ
6. Ⓐ Ⓑ Ⓒ Ⓓ Ⓔ	16. Ⓐ Ⓑ Ⓒ Ⓓ Ⓔ	26. Ⓐ Ⓑ Ⓒ Ⓓ Ⓔ	36. Ⓐ Ⓑ Ⓒ Ⓓ Ⓔ
7. Ⓐ Ⓑ Ⓒ Ⓓ Ⓔ	17. Ⓐ Ⓑ Ⓒ Ⓓ Ⓔ	27. Ⓐ Ⓑ Ⓒ Ⓓ Ⓔ	37. Ⓐ Ⓑ Ⓒ Ⓓ Ⓔ
8. Ⓐ Ⓑ Ⓒ Ⓓ Ⓔ	18. Ⓐ Ⓑ Ⓒ Ⓓ Ⓔ	28. Ⓐ Ⓑ Ⓒ Ⓓ Ⓔ	38. Ⓐ Ⓑ Ⓒ Ⓓ Ⓔ
9. Ⓐ Ⓑ Ⓒ Ⓓ Ⓔ	19. Ⓐ Ⓑ Ⓒ Ⓓ Ⓔ	29. Ⓐ Ⓑ Ⓒ Ⓓ Ⓔ	39. Ⓐ Ⓑ Ⓒ Ⓓ Ⓔ
10. Ⓐ Ⓑ Ⓒ Ⓓ Ⓔ	20. Ⓐ Ⓑ Ⓒ Ⓓ Ⓔ	30. Ⓐ Ⓑ Ⓒ Ⓓ Ⓔ	40. Ⓐ Ⓑ Ⓒ Ⓓ Ⓔ

right in
Section 5

wrong in
Section 5

SECTION
6

1. Ⓐ Ⓑ Ⓒ Ⓓ Ⓔ	11. Ⓐ Ⓑ Ⓒ Ⓓ Ⓔ	21. Ⓐ Ⓑ Ⓒ Ⓓ Ⓔ	31. Ⓐ Ⓑ Ⓒ Ⓓ Ⓔ
2. Ⓐ Ⓑ Ⓒ Ⓓ Ⓔ	12. Ⓐ Ⓑ Ⓒ Ⓓ Ⓔ	22. Ⓐ Ⓑ Ⓒ Ⓓ Ⓔ	32. Ⓐ Ⓑ Ⓒ Ⓓ Ⓔ
3. Ⓐ Ⓑ Ⓒ Ⓓ Ⓔ	13. Ⓐ Ⓑ Ⓒ Ⓓ Ⓔ	23. Ⓐ Ⓑ Ⓒ Ⓓ Ⓔ	33. Ⓐ Ⓑ Ⓒ Ⓓ Ⓔ
4. Ⓐ Ⓑ Ⓒ Ⓓ Ⓔ	14. Ⓐ Ⓑ Ⓒ Ⓓ Ⓔ	24. Ⓐ Ⓑ Ⓒ Ⓓ Ⓔ	34. Ⓐ Ⓑ Ⓒ Ⓓ Ⓔ
5. Ⓐ Ⓑ Ⓒ Ⓓ Ⓔ	15. Ⓐ Ⓑ Ⓒ Ⓓ Ⓔ	25. Ⓐ Ⓑ Ⓒ Ⓓ Ⓔ	35. Ⓐ Ⓑ Ⓒ Ⓓ Ⓔ
6. Ⓐ Ⓑ Ⓒ Ⓓ Ⓔ	16. Ⓐ Ⓑ Ⓒ Ⓓ Ⓔ	26. Ⓐ Ⓑ Ⓒ Ⓓ Ⓔ	36. Ⓐ Ⓑ Ⓒ Ⓓ Ⓔ
7. Ⓐ Ⓑ Ⓒ Ⓓ Ⓔ	17. Ⓐ Ⓑ Ⓒ Ⓓ Ⓔ	27. Ⓐ Ⓑ Ⓒ Ⓓ Ⓔ	37. Ⓐ Ⓑ Ⓒ Ⓓ Ⓔ
8. Ⓐ Ⓑ Ⓒ Ⓓ Ⓔ	18. Ⓐ Ⓑ Ⓒ Ⓓ Ⓔ	28. Ⓐ Ⓑ Ⓒ Ⓓ Ⓔ	38. Ⓐ Ⓑ Ⓒ Ⓓ Ⓔ
9. Ⓐ Ⓑ Ⓒ Ⓓ Ⓔ	19. Ⓐ Ⓑ Ⓒ Ⓓ Ⓔ	29. Ⓐ Ⓑ Ⓒ Ⓓ Ⓔ	39. Ⓐ Ⓑ Ⓒ Ⓓ Ⓔ
10. Ⓐ Ⓑ Ⓒ Ⓓ Ⓔ	20. Ⓐ Ⓑ Ⓒ Ⓓ Ⓔ	30. Ⓐ Ⓑ Ⓒ Ⓓ Ⓔ	40. Ⓐ Ⓑ Ⓒ Ⓓ Ⓔ

right in
Section 6

wrong in
Section 6

SECTION
7

1. Ⓐ Ⓑ Ⓒ Ⓓ Ⓔ	11. Ⓐ Ⓑ Ⓒ Ⓓ Ⓔ	21. Ⓐ Ⓑ Ⓒ Ⓓ Ⓔ	31. Ⓐ Ⓑ Ⓒ Ⓓ Ⓔ
2. Ⓐ Ⓑ Ⓒ Ⓓ Ⓔ	12. Ⓐ Ⓑ Ⓒ Ⓓ Ⓔ	22. Ⓐ Ⓑ Ⓒ Ⓓ Ⓔ	32. Ⓐ Ⓑ Ⓒ Ⓓ Ⓔ
3. Ⓐ Ⓑ Ⓒ Ⓓ Ⓔ	13. Ⓐ Ⓑ Ⓒ Ⓓ Ⓔ	23. Ⓐ Ⓑ Ⓒ Ⓓ Ⓔ	33. Ⓐ Ⓑ Ⓒ Ⓓ Ⓔ
4. Ⓐ Ⓑ Ⓒ Ⓓ Ⓔ	14. Ⓐ Ⓑ Ⓒ Ⓓ Ⓔ	24. Ⓐ Ⓑ Ⓒ Ⓓ Ⓔ	34. Ⓐ Ⓑ Ⓒ Ⓓ Ⓔ
5. Ⓐ Ⓑ Ⓒ Ⓓ Ⓔ	15. Ⓐ Ⓑ Ⓒ Ⓓ Ⓔ	25. Ⓐ Ⓑ Ⓒ Ⓓ Ⓔ	35. Ⓐ Ⓑ Ⓒ Ⓓ Ⓔ
6. Ⓐ Ⓑ Ⓒ Ⓓ Ⓔ	16. Ⓐ Ⓑ Ⓒ Ⓓ Ⓔ	26. Ⓐ Ⓑ Ⓒ Ⓓ Ⓔ	36. Ⓐ Ⓑ Ⓒ Ⓓ Ⓔ
7. Ⓐ Ⓑ Ⓒ Ⓓ Ⓔ	17. Ⓐ Ⓑ Ⓒ Ⓓ Ⓔ	27. Ⓐ Ⓑ Ⓒ Ⓓ Ⓔ	37. Ⓐ Ⓑ Ⓒ Ⓓ Ⓔ
8. Ⓐ Ⓑ Ⓒ Ⓓ Ⓔ	18. Ⓐ Ⓑ Ⓒ Ⓓ Ⓔ	28. Ⓐ Ⓑ Ⓒ Ⓓ Ⓔ	38. Ⓐ Ⓑ Ⓒ Ⓓ Ⓔ
9. Ⓐ Ⓑ Ⓒ Ⓓ Ⓔ	19. Ⓐ Ⓑ Ⓒ Ⓓ Ⓔ	29. Ⓐ Ⓑ Ⓒ Ⓓ Ⓔ	39. Ⓐ Ⓑ Ⓒ Ⓓ Ⓔ
10. Ⓐ Ⓑ Ⓒ Ⓓ Ⓔ	20. Ⓐ Ⓑ Ⓒ Ⓓ Ⓔ	30. Ⓐ Ⓑ Ⓒ Ⓓ Ⓔ	40. Ⓐ Ⓑ Ⓒ Ⓓ Ⓔ

right in
Section 7

wrong in
Section 7

Remove (or photocopy) this answer sheet and use it to complete the Practice Test.

Start with number 1 for each section. If a section has fewer questions than answer spaces, leave the extra spaces blank.

SECTION 8

1. Ⓐ Ⓑ Ⓒ Ⓓ Ⓔ   11. Ⓐ Ⓑ Ⓒ Ⓓ Ⓔ   21. Ⓐ Ⓑ Ⓒ Ⓓ Ⓔ   31. Ⓐ Ⓑ Ⓒ Ⓓ Ⓔ
2. Ⓐ Ⓑ Ⓒ Ⓓ Ⓔ   12. Ⓐ Ⓑ Ⓒ Ⓓ Ⓔ   22. Ⓐ Ⓑ Ⓒ Ⓓ Ⓔ   32. Ⓐ Ⓑ Ⓒ Ⓓ Ⓔ
3. Ⓐ Ⓑ Ⓒ Ⓓ Ⓔ   13. Ⓐ Ⓑ Ⓒ Ⓓ Ⓔ   23. Ⓐ Ⓑ Ⓒ Ⓓ Ⓔ   33. Ⓐ Ⓑ Ⓒ Ⓓ Ⓔ
4. Ⓐ Ⓑ Ⓒ Ⓓ Ⓔ   14. Ⓐ Ⓑ Ⓒ Ⓓ Ⓔ   24. Ⓐ Ⓑ Ⓒ Ⓓ Ⓔ   34. Ⓐ Ⓑ Ⓒ Ⓓ Ⓔ
5. Ⓐ Ⓑ Ⓒ Ⓓ Ⓔ   15. Ⓐ Ⓑ Ⓒ Ⓓ Ⓔ   25. Ⓐ Ⓑ Ⓒ Ⓓ Ⓔ   35. Ⓐ Ⓑ Ⓒ Ⓓ Ⓔ
6. Ⓐ Ⓑ Ⓒ Ⓓ Ⓔ   16. Ⓐ Ⓑ Ⓒ Ⓓ Ⓔ   26. Ⓐ Ⓑ Ⓒ Ⓓ Ⓔ   36. Ⓐ Ⓑ Ⓒ Ⓓ Ⓔ
7. Ⓐ Ⓑ Ⓒ Ⓓ Ⓔ   17. Ⓐ Ⓑ Ⓒ Ⓓ Ⓔ   27. Ⓐ Ⓑ Ⓒ Ⓓ Ⓔ   37. Ⓐ Ⓑ Ⓒ Ⓓ Ⓔ
8. Ⓐ Ⓑ Ⓒ Ⓓ Ⓔ   18. Ⓐ Ⓑ Ⓒ Ⓓ Ⓔ   28. Ⓐ Ⓑ Ⓒ Ⓓ Ⓔ   38. Ⓐ Ⓑ Ⓒ Ⓓ Ⓔ
9. Ⓐ Ⓑ Ⓒ Ⓓ Ⓔ   19. Ⓐ Ⓑ Ⓒ Ⓓ Ⓔ   29. Ⓐ Ⓑ Ⓒ Ⓓ Ⓔ   39. Ⓐ Ⓑ Ⓒ Ⓓ Ⓔ
10. Ⓐ Ⓑ Ⓒ Ⓓ Ⓔ   20. Ⓐ Ⓑ Ⓒ Ⓓ Ⓔ   30. Ⓐ Ⓑ Ⓒ Ⓓ Ⓔ   40. Ⓐ Ⓑ Ⓒ Ⓓ Ⓔ

right in Section 8

wrong in Section 8

SECTION 9

1. Ⓐ Ⓑ Ⓒ Ⓓ Ⓔ   11. Ⓐ Ⓑ Ⓒ Ⓓ Ⓔ   21. Ⓐ Ⓑ Ⓒ Ⓓ Ⓔ   31. Ⓐ Ⓑ Ⓒ Ⓓ Ⓔ
2. Ⓐ Ⓑ Ⓒ Ⓓ Ⓔ   12. Ⓐ Ⓑ Ⓒ Ⓓ Ⓔ   22. Ⓐ Ⓑ Ⓒ Ⓓ Ⓔ   32. Ⓐ Ⓑ Ⓒ Ⓓ Ⓔ
3. Ⓐ Ⓑ Ⓒ Ⓓ Ⓔ   13. Ⓐ Ⓑ Ⓒ Ⓓ Ⓔ   23. Ⓐ Ⓑ Ⓒ Ⓓ Ⓔ   33. Ⓐ Ⓑ Ⓒ Ⓓ Ⓔ
4. Ⓐ Ⓑ Ⓒ Ⓓ Ⓔ   14. Ⓐ Ⓑ Ⓒ Ⓓ Ⓔ   24. Ⓐ Ⓑ Ⓒ Ⓓ Ⓔ   34. Ⓐ Ⓑ Ⓒ Ⓓ Ⓔ
5. Ⓐ Ⓑ Ⓒ Ⓓ Ⓔ   15. Ⓐ Ⓑ Ⓒ Ⓓ Ⓔ   25. Ⓐ Ⓑ Ⓒ Ⓓ Ⓔ   35. Ⓐ Ⓑ Ⓒ Ⓓ Ⓔ
6. Ⓐ Ⓑ Ⓒ Ⓓ Ⓔ   16. Ⓐ Ⓑ Ⓒ Ⓓ Ⓔ   26. Ⓐ Ⓑ Ⓒ Ⓓ Ⓔ   36. Ⓐ Ⓑ Ⓒ Ⓓ Ⓔ
7. Ⓐ Ⓑ Ⓒ Ⓓ Ⓔ   17. Ⓐ Ⓑ Ⓒ Ⓓ Ⓔ   27. Ⓐ Ⓑ Ⓒ Ⓓ Ⓔ   37. Ⓐ Ⓑ Ⓒ Ⓓ Ⓔ
8. Ⓐ Ⓑ Ⓒ Ⓓ Ⓔ   18. Ⓐ Ⓑ Ⓒ Ⓓ Ⓔ   28. Ⓐ Ⓑ Ⓒ Ⓓ Ⓔ   38. Ⓐ Ⓑ Ⓒ Ⓓ Ⓔ
9. Ⓐ Ⓑ Ⓒ Ⓓ Ⓔ   19. Ⓐ Ⓑ Ⓒ Ⓓ Ⓔ   29. Ⓐ Ⓑ Ⓒ Ⓓ Ⓔ   39. Ⓐ Ⓑ Ⓒ Ⓓ Ⓔ
10. Ⓐ Ⓑ Ⓒ Ⓓ Ⓔ   20. Ⓐ Ⓑ Ⓒ Ⓓ Ⓔ   30. Ⓐ Ⓑ Ⓒ Ⓓ Ⓔ   40. Ⓐ Ⓑ Ⓒ Ⓓ Ⓔ

right in Section 9

wrong in Section 9

SECTION 1
Time—25 Minutes
ESSAY

The essay gives you an opportunity to show how effectively you can develop and express ideas. You should, therefore, take care to develop your point of view, present your ideas logically and clearly, and use language precisely.

Your essay must be written in your Answer Grid Booklet—you will receive no other paper on which to write. You will have enough space if you write on every line, avoid wide margins, and keep your handwriting to a reasonable size. Remember that people who are not familiar with your handwriting will read what you write. Try to write or print so that what you are writing is legible to those readers.

You have 25 minutes to write an essay on the topic assigned below.
DO NOT WRITE ON ANOTHER TOPIC. AN OFF-TOPIC ESSAY WILL RECEIVE A SCORE OF ZERO.

Think carefully about the issue presented in the following excerpt and the assignment below.

> "Life without memory is no life at all, just as an intelligence without the possibility of expression is not really an intelligence. Our memory is our coherence, our reason, our feeling, even our action. Without it, we are nothing."
> –Luis Buñuel, *An Unspeakable Betrayal*
>
> "Many a man fails to become a thinker for the sole reason that his memory is too good."
>
> –Friedrich Nietzsche, *Maxims*

Assignment: Is memory central to our progress, or does it merely hold us back? Plan and write an essay in which you develop your point of view on this issue. Support your position with reasoning and examples taken from your reading, studies, experience, or observations.

DO NOT WRITE YOUR ESSAY IN YOUR TEST BOOK.
You will receive credit only for what you write in your Answer Grid Booklet.

SECTION 2

Time—25 Minutes
20 Questions

Directions: For this section, solve each problem and decide which is the best of the choices given. Fill in the corresponding oval on the answer sheet. You may use any available space for scratchwork.

Notes:

(1) Calculator use is permitted.

(2) All numbers used are real numbers.

(3) Figures are provided for some problems. All figures are drawn to scale and lie in a plane UNLESS otherwise indicated.

(4) Unless otherwise specified, the domain of any function f is assumed to be the set of all real numbers x for which $f(x)$ is a real number.

Information

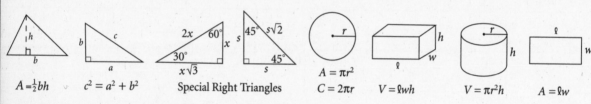

$A = \frac{1}{2}bh$ $c^2 = a^2 + b^2$ Special Right Triangles $A = \pi r^2$ $V = \ell wh$ $V = \pi r^2 h$ $A = \ell w$
                                                                    $C = 2\pi r$

The sum of the degree measures of the angles in a triangle is 180.
The number of degrees of arc in a circle is 360.
A straight angle has a degree measure of 180.

1. $\left(\frac{1}{5} + \frac{1}{3}\right) \div \frac{1}{2} =$

    (A) $\frac{1}{8}$

    (B) $\frac{1}{4}$

    (C) $\frac{4}{15}$

    (D) $\frac{1}{2}$

    (E) $\frac{16}{15}$

2. What is the value of $x^2 - 2x$ when $x = -2$?

    (A) -8

    (B) -4

    (C) 0

    (D) 4

    (E) 8

3. Vito read 96 pages in 2 hours and 40 minutes. What was Vito's average rate of pages per hour?

    (A) 24

    (B) 30

    (C) 36

    (D) 42

    (E) 48

GO ON TO THE NEXT PAGE

4. For how many integer values of x will $\frac{7}{x}$ be greater than $\frac{1}{4}$ and less than $\frac{1}{3}$?

   (A) 6
   (B) 7
   (C) 12
   (D) 28
   (E) Infinitely many

5. What is the average (arithmetic mean) of $2x + 5$, $5x - 6$, and $-4x + 2$?

   (A) $x + \frac{1}{3}$

   (B) $x + 1$

   (C) $3x + \frac{1}{3}$

   (D) $3x + 3$

   (E) $3x + 3\frac{1}{3}$

6. In a group of 25 students, 16 are female. What percent of the group is female?

   (A) 16%
   (B) 40%
   (C) 60%
   (D) 64%
   (E) 75%

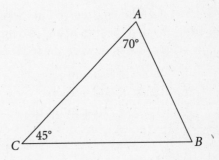

7. In the triangle above, what is the degree measure of angle B?

   (A) 45
   (B) 60
   (C) 65
   (D) 75
   (E) 80

8. For all $x \neq 0$, $\dfrac{x^2 + x^2 + x^2}{x^2} =$

   (A) 3
   (B) $3x$
   (C) x^2
   (D) x^3
   (E) x^4

9. The equation $x^2 = 5x - 4$ has how many distinct real solutions?

   (A) 0
   (B) 1
   (C) 2
   (D) 3
   (E) Infinitely many

GO ON TO THE NEXT PAGE

10. Which of the following sets of numbers has the property that the sum of any two numbers in the set is also a number in the set?

     I. The set of even integers
    II. The set of odd integers
   III. The set of prime numbers

(A) I only

(B) III only

(C) I and II only

(D) I and III only

(E) I, II, and III

11. Martin's average (arithmetic mean) score after four tests is 89. What score on the fifth test would bring Martin's average up to exactly 90?

(A) 90

(B) 91

(C) 92

(D) 93

(E) 94

12. The price s of a sweater is reduced by 25% for a sale. After the sale, the reduced price is increased by 20%. Which of the following represents the final price of the sweater?

(A) $0.80s$

(B) $0.85s$

(C) $0.90s$

(D) $0.95s$

(E) $1.05s$

13. How many distinct prime factors does the number 36 have?

(A) 2

(B) 3

(C) 4

(D) 5

(E) 6

14. If the area of a triangle is 36 and its base is 9, what is the length of the altitude to that base?

(A) 2

(B) 4

(C) 6

(D) 8

(E) 12

15. Let $a \clubsuit$ be defined for all positive integers a by the equation $a \clubsuit = \dfrac{a}{4} - \dfrac{a}{6}$. If $x \clubsuit = 3$, what is the value of x?

(A) 18

(B) 28

(C) 36

(D) 40

(E) 54

16. Joan has q quarters, d dimes, n nickels, and no other coins in her pocket. Which of the following represents the total number of coins in Joan's pocket?

(A) $q + d + n$

(B) $5q + 2d + n$

(C) $.25q + .10d + .05n$

(D) $(25 + 10 + 5)(q + d + n)$

(E) $25q + 10d + 5n$

GO ON TO THE NEXT PAGE

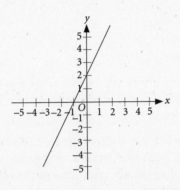

17. Which of the following is an equation for the graph above?

(A) $y = -2x + 1$

(B) $y = x + 1$

(C) $y = x + 2$

(D) $y = 2x + 1$

(E) $y = 2x + 2$

18. If an integer is divisible by 6 and by 9, then the integer must be divisible by which of the following?

    I. 12
    II. 18
    III. 36

(A) I only

(B) II only

(C) I and II only

(D) II and III only

(E) I, II, and III

19. A wooden cube with volume 64 is sliced in half horizontally. The two halves are then glued together to form a rectangular solid that is not a cube. What is the surface area of this new solid?

(A) 48

(B) 56

(C) 96

(D) 112

(E) 128

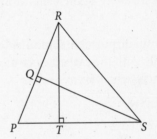

20. In $\triangle PRS$ above, RT is the altitude to side PS, and QS is the altitude to side PR. If $RT = 7$, $PR = 8$, and $QS = 9$, what is the length of PS?

(A) $5\frac{1}{7}$

(B) $6\frac{2}{9}$

(C) $7\frac{7}{8}$

(D) $10\frac{2}{7}$

(E) $13\frac{4}{9}$

IF YOU FINISH BEFORE TIME IS CALLED, YOU MAY CHECK YOUR WORK ON THIS SECTION ONLY. DO NOT TURN TO ANY OTHER SECTION IN THE TEST.

STOP

SECTION 3

Time—25 Minutes
24 Questions

Directions: For each of the following questions, choose the best answer and darken the corresponding oval on the answer sheet.

Each sentence below has one or two blanks, each blank indicating that something has been omitted. Beneath the sentence are five words or sets of words labeled (A) through (E). Choose the word or set of words that, when inserted in the sentence, <u>best</u> fits the meaning of the sentence as a whole.

EXAMPLE:

Today's small, portable computers contrast markedly with the earliest electronic computers, which were -------.

(A) effective
(B) invented
(C) useful
(D) destructive
(E) enormous

1. Finding an old movie poster that is still ------- usually proves difficult because such posters were meant to be used and then -------.

   (A) recognizable . . . returned
   (B) relevant . . . discarded
   (C) intact . . . destroyed
   (D) immaculate . . . restored
   (E) displayed . . . maintained

2. The Kemp's Ridley turtle, long considered one of the most --------- creatures of the sea, finally appears to be making some headway in its battle against extinction.

   (A) elusive
   (B) prevalent
   (C) combative
   (D) voracious
   (E) imperiled

3. Before the invention of the tape recorder, quotes from an interview were rarely --------; journalists usually paraphrased the words of their subject.

   (A) verbatim
   (B) misconstrued
   (C) pragmatic
   (D) extensive
   (E) plagiarized

4. Batchelor's reputation as --------- novelist encouraged hopes that his political thriller would offer more -------- characterizations than are usually found in the genre.

   (A) a serious . . . subtle
   (B) a maturing . . . sweeping
   (C) a prolific . . . accurate
   (D) an accomplished . . . fictional
   (E) a reclusive . . . authentic

5. Aristotle espoused a --------- biological model in which all extant species are unchanging and eternal and no new species ever come into existence.

   (A) paradoxical
   (B) morbid
   (C) static
   (D) holistic
   (E) homogeneous

GO ON TO THE NEXT PAGE

6. The agency's failure to --------- policies that it has acknowledged as flawed is a potent demonstration of its --------- approach to correcting its problems.

    (A) support . . . ambiguous
    (B) institute . . . earnest
    (C) rescind . . . lackadaisical
    (D) amend . . . devoted
    (E) chasten . . . meticulous

7. The inconsistency of the educational policies adopted by various schools across the state has been greatly --------- by the rapid turnover of school superintendents.

    (A) counteracted
    (B) stabilized
    (C) criticized
    (D) exacerbated
    (E) understated

8. The journalist's claim of --------- is belied by her record of contributing to the campaign funds of only one party's candidates.

    (A) innocence
    (B) corruption
    (C) impartiality
    (D) affluence
    (E) loyalty

GO ON TO THE NEXT PAGE

Directions: The passages below are followed by questions based on their content; questions following a pair of related passages may also be based on the relationship between the paired passages. Answer the questions on the basis of what is <u>stated</u> or <u>implied</u> in the passages and in any introductory material that may be provided.

Questions 9–12 refer to the following passage.

Passage 1

Recently, a disturbing practice has developed among book publishers. They have hired contemporary authors to write sequels to the novels of long-dead authors. If these sequels
(5) were being written for the works of relatively untalented or unknown authors, then no one would pay much attention. Unfortunately, this has not been the case. One author wrote a sequel to Margaret Mitchell's *Gone with the*
(10) *Wind*, for example. It's clear that these sequels are written in order to entice an author's or a literary work's fans to spend money. Since these counterfeits can never equal the original, however, disappointment is the only possible
(15) outcome for the reader.

Passage 2

What unalloyed delight for those who have read all of Sir Arthur Conan Doyle's stories of Sherlock Holmes to discover Nicholas Meyer's 1989 novel, *The Seven Percent Solution*. In
(20) it, the violin-playing detective and his faithful sidekick, Dr. Watson, roam the moors in search of evil-doers. Once again, readers can get lost in the cozy, yet often terrifying world of Victorian England. While Meyer's
(25) style, informed as it is by modern civilization and sensibilities, is not Sir Arthur's, the book nonetheless contains many pleasures for the avid Sherlockian. One can only hope that Meyer will continue to write novels about
(30) Watson and Holmes so that devoted followers will get lasting pleasure from reading them.

9. The author of Passage 1 would most likely agree with which of the following statements?

(A) It is easier to write a sequel to the work of an unknown author than it is to write a sequel to the work of a famous author.

(B) Modern sequels to old works should be regarded as pale imitations of the originals.

(C) Although many modern sequels to older books are of poor quality, *The Seven Percent Solution* is an exception to that rule.

(D) The works of Margaret Mitchell have caused indignation among many readers.

(E) Readers who buy sequels rarely read the original works on which the sequels are based.

10. The author of Passage 1 most likely regards Margaret Mitchell as an author

(A) who is well-known

(B) who wrote only one novel

(C) whose skills are comparable to those of Sir Arthur Conan Doyle

(D) whose book is more famous than its author

(E) who will disappoint her readers

GO ON TO THE NEXT PAGE

11. In line 16, the word "unalloyed" most nearly
means

(A) metallic

(B) effervescent

(C) plentiful

(D) pure

(E) bland

12. The author of Passage 2 would most
likely respond to the contention that
"disappointment is the only possible outcome
for the reader" (Passage 1, lines 14–15) of
sequels by

(A) reconsidering his own thesis

(B) countering that *The Seven Percent
Solution* is superior to the sequel to *Gone
with the Wind*

(C) mocking the author's rigid views in
Passage 1

(D) agreeing that while some readers will be
disappointed, some will be very pleased

(E) emphasizing the pleasure an ardent fan
gets from reading a sequel to the work of
an admired author

GO ON TO THE NEXT PAGE

Questions 13–24 refer to the following passage.

The following passage is an excerpt from a book about wolves, written by a self-taught naturalist who studied them in the wild.

My precautions against disturbing the wolves were superfluous. It had required me a week to get their measure, but they must have taken mine at our first meeting; and while there
(5) was nothing disdainful in their evident assessment of me, they managed to ignore my presence, and indeed my very existence, with a thoroughness which was somehow disconcerting.
(10) Quite by accident I had pitched my tent within ten yards of one of the major paths used by the wolves when they were going to, or coming from, their hunting paths to the westward; and only a few hours after I had
(15) taken up my residence one of the wolves came back from a trip and discovered me and my tent.

He was at the end of a hard night's work and was clearly tired and anxious to go home
(20) to bed. He came over a small rise fifty yards from me with his head down, his eyes half-closed, and a preoccupied air about him. Far from being the preternaturally alert and sus-picious beast of fiction, this wolf was so self-
(25) engrossed that he came straight on to within fifteen yards of me, and might have gone right past the tent without seeing it at all, had I not banged an elbow against the teakettle, making a resounding clank. The wolf's head
(30) came up and his eyes opened wide, but he did not stop or falter in his pace. One brief, side-long glance was all he vouchsafed to me as he continued on his way.

By the time this happened, I had learned a
(35) great deal about my wolfish neighbors, and one of the facts which had emerged was that they were not nomadic roamers, as is almost universally believed, but were settled beasts and the possessors of a large permanent estate
(40) with very definite boundaries. The territory owned by my wolf family comprised more than a hundred square miles, bounded on one side by a river but otherwise not delimited by geographical features. Nevertheless there were
(45) boundaries, clearly indicated in wolfish fashion.

Once a week, more or less, the clan made the rounds of the family lands and freshened up the boundary markers—a sort of lupine* beating of the bounds. This careful attention
(50) to property rights was perhaps made neces-sary by the presence of two other wolf fami-lies whose lands abutted on ours, although I never discovered any evidence of bickering or disagreements between the owners of the vari-
(55) ous adjoining estates. I suspect, therefore, that it was more of a ritual activity.

In any event, once I had become aware of this strong feeling of property among the wolves, I decided to use this knowledge to
(60) make them at least recognize my existence. One evening, after they had gone off for their regu-lar nightly hunt, I staked out a property claim of my own, embracing perhaps three acres, with the tent at the middle, and including a
(65) hundred yard long section of the wolves' path. This took most of the night and required fre-quent returns to the tent to consume copious quantities of tea; but before dawn brought the hunters home, the task was done and I retired,
(70) somewhat exhausted, to observe the results.

I had not long to wait. At 0814 hours, according to my wolf log, the leading male of the clan appeared over the ridge behind me, padding homeward with his usual air of
(75) preoccupation. As usual, he did not deign to look at the tent; but when he reached the point where my property line intersected the trail, he stopped as abruptly as if he had run into an invisible wall. His attitude of fatigue vanished
(80) and was replaced by one of bewilderment. Cautiously he extended his nose and sniffed at one of my marked bushes. After a minute of complete indecision he backed away a

GO ON TO THE NEXT PAGE

few yards and sat down. And then, finally, he
(85) looked directly at the tent and me. It was a
long, considering sort of look.

Having achieved my object—that of forcing
at least one of the wolves to take cognizance
of my existence—I now began to wonder if,
(90) in my ignorance, I had transgressed some
unknown wolf law of major importance and
would have to pay for my temerity. I found
myself regretting the absence of a weapon as
the look I was getting became longer, more
(95) thoughtful, and still more intent. In an effort
to break the impasse I loudly cleared my throat
and turned my back on the wolf to indicate as
clearly as possible that I found his continued
scrutiny impolite, if not actually offensive.
(100) He appeared to take the hint. Briskly, and
with an air of decision, he turned his attention away from me and began a systematic
tour of the area, sniffing each boundary
marker once or twice, and carefully placing
(105) his mark on the outside of each clump of
grass or stone. In fifteen minutes he rejoined
the path at the point where it left my property
and trotted off towards his home, leaving me
with a good deal to occupy my thoughts.

*lupine: relating to wolves

13. According to the author, why were his
precautions against disturbing the wolves
"superfluous" (line 2)?

(A) It was several weeks before he encountered his first wolf.
(B) Other wild animals posed a greater
threat to his safety.
(C) The wolves noticed him but were not
interested in harming him.
(D) He was not bothered by the wolves until
he started interfering with them.
(E) The wolves were unable to detect him
because of their poor eyesight.

14. The author mentions the wolves'
"assessment" of him (line 6) in order to

(A) account for their strange behavior
towards him
(B) convey his initial fear of being attacked
(C) emphasize his ignorance on first
encountering them
(D) indicate the need for precautions
against disturbing them
(E) suggest his courage in an unfamiliar
situation

15. In paragraph 3, the author is primarily
surprised to find that the wolf

(A) is traveling alone
(B) lacks the energy to respond
(C) is hunting at night
(D) is not more on its guard
(E) does not attack him

16. In line 19, the word "anxious" most nearly
means

(A) distressed
(B) afraid
(C) eager
(D) uneasy
(E) worried

17. In line 38, the word "settled" most nearly
means

(A) decided
(B) resolute
(C) stable
(D) inflexible
(E) confident

GO ON TO THE NEXT PAGE

18. Lines 34–40 provide

(A) a contradiction to a popular myth
(B) an explanation of a paradox
(C) a rebuttal of established facts
(D) an exception to a general rule
(E) a summary of conclusions

19. The author suggests that boundary marking was a "ritual activity" (line 56) because

(A) the wolves marked their boundaries at regular intervals
(B) no disputes over territory ever seemed to occur
(C) the boundaries were marked by geographical features
(D) the boundaries were marked at the same time each week
(E) the whole family of wolves participated in the activity

20. Which of the following discoveries would most weaken the author's thesis concerning the wolves' "strong feeling of property" (line 58)?

(A) Disputes over boundaries are a frequent occurrence.
(B) Wolf territories are typically around one hundred square miles in area.
(C) Wolf families often wander from place to place to find food.
(D) Territorial conflicts between wolves and human beings are rare.
(E) Wolves are generally alert when encountering other animals.

21. The author most likely mentions an "invisible wall" (line 79) in order to emphasize

(A) his delight in attracting the wolf's attention
(B) the wolf's annoyance at encountering a challenge
(C) the high speed at which the wolf was traveling
(D) the sudden manner in which the wolf stopped
(E) the wolf's exhaustion after a night of hunting

22. The wolf's first reaction on encountering the author's property marking is one of

(A) combativeness
(B) confusion
(C) anxiety
(D) wariness
(E) dread

23. In line 92, "temerity" means

(A) discourtesy
(B) rashness
(C) courage
(D) anger
(E) discretion

24. The author turns his back on the wolf (line 97) primarily in order to

(A) demonstrate his power over the wolf
(B) bring about some change in the situation
(C) compel the wolf to recognize his existence
(D) look for a suitable weapon
(E) avoid the wolf's hypnotic gaze

IF YOU FINISH BEFORE TIME IS CALLED, YOU MAY CHECK YOUR WORK ON THIS SECTION ONLY. DO NOT TURN TO ANY OTHER SECTION IN THE TEST.

SECTION 4
Time—25 Minutes
18 Questions

Directions: For this section, solve each problem and decide which is the best of the choices given. Fill in the corresponding oval on the answer sheet. You may use any available space for scratchwork.

Notes:

(1) Calculator use is permitted.

(2) All numbers used are real numbers.

(3) Figures are provided for some problems. All figures are drawn to scale and lie in a plane UNLESS otherwise indicated.

(4) Unless otherwise specified, the domain of any function f is assumed to be the set of all real numbers x for which $f(x)$ is a real number.

Information

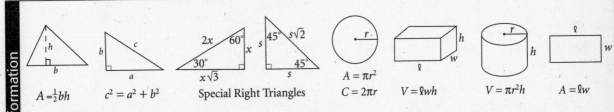

$A = \frac{1}{2}bh$ $c^2 = a^2 + b^2$ Special Right Triangles $A = \pi r^2$ $C = 2\pi r$ $V = \ell wh$ $V = \pi r^2 h$ $A = \ell w$

The sum of the degree measures of the angles in a triangle is 180.
The number of degrees of arc in a circle is 360.
A straight angle has a degree measure of 180.

---

1. If $r = 3$ and $s = 1$, then $r^2 - 2s =$

    (A) 2

    (B) 4

    (C) 6

    (D) 7

    (E) 9

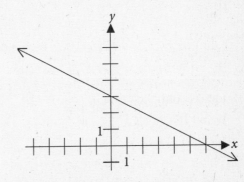

2. Which of the following equations best describes the line shown in the graph above?

    (A) $y = -2x + 6$

    (B) $y = \frac{1}{2}x + 6$

    (C) $y = -2x + 3$

    (D) $y = \frac{-1}{2}x + 3$

    (E) $y = 2x + 3$

GO ON TO THE NEXT PAGE

3. If q is 4 less than r and r is 6 more than s, what is the value of q when $s = 2$?

    (A) −8
    (B) −4
    (C) −2
    (D) 4
    (E) 8

4. On a certain planet, if each year has 9 months and each month has 15 days, how many full years have passed after 700 days on this planet?

    (A) 1
    (B) 2
    (C) 3
    (D) 5
    (E) 7

5. If $f(x) = x^2$ for all real values of x, which of the following is NOT a possible value of $f(x)$?

    I. −4
    II. 0
    III. 2.3

    (A) I only
    (B) II only
    (C) III only
    (D) I and II only
    (E) II and III only

Questions 6–8 refer to the following table, which shows the amount of trash collected by 30 participants in a litter cleanup drive.

Trash Collected in Litter Cleanup Drive

Pieces of trash	10	15	20	25	30
Number of participants	12	9	4	4	1

6. What is the mode of the number of pieces of trash collected by the participants in the litter cleanup drive?

    (A) 10
    (B) 15
    (C) 20
    (D) 25
    (E) 30

7. The goal of the litter cleanup drive was to collect 500 pieces of trash. What percent of this goal did the 30 participants achieve?

    (A) 8%
    (B) 20%
    (C) 56%
    (D) 93%
    (E) 100%

8. What was the average amount of trash collected by the 30 participants in the litter cleanup drive?

    (A) Between 10 and 11 pieces
    (B) Between 11 and 12 pieces
    (C) Between 15 and 16 pieces
    (D) Between 19 and 20 pieces
    (E) Between 20 and 21 pieces

GO ON TO THE NEXT PAGE

Directions: For student-produced response questions 9–18, use the grids at the bottom of the answer sheet page on which you have answered questions 1–8.

Each of the remaining ten questions requires you to solve the problem and enter your answer by marking the ovals in the special grid, as shown in the example below. You may use any available space for scratchwork.

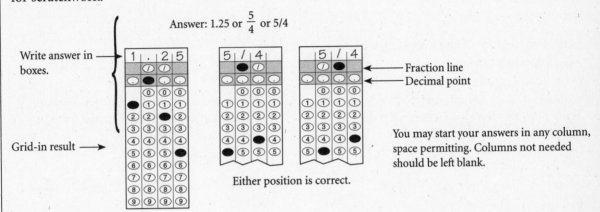

Answer: 1.25 or $\frac{5}{4}$ or 5/4

Write answer in boxes.

Grid-in result →

Either position is correct.

Fraction line
Decimal point

You may start your answers in any column, space permitting. Columns not needed should be left blank.

- It is recommended, though not required, that you write your answer in the boxes at the top of the columns. However, you will receive credit only for darkening the ovals correctly.

- Grid only one answer to a question, even though some problems have more than one correct answer.

- Darken no more than one oval in a column.

- No answers are negative.

- Mixed numbers cannot be gridded. For example: the number $1\frac{1}{4}$ must be gridded as 1.25 or 5/4.

(If $\boxed{.\,|\,1\,|\,1\,/\,|\,4}$ is gridded, it will be interpreted as $\frac{11}{4}$, not $1\frac{1}{4}$.)

- Decimal Accuracy: Decimal answers must be entered as accurately as possible. For example, if you obtain an answer such as 0.1666…, you should record the result as .166 or .167. **Less accurate values such as .16 or .17 are not acceptable.**

Acceptable ways to grid $\frac{1}{6}$ = .1666…

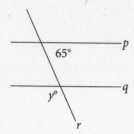

9. In the figure above, if line p is parallel to line q, what is the value of y?

10. What is $\frac{1}{4}$ percent of 16?

$$\frac{3}{a}, \frac{5}{a}, \frac{14}{a}$$

11. Each of the fractions above is in its simplest reduced form, and a is an integer greater than 1 and less than 50. Grid-in one possible value of a.

12. If there are 36 men and 24 women in a group, women make up what fraction of the entire group?

13. What is the value of $\frac{3s + 5}{4}$ when $s = 9$?

14. If the positive integer x leaves a remainder of 2 when divided by 6, what will the remainder be when $x + 8$ is divided by 6?

15. Pat deposited 15% of last week's take-home pay into a savings account. If she deposited $37.50, what was last week's take-home pay?

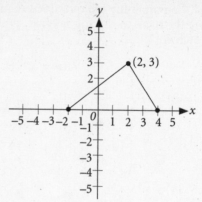

16. What is the area of the triangle in the figure above?

17. A square is divided in half to form two congruent rectangles, each with perimeter 24. What is the area of the original square?

18. The formula for converting a Fahrenheit temperature reading to a Celsius temperature reading is $C = \frac{5}{9}(F - 32)$, where C is the reading in degrees Celsius and F is the reading in degrees Fahrenheit. What is the Fahrenheit equivalent to a reading of 95° Celsius?

IF YOU FINISH BEFORE TIME IS CALLED, YOU MAY CHECK YOUR WORK ON
THIS SECTION ONLY. DO NOT TURN TO ANY OTHER SECTION IN THE TEST.

STOP

SECTION 5

Time—25 Minutes
35 Questions

Directions: For each question in this section, select the best answer from among the choices given and fill in the corresponding oval on the answer sheet.

The following sentences test correctness and effectiveness of expression. Part of each sentence or the entire sentence is underlined; beneath each sentence are five ways of phrasing the underlined material. Choice (A) repeats the original phrasing; the other four choices are different. If you think the original phrasing produces a better sentence than any of the alternatives, select choice (A); if not, select one of the other choices.

In making your selection, follow the requirements of standard written English; that is, pay attention to grammar, choice of words, sentence construction, and punctuation. Your selection should result in the most effective sentence—clear and precise, without awkwardness or ambiguity.

EXAMPLE: ANSWER:

Every apple in the baskets <u>are ripe and labeled according to the date it was picked</u>.   Ⓐ ● Ⓒ Ⓓ Ⓔ

(A) are ripe and labeled according to the date it was picked
(B) is ripe and labeled according to the date it was picked
(C) are ripe and labeled according to the date they were picked
(D) is ripe and labeled according to the date they were picked
(E) are ripe and labeled as to the date it was picked

---

1. Trekking into the deep, inactive crater, we suddenly realized that all outside sound <u>blocked by the dense rock walls</u> of the volcano.

   (A) blocked by the dense rock walls
   (B) blocked as a result of the dense rock walls
   (C) was blocked by the dense rock walls
   (D) was blocking the dense rock walls
   (E) was going to be blocking the dense and rocky walls

2. Tessa, after several lengthy phone conversations <u>who occupied most of her afternoon</u>, confirmed debate practice, an African dance class, and a part-time babysitting job.

   (A) who occupied most of her afternoon
   (B) whom occupied most of her afternoon
   (C) that occupied most afternoons
   (D) that occupied most of her afternoon
   (E) that became her afternoon occupation

3. <u>Perhaps no person was most crucial</u> to the success of the film *On the Waterfront* than the young actor Marlon Brando, who mesmerized audiences with his talent.

   (A) Perhaps no person was most crucial
   (B) Perhaps no person was crucialer
   (C) Perhaps every person was more crucial
   (D) Perhaps the most crucial person
   (E) Perhaps no person was more crucial

4. During the Renaissance, artists such as Michelangelo and Fra Angelico, <u>who have worked</u> for the Church, did not have to search far for subject matter.

   (A) who have worked
   (B) which worked
   (C) who worked
   (D) which had worked
   (E) who have always worked

GO ON TO THE NEXT PAGE ⇨

5. As we waited for the Haunted House ride to begin, we heard strange sounds that seemed to be neither of human or mechanical origin.

   (A) neither of human or mechanical origin
   (B) neither of human nor mechanical origin
   (C) either of human nor mechanical origin
   (D) neither of human nor was it mechanical in origin
   (E) either of human origin or that of mechanical

6. Artists during World War I created performances and paintings that reflected the chaos of war, the anxiety of the people, and they showed the irrational behavior that was escalating in the cities of Europe.

   (A) they showed the irrational behavior that was escalating
   (B) the irrational behavior that is escalating
   (C) they showed the irrational escalation of behavior
   (D) the irrational behavior that was escalating
   (E) the irrational behavior that should have been escalating

7. Known as one of the group of existential French writers, Simone Weil is respected as much for her philosophical ideas as for her writing.

   (A) as for her writing
   (B) as she was for writing them down
   (C) as she is for having written
   (D) and she was for her writing
   (E) as she is for her writing

8. The professor, after distributing samples of igneous rock, explained that this type of rock is formed under intense heat and pressure deep down there within the crust of the earth.

   (A) deep down there within the crust of the earth
   (B) deep within earth's crust
   (C) deeper down there within the crust of earth
   (D) deep within the earth
   (E) deep down there within the earth's crust

9. Three women in the booth of the Swan Diner were angrily discussing the terms of the lease and arguing about the level of commitment expected from each of them.

   (A) were angrily discussing the terms of the lease and arguing about
   (B) were angrily discussing the terms of the lease, but they argued about
   (C) were discussing angrily the terms of the lease and arguing for
   (D) was angrily discussing the terms of the lease and arguing with
   (E) had been angrily in discussion about the terms of the lease and arguing about

10. Although talent may be a crucial element on the road to fame, it will be difficult to get very far without a highly developed work ethic.

    (A) difficult to get very far
    (B) difficult to travel there
    (C) hard to get going
    (D) difficult to get farther
    (E) difficult to become well known

11. Unlike a root canal, which is the preferred method for saving a diseased tooth, chewing problems can result from extraction.

    (A) chewing problems can result from extraction
    (B) problems with chewing can result from an extraction
    (C) an extraction is resulting in chewing problems
    (D) an extraction can result in chewing problems
    (E) an extraction is the result of chewing problems

GO ON TO THE NEXT PAGE

Directions: The following sentences test your ability to recognize grammar and usage errors. Each sentence contains either a single error or no error at all. No sentence contains more than one error. The error, if there is one, is underlined and lettered. If the sentence contains an error, select the one underlined part that must be changed to make the sentence correct. If the sentence is correct, select choice (E). In choosing answers, follow the requirements of standard written English.

EXAMPLE:

<u>Whenever</u> one is driving late at night, <u>you</u> must take extra precautions <u>against</u>
   A   B   C

falling asleep <u>at the wheel</u>. <u>No error</u>
           D   E

12. In the <u>original</u> Star Trek series, the crew <u>defied</u> the
          A   B
    laws <u>of nature</u> because they could breathe as
          C
    easily on other planets <u>as humans</u> could breathe
                            D
    on Earth. <u>No error</u>
            E

13. Thomas <u>was</u> so proud of his <u>younger</u> brother,
          A   B
    <u>who was graduating</u> <u>from</u> college last month.
          C   D
    <u>No error</u>
        E

14. <u>Outside the barn</u>, a commotion <u>involving</u> three
          A   B
    hens and a rooster <u>woke</u> the twins, who were
                     C
    sleeping <u>deep</u>. <u>No error</u>
           D   E

15. <u>When</u> we <u>looked</u> at the photograph of the
      A   B
    lightning bolt hitting the tree, we noticed a
    <u>more smaller</u> bolt of electricity also <u>emanating</u>
          C   D
    from the ground. <u>No error</u>
                 E

16. The beaded necklaces <u>sold at</u> a local craft
                         A
    store <u>are</u> so popular <u>with customers</u> that
        B   C
    <u>they</u> can't restock the items quickly
     D
    enough. <u>No error</u>
          E

GO ON TO THE NEXT PAGE ▷

17. He could have easily <u>completed</u> the <u>unusually</u> long
                   A   B

    and complicated assignment before it was due, if

    only <u>he had started</u> it <u>earlier</u> in the week. <u>No error</u>
          C   D   E

18. Concerned <u>about</u> the playoff game <u>on</u> Saturday,
              A   B

    each of the team members <u>spent</u> most of the
                           C

    week practicing <u>their</u> plays. <u>No error</u>
                D   E

19. Studies indicate that the environment in schools

    <u>where</u> there are <u>less</u> adults on staff <u>is</u> often not
     A   B   C

    conducive <u>to</u> learning. <u>No error</u>
           D   E

20. At breakfast, Dad asked <u>Hilary and I</u> if we <u>wanted</u>
                        A   B

    to attend <u>my cousin Noah's</u> college
             C

    graduation ceremony in Nebraska <u>next spring</u>.
                             D

    <u>No error</u>
     E

21. Only after the water in the river had <u>rose</u>
                               A

    <u>to dangerous</u> levels <u>did</u> the governor order the
     B   C

    <u>evacuation of</u> the city. <u>No error</u>
       D   E

22. The list of concert-goers <u>who waited</u> hours for
                        A

    the entrance of their favorite music group

    <u>include</u> <u>more than</u> one hundred fans <u>who</u>
     B   C   D

    traveled long distances from European

    countries for the show. <u>No error</u>
                      E

23. Because the university's math department was

    reconsidering <u>its</u> degree requirements, it
               A

    <u>announced</u> that the schedule of classes <u>would be</u>
     B   C

    delayed for an <u>indecisive</u> period. <u>No error</u>
             D   E

24. Grant Parson's new book <u>is</u> more a
                    A

    compilation of stories <u>than like</u> a novel;
                 B

    characters and plot lines appear <u>and</u> disappear
                           C

    <u>from chapter to</u> chapter. <u>No error</u>
       D   E

25. If one <u>is interested</u> <u>in learning</u> <u>even more</u> about
           A   B   C

    Eleanor and Franklin Roosevelt, <u>you</u> should
                            D

    read Goodwin's biography of the couple.

    <u>No error</u>
     E

GO ON TO THE NEXT PAGE

26. Learning stations <u>in</u> elementary school
        A
classrooms <u>allow</u> students to personalize <u>their</u>
        B   C
education by reading extracurricular books

that <u>interests</u> them. <u>No error</u>
        D   E

27. The guidance counselor's recommendation

<u>included</u> a plan <u>where</u> each student was <u>to visit</u>
    A   B   C
colleges <u>throughout</u> the spring of junior year.
              D
<u>No error</u>
    E

28. <u>From 1607 until</u> 1698, Jamestown, now an
        A
<u>excavation site</u> in Virginia, was the capital of the
        B
state; <u>however</u>, by 1750 it <u>will be</u> privately
        C   D
owned. <u>No error</u>
            E

29. Throughout history, <u>both literary scholars</u>
                            A
as well as Greek historians <u>have been obsessed</u>
                                    B
<u>with discovering</u> if the lost city of Atlantis,
        C
<u>described</u> by Plato, is real or mythological.
    D
<u>No error</u>
    E

GO ON TO THE NEXT PAGE

Directions: The following passage is an early draft of an essay. Some parts of the passage need to be rewritten.

Read the passage and select the best answer for each question that follows. Some questions are about particular sentences or parts of sentences and ask you to improve sentence structure or word choice. Other questions ask you to consider organization and development. In choosing answers, follow the conventions of standard written English.

Questions 30–35 are based on the following passage.

(1) Most people seem to find the winter season dreary. (2) It is true that it is cold and snows a lot. (3) But I don't see this as bleak; I see it as beautiful. (4) Winter is my favorite season of the year for three reasons.

(5) First, I think white snow and icicles all around are magical and make winter exceptional. (6) The snow puts a beautiful blanket on the outdoors, with a certain shimmer and shine. (7) Most days, when it doesn't snow, are very bright and sunny, not bleak.

(8) Second, winter weather provides them with the opportunity for so many activities. (9) It allows us to ski down mountains, skate on frozen ponds, and sled down hills. (10) When we complain that Americans don't exercise enough, people are saying that they don't take advantage of the outdoors. (11) But winter sport are the perfect opportunity to exercise outdoors.

(12) Third, winter weather allows families to gather together and connect. (13) On winter nights my family, for instance, is always enjoying a fire in the fireplace, hot chocolate, and board games. (14) And throughout the evening we can look outside and see the beautiful white snow fall on the trees and the ground. (15) The winter weather makes us more aware of the protection our home provides, and of the companionship we can provide each other, than the rest of the year.

30. Which sentence would be most appropriate to follow sentence 1?

(A) They see it as cold, snowy, and bleak.

(B) There are three months in winter.

(C) I think they are right.

(D) People prefer the warmth of summer.

(E) In winter they don't get enough exercise.

31. In context, which is the best way to revise and combine the underlined portions of sentences 8 and 9 (reproduced below)?

Second, _winter weather provides them with the opportunity for so many activities. It allows us to_ ski down mountains, skate on frozen ponds, and sled down hills.

(A) winter weather provides them with the opportunity for so many activities, allowing us to

(B) winter weather provides the opportunity for so many activities, allowing people to

(C) providing the opportunity for so many activities, in winter weather it is allowed to

(D) winter weather provides many activities and allows them to

(E) winter weather is the opportunity for so many activities, it allows them to

GO ON TO THE NEXT PAGE

32. Which of the following is the best version of the underlined portion of sentence 10 (reproduced below)?

    When we complain that Americans don't exercise enough, people are saying that they don't take advantage of the outdoors.

    (A) (As it is now)

    (B) In fact, Americans don't exercise enough; we however

    (C) Therefore, by our complaints that Americans don't exercise enough, people

    (D) However, when Americans don't exercise enough, it is because people,

    (E) When people complain that Americans don't exercise enough, they

33. In context, which of the following revisions is necessary in sentence 13 (reproduced below)?

    On winter nights my family, for instance, is always enjoying a fire in the fireplace, hot chocolate, and board games.

    (A) Replace "and board games" with "and playing board games."

    (B) Replace "is always" with "are always."

    (C) Replace "is always enjoying" with "always enjoys."

    (D) Replace "on" with "during."

    (E) Replace "for instance" with "as an example."

34. Which of the following is the best version of the underlined portion of sentence 15 (reproduced below)?

    The winter weather makes us more aware of the protection our home provides, and of the companionship we can provide each other, than the rest of the year.

    (A) (As it is now)

    (B) than the rest of the year of the protection of our home and companionship of our family

    (C) of the protection and companionship that is provided by our home and family than the rest of the year

    (D) than we are during the rest of the year of the protection our home provides, and of the companionship we can provide each other

    (E) of home protection and companionship than we are during the rest of the year

35. Which of the following would make the most logical final sentence for the essay?

    (A) However, in the summertime I can't enjoy hot beverages.

    (B) The snow even seems to magnify the sunlight.

    (C) Most people prefer the spring or autumn months.

    (D) Increased outdoor activity improves both mental and physical health.

    (E) Winter deserves a better reputation.

SECTION 6

Time—25 Minutes
24 Questions

Directions: For each of the following questions, choose the best answer and darken the corresponding oval on the answer sheet.

Each sentence below has one or two blanks, each blank indicating that something has been omitted. Beneath the sentence are five words or sets of words labeled (A) through (E). Choose the word or set of words that, when inserted in the sentence, best fits the meaning of the sentence as a whole.

EXAMPLE:

Today's small, portable computers contrast markedly with the earliest electronic computers, which were -------.

(A) effective
(B) invented
(C) useful
(D) destructive
(E) enormous

1. The band has courted controversy before in order to get attention, and the ------- lyrics on their new album demonstrate that they found the strategy -------.

   (A) sedate . . . plausible
   (B) vacuous . . . rewarding
   (C) belligerent . . . counterproductive
   (D) scandalous . . . effective
   (E) provocative . . . comparable

2. James Joyce regarded ------- as central to the creative process, which is evident in the numerous scribbled edits that cover even his supposedly final drafts.

   (A) contrivance
   (B) revision
   (C) inspiration
   (D) obsession
   (E) disavowal

3. Fans who believe that the players' motivations are not ------- would be ------- to learn that they now charge for their signatures.

   (A) self-serving . . . vindicated
   (B) venal . . . chagrined
   (C) altruistic . . . unsurprised
   (D) atypical . . . disillusioned
   (E) tainted . . . gratified

4. Though the film ostensibly deals with the theme of -------, the director seems to have been more interested in its absence—in isolation and the longing for connection.

   (A) reliance
   (B) fraternity
   (C) socialism
   (D) privation
   (E) levity

5. Everything the candidate said publicly was -------; he manipulated the media in order to present the image he wanted.

   (A) incendiary
   (B) calculated
   (C) facetious
   (D) scrupulous
   (E) impromptu

GO ON TO THE NEXT PAGE

Directions: The passages below are followed by questions based on their content; questions following a pair of related passages may also be based on the relationship between the paired passages. Answer the questions on the basis of what is <u>stated</u> or <u>implied</u> in the passages and in any introductory material that may be provided.

Questions 6–7 refer to the following passage.

The discovery of helium required the combined efforts of several scientists. Pierre-Jules Cesar Janssen first obtained evidence for the existence of helium during a solar eclipse in
(5) 1868 when he detected a new yellow line on his spectroscope while observing the sun. This experiment was repeated by Norman Lockyer, who concluded that no known element produced such a line. However, other scientists
(10) were dubious, finding it unlikely that an element existed only on the sun. Then, in 1895, William Ramsay discovered helium on Earth after treating clevite, a uranium mineral, with mineral acids. After isolating the resulting gas,
(15) Ramsay sent samples to William Crookes and Norman Lockyer, who identified it conclusively as the missing element helium.

6. The passage indicates that Ramsay's chief contribution to the discovery of helium was to

(A) prove the validity of Janssen's experiment

(B) find helium in uranium minerals

(C) identify the element discovered by Crookes as helium

(D) detect helium on the sun without using a spectroscope

(E) discover that helium naturally occurs on Earth

7. The author of the passage suggests that the results of the work of Janssen and Lockyer were

(A) repeated incorrectly by other scientists

(B) thought by others to be the result of flawed methodologies

(C) met with skepticism by other scientists

(D) only valid during solar eclipses

(E) obtained using outdated equipment

Questions 8–9 refer to the following passage.

July 19: Loretta arrives tomorrow, and I'll pick her up at the airport. We'll spend the week exploring the city together, but first we'll visit Grandmama. It's been years since
(5) Loretta has seen her. The rift that began for reasons lost in the mists of family lore has continued to this day. I'll wager that Loretta can't even remember why she and Grandmama haven't spoken in all this time.
(10) The truth is, I think that Grandmama is angry with Uncle Martin, not his daughter. Now she seems ready for reconciliation— perhaps this is because she's getting older.

8. Based on the passage, the reason that Loretta and Grandmama have not seen each other in years is most likely

(A) due to Grandmama's treatment of Uncle Martin

(B) the sole purpose of Loretta's visit to the city

(C) the impetus for their reunion

(D) that Loretta has been too busy to visit

(E) forgotten by both of them

9. In line 5, "rift" is best understood as meaning

(A) motion

(B) break

(C) revelry

(D) clarity

(E) discussion

GO ON TO THE NEXT PAGE

Questions 10–16 refer to the following passage.

The following passage is from a discussion of the origin of the Cold War between the United States and the Soviet Union.

Revisionist historians maintain that it was within the power of the United States, in the years during and immediately after the Second World War, to prevent the Cold War with
(5) the Soviet Union. Revisionists suggest that the prospect of impending conflict with the Soviets could have been avoided in several ways. The U.S. could have officially recognized the new Soviet sphere of influence in
(10) Eastern Europe instead of continuing to call for self-determination in those countries. A much-needed reconstruction loan could have helped the Soviets recover from the war. The Americans could have sought to assuage Soviet
(15) fears by giving up the U.S. monopoly of the atomic bomb and turning the weapons over to an international agency (with the stipulation that future nuclear powers do the same).

This criticism of the post-war American
(20) course of action fails to take into account the political realities in America at the time and unfairly condemns the American policy-makers who did consider each of these alternatives and found them to be unworkable.
(25) Recognition of a Soviet Eastern Europe was out of the question. Roosevelt had promised self-determination to the Eastern European countries, and the American people, having come to expect this, were furious when Stalin
(30) began to shape his spheres of influence in the region. The President was in particular acutely conscious of the millions of Polish-Americans who would be voting in the upcoming election.
(35) Negotiations had indeed been conducted by the administration with the Soviets about a reconstruction loan, but the Congress refused to approve it unless the Soviets made enormous concessions tantamount to restruc-
(40) turing their system and withdrawing from Eastern Europe. This, of course, made Soviet

rejection of the loan a foregone conclusion. As for giving up the bomb—the elected officials in Washington would have been in deep trou-
(45) ble with their constituents had that plan been carried out. Polls showed that 82 percent of the American people understood that other nations would develop bombs eventually, but that 85 percent thought that the U.S.
(50) should retain exclusive possession of the weapon. Policy-makers have to abide by certain constraints in deciding what is acceptable and what is not. They, and not historians, are in the best position to perceive those constraints and
(55) make the decisions.

Revisionist historians tend to eschew this type of political explanation of America's supposed failure to reach a peaceful settlement with the Soviets in favor of an economic read-
(60) ing of events. They point to the fact that in the early post-war years, American businessmen and government officials cooperated to expand American foreign trade vigorously and to exploit investment opportunities in many for-
(65) eign countries. In order to sustain the lucrative expansion, revisionists assert, American policy-makers were obliged to maintain an "Open Door" foreign policy, the object of which was to keep all potential trade opportunities open.
(70) Since the Soviets could jeopardize such opportunities in Eastern Europe and elsewhere, they had to be opposed. Hence, the Cold War. But if American policy-makers were simply pawns in an economic game of expansionist capital-
(75) ism, as the revisionists seem to think, why do the revisionists hold them responsible for not attempting to reach an accord with the Soviets? The policy-makers, swept up by a tidal wave of capitalism, clearly had little control
(80) and little choice in the matter.

Even if American officials had been free and willing to make conciliatory gestures toward the Soviets, the Cold War would not have been prevented. Overtures of friend-
(85) ship would not have been reciprocated (as far as we can judge; information on the inner

GO ON TO THE NEXT PAGE

workings of the Kremlin during that time
is scanty). Soviet expert George F. Kennan
concluded that Russian hostility could not
(90) be dampened by any effort on the part of the
United States. The political and ideological
differences were too great, and the Soviets
had too long a history of distrust of for-
eigners—exacerbated at the time by Stalin's
(95) rampant paranoia, which infected his government—to embark on a process of establish-
ing trust and peace with the United States,
though it was in their interest to do so.

10. The primary purpose of the passage is to

    (A) explode a popular myth
    (B) criticize historical figures
    (C) refute an argument
    (D) analyze an era
    (E) reconcile opposing views

11. In lines 8–9, the word "recognized" most
    nearly means

    (A) identified
    (B) noticed
    (C) acknowledged
    (D) distinguished
    (E) remembered

12. The author refers to the Polish-Americans
    (lines 32–33) chiefly to illustrate that

    (A) the president had an excellent rapport
        with ethnic minorities
    (B) immigrants had fled from Eastern
        European countries to escape communism
    (C) giving up the idea of East European self-
        determination would have been costly in
        political terms
    (D) the Poles could enjoy self-determination
        only in America
    (E) the political landscape of the United
        States had changed considerably since
        the president was elected

13. A fundamental assumption underlying the
    author's argument in the second and third
    paragraphs is that

    (A) the Soviets were largely to blame for the
        failure of conciliatory U.S. initiatives
    (B) the American public was very well
        informed about the incipient Cold War
        situation
    (C) none of the proposed alternatives would
        have had its intended effect
    (D) the American public was overwhelm-
        ingly opposed to seeking peace with the
        Soviets
    (E) the government could not have been
        expected to ignore public opinion

14. The phrase "certain constraints" in lines 51–52
    most likely refers to the

    (A) etiquette of international diplomacy
    (B) danger of leaked information about
        atomic bombs
    (C) views of the electorate
    (D) potential reaction of the enemy
    (E) difficulty of carrying out a policy
        initiative

GO ON TO THE NEXT PAGE

15. Which statement best summarizes the revisionist argument concerning the origin of the Cold War (lines 56–72)?

(A) The United States started the Cold War in order to have a military cover for illegal trading activities.

(B) The Soviets were oblivious to the negative impact they had on the American economy.

(C) The economic advantage of recognizing Soviet Europe outweighed the disadvantage of an angry public.

(D) America could trade and invest with foreign countries only if it agreed to oppose the Soviet Union.

(E) American economic interests abroad would have been threatened by any Soviet expansion.

16. The question "But if American policy-makers . . . Soviets?" (lines 72–78) serves to

(A) point out an inconsistency in a position

(B) outline an area that requires further research

(C) contrast two different historical interpretations

(D) sum up a cynical view of post-war economic activity

(E) restate the central issue of the passage

GO ON TO THE NEXT PAGE

Questions 17–24 refer to the following passage.

James Weldon Johnson was a poet, diplomat, composer, and historian of black culture who wrote around the turn of the century. In this narrative passage, Johnson recalls his first experience of hearing rag-time jazz.

When I had somewhat collected my senses, I realized that in a large back room into which the main room opened, there was a young fellow singing a song, accompanied on the
(5) piano by a short, thickset black man. After each verse, he did some dance steps, which brought forth great applause and a shower of small coins at his feet. After the singer had responded to a rousing encore, the stout man
(10) at the piano began to run his fingers up and down the keyboard. This he did in a manner which indicated that he was a master of a good deal of technique. Then he began to play; and such playing! I stopped talking to listen. It
(15) was music of a kind I had never heard before. It was music that demanded physical response, patting of the feet, drumming of the fingers, or nodding of the head in time with the beat. The dissonant harmonies, the audacious reso-
(20) lutions, often consisting of an abrupt jump from one key to another, the intricate rhythms in which the accents fell in the most unexpected places, but in which the beat was never lost, produced a most curious effect . . .
(25) This was rag-time music, then a novelty in New York, and just growing to be a rage, which has not yet subsided. It was originated in the questionable resorts about Memphis and St. Louis by Negro piano players who knew no
(30) more of the theory of music than they did of the theory of the universe, but were guided by natural musical instinct and talent. It made its way to Chicago, where it was popular some time before it reached New York. These players
(35) often improvised simple and, at times, vulgar words to fit the melodies. This was the beginning of the rag-time song . . .
American musicians, instead of investigating rag-time, attempt to ignore it, or dismiss

(40) it with a contemptuous word. But that has always been the course of scholasticism in every branch of art. Whatever new thing the *people* like is pooh-poohed; whatever is *popular* is spoken of as not worth the while.
(45) The fact is, nothing great or enduring, especially in music, has ever sprung full-fledged and unprecedented from the brain of any master; the best that he gives to the world he gathers from the hearts of the people, and
(50) runs it through the alembic* of his genius. In spite of the bans which musicians and music teachers have placed upon it, the people still demand and enjoy rag-time. One thing cannot be denied; it is music which possesses at least
(55) one strong element of greatness: it appeals universally; not only the American, but the English, the French, and even the German people find delight in it. In fact, there is not a corner of the civilized world in which it is not
(60) known, and this proves its originality; for if it were an imitation, the people of Europe, anyhow, would not have found it a novelty . . .
I became so interested in both the music and the player that I left the table where I was
(65) sitting, and made my way through the hall into the back room, where I could see as well as hear. I talked to the piano player between the musical numbers and found out that he was just a natural musician, never having
(70) taken a lesson in his life. Not only could he play almost anything he heard, but he could accompany singers in songs he had never heard. He had, by ear alone, composed some pieces, several of which he played over for me;
(75) each of them was properly proportioned and balanced. I began to wonder what this man with such a lavish natural endowment would have done had he been trained. Perhaps he wouldn't have done anything at all; he might
(80) have become, at best, a mediocre imitator of the great masters in what they have already done to a finish, or one of the modern innovators who strive after originality by seeing how cleverly they can dodge about through

GO ON TO THE NEXT PAGE

(85) the rules of harmony and at the same time avoid melody. It is certain that he would not have been so delightful as he was in rag-time.

*alembic: scientific apparatus used in the process of distillation

17. In relating his initial impression of rag-time music to the reader, the narrator makes use of

    (A) comparison with the improvisations of classical music

    (B) reference to the audience's appreciative applause

    (C) description of the music's compelling rhythmic effect

    (D) evocation of poignant visual images

    (E) allusion to several popular contemporary tunes

18. In the first paragraph, the narrator portrays rag-time as a type of music that

    (A) would be a challenge to play for even the most proficient musician

    (B) satisfied the narrator's expectations regarding the genre

    (C) violated all of the accepted rules governing musical composition

    (D) made up for a lack of melody with a seductive rhythm

    (E) contained several surprises for the discerning listener

19. In line 28, "questionable" most nearly means

    (A) disreputable

    (B) ambiguous

    (C) doubtful

    (D) approachable

    (E) unconfirmed

20. The narrator's perspective during the second and third paragraphs is that of

    (A) an impartial historian of events in the recent past

    (B) a mesmerized spectator of a musical spectacle

    (C) a knowledgeable critic of the contemporary musical scene

    (D) a commentator reflecting on a unique experience

    (E) an adult reminiscing fondly about his youth

21. The discussion in paragraph 3 of the refusal of American musicians to investigate rag-time suggests that they

    (A) have little or no interest in pleasing people with their music

    (B) need to be made aware of the popularity of rag-time in Europe

    (C) are misguided in their conservative and condescending attitude

    (D) attack rag-time for being merely an imitation of an existing style

    (E) know that it would be difficult to refine rag-time as a musical form

22. Which statement best summarizes the author's argument in the third paragraph?

    (A) Any type of music that is extremely popular should be considered great.

    (B) The two criteria for musical greatness are popularity and originality.

    (C) Music that has become popular overseas cannot be ignored by American musicians.

    (D) Rag-time must be taken up by a musical master and purified to earn critical acclaim.

    (E) Mass appeal in music can be a sign of greatness rather than a stigma.

GO ON TO THE NEXT PAGE

23. The statement "Perhaps he wouldn't have done anything at all" (lines 78–79) is best interpreted as conveying

(A) doubt about the depth of the piano player's skill

(B) understanding that no amount of talent can compensate for a lack of discipline

(C) cynicism about the likelihood that a man can live up to his potential

(D) a recognition that the piano player might have wasted his talent

(E) frustration at the impossibility of knowing what might have been

24. The author's view (lines 78–87) about the rag-time piano player's lack of formal training can best be summarized as which of the following?

(A) The piano player's natural talent had allowed him to develop technically to the point where formal training would have been superfluous.

(B) Formal lessons would have impaired the piano player's native ability to play and compose by ear alone.

(C) More would have been lost than gained if the piano player had been given formal lessons.

(D) The piano player's potential to be a truly innovative rag-time artist had been squandered because he had not been formally trained.

(E) Although dazzling when improvising rag-time, the piano player could never have been more than mediocre as a classical pianist.

IF YOU FINISH BEFORE TIME IS CALLED, YOU MAY CHECK YOUR WORK ON THIS SECTION ONLY. DO NOT TURN TO ANY OTHER SECTION IN THE TEST. STOP

SECTION 7
Time—20 Minutes
16 Questions

Directions: For this section, solve each problem and decide which is the best of the choices given. Fill in the corresponding oval on the answer sheet. You may use any available space for scratchwork.

Notes:

(1) Calculator use is permitted.
(2) All numbers used are real numbers.
(3) Figures are provided for some problems. All figures are drawn to scale and lie in a plane UNLESS otherwise indicated.
(4) Unless otherwise specified, the domain of any function f is assumed to be the set of all real numbers x for which $f(x)$ is a real number.

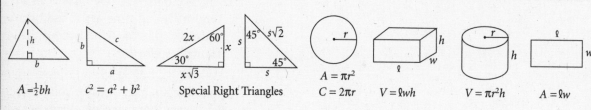

$A = \frac{1}{2}bh$ $c^2 = a^2 + b^2$ Special Right Triangles $A = \pi r^2$ $V = \ell wh$ $V = \pi r^2 h$ $A = \ell w$
$C = 2\pi r$

The sum of the degree measures of the angles in a triangle is 180.
The number of degrees of arc in a circle is 360.
A straight angle has a degree measure of 180.

1. For all values of x, $(3x+4)(4x-3) =$

   (A) $7x+1$
   (B) $7x-12$
   (C) $12x^2 - 12$
   (D) $12x^2 - 25x - 12$
   (E) $12x^2 + 7x - 12$

2. In a certain set of numbers, the ratio of integers to nonintegers is 2:3. What percent of the numbers in the set are integers?

   (A) 20%
   (B) $33\frac{1}{3}\%$
   (C) 40%
   (D) 60%
   (E) $66\frac{2}{3}\%$

3. If $xyz \neq 0$, which of the following is equivalent to $\dfrac{x^2 y^3 z^4}{(xyz^2)^2}$?

   (A) $\dfrac{1}{y}$
   (B) $\dfrac{1}{z}$
   (C) y
   (D) $\dfrac{x}{yz}$
   (E) xyz

GO ON TO THE NEXT PAGE

4. When the positive integer p is divided by 7, the remainder is 5. What is the remainder when $5p$ is divided by 7?

    (A) 0
    (B) 1
    (C) 2
    (D) 3
    (E) 4

5. What is the y-intercept of the line with the equation $2x - 3y = 18$?

    (A) −9
    (B) −6
    (C) −3
    (D)   6
    (E)   9

6. Jan types at an average rate of 12 pages per hour. At that rate, how long will it take Jan to type 100 pages?

    (A) 8 hours and 3 minutes
    (B) 8 hours and 15 minutes
    (C) 8 hours and 20 minutes
    (D) 8 hours and 30 minutes
    (E) 8 hours and $33\frac{1}{3}$ minutes

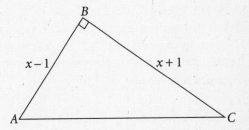

7. In the figure above, AB is perpendicular to BC. The lengths of AB and BC are given in terms of x. Which of the following represents the area of $\triangle ABC$ for all $x > 1$?

    (A) x
    (B) $2x$
    (C) x^2
    (D) $x^2 - 1$
    (E) $\dfrac{x^2 - 1}{2}$

8. If Jim and Bill have less than 15 dollars between them, and Bill has 4 dollars, which of the following could be the number of dollars that Jim has?

    I.   10
    II. 11
    III. 15

    (A) I only
    (B) II only
    (C) I and II only
    (D) II and III only
    (E) I, II, and III

GO ON TO THE NEXT PAGE

9. Angelo makes x dollars for y hours of work. Sarah makes the same amount of money for 1 less hour of work. Which of the following expressions represents the positive difference between the two people's hourly wage?

(A) $\dfrac{x}{y-1} - \dfrac{x}{y}$

(B) $\dfrac{x}{y} - \dfrac{x}{y-1}$

(C) $\dfrac{x}{y-1} + \dfrac{x}{y}$

(D) $\dfrac{y-1}{x} - \dfrac{y}{x}$

(E) $\dfrac{y}{x} - \dfrac{y-1}{x}$

10. Erica has 8 squares of felt, each with area 16. For a certain craft project, she cuts the largest circle possible from each square of felt. What is the combined area of the excess felt left over after cutting out all the circles?

(A) $4(4 - \pi)$

(B) $8(4 - \pi)$

(C) $8(\pi - 2)$

(D) $32(4 - \pi)$

(E) $16(16 - \pi)$

11. In the sequence 2, 6, 18, x, 162 ..., what is the most likely value of x?

(A) 36

(B) 48

(C) 54

(D) 81

(E) 98

12. What is the remainder when $5x^3 - 2x^2 + x + 1$ is divided by $x - 3$?

(A) -121

(B) -60

(C) 65

(D) 120

(E) 121

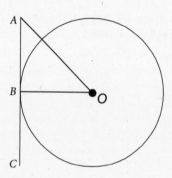

13. In the diagram above, the circle's center is at point O. $\overline{AC}$ is tangent to the circle at point B, which is the midpoint of $\overline{AC}$. If $\overline{AC} = 4$ and the area of the circle is 4π, what is the length of $\overline{AO}$?

(A) 2

(B) $2\sqrt{2}$

(C) 3

(D) 4

(E) $4\sqrt{2}$

GO ON TO THE NEXT PAGE

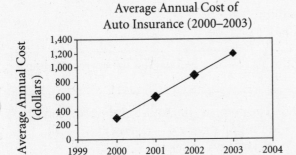

14. The graph above represents the average annual cost of automobile insurance in a certain state from 2000 to 2003. Assuming that the cost of insurance increases at the same average (arithmetic mean) rate depicted in the graph, what is the expected cost of automobile insurance in 2004?

(A) $200
(B) $550
(C) $875
(D) $1,000
(E) $1,500

15. Which of the following expressions describes the indicated values on the number line above?

(A) $x \le 1$
(B) $x \ge 1$
(C) $|x| \le 1$
(D) $|x| \ge 1$
(E) $x \ge |1|$

16. There are 3 routes from Bay City to Riverville. There are 4 routes from Riverville to Straitstown. There are 3 routes from Straitstown to Frog Pond. If a driver must pass through Riverville and Straitstown exactly once, how many possible ways are there to go from Bay City to Frog Pond?

(A) 6
(B) 10
(C) 12
(D) 24
(E) 36

IF YOU FINISH BEFORE TIME IS CALLED, YOU MAY CHECK YOUR WORK ON THIS SECTION ONLY. DO NOT TURN TO ANY OTHER SECTION IN THE TEST.

STOP

SECTION 8

Time—20 Minutes
19 Questions

Directions: For each of the following questions, choose the best answer and darken the corresponding oval on the answer sheet.

Each sentence below has one or two blanks, each blank indicating that something has been omitted. Beneath the sentence are five words or sets of words labeled (A) through (E). Choose the word or set of words that, when inserted in the sentence, <u>best</u> fits the meaning of the sentence as a whole.

EXAMPLE:

Today's small, portable computers contrast markedly with the earliest electronic computers, which were -------.

(A) effective
(B) invented
(C) useful
(D) destructive
(E) enormous

1. Although sub-Saharan Africa encompasses a large number of ------- cultures, its music is often considered an essentially ------- mass.

   (A) disparate . . . homogeneous
   (B) impoverished . . . inimitable
   (C) warring . . . concrete
   (D) interwoven . . . distinctive
   (E) proud . . . languid

2. His face was -------, his features pulled downward by the weight of heavy thoughts.

   (A) morose
   (B) onerous
   (C) contorted
   (D) ossified
   (E) inscrutable

3. The unfortunate demise of the protagonist in the final scene of the movie ------- all possibility of a sequel.

   (A) entertained
   (B) dissembled
   (C) raised
   (D) exacerbated
   (E) precluded

4. The repeated breakdown of negotiations only -------- the view that the two sides were not truly committed to the goal of --------- a military confrontation.

   (A) established . . . escalating
   (B) undermined . . . avoiding
   (C) distorted . . . financing
   (D) strengthened . . . initiating
   (E) reinforced . . . averting

5. Duncan was a modest and cooperative worker; he demonstrated none of his colleague's ------.

   (A) geniality
   (B) influence
   (C) arrogance
   (D) reluctance
   (E) humility

6. When the election results were announced, the victorious candidate's exhilaration temporarily ------- the recognition of the forthcoming ------- to improve the economic climate of the city.

   (A) accepted . . . promise
   (B) illuminated . . . campaign
   (C) admitted . . . hostility
   (D) eclipsed . . . struggle
   (E) blocked . . . inauguration

GO ON TO THE NEXT PAGE

Directions: The passages below are followed by questions based on their content; questions following a pair of related passages may also be based on the relationship between the paired passages. Answer the questions on the basis of what is <u>stated</u> or <u>implied</u> in the passages and in any introductory material that may be provided.

Questions 7–19 refer to the following passages.

These passages present two critics' perspectives on the topic of design museums.

Passage 1

City museums are places where people can learn about various cultures by studying objects of particular historical or artistic value. The increasingly popular "design museums"
(5) that are opening today perform quite a different function. Unlike most city museums, the design museum displays and assesses objects that are readily available to the general public. These museums place ignored household
(10) appliances under spotlights, breaking down the barriers between commerce and creative invention.

Critics have argued that design museums are often manipulated to serve as advertise-
(15) ments for new industrial technology. But their role is not simply a matter of merchandis-ing—it is the honoring of impressive, innova-tive products. The difference between the win-dow of a department store and the showcase
(20) in a design museum is that the first tries to sell you something, while the second informs you of the success of the attempt.

One advantage that the design museum has over other civic museums is that design
(25) museums are places where people feel familiar with the exhibits. Unlike the average art gal-lery patron, design museum visitors rarely feel intimidated or disoriented. Partly, this is because design museums clearly illustrate how and why
(30) mass-produced consumer objects work and look as they do and show how design contrib-utes to the quality of our lives. For example, an exhibit involving a particular design of chair would not simply explain how it functions as a
(35) chair. It would also demonstrate how its various features combine to produce an artistic effect or redefine our manner of performing the basic act of being seated. The purpose of such an exhibit would be to present these concepts in ways that
(40) challenge, stimulate, and inform the viewer. An art gallery exhibit, on the other hand, would provide very little information about the chair and charge the visitor with understanding the exhibit on some abstract level.

(45) Within the past decade, several new design museums have opened their doors. Each of these museums has responded in totally original ways to the public's growing interest in the field. London's Design Museum, for
(50) instance, displays a collection of mass-pro-duced objects ranging from Zippo lighters to electric typewriters to a show of Norwegian sardine-tin labels. The options open to cura-tors of design museums seem far less rigor-
(55) ous, conventionalized, and pre-programmed than those applying to curators in charge of public galleries of paintings and sculpture. The humorous aspects of our society are bet-ter represented in the display of postmodern
(60) playthings or quirky Japanese vacuum clean-ers in pastel colors than in an exhibition of Impressionist landscapes.

Passage 2

The short histories of some of the leading technical and design museums make clear an
(65) underlying difficulty in this area. The tendency everywhere today is to begin with present machines and technological processes and to show how they operate and the scientific principles on which they are based without
(70) paying much attention to their historical development, to say nothing of the society

GO ON TO THE NEXT PAGE

that produced them. Only a few of the oldest,
largest and best-supported museums collect
historical industrial objects. Most science cent-
(75) ers put more emphasis on mock-ups, graphs,
and multimedia devices. This approach of "pre-
sentism" often leads the museum to drop all attempts at study and research; if industry is called
upon to design and build the exhibits, curators
(80) may be entirely dispensed with, so that impartial
and scientific study disappears, and emphasis is
placed on the idea that progress automatically
follows technology.

   Industrialization and the machine have, of
(85) course, brought much progress; a large portion
of humankind no longer works from sun-up
to sundown to obtain the bare necessities of
life. But industrialization also creates problems—harm to the environment and ecology,
(90) neglect of social, cultural, and humanistic values, depletion of resources, and even threats of
human extinction. Thus, progress needs to be
considered critically—from a wider social and
humanitarian point of view. Unfortunately,
(95) most museums of science and technology glorify machines. Displayed in pristine condition,
elegantly painted or polished, they can make
the observer forget the noise, dirt, danger,
and frustration of machine-tending. Mines,
(100) whether coal, iron, or salt, are a favorite museum display but only infrequently is there even
a hint of the dirt, the damp, the smell, the low
headroom, or the crippling and destructive
accidents that sometimes occur in industry.
(105)   Machinery also ought to be operated to be
meaningful. Consequently, it should not be
shown in sculptured repose but in full, often
clattering, action. This kind of operation is
difficult to obtain, and few museums can com-
(110) mand the imagination, ingenuity, and manual
dexterity it requires. Problems also arise in
providing adequate safety devices for both the
public and the machine operators. These, then,
are some of the underlying problems of the
(115) technical museum—problems not solved by
the usual push buttons, cranks, or multimedia

gimmicks. Yet attendance figures show that
technical museums outdraw all the others;
the public possesses lively curiosity and a real
(120) desire to understand science and technology.

7. In line 8, the word "readily" most nearly means

(A) easily
(B) willingly
(C) instantly
(D) cheaply
(E) constantly

8. The author of Passage 1 refers to objects
displayed in design museums as "ignored"
(line 9) to emphasize that these objects were

(A) unsuccessful commercially
(B) generally unused in the household
(C) never the subject of conversation in the
household
(D) allowed to fall into disrepair
(E) not treated as objects of beauty

9. In lines 18–22, the author of Passage 1 suggests
that design museums are different from store
windows in that

(A) design museums display more
technologically advanced products
(B) store window displays are not created
with as much concern to the visual quality of the display
(C) design museums are not concerned
with the commercial aspects of a successful product
(D) design museums focus on highlighting
the artistic qualities that help sell products
(E) the objects in store displays are more
commercially successful than those in
design museums

GO ON TO THE NEXT PAGE ⟩

10. From lines 23–28, it can be inferred that the author believes that most museum visitors

    (A) are hostile toward the concept of abstract art

    (B) prefer to have a context in which to understand museum exhibits

    (C) are confused when faced with complex technological exhibits

    (D) are unfamiliar with the exhibits in design museums

    (E) undervalue the artistic worth of household items

11. Lines 23–44 suggest that one important difference between design museums and the art galleries is

    (A) the low price of admission at design museums

    (B) the amount of information presented with design museum exhibits

    (C) the intelligence of the average museum visitor

    (D) that art galleries feature exhibits that have artistic merit

    (E) the contribution that design museums make to our quality of life

12. In line 53, the word "options" most likely refers to the ability of curators of design museums to

    (A) afford large collections of exhibits

    (B) attract a wide range of visitors

    (C) put together unconventional collections

    (D) feature rare objects that interest the public

    (E) satisfy their own personal whims in planning exhibitions

13. In line 62, the author most likely mentions "Impressionist landscapes" in order to

    (A) provide an example of a typical design museum exhibit

    (B) compare postmodern exhibits to 19th-century art

    (C) point out a decline in the sophistication of the museum-going public

    (D) refute the notion that postmodern art is whimsical

    (E) emphasize the contrast between two different types of exhibits

14. Which of the following best describes the "underlying difficulty" mentioned in line 65?

    (A) Design museums rarely mention the historical origin of objects they display.

    (B) Industrial involvement often forces curators out of their jobs.

    (C) Design museums appropriate technology that is essential for study and research.

    (D) Technology almost never leads to progress.

    (E) Industry places too much emphasis on impartial research.

15. The author of Passage 2 most likely mentions "harm to the environment and ecology," line 89, in order to

    (A) encourage a critical response to the technological age

    (B) discourage the reader from visiting technology museums

    (C) describe the hazardous conditions in coal, iron, and salt mines

    (D) dissuade museum visitors from operating the machinery on display

    (E) praise museums that present an accurate depiction of technology

GO ON TO THE NEXT PAGE

16. In line 107, the author of Passage 2 uses the phrase "sculptured repose" in order to

    (A) condemn the curators of design museums for poor planning

    (B) illustrate the greatest problem inherent in design museums

    (C) present an idealized vision of a type of exhibit

    (D) describe the unrealistic way in which machinery is generally displayed

    (E) compare the shape of a machine to a work of art

17. In lines 109–110, the word "command" most nearly means

    (A) oversee

    (B) direct

    (C) control

    (D) summon

    (E) order

18. The author of Passage 2 would probably object to the statement in Passage 1 that design "contributes to the quality of our lives" (lines 31–32) on the grounds that

    (A) technical innovation has historically posed threats to our physical and social well-being

    (B) the general public would benefit more from visiting art galleries

    (C) machinery that is not shown in action is meaningless to the viewer

    (D) industry has made a negligible contribution to human progress

    (E) few people have a genuine interest in the impact of science and technology

19. The authors of both passages would probably agree that

    (A) machinery is only enjoyable to watch when it is moving

    (B) most people are curious about the factors behind the design of everyday objects

    (C) the public places a higher value on packaging than it does on quality

    (D) the very technology that is displayed in the museums is likely to cost curators their jobs

    (E) design museums are flawed because they fail to accurately portray the environmental problems that technology sometimes causes

IF YOU FINISH BEFORE TIME IS CALLED, YOU MAY CHECK YOUR WORK ON THIS SECTION ONLY. DO NOT TURN TO ANY OTHER SECTION IN THE TEST.   STOP

SECTION 9

Time—10 Minutes
14 Questions

Directions: For each question in this section, select the best answer from among the choices given and fill in the corresponding oval on the answer sheet.

The following sentences test correctness and effectiveness of expression. Part of each sentence or the entire sentence is underlined; beneath each sentence are five ways of phrasing the underlined material. Choice (A) repeats the original phrasing; the other four choices are different. If you think the original phrasing produces a better sentence than any of the alternatives, select choice (A); if not, select one of the other choices.

In making your selection, follow the requirements of standard written English; that is, pay attention to grammar, choice of words, sentence construction, and punctuation. Your selection should result in the most effective sentence—clear and precise, without awkwardness or ambiguity.

EXAMPLE: ANSWER:

Every apple in the baskets <u>are ripe and labeled according to the date it was picked</u>.   (A) ● (C) (D) (E)

(A) are ripe and labeled according to the date it was picked
(B) is ripe and labeled according to the date it was picked
(C) are ripe and labeled according to the date they were picked
(D) is ripe and labeled according to the date they were picked
(E) are ripe and labeled as to the date it was picked

---

1. A spokesman for the car company boasted that the new model was lightweight, effective, <u>and virtually indistinguishable from the expensive model commonly used in movies</u>.

    (A) and virtually indistinguishable from the expensive model commonly used in movies

    (B) and the expensive model commonly used in movies could not distinguish it

    (C) and virtually indistinguishable by the expensive model commonly used in movies

    (D) and had gone virtually indistinguished by the expensive model commonly used in movies

    (E) and the expensive model commonly used in movies virtually unable to distinguish it

2. <u>Because the polar ice caps are melting, therefore many</u> scientists and environmentalists fear that several small island nations will be completely covered by water in only a few decades.

    (A) Because the polar ice caps are melting, therefore many

    (B) Because the polar ice caps are melting, many

    (C) The polar ice caps are melting, therefore many

    (D) Because the polar ice caps are melting; many

    (E) The polar ice caps are melting; and many

GO ON TO THE NEXT PAGE ▷

3. One of the great literary artists of the 19th <u>century was Gustave Flaubert known for his obsession with the writer's craft</u>.

   (A) century was Gustave Flaubert known for his obsession with the writer's craft

   (B) century, Gustave Flaubert's obsession with the writer's craft was well known

   (C) century, Gustave Flaubert was known for his obsession with the writer's craft

   (D) century, Gustave Flaubert, known for his obsession with the writer's craft

   (E) century was Gustave Flaubert: known for his obsession with the writer's craft

4. David Hockney created <u>images and they converge</u> the art of photography with the craft of collages, giving his works a cubist effect.

   (A) images and they converge

   (B) images, being the convergence of

   (C) images, they converge

   (D) images that converge

   (E) images, and converging in them

5. The dean of students argued that although the university's professors have raised students' interest in continuing in academia, <u>the failure is in their not preparing</u> the students for the real world outside of textbooks and calculators.

   (A) the failure is in their not preparing

   (B) the failure they have is in their not preparing

   (C) they failed not to prepare

   (D) they have failed to prepare

   (E) failing in their preparation of

6. The amount of water used by Americans can be reduced by turning off faucets when not in use, decreasing time spent in showers, <u>and running washing machines</u> less frequently.

   (A) and running washing machines

   (B) and if they run washing machines

   (C) also by running washing machines

   (D) and washing machines being run

   (E) and if there ran washing machines

GO ON TO THE NEXT PAGE

7. Having exceptionally clear waters and
    active underwater life, the directors chose
    Cozumel as a prospective site for their next
    documentary on scuba diving.

    (A) Having exceptionally clear waters and
        active underwater life, the directors
        chose Cozumel

    (B) Directors who chose Cozumel for its
        exceptionally clear waters and active
        underwater life seeing it

    (C) Cozumel's exceptionally clear waters and
        active underwater life led directors to
        choose it

    (D) Because its waters are clear and it has
        active underwater life, directors chose
        Cozumel

    (E) Based on its clear waters and active under-
        water life, Cozumel, which was chosen by
        directors,

8. Several of Salvador Dali's paintings were
    inspired by his wife, featured beauty, grace,
    and femininity.

    (A) paintings were inspired by his wife,
        featured

    (B) paintings had their inspiration from
        his wife, with features

    (C) paintings, inspired by his wife, featured

    (D) paintings, which were inspired by his
        wife, and which featured

    (E) paintings, being inspired by his wife,
        featuring

9. The fire, once close to destroying another
    forest, had trickled to a small flame.

    (A) The fire, once close to destroying
        another forest, had

    (B) The fire was once close to destroying
        another forest, it had

    (C) The fire that once having been close to
        destroying another forest had

    (D) The fire, because it was once close to
        destroying a forest, had

    (E) The fire was once close to destroying a
        forest, and it had

10. Michael Ondaatje collected the anecdotes and
    memories of his family in Sri Lanka, his native
    country, and these are stories that are told in his
    memoir.

    (A) these are stories that are told

    (B) the telling of these stories is

    (C) these stories having been told

    (D) his telling of these stories

    (E) told these stories

GO ON TO THE NEXT PAGE

11. <u>The idea that women should not vote or
    express their political opinions prevailed in
    19th-century America.</u>

    (A) The idea that women should not vote or
    express their political opinions prevailed
    in 19th-century America.

    (B) The idea that prevailed about women
    during 19th-century America was that of
    not voting and not expressing their politi-
    cal opinions.

    (C) During most of 19th-century America, they
    had a prevalent idea that women should
    not vote or express political opinions.

    (D) Prevalent as the idea during 19th-century
    America was for women to not vote or
    express their political opinions.

    (E) Prevalent during 19th-century America,
    they thought that women should not vote
    or express political opinions.

12. For many an inspirational writer, <u>being free to
    create is more important</u> than having a lot of
    money.

    (A) being free to create is more important

    (B) having freedom of creation is more
    important

    (C) there is more importance in the freedom
    to create

    (D) freedom to create has more importance

    (E) to have the freedom to create is more
    important

13. <u>The peace conference that was being mediated
    by the president, but now the countries are
    adamantly refusing to compromise their
    positions.</u>

    (A) The peace conference that was being
    mediated by the president, but now the
    countries are adamantly refusing to com-
    promise their positions.

    (B) The president had mediated the peace
    conference, but the countries are now
    adamantly refusing to compromise their
    positions.

    (C) The peace conference was mediated by
    the president, and so now the countries
    are adamantly refusing to compromise
    their positions.

    (D) Though the president mediated the
    peace conference, the countries now
    adamantly refusing to compromise their
    beliefs.

    (E) Now adamantly refusing to compromise
    their beliefs, the president mediated the
    peace conference.

14. Although Internet traffic often occurs
    during the evening hours, <u>causing it to delay
    connection no more</u> than two minutes.

    (A) causing it to delay connection no more

    (B) and yet it delays connection no more

    (C) it does not delay connection more

    (D) and it does not delay connection more

    (E) yet causing it to delay no more

IF YOU FINISH BEFORE TIME IS CALLED, YOU MAY CHECK YOUR WORK ON
THIS SECTION ONLY. DO NOT TURN TO ANY OTHER SECTION IN THE TEST.   STOP

(Answers on the next page.)

Practice Test One: **Answer Key**

SECTION 1

Essay

SECTION 2

1. E
2. E
3. C
4. A
5. A
6. D
7. C
8. A
9. C
10. A
11. E
12. C
13. A
14. D
15. C
16. A
17. E
18. B
19. D
20. D

SECTION 3

1. C
2. E
3. A
4. A
5. C
6. C
7. D
8. C
9. B

10. A
11. D
12. E
13. C
14. A
15. D
16. C
17. C
18. A
19. B
20. C
21. D
22. B
23. B
24. B

SECTION 4

1. D
2. D
3. D
4. D
5. A
6. A
7. D
8. C
9. 115
10. .04
11. 11, 13, 17, 19, 23, 29, 31, 37, 41, 43, or 47
12. $\frac{2}{5}$ or .4
13. 8
14. 4
15. 250
16. 9

17. 64
18. 203

SECTION 5

1. C
2. D
3. E
4. C
5. B
6. D
7. A
8. B
9. A
10. A
11. D
12. E
13. C
14. D
15. C
16. D
17. E
18. D
19. B
20. A
21. A
22. B
23. D
24. B
25. D
26. D
27. B
28. D
29. A
30. A
31. B

32. E
33. C
34. D
35. E

SECTION 6

1. D
2. B
3. C
4. B
5. B
6. E
7. C
8. E
9. B
10. C
11. C
12. C
13. E
14. C
15. E
16. A
17. C
18. E
19. A
20. C
21. C
22. E
23. D
24. C

SECTION 7

1. E
2. C
3. C
4. E

5. B
6. C
7. E
8. A
9. A
10. D
11. C
12. E
13. B
14. E
15. D
16. E

SECTION 8

1. A
2. A
3. E
4. E
5. C
6. D
7. A
8. E
9. D
10. B
11. B
12. C
13. E
14. A
15. A
16. D
17. D
18. A
19. B

SECTION 9

1. A
2. B
3. C
4. D
5. D
6. A
7. C
8. C
9. A
10. E
11. A
12. A
13. B
14. C

ANSWERS AND EXPLANATIONS

SECTION 1

6 Essay

Luis Buñuel hits truth with this statement, bringing up one of the human condition's greatest dilemmas. I think that without memory, we would know nothing, absorb nothing, feel nothing, and be nothing. The only reason humans care about anything, feel anything, or are anything, is because of memories from their own lives.

Memories play a large role in shaping our societies, because we learn from the events of history, and we even shape our governments based on the ideas of ancient Greeks. And most importantly, memories are exactly what make us individuals. For example, our childhood shapes who we are for our whole lives, from things as vital as the thinking process, to things as trivial as eating habits and music taste. We have to remember words in order to speak and we have to remember how to walk as well as the names and faces of our parents.

I have found that love, hate, anger, happiness, sadness, are all caused by remembering what just happened to us. And these emotions would mean nothing if we forgot them an instant after we had them, because they would seem to never existed. Even the greatest suffering would mean nothing if we forgot it seconds later, and if I fell in love with someone, but I forgot about them a second later, it would mean absolutely nothing to me. It's just like the "If a tree falls in the forest and no one sees it, does it make a sound" dilemma. If we experience something and forget it instantly, we can never know and will never know if it existed.

Memory is vital to human existence. In fact, it is human existence. To quote Luis Buñuel, . . . *Memory is our coherence, our reason . . . Without it we are nothing.*

GRADER'S COMMENTS

The essay is scored based on four basic criteria: Topic, Support, Organization, and Language. This essay does well on all counts, so it has earned a 6. It demonstrates an especially strong grasp of the writing assignment, earning high points for topic, support, and organization. The author states a thesis in paragraph 1, and then provides specific, relevant examples in each paragraph that support the idea of memory shaping the individual life. The examples are explained clearly and follow logically.

The writing stays on track, using the writer's previous knowledge to discuss the topic comfortably. The writer uses key phrases such as *and most importantly, for example,* and *I have found* to link and explain connected ideas. Vocabulary is strong (*dilemmas* and *absorb,* for example). The brief discussion of philosophy in the third paragraph shows the writer's attempt to connect the argument to literature. The closing paragraph sums up the writer's opinion. The opening sentence of the third paragraph is unnecessarily passive, but this does not detract from the overall high quality of the essay.

4 ESSAY

Without memory, we are basically nothing. For instance, during the war in 2003, if we had remembered that Saddam Hussein hadn't cooperated last time, we could have gone in and removed him without the hassle of waiting for the weapons inspectors and things might have gone easier.

Another is example is to eat chocolate. Everyone knows that it tastes good. But I would never buy chocolate if I didn't remember how it tasted. In history, as well, such as the French revolution, memory is also vital. The French would not have fought for their freedom in the Revolution unless they remembered what freedom was like or what it would be like as well. Also, scientists wouldn't be able to make new discoveries without the memory, because how else would they remember complicated formulas or even their experiments? They wouldn't. Also, I remember that when I was about three years old, I burned my hand on the stove, and because then I have not placed my hand on a hot stove again. if I had no memory, I would still be burning myself. I believe people learn from their mistakes and this is because of memory.

There is another experience that tells me memory is vital. My grandfather had Alscizmers's disease. He completely lost his memory and didn't even recognize my mother, his own daughter. And this was disturbing because she was his own daughter. My mother said it was like her dad had disappeared completely because he has no memory. He also forgot how to brush his teeth and asked the same question over and over again. It was the opposite of when I burned myself. So memory is vital to human life, and so I agree with Bunuel's idea.

GRADER'S COMMENTS

The essay is scored based on four basic criteria: Topic, Support, Organization, and Language. This author attempted with some success to fulfill the assignment, and the arguments make sense overall. However, no one idea is sufficiently developed and many opinions are lacking supporting examples. The essay presents several logical arguments in the third paragraph, but organization is lacking. The final argument is the most successful as it shows the writer's understanding of the essay topic; however, the organization is confused and this detracts from the strength of the argument.

The language and vocabulary in the essay could be improved. Phrases like *as well, and how else,* and *this is because of* distract the reader from the author's meaning. The tone of the question and answer in the second paragraph is not appropriate for the essay. Many sentences could have been written with more clarity.

Overall, the essay looks like the writer is able to think about difficult issues but unable to express his or her ideas clearly. It would have been a better essay if the writer had spent a few minutes reviewing the completed essay to clarify sentences, add supporting ideas, and improve the vocabulary.

1 ESSAY

I remember songs in my head all the time and there is nothing I can do about it. My favorite songs are not the ones I remember but more than likely some advertisement I heard on the way to school this morning. It seems like things are like that. You have to remember so. Everyone does and then if we didn't remember things we wouldn't really have much thoughts or people who live wouldn't really have very much reasons to make decesions.

Once my fish died and when the fish buried, we didn't like the part when the fish didn't remind us of things. It was sad, like when Roger moved to Dallas. But memory is a funny thing, the way you can't control it or nothing when you really want to.

GRADER'S COMMENTS

The essay is scored based on four basic criteria: Topic, Support, Organization, and Language. In this essay, the author mentions memory, but does not answer the assignment. Nearly every sentence has a grammatical error (*there is nothing I can do about it, we didn't like the part when the fish didn't remind us*), and there are many spelling errors. The story about remembering songs might have been used to create an argument about memory, but the story about the fish makes no sense. The essay lacks a thesis statement and a closing summary. It might have been a better essay if the writer had focused on one story and developed a single basic argument about how memory shapes our lives.

SECTION 2

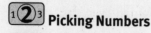 Picking Numbers

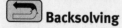 Backsolving

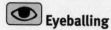 Eyeballing

1. E

Do what's in parentheses first:

$$\left(\frac{1}{5} + \frac{1}{3}\right) \div \frac{1}{2} = \left(\frac{3}{15} + \frac{5}{15}\right) \div \frac{1}{2}$$

$$= \frac{8}{15} \div \frac{1}{2}$$

Then, to divide fractions, invert the one after the division sign and multiply:

$$\frac{8}{15} \div \frac{1}{2} = \frac{8}{15} \times \frac{2}{1} = \frac{16}{15}, \text{ choice (E)}.$$

2. E

Plug in $x = -2$ and see what you get:

$$x^2 - 2x = (-2)^2 - 2(-2)$$

$$= 4 - (-4)$$

$$= 4 + 4$$

$$= 8, \text{ choice (E)}.$$

3. C

To get Vito's rate in pages per hour, take the 96 pages and divide by the time in hours.

The time is given as "2 hours and 40 minutes." Forty minutes is $\frac{2}{3}$ of an hour, so you can express Vito's time as $2\frac{2}{3}$ hours, or $\frac{8}{3}$ hours:

$$\text{Pages per hour} = \frac{96 \text{ pages}}{\frac{8}{3}} \text{ hours}$$

$$= 96 \times \frac{3}{8} = 36, \text{ choice (C)}.$$

4. A

For $\frac{7}{x}$ to be greater than $\frac{1}{4}$, the denominator x has to be less than 4 times the numerator, or 28. And for $\frac{7}{x}$ to be less than $\frac{1}{3}$, the denominator x has to be greater than 3 times the numerator, or 21. Thus, x could be any of the integers 22 through 27, of which there are 6, choice (A).

5. A ①②③

To find the average of three numbers—even if they're algebraic expressions—add them up and divide by 3:

$$\text{Average} = \frac{(2x + 5) + (5x - 6) + (-4x + 2)}{3}$$
$$= \frac{3x + 1}{3}$$
$$= x + \frac{1}{3}, \text{ choice (A)}$$

6. D

$$\text{Percent} \times \text{Whole} = \text{Part:}$$
$$(\text{Percent}) \times 25 = 16$$
$$\text{Percent} = \frac{16}{25} \times 100\% = 64\%, \text{ choice (D)}.$$

7. C 👁

The measures of the interior angles of a triangle add up to 180, so add the two *given* measures and subtract the sum from 180. The difference will be the measure of the third angle:

$$45 + 70 = 115$$
$$180 - 115 = 65$$

8. A ①②③

$$\frac{x^2 + x^2 + x^2}{x^2} = \frac{3x^2}{x^2} = 3$$

9. C

To solve a quadratic equation, put it in the "$ax^2 + bx + c = 0$" form, factor the left side (if you can), and set each factor equal to 0 separately to get the two solutions. To solve $x^2 = 5x - 4$, first rewrite it as $x^2 - 5x + 4 = 0$. Then factor the left side:

$$x^2 - 5x + 4 = 0$$
$$(x - 1)(x - 4) = 0$$
$$x = 1 \text{ or } 4, \text{ so answer choice (C) is correct.}$$

10. A

Picking numbers is the easiest, fastest way to do this problem. Choose a pair of numbers from each set and add them together. If you are unable to prove immediately that a set does not have the property described in the question stem, you may want to choose another pair. In set I, if we add 2 and 4, we get 6. Adding 12 and 8 gives us 20. Adding −2 and 8 gives us 6. Since each sum is a member of the set of even integers, set I seems to be true. For set II, adding 3 and 5 yields 8, which is not an odd integer. Therefore, II is not true. Finally, if we add two primes, say 2 and 3, we get 5. That example is true. If we add 3 and 5, however, we get 8, and 8 is not a prime number. Therefore, only set I has the property, and the answer is (A).

11. E

The best way to deal with changing averages is to use the sum. Use the old average to figure out the total of the first four scores:

Sum of first four scores = (4)(89) = 356

Use the new average to figure out the total he needs after the fifth score:

Sum of five scores = (5)(90) = 450

To get his sum from 356 to 450, Martin needs to score 450 − 356 = 94.

12. C

Don't fall for the trap choice (D): You can't add or subtract percents of different wholes. Let the original price $s = 100$. Reducing s by 25% gives you a sale price of $75. This price is then increased by 20%, so the final price is $90. Since $s = 100$, it's easy to see that this is equal to choice (C), $.90s$.

13. A

The prime factorization of 36 is $2 \times 2 \times 3 \times 3$. That factorization includes two distinct prime factors, 2 and 3.

14. D

The area of a triangle is equal to one-half the base times the height:

$$\text{Area} = \frac{1}{2}(\text{base})(\text{height})$$

$$36 = \frac{1}{2}(9)(\text{height})$$

$$36 = \frac{9}{2}h$$

$$h = \frac{2}{9} \times 36 = 8, \text{ choice (D).}$$

15. C

According to the definition, $x \clubsuit = \frac{x}{4} - \frac{x}{6}$. Set that equal to 3 and solve for x:

$$\frac{x}{4} - \frac{x}{6} = 3$$

$$12\left(\frac{x}{4} - \frac{x}{6}\right) = 12(3)$$

$$3x - 2x = 36$$

$$x = 36, \text{ choice (C)}.$$

16. A

Read carefully. This question's a lot easier than you might think at first. It's asking for the total number of coins, not the total value. q quarters, d dimes, and n nickels add up to a total of $q + d + n$ coins, answer choice (A).

17. E

Use the points where the line crosses the axes—$(-1, 0)$ and $(0, 2)$—to find the slope:

$$\text{Slope} = \frac{y_2 - y_1}{x_2 - x_1} = \frac{2 - 0}{0 - (-1)} = 2$$

The y-intercept is 2. Now plug $m = 2$ and $b = 2$ into the slope-intercept equation form:

$$y = mx + b$$
$$y = 2x + 2, \text{ choice (E)}.$$

18. B

An integer that's divisible by 6 has at least one 2 and one 3 in its prime factorization. An integer that's divisible by 9 has at least two 3s in its prime factorization. Therefore, an integer that's divisible by both 6 and 9 has at least one 2 and two 3s in its prime factorization. That means it is divisible by 2 and 3: $2 \times 3 = 6$, $3 \times 3 = 9$, and $2 \times 3 \times 3 = 18$. It's not necessarily divisible by 12 or 36, each of which includes two 2s in its prime factorization. Thus, I and III can be ruled out, so answer choice (B) is correct.

You could also do this one by picking numbers. Think of a common multiple of 6 and 9 and use it to eliminate some options. $6 \times 9 = 54$ is an obvious common multiple—and it's not divisible by 12 or 36, but it is divisible by 18. The least common multiple of 6 and 9 is 18, which is also divisible by 18. It looks like every common multiple of 6 and 9 is also a multiple of 18.

19. D

The volume of a cube is equal to an edge cubed, so $e^3 = 64$, and each edge of the cube has length 4. If the cube is sliced horizontally in two, each of the resulting solids will have two sides of length 4 and one of length 2. So when they are glued together, the resulting figure will have one edge of length 2, one of length 4, and one of length 4 + 4 or 8.

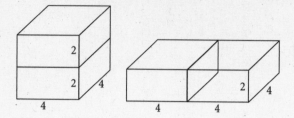

The surface area is the sum of the areas of the solid's six faces. The top and bottom each have area $8 \times 4 = 32$, the front and back each have area $8 \times 2 = 16$, and each side has area $4 \times 2 = 8$. So the surface area of the new solid is $2(32) + 2(16) + 2(8) = 64 + 32 + 16 = 112$, answer choice (D).

20. D 👁

The area of a triangle is equal to one-half the base times the height. You can use any of the three sides of a triangle for the base—each side has a height to go along with it. It doesn't make any difference which base-height pair you use—a triangle has the same area no matter how you figure it. Thus, one-half times PR times QS will be the same as one-half times PS times RT:

$$\frac{1}{2}(PR)(QS) = \frac{1}{2}(PS)(RT)$$

$$\frac{1}{2}(8)(9) = \frac{1}{2}(PS)(7)$$

$$(8)(9) = (PS)(7)$$

$$PS = \frac{72}{7} = 10\frac{2}{7}, \text{ choice (D).}$$

SECTION 3

1. C

The phrase *proves difficult* is a clue: the two missing words have to be nearly opposite in meaning. Choice (C) is correct because few posters would be *intact* if they were meant to be *destroyed*. None of the other choices makes sense: (A), being *returned,* would not stop something from being *recognizable*; (B), being *discarded,* would not necessarily stop something from being *relevant*. This is the case for choices (D) and (E), too.

2. E

The phrases *long considered* and *finally* suggest contrast. The missing word is probably the opposite of *making some headway in its battle against extinction*. Choice (E), *imperiled,* or in danger, is the best answer. (A), *elusive,* means hard to find. (B), *prevalent,* means common. (C), *combative,* means eager to fight. (D), *voracious,* means having a huge appetite.

3. A

The sentence sets up a contrast between the situation before the invention of the tape recorder and the situation after. We need a word that's the opposite of *paraphrased*, which means expressed in different words. Choice (A), *verbatim*, meaning word-for-word, is correct.

4. A

The phrase *encouraged hopes* suggests that the two missing words will be somewhat related in meaning. Choice (A) is the best answer because we expect a *serious* novelist to use *subtle* characterizations. The other choices make less sense; in fact, it's not clear what (C), *accurate*, (D), *fictional*, or (E), *authentic*, characterizations would be. (C), *prolific*, means highly productive. (D), *accomplished*, means skillful, experienced. (E), *reclusive*, means unsociable.

5. C

Words like *unchanging* and *eternal* provide a definition of the missing word, (C), *static*. (D), *holistic*, means functioning as a whole, and (E), *homogeneous*, means all of one kind; neither word implies species being unchanging and *no new species* coming into existence.

6. C

The phrase *failure to* establishes the negative tone of the sentence. An agency ought to fix or get rid of flawed policies. Possible answers for the first blank are (C), *rescind*, or remove, cancel, and (D), *amend*, or fix. Failure to do this is a bad thing, so we need a negative word for the second blank. The best choice is (C), *lackadaisical*, or careless, sloppy.

7. D

Rapid turnover would tend to increase *inconsistency*, so we need a word that means increased or worsened. Choice (D), *exacerbated*, means made worse.

8. C

What claim would be *belied* or contradicted by a record of contributing to only one party? A claim of *impartiality*, of not favoring one side over the other, or choice (C).

BOOK SEQUELS PASSAGES

9. B

When asked for information about one author, eliminate choices that discuss the other author. Be sure that you have each author's position clear in your mind before you tackle the questions. The author of Passage 1 is hostile to the idea of sequels, so you should look for an answer that reflects this attitude. (B) fits well and follows directly from the last sentence. The author of Passage 1 is not concerned with the ease of writing a sequel, (A)—she considers all sequels a bad idea. Author 1 never discusses *The Seven Percent Solution*, so (C) is out. Although the author is indignant, (D), you don't have any information that other readers feel that way. (E) is actually the opposite of the truth, since the author states that sequels are written to entice readers of the original books.

10. A

The author uses Margaret Mitchell as an example of an author who has had a sequel written to her book. The author states that if the authors and the books that are the subjects of sequels were untalented or unknown, this practice wouldn't be so bad. But, the author goes on to state, that's not the case. From this, you can infer that the author regards Margaret Mitchell as talented or well known, (A). While the author mentions only one novel, *Gone with the Wind*, you can't infer that Mitchell wrote only one book, (B). The passage doesn't discuss the relative skills of the authors she mentions, (C), or the relative fame of the author and her book, (D). (E) might be tempting for the unwary test taker; the passage says that the authors of sequels, rather than of the original books, will disappoint readers.

11. D

Always read the context in which the vocabulary word appears—the context for this word is: *What unalloyed delight for those who have read* . . . . You can tell immediately that the adjective *unalloyed* must have a positive connotation, since it modifies a positive noun—*delight*. It wouldn't make sense to say, "awful" *delight* or "unpleasant" *delight*. Since *delight* means high satisfaction or great pleasure, you need an adjective of equal intensity to modify it. Therefore, you can eliminate all negative or neutral words, like (A) and (E). (B), (C), and (D) are all positive, but (D) is the best match here. *Unalloyed* means not mixed with anything else. (You might be familiar with the term *alloy* to refer to a blend of metals.) So *unalloyed* means pure.

12. E

Remember, author 1 is against sequels; author 2 contends that fans will be delighted that there's a sequel to Arthur Conan Doyle's Sherlock Holmes stories. So author 2 would almost certainly disagree with author 1's comments that sequels are always disappointing. (E) captures this by noting the delight that readers will get when they read a sequel to a book they love. You don't have any reason to believe that author 1 will change her mind, (A), or even concede that some readers will be disappointed, (D). Since author 2 never discusses *Gone with the Wind*, there's no support for (B). Finally, you can rule out (C) since the tone is so extreme.

THE WOLVES PASSAGE

This Science passage is written by a naturalist who recounts how he went into the wilderness and, through trial and error, experimentation and observation, learned some new and surprising things about the way wolves live. For example, wolves are a lot less suspicious and aggressive than people think they are, and contrary to popular belief, wolf families are not nomadic—they live and stay in territories with very definite boundaries.

13. C

In the first paragraph, the author explains how the wolves were aware of his presence but ignored him. That's why the author's precautions were *superfluous*. (C) basically paraphrases that idea: the author's precautions were unnecessary because the wolves weren't interested in him. (A) doesn't work because the author never really says how long it was before he encountered the wolves. (B) is out because the author never mentions any wild animals other than wolves. Contrary to (D), even after the author interfered with the wolves' boundaries, they never bothered him. (E) is out because it's never suggested that the wolves have poor eyesight.

14. A

The author's basic point in the first paragraph is that he was surprised at the way the wolves behaved toward him: they sized him up quickly right at the beginning and, from then on, ignored him. He found this behavior *disconcerting*, or *strange*, as (A) puts it. (B) sounds exaggerated—the author never really suggests that he was fearful of attack. With (C), the author says that he took longer to assess the wolves than they took to assess him, but his basic point is not to emphasize his own ignorance. (D) doesn't work because the wolves left the author alone—precautions weren't necessary. (E), like (B), isn't suggested—that the author thinks he has a lot of courage.

15. D

In the third paragraph, the author describes how the wolf was so *preoccupied* that he came within 15 yards of his tent without seeing it. It wasn't until the author made noise that the wolf suddenly became aware of its surroundings. (D) paraphrases this idea: that the wolf was not *on its guard*—it was self-absorbed. The author expresses no surprise about the wolf traveling alone, (A), or hunting at night, (C). As for (B), the point is not that the wolf lacks energy—it does respond when the author startles it. (E) is out because the author doesn't mention any fear here.

16. C

The first sentence of the third paragraph describes the wolf as *anxious to go home to bed*. The idea is that he was *eager* to get home, (C). *Distressed*, (A), *afraid*, (B), *uneasy*, (D), and *worried*, (E), are other definitions of anxious, but they don't fit the idea in the sentence.

17. C

In paragraph 4, the author explains that one of the things he learned is that, contrary to popular belief, the wolves were *settled beasts* rather than *nomadic hunters*. The idea, in other words, is that the wolves were *stable*, (C)—they had established homes. *Decided*, (A), and *resolute*, (B), are other meanings of *settled*, but they don't work in the sentence. Neither *inflexible*, (D), nor *confident*, (E), fits when plugged in.

18. A

The idea at the beginning of paragraph 4 is that the wolves, contrary to what people generally think, are not nomadic. (A) catches the idea: the author is countering a *popular myth* or belief about the behavior of wolves. (B) is tricky, but there's really no *paradox* or ambiguity: the idea is that the wolves are NOT nomadic. (C) is tricky too, but the passage never says that the idea that wolves are nomadic is an *established* fact. As for (D), there's no indication that what the author observed—that the wolves live in established territories—is *an exception to a general rule*. (E) doesn't work because there's really no *summary* of any conclusions in the quoted lines. (A) is the best choice.

19. B

In the middle of paragraph 5, the author describes how the wolf family regularly made the rounds of their lands and *freshened up the boundary markers*. He guessed that this was done because there were other wolves living in adjacent areas, although he never saw any sign of trouble between the neighboring wolf families. Then you get the quoted idea: since he never witnessed any disputes, he figured that it was all basically a ritual activity. (B) catches the idea. The idea that the activity was a ritual isn't related to the fact that it was repeated, (A); that the boundaries were marked by *geographic features*, (C); that they *were marked at the same time each week*, (D)—that's never suggested—or that *the whole family* participated, (E). The wrong choices miss the point.

20. C

One of the author's discoveries is that the wolves live in territories with clearly marked boundaries. So, contrary to what most people think, they aren't nomadic—they don't travel endlessly *from place to place* looking for food and sleeping in new areas. The idea in (C), if it were true, would contradict or weaken that idea. The idea in (A) would strengthen the thesis—if there were disputes over boundaries, that would suggest that the wolves are protective of their territory. The idea in (B)—the particular size of the wolves' territory—is irrelevant—it doesn't really relate to the question. (D) is tricky, but it doesn't work: the author finds that the wolves are territorial even though they actually don't have conflicts with their neighbors. The idea in (E) is irrelevant: the passage never discusses whether or not wolves are *alert when encountering other animals*.

21. D

The phrase *invisible wall* occurs in paragraph 7, and the point is that the wolf, who was plodding home as preoccupied as usual, was suddenly stopped in its tracks when it encountered the spot where the author had left his own markings. So the idea about the invisible wall is that the wolf was stopped suddenly, (D), as if it had suddenly banged up against it. The idea of an invisible wall has nothing to do with delight in getting *the wolf's attention*, (A), *annoyance* on the part of the wolf, (B), *high speed*, (C)—the wolf was *padding*, not running—or *exhaustion after a night of hunting*, (E).

22. B

In the very same sentence in paragraph 7, the author says that the wolf, upon finding the author's marks, immediately became bewildered. (B) restates that. The passage says nothing about *combativeness*, (A), *anxiety*, (C), *wariness*, (D), or *dread*, (E).

23. B

Temerity is a tough vocabulary word—it means impetuousness or rashness, (B). But you really didn't have to know that definition to pick the right answer. All you have to do with Vocabulary-in-Context questions is plug in each of the answer choices, and eliminate the ones that don't fit the sentence's meaning. If you do that here, none of the other choices work. With (A), it's not that the author's being discourteous. That sounds strange. Rather, he's being too bold—only (B) makes sense. Remember, if you're stumped with any hard question, work backward by eliminating any wrong choices you can—and then guess.

24. B

At the end of paragraph 8, the author states that he turned his back on the wolf *in an effort to break the impasse*. In other words, he did it to bring about a *change in the situation*, (B). Nothing suggests that he did it to show *his power over the wolf*, (A); to make the *wolf recognize his existence*, (C)—the wolf already did; to look for a *weapon*, (D); or to *avoid the wolf's hypnotic gaze*, (E).

SECTION 4

1. D

This is a straightforward substitution problem. Plug in the given values and remember your order of operations (PEMDAS): $3^2 - 2(1) = 9 - 2(1) = 9 - 2 = 7$, choice (D).

2. D

The answer choices are given in the form $y = mx + b$, where m is the slope and b is the y-intercept. The y-intercept is clearly 3, so the answer must be (C), (D), or (E). You can either estimate the slope by looking at the graph, or calculate it. To calculate it, you first need the x and y values of two points on the graph, for instance, (0, 3) and (6, 0). $\frac{0-3}{6-0} = \frac{-3}{6} = \frac{-1}{2}$, so the slope of the graph must be $\frac{-1}{2}$, choice (D).

3. D

First, translate the question into a system of equations: $q = r - 4$ and $r = 6 + s$. Now plug $s = 2$ into the second equation to get $r = 6 + 2 = 8$, and plug this into the first equation to find $q = 8 - 4 = 4$, choice (D).

4. D

Each month has 15 days, so 700 days is $\frac{700}{15}$ months. Each year has 9 months, so $\frac{700}{15}$ months is $\frac{700}{(15 \times 9)} = \frac{700}{135} = 5\frac{5}{27}$. This means 5 full years have gone by.

5. A

The square of a positive number is positive. The square of a negative number is positive. The square of zero is zero. Therefore, statement I, which presents a negative number, cannot be the square of any real number x. I cannot be the value of $f(x)$ for any real value of x. II is the result of $f(0)$. III is the result of $f(\pm\sqrt{2.3})$. So answer choice (A) is correct.

6. A

The mode is the number that appears most often in a set of data. The largest number of people who collected the same amount of trash was the 12 people who collected 10 pieces of trash, so 10 is the mode of this set of data, choice (A).

7. D

The total amount of trash collected by the 30 participants was $12(10) + 9(15) + 4(20) + 4(25) + 1(30) = 120 + 135 + 80 + 100 + 30 = 465$ pieces of trash. The goal of the drive was to collect 500 pieces of trash, so we need to figure out what percent 465 is of 500. $\frac{465}{500} = .93$, so the participants reached 93% of the goal, choice (D).

8. C

The total amount of trash collected by the 30 participants was $12(10) + 9(15) + 4(20) + 4(25) + 1(30) = 120 + 135 + 80 + 100 + 30 = 465$ pieces of trash. Since there were 30 participants, the average amount of trash collected by each one was $\frac{465}{30} = 15.5$ pieces, choice (C).

9. 115

Since lines p and q are parallel, we can use the rule about alternate interior angles to fill in the following:

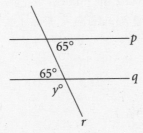

Since the angle marked $y°$ is adjacent and supplementary to a 65° angle, $y = 180 - 65 = 115$.

10. .04

Be careful. The question is not asking: "What is $\frac{1}{4}$ of 16?" It's asking: "What is $\frac{1}{4}$ *percent* of 16?" One-fourth of 1 percent is 0.25%, or 0.0025:

$$\frac{1}{4}\% \text{ of } 16 = 0.0025 \times 16 = .04$$

11. 11, 13, 17, 19, 23, 29, 31, 37, 41, 43, or 47

In order for each of these fractions to be in its simplest form, a would have to be a number that has no prime factors in common with 3, 5, or 14. So find a value between 2 and 50 that fits that description. Your best bet is to use a prime number, such as 11. That's one of 11 acceptable answers.

12. $\frac{2}{5}$ or .4

If there are 36 men and 24 women in the group, then the total number of group members is 60. The women make up $\frac{24}{60}$ of the group. Since this fraction cannot be gridded, reduce it or turn it into a decimal. To reduce it, divide both the numerator and denominator by 12, and you end up with $\frac{2}{5}$. To turn it into a decimal, divide 60 into 24, and you end up with .4.

13. 8

To evaluate this expression when $s = 9$, simply plug in 9 for s. Substituting 9 into the expression yields:

$$\frac{3(9) + 5}{4} = \frac{27 + 5}{4} = \frac{32}{4} = 8$$

14. 4 ①②③

The easiest way to get the answer here is to pick numbers. Pick a number for x that has a remainder of 2 when divided by 6, such as 8. Increase the number you picked by 8. In this case, $8 + 8 = 16$. Now divide 16 by 6, which gives you 2 remainder 4. Therefore, the answer is 4.

15. 250

Percent × Whole = Part:
(15%) × (take-home pay) = $37.50
(0.15) × (take-home pay) = $37.50
take-home pay $= \dfrac{\$37.50}{0.15} = \$250.00$

16. 9

The area of a triangle is equal to one-half the base times the height. Here, the base (along the x-axis) is 6 and the height (perpendicular to the base—i.e., parallel to the y-axis) is 3, so the area is $\frac{1}{2}bh = \frac{1}{2}(6)(3) = 9$.

17. 64

You cannot find the area of the square without finding the length of a side, so use the information you are given about the rectangles to find the length of the square's sides. Since the rectangles have the same dimensions, we know that the side of the square must be twice the length of the shorter side of either rectangle. The side of the square must also be the longer side of either rectangle. Call the length of a side of the square, which is also the length of a longer side of either rectangle, x. Then the shorter side of either rectangle is $\frac{x}{2}$. Now use the formula for the perimeter:

$$P = 2l + 2w$$

For either rectangle, you have:

$$24 = 2x + 2\left(\frac{x}{2}\right)$$
$$24 = 2x + x$$
$$24 = 3x$$
$$8 = x$$

To find the area of the square, simply multiply 8 by 8. The answer is 64.

18. 203

This looks like a physics question, but in fact it's just a "plug-in-the-number-and-see-what-you-get" question. Be sure you plug 95 in for C (not F):

$$C = \frac{5}{9}(F - 32)$$

$$95 = \frac{5}{9}(F - 32)$$

$$\frac{9}{5} \times 95 = F - 32$$

$$F - 32 = 172$$

$$F = 171 + 32 = 203$$

SECTION 5

1. C

In this sentence, the subject *sound* lacks a verb. The word *blocked* is not a verb; it's the past participle of the verb, which is used as an adjective. Look for choices that offer *was blocked*. (B) keeps the original problem. It also unnecessarily changes the preposition *by* to the longer *as a result of*. In general, the SAT prefers sentences that are more concise. (C) correctly uses *was*. (D) gives you *was*, but makes a mess of the meaning of the sentence. (E) has the same problem as (D), even though it's expressed a little differently.

2. D

Here, the pronoun *who* is incorrectly used to refer to phone conversations. For this clause, look for choices that replace *who*. (C), (D), and (E) are all possibilities. (B) uses *whom,* which should refer to people, incorrectly. (C) uses *that* but changes the meaning of the sentence. (D) correctly uses *that*. (E) changes the meaning of the sentence.

3. E

The comparative adjective *more* is used to compare two people, places, or things; *most* is used to compare more than two. Here, you are comparing Brando to any other person on the set individually. (E) is correct. (B) tries to form the comparative by adding the suffix *-er* to *crucial*. This is incorrect. (C) changes the meaning of the sentence. (D) is grammatically incorrect and distorts the meaning.

4. C

Be sure that each verb tense is the appropriate choice in the context of the sentence. Because this sentence talks about the Renaissance, which is long over, it requires simple past tenses. Look for a choice that provides it. (B) uses the incorrect pronoun to refer to people. You need the correct form of *who*. Choice (C) provides the simple past tense that you are looking for. (D) incorrectly uses *which* to refer to people. (E) uses the wrong tense.

5. B

Remember that *neither . . . nor* and *either . . . or* work in pairs. In this sentence, you have *neither . . . or*, so you need to find a choice that gives you *neither . . . nor*. Two choices start with *neither*—(B) and (D). (B) correctly pairs *neither . . . nor* and maintains the meaning of the sentence. (D) correctly pairs *neither . . . nor*, but it adds unnecessary wordiness. While (E) gives you *either . . . or*, when you read it into the sentence, you see that it makes the sentence grammatically incorrect. In (C), the incorrect pairing of *either . . . nor* makes this an easy choice to eliminate.

6. D

In this sentence, you have a series that should be written the same way to maintain parallelism— *the chaos of war, the anxiety of the people*, and *the irrational behavior*. Look for that parallel structure among the choices. (B) corrects the parallelism but adds the incorrect present tense verb *is*. Because choice (C) maintains the incorrect *they showed*, you know it's wrong. It also changes the meaning of the sentence, because here it's the escalation and not the behavior that is irrational. Choice (D) does what you predicted you'd need—it fixes the parallelism problem while keeping the meaning of the sentence intact. (E) uses an incorrect verb tense.

7. A

This sentence is correct as written because it is both grammatically structured and concise. The comparison between *ideas* and *writing* is in parallel form. (B) is wordy. (C) uses an incorrect tense, *having written*. (D) uses the past tense *was*, which is inconsistent with the non-underlined tense *is* in the sentence. (E) is grammatically correct but is less concise than (A). On the SAT, if two versions are both grammatically and logically correct, choose the more concise one as the right answer.

8. B

Be on the lookout for words and phrases that are acceptable in speech but not in writing. The expression *deep down there* is too colloquial for written English. (B) eliminates the colloquialism and also cleans up the possessive to make it less wordy. (C) uses the incorrect comparative form of the adjective. (D) changes the meaning of the sentence. (E) cleans up the possessive but doesn't correct the colloquialism.

9. A

If you think there are no errors in a sentence, there's at least a 20 percent chance that you're right. Check the sentence for common errors if you're not sure—subject-verb, pronoun agreement, parallelism, logical comparisons. If this all checks out, choose (A). (B) substitutes the incorrect conjunction *but* for the correct one. It also incorrectly changes the past progressive tense to the simple past. (C) changes the correct preposition *about* to *for*. (D), the subject, *three women*, is plural so you need the plural verb, *were*, not *was*. (E) uses the wrong verb tense and changes the meaning of the sentence by changing *discussing* to *in discussion*.

10. A

Be sure that idioms are expressed clearly and precisely. In (B), *there* is used without any proper antecedent—what place is referred to? (C) expresses a different idea. (D) makes no sense; what is *farther* a comparison to? (E) also expresses a different meaning.

11. D

This sentence meant to compare two dental procedures—root canal and extraction—instead it compares root canals to chewing problems. Only (C), (D), and (E) correctly begin with *an extraction*, eliminating (A) and (B). (B) is also wordy. (C) uses the incorrect verb tense. (D) is what you were looking for. (E) reverses the cause/effect—an extraction can lead to chewing problems according to the original sentence. This choice has chewing problems leading to an extraction.

12. E

What are the possible issues? An adjective, a past-tense verb, a prepositional phrase, and a phrase completing a comparison are underlined. (A) uses an appropriate adjective to describe the noun *series*. (B) correctly uses the past tense. (C) uses the idiomatically correct preposition. (D) correctly completes the comparison begun with *as easily*. Therefore, (E) is the right answer: No error.

13. C

You have a clear indication of time in this sentence—last month. Make sure that the verb or verbs that refer to this event are in the simple past tense. (C) is in the progressive past tense and needs to be changed to the simple past—*graduated*. (A) uses the correct simple past tense form of the verb. (B) is the correct comparative form of the adjective. (D) is the correct preposition to use with *graduate*.

14. D

The adjective *deep*, (D), is incorrectly used to modify *sleeping*. Remember, adjectives modify nouns, and adverbs modify verbs, adjectives, and other adverbs. (A) is an idiomatically correct prepositional phrase that explains where the commotion took place. (B) is correctly used to indicate that the hens and the rooster were part of an ongoing ruckus. In (C), the past tense verb *woke* is correct.

15. C

The general rule for forming comparatives is to use *more* if the adjective has more than one syllable and the suffix *-er* if the adjective has one syllable. In this sentence, (C) does both things—it places *more* in front of *small* and adds the suffix *-er* to it. Because *small* has one syllable, the correct comparative form is *smaller*. In (A), *when* is used correctly to refer to time. (B) correctly uses the past tense form of the verb *to look*. (D), *emanating,* is a good vocabulary word, correctly used. It means *to come forth*.

16. D

Whenever you see an unlined pronoun, make sure that it has a clearly defined antecedent. The sentence contains two plural nouns, *necklaces* and *customers*, that *they* might refer to. However, neither *necklaces* nor *customers* is a logical subject for the verb *restock*. (D) constitutes an ambiguous pronoun error because there is no word in the sentence that it can logically refer to.

17. E

The sentence is correct as written. In (A), *completed* is the correct form to use in *could have completed*. (B) correctly modifies the adjective *long*. (C) is in the correct tense because it happened before *he might have succeeded*. (D) is the correct form of the adverb, modifying *started*.

18. D

The pronoun *their* is plural, but it refers to the pronoun *each,* which is singular. If you were correcting this sentence, you would replace (D)'s *their* with *his* or *her* depending on who is on the team. In (A), *about* is one of the prepositions that can be used with *concerned*. In (B), the preposition *on* is used correctly. In (C), the past tense verb correctly expresses the time indicated in the sentence.

19. B

Use *fewer* for countable nouns and *less* for uncountable nouns. *Adults* is a countable noun, so (B) is incorrect. (A) is the correct word to refer to a place. (C) agrees with the singular subject *environment*. In (D), the preposition *to* is correctly used with *conducive*.

20. A

(A) is a compound object using a noun, *Hilary*, and a pronoun, *I*. Read the sentence without *Hilary*. You would never say: *Dad asked I*, so you need the objective pronoun *me*. (B) uses the correct simple past tense. (C) uses the possessive correctly. (D) is idiomatically correct.

21. A

This sentence needs a verb in the past perfect tense to indicate that an action was completed at some point in the past before something else happened, so (A) is incorrect. Here, the water rose and then the governor ordered the evacuation. The correct form of the irregular verb *rise* is *had risen.* (B) is idiomatically correct usage. (C) uses the past tense correctly. (D) is idiomatically correct.

22. B

The phrase and clause *of concert-goers who waited hours for the entrance of their favorite music group* comes between the subject and verb. The singular subject *list* needs a singular verb, and so (B) should be *includes.* (A) is the right relative pronoun to refer to people and correctly uses the past tense. (C) is idiomatically correct. (D) uses the correct pronoun.

23. D

Make sure that all underlined words are used correctly. In this sentence, the author meant to use *indeterminate* or *undetermined,* which mean not yet decided. Instead, he used *indecisive,* (D), which means uncertain or vague. (A) is the correct possessive pronoun to refer to the university. (B) correctly uses the past tense. (C) is the correct verb form.

24. B

Remember that certain words go together; for example, *not only . . . but also; more . . . than.* The addition of *like,* (B), is incorrect and it has to be omitted to make this sentence correct. (A) is correct in the present tense. (C) is the right conjunction. (D) is idiomatically correct.

25. D

The sentence begins with the impersonal pronoun *one* and then switches to the personal pronoun *you.* You have to change *you,* (D), to *one* for consistency. (A) is correctly in the present progressive. (B) uses the idiomatically correct preposition. (C) is idiomatically correct.

26. D

Make sure all subjects and verbs agree. *Books* is plural, so (D), *interests,* needs to be changed to *interest* to agree with the plural subject. Don't be confused by the relative pronoun *that.* (A) is the right preposition. (B) correctly uses the present tense. (C) is the right plural pronoun to refer to *students.*

27. B

If you're not sure there's an error, check each underlined part of the sentence. (B)'s adverb *where* means in what place. A plan is not a place, so you need to change *where* to *in which* to make this sentence correct. (A) is appropriately in the past tense. (C) is idiomatically correct. (D) is the right preposition.

28. D

Each verb must accurately express time. Something that happened in 1750 needs a past tense verb. In this sentence, (D)'s *will be* is the future tense. (A) idiomatically expresses the time period. (B) uses the correct words. (C) is an appropriate transition word.

29. A

If you find two elements in the sentence that are expressing the same thought, you need to eliminate one of them. In this sentence, *both* and *as well as* are saying the same thing, creating a redundancy. You need to eliminate one, and the only one that is underlined is *both,* (A). (B) is correctly in the perfect tense, since it is an ongoing obsession. (C) uses the idiomatically correct preposition. (D) is properly in the past tense.

30. A

To determine what logically follows the first sentence, read through the first paragraph to see what ideas are introduced. The paragraph goes on to describe how winter is viewed by some as cold, snowy, and bleak. (A) introduces this. (B) is true, but irrelevant here. (C) is opposite in meaning to the passage; the author clearly likes winter. (D) is out of scope; the author never states what season people prefer. In addition, this sentence doesn't introduce the ideas that follow in the paragraph. (E) brings in an idea from paragraph 3 that is out of place here.

31. B

To combine the sentences, you must determine their relationship. (B) correctly combines the sentences by subordinating the second clause and replacing the ambiguous pronouns *them* and *us.* (A) doesn't correct the ambiguity or the inconsistency between *them* and *us.* (C) badly distorts the meaning. (D) omits the idea that the *opportunity* for activity is provided. (E) is a run-on sentence with a comma splice.

32. E

Sentence 10 starts with the pronoun *we* and then switches to *people.* (E) correctly uses *people* as the subject of the sentence. (B) changes the meaning by stating a fact instead of stating that people *complain* about this fact. (C) inserts the transition word *therefore,* which incorrectly sets up a causal relationship with sentence 9. (D) incorrectly sets up a causal relationship within sentence 10.

33. C

Paragraph 4 generally uses present tense, but sentence 13 uses present progressive. (C) correctly uses the present tense. (A) eliminates the parallelism in the list of nouns (*a fire, hot chocolate*, and *board games*). (B) is incorrect—*family* is a singular noun. (D) and (E) make unnecessary changes.

34. D

The original sentence is unclear about what is being compared: how aware we are in winter compared to how aware we are the rest of the year. (D) clarifies this by moving the *than . . .* closer to *more . . .* and by adding *we are during* to complete the second half of that thought. (B) starts to correct the problem, but *protection of our home* is ambiguous. (C) mixes the ideas of protection and companionship together, making them less clear. (E) is another partial correction, but it loses part of the original meaning.

35. E

The essay claims most other people don't appreciate winter as much as they should and details three reasons why the writer prefers winter. (E) is a logical conclusion to this reasoning. (A) is a change of subject. (B) might be added in the second paragraph, but not here, where evening snowfall is discussed. (C) could be appropriate close to the first sentence and (D) in the third paragraph.

SECTION 6

1. D

The word in the first blank has to be similar in meaning to *controversy*: (C), *belligerent*, (D), *scandalous*, and (E), *provocative*, would fit. The band wouldn't do this if they didn't find that the strategy worked, so (B), *rewarding*, and (D), *effective*, fit for the second blank. Only (D) fits for both blanks.

2. B

The correct answer is implied by *numerous scribbled edits that cover even his supposed final drafts*. In other words, Joyce attached great importance to (B), *revision*. A *contrivance*, (A), is a gadget or an invention. A *disavowal*, (E), is a refusal to confirm the truth of something.

3. C

The key is that the players *now charge for their signatures*. Either the fans who believe that the players are not "greedy" would be "surprised" or "disappointed," or the fans who believe that the players are not "ungreedy" would be "confirmed." Choice (C) fits the former prediction.

4. B

The words *though* and *absence* indicate contrast, so the missing word has to be nearly opposite in meaning to *isolation and the longing for connection*. Choice (B), *fraternity*—brotherhood or fellowship—is the best choice. Choice (D) may be tempting, but the term *socialism* refers to a specific set of political and economic doctrines, not just to any sort of society.

5. B

The part of the sentence after the semicolon basically defines the missing word. The word is (B), *calculated*, consciously planned. (A), *incendiary*, means inflaming; (C), *facetious*, means joking; (D), *scrupulous*, means honest; and (E), *impromptu*, means unplanned.

HELIUM PASSAGE

6. E

Ramsay appears toward the middle of the passage after the author mentions that scientists doubted that helium exists only on the sun. Since Ramsay's experiment with naturally occurring Earth minerals occurs in the next sentence, the correct answer will probably be something that cites discovering helium on Earth, and (E) fits this well. The wrong answers here all misuse details from other parts of the passage. Ramsay did not repeat Janssen's experiment, Lockyer did, (A). Ramsay's chief contribution was to find helium on Earth; the fact that it was found in uranium minerals is secondary to this larger concern, (B). Ramsay did not identify the gas as being helium; Crookes did, (C). Finally, Ramsay was not involved with detecting helium on the sun; Janssen and Lockyer were, (D).

7. C

The passage states that Janssen and Lockyer observed the sun using their spectroscopes and discovered a new yellow line that belonged to an unknown element. Reading the next sentence reveals that Janssen and Lockyer's work was doubted by many other scientists, (C). Watch out for incorrectly used details: Lockyer repeated Janssen's experiment, but it is not stated that other scientists repeated the experiment incorrectly, (A). Other scientists were skeptical, but this doesn't mean they thought the methodology behind the experiments was unsound, (B); for example, perhaps they thought the results were interpreted incorrectly. Although it is mentioned that Janssen did his experiment during a solar eclipse, the author does not mention that this was necessary for the experiment, (D). (E) is pretty far out-of-scope; using outdated equipment is never mentioned in the passage.

LORETTA'S VISIT PASSAGE

8. E

In the fourth sentence, we learn that the reasons for their separation is *lost in the mists of family lore*. In other words, no one knows the original cause of the estrangement, (E). The author doesn't tell us how Grandmama treated Uncle Martin, (A). (B) is too extreme, since Loretta is also visiting the city to spend time exploring it with the author. The author doesn't tell us what led to the impending reunion between Loretta and Grandmama, (C), or anything about how busy Loretta is, (D).

9. B

The context for this word is: *The rift that began for reasons lost in the mists of family lore has continued to this day.* Reading the sentence following this one is helpful: *I'll wager that Loretta can't even remember why she and Grandmama haven't spoken in all this time.* So there's been a *break* in relations between Grandmama and Loretta, (B). A *motion*, (A), between the two doesn't make sense. *Revelry*, (C), and *clarity*, (D), are both too positive for this situation. *Discussion*, (E), also doesn't fit for people that are angry with one another.

THE COLD WAR PASSAGE

The author of this passage has one overarching strategy: Set up the arguments of the revisionist historians and then knock them down. Paragraph 1 explains the things that, according to the revisionists, could have been done to avoid the Cold War, which are 1) the U.S. could have just accepted Soviet domination in Eastern Europe, 2) the U.S. could have given them money for reconstruction, and 3) the U.S. could have given up its monopoly of the bomb. Paragraphs 2 and 3 outline the author's refutation of these arguments; he concentrates on the American political atmosphere as the main reason that the revisionists' ideas were not really workable at the time. Revisionists, he then asserts in paragraph 4, would reject this politics-based argument and claim instead that it was the economic situation that forced American policy-makers to oppose the Soviets. The author, of course, then knocks down this new argument; it is contradictory, he says, to say that American officials were caught in an economic tide and then to blame them for not doing things differently. The author concludes in the final paragraph by stating that there was essentially no way, given the climate in the Soviet Union, that the Cold War could have been avoided.

10. C

As we noted above, the author of this passage is primarily engaged in setting up and knocking down the arguments of the revisionist historians of the Cold War. This makes (C) correct and (E) wrong (the author is definitely not interested in reconciling his view with that of the revisionists). (A) is wrong because the ideas of the revisionists are not, as far as we know, a popular myth. (B) is out because the author is defending historical figures—the policy-makers—for what they did, not criticizing them. (D) is too neutral a choice for this passage; the author does engage in analysis of the era of the beginning of the Cold War, but his purpose is to do far more than just analyze events. He wants to poke holes in revisionist theories.

11. C

When revisionists say that the U.S. could have *recognized* the Soviet influence in Eastern Europe, they mean that the U.S. could have formally *acknowledged* this Soviet presence, so (C) is correct.

12. C

Look back to the second half of the second paragraph. The author says there that Roosevelt could never have recognized a Soviet Eastern Europe because the American people did not like the idea of the Soviets holding sway in that region. In particular, the president would have lost the votes of the Polish-Americans who, you can infer, did not want the Soviets controlling their *old country*. (C) spells out this point. Each of the other choices, (A), (B), (D), and (E), is a misreading of the context of the sentence about the Polish-American voters.

13. E

In the second and third paragraphs, the author refutes the suggestions of the revisionists primarily by saying that the policy-makers couldn't do what was necessary to avoid the Cold War because the American people were against it. The assumption the author makes is that the policy-makers *could not have been expected to ignore public opinion,* (E). The author never says in the second and third paragraphs that the Soviets were to blame for failed U.S. peace initiatives, (A), or that none of the alternatives would work, (C)—what he does say, in a later paragraph, is that if peace initiatives had not run aground due to American politics, then they would have run aground due to the Soviet climate. The author also does not say in the second and third paragraphs that the American public was *well informed,* (B), or *overwhelmingly opposed to seeking peace,* (D); all we know is that they opposed Soviet influence in Eastern Europe as well as the idea of giving up the atom bomb monopoly.

14. C

This question is closely linked to the previous one. The author refers to the *certain constraints* at the end of the third paragraph, in the midst of the discussion on the impact of public opinion on the policy-makers. From context, then, you know that the constraints the author is talking about are the opinions of the people—in other words, *the views of the electorate,* (C). If you didn't put the sentence about *constraints* in context, (A), (B), (D), and (E) might have looked appealing.

15. E

This question centers on the fourth paragraph, which is where the author explains the revisionists' view that American policy-makers decided to oppose the Soviet Union because Soviet expansion could jeopardize U.S. trade and investment opportunities in Eastern Europe and elsewhere. (E) captures this idea. The author says nothing about illegal trading activities, (A), nor does he indicate whether or not the Soviets knew about the negative impact they could have on the American economy, (B). (C) is out because the Soviet Union was not recognized by the United States, so this could not possibly have had anything to do with the origin of the Cold War. (D) is wrong because there is no evidence in the paragraph to support it.

16. A

The author poses the question in order to show that there is a problem with the revisionists' economic interpretation of the Cold War: You can't blame the policy-makers if they didn't have any control. Thus, the question serves to *point out an inconsistency*, (A), in the revisionists' position. (D) might be tempting since the revisionists' view is pretty cynical, but the author is questioning that view here, not summing it up.

THE JAMES WELDON JOHNSON PASSAGE

Johnson, the author of this autobiographical piece, does not just describe the experience he had watching the piano player playing rag-time; he also uses the scene as a jumping-off point from which to comment on the origin of rag-time (second paragraph), to disparage American musicians for refusing to accept rag-time (third paragraph), and to speculate on what the piano player could have amounted to under different circumstances (fourth paragraph).

17. C

The author's initial impression of rag-time can be found in the first paragraph. He emphasizes how the beat demanded a physical response and meshed with the *dissonant harmonies*, etc., to produce a *curious effect*. (C) is the correct answer. The only other choice that has anything to do with the first paragraph is (B), which is wrong because the audience is said to have applauded the singer's dance steps, not the rag-time music.

18. E

Let's go through the choices one-by-one, keeping in mind that we're focusing exclusively on the first paragraph. Although the piano player is *master of a good deal of technique*, choice (A) is too extreme to be correct. We know nothing in the first paragraph of the author's expectations of rag-time, so (B) is out, too. (C), (D), and (E) are different interpretations of the author's description of the piano player's playing. While it is certainly true that rag-time has dissonant harmonies and jumps from one key to another, you cannot infer from this that rag-time violates every rule of musical composition, (C), or that it has no melody at all, (D). (E) is correct since the narrator notes that *the accents fell in the most unexpected places.*

19. A

In the context of the phrase *questionable resorts about Memphis and St. Louis*, the word questionable means *disreputable*, (A).

20. C

Choice (B) might have jumped right out at you since the narrator's perspective in paragraph 1 is that of a mesmerized spectator, but his perspective in paragraphs 2 and 3 changes. He steps back from the description of his first encounter with rag-time and begins to discuss rag-time's history, appeal, and impact on the contemporary musical scene. Therefore, (C) is the correct answer. (A) is wrong because the author is not impartial; he thinks highly of rag-time. Watching rag-time playing is not a *unique experience*, which eliminates (D). As for (E), the narrator says nothing about his youth in the second and third paragraphs.

21. C

The narrator argues in the third paragraph that rag-time should not be ignored or dismissed by American musicians just because it is popular. All great music, he states, comes from the hearts of the people. In other words, he is saying that the *conservative and condescending attitude* of the American musicians is misguided, (C). There is no evidence in the third paragraph to support any of the other choices. (B) is perhaps the most tempting since the author talks in the third paragraph about rag-time's popularity in Europe, but it seems as though American musicians do know about rag-time's popularity and find it distasteful.

22. E

This question is a follow-up on the previous one. The author's argument in the third paragraph is that music should not be dismissed by serious musicians just because it happens to be popular. (E) paraphrases this idea. (A) stretches the author's argument way too far. (B) is wrong because the author does not try to establish criteria for musical greatness. (C) focuses too narrowly on the author's mention of the fact that rag-time was popular abroad. (D) is clearly wrong since rag-time gained popularity even though it had not been *taken up by a musical master.*

23. D

The narrator poses to himself the question about what might have become of the piano player had he been properly trained and then answers himself by saying *perhaps he wouldn't have done anything at all.* The narrator goes on to say that even if the piano player achieved some success as an imitator of the greats or as an innovator, he still would not have been as *delightful* as he was playing rag-time. Thus, the statement that *perhaps he wouldn't have done anything at all* can best be interpreted as a *recognition that the piano player might have wasted his talent*, (D), had he been formally trained.

(A) and (B) are wrong because the narrator thinks highly of the piano player's skill even if that skill is not genius-level or particularly disciplined. (C) and (E) are both far too broad and too negative to be the correct answer.

24. C

The correct answer here is going to be a paraphrase of the idea that no matter how far the piano player would have gone if trained, he would not have been as delightful as he was as a rag-time player. (C) is the choice you're looking for. (E) is the most tempting wrong answer since the author's statements at the end of the passage can easily be misconstrued to mean that the piano player could never have been more than mediocre as a classical artist. However, *never* is too strong a word here—the narrator is not, and cannot be, as sure as that—so this choice is wrong.

SECTION 7

1. E ①②③
Use FOIL:

$$(3x + 4)(4x - 3)$$
$$= (3x \times 4x) + [3x \times (-3)] + (4 \times 4x) + [4 \times (-3)]$$
$$= 12x^2 - 9x + 16x - 12$$
$$= 12x^2 + 7x - 12, \text{ choice (E)}.$$

2. C

When you know that the given parts add up to the whole, then you can turn a part-to-part ratio into two part-to-whole ratios—put each term of the ratio over the sum of the terms. In this case, since all the numbers in the set must be either integers or nonintegers, the parts do add up to the whole. The sum of the terms in the ratio 2:3 is 5, so the two part-to-whole ratios are 2:5 and 3:5.

$$\frac{\text{integers}}{\text{numbers}} = \frac{2}{5}(100\%) = \frac{200\%}{5} = 40\%, \text{ choice (C)}.$$

3. C ①②③
Get rid of the parentheses in the denominator, and then cancel factors the numerator and denominator have in common:

$$\frac{x^2 y^3 z^4}{(xyz^2)^2} = \frac{x^2 y^3 z^4}{x^2 y^2 z^4}$$
$$= \frac{x^2}{x^2} \times \frac{y^3}{y^2} \times \frac{z^4}{z^4}$$
$$= y, \text{ choice (C)}.$$

4. E [1(2)3]

If p divided by 7 leaves a remainder of 5, you can say that $p = 7n + 5$, where n represents some integer. Multiply both sides by 5 to get $5p = 35n + 25$. The remainder when you divide 7 into $35n$ is 0. The reminder when you divide 7 into 25 is 4, so the remainder when you divide $5p$ by 7 is $0 + 4 = 4$.

For most people, this one's a lot easier to do by picking numbers. Think of an example for p and try it out. p could be 12, for example, because when you divide 12 by 7, the remainder is 5. (p could also be 19, 26, 33, or any of infinitely many more possibilities.) Now multiply your chosen p by 5: $12 \times 5 = 60$. Divide 60 by 7 and see what the remainder is: 60 by 7 = 8, remainder 4. Thus, choice (E) is correct.

5. B

To find the y-intercept of a line from its equation, put the equation in slope-intercept form:

$$2x - 3y = 18$$
$$-3y = -2x + 18$$
$$y = \frac{2}{3}x - 6$$

In this form, the y-intercept is what comes after the x. In this case, it's -6, choice (B).

6. C

Set up a proportion:

$$\frac{12 \text{ pages}}{1 \text{ hour}} = \frac{100 \text{ pages}}{x \text{ hours}}$$
$$12x = 100$$
$$x = \frac{100}{12} = 8\frac{1}{3}$$

One-third of an hour is $\frac{1}{3}$ of 60 minutes, or 20 minutes. So $8\frac{1}{3}$ hours is 8 hours and 20 minutes, choice (C).

7. E [1(2)3]

With a right triangle, you can use the two legs as the base and the height to figure out the area. Here, the two leg lengths are expressed algebraically. Just plug the two expressions in for b and h in the triangle area formula:

$$\text{Area} = \frac{1}{2}(x - 1)(x + 1)$$
$$= \frac{1}{2}(x^2 - 1) = \frac{x^2 - 1}{2}, \text{ choice (E)}$$

8. A

The easiest way to do this problem is to subtract Bill's money from the total of the money that Jim and Bill have. Doing this gives you $15 - 4 = 11$. However, the problem states that they have LESS THAN 15 dollars. Therefore, Jim must have less than 11 dollars. Of I, II, and III, the only value that is less than 11 is I, so the answer must be (A).

To solve this problem algebraically, set up an inequality where J is Jim's money and B is Bill's money:

$J + B < 15$ where $B = 4$
$J + 4 < 15$
$J < 11$

Again, be wary of the fact that this is an inequality, NOT an equation.

9. A

Pick numbers for x and y. For instance, say that Angelo makes \$20 for working 5 hours and Sarah makes \$20 for working 4 hours. In this case, Angelo makes \$4 per hour and Sarah makes \$5. The difference between their wages is \$1 per hour. Now plug 20 in for x and 5 in for y in each of the answer choices. Which ones give you a result of 1? Only (A), which is the answer.

10. D

A square with area 16 has sides of length 4. Therefore, the largest circle that could possibly be cut from such a square would have a diameter of 4.

Such a circle would have a radius of 2, making its area 4π. So the amount of felt left after cutting such a circle from one of the squares of felt would be $16 - 4\pi$, or $4(4 - \pi)$. There are 8 such squares, so the total area of the leftover felt is $8 \times 4(4 - \pi) = 32(4 - \pi)$, choice (D).

11. C

When you see a question like this one on test day, look for patterns in the differences between terms. Is each term a result of adding some number to the previous term? Is each term a result of multiplying the previous term by some number? In this case, each term is the result of multiplying the previous term by 3:

$x = 18(3) = 54$

You can check this result by comparing it to later terms:

$54(3) = 162$

Thus, choice (C) is correct.

12. E

$$\begin{array}{r}
5x^2 + 13x + 40 \\
x - 3 \overline{)\, 5x^3 - 2x^2 + x + 1} \\
\underline{-(5x^3 - 15x^2)} \\
13x^2 + x \\
\underline{-(13x^2 - 39x)} \\
40x + 1 \\
\underline{-(40x - 120)} \\
121
\end{array}$$

13. B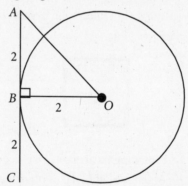

This problem requires you to put together several different pieces of information. If you don't see all the steps you need to follow at first, just write down what information you can get from the problem and that may help you figure out what to do next. Since B is the midpoint of $\overline{AC}$, which is 4 units long, $\overline{AB}$ and $\overline{BC}$ are each 2 units long. Since the area of the circle is $4\pi = \pi r^2 = \pi 2^2$, its radius is 2. $\overline{BO}$ is a radius of the circle, so it is 2 units long. $\overline{AC}$ is tangent to the circle at point B, so $\angle OBA$ is 90 degrees. The following diagram summarizes this information:

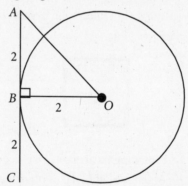

Since BO and AB both equal 2 and $\angle ABO$ is 90 degrees, triangle ABO is a 45-45-90 special right triangle, so its sides have a ratio of $1:1:\sqrt{2}$. Thus, $AO = 2\sqrt{2}$, choice (B).

14. E

Learning how to interpret a graph can be challenging. Practice this skill before test day, so you have mastered it by then. Each year, the cost increases. In 2003, insurance was $1,200. So you know that in 2004 it should be more; the only option is (E).

15. D

Be sure not to be tempted by answers that are partly right. $x \geq 1$ describes the right half of the values on the number line but leaves out the left half. The selected values on the number line consist of 1, everything greater than 1, −1, and everything less than −1. The easiest way to describe this set is that the absolute value of x, or its distance from zero on the number line, is greater than or equal to 1. This can be written in mathematical notation as $|x| \geq 1$. Thus, choice (D) is correct.

16. E

In order to find the number of possibilities, multiply the number of possibilities in each step. In other words, there are 3 routes from Bay City to Riverville and 4 routes from Riverville to Straitstown. There are 3 more routes from Straitstown to Frog Pond, so there are $12 \times 3 = 36$ total routes from Bay City to Frog Pond, choice (E).

SECTION 8

1. A

The word *although* indicates contrast, and the words *large number* and *mass* provide a clue to what's missing. We need something that means "different" for the first blank and something that means "the same" for the second blank. This is basically what *disparate* and *homogeneous* mean, so (A) is correct.

2. A

We need something here that goes with *heavy thoughts. Morose*, or gloomy, (A), is the best choice. *Onerous*, (B), means troublesome or involving hardship. *Contorted*, (C), means deformed. *Ossified*, (D), means sticking to an opinion or course of action despite arguments of persuasion. *Inscrutable*, (E), means mysterious or obscure.

3. E

The *demise* or death of the protagonist presumably eliminated all possibility of a sequel. That's what (E), *precluded*, means. *Dissembled*, (B), means pretended. *Exacerbated*, (D), means made more violent or bitter.

4. E

Repeated breakdown of negotiations would tend to support or reinforce the view that the sides *were not truly committed to* preventing or averting a military confrontation, choice (E). In (A) and (D), *established* and *strengthened* fit the first blank, but *escalating* and *initiating* are wrong for the second. In (B), *avoiding* fits the second blank, but *undermined* is wrong for the first.

5. C

The sentence contrasts Duncan with his coworker. You can, therefore, predict that the colleague is neither *modest* nor *cooperative*. (C), meaning proud contempt for others matches the prediction.

(A), meaning pleasantness, friendliness, and (E), meaning the quality of being humble, have the wrong charge. You could use those words to describe Duncan perhaps, but not the colleague. (B) and (D) do not contrast with the modest and cooperative qualities of Duncan.

6. D

Start with the second blank where you are looking for a word to suggest the effort needed to improve the economic climate. (B) and (D) both fit. (A) may be tempting because the candidate may very well have made a *promise* about the economic climate before the election. You do not, however, recognize a forthcoming (approaching, upcoming) *promise*. Note that an *inauguration* (formal acceptance into office) may be forthcoming for the candidate, but it will not improve the economic climate. (C) is too extreme for the second blank. Now look at the first blank for (B) and (D). The candidate's exhilaration (joy, elation) temporarily *illuminated* (clarified, brought to light) or *eclipsed* (surpassed, outshone) the recognition of the coming effort. (D) is the best fit.

THE DESIGN MUSEUMS PASSAGES

Passage 1: The position of the author of this passage starts to become clear in the second paragraph: She likes design museums and is willing to defend them against critics. She thinks design museums are not just advertisements for new technology but places where new products can be honored. Design museums, she asserts, are comfortable for visitors because the exhibits provide a lot of information about the objects displayed—information you wouldn't get in an art gallery. Another advantage of design museums, she says, is that their curators have more freedom than do the curators of public art galleries.

Passage 2: Author 2 does not hold technical and design museums in the same high regard as author 1 does. Author 2 complains about several things: 1) technical museums concentrate on present technology and ignore historical study and research; 2) they glorify machines and industrialization when these things do harm as well as good; and 3) they do not (and cannot safely and imaginatively) show machinery in action. Author 2 does admit at the very end, however, that the public has shown a healthy curiosity about science and technology.

7. A

To say that something is *readily available to the general public* is to say that it is *easily* available. (A) is the correct answer.

8. E

Although the question is not Vocabulary-in-Context, you must still be careful not to assume the word is used in its most common sense. Look at the context. Since these appliances are in design museums, they must have been very popular and successful. It's only as "design" that they have been ignored. (C) might have been tempting, but it's not to the point and outside the scope. People may or may not have had conversations about, say, a toaster—it's never mentioned. But the conversations might have been about how well it worked or how little it cost, not about its design attributes—the focus of the passage.

9. D

Author 1 says that department store windows try to sell you something whereas design exhibits try to give you an appreciation of the aesthetic value of something. (D) paraphrases this idea. (A), (B), and (E) can be readily eliminated. Be careful with (C), though. Even though design museums focus on the artistic qualities of products, it does not automatically follow from this that design museums are not concerned at all with the commercial aspects of a successful product. Thus, (C) is wrong.

10. B

In the third paragraph of Passage 1, the author argues that design museums make visitors feel comfortable because the exhibits illustrate the purpose behind the look and function of the displayed object; art gallery exhibits, by contrast, provide no such information. From this argument, you can infer that author 1 thinks that visitors want to be informed about the object they are viewing. This makes (B) correct. There is no evidence to support any of the other choices, all of which are misreadings of paragraph 3. (A) can be eliminated as soon as you see *hostile toward . . . abstract art*. (C) and (D) contradict the author, who says that visitors are not confused by technological exhibits since they are familiar and informative. (E) is an unwarranted inference based on the author's statement that design exhibits point out the artistic qualities of the displayed items; you cannot conclude from this that most museum visitors undervalue the artistic worth of household items.

11. B

Since you just reviewed paragraph 3 for the last question, the answer to this one should jump right out at you. The difference between a design museum exhibit and an art gallery exhibit is that a design museum exhibit provides you with information about the object being displayed, whereas the art gallery exhibit does not. (B) is correct. None of the other choices—(A), (C), (D), or (E)—have any basis in the passage.

12. C

After mentioning the collection of Zippo lighters, etc., in London's Design Museum, author 1 says that curators of design museums have options that are far less rigorous, conventionalized, and preprogrammed than those open to curators of art galleries. This is a fancy way of saying that the curators of design museums have more freedom to put together unconventional collections, (C).

(E) is the tempting wrong answer to this question. It's wrong because it goes too far: the design curators have freedom, but not, as far as we know, the freedom to satisfy *their own personal whims*.

13. E

In the very last sentence of Passage 1, the author says that design museums (*the display of postmodern playthings or quirky Japanese vacuum cleaners*) are better able to represent humor than art galleries (*an exhibition of Impressionist landscapes*). The author is emphasizing the contrast between design museum and art gallery exhibits, (E). (B) is the trickiest wrong answer. It misses the point of the last sentence because the author is not comparing *postmodern playthings* with Impressionist art; she is comparing the different ways these two things are exhibited.

14. A

The answer to this question will be the choice that summarizes paragraph 1 of Passage 2. Since the author spends paragraph 1 complaining that design museums ignore the historical aspect of technology, choice (A) is the best answer. (B) focuses too narrowly on the last part of the paragraph, where the author says that since industry builds the exhibits, curators may be dispensed with. This is not the underlying difficulty referred to at the beginning of the paragraph. Choices (C), (D), and (E) have nothing to do with the first paragraph.

15. A

Author 2's point in the second paragraph is that industrialization and *progress* have not been all good and should be considered critically, but technology museums just glorify them. He mentions industrialization's harm to the environment and ecology to support this point and to encourage a *critical response* to technology, so (A) is correct. (B) is wrong because it's too negative, even for this author. (C) is a distortion of a detail at the end of the second paragraph, whereas (D) is a distorted idea from the third paragraph. (E) is out because author 2 doesn't do any praising in the second paragraph.

16. D

Put the phrase in context. Author 2 says that displayed machinery should be in action, not in *sculptured repose*, as is the case with the machinery in technology museums. To author 2, you can infer that *sculptured repose* is meaningless and *unrealistic,* (D). (A) is out because the author is not condemning the curators for poor planning; in fact, the author admits that displaying operating machinery would be extremely difficult. (B) can be eliminated because it's too extreme. The author never says which—if any—of the problems he discusses is the *greatest problem*. (C) and (E) miss the author's point and the context in which the phrase *sculptured repose* is found.

17. D

Choices (A), (B), (C), and (E) are common synonyms for *command*, but none of them work in the context of the phrase *command the imagination, ingenuity, and manual dexterity it requires*. Only choice (D) can do the job.

18. A

Predict the answer to the question before you go looking through the choices. You know that author 2 thinks that technology has had a lot of negative consequences, so you can assume that he would point this out in response to author 1's optimistic statement. This makes (A) the best answer. We don't know what author 2's position on art galleries is, so (B) is out. (C) comes from Passage 2 but is irrelevant to the question asked in the stem. (D) and (E) contradict specific things author 2 says in the course of his passage.

19. B

In questions like this one, wrong answer choices are often statements that one author, but not both, would agree with. For example, author 2 would probably agree with choice (A) and would definitely agree with (D) and (E), but author 1 most likely would not agree with any of these three. That narrows the field to (B) and (C). (C) is a very general statement that really has no basis in either passage. (B), on the other hand, is an idea that can be found in both passages, so it is the correct answer.

SECTION 9

1. A

The sentence is correct and conforms to the rules of parallelism; all three items in the list are adjectives describing the new model.

2. B

There is an error of subordination here. To express the causal relationship between melting ice caps and flooding of islands, you need only one conjunction, *because* or *therefore*, as done correctly in choice (B). To have both is redundant. Furthermore, the word *therefore* should be preceded by a semicolon, not a comma.

3. C

This sentence fragment is best corrected by moving the verb *was* and inserting a comma after the introductory phrase describing *Flaubert*, as in choice (C).

4. D

In order for (A) to be grammatically correct, a comma is needed before the coordinating conjunction *and*. (C) adds the comma but takes away the conjunction, so it is incorrect. (B) and (E) are extremely awkward. (D) is the clearest and most concise answer.

5. D

Eliminate the excessively wordy answer choices—(A), (B), and (E). (C) might be tempting, but *failed not* creates a double negative. (D) is correct because it is clear and concise; (D) also continues the structure established in the first part of the sentence: *have raised . . . have failed.*

6. A

Make sure that all three items in the series are parallel. The first two begin with gerunds (verbs ending in *-ing*), so (A) is correct. Do not be confused by the word *washing*. It is part of the noun *washing machine* and cannot be called upon to function in any other way in this sentence.

7. C

First, eliminate any answer choices that begin with misplaced modifiers. (A) and (D) both say the *directors* have *exceptionally clear waters and active underwater life*. Next, eliminate answer choices that do not create complete sentences. (B) and (E) are long sentence fragments. (C) is correct because it is the only choice with grammatically correct structure.

8. C

(A) is a run-on; the phrase beginning with *featured* makes the sentence incorrect. (B) is nonsensical—the phrase *with features beauty* makes it incorrect. (C), (D), and (E) set apart the nonessential information with commas, so look for the choice that does this best. That choice is (C)—it is the clearest (and shortest).

9. A

(A) is the clearest answer choice because it sets apart the nonessential information with commas. (D) also uses this structure, but it unnecessarily adds *because it was*. (B), (C), and (E) are wordy.

10. E

Eliminate the answer choices that change the underlined portion to an incomplete sentence—(C) and (D). (A) and (B) are technically correct, but (E) is the clearest and most concise.

11. A

(C) and (E) lack an antecedent for the pronoun *they*. (B) is very awkward with the words *that* and *not* repeated. (D) is also awkward because of the word *as* toward the beginning of the sentence. (A), the original sentence, is the most concise and clear answer choice.

12. A

The correct answer will have to be parallel with *having a lot of money*. In other words, the underlined portion should contain a gerund (a word ending in *-ing*). The only answer choices with this structure are (A) and (B). So (C), (D), and (E) can be eliminated. (A) is much clearer and more concise, so it is the correct answer.

13. B

Some of the answer choices violate the rules of independent and dependent clauses. For example, (A) uses a comma and coordinating conjunction, calling for two independent clauses. However, the first clause is dependent because of the word *that*. In (D), the first clause is dependent, so the second should be independent, but it is not. (E) introduces a misplaced modifier, and (C) has an illogical connection between the two clauses. (B) has correct structure and makes the most sense.

14. C

The introductory phrase is a dependent clause, so the underlined portion must create an independent clause. The word *causing* in (A) and (E) does not make an independent clause, so eliminate these choices. (B) and (D) insert the coordinating conjunction *and*, which is incorrect when connecting a dependent clause and an independent clause. (The coordinating conjunction and comma are only used for connecting two independent clauses.) (C) is the only answer choice to set up a correct independent clause.

SAT Practice Test Two
Answer Sheet

**Remove (or photocopy) the answer sheet and use it to complete the Practice Test.
See the answer key following the test when finished.**

Start with number 1 for each section. If a section has fewer questions than answer spaces, leave the extra spaces blank.

SECTION

1

Section 1 is the Writing section's essay component.

SECTION

2

1. Ⓐ Ⓑ Ⓒ Ⓓ Ⓔ	11. Ⓐ Ⓑ Ⓒ Ⓓ Ⓔ	21. Ⓐ Ⓑ Ⓒ Ⓓ Ⓔ	31. Ⓐ Ⓑ Ⓒ Ⓓ Ⓔ
2. Ⓐ Ⓑ Ⓒ Ⓓ Ⓔ	12. Ⓐ Ⓑ Ⓒ Ⓓ Ⓔ	22. Ⓐ Ⓑ Ⓒ Ⓓ Ⓔ	32. Ⓐ Ⓑ Ⓒ Ⓓ Ⓔ
3. Ⓐ Ⓑ Ⓒ Ⓓ Ⓔ	13. Ⓐ Ⓑ Ⓒ Ⓓ Ⓔ	23. Ⓐ Ⓑ Ⓒ Ⓓ Ⓔ	33. Ⓐ Ⓑ Ⓒ Ⓓ Ⓔ
4. Ⓐ Ⓑ Ⓒ Ⓓ Ⓔ	14. Ⓐ Ⓑ Ⓒ Ⓓ Ⓔ	24. Ⓐ Ⓑ Ⓒ Ⓓ Ⓔ	34. Ⓐ Ⓑ Ⓒ Ⓓ Ⓔ
5. Ⓐ Ⓑ Ⓒ Ⓓ Ⓔ	15. Ⓐ Ⓑ Ⓒ Ⓓ Ⓔ	25. Ⓐ Ⓑ Ⓒ Ⓓ Ⓔ	35. Ⓐ Ⓑ Ⓒ Ⓓ Ⓔ
6. Ⓐ Ⓑ Ⓒ Ⓓ Ⓔ	16. Ⓐ Ⓑ Ⓒ Ⓓ Ⓔ	26. Ⓐ Ⓑ Ⓒ Ⓓ Ⓔ	36. Ⓐ Ⓑ Ⓒ Ⓓ Ⓔ
7. Ⓐ Ⓑ Ⓒ Ⓓ Ⓔ	17. Ⓐ Ⓑ Ⓒ Ⓓ Ⓔ	27. Ⓐ Ⓑ Ⓒ Ⓓ Ⓔ	37. Ⓐ Ⓑ Ⓒ Ⓓ Ⓔ
8. Ⓐ Ⓑ Ⓒ Ⓓ Ⓔ	18. Ⓐ Ⓑ Ⓒ Ⓓ Ⓔ	28. Ⓐ Ⓑ Ⓒ Ⓓ Ⓔ	38. Ⓐ Ⓑ Ⓒ Ⓓ Ⓔ
9. Ⓐ Ⓑ Ⓒ Ⓓ Ⓔ	19. Ⓐ Ⓑ Ⓒ Ⓓ Ⓔ	29. Ⓐ Ⓑ Ⓒ Ⓓ Ⓔ	39. Ⓐ Ⓑ Ⓒ Ⓓ Ⓔ
10. Ⓐ Ⓑ Ⓒ Ⓓ Ⓔ	20. Ⓐ Ⓑ Ⓒ Ⓓ Ⓔ	30. Ⓐ Ⓑ Ⓒ Ⓓ Ⓔ	40. Ⓐ Ⓑ Ⓒ Ⓓ Ⓔ

☐ # right in Section 2

☐ # wrong in Section 2

SECTION

3

1. Ⓐ Ⓑ Ⓒ Ⓓ Ⓔ	11. Ⓐ Ⓑ Ⓒ Ⓓ Ⓔ	21. Ⓐ Ⓑ Ⓒ Ⓓ Ⓔ	31. Ⓐ Ⓑ Ⓒ Ⓓ Ⓔ
2. Ⓐ Ⓑ Ⓒ Ⓓ Ⓔ	12. Ⓐ Ⓑ Ⓒ Ⓓ Ⓔ	22. Ⓐ Ⓑ Ⓒ Ⓓ Ⓔ	32. Ⓐ Ⓑ Ⓒ Ⓓ Ⓔ
3. Ⓐ Ⓑ Ⓒ Ⓓ Ⓔ	13. Ⓐ Ⓑ Ⓒ Ⓓ Ⓔ	23. Ⓐ Ⓑ Ⓒ Ⓓ Ⓔ	33. Ⓐ Ⓑ Ⓒ Ⓓ Ⓔ
4. Ⓐ Ⓑ Ⓒ Ⓓ Ⓔ	14. Ⓐ Ⓑ Ⓒ Ⓓ Ⓔ	24. Ⓐ Ⓑ Ⓒ Ⓓ Ⓔ	34. Ⓐ Ⓑ Ⓒ Ⓓ Ⓔ
5. Ⓐ Ⓑ Ⓒ Ⓓ Ⓔ	15. Ⓐ Ⓑ Ⓒ Ⓓ Ⓔ	25. Ⓐ Ⓑ Ⓒ Ⓓ Ⓔ	35. Ⓐ Ⓑ Ⓒ Ⓓ Ⓔ
6. Ⓐ Ⓑ Ⓒ Ⓓ Ⓔ	16. Ⓐ Ⓑ Ⓒ Ⓓ Ⓔ	26. Ⓐ Ⓑ Ⓒ Ⓓ Ⓔ	36. Ⓐ Ⓑ Ⓒ Ⓓ Ⓔ
7. Ⓐ Ⓑ Ⓒ Ⓓ Ⓔ	17. Ⓐ Ⓑ Ⓒ Ⓓ Ⓔ	27. Ⓐ Ⓑ Ⓒ Ⓓ Ⓔ	37. Ⓐ Ⓑ Ⓒ Ⓓ Ⓔ
8. Ⓐ Ⓑ Ⓒ Ⓓ Ⓔ	18. Ⓐ Ⓑ Ⓒ Ⓓ Ⓔ	28. Ⓐ Ⓑ Ⓒ Ⓓ Ⓔ	38. Ⓐ Ⓑ Ⓒ Ⓓ Ⓔ
9. Ⓐ Ⓑ Ⓒ Ⓓ Ⓔ	19. Ⓐ Ⓑ Ⓒ Ⓓ Ⓔ	29. Ⓐ Ⓑ Ⓒ Ⓓ Ⓔ	39. Ⓐ Ⓑ Ⓒ Ⓓ Ⓔ
10. Ⓐ Ⓑ Ⓒ Ⓓ Ⓔ	20. Ⓐ Ⓑ Ⓒ Ⓓ Ⓔ	30. Ⓐ Ⓑ Ⓒ Ⓓ Ⓔ	40. Ⓐ Ⓑ Ⓒ Ⓓ Ⓔ

☐ # right in Section 3

☐ # wrong in Section 3

Remove (or photocopy) this answer sheet and use it to complete the Practice Test.

Start with number 1 for each section. If a section has fewer questions than answer spaces, leave the extra spaces blank.

SECTION 4

1. Ⓐ Ⓑ Ⓒ Ⓓ Ⓔ 11. Ⓐ Ⓑ Ⓒ Ⓓ Ⓔ 21. Ⓐ Ⓑ Ⓒ Ⓓ Ⓔ 31. Ⓐ Ⓑ Ⓒ Ⓓ Ⓔ
2. Ⓐ Ⓑ Ⓒ Ⓓ Ⓔ 12. Ⓐ Ⓑ Ⓒ Ⓓ Ⓔ 22. Ⓐ Ⓑ Ⓒ Ⓓ Ⓔ 32. Ⓐ Ⓑ Ⓒ Ⓓ Ⓔ
3. Ⓐ Ⓑ Ⓒ Ⓓ Ⓔ 13. Ⓐ Ⓑ Ⓒ Ⓓ Ⓔ 23. Ⓐ Ⓑ Ⓒ Ⓓ Ⓔ 33. Ⓐ Ⓑ Ⓒ Ⓓ Ⓔ
4. Ⓐ Ⓑ Ⓒ Ⓓ Ⓔ 14. Ⓐ Ⓑ Ⓒ Ⓓ Ⓔ 24. Ⓐ Ⓑ Ⓒ Ⓓ Ⓔ 34. Ⓐ Ⓑ Ⓒ Ⓓ Ⓔ

☐ # right in Section 4

5. Ⓐ Ⓑ Ⓒ Ⓓ Ⓔ 15. Ⓐ Ⓑ Ⓒ Ⓓ Ⓔ 25. Ⓐ Ⓑ Ⓒ Ⓓ Ⓔ 35. Ⓐ Ⓑ Ⓒ Ⓓ Ⓔ
6. Ⓐ Ⓑ Ⓒ Ⓓ Ⓔ 16. Ⓐ Ⓑ Ⓒ Ⓓ Ⓔ 26. Ⓐ Ⓑ Ⓒ Ⓓ Ⓔ 36. Ⓐ Ⓑ Ⓒ Ⓓ Ⓔ
7. Ⓐ Ⓑ Ⓒ Ⓓ Ⓔ 17. Ⓐ Ⓑ Ⓒ Ⓓ Ⓔ 27. Ⓐ Ⓑ Ⓒ Ⓓ Ⓔ 37. Ⓐ Ⓑ Ⓒ Ⓓ Ⓔ
8. Ⓐ Ⓑ Ⓒ Ⓓ Ⓔ 18. Ⓐ Ⓑ Ⓒ Ⓓ Ⓔ 28. Ⓐ Ⓑ Ⓒ Ⓓ Ⓔ 38. Ⓐ Ⓑ Ⓒ Ⓓ Ⓔ

☐ # wrong in Section 4

9. Ⓐ Ⓑ Ⓒ Ⓓ Ⓔ 19. Ⓐ Ⓑ Ⓒ Ⓓ Ⓔ 29. Ⓐ Ⓑ Ⓒ Ⓓ Ⓔ 39. Ⓐ Ⓑ Ⓒ Ⓓ Ⓔ
10. Ⓐ Ⓑ Ⓒ Ⓓ Ⓔ 20. Ⓐ Ⓑ Ⓒ Ⓓ Ⓔ 30. Ⓐ Ⓑ Ⓒ Ⓓ Ⓔ 40. Ⓐ Ⓑ Ⓒ Ⓓ Ⓔ

SECTION 5

1. Ⓐ Ⓑ Ⓒ Ⓓ Ⓔ 11. Ⓐ Ⓑ Ⓒ Ⓓ Ⓔ 21. Ⓐ Ⓑ Ⓒ Ⓓ Ⓔ 31. Ⓐ Ⓑ Ⓒ Ⓓ Ⓔ
2. Ⓐ Ⓑ Ⓒ Ⓓ Ⓔ 12. Ⓐ Ⓑ Ⓒ Ⓓ Ⓔ 22. Ⓐ Ⓑ Ⓒ Ⓓ Ⓔ 32. Ⓐ Ⓑ Ⓒ Ⓓ Ⓔ
3. Ⓐ Ⓑ Ⓒ Ⓓ Ⓔ 13. Ⓐ Ⓑ Ⓒ Ⓓ Ⓔ 23. Ⓐ Ⓑ Ⓒ Ⓓ Ⓔ 33. Ⓐ Ⓑ Ⓒ Ⓓ Ⓔ
4. Ⓐ Ⓑ Ⓒ Ⓓ Ⓔ 14. Ⓐ Ⓑ Ⓒ Ⓓ Ⓔ 24. Ⓐ Ⓑ Ⓒ Ⓓ Ⓔ 34. Ⓐ Ⓑ Ⓒ Ⓓ Ⓔ

☐ # right in Section 5

5. Ⓐ Ⓑ Ⓒ Ⓓ Ⓔ 15. Ⓐ Ⓑ Ⓒ Ⓓ Ⓔ 25. Ⓐ Ⓑ Ⓒ Ⓓ Ⓔ 35. Ⓐ Ⓑ Ⓒ Ⓓ Ⓔ
6. Ⓐ Ⓑ Ⓒ Ⓓ Ⓔ 16. Ⓐ Ⓑ Ⓒ Ⓓ Ⓔ 26. Ⓐ Ⓑ Ⓒ Ⓓ Ⓔ 36. Ⓐ Ⓑ Ⓒ Ⓓ Ⓔ
7. Ⓐ Ⓑ Ⓒ Ⓓ Ⓔ 17. Ⓐ Ⓑ Ⓒ Ⓓ Ⓔ 27. Ⓐ Ⓑ Ⓒ Ⓓ Ⓔ 37. Ⓐ Ⓑ Ⓒ Ⓓ Ⓔ
8. Ⓐ Ⓑ Ⓒ Ⓓ Ⓔ 18. Ⓐ Ⓑ Ⓒ Ⓓ Ⓔ 28. Ⓐ Ⓑ Ⓒ Ⓓ Ⓔ 38. Ⓐ Ⓑ Ⓒ Ⓓ Ⓔ

☐ # wrong in Section 5

9. Ⓐ Ⓑ Ⓒ Ⓓ Ⓔ 19. Ⓐ Ⓑ Ⓒ Ⓓ Ⓔ 29. Ⓐ Ⓑ Ⓒ Ⓓ Ⓔ 39. Ⓐ Ⓑ Ⓒ Ⓓ Ⓔ
10. Ⓐ Ⓑ Ⓒ Ⓓ Ⓔ 20. Ⓐ Ⓑ Ⓒ Ⓓ Ⓔ 30. Ⓐ Ⓑ Ⓒ Ⓓ Ⓔ 40. Ⓐ Ⓑ Ⓒ Ⓓ Ⓔ

If section 5 of your test book contains math questions that are not multiple-choice, continue to item 9 below. Otherwise, continue to item 9 above.

9. 10. 11. 12. 13.

14. 15. 16. 17. 18.

Remove (or photocopy) this answer sheet and use it to complete the Practice Test.

Start with number 1 for each section. If a section has fewer questions than answer spaces, leave the extra spaces blank.

SECTION

6

1. Ⓐ Ⓑ Ⓒ Ⓓ Ⓔ   11. Ⓐ Ⓑ Ⓒ Ⓓ Ⓔ   21. Ⓐ Ⓑ Ⓒ Ⓓ Ⓔ   31. Ⓐ Ⓑ Ⓒ Ⓓ Ⓔ
2. Ⓐ Ⓑ Ⓒ Ⓓ Ⓔ   12. Ⓐ Ⓑ Ⓒ Ⓓ Ⓔ   22. Ⓐ Ⓑ Ⓒ Ⓓ Ⓔ   32. Ⓐ Ⓑ Ⓒ Ⓓ Ⓔ
3. Ⓐ Ⓑ Ⓒ Ⓓ Ⓔ   13. Ⓐ Ⓑ Ⓒ Ⓓ Ⓔ   23. Ⓐ Ⓑ Ⓒ Ⓓ Ⓔ   33. Ⓐ Ⓑ Ⓒ Ⓓ Ⓔ
4. Ⓐ Ⓑ Ⓒ Ⓓ Ⓔ   14. Ⓐ Ⓑ Ⓒ Ⓓ Ⓔ   24. Ⓐ Ⓑ Ⓒ Ⓓ Ⓔ   34. Ⓐ Ⓑ Ⓒ Ⓓ Ⓔ
5. Ⓐ Ⓑ Ⓒ Ⓓ Ⓔ   15. Ⓐ Ⓑ Ⓒ Ⓓ Ⓔ   25. Ⓐ Ⓑ Ⓒ Ⓓ Ⓔ   35. Ⓐ Ⓑ Ⓒ Ⓓ Ⓔ

right in Section 6

6. Ⓐ Ⓑ Ⓒ Ⓓ Ⓔ   16. Ⓐ Ⓑ Ⓒ Ⓓ Ⓔ   26. Ⓐ Ⓑ Ⓒ Ⓓ Ⓔ   36. Ⓐ Ⓑ Ⓒ Ⓓ Ⓔ
7. Ⓐ Ⓑ Ⓒ Ⓓ Ⓔ   17. Ⓐ Ⓑ Ⓒ Ⓓ Ⓔ   27. Ⓐ Ⓑ Ⓒ Ⓓ Ⓔ   37. Ⓐ Ⓑ Ⓒ Ⓓ Ⓔ
8. Ⓐ Ⓑ Ⓒ Ⓓ Ⓔ   18. Ⓐ Ⓑ Ⓒ Ⓓ Ⓔ   28. Ⓐ Ⓑ Ⓒ Ⓓ Ⓔ   38. Ⓐ Ⓑ Ⓒ Ⓓ Ⓔ
9. Ⓐ Ⓑ Ⓒ Ⓓ Ⓔ   19. Ⓐ Ⓑ Ⓒ Ⓓ Ⓔ   29. Ⓐ Ⓑ Ⓒ Ⓓ Ⓔ   39. Ⓐ Ⓑ Ⓒ Ⓓ Ⓔ

wrong in Section 6

10. Ⓐ Ⓑ Ⓒ Ⓓ Ⓔ   20. Ⓐ Ⓑ Ⓒ Ⓓ Ⓔ   30. Ⓐ Ⓑ Ⓒ Ⓓ Ⓔ   40. Ⓐ Ⓑ Ⓒ Ⓓ Ⓔ

SECTION

7

1. Ⓐ Ⓑ Ⓒ Ⓓ Ⓔ   11. Ⓐ Ⓑ Ⓒ Ⓓ Ⓔ   21. Ⓐ Ⓑ Ⓒ Ⓓ Ⓔ   31. Ⓐ Ⓑ Ⓒ Ⓓ Ⓔ
2. Ⓐ Ⓑ Ⓒ Ⓓ Ⓔ   12. Ⓐ Ⓑ Ⓒ Ⓓ Ⓔ   22. Ⓐ Ⓑ Ⓒ Ⓓ Ⓔ   32. Ⓐ Ⓑ Ⓒ Ⓓ Ⓔ
3. Ⓐ Ⓑ Ⓒ Ⓓ Ⓔ   13. Ⓐ Ⓑ Ⓒ Ⓓ Ⓔ   23. Ⓐ Ⓑ Ⓒ Ⓓ Ⓔ   33. Ⓐ Ⓑ Ⓒ Ⓓ Ⓔ
4. Ⓐ Ⓑ Ⓒ Ⓓ Ⓔ   14. Ⓐ Ⓑ Ⓒ Ⓓ Ⓔ   24. Ⓐ Ⓑ Ⓒ Ⓓ Ⓔ   34. Ⓐ Ⓑ Ⓒ Ⓓ Ⓔ
5. Ⓐ Ⓑ Ⓒ Ⓓ Ⓔ   15. Ⓐ Ⓑ Ⓒ Ⓓ Ⓔ   25. Ⓐ Ⓑ Ⓒ Ⓓ Ⓔ   35. Ⓐ Ⓑ Ⓒ Ⓓ Ⓔ

right in Section 7

6. Ⓐ Ⓑ Ⓒ Ⓓ Ⓔ   16. Ⓐ Ⓑ Ⓒ Ⓓ Ⓔ   26. Ⓐ Ⓑ Ⓒ Ⓓ Ⓔ   36. Ⓐ Ⓑ Ⓒ Ⓓ Ⓔ
7. Ⓐ Ⓑ Ⓒ Ⓓ Ⓔ   17. Ⓐ Ⓑ Ⓒ Ⓓ Ⓔ   27. Ⓐ Ⓑ Ⓒ Ⓓ Ⓔ   37. Ⓐ Ⓑ Ⓒ Ⓓ Ⓔ
8. Ⓐ Ⓑ Ⓒ Ⓓ Ⓔ   18. Ⓐ Ⓑ Ⓒ Ⓓ Ⓔ   28. Ⓐ Ⓑ Ⓒ Ⓓ Ⓔ   38. Ⓐ Ⓑ Ⓒ Ⓓ Ⓔ
9. Ⓐ Ⓑ Ⓒ Ⓓ Ⓔ   19. Ⓐ Ⓑ Ⓒ Ⓓ Ⓔ   29. Ⓐ Ⓑ Ⓒ Ⓓ Ⓔ   39. Ⓐ Ⓑ Ⓒ Ⓓ Ⓔ

wrong in Section 7

10. Ⓐ Ⓑ Ⓒ Ⓓ Ⓔ   20. Ⓐ Ⓑ Ⓒ Ⓓ Ⓔ   30. Ⓐ Ⓑ Ⓒ Ⓓ Ⓔ   40. Ⓐ Ⓑ Ⓒ Ⓓ Ⓔ

SECTION

8

1. Ⓐ Ⓑ Ⓒ Ⓓ Ⓔ   11. Ⓐ Ⓑ Ⓒ Ⓓ Ⓔ   21. Ⓐ Ⓑ Ⓒ Ⓓ Ⓔ   31. Ⓐ Ⓑ Ⓒ Ⓓ Ⓔ
2. Ⓐ Ⓑ Ⓒ Ⓓ Ⓔ   12. Ⓐ Ⓑ Ⓒ Ⓓ Ⓔ   22. Ⓐ Ⓑ Ⓒ Ⓓ Ⓔ   32. Ⓐ Ⓑ Ⓒ Ⓓ Ⓔ
3. Ⓐ Ⓑ Ⓒ Ⓓ Ⓔ   13. Ⓐ Ⓑ Ⓒ Ⓓ Ⓔ   23. Ⓐ Ⓑ Ⓒ Ⓓ Ⓔ   33. Ⓐ Ⓑ Ⓒ Ⓓ Ⓔ
4. Ⓐ Ⓑ Ⓒ Ⓓ Ⓔ   14. Ⓐ Ⓑ Ⓒ Ⓓ Ⓔ   24. Ⓐ Ⓑ Ⓒ Ⓓ Ⓔ   34. Ⓐ Ⓑ Ⓒ Ⓓ Ⓔ
5. Ⓐ Ⓑ Ⓒ Ⓓ Ⓔ   15. Ⓐ Ⓑ Ⓒ Ⓓ Ⓔ   25. Ⓐ Ⓑ Ⓒ Ⓓ Ⓔ   35. Ⓐ Ⓑ Ⓒ Ⓓ Ⓔ

right in Section 8

6. Ⓐ Ⓑ Ⓒ Ⓓ Ⓔ   16. Ⓐ Ⓑ Ⓒ Ⓓ Ⓔ   26. Ⓐ Ⓑ Ⓒ Ⓓ Ⓔ   36. Ⓐ Ⓑ Ⓒ Ⓓ Ⓔ
7. Ⓐ Ⓑ Ⓒ Ⓓ Ⓔ   17. Ⓐ Ⓑ Ⓒ Ⓓ Ⓔ   27. Ⓐ Ⓑ Ⓒ Ⓓ Ⓔ   37. Ⓐ Ⓑ Ⓒ Ⓓ Ⓔ
8. Ⓐ Ⓑ Ⓒ Ⓓ Ⓔ   18. Ⓐ Ⓑ Ⓒ Ⓓ Ⓔ   28. Ⓐ Ⓑ Ⓒ Ⓓ Ⓔ   38. Ⓐ Ⓑ Ⓒ Ⓓ Ⓔ
9. Ⓐ Ⓑ Ⓒ Ⓓ Ⓔ   19. Ⓐ Ⓑ Ⓒ Ⓓ Ⓔ   29. Ⓐ Ⓑ Ⓒ Ⓓ Ⓔ   39. Ⓐ Ⓑ Ⓒ Ⓓ Ⓔ

wrong in Section 8

10. Ⓐ Ⓑ Ⓒ Ⓓ Ⓔ   20. Ⓐ Ⓑ Ⓒ Ⓓ Ⓔ   30. Ⓐ Ⓑ Ⓒ Ⓓ Ⓔ   40. Ⓐ Ⓑ Ⓒ Ⓓ Ⓔ

Remove (or photocopy) this answer sheet and use it to complete the Practice Test.

Start with number 1 for each section. If a section has fewer questions than answer spaces, leave the extra spaces blank.

SECTION

9

1. Ⓐ Ⓑ Ⓒ Ⓓ Ⓔ	11. Ⓐ Ⓑ Ⓒ Ⓓ Ⓔ	21. Ⓐ Ⓑ Ⓒ Ⓓ Ⓔ	31. Ⓐ Ⓑ Ⓒ Ⓓ Ⓔ
2. Ⓐ Ⓑ Ⓒ Ⓓ Ⓔ	12. Ⓐ Ⓑ Ⓒ Ⓓ Ⓔ	22. Ⓐ Ⓑ Ⓒ Ⓓ Ⓔ	32. Ⓐ Ⓑ Ⓒ Ⓓ Ⓔ
3. Ⓐ Ⓑ Ⓒ Ⓓ Ⓔ	13. Ⓐ Ⓑ Ⓒ Ⓓ Ⓔ	23. Ⓐ Ⓑ Ⓒ Ⓓ Ⓔ	33. Ⓐ Ⓑ Ⓒ Ⓓ Ⓔ
4. Ⓐ Ⓑ Ⓒ Ⓓ Ⓔ	14. Ⓐ Ⓑ Ⓒ Ⓓ Ⓔ	24. Ⓐ Ⓑ Ⓒ Ⓓ Ⓔ	34. Ⓐ Ⓑ Ⓒ Ⓓ Ⓔ
5. Ⓐ Ⓑ Ⓒ Ⓓ Ⓔ	15. Ⓐ Ⓑ Ⓒ Ⓓ Ⓔ	25. Ⓐ Ⓑ Ⓒ Ⓓ Ⓔ	35. Ⓐ Ⓑ Ⓒ Ⓓ Ⓔ
6. Ⓐ Ⓑ Ⓒ Ⓓ Ⓔ	16. Ⓐ Ⓑ Ⓒ Ⓓ Ⓔ	26. Ⓐ Ⓑ Ⓒ Ⓓ Ⓔ	36. Ⓐ Ⓑ Ⓒ Ⓓ Ⓔ
7. Ⓐ Ⓑ Ⓒ Ⓓ Ⓔ	17. Ⓐ Ⓑ Ⓒ Ⓓ Ⓔ	27. Ⓐ Ⓑ Ⓒ Ⓓ Ⓔ	37. Ⓐ Ⓑ Ⓒ Ⓓ Ⓔ
8. Ⓐ Ⓑ Ⓒ Ⓓ Ⓔ	18. Ⓐ Ⓑ Ⓒ Ⓓ Ⓔ	28. Ⓐ Ⓑ Ⓒ Ⓓ Ⓔ	38. Ⓐ Ⓑ Ⓒ Ⓓ Ⓔ
9. Ⓐ Ⓑ Ⓒ Ⓓ Ⓔ	19. Ⓐ Ⓑ Ⓒ Ⓓ Ⓔ	29. Ⓐ Ⓑ Ⓒ Ⓓ Ⓔ	39. Ⓐ Ⓑ Ⓒ Ⓓ Ⓔ
10. Ⓐ Ⓑ Ⓒ Ⓓ Ⓔ	20. Ⓐ Ⓑ Ⓒ Ⓓ Ⓔ	30. Ⓐ Ⓑ Ⓒ Ⓓ Ⓔ	40. Ⓐ Ⓑ Ⓒ Ⓓ Ⓔ

right in
Section 9

wrong in
Section 9

SECTION 1
Time—25 Minutes
ESSAY

The essay gives you an opportunity to show how effectively you can develop and express ideas. You should, therefore, take care to develop your point of view, present your ideas logically and clearly, and use language precisely.

Your essay must be written in your Answer Grid Booklet—you will receive no other paper on which to write. You will have enough space if you write on every line, avoid wide margins, and keep your handwriting to a reasonable size. Remember that people who are not familiar with your handwriting will read what you write. Try to write or print so that what you are writing is legible to those readers.

You have 25 minutes to write an essay on the topic assigned below.
DO NOT WRITE ON ANOTHER TOPIC. AN OFF-TOPIC ESSAY WILL RECEIVE A SCORE OF ZERO.

Think carefully about the issue presented in the following excerpt and the assignment below.

> "Nothing in the world can take the place of persistence. Talent will not; nothing is more common than unsuccessful men with talent. Genius will not; unrewarded genius is almost a proverb. Education will not; the world is full of educated derelicts. Persistence and determination are omnipotent. The slogan 'Press on!' has solved and always will solve the problems of the human race."
>
> –Calvin Coolidge, *Autobiography*

Assignment: Do you agree that persistence is the major factor in success and that talent, genius, and education play, at best, secondary roles? Plan and write an essay in which you develop your point of view on this issue. Support your position with reasoning and examples taken from your reading, studies, experience, or observations.

DO NOT WRITE YOUR ESSAY IN YOUR TEST BOOK.
You will receive credit only for what you write in your Answer Grid Booklet.

_____

_____

_____

_____

_____

_____

_____

_____

_____

_____

_____

_____

_____

_____

SECTION 2

Time—25 Minutes

24 Questions

Directions: For each of the following questions, choose the best answer and darken the corresponding oval on the answer sheet.

Each sentence below has one or two blanks, each blank indicating that something has been omitted. Beneath the sentence are five words or sets of words labeled (A) through (E). Choose the word or set of words that, when inserted in the sentence, best fits the meaning of the sentence as a whole.

EXAMPLE:

Today's small, portable computers contrast markedly with the earliest electronic computers, which were -------.

(A) effective

(B) invented

(C) useful

(D) destructive

(E) enormous   Ⓐ Ⓑ Ⓒ Ⓓ ●

1. Despite their fierce appearance, caymans are rarely ------- and will not attack humans unless provoked.

   (A) extinct

   (B) timid

   (C) domesticated

   (D) amphibious

   (E) aggressive

2. Some historians claim that the concept of courtly love is a ------- that dates from the age of chivalry, while others believe it has more ------- origins.

   (A) relic . . . simultaneous

   (B) notion . . . ancient

   (C) memento . . . discovered

   (D) novelty . . . documented

   (E) doctrine . . . amorous

3. In Shakespeare's day, ------- theater audiences would often throw fruits and vegetables at actors who failed to live up to their expectations.

   (A) doting

   (B) ravenous

   (C) jingoistic

   (D) boisterous

   (E) stagnant

4. Although they physically resemble each other, the brothers could not be more ------- temperamentally; while the one is quiet and circumspect, the other is brash and--------.

   (A) inimical . . . timid

   (B) passionate . . . superficial

   (C) dissimilar . . . audacious

   (D) different . . . forgiving

   (E) alike . . . respectful

GO ON TO THE NEXT PAGE ▷

5. The retreat of Napoleon's army from Moscow quickly turned into a rout, as French soldiers, already ------- in the snow were ------- by Russian troops.

    (A) replenishing . . . ravaged
    (B) pursuing . . . joined
    (C) sinking . . . camouflaged
    (D) floundering . . . assaulted
    (E) tottering . . . upbraided

6. The Morgan Library in New York provides a ------- environment in which scholars work amidst costly tapestries, paintings, stained-glass windows, and hand-crafted furniture.

    (A) realistic
    (B) frugal
    (C) sumptuous
    (D) friendly
    (E) practical

7. The lecturer's frustration was only ------- by the audience's ------- to talk during her presentation.

    (A) compounded . . . propensity
    (B) alleviated . . . invitation
    (C) soothed . . . authorization
    (D) increased . . . inability
    (E) supplanted . . . desire

8. The proposal to build a nuclear power plant was the most ------- issue ever to come up at a council meeting; it is astonishing, therefore, that the members' vote was unanimous.

    (A) popular
    (B) contentious
    (C) concise
    (D) exorbitant
    (E) inconsequential

GO ON TO THE NEXT PAGE

Directions: The passages below are followed by questions based on their content; questions following a pair of related passages may also be based on the relationship between the paired passages. Answer the questions on the basis of what is <u>stated</u> or <u>implied</u> in the passages and in any introductory material that may be provided.

Questions 9–10 refer to the following passage.

While it is often helpful to think of humans as simply another successful type of mammal, a vital distinction remains. When a pride of lions enjoys a surfeit of food, they are likely to
(5) hunt quickly, eat all they can, then spend the remainder of the day sleeping. When people enjoy such easy living, we see a markedly different pattern—our big brains cause us to be restless, and we engage in play. This takes the
(10) form of art, philosophy, science, even government. So the intelligence and curiosity that allowed early humans to develop agriculture, and thus a caloric surplus, also led to the use of that surplus as a foundation for culture.

9. The author most likely cites the behavior of lions in order to

   (A) provide an example of an even more successful mammalian species

   (B) question the efficiency of the lion's feeding behavior

   (C) provide a contrast to the image of humans as industrious and resourceful

   (D) help illustrate the distinguishing characteristic of humans that led to the development of culture

   (E) explore the range of hunting behaviors in different successful species

10. The final sentence "the intelligence ... for culture" (lines 11–14), primarily serves to

   (A) illustrate the significance of a distinction

   (B) counter a likely objection

   (C) provide an alternative explanation

   (D) suggest future implications of a phenomenon

   (E) condone a future investigation

Questions 11–12 refer to the following passage.

Eugene O'Neill is truly a playwright of ideas, ideas that speak to a fundamental aspect of humanity. Many of O'Neill's plays are set firmly on American soil at a particular
(5) time in history, and it is easy to imagine that since the characters on stage are American, the only viable audience for such a play must be American as well. While a logical conclusion, this does not allow for the consistently
(10) strong record of production of O'Neill plays in Europe. His plays encompass ideas relevant to everyone, not just Americans.

11. The "logical conclusion" (lines 8–9) is contradicted by O'Neill's

   (A) primarily American audiences

   (B) knowledge of American humanity

   (C) mastery of playwriting

   (D) authentically American characters

   (E) popularity in Europe

12. Which of the following, if true, would most seriously undermine the conclusion of the passage?

   (A) O'Neill's plays, once popular in American theaters, are rarely performed there today.

   (B) In order to be a successful playwright, it is important to cultivate a specific and loyal following.

   (C) When O'Neill's plays are staged in Europe, they are generally performed in English.

   (D) The audiences attending O'Neill's plays in Europe are, for the most part, Americans traveling or living in Europe.

   (E) O'Neill never traveled to Europe.

GO ON TO THE NEXT PAGE

Questions 13–24 refer to the following passage.

In the following passage, a famous zoologist discusses the origins of the domesticated animal.

The relationship between humans and animals dates back to the misty morning of history. The caves of southern France and northern Spain are full of wonderful depictions
(5) of animals. Early African petroglyphs depict recognizable mammals and so does much American Indian art. But long before art, we have evidence of the closeness of humans and animals. The bones of dogs lie next to those of
(10) humans in the excavated villages of northern Israel and elsewhere. This unity of death is terribly appropriate. It marks a relationship that is the most ancient of all, one that dates back at least to the Mesolithic Era.* With the
(15) dog, the hunter acquired a companion and ally very early on, before agriculture, and long before the horses and the cat. The companion animals were followed by food animals, and then by those that provided enhanced speed
(20) and range, and those that worked for us.

How did it all come about? A dog of some kind was almost inevitable. Consider its essence: a social carnivore, hunting larger animals across the broad plains it shared with
(25) our ancestors. Because of its pack structure it is susceptible to domination by, and attachment to, a pack leader—the top dog. Its young are born into the world dependent, rearable, without too much skill, and best of all, they
(30) form bonds with the rearers. Dogs have a set of appeasement behaviors that elicit affective reactions from even the most hardened and unsophisticated humans. Puppies share with human babies the power to transform cynics
(35) into cooing softies. Furthermore, the animal has a sense of smell and hearing several times more acute than our own, great advantages to a hunting companion and intrusion detector. The dog's defense behavior makes it an
(40) instinctive guard animal.

No wonder the dog was first and remains so close to us. In general, however, something else was probably important in narrowing the list—the candidates had to be camp followers
(45) or cohabitants. When humankind ceased to be continually nomadic, when we put down roots and established semi-permanent habitations, hut clusters, and finally villages, we created an instant, rich food supply for guilds
(50) of opportunistic feeders. Even today, many birds and mammals parasitize our wastes and feed from our stores. They do so because their wild behaviors provide the mechanisms for opportunistic exploitation. A striking example
(55) occurred in Britain during the 1940s and '50s. In those days, milk was delivered to the homeowners' doorstep in glass bottles with aluminum foil caps. Rich cream topped the milk, the paradise before homogenization. A chicka-
(60) dee known as the blue tit learned to puncture the cap and drink the cream. The behavior soon spread among the tits, and soon milk bottles were being raided in the early morning throughout Britain. If the birds had been so
(65) specialized that they only fed in deep forest, it never would have happened. But these were forest-edge opportunists, pioneers rather than conservatives. It is from animals of this ilk that we find our allies and our foes.
(70) Returning to the question of how it all came about, my instincts tell me that we first domesticated those individual animals that were orphaned by our hunting ancestors. In my years in the tropics, I have seen many wild
(75) animals raised by simple people in their houses. The animals were there, without thought of utility or gain, mainly because the hunter in the family had brought the orphaned baby back for his wife and children. In Panama it
(80) was often a beautiful small, spotted cat that bounced friskily out of a peasant's kitchen to

GO ON TO THE NEXT PAGE

play at my feet. The steps from the
home-raised wolfling to the domestic dog
probably took countless generations. I bet it
(85) started with affection and curiosity. Only later
did it become useful.

When we consider that there are more
than 55 million domestic cats and 50 million
dogs in this country, and that they support
(90) an industry larger than the total economy
of medieval Europe, we must recognize the
strength of the ancient bond.

Without the "aid" of goats, sheep, pigs, cattle, and horses we would never have reached
(95) our present population densities. Our parasiti-
zation of some species and symbiosis
with others made civilization possible. That
civilization, in turn, is increasingly causing
the extinction of many animals and plant
(100) species—an ironic paradox indeed.

*Mesolithic Era: the Middle Stone Age, between
8,000 and 3,000 B.C.

13. The author most likely describes the
archeological discoveries mentioned in lines
9–11 as "terribly appropriate" because

(A) dogs were always buried next to their
owners in the Mesolithic Era

(B) few animals were of religious significance
in prehistoric cultures

(C) they illustrate the role of dogs on a typical hunting expedition

(D) our relationship with dogs goes back farther than with any other animal

(E) they indicate the terrible speed of natural
disasters

14. According to the first paragraph, the first
animals that humans had a close relationship
with were those that

(A) acted as companions
(B) provided a source of food
(C) helped develop agriculture
(D) enabled humans to travel farther
(E) raided our food supply

15. According to the author, why was some kind
of dog "inevitable" (line 22) as a companion
animal for humans?

(A) It survived by maintaining its
independence.
(B) It was stronger than other large animals.
(C) It shared its prey with our ancestors.
(D) It was friendly to other carnivores.
(E) It was suited for human domination.

16. In line 23, "essence" means

(A) history
(B) nature
(C) scent
(D) success
(E) aggression

17. Judging from lines 31–32, "affective reactions"
most probably means

(A) callous decisions
(B) rational judgements
(C) emotional responses
(D) juvenile behavior
(E) cynical comments

GO ON TO THE NEXT PAGE

18. The author most likely compares puppies with human babies in lines 33–35 in order to

    (A) criticize an uncaring attitude toward animals

    (B) point out ways in which animals dominate humans

    (C) support the idea that dogs form bonds with their owners

    (D) dispel some misconceptions about the innocence of puppies

    (E) show how rewarding the ownership of a dog can be

19. In lines 43–44, "the list" most likely refers to the

    (A) types of birds that scavenge human food supplies

    (B) number of animals that developed relationships with humans

    (C) group of species that are able to communicate with dogs

    (D) variety of attributes that make dogs good hunters

    (E) range of animals depicted in cave paintings

20. The author most likely discusses the case of the British blue tit (lines 59–64) in order to

    (A) highlight a waste of valuable food supplies

    (B) indicate the quality of milk before homogenization

    (C) explain how unpredictable animal behavior can be

    (D) point out the disadvantages of living in rural areas

    (E) provide one example of an opportunistic feeder

21. In line 68, "animals of this ilk" refers to animals that are

    (A) good companions

    (B) forest inhabitants

    (C) adaptable feeders

    (D) efficient hunters

    (E) persistent pests

GO ON TO THE NEXT PAGE

22. The author most likely describes his experience in the tropics (lines 73–82) in order to

 (A) portray the simple life led by a hunter's family

 (B) show how useful animals can be in isolated places

 (C) underline the effort involved in training a wild animal

 (D) illustrate how the first domesticated animals were created

 (E) indicate the curious nature of the domestic cat

23. In line 93, the use of "aid" in quotation marks emphasizes the point that

 (A) the animals' help was involuntary

 (B) population levels are dangerously high

 (C) the contribution of animals is rarely recognized

 (D) many animals benefited from the relationship

 (E) livestock animals are not as loyal as dogs

24. Which of the following best describes the "ironic paradox" mentioned in line 100?

 (A) More money is now spent on domestic animals than on animal livestock.

 (B) Pet ownership will become impractical if population density continues to increase.

 (C) The pet care industry in the U.S. today is larger than the total economy of medieval Europe.

 (D) Many parasitical species have a beneficial effect on the human population.

 (E) Human civilization is currently making extinct many of the other life forms that enabled it to grow.

IF YOU FINISH BEFORE TIME IS CALLED, YOU MAY CHECK YOUR WORK ON THIS SECTION ONLY. DO NOT TURN TO ANY OTHER SECTION IN THE TEST.

STOP

SECTION 3

Time—25 Minutes
20 Questions

Directions: For this section, solve each problem and decide which is the best of the choices given. Fill in the corresponding oval on the answer sheet. You may use any available space for scratchwork.

Notes:

(1) Calculator use is permitted.

(2) All numbers used are real numbers.

(3) Figures are provided for some problems. All figures are drawn to scale and lie in a plane UNLESS otherwise indicated.

(4) Unless otherwise specified, the domain of any function f is assumed to be the set of all real numbers x for which $f(x)$ is a real number.

Information

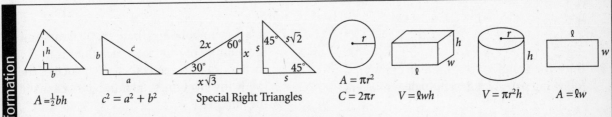

$A = \frac{1}{2}bh$ $\qquad c^2 = a^2 + b^2$ $\qquad$ Special Right Triangles $\qquad$ $A = \pi r^2$ $\qquad$ $V = \ell wh$ $\qquad$ $V = \pi r^2 h$ $\qquad$ $A = \ell w$

$\qquad\qquad\qquad\qquad\qquad\qquad\qquad\qquad\qquad\qquad\qquad\qquad$ $C = 2\pi r$

The sum of the degree measures of the angles in a triangle is 180.
The number of degrees of arc in a circle is 360.
A straight angle has a degree measure of 180.

1. If $2(x + y) = 8 + 2y$, then $x =$

    (A) 1
    (B) 2
    (C) 3
    (D) 4
    (E) 8

2. On the number line above, what is the distance from point B to the midpoint of AC?

    (A) 1
    (B) 2
    (C) 3
    (D) 4
    (E) 5

GO ON TO THE NEXT PAGE

3. A certain machine caps 5 bottles every 2 seconds. At this rate, how many bottles will be capped in 1 minute?

   (A) 10
   (B) 75
   (C) 150
   (D) 225
   (E) 300

4. If $2n + 3 = 5$, then $4n =$

   (A) 1
   (B) 2
   (C) 4
   (D) 8
   (E) 16

5. If $a + b < 5$, and $a - b > 6$, which of the following pairs could be the values of a and b?

   (A) (1, 3)
   (B) (3, –2)
   (C) (4, –2)
   (D) (4, –3)
   (E) (5, –1)

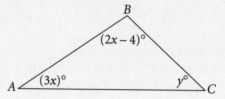

Note: Figure not drawn to scale.

6. In the triangle, if the measure of angle B is 60 degrees, then what is the value of y?

   (A) 24
   (B) 26
   (C) 28
   (D) 30
   (E) 32

7. In a certain building, there are 10 floors and the number of rooms on each floor is R. If each room has exactly C chairs, which of the following gives the total number of chairs in the building?

   (A) $10R + C$
   (B) $10R + 10C$
   (C) $\dfrac{10}{RC}$
   (D) $10RC$
   (E) $100RC$

8. If a "sump" number is defined as one in which the sum of the digits of the number is greater than the product of the digits of the same number, which of the following is a "sump" number?

   (A) 123
   (B) 234
   (C) 332
   (D) 411
   (E) 521

GO ON TO THE NEXT PAGE

9. If 4 percent of r is 6.2, then 20 percent of $r =$

    (A) 25

    (B) 26

    (C) 30

    (D) 31

    (E) 35

10. At a certain school, if the ratio of teachers to students is 1 to 10, which of the following could be the total number of teachers and students?

    (A) 100

    (B) 121

    (C) 144

    (D) 222

    (E) 1,011

11. If $x \wedge y$ is defined by the expression $(x - y)^x + (x + y)^y$, what is the value of $4 \wedge 2$?

    (A) 16

    (B) 20

    (C) 28

    (D) 44

    (E) 52

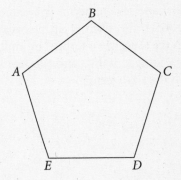

12. In pentagon $ABCDE$ shown above, each side is 1 centimeter. If a particle starts at point A and travels clockwise 723 centimeters along $ABCDE$, the particle will stop on which point?

    (A) A

    (B) B

    (C) C

    (D) D

    (E) E

13. Which of the following values of s would yield the smallest value for $4 + \dfrac{1}{s}$?

    (A) $\dfrac{1}{4}$

    (B) $\dfrac{1}{2}$

    (C) 1

    (D) 2

    (E) 4

GO ON TO THE NEXT PAGE

14. The first and seventh terms in a sequence are 1 and 365, respectively. If each term after the first in the sequence is formed by multiplying the preceding term by 3 and subtracting 1, what is the sixth term?

(A)   40

(B)   41

(C) 121

(D) 122

(E) 123

15. If an integer is randomly chosen from the first 50 positive integers, what is the probability that an integer with a digit of 3 is selected?

(A) $\frac{7}{25}$

(B) $\frac{3}{10}$

(C) $\frac{8}{25}$

(D) $\frac{2}{5}$

(E) $\frac{3}{5}$

16. In a certain triangle, the measure of the largest angle is 40 degrees more than the measure of the middle-sized angle. If the measure of the smallest angle is 20 degrees, what is the degree measure of the largest angle?

(A)   60

(B)   80

(C) 100

(D) 120

(E) 160

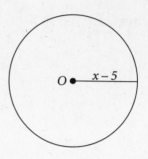

17. In the circle with center O above, for what value of x does the circle have a circumference of 20π?

(A)   5

(B) 10

(C) 15

(D) 20

(E) 25

18. In a coordinate plane, if points $A\,(p, 3)$ and $B\,(6, p)$ lie on a line with a slope of 2, what is the value of p?

(A) 1

(B) 2

(C) 3

(D) 4

(E) 5

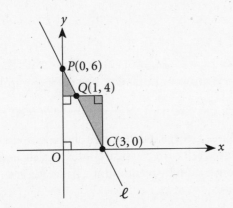

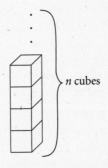

n cubes

19. In the coordinate plane above, points $P(0, 6)$, $Q(1, 4)$, and $C(3, 0)$ are on line ℓ. What is the sum of the areas of the shaded triangular regions?

(A) $\dfrac{7}{2}$

(B) 4

(C) $\dfrac{9}{2}$

(D) 5

(E) $\dfrac{11}{2}$

20. In the figure above, there is a total of n cubes, each with an edge of 1 inch, stacked directly on top of each other. If $n > 1$, what is the total surface area, in square inches, of the resulting solid, in terms of n?

(A) $2n$

(B) $2n^2 + 2$

(C) $4n + 2$

(D) $4n^2$

(E) $5n$

IF YOU FINISH BEFORE TIME IS CALLED, YOU MAY CHECK YOUR WORK ON THIS SECTION ONLY. DO NOT TURN TO ANY OTHER SECTION IN THE TEST.

STOP

SECTION 4

Time—25 Minutes
24 Questions

Directions: For each of the following questions, choose the best answer and darken the corresponding oval on the answer sheet.

Each sentence below has one or two blanks, each blank indicating that something has been omitted. Beneath the sentence are five words or sets of words labeled (A) through (E). Choose the word or set of words that, when inserted in the sentence, <u>best</u> fits the meaning of the sentence as a whole.

EXAMPLE:

Today's small, portable computers contrast markedly with the earliest electronic computers, which were -------.

(A) effective
(B) invented
(C) useful
(D) destructive
(E) enormous

1. Ozone in the upper layers of Earth's atmosphere is beneficial, ------- animal and plant life from dangerous ultraviolet radiation.

(A) reflecting
(B) withdrawing
(C) displacing
(D) thwarting
(E) protecting

2. While George Balanchine's choreography stayed within a classical context, he challenged convention by recombining ballet idioms in ------- ways.

(A) unexpected
(B) familiar
(C) redundant
(D) naive
(E) awkward

3. All of today's navel oranges are ------- of a single mutant tree that began bearing seedless fruit 200 years ago.

(A) progenitors
(B) combinations
(C) descendants
(D) conglomerations
(E) spores

GO ON TO THE NEXT PAGE

4. Because he consumed ------- quantities of food and drink at feasts given in his honor, King Henry VIII was considered a ------- by his subjects.

   (A) enormous . . . glutton
   (B) prodigious . . . peer
   (C) minute . . . luminary
   (D) unhealthy . . . fraud
   (E) unknown . . . dolt

5. The prime minister ordered the cabinet to stay on as ------- administration until a new government could be formed.

   (A) an interim
   (B) a political
   (C) an invalid
   (D) a premature
   (E) a civilian

GO ON TO THE NEXT PAGE

Directions: The passages below are followed by questions based on their content; questions following a pair of related passages may also be based on the relationship between the paired passages. Answer the questions on the basis of what is <u>stated</u> or <u>implied</u> in the passages and in any introductory material that may be provided.

Questions 6–9 refer to the following passages.

Passage 1

　　Miles Davis, though noteworthy as a jazz trumpet player, can best be understood instead as the ultimate musical iconoclast—a constant defier of popular and critical expec-
(5) tations. He first came to prominence as the young trumpeter in Charlie Parker's quintet in the late 1940s. In the early 50s, however, Davis led his own band in a completely different direction, using elaborate and original
(10) arrangements to explore a cool, subdued sound more in keeping with Davis's own personality. Characteristically, Davis soon abandoned this increasingly popular sound, pioneering the less harmonically sophisticated
(15) "modal" movement. Each decade brought more surprises, as Davis was at the forefront of free jazz, Fusion, and electronic instrumentation.

Passage 2

　　Great art often comes from limitations, and
(20) one can find no better example of this maxim than jazz great Miles Davis. Davis entered the jazz world when bebop music was at its peak. This style, pioneered by alto saxophonist Charlie Parker, demanded acrobatic facility,
(25) as soloists improvised dizzying melodies at break-neck speeds. Davis, though supremely expressive, didn't have the range or technique to play convincingly in this style. Rather than giving up, or continuing his career as a sec-
(30) ond-rate footnote, Davis evolved a unique style in which a few well-chosen notes were surrounded by artful silences that spoke volumes.

6. The author of Passage 1 most likely uses the word "characteristically" (line 12) in order to convey that

(A) like many artists, Davis creatively overcame technical limitations to create original art
(B) Davis's development of the new "modal" sound was part of a larger pattern of innovation
(C) Davis's inability to dedicate himself to a single style of jazz compromised his ultimate contribution to the art form
(D) Davis's skill as an instrumentalist is secondary to his role as a stylistic pioneer
(E) the modal movement, like Davis's other innovations, occurred about a decade after his previous stylistic advance

7. As used in line 30, "footnote" most nearly means

(A) unexpressive technician
(B) bibliographic citation
(C) unskilled artist
(D) stylistic innovator
(E) incidental participant

GO ON TO THE NEXT PAGE

8. Which of the following is most like Davis's "unique style" as described in lines 30–33?

  (A) A writer who explores poetry, short stories, and novels over the course of her career

  (B) A chef who carefully selects ingredients to create a balanced flavor

  (C) A photographer who purposely leaves his subject unfocused

  (D) A painter who uses a simple background to highlight her subject

  (E) A playwright who writes fast-paced, witty dialogue to advance the play's plot

9. The author of Passage 1 would most likely regard the description of Davis's departure from "bebop music" described in Passage 2 as

  (A) illustrative of Davis's ability to overcome technical obstacles

  (B) an example of limitations facilitating artistic progress

  (C) characteristic of Davis's stylistic innovations

  (D) a surprising though important development in Davis's career

  (E) the most significant of Davis's contributions to jazz music

Questions 10–17 refer to the following passage.

The passage below is adapted from a short story set in the wilderness of Alaska.

Day had broken cold and gray, exceedingly cold and gray, when the man turned away from the main Yukon trail and climbed the high earth-bank, where a dim and little-
(5) traveled trail led eastward through the spruce timberland. It was a steep bank, and he paused for breath at the top, excusing the act to himself by looking at his watch. It was nine o'clock. There was no hint of sun, though
(10) there was not a cloud in the sky. It was a clear day, and yet there seemed an intangible pall over the face of things that made the day dark. This fact did not worry the man.

In fact, all this—the dim trail, the absence
(15) of sun from the sky, the tremendous cold, and the strangeness and weirdness of it all—made no impression on the man. It was not because he was used to it. He was a newcomer in the land, and this was his first winter. The trou-
(20) ble was that he was without imagination. He was young and quick and alert in the things of life, but only in the things, and not in the significances. It was fifty degrees below zero, he judged. That impressed him as being cold
(25) and uncomfortable, but it did not lead him to meditate upon his frailty as a creature of temperature, and upon human frailty in general, able only to live within narrow limits of heat and cold; and from there on it did not
(30) lead him to the conjectural field of immortality and humanity's place in the universe. Fifty degrees below zero stood for a bite of frost that hurt and that must be guarded against. Nothing more than that entered his head.
(35) He plunged in among the trees with determination. The trail was faint. A foot of snow had fallen since the last sled had passed, and

GO ON TO THE NEXT PAGE

he was glad he was traveling light. In fact, he
carried nothing but the lunch wrapped in his
(40) handkerchief. He was surprised, however, at
the cold. It certainly was cold, he concluded,
as he rubbed his numb nose and cheekbones
with his mittened hand. He was bearded, but
that did not protect the high cheekbones and
(45) the eager nose that thrust itself aggressively
into the frosty air.

At his heels walked a dog, a big native husky,
gray-coated, without any visible or tempera-
mental difference from its close relative, the
(50) wild wolf. The animal was depressed by the
tremendous cold. It knew that it was no time
for traveling. Its instinct told it a truer tale
than was told by the man's judgment. In reality, it was not merely colder than fifty below
(55) zero; it was colder than sixty below, than
seventy below. It was seventy-five below zero.
The dog knew nothing of thermometers.
Possibly in its brain there was no sharp consciousness of a condition of very cold such as
(60) was in the human brain. But the brute had its
instinct. It experienced a vague but menac-
ing apprehension that subdued it and made it
slink along at the man's heels, and that made
it question every unusual movement of the
(65) man as if expecting him to go into camp or to
seek shelter somewhere and build a fire. The
dog had learned fire, and it wanted fire, or
else to burrow under the snow and cuddle its
warmth away from the air.

10. By using the phrase "excusing the act to
himself" (lines 7–8), the author suggests that
the man

(A) is annoyed that it is already nine o'clock
in the morning

(B) distrusts his own intuitive reactions to
things

(C) finds fault with others more readily than
with himself

(D) doubts that the time of day has any real
bearing on things

(E) dislikes admitting to personal weaknesses

11. The author identifies the man as "a newcomer
in the land" (lines 18–19) most likely in order
to suggest that the man was

(A) excited at being in a new place with
many opportunities

(B) nervous about being alone in an unfamiliar place

(C) lacking in knowledge and experience
about the things around him

(D) trying hard to forget something in his
past

(E) unsure about why he chose to come to
the new place

12. In lines 26–27, the phrase "a creature of
temperature" refers to

(A) the man's preference for cold climates

(B) the innate human ability to judge
temperature

(C) the fact that one's personality is shaped
by the environment

(D) the human body's physical vulnerability
in extreme climates

(E) the man's unfamiliarity with wilderness
survival techniques

GO ON TO THE NEXT PAGE

13. Judging from lines 20–31, the man does not see that

    (A) he should appreciate the immense beauty of nature

    (B) humans cannot survive in the Alaskan wilderness

    (C) there is no way to accurately judge the temperature

    (D) the extreme cold could potentially be fatal

    (E) he has undertaken to do something which most people could not

14. The man's opinion of the temperature (lines 31–33) reveals which aspect of his character?

    (A) determination to succeed against all odds

    (B) lack of concern about personal welfare

    (C) pragmatic approach to travel

    (D) absence of insight and understanding

    (E) apprehension about the extreme cold

15. In lines 50–60, by discussing the dog's reaction to the "tremendous cold," the author suggests that

    (A) animal instinct can prove to be superior to human intelligence

    (B) animals can judge temperature more accurately than humans can

    (C) humans are ill-equipped to survive in the wilderness

    (D) there is little difference between animal instinct and human judgment

    (E) animals and humans have different reactions to extreme temperatures

16. The statement "the dog knew nothing of thermometers" (line 57) means that

    (A) dogs need not be as concerned about temperature as humans do

    (B) the dog's awareness of its environment is on a different level from the man's

    (C) a dog's mental faculties are not very well developed

    (D) the dog's experience of humans had been rather limited

    (E) the dog could not rely on the technological devices that the man could

17. Which of the following best explains why the dog would "question every unusual movement of the man" (lines 64–65)?

    (A) The dog senses that it cannot rely on the man for survival.

    (B) The man is beginning to be visibly affected by the cold.

    (C) The dog recognizes the need for protection from the cold.

    (D) The dog worries that the man intends to leave it behind.

    (E) The dog understands that the man does not realize how cold it is.

GO ON TO THE NEXT PAGE

Questions 18–24 refer to the following passage.

The Social Science passage below was adapted from an article written by a health scientist.

For people in Southeast Asian refugee families, the experience of aging in America is very different from what they had expected for their second half of life. Older Southeast Asian
(5) refugees must cope with their rapidly acculturating younger family members, while taking on new roles and expectations in a foreign culture.

Many Southeast Asian immigrants are
(10) surprised to find that by American standards, they are not even considered elderly. Migration to a new culture often changes the definition of life stages. In the traditional Hmong culture of Vietnam, one can become
(15) an elder at 35 years of age when one becomes a grandparent. With grandparent status, elder Hmong can retire and expect their children to take financial responsibility for the family. Retiring at 35, of course, is not common in
(20) the United States.

There is a strong influence of Confucianism in traditional Vietnamese society. Confucianism, an ancient system of moral and religious thought, fosters strong filial
(25) piety and respect for family elders. In many Southeast Asian societies, age roles are hierarchical, with strict rules for social interaction. In America, however, because older refugees lack facility with the English language and
(30) knowledge of American culture, their credibility decreases when advising younger family members about important decisions. As younger family members take on primary roles as family mediators with American insti-
(35) tutions—schools, legal systems, and social service agencies, for example—the leadership position of elders within the family is gradually eroded.

Refugee elders must also cope with differ-
(40) ences in gender roles in the United States.

Even before migration, traditional gender roles were changing in Southeast Asia. During the Vietnam War, when men of military age were away, women took responsibility for
(45) tasks normally divided along gender lines. When Vietnamese families came to this country, these changes became more pronounced. There were more employment opportunities for younger refugees and middle-aged refugee
(50) women because their expectations often fit with the lower status jobs that were among the few opportunities open to refugees. Many middle-aged women and younger refugees of both sexes became family breadwinners. This
(55) was a radical change for middle-aged men, who had been the major breadwinners of the family.

Although the pattern for long-term adaptation of middle-aged and older Southeast
(60) Asian refugees is still unknown, there are indications that the outlook for women is problematic. Many older women provide household and childcare services in order to allow younger family members to hold jobs
(65) or go to school. While these women are helping younger family members to succeed in America, they themselves are often isolated at home and cut off from learning English or other new skills, or becoming more familiar
(70) with American society. Thus, after the immigrant family passes through the early stages of meeting basic survival needs, older women may find that they are strangers in their own families as well as in their new country.

GO ON TO THE NEXT PAGE ⇨

18. The major purpose of the passage is to discuss

   (A) the reasons why Southeast Asian people move to the United States

   (B) educational challenges facing young refugees in America today

   (C) problems that elderly Southeast Asian people encounter in America

   (D) the influence of Confucianism in Southeast Asian cultures

   (E) changing gender relationships in Southeast Asian refugee families

19. In lines 4–6, "Older Southeast Asian refugees must cope with their rapidly acculturating younger family members" refers to

   (A) middle-aged men's embarrassment at not being the principal breadwinner

   (B) middle-aged women's isolation in the home

   (C) the high crime rate among younger refugees

   (D) younger refugees' better educational and social opportunities in America

   (E) the tendency of younger refugees to join non-Asian gangs

20. The author mentions "the traditional Hmong culture" (lines 13–14) in order to

   (A) show that social expectations may vary greatly from one country to another

   (B) suggest the lessening importance of traditional values in Vietnamese society

   (C) indicate that modern Vietnam encompasses a number of ancient cultures

   (D) illustrate the growing influence of Confucianism in Vietnamese society

   (E) compare the religious beliefs of the Vietnamese to those of other Southeast Asian peoples

21. The author uses the term "family mediators" (line 34) to mean the

   (A) traditional role of elders in Vietnamese families

   (B) responsibilities that young refugees assume in a new country

   (C) help that newly arrived refugees get from friends who migrated earlier

   (D) professional help available to refugee families in U.S. communities

   (E) benefits that American society derives from immigrant people

22. The word "pronounced" in line 47 most nearly means

   (A) delivered

   (B) noticeable

   (C) famous

   (D) acceptable

   (E) declared

23. The phrase "radical change" (line 55) refers to the fact that

   (A) older refugees find that retirement ages are very different in America

   (B) women filled men's jobs during the Vietnam War

   (C) the education of their children is considered crucial by refugee parents

   (D) refugee men are often displaced as primary income earners in their families

   (E) it is difficult for young refugees of both sexes to find jobs in America

GO ON TO THE NEXT PAGE

24. The author's point about the problematic long-term outlook for refugee women is made primarily through

    (A) personal recollection
    (B) historical discussion
    (C) case study analysis
    (D) philosophical commentary
    (E) informed speculation

IF YOU FINISH BEFORE TIME IS CALLED, YOU MAY CHECK YOUR WORK ON THIS SECTION ONLY. DO NOT TURN TO ANY OTHER SECTION IN THE TEST.

STOP

SECTION 5
Time—25 Minutes
18 Questions

Directions: For this section, solve each problem and decide which is the best of the choices given. Fill in the corresponding oval on the answer sheet. You may use any available space for scratchwork.

Notes:

(1) Calculator use is permitted.

(2) All numbers used are real numbers.

(3) Figures are provided for some problems. All figures are drawn to scale and lie in a plane UNLESS otherwise indicated.

(4) Unless otherwise specified, the domain of any function f is assumed to be the set of all real numbers x for which $f(x)$ is a real number.

Information

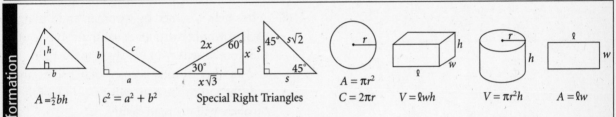

$A = \frac{1}{2}bh$ $\qquad$ $c^2 = a^2 + b^2$ $\qquad$ Special Right Triangles $\qquad$ $A = \pi r^2$ $\qquad$ $C = 2\pi r$ $\qquad$ $V = \ell wh$ $\qquad$ $V = \pi r^2 h$ $\qquad$ $A = \ell w$

The sum of the degree measures of the angles in a triangle is 180.
The number of degrees of arc in a circle is 360.
A straight angle has a degree measure of 180.

1. If $r = 3$, then $(r^2 - 2)(4 + r) =$

   (A) 5
   (B) 7
   (C) 49
   (D) 77
   (E) 91

2. If $f(x) = x^2 + x$, what is the value of $f(3)$?

   (A) 0
   (B) 3
   (C) 6
   (D) 9
   (E) 12

3. If Set A is the set of prime numbers between 10 and 20, Set B is the set of integers between -10 and 15, and Set C is the intersection of Set A and Set B, then how many elements does Set C contain?

   (A) 2
   (B) 4
   (C) 25
   (D) 29
   (E) 30

GO ON TO THE NEXT PAGE

4. What is the greatest prime factor of 87?

   (A) 3
   (B) 17
   (C) 29
   (D) 43
   (E) 87

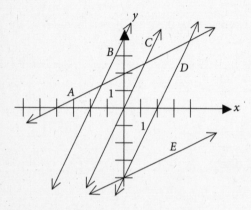

5. The graph above shows five lines, lettered A through E. Which of these lines can be represented as $y = 2x - 4$?

   (A) A
   (B) B
   (C) C
   (D) D
   (E) E

6. The statement $(y - 3)^2 = (y + 1)^2$ is true for which of the following values of y?

   (A) −1 only
   (B) 1 only
   (C) 3 and 1
   (D) −3 and −1
   (E) $\sqrt{3}$ only

7. A circular frame with a width of 2 inches surrounds a circular photo with a diameter of 8 inches. Assuming that the area of the frame does not overlap the area of the photo, what is the area of the frame?

   (A) 4π
   (B) 12π
   (C) 16π
   (D) 20π
   (E) 36π

8. A business is owned by 4 women and 1 man, each of whom owns an equal share. If one of the women sells $\frac{1}{2}$ of her share to the man, and another woman keeps $\frac{1}{4}$ of her share and sells the rest to the man, what fraction of the business will the man own?

   (A) $\frac{1}{3}$
   (B) $\frac{9}{20}$
   (C) $\frac{11}{20}$
   (D) $\frac{2}{3}$
   (E) $\frac{4}{5}$

GO ON TO THE NEXT PAGE

Directions: For Student-Produced Response questions 9–18, use the grids at the bottom of the answer sheet page on which you have answered questions 1–8.

Each of the remaining ten questions requires you to solve the problem and enter your answer by marking the ovals in the special grid, as shown in the example below. You may use any available space for scratchwork.

Answer: 1.25 or $\frac{5}{4}$ or 5/4

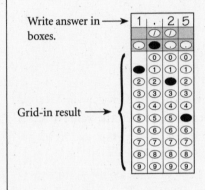

Write answer in boxes.

Grid-in result

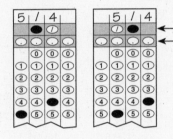

Fraction line
Decimal point

Either position is correct.

You may start your answers in any column, space permitting. Columns not needed should be left blank.

- It is recommended, though not required, that you write your answer in the boxes at the top of the columns. However, you will receive credit only for darkening the ovals correctly.

- Grid only one answer to a question, even though some problems have more than one correct answer.

- Darken no more than one oval in a column.

- No answers are negative.

- Mixed numbers cannot be gridded. For example: the number $1\frac{1}{4}$ must be gridded as 1.25 or 5/4.

(If $\boxed{1\ 1\ /\ 4}$ is gridded, it will be interpreted as $\frac{11}{4}$, not $1\frac{1}{4}$.)

- <u>Decimal Accuracy:</u> Decimal answers must be entered as accurately as possible. For example, if you obtain an answer such as 0.1666…, you should record the result as **.166 or .167. Less accurate values such as .16 or .17 are not acceptable.**

Acceptable ways to grid $\frac{1}{6}$ = .1666…

GO ON TO THE NEXT PAGE

9. If $y = 2$, then $(5 - y)(y + 3) =$

10. At a certain car rental company, the daily rental rate for a midsize car is $18.99. If the weekly rental rate for the same car is $123.50, how much money, in dollars, is saved by renting this car by the week instead of renting daily for seven days? (Exclude the $ when gridding your answer.)

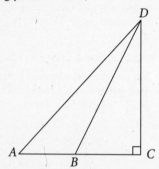

Note: Figure not drawn to scale.

11. In the figure above, $AB = 4$, $BC = 5$, and $DC = 12$. If point E lies somewhere between points A and B on line segment AB, what is one possible length of DE?

12. If $\frac{3}{4}$ of a cup of a certain drink mix is needed for every 2 quarts of water, how many cups of this drink mix is needed for 10 quarts of water?

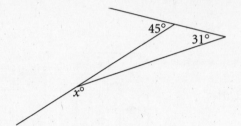

13. In the figure above, what is the value of x?

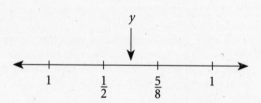

Note: Figure not drawn to scale.

14. On the number line above, what is one possible value for y?

GO ON TO THE NEXT PAGE

15. Melanie drove at an average rate of 40 miles per hour for 2 hours and then increased her average rate by 25% for the next 3 hours. Her average rate of speed for the 5 hours was t miles per hour. What is the value of t?

16. At a convention of 500 dealers, each dealer sold coins or stamps or both. If 127 dealers sold both coins and stamps, and 198 dealers sold *only* stamps, how many dealers sold *only* coins?

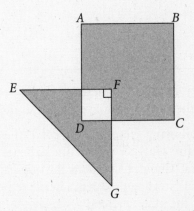

Note: Figure not drawn to scale.

17. In the figure above, square $ABCD$ and right triangle EFG overlap to form a smaller square. The length of each side of the smaller square is 2. If $AB = EF = FG = 6$, what is the sum of the areas of the shaded regions?

$$
\begin{array}{r}
NR \\
+RN \\
\hline
ABC
\end{array}
$$

18. The addition problem above is correct. If N, R, A, B, and C are different digits, what is the greatest possible value of $B + C$?

SECTION 6
Time—25 Minutes
35 Questions

Directions: For each question in this section, select the best answer from among the choices given and fill in the corresponding oval on the answer sheet.

The following sentences test correctness and effectiveness of expression. Part of each sentence or the entire sentence is underlined; beneath each sentence are five ways of phrasing the underlined material. Choice (A) repeats the original phrasing; the other four choices are different. If you think the original phrasing produces a better sentence than any of the alternatives, select choice (A); if not, select one of the other choices.

In making your selection, follow the requirements of standard written English; that is, pay attention to grammar, choice of words, sentence construction, and punctuation. Your selection should result in the most effective sentence—clear and precise, without awkwardness or ambiguity.

EXAMPLE: ANSWER:

Every apple in the baskets <u>are ripe and labeled according to the date it was picked</u>.   (A) ● (C) (D) (E)

(A) are ripe and labeled according to the date it was picked
(B) is ripe and labeled according to the date it was picked
(C) are ripe and labeled according to the date they were picked
(D) is ripe and labeled according to the date they were picked
(E) are ripe and labeled as to the date it was picked

---

1. By the time I graduate from college three years from now, my brother <u>has practiced</u> law for five years.

   (A) has practiced
   (B) has been practicing
   (C) will have been practicing
   (D) would have practiced
   (E) is practicing

2. The historians at the university who are researching the Napoleonic Wars from the Russian perspective <u>includes more than two professors who emigrated from Russia</u> to the United States.

   (A) includes more than two professors who emigrated from Russia
   (B) included more than two professors who emigrated from Russia
   (C) include more than two professors who emigrated from Russia
   (D) include more than two professors whom emigrated from Russia
   (E) includes at least two professors who emigrated from Russia

GO ON TO THE NEXT PAGE

3. In her Comparative Literature class, Nancy enjoyed reading Marcel Proust's groundbreaking novel, <u>which she considered to be more brilliant than the other writers we read</u>.

   (A) which she considered to be more brilliant than the other writers we read

   (B) whom she considered to have been more brilliant than the other writers we read

   (C) which she considered to be more brilliant than the other novels we read

   (D) which she considered to be brilliant opposed to the other novels we read

   (E) whom she considered to be more brilliant than the other novels we read

4. Many people <u>watching the baseball series seen the hometown hero arriving</u> at the stadium before the game.

   (A) watching the baseball series seen the hometown hero arriving

   (B) watching the baseball series saw the hometown hero arriving

   (C) who watch the baseball series seen the hometown hero arriving

   (D) watching the baseball series saw the hometown hero have arrived

   (E) who watch the baseball series seen the hometown hero arrived

5. The oxygen tank's increased capacity allows divers <u>to discover new species that congregate and feed close to</u> the bottom of the ocean.

   (A) to discover new species that congregate and feed close to

   (B) to have discovered new species that congregate and feed close to

   (C) to discover new species that congregate in and feed close to

   (D) to discover new species that congregate in and feed from close to

   (E) to discover new species who congregate and feed close to

6. The referee halted play in an effort <u>at avoiding serious altercations in the stadium between fans of</u> the opposing teams.

   (A) at avoiding serious altercations in the stadium between fans of

   (B) at avoiding a serious altercation in the stadium between fans of

   (C) to avoid serious altercations in the stadium between fans of

   (D) to avoid serious altercations in the stadium between fans on

   (E) to avoid serious altercations between fans in the stadium of

7. <u>Primarily a strategy to attract the votes of the elderly</u>, the Social Security adjustment carried great weight among the entire voting public of the day.

   (A) Primarily a strategy to attract the votes of the elderly

   (B) Primarily a strategy of attracting the votes of the elderly

   (C) Primarily the strategy to attract the votes of the elders

   (D) Primarily strategic to attracting the votes of the elderly

   (E) Primarily elderly voters' votes were attracted

GO ON TO THE NEXT PAGE ▷

8. A group of experts researching the bizarre occurrences theorized that the configuration of bright lights <u>were rather unusual but probably due to optical illusion</u>.

(A) were rather unusual but probably due to optical illusion

(B) were hardly unusual but probably due to optical illusion

(C) were rather unusual and probably due to optical illusion

(D) was rather unusual but probably due to optical illusion

(E) was rather unusual probably due to optical illusion

9. The school's new retro rock-and-roll band has drawn such huge crowds that an entirely new team has been hired <u>to determine new methods of providing security for their concerts</u>.

(A) to determine new methods of providing security for their concerts

(B) to determine new methods of providing security for its concerts

(C) to determine new methods for providing security for its concerts

(D) to be determining new methods for providing security for the concerts they give

(E) to be determining new methods of providing security for their concerts

10. <u>If the concert had begun later, the conductor might have succeeded in giving the difficult last-minute corrections for the symphony to the orchestra.</u>

(A) If the concert had begun later, the conductor might have succeeded in giving the difficult last-minute corrections for the symphony to the orchestra.

(B) If the concert had began later, the conductor might have succeeded in giving the difficult last-minute corrections for the symphony to the orchestra.

(C) If the concert had begun later, the conductor will succeed in giving last-minute corrections to the difficult orchestra for the symphony.

(D) If the concert had begun afterwards, the conductor might have succeeded in having given last-minute corrections for the difficult symphony to the orchestra.

(E) If the concert begun later, the orchestra would have succeeded in having difficult last-minute corrections for the symphony from the conductor.

11. Igor Stravinsky created innovative musical <u>works and they superimposed</u> beautiful melodies over discordant harmonies.

(A) works and they superimposed

(B) works, which superimposing

(C) works, they superimposed

(D) works that superimposed

(E) works, but superimposed

Directions: The following sentences test your ability to recognize grammar and usage errors. Each sentence contains either a single error or no error at all. No sentence contains more than one error. The error, if there is one, is underlined and lettered. If the sentence contains an error, select the one underlined part that must be changed to make the sentence correct. If the sentence is correct, select choice (E). In choosing answers, follow the requirements of standard written English.

EXAMPLE:

<u>Whenever</u> one is driving late at night, <u>you</u> must take extra precautions <u>against</u>
        A   B   C

falling asleep <u>at the wheel</u>. <u>No error</u>
               D   E

(A) ● (C) (D) (E)

12. The great blue heron, perhaps the most elegant

    species among birds, <u>live</u> in <u>most</u> parts of the
                          A   B
    United States, <u>at home</u> in wetland habitats
                    C
    in <u>both</u> inland and coastal regions. <u>No error</u>
        D   E

13. At the football stadium, Susan <u>liked watching</u>
                                    A
    the home team's pre-game warm-ups, <u>which</u>
                                        B
    she considered <u>more interesting</u> <u>than the</u>
    C
    <u>visiting team</u>. <u>No error</u>
     D   E

14. <u>By tracing</u> the source of artifacts found in
     A
    Europe, researchers <u>determined</u> that the
                         B
    pattern of Viking settlements <u>were</u> <u>generally</u>
                                   C   D
    similar, but varied in response to different

    climates. <u>No error</u>
               E

15. The cake recipe <u>actually called</u> for a generous
                     A
    amount of sugar, <u>and</u> Chad used a sugar
                      B
    substitute instead <u>since</u> he wanted to <u>lower</u>
                        C   D
    the cake's calorie count. <u>No error</u>
                               E

16. <u>Although</u> Luther Burbank <u>conducted</u>
     A   B
    experiments that led to many new or

    improved plants, <u>such as</u> the blight-resistant
                      C
    potato, his attempt <u>to develop</u>
                         D
    a spineless cactus was not a success. <u>No error</u>
                                           E

17. <u>They</u> were relieved <u>when</u> monsoons <u>carried</u>
     A   B   C
    rain from the southern seas <u>and</u> replenished
                                 D
    India's drought-stricken water supply.

    <u>No error</u>
     E

GO ON TO THE NEXT PAGE

18. All of the children <u>waiting</u> for the school
                        A
    bus <u>seen</u> the crossing guard <u>walking out</u> into
          B   C
    the street <u>to stop traffic</u>. <u>No error</u>
                 D   E

19. Arthur Miller's moral viewpoint allows him

    <u>to produce</u> plays <u>that</u> uniquely and
         A   B
    dramatically <u>expresses</u> the damaging effect
                 C
    modern life <u>has had</u> on Americans. <u>No error</u>
              D   E

20. <u>While</u> many small children <u>claim hearing</u>
        A   B
    Santa and his reindeer on the roof, few teen-

    agers believe that <u>such a person</u> <u>truly</u> exists.
                     C   D
    <u>No error</u>
        E

21. This week, the company <u>initiated</u> Hawaiian
                        A
    Shirt Day in an attempt <u>at creating</u> a higher
                        B
    degree <u>of team spirit</u> <u>in the office</u>. <u>No error</u>
            C   D   E

22. <u>As Shirin Abadi was awarded</u> the Nobel Peace
        A   B
    Prize, many of her colleagues <u>praised</u> her
                         C
    exceptional efforts <u>about</u> democracy
                 D
    and human rights in Iran. <u>No error</u>
                        E

23. Although the San Francisco earthquake

    <u>in the spring</u> of 1906 <u>was leveling</u> many
        A   B
    buildings, the subsequent <u>series of fires</u>
                        C
    actually <u>destroyed</u> most of the city. <u>No error</u>
            D   E

24. The quarterback, after his startling <u>failure to</u>
                           A
    throw a complete pass, <u>went about</u>
                      B
    <u>absolute shamefaced</u> and was available to
        C
    <u>only a few</u> of his teammates. <u>No error</u>
         D   E

25. <u>While</u> the effect of disease-causing agents on
        A
    cigarette smokers <u>has been known</u> for years,
                   B
    only recently <u>has</u> the damaging effects of
                C
    cigarette smoke on secondhand smokers

    <u>become</u> widely recognized. <u>No error</u>
        D   E

26. The FBI <u>maintains</u> strict <u>requirements for</u>
             A   B
    citizens when <u>they are</u> <u>interested in</u> joining
               C   D
    the Bureau. <u>No error</u>
              E

GO ON TO THE NEXT PAGE

27. <u>Although</u> James Joyce, Samuel Beckett, and
       A
Seamus Deane <u>drew on similar</u> aspects of
                        B
Irish culture in their novels, Beckett

<u>was</u> <u>more abstract</u> in his interpretations.
 C   D
<u>No error</u>
      E

28. José Limón, <u>assuredly</u> one of today's
                   A
<u>most inventive</u> modern dance
      B
choreographers, <u>brought</u> to the stage a star-
                     C
tling <u>approach to</u> movement and musicality.
         D
<u>No error</u>
      E

29. Among the great moments in twentieth

century history, the toppling of the Berlin

Wall by East Germans <u>are</u> <u>probably seen</u> by
                        A   B
<u>them</u> as one of the <u>most felicitous</u>. <u>No error</u>
 C   D   E

GO ON TO THE NEXT PAGE

Directions: The following passage is an early draft of an essay. Some parts of the passage need to be rewritten.

Read the passage and select the best answer for each question that follows. Some questions are about particular sentences or parts of sentences and ask you to improve sentence structure or word choice. Other questions ask you to consider organization and development. In choosing answers, follow the conventions of standard written English.

Questions 30–35 refer to the following passage.

(1) When I visited England last year, I wanted to attend a football match (football in England is what is called soccer in the U.S.). (2) My mother wouldn't let me. (3) She tells me, "The fans are much too violent." (4) I really wanted to go so I did some research on English fans' violence.

(5) Through my research I realized that my mother would never let me go to a game. (6) But beyond that, I felt sad that hooliganism was such a reality in the English game. (7) They cause riots, and innocent football fans are sometimes injured by them when football-related fights get out of control.

(8) England had tried all sorts of remedies to stop the violence, but they couldn't stop hooliganism from increasing. (9) The officials tried creating lists of people banned from stadiums. (10) At international matches some known hooligans weren't even allowed into the country. (11) Some say that the older generation of hooligans was teaching the younger. (12) It is just human nature and crowd mentality. (13) But there was an argument that rang even more true for me: poverty was an underlying cause. (14) Economic data indicating that the football teams with the highest rate of violence were situated in the poorest areas.

30. In context, which is the best version of the underlined portion of sentence 3 (reproduced below)?

She tells me, "The fans are much too violent."

(A) (As it is now)

(B) My mother tells me,

(C) This was because she tells me,

(D) She told me,

(E) She suggests,

31. In context, which is the best version of the underlined portion of sentence 7 (reproduced below)?

They cause riots, and innocent football fans are sometimes injured by them when football-related fights get out of control.

(A) (As it is now)

(B) They caused riots, and innocent football fans were sometimes injured by them

(C) Causing riots and injuring innocent football fans, the hooligans caused problems

(D) The hooligans cause riots and sometimes injure innocent football fans

(E) Innocent football fans sometimes cause riots and are injured

GO ON TO THE NEXT PAGE ⟶

32. In context, which of the following phrases is the most logical to insert at the beginning of sentence 12 (reproduced below)?

It is just human nature and crowd mentality.

(A) I see that
(B) They say that
(C) Others say that
(D) In contrast,
(E) As a result,

33. In context, which is the best version of the underlined portion of sentence 14 (reproduced below)?

Economic data indicating that the football teams with the highest rate of violence were situated in the poorest areas.

(A) (As it is now)
(B) seeming to indicate that the football teams
(C) are indicating that the football teams
(D) indicated that the football teams
(E) had indicated that the football teams

34. Which of the following best describes the relationship between sentences 13 and 14?

(A) Sentence 14 provides the conclusion supported by evidence in sentence 13.
(B) Sentence 14 adds to information reported in sentence 13.
(C) Sentence 14 poses an argument that contradicts the point made in sentence 13.
(D) Sentence 14 provides supporting evidence for the conclusion in sentence 13.
(E) Sentence 14 concludes that the theory proposed in sentence 13 is wrong.

35. Where is the best place to insert the following sentence?

Instead of just punishing acts of hooliganism, England should attack its source, poverty.

(A) After sentence 5
(B) After sentence 7
(C) After sentence 9
(D) After sentence 12
(E) After sentence 14

SECTION 7

Time—20 Minutes
19 Questions

Directions: For each of the following questions, choose the best answer and darken the corresponding oval on the answer sheet.

Each sentence below has one or two blanks, each blank indicating that something has been omitted. Beneath the sentence are five words or sets of words labeled (A) through (E). Choose the word or set of words that, when inserted in the sentence, best fits the meaning of the sentence as a whole.

EXAMPLE:

Today's small, portable computers contrast markedly with the earliest electronic computers, which were -------.

(A) effective
(B) invented
(C) useful
(D) destructive
(E) enormous

1. The itinerary set by their travel agent included so many stops in ------- amount of time that they received only the most ------- impressions of places visited.

    (A) a limited . . . lasting
    (B) a brief . . . cursory
    (C) a generous . . . favorable
    (D) a sufficient . . . fleeting
    (E) an unnecessary . . . preliminary

2. Many formerly ------- peoples have moved into ------- settlements as urban areas have encroached upon their land.

    (A) roving . . . vulnerable
    (B) despondent . . . stable
    (C) transitory . . . covert
    (D) fervid . . . enduring
    (E) nomadic . . . permanent

3. The ------- effect of the sleeping tablets was so ------- that she still felt groggy the next day.

    (A) toxic . . . erratic
    (B) soporific . . . pronounced
    (C) salubrious . . . dependable
    (D) pharmaceutical . . . peculiar
    (E) stimulating . . . unreliable

GO ON TO THE NEXT PAGE

4. For many years Davis had difficulty in accepting those who were in positions of authority; in fact, when he was in high school his teachers described him as a ------- student.

(A) compliant
(B) slothful
(C) conscientious
(D) model
(E) recalcitrant

5. Although the actress had lived in a large city all her life, she was such a ------- performer that she became the virtual ------- of the humble farm girl she portrayed in the play.

(A) versatile . . . opposite
(B) melodramatic . . . understudy
(C) natural . . . nemesis
(D) consummate . . . incarnation
(E) drab . . . caricature

6. The chairman ------- the decision of the board members, describing it as a ------- of every worthy ideal that the organization had hitherto upheld.

(A) defended . . . denial
(B) lamented . . . negation
(C) criticized . . . fulfillment
(D) endorsed . . . renunciation
(E) applauded . . . repudiation

GO ON TO THE NEXT PAGE

Directions: The passages below are followed by questions based on their content; questions following a pair of related passages may also be based on the relationship between the paired passages. Answer the questions on the basis of what is <u>stated</u> or <u>implied</u> in the passages and in any introductory material that may be provided.

Questions 7–19 refer to the following passages.

The two excerpts below are from speeches that were made by outstanding American leaders of the 19th century. The first excerpt is from Thomas Jefferson's first Inaugural Address in 1801; the second was delivered by Frederick Douglass during the Fourth of July celebration in Rochester, New York, in 1852.

Passage 1

Let us then, with courage and confidence, pursue our own federal and republican principles; our attachment to union and representative government. Kindly separated by nature
(5) and a wide ocean from the exterminating havoc of one quarter of the globe; too high-minded to endure the degradation of others, possessing a chosen country, with room enough for our descendants to the thousandth
(10) and thousandth generation, entertaining a due sense of our equal right to the use of our own faculties, to the acquisition of our own industry, to honor and confidence from our fellow-citizens, resulting not from birth, but
(15) from our actions and their sense of them, enlightened by a benign religion, professed in deed and practiced in various forms, yet all of them inculcating honesty, truth, temperance, gratitude, and the love of man . . . Still
(20) one thing more, fellow citizens, a wise and frugal government, which shall restrain men from injuring one another, shall leave them otherwise free to regulate their own pursuits of industry and improvement, and shall not
(25) take from the mouth of labor the bread it has earned. This is the sum of good government; and this is necessary to close the circle of our felicities.

About to enter, fellow citizens, upon the
(30) exercise of duties which comprehend everything dear and valuable to you, it is proper you should understand what I deem the essential principles of our government, and consequently, those which ought to shape its
(35) administration. I will compress them within the narrowest compass they will bear, stating the general principle, but not all its limitations. Equal and exact justice to all men, of whatever state or persuasion, religious or
(40) political . . .

Passage 2

I say it with a sad sense of disparity between us. I am not included within the pale of this glorious anniversary! Your high independence only reveals the immeasurable distance
(45) between us. The blessings in which you this day rejoice are not enjoyed in common. The rich inheritance of justice, liberty, prosperity, and independence bequeathed by your fathers is shared by you, not by me. The sunlight that
(50) brought life and healing to you has brought stripes and death to me. This Fourth of July is yours, not mine. You may rejoice, I must mourn. To drag a man in fetters into the grand illuminated temple of liberty, and call
(55) upon him to join you in joyous anthems, were inhuman mockery and sacrilegious irony. Do you mean, citizens, to mock me by asking me to speak today?
. . . Fellow citizens, above your national,
(60) tumultuous joy, I hear the mournful wail of millions, whose chains, heavy and grievous

GO ON TO THE NEXT PAGE

yesterday, are today rendered more intolerable
by the jubilant shouts that reach them. If I do
forget, if I do not remember those bleeding
(65) children of sorrow this day, "may my right
hand forget her cunning, and may my tongue
cleave to the roof of my mouth!" To forget
them, to pass lightly over their wrongs, and to
chime in with the popular theme, would be
(70) treason most scandalous and shocking, and
would make me a reproach before God and
the world. My subject, then, fellow citizens, is
"American Slavery . . ."
   . . . Would you have me argue that man
(75) is entitled to liberty? That he is the rightful
owner of his own body? You have already
declared it. Must I argue the wrongfulness of
slavery? Is that a question for republicans? Is
it to be settled by the rules of logic and argu-
(80) mentation, as a matter beset with great difficulty, involving a doubtful application of the
principle of justice, hard to understand? . . .
   . . . What to the American slave is your
Fourth of July? I answer, a day that reveals
(85) more to him than all other days of the year,
the gross injustice and cruelty to which he
is the constant victim. To him your celebration is a sham; your boasted liberty an unholy
license; your national greatness, swelling van-
(90) ity; your sounds of rejoicing are empty and
heartless; your denunciation of tyrants, brass-
fronted impudence; your shouts of liberty and
equality, hollow mockery; your prayers and
hymns, your sermons and thanksgivings, with
(95) all your religious parade and solemnity, are to
him mere bombast, fraud, deception, impiety,
and hypocrisy—a thin veil to cover up crimes
which would disgrace a nation of savages.
There is not a nation of the earth guilty of
(100) practices more shocking and bloody than are
the people of the United States at this very
hour.

7. By "our equal right . . . to honor and confidence
from our fellow-citizens, resulting not from
birth, but from our actions and their sense of
them" (Passage 1, lines 11–15), Jefferson means
that

(A) members of all nations are welcome to
come to America

(B) citizens have the right to demand respect
from each other

(C) citizens should judge each other by
their accomplishments rather than their
ancestry

(D) one can build trust by doing things for
others

(E) one should rely not only on one's family
but also on other citizens

8. In line 30, the word "comprehend" most
nearly means

(A) include

(B) understand

(C) perceive

(D) outline

(E) realize

GO ON TO THE NEXT PAGE

9. By "I will compress them within the narrowest compass they will bear" (Passage 1, lines 35–36), Jefferson means that

   (A) he intends to limit the role of government

   (B) those who oppose justice will be imprisoned

   (C) the general principles of government have boundaries

   (D) he will speak concisely about the principles of government

   (E) government bureaucracy has become too inflated

10. The word "persuasion" in line 39 most nearly means

    (A) enticement

    (B) influence

    (C) cajolery

    (D) authority

    (E) opinion

11. The statement "To drag a man . . . sacrilegious irony" (lines 53–56) conveys a sense of

    (A) indignation at the hypocrisy of Fourth of July celebrations

    (B) sorrow over the way the slaves had been treated

    (C) anger that slavery had not yet been abolished

    (D) disbelief that Fourth of July celebrations could even take place

    (E) amazement that slaves were being forced to join in the celebration

12. The references to the "mournful wail" and the "jubilant shouts" (lines 60–63) serve to

    (A) remind the audience of difficulties in the past that have been overcome

    (B) indicate the importance of commemorating the Fourth of July

    (C) warn that the future of the country looks deceptively bright

    (D) emphasize the different outlooks of two groups in the country

    (E) suggest that some are faced with an unsolvable problem

13. In line 70, the author uses the word "treason" to refer to the act of

    (A) rebelling against authority

    (B) betraying the needs of a social group

    (C) renouncing one's own principles

    (D) expressing unpopular views

    (E) acting upon irrational impulses

14. The author of Passage 2 most likely describes "American Slavery" as "my subject" (lines 72–73) in order to

    (A) underline an unexpected new direction in his argument

    (B) indicate the broad historical scope of his address

    (C) emphasize his intent to discuss an apparent contradiction

    (D) highlight the answer to a problem facing the United States

    (E) underscore his eagerness to learn more about the topic of slavery

GO ON TO THE NEXT PAGE

15. In lines 91–92, the phrase "brass-fronted impudence" is primarily used to convey the author's

(A) outrage at the contrast between political speeches and social reality

(B) exasperation at the many obstacles to racial equality

(C) resentment at the number of people excluded from Fourth of July celebrations

(D) belief that resistance to authority is ultimately futile

(E) anger at the acts of tyrants throughout the world

16. The author of Passage 1 would most likely react to the questions at the beginning of paragraph 3 of Passage 2 (lines 74–82) by commenting that

(A) a nation's political ideals are not always consistent with its actions

(B) the doctrine of equality is necessary for good government

(C) political views must be expressed through the proper democratic channels

(D) the goal of liberty for all may not be practical to attain

(E) the degradation of others must sometimes be endured

17. The author of Passage 2 would most likely react to the general principle of government in the last sentence of Passage 1 by pointing out that

(A) this general principle is hopelessly naive

(B) the real situation strongly contradicts this principle

(C) experience has proven this principle to be unattainable

(D) this principle is meaningless because it is vaguely worded

(E) the government never intended to adhere to this principle

18. Which statement is best supported by a comparison of the excerpts from the two speeches?

(A) Both excerpts denounce the degradation of some men and women in America.

(B) The purpose of both excerpts is to urge citizens to critically evaluate themselves.

(C) Both excerpts emphasize the necessity of justice for all citizens.

(D) Both excerpts argue that slavery is a violation of human rights.

(E) Both excerpts present a hopeful vision of the future.

19. The attitudes expressed in Passage 1 and Passage 2 toward equality in the United States might best be described as

(A) cautious versus angry

(B) disappointed versus adulated

(C) optimistic versus critical

(D) hopeful versus promising

(E) indulgent versus prudent

IF YOU FINISH BEFORE TIME IS CALLED, YOU MAY CHECK YOUR WORK ON THIS SECTION ONLY. DO NOT TURN TO ANY OTHER SECTION IN THE TEST.

SECTION 8
Time—20 Minutes
16 Questions

Directions: For this section, solve each problem and decide which is the best of the choices given. Fill in the corresponding oval on the answer sheet. You may use any available space for scratchwork.

Notes:

(1) Calculator use is permitted.

(2) All numbers used are real numbers.

(3) Figures are provided for some problems. All figures are drawn to scale and lie in a plane UNLESS otherwise indicated.

(4) Unless otherwise specified, the domain of any function f is assumed to be the set of all real numbers x for which $f(x)$ is a real number.

Information

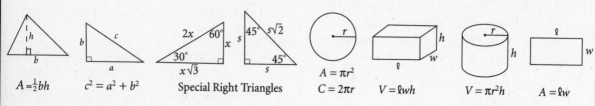

$A = \frac{1}{2}bh$ $\quad$ $c^2 = a^2 + b^2$ $\quad$ Special Right Triangles $\quad$ $A = \pi r^2$ $\quad$ $C = 2\pi r$ $\quad$ $V = \ell w h$ $\quad$ $V = \pi r^2 h$ $\quad$ $A = \ell w$

The sum of the degree measures of the angles in a triangle is 180.
The number of degrees of arc in a circle is 360.
A straight angle has a degree measure of 180.

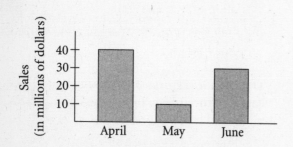

1. According to the graph above, April sales accounted for approximately what percent of the total sales?

   (A) $12\frac{1}{2}$

   (B) 25

   (C) $37\frac{1}{2}$

   (D) 50

   (E) 60

2. If xy is negative, which of the following CANNOT be negative?

   (A) $y - x$

   (B) $x - y$

   (C) $x^2 y$

   (D) xy^2

   (E) $x^2 y^2$

GO ON TO THE NEXT PAGE

3. If 1 bora = 2 fedis and 1 fedi = 3 glecks, how many boras are equal to 48 glecks?

(A)   4
(B)   8
(C)   16
(D)   48
(E)   96

4. A college class is made up of f freshmen and s sophomores. If 5 freshmen drop this class, then the number of sophomores in the class is 3 times the number of freshmen. Which of the following equations represents s in terms of f?

(A) $s = \dfrac{f-5}{3}$

(B) $s = \dfrac{f+5}{3}$

(C) $s = 3(f-5)$

(D) $s = 3(f+5)$

(E) $s = 5(f-3)$

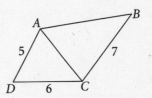

5. In the figure above, if the perimeter of triangle ABC is 4 more than the perimeter of triangle ACD, what is the perimeter of quadrilateral $ABCD$?

(A)   20
(B)   22
(C)   24
(D)   25
(E)   26

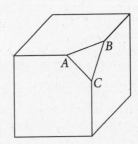

6. The figure above shows a cube-shaped stone with edges of 3 centimeters. Points A, B, and C are on three different edges of the cube, each 1 centimeter away from the same vertex. A jeweler slices off the corner with a straight cut through A, B, and C, as shown, and slices pieces of the same size off all the other corners of the stone. What is the total number of faces on the resulting stone?

(A)   7
(B)   10
(C)   12
(D)   14
(E)   16

GO ON TO THE NEXT PAGE

7. What is the average of the first 30 positive integers?

    (A) 14
    (B) 14.5
    (C) 15
    (D) 15.5
    (E) 16

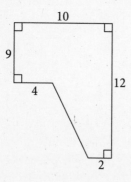

Note: Figure not drawn to scale.

8. What is the area of the figure above?

    (A) 96
    (B) 102
    (C) 104
    (D) 108
    (E) 110

9. Sixty cookies were to be equally distributed to x campers. When 8 campers did not want the cookies, the other campers each received 2 more cookies. Which of the following equations could be used to find the number of campers x?

    (A) $x^2 - 8x - 240 = 0$
    (B) $x^2 - 8x + 240 = 0$
    (C) $x^2 + 8x - 240 = 0$
    (D) $x^2 + 8x + 240 = 0$
    (E) $x^2 - 4x - 120 = 0$

10. If 6 students are eligible for 2 scholarships worth $1,000 each how many different combinations of 2 students winning the 2 scholarships are possible?

    (A) 6
    (B) 9
    (C) 12
    (D) 15
    (E) 30

11. If $q \neq 0$ and $q = q^{-2}$, what is the value of q?

    (A) -1
    (B) 0
    (C) $\dfrac{1}{2}$
    (D) 1
    (E) 2

Price of One Can	Projected Number of Cans Sold
$0.75	10,000
$0.80	9,000
$0.85	8,000
$0.90	7,000
$0.95	6,000
$1.00	5,000

GO ON TO THE NEXT PAGE

12. The previous chart describes how many cans of a new soft drink a company expects to sell at a number of possible prices per can. Which of the following equations best describes the relationship shown in the chart, where n indicates the number of cans sold and p represents the price in dollars of one can?

(A) $n = -20,000p - 25,000$

(B) $n = -20,000p + 25,000$

(C) $n = -200p - 250$

(D) $n = 200p + 250$

(E) $n = 20,000p - 25,000$

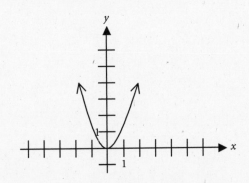

13. Which of the following equations best describes the curve shown in the graph?

(A) $y = x$

(B) $y = x^2$

(C) $y = x^3$

(D) $y = \sqrt{x}$

(E) $y = \frac{1}{2}x$

14. In a game, all tokens of the same color are worth the same number of points. If one player won 4 green tokens and 8 yellow tokens for a total score of 48 points, and another player won 6 green tokens and 4 yellow tokens for a total score of 32 points, how many points is a yellow token worth?

(A) 2

(B) 4

(C) 5

(D) 8

(E) 10

15. Pablo has c grams of cherries. He uses 30% of the cherries to make muffins, each of which requires m grams of cherries. He uses the rest of the cherries to make preserves, each pint of which requires p grams of cherries. Which of the following describes the number of pints of preserves Pablo can make?

(A) $\frac{3c}{10m}$

(B) $\frac{3c}{10p}$

(C) $\frac{7c}{10p}$

(D) $\frac{7c}{10m}$

(E) $\frac{3cp}{10}$

GO ON TO THE NEXT PAGE

16. At a fruit stand, the price of 1 pound of cherries is twice the price of 1 pound of grapes. If 32 pounds of cherries and 8 pounds of grapes were sold and sales totaled $90.00, how much more money was made on the cherries than on the grapes?

    (A) $75.00
    (B) $70.00
    (C) $65.00
    (D) $60.00
    (E) $55.00

IF YOU FINISH BEFORE TIME IS CALLED, YOU MAY CHECK YOUR WORK ON THIS SECTION ONLY. DO NOT TURN TO ANY OTHER SECTION IN THE TEST.

STOP

SECTION 9

Time—10 Minutes
14 Questions

Directions: For each question in this section, select the best answer from among the choices given and fill in the corresponding oval on the answer sheet.

The following sentences test correctness and effectiveness of expression. Part of each sentence or the entire sentence is underlined; beneath each sentence are five ways of phrasing the underlined material. Choice (A) repeats the original phrasing; the other four choices are different. If you think the original phrasing produces a better sentence than any of the alternatives, select choice (A); if not, select one of the other choices.

In making your selection, follow the requirements of standard written English; that is, pay attention to grammar, choice of words, sentence construction, and punctuation. Your selection should result in the most effective sentence—clear and precise, without awkwardness or ambiguity.

EXAMPLE: ANSWER:

Every apple in the baskets <u>are ripe and labeled according to the date it was picked</u>.   Ⓐ ● Ⓒ Ⓓ Ⓔ

(A) are ripe and labeled according to the date it was picked
(B) is ripe and labeled according to the date it was picked
(C) are ripe and labeled according to the date they were picked
(D) is ripe and labeled according to the date they were picked
(E) are ripe and labeled as to the date it was picked

---

1. Lost items can be found <u>at the admissions booth they can be picked up until one hour after the museum's closing.</u>

    (A) at the admissions booth they can be picked up until one hour after the museum's closing

    (B) at the admissions booth; they can be picked up until one hour after the museum's closing

    (C) until one hour after the museum's closing, they can be picked up at the admissions booth

    (D) and that can be picked up at the admissions booth until one hour after the museum's closing

    (E) at the admissions booth, until one hour after the museum's closing is when they can be picked up

2. By utilizing cacophony and inconsistent rhythms, <u>the shock value of postmodern music was raised by Webern to a higher level</u> than ever before.

    (A) the shock value of postmodern music was raised by Webern to a higher level

    (B) Webern raised the shock value of postmodern music to a higher level

    (C) a higher level of postmodern music was reached by Webern

    (D) postmodern music's shock value was raised to a higher level by Webern

    (E) Webern's postmodern music shock value rose to a higher level

GO ON TO THE NEXT PAGE

3. The electric fan was an ingenious invention for keeping people cool during the summer; it was popular only briefly, however, until the air conditioner made it old-fashioned.

   (A) summer; it was popular only briefly, however

   (B) summer, for it was popular only briefly, however

   (C) summer; however, popular only briefly

   (D) summer, having been popular only briefly

   (E) summer, but was popular only briefly

4. Even the play's most tragic characters are delivered with a comic touch, this dramatic effect results in a very unconventional story.

   (A) this dramatic effect results in a very unconventional story

   (B) this dramatic effect resulting in a very unconventional story

   (C) and a very unconventional story being the result of this dramatic effect

   (D) and this dramatic effect results in a very unconventional story

   (E) a very unconventional story results from this dramatic effect

5. The strict training schedule allowed the marathon runner to eventually run for 20 miles and she could scale steep hills without stopping for rest.

   (A) and she could scale

   (B) as well as scale

   (C) so she could scale

   (D) and a scaling

   (E) and to scale

6. Joseph Campbell espoused definitive ideas about the art of storytelling and the heroes and villains were defined through his work.

   (A) the heroes and villains were defined

   (B) the heroes and villains were defined by him

   (C) had defined the heroes and villains

   (D) defined the heroes and villains

   (E) the definition of the heroes and villains

7. In the past, many renowned singers wrote their own songs, a trademark of originality that is now rarely found.

   (A) a trademark of originality that is now rarely found

   (B) inasmuch as they displayed trademark of originality, it is now rarely found

   (C) this found rarely now in displaying their trademarks of originality

   (D) a trademark that is now rarely found in displaying their originality

   (E) which is now rarely found and it displays a trademark of originality

8. Thomas Jefferson was known as a brilliant politician and he was also known as an accomplished architect.

   (A) politician and he was also known as an accomplished architect

   (B) politician, and he was also an accomplished architect

   (C) politician; also he was known as an accomplished architect

   (D) politician and, furthermore, he was known as an accomplished architect

   (E) politician and an accomplished architect

GO ON TO THE NEXT PAGE

9. Although liquor companies are now
    introducing low-alcohol and alcohol-
    free beverages, litigation against distillers
    continues to increase year after year.

    (A) Although liquor companies are now
        introducing low-alcohol and alcohol-free
        beverages, litigation against distillers con-
        tinues to increase year after year.

    (B) Litigation against distillers year after year
        continues to increase even though liquor
        companies are now introducing low-
        alcohol and alcohol-free beverages.

    (C) Although introducing low-alcohol and
        alcohol-free beverages are liquor compa-
        nies now, litigation against distillers con-
        tinues to increase year after year.

    (D) Increasing year after year, liquor com-
        panies are now introducing low-alcohol
        and alcohol-free beverages, but litigation
        against distillers continues.

    (E) Liquor companies are now introducing
        low-alcohol and alcohol-free beverages,
        litigation against distillers continues to
        increase year after year.

10. The domestic cat is including more than 40
    breeds, is a member of the feline family.

    (A) cat is including more than 40 breeds

    (B) cat, of which there are more than 40
        breeds

    (C) cat to which there belongs more than
        40 breeds

    (D) cat, which there are more than 40 breeds
        of

    (E) cat, of which more than 40 breeds in
        existence

11. The Nobel Foundation was established in
    1900; since then it has awarded prizes for
    achievements in literature and science.

    (A) was established in 1900; since then
    (B) was established in 1900, since then
    (C) was established in 1900, then
    (D) established in 1900; since then
    (E) was established in 1900; and since then

12. Women are not rejecting the idea of raising
    children, but many taking jobs as well.

    (A) many taking jobs
    (B) many are taking jobs
    (C) jobs are taken by many of them
    (D) jobs are being taken
    (E) many having taken jobs

13. Changing over from a military to a peace-time economy means producing tractors rather than tanks, radios rather than rifles, and <u>to produce running shoes rather than combat boots</u>.

    (A) to produce running shoes rather than combat boots

    (B) to the production of running shoes rather than combat boots

    (C) running shoes rather than combat boots

    (D) replacing combat boots with running shoes

    (E) to running shoes rather combat boots

14. The protest movement's impact will depend on both how many people it touches and <u>its durability</u>.

    (A) its durability

    (B) is it going to endure

    (C) if it has durability

    (D) how long it endures

    (E) the movement's ability to endure

IF YOU FINISH BEFORE TIME IS CALLED, YOU MAY CHECK YOUR WORK ON THIS SECTION ONLY. DO NOT TURN TO ANY OTHER SECTION IN THE TEST.   STOP

(Answers on the next page.)

Practice Test Two: **Answer Key**

SECTION 1

Essay

SECTION 2

1. E
2. B
3. D
4. C
5. D
6. C
7. A
8. B
9. D
10. A
11. E
12. D
13. D
14. A
15. E
16. B
17. C
18. C
19. B
20. E
21. C
22. D
23. A
24. E

SECTION 3

1. D
2. A
3. C
4. C
5. D
6. A
7. D
8. D
9. D
10. B
11. E
12. D
13. E
14. D
15. A
16. C
17. C
18. E
19. D
20. C

SECTION 4

1. E
2. A
3. C
4. A
5. A
6. B
7. E
8. D
9. C
10. E
11. C
12. D
13. D
14. D
15. A
16. B
17. C
18. C
19. D
20. A
21. B
22. B
23. D
24. E

SECTION 5

1. C
2. E
3. A
4. C
5. D
6. B
7. D
8. B
9. 15
10. 9.43
11. 13 < length < 15
12. 15/4 or 3.75
13. 166
14. .5 < y < .625
15. 46
16. 175
17. 46
18. 11

SECTION 6

1. C
2. C
3. C
4. B
5. A
6. C
7. A
8. D
9. B
10. A
11. D
12. A
13. D
14. C
15. B
16. E
17. A
18. B
19. C
20. B
21. B
22. D
23. B
24. C
25. C
26. E
27. D
28. E
29. A
30. D
31. D
32. C
33. D
34. D
35. E

SECTION 7

1. B
2. E
3. B
4. E
5. D
6. B
7. C
8. A
9. D
10. E
11. A
12. D
13. B
14. C
15. A
16. B
17. B
18. C
19. C

SECTION 8

1. D
2. E
3. B
4. C
5. E
6. D
7. D
8. B
9. A
10. D
11. D
12. B
13. B
14. C
15. C
16. B

SECTION 9

1. B
2. B
3. A
4. D
5. E
6. D
7. A
8. E
9. A
10. B
11. A
12. B
13. C
14. D

ANSWERS AND EXPLANATIONS

SECTION 1

6 ESSAY

The first time I encountered a thought similar to the one expressed above by Calvin Coolidge was when I read a quote by Benjamin Franklin: "Energy and persistence conquer all things." The truth that Franklin expressed continues to affect me. I agree, therefore, that persistence is the major factor in someone's success. In fact, I know it's true because I've witnessed it first hand.

When I was 10 years old, my mother was in a car accident that left her a paraplegic; she is paralyzed from the waist down. I have watched her struggle from that day to this to reclaim a normal life and to be a mother to me and a wife to my father. She has come so far because she never gives up. She is a model of persistence. After the initial trauma she suffered from the accident faded she had to begin a long period of training to strengthen her upper body and to gain whatever strength she could in her legs. It was hard work. I used to go with her to the training room in the hospital and watch her sweat through the routines the therapist gave her.

Even today, almost 7 years since the accident, she trains three times a week. She also had to learn to use a wheelchair and how to drive a car using hand controls. She had to re-learn things she knew how to do before the accident like cooking and gardening. In fact, she had to learn how to do almost everything all over again, and she did.

I once asked her how she did all this and she said she did it because she was grateful that she survived the accident and could still be part of my father's and my life. So, Coolidge was right, and so was Franklin; persistence pays off. My mother is persistent and I'm so proud of her and so happy that her persistence means that she is still part of my life.

GRADER'S COMMENTS

All essays are evaluated on four basic criteria: Topic, Support, Organization, and Language. This is a strongly written essay in which the writer sticks to the assigned topic and develops it in a creative way. She has a stirring story to tell and she tells it very well. She never strays from her main idea, which is that persistence pays off and her mother is living proof of that. The author's clear recounting of her mother's heroic actions since the accident offers much support for her thesis.

The essay has an interesting and strong organization. The first paragraph offers another quote that is similar to the statement given. The author whets the reader's appetite by not jumping immediately into her main point. The last sentence keeps the reader's interest going. The remaining three paragraphs support her thesis.

The essay exhibits a high degree of skill with language. Both the sentence structure and the vocabulary indicate that the essay is written by an adept writer. The sentence structure is varied and even long and complex sentences are correctly punctuated. This is particularly apparent throughout the second paragraph. Some words that indicate the author's solid vocabulary: reclaim, initial, trauma, encountered, witnessed, factor.

4 ESSAY

I think that Pres. Coolidge is right. It seems to me that if your persistent you do well in life. An example I can think of is Albert Einstein who said something like 99% of genius was hard work and the remaining 1% was because you are a genius. This shows that Einstein agreed that you need more persistence than genius to succeed. Of course, Albert Einstein was a genius, too, but as the quote above says a lot of geniuses don't get rewarded. Einstein is famous because he was a persistent genius.

When Einstein was young he failed some math tests and he didn't always get great grades. He didn't let this stop him, though. He knew he wanted to be a mathematician and a physics professor and he worked hard to get to these goals. His persistence paid off. He became a teacher and later he won the Nobel Prize.

Later on Einstein came to America where he taught at Princeton University. In this way he fulfilled his dream of being a teacher of physics and mathematics. This was what he said he wanted to do when he was young and he did it because he persisted until he reached his goal. I believe that his persistence more than his genius is what brought Einstein the things he wanted.

In conclusion, Einstein is a great example of why I agree with Calvin Coolidge that persistence is the most important quality a person can have to be successful.

GRADER'S COMMENTS

All essays are evaluated on four basic criteria: Topic, Support, Organization, and Language. This writer sticks to the topic, agreeing with the quote. The writer's use of Einstein's life is great support for his agreement; however, the writer misattributes the quote about genius. Thomas Edison actually said that, not Einstein. But the essay is not testing for content; a mistake like this won't hurt the score.

The essay is well organized with an introduction, body, and conclusion. The writer's use of "In conclusion" in the last paragraph helps the sense of organization. Using words and phrases that indicate to the reader what your intentions are is a good technique for SAT essays.

The writer's language is generally good, though not very challenging. He makes a common error in the second sentence of the first paragraph—using "your" when he meant "you're." He also should not have abbreviated "President."

2 ESSAY

It's good to be persistent as the statement above says. I seen this many times. For example, my brother was not very good at basketball but he kept on shooting hoops in our backyard and after a while he got better he made the team. He not good enough to be on the varsity but he plays intrmurels.

I think persistent is important but I also think being a genius is pretty cool. I'd like to be a genius but I guess its not gonna happen. I guess I will have to just be persistent and see if that works. I think it will because as I said above I agree with the statement of Calvin Coolidge.

GRADER'S COMMENTS

All essays are evaluated on four basic criteria: Topic, Support, Organization, and Language. The author starts out pretty strongly by agreeing with the statement and using her brother as an example. However, she strays in the first part of the second paragraph and then returns to the topic at the end. The development of the topic is rudimentary. This contributed to her low score. The writer's example is good support for her opinion. She doesn't, however, develop her support enough. The essay meanders on and off topic, making the organization too loose.

The writer's language is generally below standard. There are grammatical and spelling errors. The grammar is particularly poor. There are numerous verb tense errors, run-on sentences, and slang words. Here's a sampling: "I seen" instead of "I've seen"; "He not good enough" instead of "He's not good enough"; "persistent" for "persistence"; "gonna" instead of "going to." The third sentence of the first paragraph is a long run-on. In addition, *intramurals* and *important* are misspelled.

SECTION 2

1. E

Despite is our first clue word, signaling a contrast coming up. *Despite their fierce appearance, caymans are actually rarely -------, to the point at which they won't attack humans unless provoked.* So for the blank we need a word that means the same as *fierce*. The closest word here is choice (E), *aggressive.* Choice (B) is the exact opposite of what we wanted. Choice (C), *domesticated,* means tame and usually refers to animals treated as house pets.

2. B

There are two different schools of thought competing in this sentence. One group believes one thing *while* another believes something else. So, clearly, we want words that help create a sense of the opposition between these two viewpoints. Let's start with the second blank. One group argues that courtly love *dates from the age of chivalry.* In other words, they think it's a fairly old idea, dating back from the days of knights and fair maidens. Another group thinks something else though, so they must feel it's either an even older idea or a more recent idea. A quick check through the answer choices for the second blank leads us to choice (B), *ancient. Notion,* or idea, fits quite nicely into the first blank, fitting with the word *concept* in the first half of the sentence.

3. D

Here we want a word that would describe the sort of people who might throw fruits and vegetables at those whose performances dissatisfied them. People like this are surely not *doting,* (A), meaning overindulgent or excessively fond, nor are they *ravenous,* (B), or extremely hungry. If they were hungry, they'd eat the food instead of throwing it at the stage. There's nothing to imply that the audience is (C), *jingoistic,* or excessively nationalistic. However, the audience might certainly be described as (D), *boisterous,* or rowdy. (E), *stagnant,* means dead or lifeless, which is illogical in the blank.

4. C

Although two brothers look alike, they *could not be more ------- in terms of their personalities.* "Not alike" or "different" or some such word must go into this first blank, something that helps convey that they look alike, but their behavior is not alike. The semicolon is our hint that the information following it will be more or less in line with what preceded it. So *while* one is circumspect, or cautious, the other is *brash,* or the opposite of cautious. For this second blank, you should predict something that means the opposite of quiet, something that's sort of synonymous with brash. The best answer is choice (C), because *dissimilar* fits our prediction for the first blank, while *audacious* means bold—it's kind of a synonym for brash. (A), *inimical,* is related to the word *enemy. Inimical* means hostile.

5. D

Napoleon's army was hightailing it out of Moscow. The retreat *quickly turned into a rout*, a state of wild confusion, a disastrous defeat. Why did it turn into an even bigger defeat? Probably because the French were stuck or struggling in the snow—if they were doing well traveling through snow, it's unlikely they'd end up being such big losers. Then something was done to them by Russian troops. Well, if you know that Napoleon's army was routed by the opposing side, then it seems that we want a second-blank word that means something like clobbered. Choices (A) and (D) come close to that prediction. *Ravage* means to violently destroy. Now, going back to the first blank, we know we want something that implies the troops were stuck or struggling in the snow. Only choice (D) fits both blanks: The retreat of Napoleon's army turned into a *rout* as French troops, already *floundering* in the snow, were *assaulted* by Russian soldiers. To *flounder* is to struggle awkwardly and stumble about. In (A), *replenishing* in the snow sounds a bit weird—*replenishing* means replacing something that was used up. In (E), *tottering* means walking unsteadily, and *upbraided* means scolded or reprimanded—a little mild-mannered for our purposes here.

6. C

The word that will fill in the blank is defined here in the sentence—we want a word that describes an environment composed of *tapestries, paintings, stained-glass windows, and hand-crafted furniture.* A quick survey of the answer choices leads us to choice (C), because *sumptuous* means costly or lavish, particularly with regard to furnishings and decor. While you might have been tempted to think that *friendly* in choice (D) was a plausible answer, it's hard to say for sure that an environment filled with rich, arty items is a *friendly* environment. For some people, such surroundings might be quite intimidating. *Frugal*, in choice (B), means thrifty or careful with money, which is quite the opposite of what we wanted here.

7. A

In this sentence, a lecturer is frustrated by something her audience has done. This *frustration was only ------- by some connection between the audience and talking. It sounds like the lecturer was frustrated by her audience's desire or tendency to talk during her presentation. Lecturers want to be heard; an audience's inability or lack of desire to talk would not frustrate a lecturer. So for the second blank, we want something like desire—choice (A), *propensity*, or tendency, and choice (E), *desire*, could work. (C) makes no sense. What's an audience's *authorization*? To choose between (A) and (E), let's look at the second blank. (E), *supplanted*, or replaced, is illogical. So (A) has to be correct. In fact, it makes the most sense: The lecturer's frustration was *compounded*, or increased, by the audience's *propensity*, or tendency, to talk.

8. B

There's something about the issue of the nuclear power plant that makes it surprising the council all voted in agreement. If it was shocking that there was agreement, the issue must have been divisive or controversial. The answer here is (B), because *contentious* means causing controversy and disagreement. *Concise,* (C), means brief and to the point, while *exorbitant,* (D), means extravagant or excessive.

Humans vs. Other Mammals Passage

9. D

The author says that there's a difference between humans and other mammals and uses the lions to illustrate this point. Lions sit around or nap after they eat a lot. People get bored and do stuff. Why is this important? Because this led to the ultimate development of culture. (C) and (D) both look okay, but only (D) includes the author's larger point about culture. Also, the language of (C) is not quite in keeping with the tone of the passage. *Industrious* means hardworking, but the actions of people are described as play, not work. (A) is the opposite of what you're looking for—the author seems to regard the achievements of humans as pretty positive and so wouldn't think that lions are more successful. The author never introduces the idea of efficiency, (B). (E) is too broad; the passage focuses on what animals and humans do after they eat and never discusses the hunting that precedes the eating.

10. A

The general purpose of the passage is to explain something, so look for this direction. (A) and (C) both look feasible. On further consideration, (C) doesn't quite work, since only one thesis is presented—the author is not providing an *alternative* to anything. (A), however, fits well. The author shows a *distinction* between the behavior of people and other mammals, and then shows the *significance* of this distinction (it led to culture). (B) is off base, since the author never indicates that there might be an objection to the thesis. (D) and (E) are out of the scope of the passage—what will (or should) happen in the future is never discussed.

Eugene O'Neill Passage

11. E

First, you need to identify the *logical conclusion*—O'Neill's plays are very American, so the audience must also be American. The author then goes on to say that this is not true. The plays are also quite popular in Europe. This matches (E) quite well. (A) actually expresses the opposite of what you're looking for. It describes the *logical conclusion* rather than the contradiction of that conclusion. (B) is a distortion of several ideas in the passage, but does nothing to contradict the *logical assumption.* (C) is in keeping with the tone of the passage, but is also not offered as a contradiction of the *logical assumption*. (D) is a detail from the passage but appears earlier and doesn't disprove the assumption that Americans are the sole audience of O'Neill's plays.

12. D

The conclusion of the passage is that O'Neill's plays are relevant to everyone, including non-Americans, and we know this because the plays are popular with Europeans. (D) weakens the argument, because if it's mostly Americans going to the European performances, then there's no evidence that the plays are popular with non-Americans. (A) is out of scope, since the passage discusses European, not American productions. (B) could be tempting if you thought that O'Neill didn't have an American audience, and so couldn't be considered a successful playwright. This is going too far, however, since there's no evidence that O'Neill is not also popular in America. (C) doesn't hurt the author's conclusion, since the plays could still be popular with non-Americans when performed in English. There's no reason that O'Neill couldn't be popular with Europeans, even if he'd never gone to Europe himself, so (E) doesn't affect the conclusion.

DOMESTICATED ANIMALS PASSAGE

If you're an animal lover, you might enjoy this passage. Actually, it's not a bad passage, but it's long, so be sure to keep up a good pace. You should aim at getting the main points of paragraphs and moving on. Basically, the author says that the dog was the first domesticated animal, which makes sense because of the dog's nature (it comes from a pack and likes to have a leader; as a puppy it is cute and trainable; and it has better senses of hearing and smell than humans do, which makes it a valuable hunting companion). Then the author wonders how domestication occurred, which sends him off on a tangent about animals that *parasitize* human wastes or food stores. He speculates that domestication began because baby animals were cute—only later did domesticated animals actually become useful. He concludes that it's ironic that human civilization is destroying many species, since our learning to live with them is what made civilization possible.

13. D

The *archaeological discoveries* mentioned in the question stem are human and dog bones lying next to each other in ancient burial sites. The reason the author feels it's *terribly appropriate* that these bones are found together comes a few lines later, when he says *it marks a relationship that is the most ancient of all*. (D) paraphrases that idea. You can see from this how important it is to read a few lines before and after the line reference in the stem. The author says nothing about burial habits in the Mesolithic Era, (A), or the religious significance of animals in prehistoric cultures, (B). He says nothing about *natural disasters*, (E), either. He does mention hunting, (C), but the bone finds are not *appropriate* because they *illustrate the role of dogs in hunting expeditions*. (D) is the only possibility.

14. A

The end of the first paragraph provides the answer. The author says that the dog was the first domesticated animal because it served as *a companion and an ally*, (A). Only *after* domesticating animals as companions did humans domesticate *food animals*, (B), and then *those that provide enhanced speed and range*, (D), and then those that helped us farm, (C). The key thing is to see that all these other types of domesticated animals came after animals were domesticated as companions.

15. E

The line reference takes you to the beginning of paragraph 2. The author says that having a dog as a companion animal was almost *inevitable*, and then lists several reasons why. One of these is that the dog *is susceptible to domination by, and attachment to, a pack leader—the top dog*. The implication is that humans formed bonds with dogs because they could dominate them, (E). Choices (A), (B), (C), and (D) do not give characteristics that make sense in answer to the question.

16. B

As with all Vocabulary-in-Context questions, you should go back to the sentence to see how the word is used. The author asks us to consider the *essence* of the dog in order to understand why it became a companion. He then lists several of the dog's characteristics that made it easy to domesticate. In other words, we're looking at the dog's *nature*, (B). The only other choice that might seem to make sense in this context is (A), *history*—but what follows the line *consider its essence* is not a history; rather, it's a list of characteristics that make up the dog's nature.

17. C

This is definitely a question you need to return to the passage to answer. In paragraph 2, the author lists the characteristics that made dogs *inevitable* companions for humans. In addition to being born dependent and forming bonds with their rearers, dogs *have a set of appeasement behaviors* that elicit *affective reactions* from even the most *hardened* humans. The author goes on to talk about puppies transforming *cynics* into *cooing softies*. Even if you weren't sure what *appeasement behaviors* were, you can get the gist of the author's point here: humans form bonds with dogs largely because dogs are cute and loveable. So would it make sense if *affective reactions* were *callous*, (A), *rational*, (B), or *cynical*, (E)? No. (D) goes too far. The author isn't saying humans become childish around dogs, but that dogs arouse human emotions. (C) is the best answer.

18. C

The easiest way to understand the point of a comparison is to understand the context. What's the author saying in these lines? He's trying to show why it was inevitable that dogs became human companions. One reason is that dogs *form bonds with their owners*, (C). That's the only reason he compares puppies with babies—to show how emotional people get about dogs. The author's point has nothing to do with *criticizing an uncaring attitude*, (A), so that can't be the point of his comparing puppies and babies. The same is true for the choices, (B), (D), and (E), so (C) is correct.

19. B

Again, go back to the passage. Notice that the start of paragraph 3 actually refers back to the end of the *first* paragraph. Paragraph 1 ended with the author listing the dog as the first domesticated animal, followed by food animals, work animals, etc. Paragraph 2 talks about *why* the dog came first. So when paragraph 3 begins with *no wonder the dog was first*, it's referring to the dog's status as the first domesticated animal. Similarly, *the list* refers to other domesticated animals, or *the number of animals that developed relationships with humans*, (B). The author hasn't yet mentioned *birds that scavenge human food supplies*, and when he does, he only mentions one, not many *types*, (A). The passage never mentions *species that are able to communicate with dogs*, (C), or the *variety of attributes that make dogs good hunters*, (D). Finally, if you chose (E), you were losing track of the author's main points. Read over the first three paragraphs to see what's going on, and give a closer reading next time.

20. E

This question might seem more complicated than it really is. If you were confused by the digression the author made to talk about the blue tit, taking a look at the choices first probably would've saved you time. (A), (B), and (D) are fairly easy to eliminate—they have nothing to do with any of the author's main points. Good—now that you've eliminated three choices, you can always guess. But first let's go back to the passage. In line 50, the author mentions *opportunistic feeders*. He goes on, saying, *even today, many birds . . . feed from our stores*. So (E) must be right; the blue tit is an example of an opportunistic feeder. The question doesn't go any more into depth than that, so you're done.

21. C

This is a clear reference question. Go back to the lines you're given to see what kind of animals are being referred to. You have to read above a little to find the answer. The author has just finished describing the blue tit as an example of an opportunistic feeder. He reinforces the idea that the tit is an animal that feeds when and where it can by saying, *If all birds had been so specialized that they only fed in deep forest, it never would have happened.* In other words, they are *not* so specialized—they'll eat wherever they find a food source, (C). The author isn't talking here about *companion animals*, (A). *Forest inhabitants*, (B), is too broad. (D) is out because the birds are not hunting, they're feeding. And the point about the birds is not to give an example of *persistent pests*, (E).

22. D

Go back to the passage to see in what context the author discusses his experiences in the tropics. At the beginning of paragraph 4, the author says that he thinks that the very first domesticated animals were orphaned as a result of hunting. He then tells how, in the tropics, he saw many instances of wild animals raised in homes of hunters. So his experiences illustrate his theory about how *the first domesticated animals were created*, (D). Choices (A), (B), (C), and (E) do not relate to the author's argument here (or anywhere in the passage).

23. A

This one's a little tricky. If you thought so, you should've jumped ahead and come back later if you had time. Remember, reading questions don't go from easy to hard, so the next one could be easier. Check out the line *aid* is in to see what's going on. The author says that without domesticated animals—goats, sheep, pigs, cattle, and horses—we never would've achieved civilization. These animals helped or *aided* us—but they didn't have much choice in the matter. We dominated them, and then used them for food or labor. That's why *aid* is in quotes, and (A) is correct. The passage never says *population levels are dangerously high,* (B). (C) is a better possibility—but it's not a point the author makes; you're inferring too much if you chose (C). It's not clear that animals *benefited* at all from domestication, (D). (E) is really far-out, and not supported by the passage.

24. E

The *ironic paradox* is found in the last four lines of the passage. The author says our living with other species—using them for food and labor—is what made our civilization possible. It is ironic then, that our civilization is presently wiping out many plant and animal species, (E). Nowhere does the author say anything about (A) or (B). With (C), the author does talk about the pet care industry in the final paragraph, but not to say its size is *ironic*. His point is just to show how big it is. (D) twists the author's point; it's by being parasites on other species that humans benefit, not the other way around.

SECTION 3

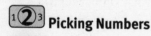 Picking Numbers

 Backsolving

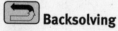 Eyeballing

1. D

We want the value of x. Let's begin by distributing the 2 over the terms inside the parentheses on the left side of the equation. This gives us $2x + 2y = 8 + 2y$. Subtracting $2y$ from both sides results in $2x = 8$. Dividing both sides by 2 gives us $x = 4$, choice (D).

2. A

Since point A is at 1 on the number line and point C is at 7, the distance between them is $7 - 1$, or 6. Half the distance from A to C is $\frac{1}{2}$ of 6, or 3, and 3 units from either point A or point C is 4, since $1 + 3 = 4$ and $7 - 3 = 4$. Therefore, the point at 4 on the number line is the midpoint of AC, since a midpoint by definition divides a line in half. Point B is at 3 and the midpoint of AC is at 4, so the distance between them is 1, answer choice (A).

3. C

The machine caps 5 bottles every 2 seconds, and we want to know how many bottles it caps in 1 minute, or 60 seconds. Multiplying 2 seconds by 30 gives you 60 seconds. If the machine caps 5 bottles in 2 seconds, how many bottles does it cap in 30 times 2 seconds? 30×5, or 150 bottles, answer choice (C).

4. C

All you have to do here is solve the equation, but instead of solving it for n, you have to solve it for $4n$. If $2n + 3 = 5$, then you can subtract 3 from both sides of the equation to get $2n = 2$. Multiplying both sides of this equation by 2 gives you $4n = 4$, choice (C).

5. D

The easiest way to do this problem is just to backsolve. Since each pair of numbers in the answer choices represents possible values of a and b, just add up each a and b to see if $a + b < 5$, and subtract each b from each a to see if $a - b > 6$. If you do this, you'll find that in all five cases $a + b < 5$, but only in choice (D) is $a - b > 6$. In choice (D), $a + b = 4 + (-3) = 1$ and $a - b = 4 - (-3) = 7$.

If you think about the properties of negative and positive numbers (drawing a number line can help), you'll probably realize that the only way $a - b$ could be larger than $a + b$ is if b is a negative number, but that would only eliminate choice (A). In some problems, your knowledge of math only helps you a little bit. In those cases, you just have to play with the given answer choices in order to solve.

6. A

In the figure, angle B is labeled $(2x - 4)°$, and in the question stem you're told that angle B measures 60°. So $2x - 4 = 60$, and $x = 32$. That means that angle A, which is labeled $(3x)°$, must measure 3×32, or 96°. Since the three angles of a triangle must add up to 180°, $60° + 96° + y° = 180°$, and $y = 24$, choice (A).

7. D ①②③

This one is easier if you plug in numbers for C and R. Suppose R is 2. Then there would be 2 rooms on each floor, and since there are 10 floors in the building, there would be 2×10 or 20 rooms altogether. If $C = 3$, then there are 3 chairs in each room. Since there are 20 rooms and 3 chairs per room, there are $20 \times 3 = 60$ chairs altogether. Which answer choices are 60 when R is 2 and C is 3? Only $10RC$, choice (D).

You don't have to plug in numbers here if you think about the units of each variable. There are 10 floors, R rooms per floor, and C chairs per room. If you multiply 10 floors by $R \frac{\text{rooms}}{\text{floor}}$, the unit "floors" will cancel out, leaving you with $10R$ rooms, and if you multiply $10R$ rooms by $C \frac{\text{chairs}}{\text{room}}$, the unit "rooms" will cancel out, leaving $10RC$ chairs in the building, again choice (D).

8. D

Here you have a strange word, "sump," which describes a number that has a certain relationship between the sum and the product of its digits. To solve this one, just find the sum and the product of the digits for each answer choice. You're told that for a "sump" number, the sum should be greater than the product. Choice (D), 411, has a sum of 6 and a product of 4, so that's the one you're looking for.

9. D

In this question, if you think about the relationship between the information you're given and the information you have to find, it becomes very easy. You're given 4% of a number and you have to find 20% of that same number. 4% of r is just a certain fraction, $\frac{4}{100}$ to be exact, times r; and 20% of r is just $\frac{20}{100}$ times r. That means that 20% of r is 5 times as great as 4% of r, since $\frac{4}{100}$ times 5 is $\frac{20}{100}$. So if you're given that 4% of r is 6.2, then 20% of r must be 5 times 6.2, or 31, choice (D). You could also have figured out the value of r and then found 20% of that value, but this takes a bit longer. 4% of r is the same as 4% times r, or $.04r$. If $.04r = 6.2$, then $r = \frac{6.2}{.04} = 155$, and 20% of 155 is $0.2 \times 155 = 31$, choice (D) again.

10. B

The ratio of teachers to students is 1 to 10, so there might be only 1 teacher and 10 students, or there might be 50 teachers and 500 students, or just about any number of teachers and students that are in the ratio 1 to 10. That means that the teachers and the students can be divided into groups of 11: 1 teacher and 10 students in each group. Think of it as a school with a large number of classrooms, all with 1 teacher and 10 students, for a total of 11 people in each room. So the total number of teachers and students in the school must be a multiple of 11. If you look at the answer choices, you'll notice that 121, choice (B), is the only multiple of 11, so (B) must be correct.

11. E

Since x and y with a funny symbol between them is equal to $(x - y)^x + (x + y)^y$, to find 4 and 2 with a funny symbol between them just plug in 4 for x and 2 for y. That gives you $(4 - 2)^4 + (4 + 2)^2$, or $2^4 + 6^2$, or $16 + 36$, or 52, answer choice (E).

12. D

If the particle travels from A to B to C to D to E and then back to A, it has traveled 5 centimeters, since each side of the pentagon measures 1 centimeter. If it goes all the way around the pentagon again, it's traveled another 5 centimeters, for a total of 10 centimeters. In fact, every time the particle makes a complete revolution around the pentagon (from point A back to point A again), it travels an additional 5 centimeters. So if the number of centimeters the particle has traveled is a multiple of 5, the particle must be at point A. The number 723 is 3 more than a multiple of 5. If the particle had gone 720 centimeters, it would be at point A; since it has gone 3 more centimeters, it must be at point D, answer choice (D).

13. E ①②③

When would $4 + \dfrac{1}{s}$ have the smallest possible value? Certainly if s, and its reciprocal $\dfrac{1}{s}$, were negative, $4 + \dfrac{1}{s}$ would be smaller than 4, since adding a negative number is like subtracting a positive number. However, none of the answer choices are negative, so $4 + \dfrac{1}{s}$ will be greater than 4. However, it will be as small as possible when $\dfrac{1}{s}$ is as small as possible. If you look at the answer choices, you can find the values for $\dfrac{1}{s}$. If $s = \dfrac{1}{4}$, then $\dfrac{1}{s} = 4$, etc. If you do that, you'll probably notice that as s gets larger its reciprocal gets smaller, so $\dfrac{1}{s}$ is smallest when s is largest, in this case when $s = 4$, choice (E).

14. D ①②③

Since you're looking for the sixth term of the sequence, let's call the sixth term x. Every term in this sequence is formed by multiplying the previous term by 3 and then subtracting 1, so the seventh term must be formed by multiplying the sixth term, x, by 3, and then subtracting 1; in other words, the seventh term is equal to $3x - 1$. Since the seventh term is 365, $365 = 3x - 1$, you can solve for x to get $x = 122$, choice (D).

15. A

If an integer is chosen randomly from the first 50 integers, the probability of choosing any particular number is 1 divided by 50, and the probability of choosing an integer with a digit of 3 is the number of integers with a digit of 3 divided by 50. The integers 3, 13, 23, 30, 31, 32, 33, 34, 35, 36, 37, 38, 39, and 43 are the only integers with 3's in them, for a total of 14 different integers, so the probability is $\dfrac{14}{50}$, or $\dfrac{7}{25}$, choice (A).

16. C

Let's call the degree measure of the largest angle x. Since the degree measure of the middle-sized angle is 40 degrees less than the degree measure of the largest angle, the degree measure of the middle-sized angle is $x - 40$. We also know that the smallest angle is 20 degrees. We know that the sum of the measures of the three interior angles of any triangle is 180 degrees. So we can write an equation for our triangle: $x + (x - 40) + 20 = 180$.

Now let's solve for x:

$$x + x - 40 + 20 = 180$$
$$2x - 20 = 180$$
$$2x = 200$$
$$x = 100, \text{ choice (C)}.$$

17. C

The diagram tells you that the radius of the circle is $x - 5$, and the question stem tells you that the circumference of the circle is 20π. Since the circumference of a circle is 2π times the radius, 20π must equal 2π times $(x - 5)$, which gives you the equation $20\pi = 2\pi(x - 5)$. Solving this equation gives you $x = 15$, answer choice (C).

18. E

The slope of a line is defined as the change in the y-coordinate divided by the change in the x-coordinate. As you go from point A to point B, the x-coordinate goes from p to 6 and the y-coordinate goes from 3 to p, so the change in the x-coordinate is $6 - p$ and the change in the y-coordinate is $p - 3$. You can make this into an equation: $\frac{p - 3}{6 - p} = 2$, and solve this equation for p. That would give you $p = 5$, choice (E). You could also plug the 5 possible values for p into the expression $\frac{p - 3}{6 - p}$ to see which one gives you 2 as a result. Either way, choice (E) is correct.

19. D

In order to find the areas of the shaded triangles, you have to find the coordinates of all the vertices of the triangles. You know where points P, Q, and C are in the coordinate plane, but what about the rest of them? Well, first, let's label all the other points that are vertices of the triangles. The triangle on top has two labeled vertices, P and Q. The third vertex of that triangle is on the y-axis between P and the origin. Let's call it point A. The other triangle has vertices Q, C, and an unlabeled point that is also the upper-right-hand corner of the rectangle. Call that point B. Points A and B are both on the same horizontal line that point Q is on, so all three points must have the same y-coordinate of 4. The x-coordinate of point A is 0 since it is on the y-axis, and the x-coordinate of B must be 3, the same as point C's x-coordinate, since points B and C lie on the same vertical line. So point A's coordinates are $(0, 4)$ and point B's coordinates are $(3, 4)$. Since triangles PQA and QBC are right triangles, we just need to know the lengths of their legs in order to find their areas. In the coordinate plane, the length of a horizontal line segment is the difference of the x-coordinates of its endpoints and the length of a vertical line segment is the difference of the y-coordinates of its endpoints. So the length of PA is $6 - 4$, or 2, and the length of AQ is $1 - 0$, or 1, so the area of triangle PQA is $\frac{1}{2} \times 2 \times 1 = 1$. The length of QB is $3 - 1$, or 2, and the length of BC is $4 - 0$, or 4, so the area of triangle QBC is $\frac{1}{2} \times 2 \times 4 = 4$. The sum of those areas is $1 + 4 = 5$, answer choice (D).

20. C ⟨1 ②₃⟩

No matter what the value of n is, this figure will be a rectangular solid. All rectangular solids have six faces. You just have to figure out the area of each of the six faces. The face on the bottom, which is the face up against the table or whatever this stack of cubes is sitting on, is a square, and it will have an area of 1 square inch, since the edge of each cube has a length of 1 inch. The face on the top of the stack of cubes is also a square, and it will also have a surface area of 1 square inch. The other four faces making up the stack are identical rectangles, each with dimensions of 1 inch by n inches. So the area of one of these rectangles is $1 \times n$, or n, square inches, and these four identical rectangular faces have a total area of $4 \times n$, or $4n$, square inches. So the total surface area of the solid is the sum of the areas of the square top, the square bottom, and the four identical rectangular faces, which is $1 + 1 + 4n$, or $4n + 2$ square inches.

If you found that confusing, it might be easier just to pick a value for n. Suppose $n = 4$ and there are 4 cubes, as in the figure shown. Then just add up the areas of the faces of the stack in the figure, but don't forget the faces that aren't shown in the drawing. Since each face of each cube has an area of 1, in square inches, the figure shown has an area of 4 in the front plus 4 on the right side plus 4 on the left side (not shown in the drawing) plus 4 in the back (not shown in the drawing) plus 1 on the top and finally 1 on the bottom (not shown in the drawing), for a total of 18. Only choice (C) has a value of 18 when $n = 4$, so choice (C) must be correct.

SECTION 4

1. E

The key here is the word *beneficial*, or helpful. If you don't know *beneficial*, a knowledge of word roots would help you. *Beneficial* contains the root BENE, meaning good, which indicates to you that it's a positive word. Well, if in one breath we are told that the ozone layer is positive, and in the next, that it does something for plant and animal life relating to dangerous ultraviolet radiation, we know we need a fairly positive word in the blank. The only choice that fits this requirement is choice (E), *protecting*. (D), *thwarting*, means impeding or preventing.

2. A

While is our tip-off that this sentence will in some way contain a contrast. *While George Balanchine's choreography stayed within a classical context, he challenged convention by recombining ballet idioms.* (If you don't know exactly what this means, it doesn't matter—you just need to grasp that this is how he challenged convention.) He's challenging convention by *recombining* typical ballet moves or whatever in some ---- way. The word in the blank must mean something like unconventional. The best choice here is (A), *unexpected*. Choice (C), *redundant*, means needlessly repetitive or excessive.

3. C

All of today's navel oranges have some common relationship to a single mutant tree that produced *seedless fruit 200 years ago.* They must all be descended from this one mutant. So the word in the blank must mean descended from. Choice (C), *descendants*, jumps out as the correct choice. *Progenitors*, in choice (A), is meant to fool you since it has something to do with genetics. If you break *progenitor* down, *PRO* means *for* or *before* while the GENUS root is related to the word *gene*. So *progenitors* are ancestors—people (or things) that are related but came before—like grandparents. *Progenitors* are the opposite of descendants. Choice (E) is another word trap—just because *spores* have something to do with plants doesn't mean this is right. A *spore* is a reproductive body found in simpler forms of life. But you don't need to know biology to figure this one out. Just use your reasoning skills. While a seed could be a spore, it makes no sense to say that all of today's navel oranges are the actual *spores* of a 200-year-old tree. But it is more plausible that this one tree produced a number of seeds, which in turn produced more of their own seeds, and so on.

4. A

In this sentence, there's a relationship between the quantities of food and drink Henry VIII consumed and the type of person he was seen as. Either he consumed minimal quantities of food and drink and was considered a spartan of sorts, or he consumed large amounts and was considered a pig. Choice (A) is the only one that fits either one of these predictions. A *glutton* is one who overindulges in the consumption of food and drink. This option is the only one that fits, where there's a connection between the type of person his subjects saw him as and the amount of food and drink he scarfed up. (C)'s first word, *minute,* or very small, fits okay, but a *luminary*, a famous or important person, doesn't. Consuming small quantities of food wouldn't make someone famous. In (B), *prodigious* means either extraordinary or enormous, while a *peer* is an equal or a member of nobility.

5. A

You want a vocabulary word that means something like transition or temporary—some word that describes a government that no longer is in power, but is staying in power just *until a new government* is ready to take over the reins. Choice (A), *interim*, means temporary or provisional, so this is the answer. INTER is a root you should know—it means between.

MILES DAVIS PASSAGES

6. B

Author 1's point is that Davis was a musical innovator. So when the author says that Davis's change of musical direction was *characteristic*, she's making the point that this change was typical of Davis's innovation. That matches (B) quite well. (A) is the thesis of Passage 2, not Passage 1. (C) is far too negative; author 1 thinks that the stylistic innovation was a positive attribute. (D) is a paraphrase of the first sentence, but that occurs earlier and is unrelated to the word *characteristically*. (E) is too literal. The author says that *each decade brought more surprises*, but that doesn't mean the innovations were spaced ten years apart, and it certainly doesn't follow from the word *characteristically*.

7. E

Davis couldn't play in Charlie Parker's style very well, so he created a new one to avoid becoming a *second-rate footnote*. The term *footnote* usually means a note at the bottom of the page that supplements the body of a test. Here, it refers to a person who is not the main focus, an unimportant person, choice (E).

The author says that Davis was *supremely expressive*, so the author wouldn't think that he was in danger of becoming *unexpressive*, (A). (B) is a literal meaning of footnote, but doesn't refer to a person. Even though Davis was not as technically skilled as Parker, it seems unlikely that the author would refer to him as *unskilled*, (C). (D) is the opposite of what you're looking for; Davis became a *stylistic innovator* in order to avoid being a *footnote*.

8. D

Right after the phrase *unique style*, the author offers a description: *a few well-chosen notes were surrounded by artful silences that spoke volumes.* So you're looking for a description of someone who uses a little to say a lot. That matches (D) pretty well. The painter is surrounding her subject with empty space in the same way that Davis surrounded his notes with silence.

(A) might fit well with the description in Passage 1 of Davis as a stylistic innovator, but the question is asking about Passage 2, not Passage 1. (B) is not too bad, since we do get the sense that Davis carefully selected his notes, but (B) doesn't convey the sense that the chef was as spare as Davis. (Maybe the chef uses tons of different ingredients.) If anything, Davis was more focused than his predecessors, so (C) doesn't fit here. (E) sounds more like the description of the highly technical Parker than the spare and elegant Davis, so it's the opposite of what you're looking for.

9. C

Author 1 characterizes Davis as an innovator, so he would see Davis's development of a new style as typical of his entire career. That's right in line with (C).

(A) and (B) both fit pretty well with Passage 2, but author 1 never discusses technique or technical limitations, so they don't work for this question. (D) is half right, because author 1 does think the development is important, but the word *surprising* makes this the opposite of what you're looking for. The development was typical, not *surprising*. There's no real evidence that author 1 would think this particular innovation was more important than the many others described in Passage 1, (E).

To Build a Fire Passage

This fiction passage shouldn't pose too many problems: it's short, clear, and straightforward. If you enjoy reading fiction, be careful not to relax too much while reading the passage—you may slow down and lose time. Save pleasure reading for when you're not taking the SAT! The passage describes a man and a dog entering a little-traveled path in Alaska. A comparison is set up between the man, who *lacks imagination* and isn't alarmed by the extreme cold, and his dog who, going on instinct, is alarmed.

10. E

Review the beginning of the passage to see what *act* the man is *excusing to himself.* It turns out he stopped because he was out of breath, but doesn't want to admit it (to himself, since he's alone), so he plays it off by looking at his watch. That makes choice (E) correct. He shows no reaction to what time it is, (A). You may have been confused by choice (B) because the narrator (later in the passage) implies that the dog's instincts are more accurate than the man's. However, the man never shows distrust of himself, (B). You're overinterpreting if you chose (C)—there's no evidence in the passage to support this inference. The point of the man's *excusing the act to himself* has nothing to do with *the time of day*, (D); it has to do with him not admitting why he stopped in the first place.

11. C

Watch for the tone in the lines around the quote—it'll help you eliminate choices. For example, does the man seem at all *excited*? No, so (A) is out. He also doesn't seem *nervous*, (B), although by the end of the passage there's an ominous feeling of danger in the air. (C) is right because it's a straightforward description of what's going on. There's no evidence in the passage to support choice (D). (E) is similarly wrong—there's no discussion of why the man is in the wilderness. Remember, most inferences (or *suggestions*, as the question phrases it) are very mild and are always supported by the passage.

12. D

Reread the lines the quote appears in. The man's being a creature of temperature is the same *frailty* that all humans have: we're *able only to live within narrow limits of heat and cold*. In other words, if it's too cold, we'll freeze to death. Choice (D) is correct. *A creature of temperature* does not imply the man prefers cold climates, (A), because *temperature* includes hot and cold. The author shows later in the passage how wrong the man's judgment of the temperature is, so (B) is unlikely. There's no discussion of *personality being shaped by the environment*, (C). The man may or may not know wilderness survival techniques, (E), but in any case, that's not what *a creature of temperature* refers to.

13. D

This question refers you to a big chunk of text, so save time by reviewing your notes and scanning the choices before you go to the passage. Choice (A) implies the wrong thing. This wilderness must be immensely beautiful, but whether the man notices it is not the point. The point is the judgment the man makes about the temperature. (B) overstates the case. The author isn't flatly declaring *humans can't survive in the Alaskan wilderness*. Instead, he's describing a man who is underestimating the potential danger. That makes (D) correct. Just because this character can't judge the temperature accurately doesn't mean *there's no way to accurately judge the temperature*, (C). There's no evidence that *most people could not do* what this guy is doing, even though it's obviously a difficult thing, (E).

14. D

All of paragraph 2 leads up to the lines you're sent to for this question. After a discussion of the potential danger extreme temperatures pose to humans, the paragraph concludes by saying none of this entered the man's head. In other words, he lacks *insight and understanding*, (D). The man thinks the cold *must be guarded against*, so (B) can't be right. At the same time, (A) is too strong—the man doesn't even acknowledge that there are *odds* to succeed against. (C) is too general. *Apprehension* in (E) means fearfulness, which we've already seen the man lacks.

15. A

Again, you have a lot of lines to review, so save time by reviewing your notes and scanning the answer choices before you check the passage. It's in these lines that the author introduces the dog and its *instinct*—which tells it to take shelter from the cold. Choice (A) restates what's in lines 50–60, so it is the correct choice. The dog isn't judging the temperature, (B), it's just reacting to an instinct of danger. Choice (C) is an inference that goes too far—it's too general for these lines. (D) contradicts the point the author's making. (E) is partially true, but it captures only a small part of what the author suggests.

16. B

This question doesn't require too much interpretation, so don't go digging for difficult answers. The passage says that the dog *knew nothing of thermometers*, but that it *had its instinct*. In other words, it didn't read the temperature with a device as humans do, and it didn't need to—it knew instinctively how cold it was. The answer is (B)—the dog's awareness of its environment is different from the man's. Nothing implies that dogs *need not be concerned about temperature*, (A); the point is that they perceive it differently than people do. (C) is too negative. Although the author calls the dog a *brute* at one point, it is done with respect, since the dog's instincts prove to be more valuable than the man's intelligence. (D) is too literal, and the point is not that the dog *could not rely on technological devices*, (E), but that the dog has no need of them.

17. C

Reread the lines at the end of the passage to see what's going on. We've seen that the dog fears the cold, and the end of the passage describes the dog watching the man for a sign that they are heading for protection, (C). Choices (A) and (E) miss the mark because the author never says that the dog recognizes the man's mistaken estimation of the cold. There is also no sign that the man is being visibly affected by the cold, (B). Choice (D) invents something not found in the passage.

ELDERLY ASIANS PASSAGE

This is a passage about Southeast Asian immigrants' experience of aging in America. This passage may be a little dry, but it's not complex. The discussion focuses on the problems older immigrants have when they come to America, which include different standards of what's considered *elderly* not getting the kind of respect they would in their homelands, dealing with different gender roles, and elderly women being isolated in the home and becoming estranged from their families. Don't worry about any more detail than this until you get to the questions.

18. C

Remember this strategy for dealing with main idea questions: Look for an answer that's not too broad or too narrow, but that encompasses the whole passage. In this case, (A) is too broad. From the first paragraph, you know that the focus is more specific than *the reasons why Southeast Asian people move to the United States*. This helps you eliminate (B) as well; from the start you're told the passage is concerned with the problems of the elderly, not the young. (C) covers the whole passage and is correct. (D) picks up on a detail—Confucianism—and expands it beyond the scope of the passage. And (E) is just one topic discussed in the passage, not the focus of it.

19. D

Even if the word *acculturating* was unfamiliar to you, the rest of the passage should have made it clear that the differences between generations, once the family came to America, had to do with differences in language ability, different cultural attitudes toward and definitions of age, better employment opportunities, and obstacles to older refugees mixing in their new society. The closest answer to capturing all that is (D). (A) and (B) are too narrow, focusing on single issues that affect only a portion of the refugees, while this quotation applies generally to older refugees. (C) and (E) are out of the scope of the passage.

20. A

Review paragraph 2 to understand why the author mentions the *traditional Hmong culture*. There, the author says that American and Asian cultures define *elderly* differently. In the Hmong culture, people become elders and retire at 35; obviously, in American culture, this is not the case. So Hmong culture is mentioned to illustrate the paragraph's main point—that *social expectations vary greatly from one country to another*, (A). There's no mention of traditional values in Vietnamese society *lessening*, (B). No other ancient cultures are mentioned in paragraph 2, so (C) is out. (D) is out because Confucianism isn't mentioned until paragraph 3. Likewise, no other Southeast Asian peoples are mentioned, (E).

21. B

Go back to the line in which *family mediators* appears. This part of paragraph 3 says that younger members of immigrant families deal with schools and other institutions because they have better English language skills than older family members. So being a *family mediator* is a responsibility that young refugees assume in a new country, (B). (A) might've confused you because a hasty reading of the passage makes it sound like this is a role older people used to fill—but in fact, it's not. The passage really says that in the traditional culture there are strict rules for social interaction based on age, which the new role of family mediator gradually erodes. The passage says nothing about getting help from friends, (C), or professionals, (D). The author doesn't write about the benefits American society derives from immigrant people, (E).

22. B

After rereading the line that *pronounced* is in, the first thing you should do is eliminate the obvious choice. In this case, that's (E), *declared*. The author uses *pronounced* to mean (B), *noticeable*. Gender roles changed somewhat in Southeast Asia during the Vietnam War, but they changed even more drastically for families that emigrated to the United States. None of the other choices fits this context. The author doesn't imply that these changes became more *acceptable*, (D); she implies that they happened out of necessity and says they were a *radical change*.

23. D

The *radical change* the author refers to is the fact that women often become the main source of income in immigrant families in the United States. This is a major change in gender roles, because in Southeast Asia men were usually the breadwinners. (D) is correct. (A) is an unlikely answer because retirement ages were discussed back in paragraph 2. (B) might've been tempting, because the Vietnam War is mentioned in paragraph 4, along with the answer. But the author says that while gender roles are changing in Southeast Asia due to the Vietnam War, the *radical change* occurs when families emigrate. *Education*, (C), is not discussed in these lines. (E) is out because the author says there are more jobs for younger refugees, not that it's hard for young refugees to find them.

24. E

When you're not given a line reference, it makes sense to look in the passage where the previous question left off because Critical Reading questions are ordered sequentially. So that takes you to the last paragraph, which is indeed where the author makes a point about the *long-term outlook for refugee women*. The author starts off by saying that although the long-term outlook is *unknown*, there are *indications* about it. Now look at the choices. There's no evidence that this is a *personal recollection*, (A), or a *historical discussion*, (B). No specific *case* is mentioned or analyzed, (C). The author isn't being *philosophical*, (D); if anything, she's being as scientific as possible, given the lack of data. That leaves (E), *informed speculation*. Since the author is knowledgeable about the subject matter, but has to go on *indications* to make her final point, (E) is the best answer.

SECTION 5

1. C

This is a straightforward substitution problem, but be sure to remember order of operations. First plug in 3 for r to get $(3^2 - 2)(4 + 3)$. Simplify the expressions within the parentheses to get $(9 - 2)(4 + 3)$, which is 7×7, or 49, choice (C).

2. E

Work carefully and follow the order of operations, and problems like this one will be easy points: $f(3) = 3^2 + 3 = 9 + 3 = 12$, choice (E).

3. A

The intersection of two sets consists of all the elements that are common to both sets. Be sure to read the question carefully; there are many different questions that could be asked about these sets. Set A consists of the numbers 11, 13, 17, and 19. Set B consists of the numbers $-7, -5, -4, -3, -2,$ 2, 3, 4, 5, 7, 11, 13. Only two of these are also in Set B, choice (A).

4. C

The factors of 87 are 1, 3, 29, and 87; 87 is a factor of 87, but it is not prime, so (E) is incorrect. 29 and 3 are both factors of 87 and prime, so the greater of these, (C), is correct.

5. D

In equations of the form $y = mx + b$, m represents the slope of the line and b represents the y-intercept of the line. The slope of a line is the rise over the run, or the difference between the values of y at two different points on the line over the difference between the values of x at those same points—a shorthand way of expressing this is $\frac{\Delta Y}{\Delta X}$. A good way to double-check your answer is to plug the values of x and y at some point on your chosen line into the equation to see if they work. You need to figure out which line in the figure changes two units in the y-direction for every one it changes in the x-direction. Lines B, C, and D all do this, so they all have a slope of 2. However, only line D also has the correct y-intercept, -4, so (D) is correct.

6. B

Backsolving is a good strategy for this question. Plug in all the numbers in the choices for y, and see which ones work; -1 gives you $(-1 - 3)^2 = (-1 + 1)^2$, which simplifies to $(-4)^2 = (0)^2$ or $16 = 0$. This isn't true, so eliminate (A) and (D). 1 gives you $(1 - 3)^2 = (1 + 1)^2$, which is $(-2)^2 = (2)^2$ or $4 = 4$. This is true, so (B) or (C) must be the answer. Try 3: $(3 - 3)^2 = (3 + 1)^2$, $(0)^2 = (4)^2$ or $0 = 16$. This isn't true, so the answer must be (B).

7. D

First, find the area of the frame and photo combined, then find the area of the photo alone, and finally, find the difference. Since we know that the diameter of the photo is 8, its radius must be 4, and the area of the photo is $\pi r^2 = \pi 4^2 = 16\pi$. We are given that the frame is 2 inches wide, so we can say that the radius of the frame and photo combined is $4 + 2 = 6$. So the area of the frame and photo combined must be $\pi r2 = \pi 62 = 36\pi$. Finally, to get the area of only the frame, we subtract the area of the photo from the area of the frame and photo combined, giving us $36\pi - 16\pi = 20\pi$, choice (D).

8. B

Picking numbers makes this problem easier to work with. Rather than dealing with fractions of the business, say that there are 100 total shares. At the beginning of the problem, the 4 women each own 20 shares and the man owns 20 shares. One woman sells $\frac{1}{2}$ of her part of the business, 10 shares, to the man, and another woman sells $1 - \frac{1}{4} = \frac{3}{4}$ of her part of the business, $20(\frac{3}{4}) = 15$ shares to the man. Now the man owns $20 + 10 + 15 = 45$ shares out of the total 100 shares in the business. $\frac{45}{100} = \frac{9}{20}$, so the man now owns $\frac{9}{20}$ of the business, choice (B).

9. 15

This is a simple plug-in, but make sure you write out every step so as to avoid a careless error. This is especially important in the Grid-ins. If $y = 2$, the expression $(5 - y)(y + 3)$ becomes $(5 - 2)(2 + 3)$. Remember to do the calculations inside the parentheses first: $5 - 2$ is 3 and $2 + 3$ is 5, so $(5 - 2)(2 + 3) = 3 \times 5 = 15$, so put 15 in the grid.

10. 9.43

If the daily rate is $18.99, then the price for a week, or 7 days, is $7 \times \$18.99 = \$132.93$. Since the weekly rate is less, only $123.50, you can save $\$132.93 - \$123.50 = \$9.43$ by renting at the weekly rate.

11. 13 < length < 15

The first thing to do is to put the numbers 4, 5, and 12 in the appropriate places in the figure. Now you should see that you have the lengths of two sides of triangle BCD. Since BCD is a right triangle, you can use the Pythagorean theorem to figure out the length of the hypotenuse, but if you've memorized the common Pythagorean triplets you don't have to do that—you'll immediately recognize that this is a 5-12-13 right triangle, and so the length of BD is 13. The length of AC is $4 + 5 = 9$, so the triangle ACD has legs of lengths 9 and 12. Again, you can use the Pythagorean theorem to find the length of the hypotenuse, but you should notice that ACD is a multiple of the 3-4-5 right triangle, and AD has length 15. If you draw in point E in the figure between A and B, you'll see that DE will be longer than BD but shorter than AD, or greater than 13 but less than 15. So any number between 13 and 15, such as 14, is a possible answer.

12. 15/4 or 3.75

If you need $\frac{3}{4}$ of a cup of drink mix for 2 quarts of water, then you need more than $\frac{3}{4}$ of a cup of drink mix for 10 quarts of water. How much more? Since $2 \times 5 = 10$, you have 5 times as much water, so you also need 5 times as much drink mix: $5 \times \frac{3}{4} = \frac{15}{4}$, so grid in $\frac{15}{4}$ (in the form of $\frac{15}{4}$).

13. 166

The sum of the three angles of the triangle must be 180°. One angle measures 31°, but you don't know the measures of the other two angles in the triangle. However, the interior angle of the triangle on top lies on a straight line with an angle measuring 45°, so that interior angle must measure $180° - 45° = 135°$. If two angles of a triangle measure 135° and 31°, then the third angle measures $180° - 135° - 31° = 14°$. The 14° angle lies on a straight line with the $x°$ angle, so $14° + x° = 180°$, and $x = 166$.

If you remembered that any exterior angle of a triangle has the same measure as the sum of the two opposite interior angles, you could have saved a few steps. Once you figure out that the top angle of the triangle is 135°, you know that $x° = 135° + 31°$, and therefore $x = 166°$.

14. .5 < y < .625

The only thing you know about y is that it is between $\frac{1}{2}$ and $\frac{5}{8}$. $\frac{1}{2}$ is the same as $\frac{4}{8}$, so y is between $\frac{4}{8}$ and $\frac{5}{8}$. You can't grid a fraction like $\frac{4\frac{1}{2}}{8}$, but you can change $\frac{4}{8}$ to $\frac{8}{16}$ and $\frac{5}{8}$ to $\frac{10}{16}$. That gives you an obvious value for y; since y is between $\frac{8}{16}$ and $\frac{10}{16}$, it could be $\frac{9}{16}$, so that's one possible number to grid in. You could also solve this question by converting $\frac{1}{2}$ and $\frac{5}{8}$ to decimals. If you convert $\frac{1}{2}$ to .5 and $\frac{5}{8}$ to .625, you can grid in any number greater than .5 and less than .625. For example, you can grid in .6.

15. 46

The average rate of speed is the total distance traveled divided by the total hours traveled. Melanie drove at 40 miles per hour for 2 hours, for a total of 40×2, or 80, miles. If she increased her speed by 25%, then she increased her speed by 25% of 40, or 10, so her new speed was $40 + 10 = 50$. So she drove at 50 miles per hour for the next 3 hours, for a total of $50 \times 3 = 150$ miles. She went 80 miles and then 150 miles, for a total of 230 miles, and she drove for 2 hours and then for 3 hours, for a total of 5 hours. Her average rate for the trip was 230 miles divided by 5 hours, or 46 miles per hour.

16. 175

There are three types of dealers at this convention—dealers who sell only stamps, dealers who sell only coins, and dealers who sell both stamps and coins. The total number of dealers is 500.

You're given the number of two out of the three types of dealers—there are 127 that sell both stamps and coins and 198 that sell only stamps. Since there are only three types of dealers, 127 + 198 + the number of dealers who sell only coins = 500, and so the number of dealers who sell only coins is 500 − 198 − 127 = 175.

17. 46

Since the small square has a side of length 2, the area of the square must be 2^2, or 4. The larger square has a side of length 6, so its area is 6^2, or 36. The shaded part of square $ABCD$ is then 36 − 4, or 32. The triangle is a right triangle with both legs of length 6, so the area of the triangle is $\frac{1}{2} \times 6 \times 6$, or 18. The shaded area of the triangle is then 18 − 4 = 14. The total shaded area is 32 + 14, or 46, so grid in 46.

18. 11

If N and R added up to a number less than 10, the problem would look different, something like:

$$+\begin{array}{r} NR \\ \underline{RN} \\ XX \end{array}$$

Since it doesn't look like that, $N + R$ must be greater than 10. The best way to proceed from here is to try different pairs of numbers for R and N, and see what you get for B and C (keeping in mind that N, R, A, B, and C are different digits). If you try setting either N or R equal to 9, you'll notice that you won't get different digits for all five variables. For example, if $R = 9$ and $N = 7$:

$$+\begin{array}{r} 79 \\ \underline{97} \\ 176 \end{array}$$

Since there is always a 1 carried over into the tens' place, if $R = 9$, then the tens' column will add up to $9 + N + 1$, or $10 + N$. The sum $10 + N$ has the same units' digit as N, so B and N will be the same if $R = 9$. The same thing happens if $N = 9$, only R and B turn out to be the same. If you try the next largest combination of numbers for N and R, which is 7 and 8, B and C turn out to be 6 and 5, so $B + C = 11$. Any smaller values for N and R will result in smaller values for B and C, so the greatest possible value of $B + C$ is 11.

SECTION 6

1. C

This sentence tests your knowledge of the sequence of tenses. *By the time* the speaker graduates from college in the future, her brother *will have been* practicing law—you need the future perfect tense. (C) expresses the sequence correctly. All the remaining choices have incorrect tenses. (B) places this action in the past; (D) makes it inappropriately conditional, and (E) places it in the present.

2. C

The intervening phrase and clause make it difficult to see that the subject and verb don't agree. The plural subject *historians* needs a plural verb, so *includes* should be *include*. (B) incorrectly changes *includes* to the past tense. (C) and (D) both correct this problem, but only (C) keeps the correct relative pronoun. (D) incorrectly changes the subjective *who* to the objective *whom*. (E) doesn't correct the subject-verb problem and changes the idiomatically correct *more than* to *at least*, which changes the meaning.

3. C

Nancy illogically compares Marcel Proust's *novel* with *other writers*. Nancy should compare Proust's novel with other novels, as in (C), (D), and (E). Only (C) makes that change without introducing new errors. (D) illogically changes the comparison *more brilliant* (which is correct because two things are compared) to *brilliant opposed to*. (E) changes the correct relative pronoun *which* to *whom*—perhaps thinking that the authors, not the books, are compared. (B) also introduces that mistake and incorrectly changes the second clause to the past tense.

4. B

The past tense of the irregular verb *to see* is *saw*. (B) and (D) correct this problem, but (D) introduces another error by changing *arriving* to *have arrived*. (C) and (E) illogically change the correct *watching* to *who watch*. (C) also doesn't correct the original problem, and (E) incorrectly changes *arriving* to *arrived*.

5. A

This sentence is correct as written. (B) illogically changes *to discover* to the past tense *to have discovered*. (C) incorrectly adds the preposition *in* (the species don't congregate in the floor). (D) needlessly adds the preposition *from*. (E) incorrectly changes *that* to *who*.

6. C

In this sentence, we must sort through all the prepositions to see that *in an effort at avoiding* is not good, idiomatic English. The correct phrase is *in an effort to avoid*. (C), (D), and (E) all make this change; however, (D) and (E) distort the meaning. (D) is incorrect because fans are not on the team. (E) switches the phrases *in the stadium* and *between fans*, which would mean that the altercations happen in more than one stadium.

7. A

Look through the answer choices: all except (E) focus on the phrase *a strategy to attract*. Is that idiomatically correct? Yes, *a strategy to attract* is correct. (B), (C), and (D) alter the phrase. (C) also changes the adjective *elderly* to *elders*. (E) rearranges the introductory phrase so that the votes incorrectly modify the Social Security adjustment.

8. D

The subject, *group,* is separated from the verb, *were,* making the agreement problem difficult to see. The singular subject *configuration* agrees with the singular verb *was*. (D) and (E) make this change, but (E) omits the transition word *but*, so (D) is the correct choice. (B) and (C) don't address the agreement problem, and (C) changes the contrasting transition word *but* to *and*.

9. B

The plural pronoun *their* actually refers to the singular subject *band*. (B) and (C) correctly change *their* to *its*, but (C) incorrectly changes the preposition *of* to *for*. The expression *methods of providing* is idiomatically correct. Neither (D) nor (E) addresses the pronoun problem. They both also change the infinitive *to determine* to *to be determining*, which is not standard English.

10. A

This is a complex sentence, so break it down to see if it is correct. (B) changes *had begun* (which is correctly in the past perfect tense) to the incorrect form *had began*. (C) illogically puts the second clause in the future tense. (D) incorrectly changes *later* (which is good, standard written English) to the illogical *afterwards*. (E) changes the subject of the sentence from the *conductor* to the *orchestra,* altering the meaning.

11. D

The sentence is a run-on. (B) is ungrammatical. (C) is a run-on. (E) uses the illogical transition *but*. (D) is clear and concise and, thus, the correct answer.

12. A

It's especially important to check subject-verb agreement when a verb is separated from its subject. The subject is the singular *heron*, but the verb is the plural *live*, (A). To correct this, you would change *live* to *lives*. *Most*, (B), is correctly in the superlative form, since all parts of the United States are compared. (C) is idiomatically correct. (D) uses *both* correctly with *and*.

13. D

Susan compares the home team's warm-ups with the visiting team. She should compare the *warm-ups* of both teams. (D) is your answer. The phrase *liked watching* in (A) is correctly in the past tense. (B) uses the correct relative pronoun. In (C), the phrase *more interesting* works because two things are compared.

14. C

The intervening phrase *of Viking settlements* interrupts the subject and verb. The singular subject *pattern* doesn't agree with the plural verb *were*, (C). The phrase *by tracing*, (A), is idiomatically correct. The verb *determined*, (B), is correctly in the past tense. The adverb *generally*, (D), correctly modifies the adjective *similar*.

15. B

This sentence sets up a contrast between what the recipe required and what Chad did; however, the conjunction *and*, (B), indicates an addition rather than a contrast and should be replaced with a word like *but*. In (A), *actually* is an adverb correctly used to modify the verb, and *called for* is an idiomatic expression meaning *needed in the circumstances*. (C) sets up the right causal relationship required by the meaning of the sentence. (D) is idiomatically correct.

16. E

Read all sentences carefully looking for common errors, but remember that about 20 percent will be error-free. (A) is the correct word to express the contrast that the sentence sets up. (B) is correctly the past tense. (C) is a phrase that indicates an example is being given. (D) is idiomatically correct after the verb *attempt*. (E) is the correct choice since this sentence is correct as written.

17. A

When there are underlined pronouns in a Usage question, check to see that they have clear antecedents. The pronoun *they*, (A), doesn't. You can guess that *they* are the people of India, but that would be only a guess since the sentence doesn't provide that information. (B) is correctly used here. In (C), the past tense verb is correct. In (D), the conjunction *and* correctly expresses a continuation of the idea that precedes it.

18. B

The action took place in the past and should use the simple past tense *saw* instead of the past participle of the verb *to see* (*seen*), (B). The verbs *waiting*, (A), and *walking*, (C), are in the correct form, and the phrase *to stop traffic*, (D), is idiomatically correct.

19. C

The plural subject *plays* doesn't agree with the singular verb *expresses,* (C), which should read *express*. The infinitive verb *to produce*, (A), is correct. The phrases *that expresses*, (B), and *has had*, (D), are in the correct tense and idiomatically correct.

20. B

The phrase *claim hearing* is not idiomatically correct, so (B) should read *claim to have heard*. The contrasting transition word *while*, (A), is used appropriately as is the adverb *truly*, (D). The phrase *such a person*, (C), is idiomatically correct.

21. B

The preposition *to* should follow the phrase *in an attempt*. The phrase *at creating*, (B), should read *to create*. The verb *initiated*, (A), is correctly in the present tense. The phrases *of team spirit*, (C), and *in the office*, (D), use the correct prepositions.

22. D

Did efforts *about*, (D), democracy sound correct when you read this sentence? Probably not. What you would need is something like *efforts on behalf of*. In (A), the adverb *as* is correctly used to modify the verb. In (B), the verb tense is correct—past perfect, which indicates that something happened before something else happened: Abadi got the Nobel Prize before her colleagues praised her. (C) correctly uses the simple past.

23. B

Be sure that the verbs in the sentence correctly express the time of the action. This sentence contains a clear indication of time—1906, which is in the past. Anything that happened in 1906 is done. The verb tenses should express this completeness. (B) should be in the simple past tense—*leveled*. (A) is idiomatically correct. (C) uses the right words and the correct preposition. (D) uses the correct tense—the simple past.

24. C

The phrase *absolute shamefaced*, (C), has an adjective modifying an adjective (*shamefaced*). The phrase should read *absolutely shamefaced*. The phrases *failure to*, (A), *went about*, (B), and *only a few*, (D), are all idiomatically correct.

25. C

Reversing the sentence order can help you find the error. Does it make sense to say *the damaging effects of cigarette smoking has become recognized*? No. The plural subject *effects* takes the plural verb *have*, rather than *has*, (C). The transition word *while*, (A), correctly sets up a contrast. The verb *has been known*, (B), is in the correct tense because it takes place before the second part of the sentence. Therefore, the past participle *become*, (D), is also in the correct tense (you can also reverse the order to say *the damaging effects have become known*).

26. E

The sentence is correct as written. The verb *maintains*, (A), agrees with the singular subject *FBI* and is correctly in the present tense. The prepositions *for*, (B), and *in*, (D), correctly follow *maintains* and *interested*, respectively. The pronoun *they*, (C), clearly refers to *citizens*.

27. D

When three people are being compared, the superlative phrase *most* should be used. (D) should read *most abstract*, rather than *more abstract*. The phrase *in many ways*, (A), is idiomatically correct. (B) is an idiomatically correct phrase, and *similar* is correctly used to modify *aspects*. The verb *was*, (C), is correctly in the past tense.

28. E

The sentence is correct as written. (A) correctly uses the adverb. (B) correctly uses the superlative, since all choreographers are compared, and *inventive* correctly modifies the noun *choreographers*. (C) is correctly in the past tense and is the correct form of the irregular verb, and the noun *approach* takes the preposition *to*, (D).

29. A

The plural noun *Germans* is close to the verb but is not the subject. The subject *toppling* is singular, and so (A) should be the singular *is*. The phrases *probably seen*, (B), and *most felicitous*, (D), are idiomatically correct, and the pronoun *them*, (C), is correctly plural and in the objective case (*they* wouldn't work).

30. D

The paragraph is in the past tense but *she tells me* is present tense. The author is telling a story about what happened last year so the mother's action should be in past tense. (D) is correct. (B) and (C) don't address the tense issue. (B) unnecessarily substitutes *my mother* for *she*, and (C) incorrectly uses the causal word *because*.

31. D

Sentence 7 introduces the ambiguous pronoun *they* and uses the passive voice. (D) correctly substitutes *the hooligans* for *they* and uses the present tense. (B) doesn't address the pronoun problem. (C) is redundant and uses the past tense. (E) substitutes *football fans,* instead of the hooligans, for *they*.

32. C

The correct answer should clarify sentence 12's relationship with sentence 11. Sentence 11 offers one explanation offered by *some*. Sentence 12 is another possibility, and (C) indicates that. (A) is incorrect because there is no indication this is the author's opinion. (B) introduces the ambiguous pronoun *they*. (D) and (E) set up incorrect relationships: contrasting and causal, respectively.

33. D

Sentence 14 is a fragment, with no verb in an independent clause. (D) uses the past tense *indicated*, which agrees with the prior sentence. (B) is still a fragment. (C) incorrectly uses the present progressive tense, and (E) incorrectly uses the past perfect tense.

34. D

In sentence 13, the words *one argument . . . rang . . . true* tell you the author is offering a conclusion. What is the conclusion? It's set off by the colon: *poverty was an underlying cause.* Sentence 14, adding data about the connection between poverty and violence, supports that conclusion, choice (D).

35. E

The sentence offers a conclusion based on the economic data in sentence 14, so it should conclude the passage, choice (E). (A) would interrupt the related ideas in sentences 5 and 6. (B) is too soon; the problem has just been introduced, but the ways England has tried to solve the problem haven't been discussed. (C) is still too early—poverty isn't mentioned again until sentence 13. (D) is incorrect because the next sentence begins with the contrasting transition word *but*; however, the inserted sentence and sentence 14 do not contrast.

SECTION 7

1. B

There's a connection between the amount of time spent visiting and the impression of the *places visited,* so the two words that will fill in the blanks here must be roughly synonymous. Only choice (B) works here. There were so many stops in such a *brief* amount of time that only a *cursory* (superficial or hasty) impression of places was gained. (D)'s second word fits the blank, but (D)'s first word, *sufficient,* isn't a rough synonym and doesn't fit. In (A), many stops probably wouldn't leave a *lasting* impression, nor would a tour at breakneck speed necessarily leave a *favorable,* (C), impression on travelers.

2. E

In this sentence, we need two adjectives that are roughly the opposite of each other, so the answer here is (E). Peoples who were once *nomadic,* or roaming freely without a permanent home, have moved into *permanent* settlements as their land got swallowed up by growing cities. *Fervid,* in choice (D), means passionate.

3. B

For the first blank, we want something that describes *sleeping tablets*—that rules out (E) right away, since *stimulating* is the one word here that most definitely would not describe sleeping tablets. For the second blank, we want a word that characterizes the effect of those sleeping tablets, an effect that resulted in a woman feeling *groggy* the day after taking them. Something like "strong" or "intense" would be good. The best choice here is (B), because *soporific* means sleep-inducing— what word could be better to describe sleeping pills? *Pronounced,* meaning unmistakable or obvious, fits closely with our prediction. *Salubrious* in choice (C) means healthful.

4. E

Here we want a vocabulary word meaning something like "unable to accept the authority of others." Choice (A), *compliant,* means the exact opposite of this; a *compliant* person is one who bends easily to the will of others. (B), *slothful,* means lazy. In choice (C), *conscientious* means responsible, hardly a word to describe Davis. (E) is correct because *recalcitrant* describes someone who refuses to obey authority.

5. D

Although tells us that there will be some sort of contrast with the fact that the actress has *lived in a large city* her whole life. The contrast will be that, despite her upbringing in a city, she still manages to be successful at portraying a *humble farm girl.* Therefore, she must be quite a good performer—the first blank will be a positive word, describing what a good actress she is. The second blank must be a word that explains how successfully she portrays the farm girl. The best choice here is (D), because a *consummate* actress is very skilled, while an *incarnation* is the embodiment of something or someone—you'd have to be a pretty good actress to become the embodiment of the character you're playing. In choice (C), *nemesis* means enemy.

6. B

Notice the word *hitherto* in this sentence, which means previously. The board members had previously upheld worthy ideals. This implies that they no longer do. For the second blank, then, we need a word like "rejection": the board's recent decision must be a rejection of the previous worthy ideals. In the first blank, we need a word to describe what the chairman was doing as he described the board's decision so negatively. So the first blank must mean something like "criticized." (C) fits in the first blank, but not in the second. Remember to try both words in the blanks! Choice (B) works with both blanks: to *lament* is to regret, while a *negation* is what it sounds like, a rejection. The chairman lamented the decision of the board, describing it as a *negation* of worthy ideals. This is the only choice with two negative words that fit the context. To *endorse*, in choice (D), is to offer one's support, while a *renunciation* is a giving up or casting off of something like values. Finally, in (E), a *repudiation* is similar to a *renunciation*—it is a denial or rejection of something or someone.

THE JEFFERSON/DOUGLASS PASSAGES

These two passages may seem hard because of their old-fashioned language, but the main points should be clear on a quick read-through. Jefferson emphasizes the natural and social riches of the United States (paragraph 1), supports the idea of limited government (end of paragraph 1), and states the principle of equal justice for all (paragraph 2). Douglass, speaking as an escaped slave, stresses that slaves do not have the freedoms celebrated on the Fourth of July. (If you don't remember who Douglass was, you may not catch the point of his speech until the end of paragraph 2, where it is stated directly. Always be patient—the drift of a passage often becomes clearer as you go along.) In paragraph 2, Douglass says that the case against slavery should not have to be argued, because freedom and liberty are basic American principles. In paragraph 3, he concludes that as long as slavery exists, the Fourth of July is a *sham.*

Before going to the questions, it can be helpful to think for a second about how the two passages relate—an important paired-passage strategy. You should come up with something like: Jefferson is stating American principles, but Douglass is saying they haven't been applied in practice. In a double passage, you'll have several questions on Passage 1, followed by several on Passage 2, followed by some asking for comparisons. Since answering the questions is the priority, be sure to read the first passage, do the questions that relate to it, then read the second passage and answer the rest of the questions.

7. C

In the cited lines, Jefferson is saying that Americans feel entitled to respect, or *honor and confidence*, on the basis of *actions* rather than *birth*. (C) is a paraphrase of this idea. Remember that the United States didn't have a hereditary aristocracy like European countries—that's what Jefferson is talking about. (A), (D), and (E) bring in ideas not mentioned in the excerpt—immigration, (A), mutual help, (D), or family, (E). (B)'s idea of demanding respect is wrong; Jefferson feels respect has to be based on actions.

8. A

In this Vocabulary-in-Context question, choice (B) might've jumped out at you, but remember, the correct answer is probably not going to be the most common or familiar definition of the word, so don't be too hasty. Find the word in the passage and see how it's used there. In this case, Jefferson is talking about what his duties as president involve, or *include*, choice (A). Choices (C) and (E) give you other common synonyms for *comprehend*, but they don't fit the context. (D) does not mean comprehend.

9. D

Again, look at the context. Read the rest of the sentence in question and the sentence before it. This should clarify that Jefferson is about to state what he believes to be the essential principles of government. Further, he's going to state them in the briefest possible way, which is what choice (D) says. (A) and (C) refer to Jefferson's mention of *limitations*, but all Jefferson says is that he won't mention *limitations* or exceptions to the general principles. (B) is wrong because *them* in Jefferson's sentence refers to the principles of government, not to people who oppose the principles. Finally, Jefferson never mentions *bureaucracy*, choice (E).

10. E

Ignore the choices for the moment and look at the context: Jefferson is talking about equal justice for all, regardless of something religious or political. This suggests that Jefferson is talking about people's beliefs, creeds, opinions, or convictions. (E) gives you the word that fits this context. (A), (B), and (C) are all vocabulary-list meanings for *persuasion*, but they don't fit the context. *Authority*, (D), is often seen as the opposite of *persuasion*; it has nothing to do with Jefferson's meaning here.

11. A

The next two questions take us through the Douglass excerpt. This one asks about paragraph 1, in which Douglass is contrasting the American celebration of independence and liberty with the bondage of slaves. The overall idea is that the celebrations are a *mockery* and an *irony* (line 56) because they don't apply to everyone. In other words, they are hypocritical, (A). (B) and (C) refer to emotions Douglass undoubtedly feels, but that he is not expressing here. (D) is an idea he never expresses at all. (E) interprets *drag a man in fetters* (chains) literally—force a slave to attend. Don't go for a simple paraphrase like this. Go back and get the meaning in context. Douglass is speaking figuratively; he doesn't mean he's actually being dragged to the celebration in chains.

12. D

In the cited sentence, the *millions* who are wailing are the slaves, while the *shouts* come from the Fourth of July celebrants. Douglass uses this contrast to emphasize the differences between the lives and attitudes of slaves and free Americans, (D). (A) and (C) twist the meaning of Douglass's mention of *yesterday* and *today* in these lines. Choice (B) goes against Douglass's overall point, which is to point out the hypocrisy of Fourth of July celebrations. And while the problem of slavery is not yet solved, Douglass doesn't imply it is *unsolvable*, (E).

13. B

Always put the detail in context by rereading the surrounding lines. Here, the author's referring to the *treason* of betraying the American slaves by failing to protest during Fourth of July celebrations. Douglass is saying that he'd be committing *treason* to them by not speaking out. So in this example, *treason* refers to acting against the needs of a social group, in this case, the slaves, choice (B). (A) and (D) may sound tempting as common definitions of *treason*, but they don't express what the author means in this context.

14. C

Rereading the context, you can see that throughout paragraph 2 Douglass is emphasizing the contradiction between Fourth of July celebrations and the condition of the slaves. When he describes *American Slavery* as *my subject*, he's highlighting this paradox and also describing what he's about to talk about next—literally outlining what the subject of the rest of his speech is. (A) is wrong because the topic of slavery is not unexpected—it's what Douglass has been discussing all along. (B) is wrong because Douglass isn't talking about slavery through the ages. (D) is wrong because Douglass suggests no immediate answer to the problem. Finally, there's no suggestion that Douglass has to learn more about his topic, (E). Thus, (C) is the correct choice.

15. A

Again, put the detail in context—who or what is *impudent* here? Douglass is contrasting political speeches with the actual conditions that slaves endured, making (A) the correct answer. (B) is too general; (C) is off the point. (D) actually contradicts Douglass's explicit point of view. Finally, (E) is a distortion—according to the passage, it's the hypocritical speeches of politicians that railed against tyrants.

16. B

In Passage 1, Jefferson deals with the themes of liberty and equality as the necessary principles of good government—he's describing these qualities as the bedrock of the Constitution. Based on Passage 1, you can infer that he would respond to Douglass's questions about liberty in a similar manner—by agreeing that these are staples in any democracy, choice (B). None of the other choices—(A), (C), (D), or (E)—are consistent with any statement made in Passage 1. Remember, you've always got to find evidence for your answer in the passage.

17. B

The last three questions ask for comparisons. In this one, you're asked how Douglass would respond to Jefferson's stated principle, *equal and exact justice to all men*. Douglass gives the answer when he says slaves do not enjoy the liberties of other Americans (paragraph 1). So he would respond that the principle is not being carried out in reality, (B). (A), (C), and (E) all imply that the principle is invalid. But Douglass's argument is that a principle that is valid in general isn't being followed for African Americans. (E) is a possible response, but (B) sums up Douglass's overall point better.

18. C

Since each of the answer choices uses the word *both*, you should be looking for a similarity between the speeches. Jefferson states a general principle; Douglass points out how it has been violated. The only point that both agree on is that equal justice is desirable, choice (C). Choices (A) and (D) describe Douglass's speech as a whole; (B) is implied in Douglass's final sentence—but Jefferson's speech never discusses these topics. (E), on the other hand, is true of Jefferson's speech, but not Douglass's.

19. C

Summarizing each passage's point of view, you'd probably argue that Jefferson was optimistic about equality in the United States (having just established the Constitution), but that Douglass was critical of United States standards on equality 50 years later. Choice (C) picks up this contrast. Choices (A), (B), (D), and (E) do not capture the appropriate positive/negative answer required.

SECTION 8

1. D

The graph shows you the sales of all the toys for the months April, May, and June. If you look at the sales for those three months, you'll see that the bar for April goes up to 40, the bar for May goes up to 10, and the bar for June goes up to 30. The title on the vertical axis is "Sales (in millions of dollars)," so that's what those numbers represent: $40 million in sales for April, $10 million for May, and $30 million for June, for a total of $40 + 10 + 30$, or $80 million dollars total in sales for those months. The total sales were $80 million and the April sales were $40 million, and you want to know what percent of the total the April sales were. Since it says "of the total," $80 million is the whole and the $40 million is the part, so using the formula *Percent* × *Whole* = *Part*, you get Percent × 80 = 40, or Percent = $\frac{40}{80} = \frac{1}{2} = 50$, answer choice (D).

2. E [1(2)3]

If you remembered that any number squared is positive, a quick look at the answer choices would tell you that choice (E), x^2y^2, will be positive for any nonzero values of x and y. If you didn't remember that, you should make a note of it, since it's a very important concept. You can also solve this one by picking numbers. If xy is negative, then either x or y is negative and the other is positive since a negative times a positive equals a negative. Picking a couple of pairs of numbers for x and y will tell you that both $x - y$ and $y - x$ can be either positive or negative depending on the exact values of x and y; x^2y can be negative if y is negative, and xy^2 can be negative if x is negative. However, any values you pick for x and y will give you a positive number for x^2y^2, so again, choice (E) is correct.

3. B

Don't get confused by the strange words! They're just symbols for an unknown quantity, the same as the letters x and y, which we usually use as symbols for unknown quantities. If 1 fedi = 3 glecks, then multiplying both sides by 2 tells you that 2 fedis = 6 glecks. You're given that 1 bora = 2 fedis, so 1 bora must be equal to 6 glecks. Now that we know the relationship between boras and glecks (whatever they are), the rest is easy. If 1 bora is equal to 6 glecks, then how many boras equal 48 glecks? Since $6 \times 8 = 48$, just multiply both sides of the equation (1 bora = 6 glecks) by 8 to get 8 boras = 48 glecks. So the correct answer is 8, answer choice (B).

4. C [1(2)3]

If algebra confuses you, try picking numbers. If $f = 10$ then there are 10 freshmen in the class. If 5 freshmen drop the class, then there are $10 - 5 = 5$ freshmen left in the class. The number of sophomores is 3 times the number of freshmen left, or $3 \times 5 = 15$. So there are 15 sophomores in the class and $s = 15$. Which of the answer choices work with $f = 10$ and $s = 15$? All you have to do is plug those numbers into the five choices and you'll find that only choice (C) works and is therefore correct.

To do it algebraically, just translate one step at a time. There are f freshmen in the class. If 5 freshmen drop the class, there are $f - 5$ freshmen left. The number of sophomores is 3 times the number of freshmen left, or 3 times $f - 5$, or $3(f - 5)$. So $s = 3(f - 5)$, answer choice (C).

5. E

The perimeter of triangle ABC is $AC + AB + 7$, and the perimeter of triangle ACD is $AC + 5 + 6$. You can combine that with the given information that the perimeter of triangle ABC is 4 more than the perimeter of triangle ACD to get $AC + AB + 7 = AC + 5 + 6 + 4$. Adding the numbers on the right side of the equation gives you $AC + AB + 7 = AC + 15$, and subtracting 7 from both sides gives you $AC + AB = AC + 8$. If you subtract AC from both sides, you get $AB = 8$. That's all you need to find the perimeter of $ABCD$, which is $5 + 6 + 7 + 8$, or 26, answer choice (E).

6. D

Notice that at each corner of the cube, a triangular face like triangular face ABC is being made. How many corners are there? There are 8 corners; 4 of the corners are on the top and 4 are on the bottom. After all 8 triangular faces are made, a part of each of the original 6 faces of the cube remains. The total number of faces of the resulting stone must be $6 + 8$, or 14.

7. D

We want the average of the first 30 positive integers. Whenever we want the average of a group of evenly spaced numbers, we just have to take the average of the smallest number and the largest number. If you have difficulty seeing this, consider a simpler problem. Consider the average of 1, 2, 3, and 4. The average of 1, 2, 3, and 4 is $\frac{1 + 2 + 3 + 4}{4} = \frac{10}{4} = \frac{5}{2} = 2\frac{1}{2}$, using the average formula: Average $= \frac{\text{Sum of the terms}}{\text{Numbers of terms}}$. What happens if we just take the average of the smallest number, 1, and the largest number, 4? We get $\frac{1 + 4}{2} = \frac{5}{2} = 2\frac{1}{2}$, which is what we got by finding the average the other way. So the average of the first 30 positive integers is just the average of 1 and 30, which is $\frac{1 + 30}{2} = \frac{31}{2} = 15\frac{1}{2}$. None of the answer choices is $15\frac{1}{2}$, but $15\frac{1}{2}$ is 15.5, choice (D).

8. B

You may notice that the figure looks like a rectangle with a quadrilateral piece hanging off of it. That means that you can find the area of the figure by adding the area of the rectangle and the area of the quadrilateral. The quadrilateral piece can be divided into a rectangle and a triangle. It may help to draw in some dotted lines to represent this:

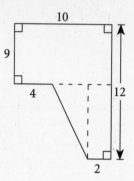

The larger rectangle on the top has length 10 and width 9. Since the vertical line segment on the right is labeled 12, the length of the part of that line that is not part of the larger rectangle must be 12 − 9, or 3, so write that on your figure. The short horizontal line in the middle of the figure has length 4, the small rectangle on the bottom has length 2, and the entire figure has a top horizontal length of 10, so the dotted horizontal line that is a leg of the right triangle must have length 10 − 4 − 2, or 4.

Now we've got the lengths of all the pieces of the figure:

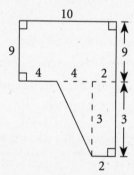

The rectangle on the top has an area of 9 × 10 = 90. The small rectangle on the bottom right has length 3 and width 2, so its area is 6, and the triangle has legs 4 and 3, so its area is also 6. The total area of the figure is 90 + 6 + 6 = 102, answer choice (B).

9. A

If 60 cookies are distributed among x campers, then each camper gets $\frac{60}{x}$ cookies. When the same number of cookies is divided among fewer campers, then each camper gets 2 more than $\frac{60}{x}$ cookies, or $\frac{60}{x} + 2$. This number of cookies per camper is also equal to 60 cookies divided by 8 less than the original number of campers, or $\frac{60}{x-8}$. This gives us the equation $\frac{60}{x} + 2 = \frac{60}{x-8}$. Unfortunately, this equation is not in the same form as the equations in the answer choices, so you'll have to do some algebra:

$$\frac{60}{x} + 2 = \frac{60}{x-8}$$

$$\frac{60 + 2x}{x} = \frac{60}{x-8}$$

$$(60 + 2x)(x-8) = 60x$$

$$60x - 480 + 2x^2 - 16x = 60x$$

$$2x^2 - 16x - 480 = 0$$

$$x^2 - 8x - 240 = 0, \text{ answer choice (A).}$$

10. D

All they're asking here is: How many different pairs can you make from a group of 6? Let's call the 6 students A, B, C, D, E, and F; A can be joined with the others to make the 5 pairs AB, AC, AD, AE, and AF. Since you've already paired A and B, you don't have to do it again, so just pair B up with the rest of the group to get BC, BD, BE, and BF. That's 4 new pairs. C has already been matched up with A and B, so the new pairs that involve C are CD, CE, and CF, for 3 new pairs. There are only 2 new pairs left for D, DE, and DF, and finally 1 more, EF. So there's a total of $5 + 4 + 3 + 2 + 1 = 15$, choice (D).

11. D

$$q = q^{-2} = \frac{1}{q^2}$$

If $q = \frac{1}{q^2}$, then $q^3 = 1$ and $q = 1$.

12. B

Backsolving is a great way to answer this question. Pick a set of p and n from the chart, then plug them into each given equation to see whether the pair works. If you would rather see how the equation was derived, you can follow the steps that follow. On test day, follow whichever approach gets you to the answer faster. The relationship between n and p can be expressed in the form $n = -kp + b$, where k and b are constants. There is a negative sign before k to indicate that as the price increases, the number of expected sales decreases. Pick two points from the chart and insert those values of p and n into this equation, then solve for k and b:

First point:

$10,000 = -k(.75) + b$

Second point:

$5,000 = -k(1.00) + b$

$5,000 = -k + b$

$5,000 + k = b$

Substitute:

$10,000 = -k(.75) + 5,000 + k$

$5,000 = k - .75k$

$5,000 = .25k$

$20,000 = k$

$25,000 = b$

$n = -20,000p + 25,000$, choice (B).

13. B

It's a good idea to know what the graphs of common equations such as $y = x^2$ look like, but if you forget or would like to double-check your answer, you can plug in the x and y values of a few points on the graph into the given equations to see which one works. Be careful of using points like (0, 0), as they may work for several (or, in this case, all) of the answer choices. In this case, some useful points to check are (−2, 4) and (2, 4): $4 = (-2)^2$ and $4 = 2^2$.

14. C

Let g = number of green tokens, and y = number of yellow tokens. The scores given in the problem can be written as $4g + 8y = 48$ and $6g + 4y = 32$. Both sides of the first equation can be divided by 4 to get $g + 2y = 12$. Subtract $2y$ from both sides to find $g = 12 - 2y$. Substitute this into the second equation to get $6(12 - 2y) + 4y = 72 - 12y + 4y = 32$. Solving for y, you find that $40 = 8y$, and $y = 5$, choice (C).

15. C ①②③

Since there are variables in the answer choices, picking numbers is a good strategy for solving this problem. Since the question deals with percentages, 100 is a good number to pick for c. Pablo uses 30% of 100 cherries, that is $100(0.3) = 30$ grams of cherries to make muffins. You don't need to know how many grams of cherries it takes to make a muffin or how many muffins Pablo makes. All you need to know is how many grams of cherries are available to make preserves with: $100 - 30 = 70$ grams of cherries are available to make preserves with. If each pint of preserves requires 7 grams of cherries (that is, if $p = 7$), Pablo can make 10 pints of preserves. Plug $c = 100$ and $p = 7$ into the answer choices to see which yields 10. $\frac{7c}{10p} = \frac{7(100)}{10(7)} = \frac{700}{70} = 10$, so (C) is correct.

16. B

If C is the price of one pound of cherries and G is the price of one pound of grapes, then $C = 2G$. The total cost of 32 pounds of cherries and 8 pounds of grapes is $32C + 8G$, and is also equal to $90. You can use the equations $C = 2G$ and $32C + 8G = 90$ to solve for C and G. Plugging $2G$ for C into the equation $32C + 8G = 90$, we have $32(2G) + 8G = 90$, $64G + 8G = 90$, $72G = 90$, and $G = \frac{90}{72} = \frac{5}{4} = 1.25$. $C = 2G$, so $C = 2(1.25) = 2.50$. Since 32 pounds of cherries and 8 pounds of grapes were sold, $2.50 \times 32 = 80$ was made on the cherries, and $1.25 \times 8 = 10$ was made on the grapes. That means that $80 - 10 = 70$ more was made on the cherries than on the grapes, answer choice (B).

SECTION 9

1. B

This sentence is a run-on—the part beginning with *they* starts an entirely new sentence. Therefore, look for the answer choice that fixes the run-on. (B) does so by simply inserting a semicolon. (A), (C), (D), and (E) are also run-ons.

2. B

All of the incorrect answer choices contain misplaced modifiers. (A), (D), and (E) say the *shock value utilized cacophony*. (C) says *a higher level utilized cacophony*. Clearly, you want the sentence to say that Webern or Webern's music utilized cacophony—the only answer choice to accomplish this is (B).

3. A

The answer choices that utilize semicolons must have independent clauses on both sides of the semicolon. (A) is the only choice that meets the requirement. (D) and (E) exchange the semicolon for a comma, but they are both incorrect. (D) adds a tense shift with the words *having been*, and (E) incorrectly uses a coordinating conjunction and a comma to separate an independent clause and a dependent clause.

4. D

(A) and (E) are comma splices—two independent clauses separated only by a comma. (C) adds the coordinating conjunction *and*, but it also adds *being*, which makes the second clause dependent and incorrect. (B) uses incorrect clause structure. (D) is the best choice because it simply fixes the comma splice by adding the coordinating conjunction *and*.

5. E

(A) and (C) are run-on sentences; a coordinating conjunction separates two independent clauses without a comma. Look for the answer choice that is parallel with to *eventually run*. That answer choice is (E) because of the word *scale*.

6. D

(A) and (B) are run-on sentences because they have two independent clauses separated by *and* but do not have a comma before that conjunction. (E) does not make sense because the verb *defined* was changed to a noun, *definition*. Between (C) and (D), (D) is correct. (C) adds the word *had*, indicating that the Campbell's definition of the heroes and villains happened before his espousal of definitive ideas. Without a broader context, this does not make sense. (D) is correct because it extends the simple past tense structure of *espoused* to *defined*.

7. A

Look for the simplest (and shortest) answer choice. As long as that choice is grammatically correct, you can be sure it is the correct answer. In this case, that choice is (A). (B), (C), (D), and (E) are all too wordy or overly complex.

8. E

(A) is incorrect because this sentence is wordy as written. (B), (C), and (D) are grammatically correct but are less concise than (E). If more than one choice is grammatically correct, always look for the one that is most concise.

9. A

The original sentence is the best choice because it has a dependent clause that is related to the complete independent clause. Choices (B), (C), (D), and (E) do not have as good sentence structure.

10. B

The phrase *of which there are more than 40 breeds* is nonessential information and should be set apart with commas on both sides as in choice (B). The words *of which* are correct in starting the phrase, so (C) and (D) are incorrect. The words *in existence* in (E) are unnecessary.

11. A

The semicolon is used correctly with two independent clauses on both sides of the punctuation mark. (B) and (C) are run-on sentences. (D) and (E) do not contain two independent clauses.

12. B

This sentence uses a *not . . . but* word pair, so it requires parallel blocks of words around each half of the pair. The first block is *are not rejecting*, so the second block must be *are taking* as in choice (B). Don't be misled because *are* and *rejecting* are separated by the word *not*. *Are* is still a helping verb that works together with *rejecting*.

13. C

This sentence presents a list of comparisons. All items in a list must have parallel construction. Only (C) gives the last comparison an appearance parallel to the previous two comparisons. The word *producing* could have been repeated in all three comparisons, but since it wasn't repeated in the second comparison, it can't be repeated in the third one either.

14. D

This sentence uses a *both . . . and* pair, so it requires parallel blocks of words following each half of the pair. Only (D) has a second block of words—*how long it endures*—similar to the first block—*how many people it touches*.

SAT Practice Test Three
Answer Sheet

Remove (or photcopy) the answer sheet and use it to complete the Practice Test.
See the answer key following the test when finished.

Start with number 1 for each section. If a section has fewer questions than answer spaces, leave the extra spaces blank.

SECTION

1

Section 1 is the Writing section's essay component.

SECTION

2

1. Ⓐ Ⓑ Ⓒ Ⓓ Ⓔ	11. Ⓐ Ⓑ Ⓒ Ⓓ Ⓔ	21. Ⓐ Ⓑ Ⓒ Ⓓ Ⓔ	31. Ⓐ Ⓑ Ⓒ Ⓓ Ⓔ	
2. Ⓐ Ⓑ Ⓒ Ⓓ Ⓔ	12. Ⓐ Ⓑ Ⓒ Ⓓ Ⓔ	22. Ⓐ Ⓑ Ⓒ Ⓓ Ⓔ	32. Ⓐ Ⓑ Ⓒ Ⓓ Ⓔ	
3. Ⓐ Ⓑ Ⓒ Ⓓ Ⓔ	13. Ⓐ Ⓑ Ⓒ Ⓓ Ⓔ	23. Ⓐ Ⓑ Ⓒ Ⓓ Ⓔ	33. Ⓐ Ⓑ Ⓒ Ⓓ Ⓔ	
4. Ⓐ Ⓑ Ⓒ Ⓓ Ⓔ	14. Ⓐ Ⓑ Ⓒ Ⓓ Ⓔ	24. Ⓐ Ⓑ Ⓒ Ⓓ Ⓔ	34. Ⓐ Ⓑ Ⓒ Ⓓ Ⓔ	# right in Section 2
5. Ⓐ Ⓑ Ⓒ Ⓓ Ⓔ	15. Ⓐ Ⓑ Ⓒ Ⓓ Ⓔ	25. Ⓐ Ⓑ Ⓒ Ⓓ Ⓔ	35. Ⓐ Ⓑ Ⓒ Ⓓ Ⓔ	
6. Ⓐ Ⓑ Ⓒ Ⓓ Ⓔ	16. Ⓐ Ⓑ Ⓒ Ⓓ Ⓔ	26. Ⓐ Ⓑ Ⓒ Ⓓ Ⓔ	36. Ⓐ Ⓑ Ⓒ Ⓓ Ⓔ	
7. Ⓐ Ⓑ Ⓒ Ⓓ Ⓔ	17. Ⓐ Ⓑ Ⓒ Ⓓ Ⓔ	27. Ⓐ Ⓑ Ⓒ Ⓓ Ⓔ	37. Ⓐ Ⓑ Ⓒ Ⓓ Ⓔ	
8. Ⓐ Ⓑ Ⓒ Ⓓ Ⓔ	18. Ⓐ Ⓑ Ⓒ Ⓓ Ⓔ	28. Ⓐ Ⓑ Ⓒ Ⓓ Ⓔ	38. Ⓐ Ⓑ Ⓒ Ⓓ Ⓔ	# wrong in Section 2
9. Ⓐ Ⓑ Ⓒ Ⓓ Ⓔ	19. Ⓐ Ⓑ Ⓒ Ⓓ Ⓔ	29. Ⓐ Ⓑ Ⓒ Ⓓ Ⓔ	39. Ⓐ Ⓑ Ⓒ Ⓓ Ⓔ	
10. Ⓐ Ⓑ Ⓒ Ⓓ Ⓔ	20. Ⓐ Ⓑ Ⓒ Ⓓ Ⓔ	30. Ⓐ Ⓑ Ⓒ Ⓓ Ⓔ	40. Ⓐ Ⓑ Ⓒ Ⓓ Ⓔ	

SECTION

3

1. Ⓐ Ⓑ Ⓒ Ⓓ Ⓔ	11. Ⓐ Ⓑ Ⓒ Ⓓ Ⓔ	21. Ⓐ Ⓑ Ⓒ Ⓓ Ⓔ	31. Ⓐ Ⓑ Ⓒ Ⓓ Ⓔ	
2. Ⓐ Ⓑ Ⓒ Ⓓ Ⓔ	12. Ⓐ Ⓑ Ⓒ Ⓓ Ⓔ	22. Ⓐ Ⓑ Ⓒ Ⓓ Ⓔ	32. Ⓐ Ⓑ Ⓒ Ⓓ Ⓔ	
3. Ⓐ Ⓑ Ⓒ Ⓓ Ⓔ	13. Ⓐ Ⓑ Ⓒ Ⓓ Ⓔ	23. Ⓐ Ⓑ Ⓒ Ⓓ Ⓔ	33. Ⓐ Ⓑ Ⓒ Ⓓ Ⓔ	
4. Ⓐ Ⓑ Ⓒ Ⓓ Ⓔ	14. Ⓐ Ⓑ Ⓒ Ⓓ Ⓔ	24. Ⓐ Ⓑ Ⓒ Ⓓ Ⓔ	34. Ⓐ Ⓑ Ⓒ Ⓓ Ⓔ	# right in Section 3
5. Ⓐ Ⓑ Ⓒ Ⓓ Ⓔ	15. Ⓐ Ⓑ Ⓒ Ⓓ Ⓔ	25. Ⓐ Ⓑ Ⓒ Ⓓ Ⓔ	35. Ⓐ Ⓑ Ⓒ Ⓓ Ⓔ	
6. Ⓐ Ⓑ Ⓒ Ⓓ Ⓔ	16. Ⓐ Ⓑ Ⓒ Ⓓ Ⓔ	26. Ⓐ Ⓑ Ⓒ Ⓓ Ⓔ	36. Ⓐ Ⓑ Ⓒ Ⓓ Ⓔ	
7. Ⓐ Ⓑ Ⓒ Ⓓ Ⓔ	17. Ⓐ Ⓑ Ⓒ Ⓓ Ⓔ	27. Ⓐ Ⓑ Ⓒ Ⓓ Ⓔ	37. Ⓐ Ⓑ Ⓒ Ⓓ Ⓔ	
8. Ⓐ Ⓑ Ⓒ Ⓓ Ⓔ	18. Ⓐ Ⓑ Ⓒ Ⓓ Ⓔ	28. Ⓐ Ⓑ Ⓒ Ⓓ Ⓔ	38. Ⓐ Ⓑ Ⓒ Ⓓ Ⓔ	# wrong in Section 3
9. Ⓐ Ⓑ Ⓒ Ⓓ Ⓔ	19. Ⓐ Ⓑ Ⓒ Ⓓ Ⓔ	29. Ⓐ Ⓑ Ⓒ Ⓓ Ⓔ	39. Ⓐ Ⓑ Ⓒ Ⓓ Ⓔ	
10. Ⓐ Ⓑ Ⓒ Ⓓ Ⓔ	20. Ⓐ Ⓑ Ⓒ Ⓓ Ⓔ	30. Ⓐ Ⓑ Ⓒ Ⓓ Ⓔ	40. Ⓐ Ⓑ Ⓒ Ⓓ Ⓔ	

SECTION 4

1. Ⓐ Ⓑ Ⓒ Ⓓ Ⓔ 11. Ⓐ Ⓑ Ⓒ Ⓓ Ⓔ 21. Ⓐ Ⓑ Ⓒ Ⓓ Ⓔ 31. Ⓐ Ⓑ Ⓒ Ⓓ Ⓔ
2. Ⓐ Ⓑ Ⓒ Ⓓ Ⓔ 12. Ⓐ Ⓑ Ⓒ Ⓓ Ⓔ 22. Ⓐ Ⓑ Ⓒ Ⓓ Ⓔ 32. Ⓐ Ⓑ Ⓒ Ⓓ Ⓔ
3. Ⓐ Ⓑ Ⓒ Ⓓ Ⓔ 13. Ⓐ Ⓑ Ⓒ Ⓓ Ⓔ 23. Ⓐ Ⓑ Ⓒ Ⓓ Ⓔ 33. Ⓐ Ⓑ Ⓒ Ⓓ Ⓔ
4. Ⓐ Ⓑ Ⓒ Ⓓ Ⓔ 14. Ⓐ Ⓑ Ⓒ Ⓓ Ⓔ 24. Ⓐ Ⓑ Ⓒ Ⓓ Ⓔ 34. Ⓐ Ⓑ Ⓒ Ⓓ Ⓔ
5. Ⓐ Ⓑ Ⓒ Ⓓ Ⓔ 15. Ⓐ Ⓑ Ⓒ Ⓓ Ⓔ 25. Ⓐ Ⓑ Ⓒ Ⓓ Ⓔ 35. Ⓐ Ⓑ Ⓒ Ⓓ Ⓔ
6. Ⓐ Ⓑ Ⓒ Ⓓ Ⓔ 16. Ⓐ Ⓑ Ⓒ Ⓓ Ⓔ 26. Ⓐ Ⓑ Ⓒ Ⓓ Ⓔ 36. Ⓐ Ⓑ Ⓒ Ⓓ Ⓔ
7. Ⓐ Ⓑ Ⓒ Ⓓ Ⓔ 17. Ⓐ Ⓑ Ⓒ Ⓓ Ⓔ 27. Ⓐ Ⓑ Ⓒ Ⓓ Ⓔ 37. Ⓐ Ⓑ Ⓒ Ⓓ Ⓔ
8. Ⓐ Ⓑ Ⓒ Ⓓ Ⓔ 18. Ⓐ Ⓑ Ⓒ Ⓓ Ⓔ 28. Ⓐ Ⓑ Ⓒ Ⓓ Ⓔ 38. Ⓐ Ⓑ Ⓒ Ⓓ Ⓔ
9. Ⓐ Ⓑ Ⓒ Ⓓ Ⓔ 19. Ⓐ Ⓑ Ⓒ Ⓓ Ⓔ 29. Ⓐ Ⓑ Ⓒ Ⓓ Ⓔ 39. Ⓐ Ⓑ Ⓒ Ⓓ Ⓔ
10. Ⓐ Ⓑ Ⓒ Ⓓ Ⓔ 20. Ⓐ Ⓑ Ⓒ Ⓓ Ⓔ 30. Ⓐ Ⓑ Ⓒ Ⓓ Ⓔ 40. Ⓐ Ⓑ Ⓒ Ⓓ Ⓔ

☐ # right in Section 4

☐ # wrong in Section 4

SECTION 5

1. Ⓐ Ⓑ Ⓒ Ⓓ Ⓔ 11. Ⓐ Ⓑ Ⓒ Ⓓ Ⓔ 21. Ⓐ Ⓑ Ⓒ Ⓓ Ⓔ 31. Ⓐ Ⓑ Ⓒ Ⓓ Ⓔ
2. Ⓐ Ⓑ Ⓒ Ⓓ Ⓔ 12. Ⓐ Ⓑ Ⓒ Ⓓ Ⓔ 22. Ⓐ Ⓑ Ⓒ Ⓓ Ⓔ 32. Ⓐ Ⓑ Ⓒ Ⓓ Ⓔ
3. Ⓐ Ⓑ Ⓒ Ⓓ Ⓔ 13. Ⓐ Ⓑ Ⓒ Ⓓ Ⓔ 23. Ⓐ Ⓑ Ⓒ Ⓓ Ⓔ 33. Ⓐ Ⓑ Ⓒ Ⓓ Ⓔ
4. Ⓐ Ⓑ Ⓒ Ⓓ Ⓔ 14. Ⓐ Ⓑ Ⓒ Ⓓ Ⓔ 24. Ⓐ Ⓑ Ⓒ Ⓓ Ⓔ 34. Ⓐ Ⓑ Ⓒ Ⓓ Ⓔ
5. Ⓐ Ⓑ Ⓒ Ⓓ Ⓔ 15. Ⓐ Ⓑ Ⓒ Ⓓ Ⓔ 25. Ⓐ Ⓑ Ⓒ Ⓓ Ⓔ 35. Ⓐ Ⓑ Ⓒ Ⓓ Ⓔ
6. Ⓐ Ⓑ Ⓒ Ⓓ Ⓔ 16. Ⓐ Ⓑ Ⓒ Ⓓ Ⓔ 26. Ⓐ Ⓑ Ⓒ Ⓓ Ⓔ 36. Ⓐ Ⓑ Ⓒ Ⓓ Ⓔ
7. Ⓐ Ⓑ Ⓒ Ⓓ Ⓔ 17. Ⓐ Ⓑ Ⓒ Ⓓ Ⓔ 27. Ⓐ Ⓑ Ⓒ Ⓓ Ⓔ 37. Ⓐ Ⓑ Ⓒ Ⓓ Ⓔ
8. Ⓐ Ⓑ Ⓒ Ⓓ Ⓔ 18. Ⓐ Ⓑ Ⓒ Ⓓ Ⓔ 28. Ⓐ Ⓑ Ⓒ Ⓓ Ⓔ 38. Ⓐ Ⓑ Ⓒ Ⓓ Ⓔ
9. Ⓐ Ⓑ Ⓒ Ⓓ Ⓔ 19. Ⓐ Ⓑ Ⓒ Ⓓ Ⓔ 29. Ⓐ Ⓑ Ⓒ Ⓓ Ⓔ 39. Ⓐ Ⓑ Ⓒ Ⓓ Ⓔ
10. Ⓐ Ⓑ Ⓒ Ⓓ Ⓔ 20. Ⓐ Ⓑ Ⓒ Ⓓ Ⓔ 30. Ⓐ Ⓑ Ⓒ Ⓓ Ⓔ 40. Ⓐ Ⓑ Ⓒ Ⓓ Ⓔ

☐ # right in Section 5

☐ # wrong in Section 5

If section 5 of your test book contains math questions that are not multiple-choice, continue to item 9 below. Otherwise, continue to item 9 above.

9.   10.   11.   12.   13.

14.   15.   16.   17.   18.

Remove (or photocopy) this answer sheet and use it to complete the Practice Test.

Start with number 1 for each section. If a section has fewer questions than answer spaces, leave the extra spaces blank.

SECTION

6

1. Ⓐ Ⓑ Ⓒ Ⓓ Ⓔ	11. Ⓐ Ⓑ Ⓒ Ⓓ Ⓔ	21. Ⓐ Ⓑ Ⓒ Ⓓ Ⓔ	31. Ⓐ Ⓑ Ⓒ Ⓓ Ⓔ
2. Ⓐ Ⓑ Ⓒ Ⓓ Ⓔ	12. Ⓐ Ⓑ Ⓒ Ⓓ Ⓔ	22. Ⓐ Ⓑ Ⓒ Ⓓ Ⓔ	32. Ⓐ Ⓑ Ⓒ Ⓓ Ⓔ
3. Ⓐ Ⓑ Ⓒ Ⓓ Ⓔ	13. Ⓐ Ⓑ Ⓒ Ⓓ Ⓔ	23. Ⓐ Ⓑ Ⓒ Ⓓ Ⓔ	33. Ⓐ Ⓑ Ⓒ Ⓓ Ⓔ
4. Ⓐ Ⓑ Ⓒ Ⓓ Ⓔ	14. Ⓐ Ⓑ Ⓒ Ⓓ Ⓔ	24. Ⓐ Ⓑ Ⓒ Ⓓ Ⓔ	34. Ⓐ Ⓑ Ⓒ Ⓓ Ⓔ
5. Ⓐ Ⓑ Ⓒ Ⓓ Ⓔ	15. Ⓐ Ⓑ Ⓒ Ⓓ Ⓔ	25. Ⓐ Ⓑ Ⓒ Ⓓ Ⓔ	35. Ⓐ Ⓑ Ⓒ Ⓓ Ⓔ
6. Ⓐ Ⓑ Ⓒ Ⓓ Ⓔ	16. Ⓐ Ⓑ Ⓒ Ⓓ Ⓔ	26. Ⓐ Ⓑ Ⓒ Ⓓ Ⓔ	36. Ⓐ Ⓑ Ⓒ Ⓓ Ⓔ
7. Ⓐ Ⓑ Ⓒ Ⓓ Ⓔ	17. Ⓐ Ⓑ Ⓒ Ⓓ Ⓔ	27. Ⓐ Ⓑ Ⓒ Ⓓ Ⓔ	37. Ⓐ Ⓑ Ⓒ Ⓓ Ⓔ
8. Ⓐ Ⓑ Ⓒ Ⓓ Ⓔ	18. Ⓐ Ⓑ Ⓒ Ⓓ Ⓔ	28. Ⓐ Ⓑ Ⓒ Ⓓ Ⓔ	38. Ⓐ Ⓑ Ⓒ Ⓓ Ⓔ
9. Ⓐ Ⓑ Ⓒ Ⓓ Ⓔ	19. Ⓐ Ⓑ Ⓒ Ⓓ Ⓔ	29. Ⓐ Ⓑ Ⓒ Ⓓ Ⓔ	39. Ⓐ Ⓑ Ⓒ Ⓓ Ⓔ
10. Ⓐ Ⓑ Ⓒ Ⓓ Ⓔ	20. Ⓐ Ⓑ Ⓒ Ⓓ Ⓔ	30. Ⓐ Ⓑ Ⓒ Ⓓ Ⓔ	40. Ⓐ Ⓑ Ⓒ Ⓓ Ⓔ

☐ # right in Section 6

☐ # wrong in Section 6

SECTION

7

1. Ⓐ Ⓑ Ⓒ Ⓓ Ⓔ	11. Ⓐ Ⓑ Ⓒ Ⓓ Ⓔ	21. Ⓐ Ⓑ Ⓒ Ⓓ Ⓔ	31. Ⓐ Ⓑ Ⓒ Ⓓ Ⓔ
2. Ⓐ Ⓑ Ⓒ Ⓓ Ⓔ	12. Ⓐ Ⓑ Ⓒ Ⓓ Ⓔ	22. Ⓐ Ⓑ Ⓒ Ⓓ Ⓔ	32. Ⓐ Ⓑ Ⓒ Ⓓ Ⓔ
3. Ⓐ Ⓑ Ⓒ Ⓓ Ⓔ	13. Ⓐ Ⓑ Ⓒ Ⓓ Ⓔ	23. Ⓐ Ⓑ Ⓒ Ⓓ Ⓔ	33. Ⓐ Ⓑ Ⓒ Ⓓ Ⓔ
4. Ⓐ Ⓑ Ⓒ Ⓓ Ⓔ	14. Ⓐ Ⓑ Ⓒ Ⓓ Ⓔ	24. Ⓐ Ⓑ Ⓒ Ⓓ Ⓔ	34. Ⓐ Ⓑ Ⓒ Ⓓ Ⓔ
5. Ⓐ Ⓑ Ⓒ Ⓓ Ⓔ	15. Ⓐ Ⓑ Ⓒ Ⓓ Ⓔ	25. Ⓐ Ⓑ Ⓒ Ⓓ Ⓔ	35. Ⓐ Ⓑ Ⓒ Ⓓ Ⓔ
6. Ⓐ Ⓑ Ⓒ Ⓓ Ⓔ	16. Ⓐ Ⓑ Ⓒ Ⓓ Ⓔ	26. Ⓐ Ⓑ Ⓒ Ⓓ Ⓔ	36. Ⓐ Ⓑ Ⓒ Ⓓ Ⓔ
7. Ⓐ Ⓑ Ⓒ Ⓓ Ⓔ	17. Ⓐ Ⓑ Ⓒ Ⓓ Ⓔ	27. Ⓐ Ⓑ Ⓒ Ⓓ Ⓔ	37. Ⓐ Ⓑ Ⓒ Ⓓ Ⓔ
8. Ⓐ Ⓑ Ⓒ Ⓓ Ⓔ	18. Ⓐ Ⓑ Ⓒ Ⓓ Ⓔ	28. Ⓐ Ⓑ Ⓒ Ⓓ Ⓔ	38. Ⓐ Ⓑ Ⓒ Ⓓ Ⓔ
9. Ⓐ Ⓑ Ⓒ Ⓓ Ⓔ	19. Ⓐ Ⓑ Ⓒ Ⓓ Ⓔ	29. Ⓐ Ⓑ Ⓒ Ⓓ Ⓔ	39. Ⓐ Ⓑ Ⓒ Ⓓ Ⓔ
10. Ⓐ Ⓑ Ⓒ Ⓓ Ⓔ	20. Ⓐ Ⓑ Ⓒ Ⓓ Ⓔ	30. Ⓐ Ⓑ Ⓒ Ⓓ Ⓔ	40. Ⓐ Ⓑ Ⓒ Ⓓ Ⓔ

☐ # right in Section 7

☐ # wrong in Section 7

SECTION

8

1. Ⓐ Ⓑ Ⓒ Ⓓ Ⓔ	11. Ⓐ Ⓑ Ⓒ Ⓓ Ⓔ	21. Ⓐ Ⓑ Ⓒ Ⓓ Ⓔ	31. Ⓐ Ⓑ Ⓒ Ⓓ Ⓔ
2. Ⓐ Ⓑ Ⓒ Ⓓ Ⓔ	12. Ⓐ Ⓑ Ⓒ Ⓓ Ⓔ	22. Ⓐ Ⓑ Ⓒ Ⓓ Ⓔ	32. Ⓐ Ⓑ Ⓒ Ⓓ Ⓔ
3. Ⓐ Ⓑ Ⓒ Ⓓ Ⓔ	13. Ⓐ Ⓑ Ⓒ Ⓓ Ⓔ	23. Ⓐ Ⓑ Ⓒ Ⓓ Ⓔ	33. Ⓐ Ⓑ Ⓒ Ⓓ Ⓔ
4. Ⓐ Ⓑ Ⓒ Ⓓ Ⓔ	14. Ⓐ Ⓑ Ⓒ Ⓓ Ⓔ	24. Ⓐ Ⓑ Ⓒ Ⓓ Ⓔ	34. Ⓐ Ⓑ Ⓒ Ⓓ Ⓔ
5. Ⓐ Ⓑ Ⓒ Ⓓ Ⓔ	15. Ⓐ Ⓑ Ⓒ Ⓓ Ⓔ	25. Ⓐ Ⓑ Ⓒ Ⓓ Ⓔ	35. Ⓐ Ⓑ Ⓒ Ⓓ Ⓔ
6. Ⓐ Ⓑ Ⓒ Ⓓ Ⓔ	16. Ⓐ Ⓑ Ⓒ Ⓓ Ⓔ	26. Ⓐ Ⓑ Ⓒ Ⓓ Ⓔ	36. Ⓐ Ⓑ Ⓒ Ⓓ Ⓔ
7. Ⓐ Ⓑ Ⓒ Ⓓ Ⓔ	17. Ⓐ Ⓑ Ⓒ Ⓓ Ⓔ	27. Ⓐ Ⓑ Ⓒ Ⓓ Ⓔ	37. Ⓐ Ⓑ Ⓒ Ⓓ Ⓔ
8. Ⓐ Ⓑ Ⓒ Ⓓ Ⓔ	18. Ⓐ Ⓑ Ⓒ Ⓓ Ⓔ	28. Ⓐ Ⓑ Ⓒ Ⓓ Ⓔ	38. Ⓐ Ⓑ Ⓒ Ⓓ Ⓔ
9. Ⓐ Ⓑ Ⓒ Ⓓ Ⓔ	19. Ⓐ Ⓑ Ⓒ Ⓓ Ⓔ	29. Ⓐ Ⓑ Ⓒ Ⓓ Ⓔ	39. Ⓐ Ⓑ Ⓒ Ⓓ Ⓔ
10. Ⓐ Ⓑ Ⓒ Ⓓ Ⓔ	20. Ⓐ Ⓑ Ⓒ Ⓓ Ⓔ	30. Ⓐ Ⓑ Ⓒ Ⓓ Ⓔ	40. Ⓐ Ⓑ Ⓒ Ⓓ Ⓔ

☐ # right in Section 8

☐ # wrong in Section 8

Remove (or photocopy) this answer sheet and use it to complete the Practice Test.

Start with number 1 for each section. If a section has fewer questions than answer spaces, leave the extra spaces blank.

SECTION

9

1. Ⓐ Ⓑ Ⓒ Ⓓ Ⓔ   11. Ⓐ Ⓑ Ⓒ Ⓓ Ⓔ   21. Ⓐ Ⓑ Ⓒ Ⓓ Ⓔ   31. Ⓐ Ⓑ Ⓒ Ⓓ Ⓔ
2. Ⓐ Ⓑ Ⓒ Ⓓ Ⓔ   12. Ⓐ Ⓑ Ⓒ Ⓓ Ⓔ   22. Ⓐ Ⓑ Ⓒ Ⓓ Ⓔ   32. Ⓐ Ⓑ Ⓒ Ⓓ Ⓔ
3. Ⓐ Ⓑ Ⓒ Ⓓ Ⓔ   13. Ⓐ Ⓑ Ⓒ Ⓓ Ⓔ   23. Ⓐ Ⓑ Ⓒ Ⓓ Ⓔ   33. Ⓐ Ⓑ Ⓒ Ⓓ Ⓔ
4. Ⓐ Ⓑ Ⓒ Ⓓ Ⓔ   14. Ⓐ Ⓑ Ⓒ Ⓓ Ⓔ   24. Ⓐ Ⓑ Ⓒ Ⓓ Ⓔ   34. Ⓐ Ⓑ Ⓒ Ⓓ Ⓔ

right in Section 9

5. Ⓐ Ⓑ Ⓒ Ⓓ Ⓔ   15. Ⓐ Ⓑ Ⓒ Ⓓ Ⓔ   25. Ⓐ Ⓑ Ⓒ Ⓓ Ⓔ   35. Ⓐ Ⓑ Ⓒ Ⓓ Ⓔ
6. Ⓐ Ⓑ Ⓒ Ⓓ Ⓔ   16. Ⓐ Ⓑ Ⓒ Ⓓ Ⓔ   26. Ⓐ Ⓑ Ⓒ Ⓓ Ⓔ   36. Ⓐ Ⓑ Ⓒ Ⓓ Ⓔ
7. Ⓐ Ⓑ Ⓒ Ⓓ Ⓔ   17. Ⓐ Ⓑ Ⓒ Ⓓ Ⓔ   27. Ⓐ Ⓑ Ⓒ Ⓓ Ⓔ   37. Ⓐ Ⓑ Ⓒ Ⓓ Ⓔ
8. Ⓐ Ⓑ Ⓒ Ⓓ Ⓔ   18. Ⓐ Ⓑ Ⓒ Ⓓ Ⓔ   28. Ⓐ Ⓑ Ⓒ Ⓓ Ⓔ   38. Ⓐ Ⓑ Ⓒ Ⓓ Ⓔ

wrong in Section 9

9. Ⓐ Ⓑ Ⓒ Ⓓ Ⓔ   19. Ⓐ Ⓑ Ⓒ Ⓓ Ⓔ   29. Ⓐ Ⓑ Ⓒ Ⓓ Ⓔ   39. Ⓐ Ⓑ Ⓒ Ⓓ Ⓔ
10. Ⓐ Ⓑ Ⓒ Ⓓ Ⓔ   20. Ⓐ Ⓑ Ⓒ Ⓓ Ⓔ   30. Ⓐ Ⓑ Ⓒ Ⓓ Ⓔ   40. Ⓐ Ⓑ Ⓒ Ⓓ Ⓔ

SAT Practice Test Three

SECTION 1
Time—25 Minutes
ESSAY

The essay gives you an opportunity to show how effectively you can develop and express ideas. You should, therefore, take care to develop your point of view, present your ideas logically and clearly, and use language precisely.

Your essay must be written in your Answer Grid Booklet—you will receive no other paper on which to write. You will have enough space if you write on every line, avoid wide margins, and keep your handwriting to a reasonable size. Remember that people who are not familiar with your handwriting will read what you write. Try to write or print so that what you are writing is legible to those readers.

You have 25 minutes to write an essay on the topic assigned below.
DO NOT WRITE ON ANOTHER TOPIC. AN OFF-TOPIC ESSAY WILL RECEIVE A SCORE OF ZERO.

Think carefully about the issue presented in the following excerpt and the assignment below.

> "I don't know the key to success, but the key to failure is to try to please everyone."
> –Bill Cosby

Assignment: Is trying to please people a way to achieve success or a route to failure? Plan and write an essay in which you develop your point of view on this issue. Support your position with reasoning and examples taken from your reading, studies, experience, or observations.

DO NOT WRITE YOUR ESSAY IN YOUR TEST BOOK.
You will receive credit only for what you write in your Answer Grid Booklet.

_____

_____

_____

_____

_____

_____

_____

_____

_____

_____

_____

_____

_____

_____

_____

IF YOU FINISH BEFORE TIME IS CALLED, YOU MAY CHECK YOUR WORK ON
THIS SECTION ONLY. DO NOT TURN TO ANY OTHER SECTION IN THE TEST.

SECTION 2
Time—25 Minutes
20 Questions

Directions: For this section, solve each problem and decide which is the best of the choices given. Fill in the corresponding oval on the answer sheet. You may use any available space for scratchwork.

Notes:

(1) Calculator use is permitted.

(2) All numbers used are real numbers.

(3) Figures are provided for some problems. All figures are drawn to scale and lie in a plane UNLESS otherwise indicated.

(4) Unless otherwise specified, the domain of any function f is assumed to be the set of all real numbers x for which $f(x)$ is a real number.

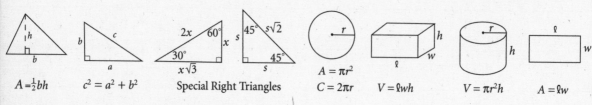

$A = \frac{1}{2}bh$ $c^2 = a^2 + b^2$ Special Right Triangles $A = \pi r^2$ $V = \ell wh$ $V = \pi r^2 h$ $A = \ell w$
                                            $C = 2\pi r$

The sum of the degree measures of the angles in a triangle is 180.
The number of degrees of arc in a circle is 360.
A straight angle has a degree measure of 180.

1. If $x^6 + 4 = x^6 + w$, then $w =$

   (A) -4
   (B) $-\sqrt[6]{4}$
   (C) $\sqrt[6]{4}$
   (D) 4
   (E) 4^6

2. Depending on the cycle, washing a load of clothes takes from 22 to 28 minutes. Drying takes an additional 20 to 30 minutes. What are the minimum and maximum total times to complete a load of laundry?

   (A) 22 minutes and 28 minutes
   (B) 28 minutes and 48 minutes
   (C) 28 minutes and 58 minutes
   (D) 42 minutes and 48 minutes
   (E) 42 minutes and 58 minutes

GO ON TO THE NEXT PAGE

3. If $\frac{a}{b} = 4$, $\frac{a}{c} = 8$, and $c = 9$, what is the value of b?

(A) 2

(B) 8

(C) 18

(D) 36

(E) 72

4. Between which two digits of 4567890 should a decimal point be placed so that the value of the resulting number is 4.567890×10^2?

(A) 5 and 6

(B) 6 and 7

(C) 7 and 8

(D) 8 and 9

(E) 9 and 0

5. Set A is the set of all prime numbers. Set B is the set of all numbers equal to a prime number plus 2. Which of the following are in the intersection of set A and set B?

   I. 2
   II. 4
   III. 5

(A) I only

(B) II only

(C) III only

(D) I and III only

(E) II and III only

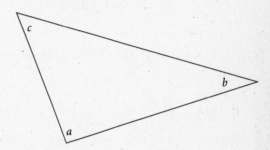

Note: Figure not drawn to scale.

6. In the figure above, if $a = 7c$ and $b = 2c$, what is the value of c?

(A) 18

(B) 20

(C) 28

(D) 34

(E) 36

GO ON TO THE NEXT PAGE

7. After 21 kids were added to a class, there were 4 times as many students as before. How many kids were in the class before the addition?

(A) 3

(B) 7

(C) 11

(D) 14

(E) 17

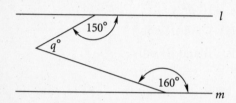

8. In the figure above, $l \parallel m$. What is the value of q?

(A) 40°

(B) 50°

(C) 60°

(D) 70°

(E) 80°

9. The value of $3x + 9$ is how much more than the value of $3x - 2$?

(A) 7

(B) 11

(C) $3x + 7$

(D) $3x + 11$

(E) $6x + 7$

10. If $a < b < 0 < c$, which of the following must be true?

    I. $-b > -a$
    II. $a + c < b + c$
    III. $a + b < c$

(A) I only

(B) II only

(C) III only

(D) II and III only

(E) I, II, and III

11. Set C includes all numbers between 0 and 5, inclusive. Set D includes all numbers between 3 and 7, inclusive. Which of the following sets of inequalities correctly describes x, where x is the union of set C and set D?

(A) $0 \le x \le 3$

(B) $0 \le x \le 5$

(C) $0 \le x \le 7$

(D) $3 \le x \le 5$

(E) $3 \le x \le 7$

12. If $\frac{10}{a+b} = \frac{4}{a}$, $\frac{b^2}{18} = \frac{a}{2}$, and $ab \ne 0$, what is the value of b?

(A) 0

(B) 2

(C) 4

(D) 6

(E) 8

GO ON TO THE NEXT PAGE

13. If $c^{-\frac{1}{2}} = 3$, what is the value of c^2?

   (A) -9

   (B) -3

   (C) $\dfrac{1}{81}$

   (D) $\dfrac{1}{9}$

   (E) $\dfrac{1}{\sqrt{3}}$

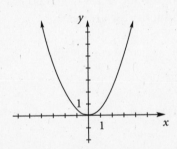

14. Which of the following equations best describes the curve in the figure above?

   (A) $y = -2x^2$

   (B) $y = -x^2$

   (C) $y = |x|$

   (D) $y = \dfrac{1}{2}x^2$

   (E) $y = 2x^2$

Questions 15 and 16 refer to the following figure.

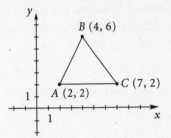

15. What is the area of triangle ABC?

   (A) 5

   (B) 6

   (C) 8

   (D) 9

   (E) 10

16. What is the perimeter of triangle ABC?

   (A) 10

   (B) 11

   (C) $10 + \sqrt{5}$

   (D) 13

   (E) $10 + 2\sqrt{5}$

GO ON TO THE NEXT PAGE

17. Which of the following represents the statement: When the sum of the squares of $2a$ and $3b$ are added to the difference between $8c$ and $7d$, the result is 3 more than e?

   (A) $(2a)^2 + (3b)^2 + (8c - 7d) = e + 3$
   (B) $(2a)^2 + (3b)^2 + (8c - 7d) + 3 = e$
   (C) $(2a + 3b)^2 + (8c - 7d) + 3 = e$
   (D) $(2a + 3b)^2 + (8c - 7d) = e + 3$
   (E) $2a^2 + 3b^2 + (8c - 7d) + 3 = e$

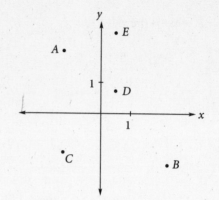

18. Line l has an undefined slope and contains the point $(-2, 3)$. Which of the following points is also on line l?

   (A) $(0, 3)$
   (B) $(5, 5)$
   (C) $(0, 0)$
   (D) $(3, -2)$
   (E) $(-2, 5)$

19. In the figure above, for which point (x, y) is the product xy the greatest?

   (A) A
   (B) B
   (C) C
   (D) D
   (E) E

20. If $a = 3n + 4$ and $b = 7 + 9n^2$, what is b in terms of a?

   (A) $a^2 + 8a + 23$
   (B) $a^2 - 8a + 23$
   (C) $9a^2 - 108a + 144$
   (D) $9a^2 - 108a + 148$
   (E) $9a^2 + 108a + 148$

IF YOU FINISH BEFORE TIME IS CALLED, YOU MAY CHECK YOUR WORK ON THIS SECTION ONLY. DO NOT TURN TO ANY OTHER SECTION IN THE TEST.

STOP

SECTION 3

Time—25 Minutes

25 Questions

Directions: For each of the following questions, choose the best answer and darken the corresponding oval on the answer sheet.

Each sentence below has one or two blanks, each blank indicating that something has been omitted. Beneath the sentence are five words or sets of words labeled (A) through (E). Choose the word or set of words that, when inserted in the sentence, best fits the meaning of the sentence as a whole.

Example:

Today's small, portable computers contrast markedly with the earliest electronic computers, which were -------.

(A) effective
(B) invented
(C) useful
(D) destructive
(E) enormous

1. Leonardo Da Vinci was a ------- artist; he was a painter, sculptor, draftsman, architect, and inventor.

    (A) demonstrative
    (B) nebulous
    (C) meticulous
    (D) versatile
    (E) metaphoric

2. Although the class was told by their math teacher that the exercises in the chapter review were -------, the students knew that some questions on the exam would be the same as those found in the review.

    (A) pivotal
    (B) ritualistic
    (C) salient
    (D) supplementary
    (E) solemn

3. Renowned buildings such as "Fallingwater" and the eminent Solomon R. Guggenheim Museum in New York City ------- Frank Lloyd Wright as one of the most ------- architects of the 20th century.

    (A) buoyed . . . irrelevant
    (B) established . . . prominent
    (C) surrendered . . . prolific
    (D) decried . . . cynical
    (E) categorized . . . mundane

4. Although he was not particularly talented, his years of experience as a plumber at least solidified his status as a ------- of the profession.

    (A) novice
    (B) neighbor
    (C) interpreter
    (D) practitioner
    (E) detractor

GO ON TO THE NEXT PAGE

5. Known as a skilled mediator, Ms. Poole was able to ------- the couple's relationship by carefully ------- their numerous differences.

    (A) reinforce . . . strengthening
    (B) preserve . . . bridging
    (C) convey . . . widening
    (D) overcome . . . plugging
    (E) disregard . . . destroying

6. The ------- that plagued the once venerable institution was so entrenched and highly publicized that few imagined its reputation could ever be -------.

    (A) integrity . . . discredited
    (B) conviction . . . justified
    (C) corruption . . . redeemed
    (D) dignity . . . excused
    (E) degradation . . . convicted

7. The waiter performs his job with ------- and hopes that if he continues to work ------- he will eventually be promoted to maitre d'.

    (A) sagacity . . . unscrupulously
    (B) leniency . . . decorously
    (C) nonchalance . . . tenaciously
    (D) acrimony . . . cheerfully
    (E) ardor . . . assiduously

8. Even though we are supposed to be more evolved than animals, the human tendency toward ------- and egocentrism shows that sometimes people can carry a narrow view of the universe.

    (A) irrationality
    (B) humanity
    (C) temerity
    (D) serendipity
    (E) anthropocentrism

GO ON TO THE NEXT PAGE

Directions: The passages below are followed by questions based on their content; questions following a pair of related passages may also be based on the relationship between the paired passages. Answer the questions on the basis of what is <u>stated</u> or <u>implied</u> in the passages and in any introductory material that may be provided.

Questions 9–10 refer to the following passage.

With my months of anticipation finally satisfied and the long-awaited bundle of fur fast asleep in my lap, I could not have then imagined the trials to come. Yet, by the time I
(5) arrived home from the breeder's with slightly scored shins and puppy urine coating my shoes, I had some idea. I suppose my mother had provided something of a warning with her constant refrain that came every time I crossed
(10) another day off my calendar: "Just make sure he stays your responsibility, not mine." But looking back, with that once tiny menace now a snoring beast asleep at my feet, I feel a hint of what must be parental satisfaction.

9. In line 6, "scored" most nearly means

   (A) counted
   (B) indented
   (C) acquired
   (D) scratched
   (E) slashed

10. The author uses the words "snoring beast" (line 13) in order to

   (A) suggest that her puppy grew to be too large
   (B) imply that her once energetic puppy is now rather lazy
   (C) indicate that her decision to get a puppy was a mistake
   (D) emphasize how much she has grown to love her puppy
   (E) underscore how much her puppy has matured

Questions 11–12 refer to the following passage.

When the revolutionary American chocolate-maker Milton Hershey enthusiastically opened his first candy shop in Philadelphia at the age of 18, he knew little of the busi-
(5) ness, and his inexperience caused his endeavor to fold six years later. Nonetheless, getting his feet wet in the industry proved enough to keep him hooked on it, for he went on to work as an intern for a local caramel manu-
(10) facturer. There he learned that superior results could only be achieved when the freshest milk was used, and thus was born a lifelong dedi-cation to quality ingredients upon which he would later build his chocolate empire.

11. As indicated in the first sentence of the passage, Milton Hershey was

   (A) quite industrious
   (B) something of a child prodigy
   (C) an untalented entrepreneur
   (D) a groundbreaking candy producer
   (E) committed to using high-quality ingredients

GO ON TO THE NEXT PAGE

12. The passage implies that Hershey

   (A) was the first to make candy from quality ingredients

   (B) had a persisting interest in candy manufacturing

   (C) tried to apply caramel-making techniques to chocolate production

   (D) was well-suited for a career only in candy making

   (E) had been fascinated by candy-making since early childhood

Questions 13–24 refer to the following passage.

The following passage is from a 2004 essay that discusses the decline in artistic awareness, appreciation, and taste in America.

While many of us express disdain at the declining condition of artistic awareness, let alone appreciation, in this country, we cannot honestly express surprise. This general
(5) decline in tastes has not escaped the commentary and analysis of cultural critics who have warned us that we may be turning into a nation of Philistines. These same critics have pointed to a pair of causes for this cul-
(10) tural decline. Perhaps, they note, the decline is due to the crumbling state of our educational system, or to the media's focus on pop culture and the general decline of taste this breeds. Nevertheless, this type of scholarly
(15) discussion about the roots of the decline, while relevant to sociological and cultural historical analysis, does nothing to solve the problem. Understanding the causes does not change the sad fact that the same coun-
(20) try that gave the world film noir, jazz, and abstract expressionism now mostly concerns itself with teen movies and boy bands. We must use our understanding and analysis of

the causes to address the problem of artistic
(25) decline in America.

   Before we can begin a discussion of artistic decline, we must first define the word "art," an endeavor that has proven problematic, especially after the introduction of modern art
(30) forms during the twentieth century. Indeed, some may argue that the entire debate about artistic decline in this country is flawed due to our exclusion of modern forms of art such as pop music. Many claim that such discus-
(35) sion can be seen as snobby, even culturally imperious. Without entering the debate on the validity of the post-modern conception of art as an idea, the question of "what is art" must be addressed. But it should be addressed
(40) expeditiously. Far too much time has been spent arguing over whether a teen movie is more or less art than *Citizen Kane* is, or whether the music of a boy band is more or less art than are the works of Sondheim. To
(45) be fair, society should not adopt an exclusionary definition or attitude. Indeed, history has proven that today's pop music can be tomorrow's great art in retrospect. Thus, we should accept all artistic endeavors as art. Individuals
(50) and critics should judge the quality of such endeavors. But this does not change the fact that today, people are unaware of and uneducated about the classics, or even about recent movements in art apart from cinema, televi-
(55) sion, and pop music.

   Imagine a United States of America in which artistic education, and thus appreciation, flourishes, a place where parents read books on art and listen to classical music and
(60) opera, as well as pop music. Children observe these adult activities and mimic them. Parents read to their children and educate them. These parents also give their children art books, classical recordings, and plays as
(65) gifts. These parents underwrite, with their tax

GO ON TO THE NEXT PAGE ⇨

dollars, public art, public broadcasting, and community art groups. In school, students receive an education in art history, classical music, and opera. This curriculum can also
(70) include pop culture such as the music videos, teen movies, and pop music students enjoy in their free time. In fact, a better education in art will better equip them to judge the artistic merit of these newer, more trendy art forms,
(75) or at least place these art forms in historical context and analyze them as an outgrowth of societal and sociological trends—an important aspect of artistic knowledge that has been lost by the general public. When these
(80) children grow up, some may produce their own art, which would likely be higher in quality than the pop music and movies produced today. Imagine a land of such developed artistic production and taste! How can
(85) we achieve such a society?

Having noted that the proliferation of low quality art in pop culture can be addressed effectively by education, there remains one fundamental cause for the decline in artistic
(90) taste: the crumbling state of our educational system. The society dreamed of above can only be achieved by sustained efforts to improve the American educational system. Unfortunately, with tightening budgets due
(95) to increased levels of government debt, often the first programs cut are those that provide art and music classes. Often these cuts are viewed as easy ones by the public since they do not compromise the fundamentals sup-
(100) posedly required for an adequate education: reading, writing, history, science, and math. However, what the public often misses is that art, music, and culture are inextricably tied to literary and historical developments that
(105) themselves stem from changes in society and culture. A holistic approach to the arts would both redefine their role in education (thereby

subsuming the argument of those who want to focus on fundamentals) and improve the
(110) state of artistic education by teaching students in an intertextual and multidisciplinary manner. The first step in improving artistic awareness and taste in this country will be not only to reinstate and improve art, music,
(115) and other cultural classes but also to restructure the curriculum to provide a more holistic education in which art, music, and culture become a part of the fundamental education in history, literature, and society. This system
(120) would require more funding and most likely higher taxes. However, such an investment would pay dividends by ensuring a more educated populace, one which is better equipped to analyze its surroundings in an analytically
(125) balanced manner and one which appreciates all forms of human artistic endeavor.

13. According to the author, which endeavor has proven problematic?

(A) Improving the education system
(B) Making art seem relevant
(C) Defining the word "art"
(D) Deciding what students should learn in school
(E) Deciding whether or not to teach art

GO ON TO THE NEXT PAGE

14. In paragraph 2 of the passage (lines 26–55), the author suggests that too much time has been spent

    (A) debating the artistic merits of so-called "classics"

    (B) debating the artistic merits of modern works

    (C) debating whether or not art education can be improved

    (D) debating whether or not a historical perspective should be used in art education

    (E) comparing the artistic merits of different works traditionally considered classics

15. The author mentions "film noir, jazz, and abstract expressionism" (lines 20–21) chiefly in order to

    (A) appeal to the reader's sense of nostalgia

    (B) introduce a historical parallel

    (C) examine the history of art

    (D) remind the reader how tastes change over time

    (E) suggest that current artistic works are inferior to older ones

16. In line 36, "imperious" most nearly means

    (A) imperative

    (B) arbitrary

    (C) regal

    (D) urgent

    (E) arrogant

17. According to the author, which important aspect of artistic knowledge has been lost by the general public?

    (A) The ability to place art works in a historical context

    (B) The ability to define the word "art"

    (C) The ability to produce art that rivals the classics

    (D) The ability to judge the merits of current art works

    (E) The ability to value all forms of art

18. In lines 56–65 ("Imagine . . . gifts"), the hypothetical United States described is noteworthy because

    (A) people have allowed new interests to develop

    (B) parents share their interest in and enjoyment of art

    (C) children learn about art in school

    (D) children and parents share many activities

    (E) artistic skill is valued by and expected of everyone

19. Lines 67–72 ("In school . . . time") present a model of education where students learn to

    (A) value artistic diversity over tradition

    (B) respect the views of all artists

    (C) reflect critically on the nature of art education

    (D) appreciate classic art works over contemporary ones

    (E) encounter art through a wide-ranging exploration

GO ON TO THE NEXT PAGE

20. The author includes paragraph 3 (lines 56–85) primarily in order to

   (A) propose a vision of a utopian society

   (B) propose a vision of an artistically educated society

   (C) argue that pop culture leaves no lasting impact on society

   (D) observe that classic literature has great appeal for even reluctant students

   (E) indicate that contemporary and classical works are interchangeable

21. In lines 102–119 ("However . . . society"), the education illustrated is best described as

   (A) elitist

   (B) philanthropic

   (C) eclectic

   (D) comprehensive

   (E) rudimentary

22. In lines 112–119 ("The first step . . . society"), the author describes an education system that would be more

   (A) expensive than the current system

   (B) celebrated than the current system

   (C) controversial than the current system

   (D) interesting than the current system

   (E) likely to inspire than the current system

23. The main purpose of the passage is to

   (A) shift the focus of a debate from causes to effects

   (B) outline a debate and support one side

   (C) present a problem and suggest a solution

   (D) revive a discredited idea that might be able to solve a current problem

   (E) promote certain kinds of art

24. In the hypothetical United States the author discusses, why does the author imply that children will grow up to produce art that may be higher in quality than the pop music and movies produced today?

   (A) They would not want to disappoint their parents.

   (B) Society would not accept low-quality art.

   (C) Their education would provide them with more artistic knowledge.

   (D) They would have more free time to experiment with their art.

   (E) Critics would judge the merits of the art more harshly.

25. The author's attitude toward pop music is that

   (A) he admires it

   (B) he has no feelings about it

   (C) he is not a fan

   (D) he wants to see more pop-influenced education

   (E) he believes it is more important than classical music

SECTION 4

Time—25 Minutes

35 Questions

Directions: For each question in this section, select the best answer from among the choices given and fill in the corresponding oval on the answer sheet.

The following sentences test correctness and effectiveness of expression. Part of each sentence or the entire sentence is underlined; beneath each sentence are five ways of phrasing the underlined material. Choice (A) repeats the original phrasing; the other four choices are different. If you think the original phrasing produces a better sentence than any of the alternatives, select choice (A); if not, select one of the other choices.

In making your selection, follow the requirements of standard written English; that is, pay attention to grammar, choice of words, sentence construction, and punctuation. Your selection should result in the most effective sentence—clear and precise, without awkwardness or ambiguity.

EXAMPLE: ANSWER:

Every apple in the baskets <u>are ripe and labeled according to the date it was picked</u>.   Ⓐ ● Ⓒ Ⓓ Ⓔ

(A) are ripe and labeled according to the date it was picked
(B) is ripe and labeled according to the date it was picked
(C) are ripe and labeled according to the date they were picked
(D) is ripe and labeled according to the date they were picked
(E) are ripe and labeled as to the date it was picked

1. <u>Nora would like to fly to Egypt, but flying is unable to be afforded by her.</u>

   (A) Nora would like to fly to Egypt, but flying is unable to be afforded by her.

   (B) Nora would like to fly to Egypt, but she cannot afford to do so.

   (C) Nora would like to fly to Egypt, but she is unable to afford that.

   (D) Flying to Egypt is what Nora would like to do, but she cannot afford it.

   (E) Flying to Egypt appeals to Nora, but she cannot afford to buy the plane ticket.

2. The state of <u>New Jersey is one of the smallest states in the union, being also</u> the most densely populated.

   (A) New Jersey is one of the smallest states in the union, being also

   (B) New Jersey, although one of the smallest states in the union, is also

   (C) New Jersey, being one of the smallest states in the union makes it

   (D) New Jersey, which is one of the smallest states in the union, although it is

   (E) New Jersey, whose size is the smallest in the union, makes it

GO ON TO THE NEXT PAGE ⟩

3. <u>The love story of Romeo and Juliet was the subject of a teen movie, being popular among high school students in the 90s.</u>

   (A) The love story of Romeo and Juliet was the subject of a teen movie, being popular among high school students in the 90s.

   (B) The love story of Romeo and Juliet was popular among high school students in the 90s, where it is being made the subject of a teen movie.

   (C) The love story of Romeo and Juliet was popular among high school students in the 90s, when it was the subject of a teen movie.

   (D) Romeo and Juliet, whose love story was the subject of a popular teen movie among high school students in the 90s.

   (E) Being the subject of a teen movie, the love story of Romeo and Juliet having been popular among high school students in the 90s.

4. <u>One consequence of the university's new bylaws is that they can no longer pay reduced wages to lecturers.</u>

   (A) One consequence of the university's new bylaws is that they can no longer pay reduced wages to lecturers.

   (B) Once consequence of its new bylaws is that the university can no longer pay reduced wages to lecturers.

   (C) One consequence of the university's new bylaws is that reduced wages to lecturers can no longer be paid by them.

   (D) The university's new bylaws result in their no longer being able to pay lecturers reduced wages.

   (E) One consequence of the university's new bylaws are that paying reduced wages to lecturers is no longer possible.

5. Photographer Andrea Valerai permitted only a few friends to view her work <u>because her strict standards caused her to doubt</u> that her pictures were worth looking at.

   (A) because her strict standards caused her to doubt

   (B) her standards being strict, she doubted

   (C) because of her standards being strict, which she doubted

   (D) from having strict standards causing her to doubt

   (E) having strict standards causing her doubting

6. It is hard for me to imagine that 100 years ago this area was undeveloped swamp <u>land, but it has since become the site of high-rise apartment buildings</u>.

   (A) land, but it has since become the site of high-rise apartment buildings

   (B) land, because it is now the site of high-rise apartment buildings

   (C) land, and has since become high-rise apartment buildings

   (D) land that has since become the site of high-rise apartment buildings

   (E) land, since becoming high-rise apartment buildings on the site

GO ON TO THE NEXT PAGE ⟩

7. <u>Gorbachev started the opening of Soviet society, and he</u> was raised in the relative freedom of thought under Khrushchev.

   (A) Gorbachev started the opening of Soviet society, and he

   (B) Gorbachev, who started the opening of Soviet society,

   (C) Starting the opening of Soviet society was Gorbachev, and he

   (D) Gorbachev started the opening of Soviet society, and that is why he

   (E) A start of the opening of Soviet society, Gorbachev

8. The cost of attending college has been affected by an increase in scholarships and <u>because there has been a decrease in large alumni donations</u>.

   (A) because there has been a decrease in large alumni donations

   (B) because of the decrease in large alumni donations

   (C) by alumni who have decreased large donations

   (D) decreasing large alumni donations

   (E) a decrease in large alumni donations

9. Airlines such as Ryan Air and Easy Jet are able to find alternative, cheap landing strips <u>and are therefore able to pass savings on to their customers</u>.

   (A) and are therefore able to pass savings on to their customers

   (B) and savings are passed on as a result to their customers

   (C) so that their customers could have savings passed to them

   (D) so, therefore, savings would be gained by their customers

   (E) and therefore have savings gained in their customers

10. The first hand transplant was performed in 1998, made possible <u>by their fuller understanding of</u> immunobiology.

    (A) by their fuller understanding of

    (B) by their understanding more fully

    (C) by their more fully understanding

    (D) by a fuller understanding of

    (E) by its fuller understanding of

11. Some speedometers register <u>high speeds as</u> two hundred miles per hour, even though few cars will ever go faster than one hundred.

    (A) high speeds as

    (B) speeds as high as

    (C) speeds that are high

    (D) high speeds that are capable of exceeding

    (E) a speed as

GO ON TO THE NEXT PAGE

12. <u>That</u> the team with the worst record won the
    A
    game <u>easily</u> using players <u>whom</u> had previously
          B   C
    scored only two goals <u>came</u> as a shock to the
                              D
    sportscasters. <u>No error</u>
                      E

13. Acknowledging that her performance in class
    <u>was</u> not up to her usual standards, Stacy
    A
    <u>had worked</u> <u>to raise</u> her test score average
       B   C
    <u>for the third marking period</u>. <u>No error</u>
              D   E

14. <u>Although</u> he <u>knows</u> his own life was <u>in danger</u>,
       A   B   C
    the mayor insisted on going downtown to see
    the site of the attack <u>for himself</u>. <u>No error</u>
                               D   E

15. The director was <u>annoyed by</u> Tom's inability
                         A
    <u>to learn</u> his line <u>because</u> his lack of preparation
       B   C
    forced her to schedule an extra rehearsal
    <u>for the next day</u>. <u>No error</u>
            D   E

16. The professor wanted <u>to be sure that</u> his
                            A
    students <u>come</u> to class <u>on time</u>, so he posted a
             B   C
    <u>schedule on</u> the Spanish department's bulletin
       D
    board. <u>No error</u>
              E

17. Henley decorated her plain white kitchen walls
    <u>with</u> colorful posters <u>because</u> she knew she
    A   B
    <u>would enjoy</u> looking at the bright reds, blues,
       C
    and yellows <u>every morning</u>. <u>No error</u>
                    D   E

GO ON TO THE NEXT PAGE

18. Paula, <u>who</u> loved <u>to see</u> new places but
        A   B
<u>had never enjoyed</u> flying, grew <u>increasing</u>
      C   D
nervous as the day of her first overseas

vacation approached. <u>No error</u>
                    E

19. In the <u>anticipatory</u> hush of the dark theater,
         A
we <u>could hear</u> the <u>rustling of</u> the costumes as
     B   C
the dancers took <u>their place</u> on the stage.
                D
<u>No error</u>
  E

20. The neighbors got <u>into their car</u> and <u>driving</u>
              A   B
off toward the main street as Katie <u>looked</u> out
                      C
the window, <u>sipping her hot chocolate</u>.
             D
<u>No error</u>
  E

21. The <u>heroine of</u> Dorothy Parker's short story
     A
"The Telephone Call" waits <u>feverishly</u> for the
                   B
telephone to ring, <u>refuses</u> to face her knowledge
              C
that the boy <u>will never call</u>. <u>No error</u>
          D   E

22. As we walked <u>through</u> the South Philadelphia
          A
neighborhood <u>known as</u> the Italian Market,
          B
a <u>number of</u> appetizing smells <u>greeting</u> our
    C   D
nostrils. <u>No error</u>
       E

23. Kyoko took <u>every opportunity</u> to practice
         A
<u>speaking</u> English, <u>even though</u> her friends
  B   C
<u>prefer</u> to speak Japanese together. <u>No error</u>
 D   E

24. The Berlin Wall, <u>which</u> became the <u>most potent</u>
            A   B
symbol <u>of the Cold War</u>, <u>constructed</u> in 1961.
       C   D
<u>No error</u>
 E

25. Larry McMurtry's <u>short</u> novel *The Last Picture*
               A
Show <u>perfectly</u> captures the atmosphere of a
      B
small Texas town <u>and</u> the loneliness
             C
<u>of its inhabitants</u>. <u>No error</u>
  D   E

26. Mrs. Ramsay told us that, since only one <u>slice of</u>
                            A
apple pie was left, <u>she</u> <u>would not be able</u> <u>to offer</u>
             B   C   D
us any dessert. <u>No error</u>
          E

27. Today's student <u>frequently choose</u> a college
             A
degree program <u>that</u> <u>leads to</u> a <u>specific</u> career.
          B   C   D
<u>No error</u>
 E

GO ON TO THE NEXT PAGE

28. This Tibetan restaurant <u>serving</u> several
                           A
    varieties of stuffed dumplings <u>as well as</u> some
                                   B
    <u>excellent</u> and hearty soups, unlike the
    C
    restaurant <u>around the corner</u>. <u>No error</u>
               D   E

29. In the 1950s, painters Jackson Pollock and

    James Brooks <u>developed</u> <u>the idea of</u>
                 A   B
    automatism: <u>to drip</u> and throwing paint
                C
    <u>spontaneously</u> across an unprimed canvas.
    D
    <u>No error</u>
    E

GO ON TO THE NEXT PAGE ⟩

<u>**Directions:**</u> The following passage is an early draft of an essay. Some parts of the passage need to be rewritten.

Read the passage and select the best answer for each question that follows. Some questions are about particular sentences or parts of sentences and ask you to improve sentence structure or word choice. Other questions ask you to consider organization and development. In choosing answers, follow the conventions of standard written English.

(1) It is generally accepted as a theory among scientists that a change in atmospheric phenomena may signal pending changes to the Earth's climate. (2) Consequently, when NASA began to document increased sightings of noctilucent clouds in the latter half of the twentieth century, the agency institutes plans for a study to determine the cause and to learn what effect, if any, this may have on future weather patterns.

(3) Noctilucent, or night-shining, clouds are virtually unknown to most people, even those that star-gaze on a regular basis. (4) This is because NLCs (as they are known in the scientific community) generally occur north of 50° latitude, above the polar region. (5) These clouds, however, are becoming increasingly visible in areas farther south. (6) In 1999, a dramatic display of NLCs appearing over Colorado and Utah, nearly 10° below the latitudes where scientists have come to expect them. (7) Sightings in Europe have also become more frequent in the past 50 years, for reasons that remain unclear.

(8) Ordinary clouds occur approximately 10 kilometers from the Earth's surface. (9) Noctilucent clouds are found at about 82 kilometers. (10) This is more than seven times higher than commercial airlines fly. (11) Although most scientists believe NLCs are formed of ice crystals, but some are convinced that they are composed of cosmic or volcanic dust. (12) This theory is most likely attributable to the fact that the first NLC sightings were documented following a large volcanic explosion in Indonesia.

30. In context, what is the best version of sentence 1 (reproduced below)?

It is generally accepted as a theory among scientists that a change in atmospheric phenomena may signal pending changes to the Earth's climate.

(A) (As it is now)

(B) Generally accepted by scientists as a theory, a change in atmospheric phenomena may signal pending changes to the Earth's climate.

(C) Scientists generally accepting the theory that a change in atmospheric phenomena may signal pending changes to the Earth's climate.

(D) Scientists generally accept the theory that a change in atmospheric phenomena may signal pending changes to the Earth's climate.

(E) Scientists, having generally accepted the theory that a change in atmospheric phenomena may signal pending changes to the Earth's climate.

GO ON TO THE NEXT PAGE ⟶

31. In context, what revision is required in sentence 2 (reproduced below)?

    Consequently, when NASA began to document increased sightings of noctilucent clouds in the latter half of the twentieth century, the agency institutes plans for a study to determine the cause and to learn what effect, if any, this may have on future weather patterns.

    (A) Eliminate "Consequently."
    (B) Change "institutes" to "instituted."
    (C) Change "for a study" to "for studying."
    (D) Change "and" to "but."
    (E) Change "may have" to "may have had."

32. Which of the following is the best version of the underlined portion of sentence 3 (reproduced below)?

    Noctilucent, or night-shining, clouds are virtually unknown to <u>most people, even those that star-gaze on a regular basis</u>.

    (A) (As it is now)
    (B) more people, even those that star-gaze on a regular basis
    (C) most people, even them that star-gaze on a regular basis
    (D) most people, even those who on a regular basis do star-gazing
    (E) most people, even those who star-gaze on a regular basis

33. In context, which of the following is the best way to phrase the underlined portion of sentence 6 (reproduced below)?

    In 1999, <u>a dramatic display of NLCs appearing over Colorado and Utah</u>, nearly 10° below the latitudes where scientists have come to expect them.

    (A) (As it is now)
    (B) a dramatic display of NLCs appears over Colorado and Utah
    (C) a dramatic display of NLCs appeared over Colorado and Utah
    (D) appearing over Colorado and Utah was a dramatic display of NLCs
    (E) over Colorado and Utah there appeared a dramatic display of NLCs

GO ON TO THE NEXT PAGE

34. Which of the following is the best way to combine sentences 8, 9, and 10 (reproduced below)?

    Ordinary clouds occur approximately 10 kilometers from the Earth's surface. Noctilucent clouds are found at about 82 kilometers. This is more than seven times higher than commercial airlines fly.

    (A) Ordinary clouds occur approximately 10 kilometers from the Earth's surface, noctilucent clouds are found at about 82 kilometers, and this is more than seven times higher than commercial airlines fly.

    (B) Ordinary clouds occur approximately 10 kilometers from the Earth's surface; while noctilucent clouds, being found at about 82 kilometers, which is more than seven times higher than commercial airlines fly.

    (C) Ordinary clouds occur approximately 10 kilometers from the Earth's surface, but noctilucent clouds are found at about 82 kilometers, which is more than seven times higher than commercial airlines fly.

    (D) Ordinary clouds occur approximately 10 kilometers from the Earth's surface, so noctilucent clouds are found at about 82 kilometers, which is more than seven times higher than commercial airlines fly.

    (E) Ordinary clouds occurring approximately 10 kilometers from the Earth's surface, and noctilucent clouds at about 82 kilometers, more than seven times higher than commercial airlines fly.

35. In context, what revision is necessary in sentence 11 (reproduced below)?

    Although most scientists believe NLCs are formed of ice crystals, but some are convinced that they are composed of cosmic or volcanic dust.

    (A) Eliminate "Although" and change "but" to "or."

    (B) Eliminate "Although" and change "but" to "because."

    (C) Change "but" to "or."

    (D) Change "but" to "while."

    (E) Eliminate "but."

SECTION 5

Time—25 Minutes

18 Questions

Directions: For this section, solve each problem and decide which is the best of the choices given. Fill in the corresponding oval on the answer sheet. You may use any available space for scratchwork.

Notes:

(1) Calculator use is permitted.

(2) All numbers used are real numbers.

(3) Figures are provided for some problems. All figures are drawn to scale and lie in a plane UNLESS otherwise indicated.

(4) Unless otherwise specified, the domain of any function f is assumed to be the set of all real numbers x for which $f(x)$ is a real number.

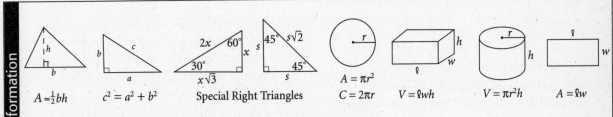

$A = \frac{1}{2}bh$ $c^2 = a^2 + b^2$ Special Right Triangles $A = \pi r^2$ $V = \ell wh$ $V = \pi r^2 h$ $A = \ell w$
$C = 2\pi r$

The sum of the degree measures of the angles in a triangle is 180.
The number of degrees of arc in a circle is 360.
A straight angle has a degree measure of 180.

1. If $3\sqrt{x} - 31 = -13$, what is x?

    (A) 6
    (B) 18
    (C) 36
    (D) 49
    (E) 72

2. Find the value of x if $\frac{3x-9}{2x+7} = 8$.

    (A) −5
    (B) −3
    (C) 1
    (D) 4
    (E) 5

3. Points P and Q are on the standard xy-plane. P has coordinates $(-2, 4)$, and Q has coordinates $(5, -2)$. What is the distance between P and Q?

    (A) 4
    (B) 7
    (C) $3\sqrt{5}$
    (D) $\sqrt{13}$
    (E) $\sqrt{85}$

GO ON TO THE NEXT PAGE

4. For all u and v, let ∇ be defined by $u \nabla v = u - v + 2$. What is the value of $(2 \nabla 3) \nabla 1$?

   (A) 0
   (B) 1
   (C) 2
   (D) 3
   (E) 4

5. If a and b are multiples of 3, which of the following CANNOT also be a multiple of 3?

   (A) $a + b$
   (B) $a - b$
   (C) $a + b + 1$
   (D) ab
   (E) $ab + 3$

6. If the length of one side of a triangle is 5, which of the following CANNOT be the lengths of the other two sides of the triangle?

   (A) 3 and 3
   (B) 3 and 5
   (C) 7 and 8
   (D) 7 and 3
   (E) 7 and 12

7. If k and s are positive integers and the ratio of $2k$ to $6s$ is the same as the ratio of $6k + 5$ to $18s + 10$, which of the following must be true?

   I. $k = s$
   II. $k = 1.5$
   III. $k = 1.5s$

   (A) None
   (B) I only
   (C) II only
   (D) III only
   (E) I and II

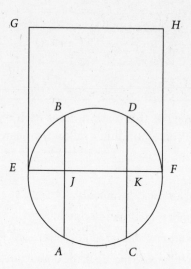

Note: Figure not drawn to scale.

8. In the figure above $\overline{BA}$ and $\overline{DC}$ have equal length and are perpendicular to $\overline{EF}$, which passes through the center of the circle. If the area of square $GEFH$ is 81, and $JK = 5$, what is the length of $\overline{EJ}$?

   (A) 2
   (B) 3
   (C) 4
   (D) 6
   (E) 9

GO ON TO THE NEXT PAGE

Directions: For Student-Produced Response questions 9–18, use the grids at the bottom of the answer sheet page on which you have answered questions 1–8.

Each of the remaining ten questions requires you to solve the problem and enter your answer by marking the ovals in the special grid, as shown in the example below. You may use any available space for scratchwork.

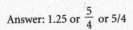

Answer: 1.25 or $\frac{5}{4}$ or 5/4

Write answer in boxes.

Grid-in result

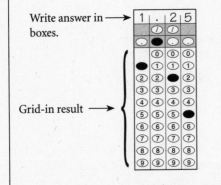

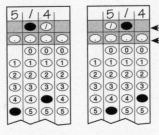

Either position is correct.

Fraction line
Decimal point

You may start your answers in any column, space permitting. Columns not needed should be left blank.

- It is recommended, though not required, that you write your answer in the boxes at the top of the columns. However, you will receive credit only for darkening the ovals correctly.

- Grid only one answer to a question, even though some problems have more than one correct answer.

- Darken no more than one oval in a column.

- No answers are negative.

- Mixed numbers cannot be gridded. For example: the number $1\frac{1}{4}$ must be gridded as 1.25 or 5/4.

(If ⟦1 1 / 4⟧ is gridded, it will be interpreted as $\frac{11}{4}$, not $1\frac{1}{4}$.)

- Decimal Accuracy: Decimal answers must be entered as accurately as possible. For example, if you obtain an answer such as 0.1666..., you should record the result as .166 or .167. **Less accurate values such as .16 or .17 are not acceptable.**

Acceptable ways to grid $\frac{1}{6}$ = .1666...

GO ON TO THE NEXT PAGE

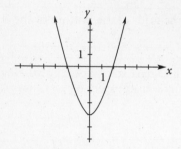

9. The figure above shows $f(x)$, a quadratic function. What is one solution of this function?

10. To borrow a single book from a lending library, Mr. Brown was charged $2 for two weeks, plus a fine of $.15 per day for every day he was late returning it. If he paid a total of $4.55, how many days did he have the book?

11. Points V, W, X, Y, and Z lie on a line in that order. VW is twice as long as WX, and XY is half as long as YZ. If the length of segment $\overline{WY}$ is 6, what is the length of segment $\overline{VZ}$?

$$\boxed{} - AA = AA$$

12. In the equation above, AA represents a positive two-digit number in which both digits are the same. If the number that has been covered by the box is a positive three-digit number that is divisible by 3, what is one possible value of the covered number?

13. Kelly has 25 pairs of pants and 32 shirts in her closet. If she wants to pick out an outfit consisting of a pair of pants and a shirt, how many different outfits could she wear?

14. The last Monday of a 31-day month must be at least how many days after the first Friday of the same month?

15. For positive integers a and b, let $a \sim b$ be defined by $a \sim b = a + (a-1) + (a-2) + \cdots + b$. For example, $9 \sim 4 = 9 + 8 + 7 + 6 + 5 + 4 = 39$. What is the value of $(100 \sim 5) - (98 \sim 3)$?

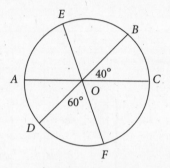

16. In the circle above, $\overline{AC}$, $\overline{BD}$, and $\overline{EF}$ pass through center O. The area of sector AOE is equal to what fraction of the total area of the circle?

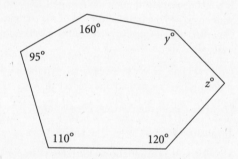

17. In the figure above, what is the sum of y and z?

18. Tameka cleans her house every 7 days and does laundry every 5 days. In the next 315 days, how many times will she have to clean her house *and* do laundry on the same day?

IF YOU FINISH BEFORE TIME IS CALLED, YOU MAY CHECK YOUR WORK ON THIS SECTION ONLY. DO NOT TURN TO ANY OTHER SECTION IN THE TEST.

SECTION 6

Time—25 Minutes

24 Questions

Directions: For each of the following questions, choose the best answer and darken the corresponding oval on the answer sheet.

Each sentence below has one or two blanks, each blank indicating that something has been omitted. Beneath the sentence are five words or sets of words labeled (A) through (E). Choose the word or set of words that, when inserted in the sentence, best fits the meaning of the sentence as a whole.

EXAMPLE:

Today's small, portable computers contrast markedly with the earliest electronic computers, which were -------.

(A) effective
(B) invented
(C) useful
(D) destructive
(E) enormous   Ⓐ Ⓑ Ⓒ Ⓓ ●

1. Jamal found the movie stubs lying on the counter to be ------- evidence that his friends had gone to the cinema without him; it was unquestionable that they had seen *Spider-Man*.

   (A) immaterial
   (B) potential
   (C) incriminating
   (D) nominal
   (E) indisputable

2. When training for a marathon, runners prepare themselves for a challenge that is both ------- and mentally -------.

   (A) illusory . . . taxing
   (B) exaggerated . . . balanced
   (C) physically . . . demanding
   (D) appealing . . . indulgent
   (E) strenuous . . . dubious

3. Healthy lifestyle choices such as exercising regularly and maintaining a nutritious diet can promote ------- yet are often ------- by the busy lives people today lead.

   (A) extinction . . . enhanced
   (B) longevity . . . hampered
   (C) behavior . . . belied
   (D) mortality . . . bolstered
   (E) reproduction . . . confirmed

4. Despite his apparently ------- lifestyle, the old man was known to drink to excess when visited by friends.

   (A) temperate
   (B) laconic
   (C) duplicitous
   (D) aesthetic
   (E) voluble

5. Nostradamus gained a reputation for ------- as he accurately predicted events such as wars complete with descriptions of vehicles that were not invented until after the sixteenth century, when he wrote about his presages.

   (A) prescience
   (B) sincerity
   (C) avarice
   (D) complicity
   (E) mendacity

GO ON TO THE NEXT PAGE

Directions: The passages below are followed by questions based on their content; questions following a pair of related passages may also be based on the relationship between the paired passages. Answer the questions on the basis of what is <u>stated</u> or <u>implied</u> in the passages and in any introductory material that may be provided.

Questions 6–9 refer to the following passages.

Passage 1

Acid rain clouds, formed by the release of gases from burning fossil fuels, join with existing weather patterns and eventually pour down toxic, highly acidic water droplets that
(5) can cause significant and often irreversible environmental damage. However, nuclear power and renewable energy technologies—those that take advantage of continuously available resources such as the sea, sun,
(10) and various biofuels—can generate electricity without giving off the gases that contribute to acid rain, and there are even proven ways to effectively sequester the harmful gases generated by fossil fuel plants. Yet as acid
(15) rain continues to seriously damage countless waterways, forests, crops, and even to erode buildings, senselessly little is being done to take advantage of these new technologies.

Passage 2

While the world's most-developed nations
(20) have the luxury of squabbling over the political and environmental questions raised by those who actually have energy choices, the developing world usually has only one resource to turn to: coal. One of the cheap-
(25) est and most plentiful sources of energy in the world, coal is used to generate nearly 40 percent of the world's electricity. But when burned, coal releases large amounts of carbon dioxide—a gas that, when present in excess,
(30) can cause a whole host of serious respiratory diseases. So while wealthy nations can complain about global warming and acid rain, the rest of the world must struggle to cope with the immediate human damage caused by the
(35) only natural resource they can afford.

6. In Passage 1, the author's attitude toward the continuing presence of acid rain is best described as

(A) astonishment that acid rain remains a problem in the developed world

(B) frustration that the use of cleaner technologies is not more widespread

(C) irritation that nothing is being done to curb the creation of acid rain

(D) impatience toward plants that refuse to adopt experimental technologies

(E) skepticism that irreversible damage is really being done to the environment

7. In Passage 2, the author characterizes "the world's most-developed nations" (line 19) as which of the following?

(A) Insensitive

(B) Responsible

(C) Privileged

(D) Reckless

(E) Impoverished

GO ON TO THE NEXT PAGE

8. How would the author of Passage 2 most likely respond to the assertion in Passage 1 that "senselessly little" (line 17) is being done to take advantage of new and cleaner energy-generation technologies?

(A) Wealthier nations have a responsibility to create opportunities for those less fortunate.

(B) Most countries would adopt these technologies if they were affordable.

(C) The environmental impact of an energy source is just as important as the cost of energy.

(D) Environmental damage is less significant than damage to humans.

(E) Not all countries can afford these technologies.

9. The authors of both passages agree that

(A) clean energy technologies are more expensive than conventional methods

(B) acid rain is a problem inevitably created by energy generation

(C) the burning of fossil fuels can release harmful gases

(D) the environmental debate over energy generation is only intensifying

(E) the human and environmental impacts of energy generation are equally important

Questions 10–15 refer to the following passage.

When I accepted a volunteer position as a social worker at a domestic violence shelter in a developing nation, I imagined the position for which my university experience
(5) had prepared me. I envisioned conducting intake interviews and traipsing around from organization to organization seeking the legal, psychological, and financial support that the women would need to rebuild their
(10) lives. When I arrived, I felt as if I already had months of experience, experience garnered in the hypothetical situations I had invented and subsequently resolved single-handedly and seamlessly. I felt thoroughly prepared to
(15) tackle head-on the situation I assumed was waiting for me.

I arrived full of zeal, knocking at the shelter's door. Within moments, my reality made a sharp break from that which I had
(20) anticipated. The coordinator explained that the shelter's need for financial self-sufficiency had become obvious and acute. To address this, the center was planning to open a bakery. I immediately enthused about the project,
(25) making many references to the small enterprise case studies I had researched at the university. In response to my impassioned reply, the coordinator declared me in charge of the bakery and left in order to "get out of my
(30) way." At that moment, I was as prepared to bake bread as I was to run for political office. The bigger problem, however, was that I was completely unfamiliar with the for-profit business models necessary to run the bakery.
(35) I was out of my depth in a foreign river with only my coordinator's confidence to keep me afloat.

They say that necessity is the mother of invention. I soon found that it is also the
(40) mother of initiative. I began finding recipes and appropriating the expertise of friends.

GO ON TO THE NEXT PAGE

With their help making bread, balancing
books, printing pamphlets and making con-
tacts, the bakery was soon running smoothly
(45) and successfully. After a short time it became
a significant source of income for the house.

In addition to funds, baking bread provided
a natural environment in which to work with
and get to know the women of the shelter.
(50) Kneading dough side by side, I shared in the
camaraderie of the kitchen, treated to stories about their children and the towns and
jobs they had had to leave behind to ensure
their safety. Baking helped me develop strong
(55) relationships with the women and advanced
my understanding of their situations. It also
improved the women's self-esteem. Their ability to master a new skill gave them confidence
in themselves, and the fact that the bakery
(60) contributed to the upkeep of the house gave
the women, many of them newly single, a
sense of pride and the conviction that they
had the capability to support themselves.

Baking gave me the opportunity to work in
(65) a capacity I had not at all anticipated, but one
that proved very successful. I became a more
sensitive and skillful social worker, capable
of making a mean seven-grain loaf. Learning
to bake gave me as much newfound self-con-
(70) fidence as it gave the women, and I found
that sometimes quality social work can be as
simple as kneading dough.

10. The primary purpose of the passage is to show
how the author

(A) was shocked by the discrepancy between
her earlier ideas about her work and the
reality she faced

(B) discovered a talent her overly focused
mind had never allowed her to explore

(C) broadened how she defined the scope of
her work

(D) developed her abilities to orchestrate
a for-profit business enterprise

(E) was abroad when she encountered and
overcame a challenging situation

11. The statement that the author arrived "full of
zeal" (line 17) indicates that she was

(A) anxious and insecure
(B) eager and interested
(C) confident but uninformed
(D) cheerful but exhausted
(E) enthusiastic but incompetent

12. The author was initially enthusiastic about the
idea of the bakery because she

(A) considered it from a theoretical point of
view

(B) hoped to obtain a leadership position in
the bakery

(C) wanted to demonstrate her baking
knowledge to her new coordinator

(D) believed it would be a good way to build
the women's self-esteem

(E) was a strong proponent of self-
sufficiency projects for nonprofit
organizations

GO ON TO THE NEXT PAGE

13. The comparison in lines 30–31 ("At that moment ... political office") demonstrates the author's belief that

(A) the bakery would never be a success

(B) social workers should not be involved in either baking or politics

(C) it was unfair of the coordinator to ask the author to run the bakery

(D) similar skills were involved in both baking and politics

(E) she was unqualified for a job baking bread

14. Lines 32–34 ("The bigger...models") suggest that the author believed that

(A) learning the necessary business practices would be a more daunting challenge than learning to bake bread

(B) good business practices are more important to running a successful bakery than is the quality of the bread

(C) her coordinator's confidence in for-profit business models was misplaced

(D) for-profit business models are significantly more complex than the nonprofit models with which she was familiar

(E) her coordinator would be unwilling to help her

15. The last sentence ("Learning ... dough") indicates that the author

(A) lacked self-confidence just as much as the women with whom she worked

(B) found that performing social work is surprisingly easy with no education

(C) underestimated her own ability to learn new skills

(D) discovered that social work is more effective when it includes tactile activities

(E) derived a benefit from her work while helping others

GO ON TO THE NEXT PAGE

Questions 16–24 refer to the following passage.

This passage discusses some recreational options and reasons for making good use of leisure time.

Recreation is a vital aspect of human life, because it provides one with opportunities to recreate oneself. Recreation can be defined as the refreshment of mind or body through
(5) activity that stimulates or amuses. This definition invites one to both contemplate the myriad options for recreational activity and evaluate these options for their potential to enrich one's life and enhance personal growth
(10) and development.

The modern economic system has freed people from the necessity to relentlessly seek daily sustenance, and thus has augmented leisure, or recreational, time. Many choose
(15) to recreate by engaging in physical competition, namely sports. Former athletes cite their experiences in wrestling, tennis, football, or soccer by way of elucidating their successes in business, government, or academia. For
(20) instance, they commend coaches who taught them to gracefully handle conflict and disappointment; or they vividly recount a specific moment of competition that transformed their lives forever.

(25) Competition, proponents say, gives athletes a profound understanding of both their limits and their abilities. The ability to candidly analyze one's strengths and weaknesses confers resilience in the face of life's vicissitudes
(30) and thus the ability to overcome obstacles.

On the other hand, some athletes shun organized sports, preferring to test themselves physically without the element of competition. They may hike or bike, snowboard or ski, or run or
(35) ride alone or with companions. They contend that their bodies and spirits are best refreshed without the distraction of needless comparison with others.

Taking a different approach, many people
(40) engage in artistic and creative pursuits as a means of recreating themselves. In an academic environment of standardized testing, which directs minds down ever-narrowing avenues of thought, proponents of the arts
(45) point to the mental and emotional flexibility developed by creative activity. For example, art teaches one how to exercise the exquisite faculty of judgment in the absence of rules. It sets forth dilemmas to be resolved, dem-
(50) onstrating that every problem has more than one solution. Practitioners of the arts learn to swim in a turbulent sea of ambiguity and chance without the lifejacket of standard procedure; in other words, art prepares them for
(55) the exigencies of life.

Productive leisure activities amplify one's vocational efforts and increase chances of success. They enhance an understanding of one's place in the world. They facilitate full use
(60) of one's capacities and provide pleasure that enhances all of life's experiences.

16. The author's primary purpose in writing this passage is to

(A) describe the propensity of successful people for athletic participation

(B) compare the theoretical benefits of physical versus artistic activities

(C) convince the reader of the pleasurable nature of recreational pursuits

(D) promote the tangible and intangible benefits of productive leisure activities

(E) engage in speculation about the requisites for vocational success

GO ON TO THE NEXT PAGE

17. The author's statement "The modern economic system has freed people from the necessity to relentlessly seek daily sustenance" (lines 11–13) suggests that increased leisure time is

    (A) always preferable to work
    (B) a consequence of shortened work days
    (C) becoming more scarce, and hence more valuable
    (D) closely related to democratic forms of government
    (E) ideally engaged in on a daily basis

18. According to paragraph 2 of the passage, which of the following is a lifelong benefit of engaging in competition?

    (A) Increased persistence in surmounting difficulties
    (B) Heightened sensitivity to inherent lack of ability
    (C) The capacity to always prevail in life's struggles
    (D) A lifelong engagement with physical activity
    (E) Gratitude to those who help one, such as coaches

19. The concept of "competition" is mentioned in lines 15–16 for which of the following reasons?

    (A) To strengthen the case for competition as an element of proper recreation
    (B) To distract the reader from the importance of comparative physical activities
    (C) To acknowledge that enjoyment is more important than competition in recreation
    (D) To contend that athletics without competition is meaningless
    (E) To emphasize that the benefits of physical recreation do not necessarily have to include competition

20. According to the passage, advantages of recreational pursuit of the arts include which of the following?

    I. Tolerance of uncertainty
    II. Ability to exercise independent judgment in unanticipated situations
    III. Appreciation of aesthetic presentation

    (A) I only
    (B) II only
    (C) I and II only
    (D) II and III only
    (E) I, II, and III

21. In line 55, "exigencies" most nearly means

    (A) crises
    (B) waves
    (C) situations
    (D) motivations
    (E) rules

GO ON TO THE NEXT PAGE

22. The author's statement about standardized testing in schools "direct[ing] minds down ever-narrowing avenues of thought" (lines 43–44) suggests a conviction that such testing is

(A) necessary

(B) irrelevant

(C) limiting

(D) productive

(E) creative

23. The author of this passage is primarily interested in which of the following aspects of recreation?

(A) Its benefits for society at large

(B) The physical and emotional flexibility it confers

(C) Its role as requisite for vocational success

(D) Its benefits for the whole life of the individual

(E) Its ubiquitous position in the human psyche

24. The author uses the metaphor "learn to swim in a turbulent sea of ambiguity and chance without the lifejacket of standard procedure" (lines 51–54) for what purpose?

(A) To show that artists know how to swim

(B) To show that artists live according to strict rules

(C) To show that artists and athletes see the world the same way

(D) To show that artists do not always need precise rules

(E) To show the need for a life jacket

IF YOU FINISH BEFORE TIME IS CALLED, YOU MAY CHECK YOUR WORK ON THIS SECTION ONLY. DO NOT TURN TO ANY OTHER SECTION IN THE TEST.   STOP

SECTION 7

Time—20 Minutes
16 Questions

Directions: For this section, solve each problem and decide which is the best of the choices given. Fill in the corresponding oval on the answer sheet. You may use any available space for scratchwork.

Notes:

(1) Calculator use is permitted.

(2) All numbers used are real numbers.

(3) Figures are provided for some problems. All figures are drawn to scale and lie in a plane UNLESS otherwise indicated.

(4) Unless otherwise specified, the domain of any function f is assumed to be the set of all real numbers x for which $f(x)$ is a real number.

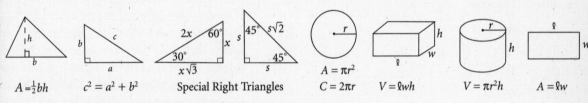

$A = \frac{1}{2}bh$ $c^2 = a^2 + b^2$ Special Right Triangles $A = \pi r^2$ $C = 2\pi r$ $V = \ell wh$ $V = \pi r^2 h$ $A = \ell w$

The sum of the degree measures of the angles in a triangle is 180.
The number of degrees of arc in a circle is 360.
A straight angle has a degree measure of 180.

1. If $8a < 3b$ and $3b < 10c$, which of the following must be true?

    (A) $8a < 10c$

    (B) $10c < 8a$

    (C) $c < a$

    (D) $8a = 10c$

    (E) $8a + 1 = 10c$

Department	Number of Teams	Employees per Team
Development	1	4
Marketing	2	3
Accounting	3	2
Public Relations	5	5

2. The chart above shows the distribution of employees at a company into different teams in different departments. According to the chart, how many total employees are there?

    (A) 14

    (B) 25

    (C) 41

    (D) 84

    (E) 154

GO ON TO THE NEXT PAGE

3. If the average (arithmetic mean) of seven numbers is greater than 7 and less than 12, which of the following could be the sum of the seven numbers?

   (A) 84
   (B) 77
   (C) 49
   (D) 42
   (E) 35

4. Carmel is spinning a basketball on his finger so that it turns around completely every 1.5 seconds. How many degrees does the logo on the ball turn in 10 seconds, assuming it is not on the spinning axis?

   (A)   54°
   (B)   240°
   (C)   720°
   (D) 2,160°
   (E) 2,400°

Questions 5 and 6 refer to the following figure.

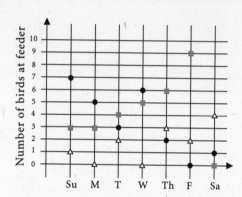

5. Joe kept a record of the birds that visited his backyard for one week. He set out three types of feeders and counted the number of birds that visited each feeder each day. In the graph above, each feeder is represented by a different colored shape. The black circles indicate the feeder with sunflower seeds. The gray squares represent the feeder with thistle seeds. The white triangles represent the feeder with suet. Approximately what percentage of the birds in Joe's yard on Thursday visited the suet feeder?

   (A) 18%
   (B) 27%
   (C) 36%
   (D) 48%
   (E) 55%

6. On what day did the greatest number of birds eat sunflower seeds?

   (A) Sunday
   (B) Tuesday
   (C) Wednesday
   (D) Friday
   (E) Saturday

GO ON TO THE NEXT PAGE

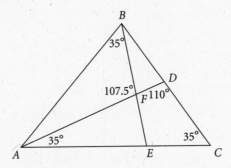

Note: Figure not drawn to scale.

7. In triangle *ABC* above, $\overline{AD}$ and $\overline{BE}$ are line segments. All of the following are isosceles triangles, EXCEPT

(A) $\triangle AFE$

(B) $\triangle ABE$

(C) $\triangle ADC$

(D) $\triangle BFD$

(E) $\triangle ABC$

Questions 8–10 refer to the following sequence of steps.

Choose a number between 0 and 9.9.

Multiply the number from the previous step by 100.

Determine the smallest integer greater than or equal to the number obtained from the previous step.

Add 12 to the number found in the previous step.

Print the resulting number.

8. If 6.127 is the number chosen in step 1, what is the number printed in step 5?

(A) 12

(B) 74

(C) 624

(D) 624.7

(E) 625

9. Which of the following could be a number printed in step 5 after steps 1 through 4 are performed?

(A) −1

(B) 10

(C) 27.3

(D) 674

(E) 1,050

10. Which change, if any, could be made in the order of the steps without changing the number printed in step 5?

(A) Only steps 2 and 3 could be switched.

(B) Only steps 2 and 4 could be switched.

(C) Only steps 3 and 4 could be switched.

(D) Steps 2, 3, and 4 can be done in any order.

(E) None of the above changes can be made.

11. If $x = 3^5$, which of the following expressions is equal to 3^{11}?

(A) $243x$

(B) $3x^2$

(C) $9x^4$

(D) $27x^3$

(E) x^6

12. If $n - 3 = 7 + m$, what is the value of $2(n - m) + 4$?

(A) 8

(B) 12

(C) 17

(D) 24

(E) 29

GO ON TO THE NEXT PAGE

13. If $x = -5$ satisfies the equation $x^2 + 3x + c = 0$, where c is a constant, what is another value of x that satisfies the equation?

(A) -2

(B) 2

(C) 5

(D) 7

(E) 10

14. The sum of three consecutive odd integers is 1,089. What is the greatest integer of the three?

(A) 185

(B) 299

(C) 317

(D) 365

(E) 423

15. Jan can mow her lawn in 60 minutes by herself. If she hires Wally to do it, he takes 30 minutes, while Peter can do it in 40 minutes. If Jan starts mowing the lawn for 15 minutes, then decides to hire Wally and Peter to help her finish, how long will it take (in hours), from when Jan started to when the three finished together?

(A) $\dfrac{1}{6}$ hours

(B) $\dfrac{5}{12}$ hours

(C) $\dfrac{7}{12}$ hours

(D) $\dfrac{3}{4}$ hours

(E) $\dfrac{5}{6}$ hours

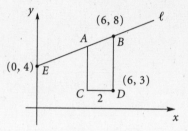

Note: Figure not drawn to scale.

16. In the figure above, quadrilateral $ABDC$ has vertices A and B on line ℓ, point E is also on line ℓ, and the coordinates of B, D, and E are as indicated. What is the area of $ABDC$?

(A) $\dfrac{1}{2}$

(B) $\dfrac{4}{3}$

(C) $\dfrac{11}{3}$

(D) $\dfrac{22}{3}$

(E) $\dfrac{26}{3}$

SECTION 8

Time—20 Minutes

19 Questions

Directions: For each of the following questions, choose the best answer and darken the corresponding oval on the answer sheet.

Each sentence below has one or two blanks, each blank indicating that something has been omitted. Beneath the sentence are five words or sets of words labeled (A) through (E). Choose the word or set of words that, when inserted in the sentence, best fits the meaning of the sentence as a whole.

Example:

Today's small, portable computers contrast markedly with the earliest electronic computers, which were -------.

(A) effective

(B) invented

(C) useful

(D) destructive

(E) enormous

1. ------ two doses of the Hepatitis A vaccine over a period of 6 to 12 months is ------- providing protection from the disease for ten years.

   (A) Constraining . . . required for

   (B) Distributing . . . unsuccessful in

   (C) Reconstituting . . . instrumental in

   (D) Administering . . . effective in

   (E) Disseminating . . . unverified for

2. After all of the passengers were safely aboard lifeboats, the crew of the King Cruiser made every attempt to ------- what scuba diving equipment they could off of the ------- dive boat before it sank.

   (A) qualify . . . obsolete

   (B) salvage . . . floundering

   (C) exacerbate . . . defunct

   (D) revitalize . . . prosperous

   (E) commandeer . . . lucrative

3. Many towns bordering two different countries have a heterogeneous population and can boast of ------- of different foods that incorporate a ------- of various ingredients.

   (A) a multiplicity . . . variety

   (B) a proliferation . . . moderation

   (C) an ambivalence . . . focus

   (D) a dearth . . . depletion

   (E) an abridgment . . . imitation

4. Despite the markings that ranked the trail as moderately difficult, the hikers found the trek to be challenging, as the path was -------; it meandered ceaselessly around the riverbank for miles.

   (A) panoramic

   (B) precipitous

   (C) serpentine

   (D) circumscribed

   (E) retrograde

GO ON TO THE NEXT PAGE

5. After the accident, Jidapa's friends found that her behavior had changed drastically; once sprightly and friendly, she now seemed disheartened and unsociable, the ------- of her former self.

   (A) naysayer
   (B) antithesis
   (C) consequence
   (D) extremity
   (E) mainstay

6. The detectives knew they had to work ------- because any mistakes, even the slightest misstep, would compromise their endeavor.

   (A) perpetually
   (B) temperamentally
   (C) meticulously
   (D) erroneously
   (E) sanguinely

GO ON TO THE NEXT PAGE

Directions: The passages below are followed by questions based on their content; questions following a pair of related passages may also be based on the relationship between the paired passages. Answer the questions on the basis of what is <u>stated</u> or <u>implied</u> in the passages and in any introductory material that may be provided.

Questions 7–19 refer to the following passages.

The following passages represent two points of view about the future of cinema. The first is by a screenwriter arguing for a change in methodology. The second is by a film critic expressing his views on the changing world of film.

Passage 1

Ancient Greek drama, often cited as the crucible of all Western drama, consisted of three types of plays. Comedy was a form greatly affected by changing times and fash-
(5)   ions; tragedy was inspired by mythology and history. The ancient Greeks believed that the dark and brooding form of tragedy required a "relief." Still common today, a relief is designed to be a moment of respite from the
(10) seriousness of the tragic theme. Satyr plays fulfilled that function in ancient Greece. Of these three forms, tragedy has received the most critical and scholarly attention in modern times. It is the Satyr play, however, that
(15) will capture the imagination of the rising generation.
          A Satyr is a mythological creature—half-human and half-beast. This creature appears on stage in the Satyr plays as a character
(20) whose main function is to be part of the coterie of the god Dionysus, a central figure in the Greek theater. Even without the exact characters of Dionysus or the Satyrs, the ideas they embody can still be used in playwriting
(25) or screenwriting today. As ardent followers of their leader, the Satyrs in the plays display a curious mix of cowardice and boldness similar to what we see in Shakespeare's Falstaff.

          The chorus is another dynamic element
(30) of the Satyr play that is full of potential. The chorus, sometimes dancing or singing, can be invisible to the central characters. In this mode, members of the chorus are free to engage the audience without interfering
(35) with the action of the play. At any moment, though, they can step into the world of the play and interact with the other characters. This fundamental boundary crossing is a central reason that this form lends itself to the
(40) modern cinema.
          The Satyr form is widely ignored and has barely been acknowledged by critics and scholars. Screenwriters today persist in looking to tragic and comic forms for inspiration
(45) when there are volumes of untapped potential in the Satyr form. The example of the chorus, "unseen" by the central players at one moment and then jumping in to the center of the scene in the next, gives just a hint of what
(50) the Satyr form has to offer. If you seek an even more unpredictable inspiration, imagine the chorus jumping into the action singing and dancing.

Passage 2

          Of the two primary forms of drama—com-
(55) edy and tragedy—comedy is the more promising form for the future of cinema. Comedy has always been the more stylistically forward form, because it looks to current events for topics and is quick to respond to trends.
(60) While some subject matter has been consistent over the centuries (for example, the lampooning of leaders or the misadventures

GO ON TO THE NEXT PAGE

of husbands and wives), the forms employed
in comedy today can only be described as
(65) sophisticated. Tragedy, on the other hand, has
always looked to the past for subject matter
and the form is consequently nostalgic.

In general, the forms of cinema have become predictable, to the point that the spoof-
(70) ing of some forms has become commonplace.
Modern filmmakers' overuse of a small number of narrative devices has produced a generation of moviegoers who are compelled by
twists and turns. Jaded by their overexposure
(75) to form, they seek out the new and surprising. It is a difficult task indeed to surprise this
generation of media-saturated spectators. But
the comedic form has the requisite flexibility.

There is no limit to the ways in which
(80) comedy can transform and conform itself
to the requirements of any generation. This
assertion is confirmed by the fact that even
in ancient Greece, comedy responded to
fashion and changing aesthetics. History
(85) has proven that comedy suits itself to all
times and circumstances. The only theatrical tradition to survive the fall of Rome was
comic. Even in the darkest times, or perhaps
especially in the darkest times, comedy shines
(90) on. The basic human need for comedy and
comic relief is one thing that has forced the
form toward flexibility. Since people crave
comedy, they do whatever they can, using
form and structure, to create the kind of
(95) comedy they need at the time.

All of this is not to say that making comedy
is easy. Although the comic "form" is wildly
loose, it is not the least bit forgiving. For
this reason, the most impressive work is in
(100) the comic form. The discriminating viewer
of today's cinema recognizes this fact and
rewards successful filmmakers with loyalty.
Today's audience seeks variety, excitement,
and surprise. The filmmakers most likely to
(105) succeed in this market will be those skilled in
the comic form and willing to exploit all of its
potential.

7. The overall tone of Passage 1 is

    (A) muted
    (B) strident
    (C) whimsical
    (D) grateful
    (E) enthusiastic

8. As used in line 34, "engage" most nearly means

    (A) contract with
    (B) propose marriage to
    (C) hire
    (D) lock together with
    (E) hold the attention of

9. The statement that "there are volumes of
   untapped potential in the Satyr form" (lines
   45–46) suggests that

    (A) there are books of Satyr plays not yet
        translated
    (B) numerous movies can be made about
        Greek drama
    (C) many ideas in Satyr plays have not yet
        been explored
    (D) the noise level in Satyr plays is extremely
        high
    (E) there is dormant inspiration in music

GO ON TO THE NEXT PAGE

10. The author of Passage 1 refers to the chorus in paragraph 4 primarily in order to

(A) prove the superiority of the comic form

(B) underline the variety and surprise provided by the Satyr form

(C) emphasize the importance of dancing to the future of cinema

(D) contrast the Satyr character with the chorus

(E) explain why the Satyr form is widely ignored

11. In lines 62–63, "the misadventures of husbands and wives" is an example of

(A) a consistent form of Greek comedy

(B) sophisticated subject matter for comedy

(C) nostalgic subject matter for tragedy

(D) traditional subject matter for comedy

(E) a typical Satyric plot

12. As used in line 74, the word "Jaded" most nearly means

(A) satisfied

(B) rocked

(C) conceited

(D) dulled

(E) surprised

13. In Passage 2, the main purpose of paragraph 3 is to

(A) explain the flexibility of the comedic form

(B) emphasize the importance of ancient Greek civilization

(C) illustrate the tragedy of the fall of Rome

(D) correct a general misunderstanding about the rigidity of comedy

(E) illuminate the significance of intergenerational traditions

14. The word "form" (line 97) is in quotation marks primarily to

(A) emphasize that the author is using the exact definition of the word

(B) indicate that the structure of comedy is not as strict as the word suggests

(C) show that the author intended to use another word

(D) highlight the difference between theater and cinema

(E) refer the reader to a previously mentioned definition of the word

15. Both authors would most likely agree that

(A) ancient Greek theater is relevant to modern cinema

(B) comedy is the most resilient form of drama

(C) tragedy is an irrelevant form in entertainment today

(D) Satyr plays represent a more adaptable form than comedy

(E) modern audiences are bored by the current cinema

GO ON TO THE NEXT PAGE

16. Both authors would most likely the views of the

    (A) chorus
    (B) audience
    (C) critic
    (D) screenwriter
    (E) characters

17. The main idea of Passage 2 is that

    (A) comedy and tragedy are superior to the Satyr form
    (B) American cinema has become too predictable
    (C) comedy is superior to tragedy as a form of drama
    (D) the comic form has the greatest promise for reinvigorating cinema
    (E) American moviegoers are anxious for the release of high-quality comedies

18. The author of Passage 2 might respond to the reference to "Shakespeare's Falstaff" (line 28) in Passage 1 by

    (A) criticizing the misuse of such a famous character in support of an unknown art form
    (B) highlighting the added relevance given to Falstaff by comic aspects Shakespeare accords to him
    (C) contending that characters of Greek and Roman drama are more applicable than those of Elizabethan drama
    (D) arguing that Falstaff would make an excellent template for the hero of a Satyr play
    (E) citing Falstaff as an example of the sophistication of the comic form

19. Which statement best describes the way the authors of Passage 1 and Passage 2 view tragedy?

    (A) The author of Passage 1 considers it to be a depressing form, while the author of Passage 2 considers it to be a sophisticated form.
    (B) Both authors agree that tragedy is the most exalted form of drama.
    (C) The author of Passage 1 believes that tragedy is inferior to the Satyr play, while the author of Passage 2 believes it is superior to the Satyr play.
    (D) Both authors agree that tragedy is likely to receive less attention in the future than other dramatic forms.
    (E) The author of Passage 1 contends that the chorus is an essential element of tragedy, while the author of Passage 2 holds that the chorus is unnecessary in tragedy.

IF YOU FINISH BEFORE TIME IS CALLED, YOU MAY CHECK YOUR WORK ON THIS SECTION ONLY. DO NOT TURN TO ANY OTHER SECTION IN THE TEST.

SECTION 9

Time—10 Minutes

14 Questions

Directions: For each question in this section, select the best answer from among the choices given and fill in the corresponding oval on the answer sheet.

The following sentences test correctness and effectiveness of expression. Part of each sentence or the entire sentence is underlined; beneath each sentence are five ways of phrasing the underlined material. Choice (A) repeats the original phrasing; the other four choices are different. If you think the original phrasing produces a better sentence than any of the alternatives, select choice (A); if not, select one of the other choices.

In making your selection, follow the requirements of standard written English; that is, pay attention to grammar, choice of words, sentence construction, and punctuation. Your selection should result in the most effective sentence—clear and precise, without awkwardness or ambiguity.

EXAMPLE: ANSWER:

Every apple in the baskets <u>are ripe and labeled according to the date it was picked</u>.   Ⓐ ● Ⓒ Ⓓ Ⓔ

(A) are ripe and labeled according to the date it was picked
(B) is ripe and labeled according to the date it was picked
(C) are ripe and labeled according to the date they were picked
(D) is ripe and labeled according to the date they were picked
(E) are ripe and labeled as to the date it was picked

---

1. For a hospital, a backup generator is <u>invaluable so that it</u> provides power in the event of an emergency that disrupts local electrical service.

   (A) invaluable so that it
   (B) invaluable because it
   (C) invaluable, although it
   (D) invaluable in order that
   (E) invaluable because they

2. In his press release, the actor <u>asserted that the media had unfairly biased</u> potential jurors before his trial had even begun.

   (A) asserted that the media had unfairly biased
   (B) asserted of how the media had unfairly biased
   (C) made an assertion of the media having unfairly biased
   (D) made an assertion that the media had unfairly biased
   (E) asserted that unfair bias had been made by the media of

GO ON TO THE NEXT PAGE ▷

3. During the harvest, French <u>vineyards hiring many temporary workers</u>, a large percentage of whom come from Spain.

(A) vineyards hiring many temporary workers

(B) vineyards hires many temporary workers

(C) vineyards hiring many workers who are temporary

(D) vineyards hire many temporary workers

(E) vineyards hire many people who work temporarily

4. <u>In most cases, in the election of a president, the results are determined by a small number of "swing states."</u>

(A) In most cases, in the election of a president, the results are determined by a small number of "swing states."

(B) Generally, the results of a president election are determined by a small number of "swing states" most of the time.

(C) A few "swing states" decide the results of most presidential elections.

(D) A presidential election, as to results, is most often determined by "swing states," of which there are a small number.

(E) Presidential elections generally have a small number of "swing states" that determine their results.

5. Vocational and technical schools offer teenagers the opportunity <u>to start working as electricians, plumbers, auto mechanics, and other jobs</u> immediately after graduation.

(A) to start working as electricians, plumbers, auto mechanics, and other jobs

(B) to start work as electricians, plumbers, auto mechanics, and other jobs

(C) to work as electricians, plumbers, auto mechanics, and other jobs

(D) to start working as electricians, plumbers, and auto mechanics, and in other jobs

(E) to start their careers as electricians, plumbers, auto mechanics, and other jobs

6. In a police lineup, witnesses see several people, <u>there is one who is</u> the suspect.

(A) there is one who is

(B) because one is

(C) one is

(D) one of whom is

(E) of which one is

7. In the nineteenth century, European politicians sought to establish a balance of power in the hope that <u>this had prevented war on the continent</u>.

(A) this had prevented war on the continent

(B) this would prevent war on the continent

(C) war on the continent will be prevented

(D) the continent will find war prevented

(E) this will prevent war on the continent

GO ON TO THE NEXT PAGE

8. <u>Vatican City is one of the most popular tourist destinations in Italy, since it is technically its own country.</u>

(A) Vatican City is one of the most popular tourist destinations in Italy, since it is technically its own country.

(B) Vatican City, one of the most popular tourist destinations in Italy, is technically its own country.

(C) Of the most popular tourist destinations in Italy, Vatican City is technically its own country.

(D) Since it is its own country, Vatican City is technically one of the most popular tourist destinations in Italy.

(E) Since it is technically its own country, one of the most popular tourist destinations in Italy is Vatican City.

9. In the United States, a candidate must be 35 years old before <u>you can run</u> for president.

(A) you can run

(B) it can run

(C) he or she can run

(D) one runs

(E) he or she is running

10. Among the most complex musical compositions of the era, <u>Chopin wrote his Etudes to be performed on the piano.</u>

(A) Chopin wrote his Etudes to be performed on the piano

(B) the piano is what Chopin wrote his Etudes to be performed on

(C) Chopin's Etudes, written to be performed on the piano

(D) Chopin's Etudes were written to be performed on the piano

(E) Chopin, having written his Etudes to be performed on the piano

11. The defendant's lawyer told the jury that <u>he was sorry for the damage he had caused and the people he had hurt.</u>

(A) he was sorry for the damage he had caused and the people he had hurt

(B) his client was sorry for the damage he had caused and the people he had hurt

(C) given the damage caused and the people hurt, he was sorry

(D) his client, sorry for the damage he had caused and the people he had hurt

(E) the damage he had caused and the people he had hurt were what his client was sorry for

GO ON TO THE NEXT PAGE

12. <u>Although the first phase of construction was completed last month and the new wing has opened</u>, the hospital still suffers from a shortage of rooms.

(A) Although the first phase of construction was completed last month and the new wing has opened

(B) Although the new wing has opened, following the completion of the first phase of construction which occurred last month

(C) The first phase of construction was completed last month and the new wing has opened

(D) The first phase of construction was completed last month, resulting in the new wing being open but, even so

(E) The first phase of construction, being completed last month, and the new wing has opened

13. When washing a car, rinse it to remove excess dirt, wipe it with a soapy sponge, and <u>then the car is dried with a clean cloth</u>.

(A) then the car is dried with a clean cloth

(B) dry it with a clean cloth

(C) then drying it with a clean cloth

(D) finally, it is dried with a clean cloth

(E) as a final step, then, you dry the car with a clean cloth

14. <u>Images transmitted by email, sharper and clearer than fax, are</u> quickly making obsolete technologies that were once considered state-of-the-art.

(A) Images transmitted by email, sharper and clearer than fax, are

(B) Sharper and clearer than the fax, images transmitted by email are

(C) Images transmitted by email, sharper and clearer than those transmitted by fax, are

(D) Images transmitted by email, which are sharper and clearer than fax, are

(E) Email transmission of images, sharper and clearer than the fax, are

IF YOU FINISH BEFORE TIME IS CALLED, YOU MAY CHECK YOUR WORK ON THIS SECTION ONLY. DO NOT TURN TO ANY OTHER SECTION IN THE TEST.

STOP

(Answers on the next page.)

Practice Test Three: **Answer Key**

SECTION 1

Essay

SECTION 2

1. D
2. E
3. C
4. B
5. C
6. A
7. B
8. B
9. B
10. D
11. C
12. D
13. C
14. D
15. E
16. E
17. A
18. E
19. C
20. B

SECTION 3

1. D
2. D
3. B
4. D
5. B
6. C
7. E
8. E
9. D

10. E
11. D
12. B
13. C
14. B
15. E
16. E
17. A
18. B
19. E
20. B
21. D
22. A
23. C
24. C
25. C

SECTION 4

1. B
2. B
3. C
4. B
5. A
6. B
7. B
8. E
9. A
10. D
11. B
12. C
13. B
14. B
15. E
16. B
17. E

18. D
19. D
20. B
21. C
22. D
23. D
24. D
25. E
26. E
27. A
28. A
29. C
30. D
31. B
32. E
33. C
34. C
35. E

SECTION 5

1. C
2. A
3. E
4. C
5. C
6. E
7. D
8. A
9. 2
10. 31
11. 18
12. 132 or 198
13. 800
14. 24

15. 192
16. 8/36 or 2/9
17. 235°
18. 9

SECTION 6

1. E
2. C
3. B
4. A
5. A
6. B
7. C
8. E
9. C
10. C
11. B
12. A
13. E
14. A
15. E
16. D
17. B
18. A
19. E
20. C
21. A
22. C
23. D
24. D

SECTION 7

1. A
2. C

3. B
4. E
5. B
6. A
7. D
8. E
9. D
10. C
11. B
12. D
13. B
14. D
15. B
16. E

SECTION 8

1. D
2. B
3. A
4. C
5. B
6. C
7. E
8. E
9. C
10. B
11. D
12. D
13. A
14. B
15. A
16. B
17. D
18. B
19. D

SECTION 9

1. B
2. A
3. D
4. C
5. D
6. D
7. B
8. B
9. C
10. D
11. B
12. A
13. B
14. C

ANSWERS AND EXPLANATIONS

SECTION 1

6 ESSAY

Most people are taught as children that it is important to do things to make other people happy. I remember how great I felt when I brought home the Valentine's Day card I made my mother in first grade. She was thrilled with the sparkly red heart and I was proud that my art project had made her so happy. This is just a small example of the positive reinforcement we receive when we make other people happy, but in the long run pleasing others can be have a negative effect on your life. If you are always guided by other people's desires, instead of discovering what makes you happy, you are more likely to fail than succeed.

I come from a football family, in a football town. My brother had been a star quarterback, and my whole family is very involved in the high school football team. My younger sister is a cheerleader; my mother works at the concession stand during games; and my father is good friends with the coach. I had played football since I was seven, and I was good enough to make the squad of our Division-A team. My parents were thrilled when I made the team in my sophomore year. My father took me aside to tell me how proud he was of me.

My decision to play football was completely motivated by my desire to please my family. What I really wanted to do was run for the cross country team. During football practice, I used to see the cross country team heading off on a long run and I felt so envious. I found the football drills boring, and I began to dread going to practice. During the season, the coach stopped playing me in games because he said I was not trying. He was right; my heart was not in the game. My father got very angry with the coach because he was not putting me in the games, and their friendship suffered. My grades even dropped because I found the situation with football so stressful.

At the end of the season I vowed that I would not play the following year. This summer when I told my parents that I was not going out for football they were not as upset as I thought they might be. I joined the cross country team and have started winning races. I look forward to practice and have made some great friends on the team. My grades are better than they have ever been. My parents still love football, and I discovered that their interest in the local team does not revolve around me. They go to games and cheer as loudly as ever. I even enjoy going to the games, when I don't have a race.

When I was guided by what I thought would make my parents happy, I made myself miserable. When I followed my own interests, I not only succeeded, I think my family is actually happier than when I was trying to please them. You have to seek your own happiness first, as you can only truly succeed at something that you enjoy. Then, as I discovered, you will probably find that the people you are most interested in pleasing will take pleasure in your success.

GRADER'S COMMENTS

All essays are evaluated on four basic criteria: Topic, Support, Organization, and Language. This is a very well-written essay. The writer shows that he understood the topic and took the time to think about it before beginning to write. He sticks to the topic and uses a personal experience to support his stance. His argument is well developed and strongly supported. He never leaves the main point of his example by wandering into another story. He further completes his argument by referring back to his opening remarks about making people happy in the conclusion. Furthermore, the essay has strong organization and is interesting.

The language used by the writer is straightforward and mature. He does not slip into slang or use awkward language in an attempt to impress the reader. His writing style and vocabulary use indicate that he is educated and capable of expressing his position in a constructive manner. He uses different structures for his sentences and paragraphs, and despite a few minor errors, stays in the same tense throughout the essay.

4 ESSAY

To borrow a phrase from President Lincoln, "You can make some of the people happy all the time, and you can make all the people happy some of the time, but you can't make all the people happy all the time." This is especially true in politics. This fall I volunteered on the campaign of a man who was running for mayor of my town. It was the first time I had volunteered on a campaign and I was really excited by what the candidate wanted to accomplish. I really believed in his ideas. For example, he wanted to add money to the school budget so we can have arts classes again. He also wanted to improve public transportation, which was important to me because I have to take the bus.

When the campaign started, the candidate was very idealistic. He was very committed to his ideas. Later into the campaign, however, he started to compromise in order to win more votes. He stopped emphasizing public transportation in his campaign when it seemed unpopular with voters. He even backed away from his proposal for the school budget when it seemed that people weren't willing to support even the smallest increase in taxes. I was very disillusioned by his failure to stick by his ideas and principles. My candidate lost the mayoral race. I think his failure can be attributed to his attempt to please all the voters instead of sticking up for his own ideas.

Instead of trying to win people over to his platform, the candidate tried to accommodate everything all the voters wanted. Even though a politicians job is to represent the people, so in some ways, his or job is to make people happy, a politician has to stand for something otherwise nobody will vote for them. In politics, you cannot please everyone and if you try you will fail. To succeed in politics you have to stick by your own ideas and try to convince other people that you are right.

GRADER'S COMMENTS

All essays are evaluated on four basic criteria: Topic, Support, Organization, and Language. The writer begins by using a quote to express his position on the topic and to preface his argument. In fact, the writer misquotes Lincoln. However, the essay is not about content, so this mistake does not affect the score. The writer uses an example that covers the topic and supports his position. His personal account of the way political success is attributed to the candidate's desire to please all of the voters speaks directly to the heart of the question. The essay is well organized, with an introduction, a body, and a conclusion.

The writer's language is good and mostly grammatically correct; however, the description is very basic and uninteresting. The tone is often very standard and conversational. He could have used more expressive terminology to help prove his point, and the conclusion is not as strong as it could be.

2 ESSAY

It is not easy to be successful. If you are not going to try, you will never be successfull. You have to do things your own way. One time I was friends with a bunch of girls who did everything together. We would call each other everynight to see who was going to where what the next day so we would not wear the same stuff. If everyone was going to the mall then there was no way you could say you were going to go to the do something else. These girls were really into clothes and makeup and jewelry. This was not the only things I was interested in but I went along with the other girls because I wanted to fit in. Then one time I wanted to join the drama club and the other girls said that drama club was not cool and they would never join drama club. I really wanted to be in the play but I didn't want to make my friends mad so I never tried out. When I went to see the play it looked like so much fun I was mad at myself for listening to my friends. When we moved to high school we were not friends as much just some girls stayed friends. Now I do plays and I think it is really fun and even played the lead roll last year. I learned that you shouldn't not do things because of what other people say and you do what you want and then you will be successful.

GRADER'S COMMENTS

All essays are evaluated on four basic criteria: Topic, Support, Organization, and Language. The writer is good about addressing the topic of the statement immediately in her opening sentence and using her friends as her example. However, the development of her example is not as detailed as it needs to be, and her train of thought seems random and all over the place. The organization of the writer's thoughts is loose, and she never returns to her initial stance until the last sentence.

The writer's language is juvenile and doesn't follow the principles of standard written English. She uses slang, such as "cool," and there are many spelling and diction errors. For example, she writes "where" when she meant "wear" and uses a double negative by using "shouldn't not." The last sentence is a run-on that goes nowhere.

SECTION 2

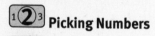 **Picking Numbers**

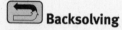 **Backsolving**

 **Eyeballing**

1. D

Don't overthink this one—the x^6 is on each side and can be subtracted from both sides. Subtract x^6 from both sides to get $4 = w$, choice (D).

2. E

To find the minimum total time, add the minimum times for each part; for the maximum total time, add the maximum times for each part:

Minimum $= 22 + 20 = 42$

Maximum $= 28 + 30 = 58$, choice (E).

3. C

Systematically solve for the variables until you have what you're looking for. Start with c, since it's defined in the question stem. Use c to find a, then a to find b:

$a = 8c = 8 \times 9 = 72$

$\dfrac{72}{b} = 4$

$72 = 4b$

$18 = b$, choice (C).

4. B

Convert the scientific notation into a simple number by multiplying it out. Then you can see where the decimal point should be:

$$4.567890 \times 10^2 = 4.567890 \times 100 = 456.7890$$

The decimal point should be between 6 and 7, choice (B).

5. C

The intersection of two sets consists of the elements that are in both sets. In this case, the intersection contains numbers that are both prime and equal to a prime number plus 2.

2 is prime, but is not equal to a prime number plus 2. It is only in set A.

4 is equal to a prime number (2) plus 2, but is not itself prime. It is only in set B.

5 is both prime and equal to a prime number (3) plus 2. Choice (C) is correct.

6. A

Whenever you see a triangle question about angles, remember that the sum of the interior angles of a triangle is 180 degrees:

$$a + b + c = 180$$
$$7c + 2c + c = 180$$
$$10c = 180$$
$$c = 18, \text{ choice (A)}.$$

7. B

Translate the words into algebra, and then let your algebra skills take you home!

Let x be the number of students at the beginning.

After the addition, there are $x + 21$ students, which is 4 times x.

So: $\quad x + 21 = 4x$
$$21 = 3x$$
$$x = 7, \text{ choice (B)}.$$

8. B 👁

Remember that you can always assume the diagram is drawn to scale, unless you're told otherwise. Use this to eliminate wrong answer choices if you get stuck.

Draw a third line parallel to l and m. Find the supplement of the given angles. The angle we want has been split into two angles, each of which is an alternate interior angle with one of the supplements, so $q = 30° + 20° = 50°$, choice (B).

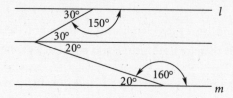

9. B ①②③

When you find the language confusing, try to put it in concrete terms. If you wanted to know how much more 9 was than 7, what would you do? You would subtract: $9 - 7 = 2$ more. So you need to subtract these two algebraic expressions:

$(3x + 9) - (3x - 2) = 3x + 9 - 3x + 2 = 11$, so choice (B) is correct.

10. D ①②③

Remember that you can always plug in numbers for the variables (being careful to follow all the rules you are given).

I. When you multiply by a negative, the inequality flips. If $b > a$, then $-b < -a$. So this statement is always false.

II. If $a < b$, you can add c to both sides to get $a + c < b + c$. Always true.

III. a and b are negative, so their sum will be negative, while c is positive. So this statement will be always true.

Thus, (D) is the correct answer choice.

11. C

The union of two sets includes all the elements that appear in either set. In this case, that means all the numbers between 0 and 5 and all the numbers between 3 and 7. You can combine these ranges and say that the union includes all the numbers between 0 and 7:

$0 \leq x \leq 7$ includes all the numbers between 0 and 7, including both 0 and 7, choice (C).

12. D

When you see fractions set equal to each other, as in this problem, you should cross-multiply to make the equations easier to work with. Next, you should solve one equation for a in terms of b and plug this into the other equation. Then solve this new equation for b. If you have extra time, you might want to double-check your answer by plugging in the values you found for a and b back into the original equations:

$$\frac{10}{a+b} = \frac{4}{a}$$

$$10a = 4(a+b) = 4a + 4b$$

$$6a = 4b$$

$$a = \frac{4b}{6} = \frac{2b}{3}$$

$$\frac{b^2}{18} = \frac{a}{2}$$

$$\frac{b^2}{18} = \frac{\left(\frac{2b}{3}\right)}{2}$$

$$2b^2 = \frac{36b}{3}$$

$$2b^2 = 12b$$

$$b^2 = 6b \quad \text{(Note that you can divide by } b \text{ since you know } b \neq 0.)$$

$$b = 6, \text{ choice (D)}.$$

13. C

Most people find it easier to work with negative exponents if they are written as fractions. Once you've solved the given equation for c, don't forget to square it to find your answer!

$$c^{-\frac{1}{2}} = \frac{1}{\sqrt{c}} = 3$$

$$1 = 3\sqrt{c}$$

$$\frac{1}{3} = \sqrt{c}$$

$$\left(\frac{1}{3}\right)^2 = \frac{1^2}{3^2} = \frac{1}{9} = c$$

$$\left(\frac{1}{9}\right)^2 = \frac{1^2}{9^2} = \frac{1}{81} = c^2, \text{ choice (C)}.$$

14. D

If you're not familiar with transformations of x^2, you can try plugging in some points from the graph into each equation to see which ones fit.

The point $(1, \frac{1}{2})$ is a great point to test—it only works for choice (D). (Even if you're not sure what the y-value of that point on the graph is, you can see that it is between 0 and 1. Choice (D) is the only equation that produces a y-value between 0 and 1 when $x = 1$.)

15. E

The area of a triangle is one-half the length of the base times the height. You need to find the base and height of this triangle. Since $\overline{AC}$ is a horizontal line (that is, A and C have the same y-coordinate), the length of the base is just the difference between the x-coordinates of A and C. The height is the vertical distance between B and the base. This is the difference between the y-coordinate of point B and the y-coordinate of the base:

Base: $7 - 2 = 5$

Height: $6 - 2 = 4$

Area: $\frac{1}{2}(5)(4) = 10$

Thus, choice (E) is correct.

16. E

The perimeter of this triangle is the sum of the lengths of its sides, $AB + BC + CA$. You can find these lengths by using the distance formula, $\sqrt{(x_1 - x_2)^2 + (y_1 - y_2)^2}$, or by sketching in the height of triangle ABC to create two right triangles, then using the Pythagorean theorem. In this case, both approaches take the same amount of time, so use whichever you prefer:

$$AB = \sqrt{(4-2)^2 + (6-2)^2}$$
$$= \sqrt{(2^2 + 4^2)} = \sqrt{(14+6)} = \sqrt{20} = 2\sqrt{5}$$
$$BC = \sqrt{(7-4)^2 + (2-6)^2}$$
$$= \sqrt{(3^2 + (-4)^2)} = \sqrt{9+16} = \sqrt{25} = 5$$

$CA = 7 - 2 = 5$. (Since this is a horizontal line, the distance between A and C is the difference between the x-coordinates of A and C. If you use the formula, you will get the same result.)

Perimeter $= 2\sqrt{5} + 5 + 5 = 10 + 2\sqrt{5}$, choice (E).

17. A

If you're stuck, focus on the differences between the answers; anything that's clearly wrong can be eliminated.

Squares of $2a$ and $3b$:

$(2a)^2$ and $(3b)^2$

Sum of those squares:

$$(2a)^2 + (3b)^2$$

Difference between $8c$ and $7d$:

$$(8c - 7d)$$

Sum of squares added to the difference:

$$(2a)^2 + (9b)^2 + (8c - 7d)$$

3 more than e:

$$e + 3$$

Sum is 3 more than e:

$$(2a)^2 + (3b)^2 + (8c - 7d) = e + 3$$

Thus, choice (A) is correct.

18. E

Remember, slope is $\frac{rise}{run}$ or $\frac{y_2 - y_1}{x_2 - x_1}$, so a slope of zero means the line is horizontal (rise $= 0$), and an undefined slope means the line is vertical (run $= 0$).

This line is vertical, so the x-coordinate stays the same. The only answer choice with the same x-coordinate is choice (E).

19. C

You should be able to immediately know where x and y are each positive and negative. Remember that a negative number times a negative number is positive.

The product will only be positive when either both coordinates are positive, or both are negative, so it must be C, D, or E. D clearly has a small product, so the answer is either C or E. Notice that E's x-coordinate is less than one, which means its product, xy, is less than y. C's x- and y-coordinates both have large values, more than making up for its y being slightly smaller than E's y (thinking in terms of absolute value, since the product gets rid of the negatives). Thus, C, choice (C), will have the largest product. You could also use your answer sheet as a ruler to estimate and confirm this.

20. B ①②③

You're looking for a way to get a and b in the same equation, without n. So solve for n in terms of a, and substitute it into the equation for b:

$$a = 3n + 4$$
$$a - 4 = 3n$$
$$\frac{a - 4}{3} = n$$
$$b = 7 + 9n^2 = 7 + 9\frac{(a-4)^2}{3^2} = 7 + 9\frac{(a-4)^2}{9}$$
$$= 7 + (a - 4)^2 = 7 + a^2 - 8a + 16 = a^2 - 8a + 23, \text{ answer choice (B).}$$

SECTION 3

1. D

The sentence states that Da Vinci was *a painter, sculptor, draftsman, architect, and inventor.* In other words, he could do many things. Therefore, predict "adaptable." This prediction matches (B), *versatile.* None of the other choices matches this prediction. (A), *demonstrative,* means showing feeling. (B), *nebulous,* means lacking form. (C), *meticulous,* means paying careful attention to detail. (E), *metaphoric,* means not literal.

2. D

The word *although* provides a clue that the sentence describes a contrasting relationship. Our prediction needs to contrast with the idea that *some questions on the exam would be the same as those found in the review.* If some review questions will show up on the exam, then those questions are important, or crucial. Predict an answer that means the opposite of this, such as "not important." (D), *supplementary,* matches this prediction because it means extra or not central to. (A), *pivotal,* and (C), *salient,* mean the opposite of our prediction. (B) and (E) do not relate at all to our prediction.

3. B

Start with the second blank. Clues in the sentence, *renowned* and *eminent,* indicate that the second blank must be positive. Predict "famous." Only (B) matches this prediction for the second blank, so it must be the right answer. *Buoyed* means supported. *Prolific* means showing high productivity. *Decried* means criticized. *Mundane* means ordinary and boring.

4. D

The words *at least* are important here. If he was *not particularly talented* as a plumber but had some *years of experience,* then he must have been working as a plumber and at the very least would have been considered a practicing professional. Look for a word that refers to one who simply practices a profession. (D), *practitioner,* is a great match. *Novice* means one who is new at an activity. *Detractor* means one who criticizes.

5. B

The phrase *skilled mediator* is a strong clue. Start with the second blank. Predict "resolving," since that is what a mediator does. Looking at the answer choices, you see that only (B), with *bridging* for the second blank, matches our prediction.

6. C

The clue *plagued* indicates that the first blank is negative. Predict something like "a bad problem." To predict for the second blank, consider the clues *once venerable institution* and *reputation*. The word *venerable* means worthy of great respect. The phrase *once venerable* suggests that the institution is no longer worthy of respect. Since the "bad problem" is *so entrenched,* which means settled or fixed, the institution's reputation would be hard to save. This is a good prediction for the second blank. (C) is the only choice that matches both predictions. *Degradation* means wearing down.

7. E

Start with the second blank. How is the waiter working if he *hopes [to] be promoted?* Predict "hard" or "diligently." The only two choices that match this are (C), *tenaciously,* and (E), *assiduously.* Now look at the first blanks in those choices. *Nonchalance* in (C) means lack of concern, while *ardor* in (E) means passion. A waiter hoping to earn a promotion would work with *ardor,* so (E) is the correct answer. *Sagacity* means wisdom. *Unscrupulously* means dishonestly. *Decorously* means with attention to rules of propriety. *Acrimony* means bitterness.

8. E

Think about the clue *egocentrism*, which means to view one's own ego as a center. The fact that the blank is joined with egocentrism by *and* shows that the two words are linked in meaning. Look for a word that means something like "human-centered." (E), *anthropomorphism,* is a great match for our prediction. *Irrationality* means lack of reason. *Temerity* means rash boldness. *Serendipity* means unexpected good luck.

PUPPY PASSAGE

9. D

In the first two sentences of the passage, the author suggests that returning from the breeder's with *slightly scored shins* and *urine coating* her shoes gave her some idea of the trials to come. In this context, you can infer that *scored* refers to something negative that the puppy did to the author's shins, such as scratching them. (A), *counted*, is a primary definition of the cited word and makes little sense in this context. (B) captures another meaning of scored—being grooved or gouged— but it's unclear what it would mean to say that shins were *indented* by the puppy. Whereas (C), *acquired*, is another meaning of the word, as in scoring a pair of basketball tickets, it makes no sense in this context. (E), *slashed*, is too extreme given the author's use of the word *slightly*. (D), *scratched*, is the best choice.

10. E

The author says that her dog used to be a *tiny menace* but is now a *snoring beast*. This comparison emphasizes how much the once-troublesome small puppy has grown and calmed down, giving the author a sense of *parental satisfaction*. (A) is too extreme; the author indicates that her dog grew, but she does not suggest that the dog became *too* large. (B) does not match the positive tone of the sentence, and it undermines the statement that the author views her dog with pride or satisfaction. (C) is a distortion; the author's reference to *parental satisfaction* in the last sentence indicates that the dog has brought her some happiness. (D) is a misused detail; whereas the passage as a whole indicates that the author feels affection for her dog, the cited words themselves do not make this point. (E) is the best answer.

HERSHEY PASSAGE

11. D

In the first sentence, the author refers to Hershey as a *revolutionary* chocolate-maker and suggests that he was enthusiastic, although his *inexperience* in the candy industry was the downfall of his first candy shop. You can expect the correct choice to match at least one of these characterizations. (A) is out of scope; this sentence does not say whether Hershey was particularly hardworking, or industrious. (B) is a distortion; while the passage indicates that Hershey opened his own business when he was quite young, this information does not necessarily suggest he was exceptionally talented or a *prodigy* for his age. (C) is also a distortion; the passage describes Hershey as *inexperienced* but does not say that he was untalented. (E) is an irrelevant detail; Hershey's commitment *to using high-quality ingredients* is mentioned in the last sentence, not the first. (D) is a good match for your prediction; *groundbreaking* is a good synonym for *revolutionary*.

12. B

Go through the choices one by one, comparing each with the evidence found in the text. Aim to work quickly, but not so quickly that you compromise accuracy. (A) is a distortion; the passage indicates that Hershey acquired this practice from another candy maker. (C) is out of scope; the passage indicates that Hershey learned to use quality ingredients from the caramel manufacturer, but it does not say that he tried to apply the *techniques* he learned there to chocolate-making. (D) is too extreme; whereas the passage suggests that Hershey was successful and that he was dedicated to the candy industry from a young age, it does not imply that he could *only* have succeeded at candy making. (E) is also out of scope; the passage only begins describing Hershey at age 18 and does not say whether his interest in candy-making originated in early childhood. (B) is the best choice; the author indicates that Hershey was *enthusiastic* about candy-making when he opened his shop at age 19 and that he was still *hooked on it* after his shop closed six years later.

ART PASSAGE

13. C

Your notes should list something like "a discussion of defining art" as the purpose of paragraph 2; if not, skim for the words *endeavor* and *problematic*. Either way, you should find that the first sentence of paragraph 2 says, *Before we can begin a discussion of artistic decline, we must first define the word "art," an endeavor that has proven problematic.* (A), (B), (C), and (D) are all distortions; the author discusses improving the education system, (A), in later paragraphs, but the author never characterizes this as a *problematic endeavor*. The author discusses how education can make art more relevant, (B), by linking it to historical and sociological developments, but the author never characterizes this as a *problematic endeavor*. Likewise, in later paragraphs, the author discusses what students should learn in school, (D), but the author never characterizes this as a *problematic endeavor*. Finally, also in later paragraphs, the author discusses whether or not to teach art, (E), but the author never characterizes this as a *problematic endeavor*. (C) is exactly as the passage states and is correct.

14. B

Since you are given the part of the passage from which you must draw the inference, skim paragraph 2 to find evidence of what the author characterizes as *too much time spent*. In lines 40–44 the author says that *far too much time has been spent arguing over whether a teen movie is more or less art than* Citizen Kane *is, or whether the music of a boy band is more or less art than are the works of Sondheim*. Now examine the answer choices by comparing them to this information and eliminating those that do not necessarily have to be true based on it. (A) is opposite; whereas the author discusses comparisons of "classics," the author does so in order to highlight the comparison of such classics to modern works, thereby judging the modern works' artistic merits. (C) and (D) are misused details; the author mentions them in later paragraphs. (E) is a distortion; the author never discusses comparisons of works traditionally considered classics to each other; the author discusses their comparison to newer works. (B) is the correct answer; the author implies that too much time has been spent comparing modern works to more established works in order to judge the modern works' artistic merits.

15. E

Your task is to determine why the author included this detail in the passage. Your notes should tell you that the author uses most of paragraph 1 to bemoan or lament the decline of artistic appreciation and awareness in America. Since the author thinks that it is *sad* that America concerns itself with *teen movies and boy bands*, then the author must think that film noir, jazz, and abstract expressionism are better. Thus, he must be mentioning them in order to draw a comparison and suggest their superiority. Look for that in the answer choices. (A) is a distortion; whereas the author does seem to be appealing to a sense of a lost golden age, he uses that as part of the comparison to newer art to suggest their inferiority. (B) is opposite; far from making a historical parallel, this author suggests that newer works are inferior. (C) is out of scope; the author never examines the history of art. (D) is a misused detail; the author uses different details in a later paragraph to remind readers of this. (E) is just as we predicted.

16. E

The sentence in question states: *Many claim that such discussion can be seen as snobby, even culturally imperious.* Since the author states that many people might think the discussion is *snobby* and then goes on to say *even culturally imperious*, the author must be using *imperious* as a higher degree of the same meaning as *snobby*. (A), *imperative*, is not a higher degree of snobbery. (B) is incorrect; when something is *arbitrary*, it is not carefully chosen, which means that it cannot relay the meaning of snobbery. (C), *regal*, simply means elegant in a royal way. While this may be associated with snobbery, it does not convey the same meaning. (D), *urgent*, is a dictionary meaning of *imperious*, but it makes no sense in the context of the original sentence. (E) is the answer; *arrogant* can be used as a higher degree of snobbery. When placed into the original sentence, it replaces *imperious* perfectly.

17. A

Both paragraphs 3 and 4 discuss aspects of artistic education. Skim for any language that might stand out of the text. In this case, the phrase *lost by the general public* should help you find the relevant detail in paragraph 3: . . . *a better education in art will better equip them to judge the artistic merit of these newer, more trendy art forms, or at least place these art forms in historical context and analyze them as an outgrowth of societal and sociological trends—an important aspect of artistic knowledge that has been lost by the general public.* Now find the answer choice that matches an ability to place art works in a *historical context and analyze them as an outgrowth of societal and sociological trends.* (B) is a misused detail; the definition of *art* is discussed earlier in the passage as a problematic endeavor for society, not an important aspect of artistic knowledge that has been lost. (C) is out of scope; the author never discusses the general public's ability to produce art that rivals the classics. (D) is a distortion; whereas the author does suggest ways the general public can better judge art works, the author never states that the general public has lost the ability to judge the merits of current art works. (E) is also a misused detail; the author discusses the value of all forms of art during the discussion of the definition of art. (A) is correct; this matches the first part of the author's detail.

18. B

Reread the lines in question in order to find evidence of what distinguishes the author's *hypothetical United States*. Parents read to their children and educate them. These parents also give their children *art books, classical recordings, and plays as gifts*. Now evaluate each answer choice, choosing the one that must be true based on the author's statements. (A) is out of scope; the author's statements deal with a new interest in art, not new interests in general. (C) is a misused detail; the author never mentions school in the piece of the paragraph mentioned by the question. (D) is out of scope; the author's statements discuss sharing enthusiasm for art, not other activities. (E) is a distortion; in the referenced lines, the author never alludes to the value of artistic skill. (B) is correct; the lines in question describe a country in which parents share their interests in and enjoyment of art with their children, so it must be true that this is what the author finds distinguishing about this hypothetical country.

19. E

Since you are given specific line numbers, your first step should be to reread the relevant lines, which state, *In school, students receive an education in art history, classical music, and opera. This curriculum can also include pop-culture such as the music videos, teen movies, and pop music students enjoy in their free time.* Now use this information to evaluate the answer choices, choosing the one that must describe such an educational model. (A), (B), (C), and (D) are all distortions; whereas the author's statements describe an education that examines a diverse body of art forms, the author never mentions which, if any, are valued, (A), over others or whether or not the students would learn to respect, (B), the views of all artists. In fact, a critical examination might lead students to disrespect the views of certain art or artists. The author's statements describe an education that reflects upon art forms, but the author never describes an education that reflects on the nature of art education, (C). Likewise, the author describes an education that examines both classical and contemporary art, (D), but the author never describes whether one would be valued over the other. (E) is correct; the author describes an education that explores both classical and contemporary art, including pop culture; such a model is wide-ranging in its exploration.

20. B

Your notes might indicate that, in paragraph 3, the author advances a vision of an artistically educated society. If your notes do not indicate this, then simply revisit the paragraph by skimming it, and then evaluate what the author does in this paragraph. The author provides a description of a more artistically educated America. Thus, the author must have included the paragraph in order to propose or provide a vision of a more artistically educated society. (A) is a distortion; the author merely provides a vision of a more artistically educated society, not a *utopian* one. (C) and (D) are out of scope; in paragraph 3, the author never examines whether pop culture leaves a *lasting impact* on society, (C), and the author never deals with *classic literature* and younger students, (D). (E) is also a distortion; whereas the author proposes studying both, the author never states that *contemporary and classical works are interchangeable.* (B) is the best answer.

21. D

Use the line numbers to locate and reread the situation described by the author. The author states that since *art, music, and culture are inextricably tied to literary and historical developments that themselves stem from changes in society and culture*, the educational system should focus on a more *holistic* approach that teaches *students in an intertextual and multidisciplinary manner*. Find the answer choice that must be characteristic of this education. (A) and (B) are distortions; the author describes an artistic education, not an *elitist* one, (A), or a *philanthropic*, meaning charitable one, (B). (C) is the opposite; *eclectic* means mixed together from various elements. This might seem true, but eclectic implies a mismatching of items. The author argues that literature, art, and history are not mismatched at all. (E) is also opposite. *Rudimentary* means basic; the education described by the author goes beyond the basics and fundamentals by contextualizing art within other developments in society, thus creating an overarching education. (D) is correct; the author describes an education that takes an overarching view. *Comprehensive* characterizes this.

22. A

In lines 119–121, the author states that *this system would require more funding, and most likely higher taxes*. Find the answer choice that must be true based on this information. (B), (C), (D), and (E) are all distortions; clearly, the author believes that the new system would be better, but the author's statements don't provide evidence that the new system would be *more celebrated,* (B), *more controversial,* (C), *more interesting,* (D), or *more likely to inspire,* (E), than the current system. (A) is correct; because the new system would require more funding and probably higher taxes, it must be true that the new system would be *more expensive.*

23. C

As you should have noted while reading the passage, the topic is the decline of artistic knowledge and appreciation in America. The author outlines causes for this decline then proposes a solution, choice (C). Look for an answer choice that says something similar to this. (A) is a distortion; in the first paragraph, the author does shift the focus of the debate from analyzing causes to proposing solutions, but the author does not attempt *to shift the focus of the debate from causes to effects.* (B), (D), and (E) are all out of scope; the author never supports a side in a debate, (B), the author does not *revive a discredited idea,* (D), or *promote certain types of art,* (E). The author promotes art education in general.

24. C

Paragraph 3 contains the discussion of the author's hypothetical United States. Skim the passage for any facts regarding the production of higher quality art. Lines 79–82 state, *When these children grow up, some may produce their own art, which would likely be higher in quality than the pop music and movies produced today.* In lines 72–79 the author states that *a better education in art will better equip them to judge the artistic merit of these newer, more trendy art forms, or at least place these art forms in historical context and analyze them as an outgrowth of societal and sociological trends . . . general public.* Now compare each answer choice to this information. (A) is a distortion; the author never links parents to the production of better art. (B) is too extreme; the author presents a more artistically educated society, but the author never goes so far as to claim that this *society would not accept lower-quality art.* (D) and (E) are also distortions; the author never mentions *free time,* (D), or discusses how *critics would judge the merits of the art more harshly* in this hypothetical society, (E). (C) is correct; the author presents children with better artistic educations, and then states that they would grow up to produce better art. Thus, their production of better art must stem from their artistic education.

25. C

In the first paragraph of the passage, the author states that the cultural decline in society has many causes, including *the media's focus on pop culture and the general decline of taste this breeds* (lines 12–14). It is clear from this statement and the continuing tone of the passage that the author believes that a narrow focus on pop culture is inappropriate, making (C) the best choice. (A) and (B) are out of scope; there is not evidence in the passage to support either statement, and quite the contrary, there is plenty of evidence against both (A) and (B). (D) and (E) are misused details. The author discusses education, but he believes society would benefit from a more artistic and classically geared music education, and this would eliminate the possibility of his feeling that pop music was more important than classical music.

SECTION 4

1. B

Although the passive voice will not always be incorrect on the SAT, when you see a passive structure, look for an active version among the answer choices. *Flying is unable to be afforded by her* is a passive (and much wordier) version of *she cannot afford to fly.* Since the first clause already mentions flying, *to do so* is an acceptable variation; (B) is correct. *That* in (C) and *it* in (D) do not have clear antecedents. (E) is unnecessarily wordy.

2. B

Transition words must express the correct relationship between ideas. As written, this sentence does not use an appropriate transition to express the contrast between ideas. (B) corrects this with the transition word *although*. (C) and (E) express a cause-and-effect relationship between the clauses that is inappropriate in context. (D) is a sentence fragment.

3. C

Sentences should be structured so that any modifying words or phrases clearly refer to one specific item. As written, this sentence does not make clear what was *popular among high school students in the 90s: the love story* or the *teen movie*. (C) clarifies the sentence's meaning. (B) introduces a verb tense that is incorrect in context. (D) and (E) are sentence fragments.

4. B

Pronouns must always have clear antecedents. Here, the only plural antecedent for the pronoun *they* is *bylaws,* but *bylaws* don't *pay . . . wages.* (B) clarifies that it is *the university* that can no longer *pay reduced wages.* The pronoun *them* in (C) has no logical antecedent. (D) is unnecessarily in the passive voice, and the pronoun *their* has no logical antecedent. The plural verb *are* in (E) does not agree with the singular subject *consequence.*

5. A

Be methodical in eliminating wrong answer choices, but if you don't spot an error, don't be afraid to choose (A). This sentence is correct as written. (B) creates a run-on sentence. (C) and (D) have incorrect grammatical structure. (E) is awkward and not very clear.

6. B

Transition words must express the correct relationship between clauses. The transition word *but* indicates contrast. In this sentence, the second clause expands on the information presented in the first, so *but* is incorrect. (B) corrects this error with an appropriate transition word, *because.* Neither the conjunction *and* in (C) nor the transition word *since* in (D) expresses the correct relationship between the clauses. (E) is awkward.

7. B

Choose the most concise answer that does not introduce any additional errors. Although not technically a run-on, this sentence consists of two independent clauses with no indication of how they are related. By making the first clause dependent, (B) indicates the relative importance of the two ideas. (C) does not address the error. (D) creates a cause-and-effect relationship between the clauses that is not present in the original. (E) is awkward and loses some of the meaning of the original.

8. E

Items in a series, list, or compound noun or verb must be parallel in structure. The object of the preposition *by* is the compound *an increase . . . and because there has been a decrease.* (E) makes the second part of the compound parallel to the first. Choices (B), (C), and (D) do not make the items parallel.

9. A

If you don't find an error, don't be afraid to choose (A). This sentence is correct as written. (B), (C), and (D) unnecessarily introduce the passive voice. (E) has grammatically incorrect structure.

10. D

A pronoun must have a clear antecedent and agree with that antecedent in gender and number. The problem here is the pronoun *their*. We don't know to whom *their* refers, since the sentence has no plural nouns. (D) is the only choice that eliminates the pronoun. (B) and (C) do not address the error. (E) replaces *their* with the singular pronoun *its,* but the pronoun's antecedent is still unclear.

11. B

Certain idioms appear regularly on the SAT; learn their proper structure. This question tests your knowledge of the idiom that compares two nouns using *as*; the correct construction is *as (adjective) as*. Only (B) correctly completes the construction. (C) is grammatically incorrect, (D) is unnecessarily wordy, and (E) does not correct the error.

12. C

The pronoun *whom* is in the objective case and cannot be used as the subject of a verb. (C) should be in the subjective case (who) because it is the subject of the verb phrase *had . . . scored.* (A) correctly uses *that* as a conjunction. (To check this, you can reverse the sentence order: "The sportscasters were shocked *that* the team with the worst record won. . . . ") The adverb in (B) correctly modifies the verb *won*. (D) is the appropriate verb tense in context.

13. B

The past perfect verb tense is only correct when used to refer to one completed action that precedes another. Since there is no other past action referred to in this sentence, (B) should simply be the past tense *worked*. The verb in (A) agrees with its singular subject *performance*. In (C), the infinitive *to raise* is appropriate in context. (D) is a correctly used prepositional phrase.

14. B

All verbs within a sentence must agree in tense, unless more than one time frame is referenced. The present tense verb in (B) is not consistent with the rest of the sentence; it should be *knew*. (A) correctly expresses the contrast between the two clauses in the sentence. (C) and (D) are properly used prepositional phrases.

15. E

The SAT writing sections will contain a total of five to eight sentences that contain no errors. (A) uses an appropriate preposition in context. (B) is a correct use of the infinitive verb form. (C) correctly shows the cause-and-effect relationship between the two clauses. (D) is a properly used prepositional phrase.

16. B

Unless context indicates that more than one time frame is referenced in a sentence, verb tenses should remain consistent. Since the rest of the sentence is in the past tense, (B) should be as well. (A) is a correct idiomatic usage. (C) and (D) use appropriate prepositions.

17. E

If you don't spot an obvious error, check each answer choice in turn. (A) is an appropriate preposition in context. (B) shows the cause-and-effect relationship between the two clauses in the sentence. (C) is the correct verb tense in context. (D) properly uses an adjective to modify a noun.

18. D

Adjectives (including participles) can only be used to modify nouns and pronouns. In (D), the participle verb form *increasing* is an adjective used to modify the adjective *nervous*. Adjectives cannot be used to modify other adjectives, however; (D) should be *increasingly*. (A) is the proper relative pronoun to refer to a person. (B) is correct use of the infinitive. (C) is appropriate use of the past perfect tense, since it refers to an action completed before another stated past action (*grew . . . nervous*).

19. D

Related nouns in a sentence must agree in number. A plural number of *dancers* would have to take a plural number of *places*; the error is in (D). (A) properly uses an adjective to modify a noun. (B) is an appropriate verb phrase in context. (C) correctly uses the gerund *rustling* and the preposition *of*.

20. B

In a compound verb, the verbs must be in parallel form. The simple predicate of the main clause in this sentence is *got . . . and driving*; (B) should be *drove*. (A) is a correctly used prepositional phrase. The verb in (C) is consistent in tense with the rest of the sentence. (D) is a correctly placed modifying phrase.

21. C

The correct verb form for a modifying phrase is the gerund (*-ing*) form. The verb *refuses* in (C) has no subject; without a conjunction to make it part of the predicate of the main clause, it would have to be changed to *refusing* to create a grammatically correct sentence. (A) uses the proper preposition in context. In (B), the adverb is used correctly to modify the verb *waits*. (D) is a correct verb phrase to describe a future action.

22. D

A sentence requires an independent clause that expresses a complete thought. Both clauses of this sentence are subordinate. Changing the gerund form in (D) to *greeted* would make the second clause independent, correcting the error. (A) is an appropriate preposition in context. (B) and (C) are idiomatically correct phrases.

23. D

All verbs within a sentence must agree in tense, unless a verb is included in a phrase that implies a different time from the rest of the sentence. The present tense verb in (D) is inconsistent with the rest of the sentence; *preferred* is the correct form here. (A) properly uses an adjective to modify a noun. In (B), the gerund is correctly used. (C) correctly expresses the contrast between the two clauses in the sentence.

24. D

Even a sentence with numerous nouns and verbs can be a fragment, if there is no independent clause. As written, this sentence is a fragment. Changing (D) to *was constructed* would remedy this. (A) is an appropriate use of the relative pronoun *which*. In (B), the superlative form is used correctly, since presumably there are more than two symbols of the Cold War. (C) is a correctly used prepositional phrase.

25. E

Expect some sentences to be correct as written. (A) and (B) are proper uses of an adjective and an adverb, respectively. (C) is the correct conjunction in context. The prepositional phrase in (D) is used correctly.

26. E

If you don't spot an obvious error, check each choice in turn. (A) is correct idiomatic usage. The pronoun in (B) clearly refers to *Mrs. Ramsay.* (C) is an appropriate verb phrase in context. (D) is proper use of the infinitive.

27. A

Verbs must agree in number with their subject nouns. (A) correctly uses an adverb to modify a verb, but the plural verb form *choose* does not agree with its singular subject *student.* (B) is the appropriate relative pronoun in context. (C) is consistent verb tense use and uses the correct preposition. (D) properly uses an adjective to modify a noun.

28. A

Make sure each sentence has an independent clause that expresses a complete thought. As written, this sentence is a fragment, since neither clause is independent. Changing (A) to *serves* would correct the error. (B) is an appropriate conjunction in context. (C) correctly uses an adjective to modify the noun *soups.* (D) is a properly used prepositional phrase.

29. C

In a compound verb construction, all verbs must be in parallel form. *To drip and throwing* is grammatically incorrect; (C) should read *dripping.* (A) is consistent verb tense usage. (B) is correct idiomatic usage. (D) properly uses an adverb to modify the compound verb.

30. D

By making *scientists* rather than *a theory* the subject, (D) puts the sentence in the active voice without changing its meaning. It also eliminates the pronoun *It,* which is used here with no antecedent. (B) eliminates the ambiguous pronoun, but does not address the passive problem. (C) and (E) correct the errors, but they are both sentence fragments.

31. B

Here, *institutes* is incorrectly in the present tense, since the sentence is talking about something that happened *in the latter half of the twentieth century.* (B) corrects the error. *Consequently,* in (A), correctly relates this sentence to the previous one. (C) is not idiomatically correct English. (D) misrepresents the relationship between the two ideas. (E) introduces a verb tense that's incorrect in context.

32. E

The relative pronoun *who* is used when referring to people; *that* and *which* are used for things. Since *people* is the noun the pronoun *that* is referring to here, the pronoun should be replaced with *who*. (E) does this, without introducing any additional errors. (B) misuses the comparative form *more*. (C) does not correct the error, and replaces the correct *those* with *them*. (D) is wordy and awkward.

33. C

As written, this sentence is a fragment, since neither of these clauses is independent. By changing the gerund (-*ing*) verb form, which can never be a predicate verb, to *appeared*, (C) corrects the error. (B) corrects the fragment error, but introduces an inappropriate verb tense. (D) does not address the error. (E) creates a complete sentence, but does so in the passive voice.

34. C

(C) combines the sentences, correctly using *but* to indicate the contrast between the first two clauses and *while* to make the third clause subordinate. (A) merely strings the sentences together without relating their ideas. (B) misuses the semicolon, since the second clause is not independent. In (D), the transition word *so* indicates an inappropriate cause-and-effect relationship between the first and second clauses. (E) is a sentence fragment, with no predicate (main) verb in an independent clause.

35. E

The transition words *although* and *but* both indicate contrast, so having one in each clause is unnecessary. The sentence could be corrected by eliminating either of them, but only (E) does this without introducing any additional errors. (A) and (B) suggest eliminating *although*, but they also involve changing *but* to another transition word, which alters the relationship of the ideas in the sentence. (C) incorrectly uses *or* to join two subordinate clauses. (D) simply replaces the second contrast transition word with a different one, but doesn't address the problem.

SECTION 5

1. C

Radical equations are not difficult, even though they may look complicated. Just remember to follow each step carefully, and you'll get the correct answer every time. Also, remember that backsolving is often a good strategy for attacking radical equations:

$$3\sqrt{x} - 31 = -13$$
$$3\sqrt{x} = 18$$
$$\sqrt{x} = 6$$
$$x = 36, \text{ choice (C)}.$$

2. A ⮌

Rational equations can be solved just like any other equation. Just remember to follow the order of operations carefully, and you can solve these equations easily:

$$\frac{3x-9}{2x+7} = 8$$
$$3x - 9 = 8(2x + 7)$$
$$3x - 9 = 16x + 56$$
$$-13x = 65$$
$$x = -5, \text{ choice (A)}.$$

3. E

This question is a simple application of the distance formula. Keep track of which points you're using for x_1 and x_2, as well as y_1 and y_2, and this will be an easy question.

Use P for (x_1, y_1) and Q for (x_2, y_2):

$$\text{Distance} = \sqrt{(x_1 - x_2)^2 + (y_1 - y_2)^2}$$

$$\sqrt{(-2-5)^2 + (4-(-2))^2}$$
$$= \sqrt{(-7)^2 + 6^2} = \sqrt{49 + 36} = \sqrt{85}, \text{ or choice (E)}.$$

4. C

Don't worry if you see a symbol you've never seen before—the operation will be defined in the problem. All you need to do is plug in the given values. Be sure to do anything in parentheses first:

$$2\nabla 3 = 2 - 3 + 2 = 1$$
$$1\nabla 1 = 1 - 1 + 2 = 2, \text{ choice (C)}.$$

5. C

You can use concrete numbers to get a handle on the situation.

Try $a = 6$ and $b = 3$:

(A) $a + b = 9$. Eliminate.

(B) $a - b = 3$. Eliminate.

(C) $a + b + 1 = 10$. Works!

(D) $ab = 18$. Eliminate.

(E) $ab + 3 = 21$. Eliminate.

6. E

Any side of a triangle must be larger than the difference between than other two sides and less than the sum of the other two sides. In choice (E), $12 = 5 + 7$, so the "triangle" would be totally flat.

7. D

Your task here is to translate English into math—what does "the ratio of $2k$ to $6s$" really mean?

The ratios described in the question can be written as:

$$\frac{2k}{6s} = \frac{6k + 5}{18s + 10}$$

Cross-multiply and simplify to get:

$$2k(18s + 10) = 6s(6k + 5)$$
$$36ks + 20k = 36ks + 30s$$
$$20k = 30s$$
$$k = 1.5s$$

You can see that statement I is never true, statement II is not necessarily true, and statement III must be true. If you're not sure about that, you can try plugging in numbers that fit each statement to see if they make the described ratios equivalent. Choice (D) is correct.

8. A

If two chords have equal length, they are the same distance from the center of the circle. Remember to add all the information from the question stem to the figure.

Because *GEFH* is a square, its area is equal to the length of a side squared:

$$81 = EF^2$$
$$9 = EF$$

Since the chords are the same distance from the center of the circle, $EJ = KF$:

$$EF = EJ + JK + KF$$
$$9 = 2(EJ) + 5$$
$$2 = EJ, \text{ choice (A) is correct.}$$

9. 2

Remember that the solutions of a quadratic function are the values of *x* where the function equals zero. Where does this function equal zero?

The function equals zero at $x = 2$ and $x = -2$. Since you can't grid a negative number, grid in 2.

10. 31

You don't even have to turn this into algebra if you don't want to—just work backwards:

$2 for the first 14 days

$4.55 – $2 = $2.55 for the rest of the days

$$\frac{\$2.55}{\$0.15} = 17 \text{ additional days}$$

$17 + 14 = 31$ days total.

11. 18

Draw a diagram so you can see what's going on:

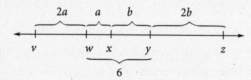

$\overline{WY} = 6 = a + b$ and $\overline{VZ} = 3a + 3b = 3(a + b) = 3(6) = 18$

12. 132 or 198

This question may look daunting, but we have two very useful pieces of information: $AA + AA$ is a 3-digit number that's divisible by 3, and it's also twice a 2-digit number where both digits are the same:

$2(AA)$ = covered number.

Knowing $2(AA)$ is 3 digits narrows the possibilities down to $AA = 55, 66, 77, 88$, or 99.

But it also must be divisible by 3, which we can only get from 66 or 99.

So the covered number is $2 \times 66 = 132$ or $2 \times 99 = 198$.

13. 800

Combinations are very similar to probabilities. How many ways can she make the first choice? How many ways can she make the second choice? Multiply these numbers to get the number of combinations:

$25 \times 32 = 800$

14. 24

Think about what has to happen for them to be as close together as possible—make the first Friday fall as late as possible.

The latest the first Friday can be is the 7th, which makes the last Friday the 28th and the last Monday the 31st. The last Monday falls $31 - 7 = 24$ days after the first Friday.

15. 192

Computing $(100 \sim 5)$ would take forever, so there must be an easier way. If a question on the SAT is taking a long time or you find yourself setting up an extremely complicated computation, you're probably missing a shortcut:

$(100 \sim 5) = 100 + 99 + 98 + \cdots + 6 + 5$

$(98 \sim 3) = 98 + 97 + \cdots + 6 + 5 + 4 + 3$

So when you subtract them, everything from 98 to 5 cancels out, leaving $100 + 99 - 4 - 3 = 192$.

16. $\dfrac{8}{36}$ or $\dfrac{2}{9}$

Don't forget that the fraction of 360 degrees a sector has is also the fraction of the circle's area it contains and the fraction of the circumference that its arc takes up. Don't stop too soon and grid the number of degrees in angle AOE—remember to make it a fraction:

$EOB = DOF = 60°$

$AOE = 180° - (60° + 40°) = 80°$

$$\frac{80°}{360°} = \frac{8}{36} = \frac{2}{9}$$

17. 235°

If you ever forget the formula for the number of degrees in a polygon, just divide it into triangles by drawing in some diagonals.

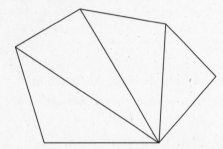

The sum of the interior angles in a polygon with n sides is $(n - 2) \times 180° = (6 - 2) \times 180° = 720°$. Or, as shown above, you can divide it into 4 triangles and deduce that the sum of the angles is $4 \times 180° = 720°$.

Since the known angles sum to $160° + 95° + 110° + 120° = 485°$, the remaining angles must sum to $720° - 485° = 235°$.

18. 9

She will clean the house on days 7, 14, 21 . . . (multiples of 7) and do laundry on days 5, 10, 15 . . . (multiples of 5). Think about what has to be true of days where both happen.

The least common multiple of 7 and 5 is 35. So every 35th day she will do both. This will happen $\frac{315}{35} = 9$ times.

SECTION 6

1. E

The semicolon in this sentence provides a structural clue: the second clause explains the first. *Unquestionable* is a clue and can in fact serve as our prediction. (E) is a perfect match. *Immaterial* means not important. *Nominal* means token or insignificant.

2. C

At least one of the blanks must describe why marathons are challenging. Think of a prediction for the second blank. Marathons are mentally "challenging" or "difficult." Both (A) and (C) match this prediction for the second blank. (C) is the right answer because *illusory*, which means appearing real, doesn't fit the context of the sentence. *Indulgent* means lenient. *Dubious* means questionable or doubtful.

3. B

The sentence provides several good clues: *healthy lifestyle, exercising regularly,* and *nutritious diet.* From these clues, we can predict something like "health" or "long life" for the first blank. Only (A) matches this prediction, and *hampered*, which means made difficult, fits the context for the second blank. *Belied* means proved false. *Bolstered* means strengthened or supported.

4. A

This sentence contains two contrast clues: *despite* and *apparently.* The man appeared to be one way, but the sentence states that he was actually *known to drink to excess.* Our prediction needs to provide a contrast that means "not drinking to excess." (A), *temperate,* means exactly this. *Laconic* means tending not to speak much. *Duplicitous* means not truthful. *Aesthetic* means relating to art or beauty. *Voluble* means talkative.

5. A

The first part of the sentence contains a great clue: *accurately predicted.* Nostradamus was able to make predictions that included knowledge of *vehicles that were not invented . . . until after . . . he wrote.* Therefore, our prediction for this blank could be "foreknowledge." (A) means precisely this. *Avarice* means greed. *Complicity* means involvement as an accomplice in a crime. *Mendacity* means untruthfulness.

ENERGY PASSAGES

6. B

What are the author's feelings or opinions about the fact that acid rain continues to exist despite the development of technologies that could eliminate it? An important clue comes in the final sentence, where the author uses the word *senselessly* to suggest that there seems to be no rational or understandable reason why the new technologies are not more widely used. (A) is a distortion; the author never expresses any *astonishment* that acid rain continues to be a problem, and Passage 1 never mentions the *developed world* in particular. (C) is too extreme; the word *nothing* in this choice goes further than the author's *little.* (D) is out of scope; although the cleaner technologies are new, the passage does not state that they are *experimental*. (E) is opposite; the author states that acid rain can produce *often irreversible environmental damage*. (B) is the best choice.

7. C

The author of Passage 2 describes how the most-developed nations *have the luxury of squabbling over* questions that the poorer countries can't afford to consider, indicating that the wealthier nations have choices and advantages not shared by others. (A) is a distortion; the author does not say whether developed nations are concerned about the energy choices available to poorer countries. (B) is out of scope; their degree of responsibility is not discussed in the passage. (D) is also a distortion; the passage does not mention any negative consequences resulting from blatant carelessness or the *squabbling* of developed nations. (E) is opposite; the author suggests that *less-developed* nations cannot afford cleaner fuels. (C) is the best answer.

8. E

The scope of Passage 2 is limited to the difference between the developed world—which has the *luxury of squabbling* over a variety of energy issues—and poorer nations, which are forced to deal with the human damage caused by the *only natural resource they can afford*. Therefore, the second author would probably reply that new and cleaner energy-generating technologies are not adopted by some countries because they can't afford them. (A) is out of scope; nowhere in Passage 2 does the author mention the responsibilities of wealthier nations. (B), (C), and (D) are distortions and are not supported by the text. (E) is the correct answer.

9. C

Passage 1 focuses on the fact that there are cleaner alternatives to the conventional burning of fossil fuels, whereas Passage 2 focuses on the fact that poorer nations are stuck with the cheaper (but more damaging) coal. However, although their emphases are different, both authors recognize the basic point that burning fossil fuels can be harmful. (A) is a distortion; only Passage 2 addresses the cost difference between clean and conventional technologies. (B) is too extreme; neither author makes such a strong statement, and the author of Passage 1 actually suggests that acid rain can be avoided. Both (D) and (E) are not supported by both passages. (C) is the correct answer.

SHELTER PASSAGE

10. C

The passage begins with a description of what the author envisioned doing in her work at the shelter: *conducting intake interviews and traipsing around from organization to organization seeking the legal, psychological, and financial support that the women would need to rebuild their lives*. At the end of the passage, she relates how her unanticipated baking endeavor made her *a more sensitive and skillful social worker*. You are looking for a choice that expresses her changed view of social work. (A) is too extreme; although the author's *reality* did differ from what she expected, the passage does not focus on her shock, but rather on how she responded to it. (B) is out of scope; the passage does not address the author's psychological constraints. (D) is a misused detail; although the bakery was for-profit, business abilities are not the focus of the passage. (E) is also a misused detail; the fact that the author was abroad in a *developing country* is not emphasized in the passage. (C) is correct; the author came to see social work as being more diverse than she originally envisioned.

11. B
The paragraph preceding the citation indicates that the author had spent a significant amount of time imagining her work and felt *thoroughly prepared*. It is thus likely that she arrived at the shelter with a positive, confident attitude. (A) is opposite; the last two sentences of the first paragraph indicate that the author felt self-assured. (C) is a misused detail; although she was uninformed about the actual content of her job, the author does not express this until later in the paragraph. (D) is also opposite; the author was energetic, not exhausted. (E) is a distortion; the author was not incompetent, only unprepared to run the bakery. (B) is the best choice.

12. A
The author's enthusiasm at the beginning of the second paragraph contrasts with her shock a few sentences later when she discovers she will be in charge of the bakery. Her references to the *case studies* she researched reveal that she was initially enthusiastic about the *concept* of the bakery, not necessarily about her practical involvement in it. (B) is opposite; initially, the author felt *out of [her] depth* at being put in charge of the bakery. (C) and (D) are distortions; initially the author had little knowledge of baking, (C), and the author only later found that the bakery *improved the women's self-esteem*, (D). (E) is out of scope; the passage does not address the author's beliefs about such projects in general. (A) is the best choice.

13. E
The author believed that starting the bakery presented a *problem*, and she never mentions any political experience or ambitions. We can infer that the author feels she is equally unsuited to perform either activity. (A) is too extreme; the fact that the author feels *unprepared* does not mean she thinks the bakery will *never* work. (B) is a distortion; although the author did not expect the bakery to be part of her job, this doesn't mean she believes it should not be. (C) and (D) are out of scope; the author's feelings about her coordinator are not discussed, (C), and no connection is made between the skills necessary for politics and those needed for baking bread, (D). (E) is correct. The comparison makes the author's lack of preparation clear.

14. A

Just before the cited sentence, the author relates one problem: she was unprepared to bake bread. In the cited sentence, the author relates a second problem: she was *completely unfamiliar with for-profit business models*. This second problem, she suggests, was the *bigger* one that might pose more of a challenge. (B) is a distortion; the author is discussing her own comparative lack of preparation for each activity, not the relative importance of each. (C) and (E) are misused details; the coordinator's confidence is mentioned in the *next* sentence, and the author does not express a belief that confidence in for-profit business models is misplaced, (C), nor does the fact that the coordinator *left* the author mean she was unwilling to help, only that she did not, (E). (D) is out of scope; the passage does not compare the relative complexity of for-profit and non-profit business models. (A) is the correct answer.

15. E

The author makes two points in this sentence: baking improved her self-confidence as well as that of the shelter residents, and simple activities can be helpful in social work. Look for a choice that picks up on one or both of these ideas. (A) and (B) are distortions; the women's self-confidence and the author's increased together, but this does not mean that their self-confidence levels were initially equal. Also, although social work can be *as simple as kneading dough*, this does not necessarily mean it is an easy profession for those who (unlike the author) have no education. (C) and (D) are out of scope; the author's prior expectations about learning new skills are not discussed, and (D) is too general because baking is the only hands-on activity discussed. (E) is the best answer. The *benefit* is increased *self-confidence*.

LEISURE PASSAGE

16. D

This passage has both introductory and concluding paragraphs. Reread those for an overview of the author's purpose. (A) is a misused detail; while the author says many successful people participate in athletics, it is not the purpose of the passage. (B) is a distortion; the author does not directly compare physical and artistic activities, nor is the passage theoretical in nature. (C) is a misused detail; pleasure is mentioned as a benefit of recreation but not as a major point of the passage. (E) is out of scope; the requisites for vocational success are not discussed in detail in this passage. (D) is the correct answer.

17. B

Limit your deliberations about meaning to the quoted clause and the sentence that contains it. (A), (D), and (E) are all out of scope; the author does not say that leisure time is preferable to work, (A), does not refer to the democratic or any other form of government, (D), and does not make a recommendation about frequency of recreational activities, (E). (C) is opposite; the passage states that leisure time has been augmented or increased. (B) is the best answer.

18. A

Follow the logical chain of benefits mentioned in the second paragraph to find the most important one. (B) is a distortion; this answer has a negative connotation that does not reflect either the question or the passage. (C) is too extreme; the word *always* exaggerates the expressed benefits of competition. (D) is out of scope; although this may be a true statement, it is not to be found in the passage. (E) is a misused detail; this relatively minor point is mentioned in passing. (A) is correct.

19. E

Match the tone of the answers to the tone of the words and sentences adjoining the word *competition*. (A) is opposite; note the words *without. . . competition* and, later in the paragraph, *needless comparison*. (B) is a distortion; the passage does not assign importance to comparative physical activities. (C) is a misused detail; whereas the author approves of enjoyment of recreation, the passage does not rank its importance. (D) is also opposite; this answer is basically a reworded version of (A) and should be eliminated for that reason alone. (E) is the best answer.

20. C

First, evaluate (for correctness) the advantage suggested after each roman numeral; then find the correct answer. (A) and (B) are limited; roman numeral I is correct but is not the only advantage mentioned in the passage, and roman numeral II is correct but is not the only advantage mentioned in the passage. (D) and (E) are out of scope; roman numerals I and II are correct, but aesthetic aspects of art are not mentioned in the passage. (C) is the best answer.

21. A

Carefully examine the context of the word, in this case, the comparison of life to a turbulent sea. (B) is a misused detail; the metaphor of the sea is not applicable in this part of the sentence. (C) is limited; *situations* is much too mild a term in this context of comparison to a sea where one might need a lifejacket. (D) misconstrues the preceding metaphor of a turbulent sea. (E) counts on your being distracted by the previous mention of rules. (A) is the best answer.

22. C

Because the answer choices are adjectives, compare each one to the adjective in the quoted phrase. (A) is out of scope; the passage does not comment on the necessity of standardized testing. (B) is a misused detail; this answer could be justified by reference to the word *ever-narrowing*, but that is very different from *irrelevant*. (D) is also out of scope; the passage does not comment on whether or not standardized testing is productive. (E) is opposite; *ever-narrowing* is the opposite of *creative*, which implies expansive. (C) is the best answer.

23. D

Notice that each paragraph of the passage discusses positive aspects of productive leisure activities in terms of their benefits to individuals. (A) is opposite; the passage addresses the benefits of productive recreation for individuals, not for society. (B) is a misused detail; *emotional flexibility* is mentioned in connection with creative activity, but physical flexibility is not discussed. (C) and (E) are too extreme; the word *requisite*, (C), means necessary, and this is an exaggeration of the author's position. Likewise, the word *ubiquitous*, (E), means everywhere or always present, not a position taken by the author. (D) is the best choice.

24. D

The statement *learn to swim in a turbulent sea of ambiguity and chance without the lifejacket of standard procedure* is being used as a metaphor for the unorthodox world that artists often live in. The author is expressing the fact that those involved in this world often make decisions and have experiences that those who live by the normal societal standards may not have, which is the opposite of (B). (A) and (E) have nothing to do with the passage, and (C) is never supported by the author. (D) is the best choice that expresses this idea.

SECTION 7

1. A

If $a < b$ and $b < c$, then $a < c$;

$8a < 3b < 10c$, so $8a < 10c$, answer choice (A).

2. C

If a problem at the beginning of a section seems easy, it probably is. All you have to do is be careful that you don't make a silly arithmetic error.

Employees by division:

Development $= 1 \times 4 = 4$

Marketing $= 2 \times 3 = 6$

Accounting $= 3 \times 2 = 6$

Public Relations $= 5 \times 5 = 25$

Overall total: $4 + 6 + 6 + 25 = 41$, choice (C).

3. B

You can rearrange the average formula to get whichever part you're missing.

For example, sum = (average) × (number of items):

$$7 < \frac{\text{sum}}{7} < 12$$

$49 < \text{sum} < 84$, choice (B).

4. E

We know that one revolution is 360°. Since this happens every 1.5 seconds, (A) and (B) are definitely too low.

The ball goes around $\frac{10}{1.5} = \frac{100}{15} = \frac{20}{3}$ times, for a total of $\frac{20}{3}$ (360°) = 2,400°, choice (E).

5. B

You need to find the total number of birds in Joe's yard on Thursday and the number of those birds that were at the suet feeder. Divide the number of birds at the suet feeder by the total number of birds, then multiply by 100 to convert this fraction into a percent.

There were 3 birds at the suet feeder on Thursday, and 6 + 3 + 2 = 11 total birds. $\frac{3}{11} \times 100\% = 27.\overline{27}\%$. The nearest answer choice is (B), 27%.

6. A

Sunflower seeds are represented by the black circles. Find the black circle that is highest on the *y*-axis, and look down to see what day it belongs to.

The greatest number of birds at the sunflower seed feeder was 7, on Sunday. Choice (A) is correct.

7. D

This problem is testing two concepts: the sum of the angles in a triangle is 180 degrees, and the definition of an isosceles triangle. Remember that if two sides of a triangle have the same length, the angles opposite them have the same measurement.

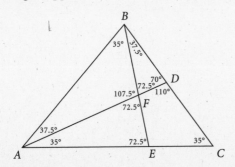

Use the facts that the interior angles of a triangle sum to 180° and that angles along a line sum to 180° to solve for the unknown angles, as in the figure. Then you can see that *ABC*, *AFE*, *ADC*, and *ABE* are all isosceles; *BFD* is not, choice (D).

8. E

This problem is designed to let you try out this procedure. Don't worry about having major insights—just plug in the given number and see what happens. This will help you gain the insight you need for the next two questions:

1. Choose 6.127
2. $6.127 \times 100 = 612.7$
3. The smallest integer greater than or equal to 612.7 is 613 (just round up)
4. $613 + 12 = 625$
5. Print 625

Thus, choice (E) is correct.

9. D

You can attack this by either trying to work backwards with each of the answers or thinking about what kinds of results you can get from the procedure:

1. Choose a number 0–9.9.
2. Result is between 0 and 990.
3. Round up to nearest integer—now number is an integer between 0 and 990.
4. Add 12—now number is an integer between 12 and 1,002.
5. Print the number from step 4.

(A) Doesn't work because it's too small.

(B) Doesn't work because it's too small.

(C) Is not an integer.

(D) Is the correct answer.

(E) Is too large.

10. C

Try plugging in a number into the reordered steps to see if you still get the same answer.

We can try 6.127 again (the number doesn't change in step 5, so we'll only show 1–4):

(A) Step 1. 6.127

Step 3. 7

Step 2. 700

Step 4. 712

This does not match with what we found in #8, so it does not work.

(B) Step 1. 6.127

Step 4. 18.127

Step 3. 19

Step 2. 1,900

This does not match with what we found in #8, so it does not work.

(C) Step 1. 6.127

Step 2. 612.7

Step 3. 624.7

Step 4. 625

This works. Notice that since we're adding an integer, it doesn't matter whether we add first or round first.

(D) Doesn't work, since (A) and (B) don't work.

(E) Not true, since (C) works.

11. B

Don't waste time trying to write fancy expressions for 3^{11} in terms of x—just convert the answer choices into powers of 3:

(A) $243x = 3^5(3^5) = 3^{10}$. Eliminate.

(B) $3x^2 = 3(3^5)^2 = 3(3^{10}) = 3^{11}$. Works!

(C) $9x^4 = 3^2(3^5)^4 = 3^2(3^{20}) = 3^{22}$. Eliminate.

(D) $27x^3 = 3^3(3^5)^3 = 3^3(3^{15}) = 3^{18}$. Eliminate.

(E) $x^6 = (3^5)^6 = 3^{30}$. Eliminate.

12. D [1 (2) 3]

In many cases you can't solve for the variables individually, but you can solve for some expression in terms of them:

$$n = 10 + m$$
$$n - m = 10$$
$$2(n - m) = 20$$
$$2(n - m) + 4 = 24, \text{ choice (D)}.$$

13. B

Use the value of x to solve for c; then find the other value by factoring:

$$(-5)^2 + 3(-5) + c = 0$$
$$25 - 15 + c = 0$$
$$c = -10$$
$$x^2 + 3x - 10 = 0$$
$$(x + 5)(x - 2) = 0$$
$$x = -5; x = 2, \text{ choice (B)}.$$

14. D

Always make sure you're answering the right question. All the good algebra in the world doesn't help if you grid in the smallest or middle number:

$$x + (x + 2) + (x + 4) = 1,089$$
$$3x + 6 = 1,089$$
$$3x = 1,083$$
$$x = 361$$
$$x + 2 = 363$$
$$x + 4 = 365$$

Numbers are 361, 363, 365, choice (D).

15. B

Work methodically, using the rate formula. Don't be discouraged by a somewhat higher level of complexity—if you understand rates, then this is simply more steps.

Their respective mowing rates are:

Jan: 1 hour per lawn or 1 lawn per hour

Wally: $\frac{1}{2}$ hours per lawn or 2 lawns per hour

Peter: $\frac{2}{3}$ hour per lawn or $\frac{3}{2}$ lawns per hour

Jan mows for $\frac{1}{4}$ hours at 1 lawn per hour, so she finishes $\frac{1}{4} \times 1 = \frac{1}{4}$ of the lawn.

Together, the three mow $1 + 2 + \frac{3}{2} = \frac{9}{2}$ lawns per hour, or $\frac{2}{9}$ hours per lawn.

The final part takes $\frac{3}{4}$ lawn $\times \frac{2}{9}$ hour per lawn $= \frac{1}{6}$ hours.

So the total time is $\frac{1}{4} + \frac{1}{6} = \frac{5}{12}$ hours, choice (B).

16. E

Use the slope of the line to find AB, then split the quadrilateral into a triangle and a rectangle:

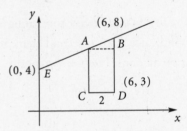

The slope of the line is $\frac{8-4}{6-0} = \frac{4}{6} = \frac{2}{3}$.

The coordinate of C is (4, 3).

When we move from E to A, the x-coordinate changes by 4, so the y-coordinate changes by $4 \times \frac{2}{3} = \frac{8}{3}$, thus the coordinates of A are $(4, 4 + \frac{8}{3}) = (4, \frac{20}{3})$.

If you split the quadrilateral, the area of the triangle is $\left(\frac{1}{2}\right) \times (2) \times \left(8 - \frac{20}{3}\right) = \left(\frac{1}{2}\right) \times (2) \times \left(\frac{4}{3}\right) = \frac{4}{3}$.

The area of the rectangle is $2 \times \left(\frac{20}{3} - 3\right) = 2 \times \frac{11}{3} = \frac{22}{3}$.

So the total area is $\frac{4}{3} + \frac{22}{3} = \frac{26}{3}$, choice (E).

SECTION 8

1. D

Start with the first blank. Vaccines can either be given or not given. If your prediction for the first blank is "giving," then the second blank should be positive in order to support this answer choice. A good prediction for the second blank would then be something that is "successful" at providing protection. This is a great match for *effective,* in (D). None of the other choices provide a good match for this prediction, so (D) is the correct answer. *Constraining* means limiting. *Reconstituting* means restoring wholeness. *Disseminating* means spreading widely. *Unverified* means not proven.

2. B

The first part of the sentence contains the clues *passengers* and *safely aboard lifeboats.* Predict that the first blank has something to do with "saving" the equipment. For the second blank, predict "sinking" or "endangered." (B) is a great match for both of these predictions. *Obsolete* means outdated. *Exacerbate* means make worse. *Defunct* means no longer functioning. *Commandeer* means seize. *Lucrative* means profitable.

3. A

The words *heterogeneous* and *different* provide good clues for the first blank. Predict something like "a large variety." Near the end of the sentence, the clue *various* indicates that the second blank also means something similar to "variety." (A) matches both of our predictions. *Proliferation* means abundance. *Dearth* means scarcity. *Depletion* means using up.

4. C

The semicolon in this sentence provides a great structural clue: it defines the blank. Using the clue words *meandered ceaselessly,* we can predict something like "curved" or "followed a winding path." (C), *serpentine,* matches our prediction perfectly. *Panoramic* means taking in a wide view. *Precipitous* means positioned as on the edge of a cliff or, simply, dangerous. *Circumscribed* means bounded or limited by constraints. *Retrograde* means moving backward.

5. B

The words *changed drastically* and *once* paired with *now* are clues that this sentence expresses opposites. In fact, the word in the blank must mean opposite, since the sentence contains two opposing pairs of clues: *sprightly* is the opposite of *disheartened,* and *friendly* is the opposite of *unsociable.* (B), *antithesis,* means polar opposite and so is a great match for our prediction. A *naysayer* is a person with a negative outlook. A *mainstay* is a source of crucial support.

6. C

The clause after *because* serves as a clue that defines the blank. Since *any mistakes . . . would compromise* the endeavor, we can predict that the detectives must work "carefully" or "in an exact and precise manner." (C) is a perfect match for this prediction. *Sanguinely* means done in a cheerful or hopeful way.

CINEMA PASSAGES

7. E

Since the author is trying to convince or persuade the reader that the Satyr form is worthy of pursuit, you can expect the correct answer to have a positive charge. The author predicts that Satyr plays will *capture the imagination of the rising generation* and sees the chorus as a *dynamic element* that contributes to the *untapped potential* of the Satyr form. Together with the exclamation point ending the passage, this phrasing gives the passage a tone of *enthusiasm* or *excitement*. (A) is opposite; the tone is excited, not dull or faint. (B) is a distortion; the author's discussion does not have a harsh tone overall. (C) is also a distortion; although the last paragraph is somewhat playful, overall the passage does not have a carefree or impulsive tone. (D) is out of scope; what the author hopes for has not taken place. He has nothing to be *grateful* for. (E) is the best answer.

8. E

Read for context. The chorus dances and sings and although *invisible* to other characters, can *engage the audience without interfering* with the main action. Predict something like *draw the attention of the audience*. (A), (B), (C), and (D) are all out of scope and relate to another meaning of the word that doesn't make sense in context. (E) is the best answer choice.

9. C

The author's main point in the passage is that the Satyr form has not received as much attention as it deserves. The cited line supports this point by suggesting that screenwriters should seek inspiration in Satyr plays because these plays have *volumes of untapped potential*. Look for a choice that notes the unexplored possibilities in Satyr plays. (A) and (B) are out of scope; translations are not discussed in the passage, (A), and possible *movies about Greek drama*, (B), are not mentioned. (D) is a distortion; in this context, volume is a matter of amount, not noise level. (E) is a misused detail; singing is mentioned elsewhere in the passage, but this is not related to the cited phrase. (C) is the best answer choice.

10. B

The chorus is first mentioned in paragraph 3, but this question asks about the *fourth* paragraph. In paragraph 4, the author suggests that the chorus provides *a hint of what the Satyr form has to offer* and says that it can embody *unpredictable inspiration*. This functions to reinforce the description from paragraph 3 of the chorus as a *dynamic element . . . that is full of potential*. Look for a choice that emphasizes the chorus's unpredictability or dynamic potential. (A) is opposite; the author is arguing that the Satyr form is worthy of more study. (C), (D), and (E) are misused details. The chorus dances, (C), but this is not the point the author is making here. Satyrs, as creatures, are mentioned earlier in the passage, but this paragraph only mentions the Satyr *form* of drama, (D). Although the author does say the form is *widely ignored*, the chorus is not mentioned in order to explain this fact, (E). (B) is the best answer.

11. D

Along with *the lampooning of leaders*, *the misadventures of husbands and wives* is given as an example of subject matter for comedy that has been *consistent over the centuries*. Look for a choice that captures the long-term use of this subject matter. (A) is a distortion; whereas this may have been tempting, there is a distinction between *form* and *subject matter* that is important in this sentence and in the passage as a whole. Also, the consistency of use is not restricted to *Greek* comedy. (B) is also a distortion; again, this choice confuses form with subject matter. The form is described in the passage as sophisticated, not the *subject matter*. (C) is incorrect because the cited detail is an example of subject matter for comedy, not tragedy. (E) is a misused detail; Satyr plays are discussed in Passage 1, not Passage 2. (D) is the best answer.

12. D

The gist of the paragraph is that, while moviegoers have become so used to common narrative devices that it's hard to surprise them, the comedic form is still flexible enough to do so. Since overexposure makes moviegoers *jaded* and unsurprised, you can infer that the word has a negative connotation. *Unsurprised* works fine as a prediction. (A) is opposite; this lacks the negative connotation required by the prediction. (B) is a distortion; this choice picks up on a similarity with jade, the mineral, but it is not the meaning in this passage. (C) is out of scope; this doesn't make sense in context. (E) is also opposite; moviegoers are *not* surprised by common narrative devices. (D) is the best answer.

13. A

The last sentence of paragraph 2 leads you to anticipate more discussion of comedy's *flexibility*, which is exactly what you get in paragraph 3. Look for a choice that mentions the changeable or *flexible nature of comedy*. (B) is a misused detail; although the comedic form originally came from ancient Greece, the purpose of this paragraph isn't to emphasize the importance of ancient Greek civilization as a whole. (C) is also a misused detail; the author mentions the fall of Rome in order to point out that comedy survived the fall, not to talk about the fall itself. (D) is a distortion; the author's focus is on the flexibility of comedy, but the passage does not suggest that there is a *general misunderstanding* of comedy as rigid. (E) is out of scope; the paragraph is about the flexibility of comedy for many generations, not intergenerational traditions beyond the sphere of comedy. (A) is the best choice.

14. B

A form is a structure, model, or mode. To say that a form is *wildly loose* is to create a contradiction. So the author puts quotation marks around the word *form* to suggest that the word shouldn't be taken too literally. (A) is the opposite; if the author were using the exact definition, there would be no need for quotation marks. (C), (D), (E) are all distortions. If the author intended to use another word, (C), presumably he would have; although the author discusses both theater and cinema, (D), the quotation marks do not highlight a difference between them; and the author frequently uses the word earlier in the passage, (E), but does not define it. (B) is the best answer.

15. A

The first author emphasizes the potential of Satyr plays, while the second author emphasizes the strengths of comedies. Despite these differences, however, both authors agree with the broad idea that current filmmakers and screenwriters can learn from the plays of antiquity. Even if this similarity doesn't occur to you right away, you can recognize it when you evaluate the choices. (B) is out of scope; the author of Passage 1 does not discuss comedy's flexibility or resilience as compared to other dramatic forms. (C) is too extreme; although neither author focuses on the potential value of tragedy, this choice is stronger than warranted by the text. (D) is also out of scope; the author of Passage 2 does not discuss Satyr plays. (E) is a distortion; both authors offer suggestions for making successful films, but they do not imply that audiences "are bored by the current cinema." (A) is correct; whereas the author of Passage 2 does not emphasize Greek theater as much as the first author does, he does reference it in the course of his argument.

16. B

Working by elimination is a good way to approach this question. The correct choice will be something discussed by both authors, and something both see as valuable. The audience fits this bill. The first author describes the chorus's ability to *engage the audience* as a strength of Satyr plays, and the second author mentions how the audience *rewards successful filmmakers with loyalty*. (A) is out of scope; the *chorus* is not mentioned in Passage 2. (C) is a distortion; the first author only mentions critics briefly in a negative light, and the second author does not directly discuss critics at all. (D) and (E) are also out of scope; screenwriters, (D), are mentioned in Passage 1, but the only job title mentioned in Passage 2 is that of filmmaker, and although this may initially seem tempting, a closer examination reveals that Passage 2 does not mention characters, (E), at all. (B) is the best answer.

17. D

Sometimes the author will state the purpose right away, as in the first sentence here—*Of the two primary forms of drama . . . comedy is the more promising form for the future of cinema.* The rest of the passage supports this thesis. Use this quote as your prediction. (A) is out of scope; Passage 2 does not discuss *the Satyr form.* (B) is a misused detail; whereas the author makes this point, it is not *the main idea* of the passage. (C) is too extreme; the author indicates that comedy is *more promising* for the cinema, not *superior* in every way. (E) is a distortion; this exaggerates points made in the text and is hardly the author's main point. (D) is the best answer.

18. B

Passage 1 describes the *mix of cowardice and boldness* in Falstaff, but says little else. The author of Passage 2 is most concerned with advocating the comic form as the best way of breathing new life into the cinema. Look for a choice that incorporates that main idea in some way. (A) is out of scope; the author of Passage 2 does not comment on the Satyr form. (C) is a distortion; the author of Passage 2 does directly mention *Greek and Roman drama*, but says nothing about *Elizabethan drama.* (D) is out of scope; the author of Passage 2 does not comment on Satyr plays. (E) is a distortion; whereas the author of Passage 2 does mention *the sophistication of the comic form,* nothing indicates that Falstaff—based on the brief comment the first author makes about him—is *an example* of that sophistication. (B) is correct; this matches well with the main idea of Passage 2.

19. D

For questions like this, keep each author's main purpose in mind as you read through the answer choices to eliminate incorrect ones. (A) is incorrect because it distorts details from both Passage 1 and Passage 2. Passage 1 states that the Greeks considered tragedy *bleak,* but that is not the view of the author. Passage 2 states that comedy, not tragedy, is a *sophisticated form.* (B) is out of scope. Neither author expresses this view. The first statement in (C) is tempting, but (C) is incorrect because its second statement is not justified; Passage 2 does not mention the Satyr play at all. (D) is correct because both authors focus on something other than tragedy as a form that is likely to receive attention in the future. (For Passage 1 it is the Satyr play; for Passage 2 it is comedy.) (E) is incorrect because Passage 2 never mentions the chorus.

SECTION 9

1. B

This sentence presents a cause (providing emergency power) and its effect (being invaluable). *Because,* in (B), best reflects this relationship. The transitions in (C) and (D) do not properly relate the clauses. (E) uses a plural pronoun to refer to a singular antecedent, *generator.*

2. A

This sentence contains no error. The pronoun *of* in (B) is idiomatically incorrect with *assertive*. (C), (D), and (E) are unnecessarily wordy.

3. D

As written, this sentence is a fragment. (D) corrects this by replacing the gerund form with *hire*. The verb in (B) doesn't agree with its plural subject, *vineyards*. (C) does not address the error. (E) is unnecessarily wordy.

4. C

As written, this sentence is unnecessarily wordy. (C) is concise, yet contains all of the information in the original. Using both *generally* and *most of the time*, as (B) does, is redundant. (D) and (E) are both unnecessarily wordy.

5. D

Technical school graduates work *in other jobs*, not *as . . . other jobs*. (D) is the correct choice here. Choices (B), (C), and (E) are not in parallel form.

6. D

As written, this is a run-on sentence. (D) corrects this by making the second clause dependent. (B) implies a causation that doesn't exist in the original. (C) does not address the error. (E) incorrectly uses the pronoun *which* to refer to a person.

7. B

The past tense is not correct for a result that had not yet happened at the time. *In the hope* indicates that the result may or may not occur, so *would prevent* is the appropriate verb phrase here; the correct choice is (B). *Will prevent* would only be appropriate if the rest of the sentence were in the present tense, so (C), (D), and (E) are incorrect; additionally, (C) unnecessarily introduces the passive voice.

8. B

The sentence as written contains a logical error. The word *since* suggests incorrectly that there is a cause-and-effect relationship between the first and second parts of the sentence. (B) corrects this problem by eliminating *since*. (C) is not grammatical, since the sentence's opening phrase *of the most popular* seems to begin a comparison that the sentence never completes. Like (A), (C), and (E) are incorrect because the word *since* creates an illogical statement.

9. C

The pronoun *you* cannot be used with the antecedent *candidate*. (C) replaces *you* with the appropriate third-person pronouns. (B) uses *it* to refer to a person. (D) and (E) use verb tenses that are inappropriate in context.

10. D

As written, this sentence says that Chopin was *among the most complex musical composition of the era*. Both (C) and (D) place the correct noun, *etudes*, after the modifying phrase (a possessive, such as *Chopin's* here, functions as an adjective), but (C) creates a sentence fragment. In (B), the introductory phrase modifies *piano*. (E) does not address the error; additionally, it creates a sentence fragment.

11. B

In this sentence, *he* could refer to either the defendant or the lawyer. (B) and (D) both make it clear about who *was sorry*, but (D) creates a sentence fragment. (C) and (E) do not address the ambiguity issue.

12. A

This sentence is correct as written. (B) and (D) are unnecessarily wordy. (C) creates a run-on sentence. (E) is incorrect grammatical structure.

13. B

The first two verbs in the series are *rinse* and *wipe*; *dry* would be the correct form for the third verb. None of the other choices make the third verb parallel.

14. C

The sentence as written compares what is being transmitted, *images*, to a method of transmission, *fax*. (C) corrects this by using the pronoun *those* to refer to *images*. (B), (D), and (E) fail to address the error.

COMPUTE YOUR SCORE

These scores are intended to give you an approximate idea of your performance. There is no way to determine your exact score for the following reasons:

- Various statistical factors and formulas are taken into account on the real test.

- For each grade, the scaled score range changes from year to year.

- There is no way to accurately grade your essay on these Practice Tests. Additionally, there will be two graders reading your essay on the real test.

The official score range for each section of the SAT will be 200–800. Taken together, the perfect total score becomes 2400.

STEP 1: SCORE YOUR ESSAY

Your essay will account for one-third of your writing grade, and the multiple-choice questions will account for two-thirds. Your essay is scored on a scale from 1–6, and that score is later calculated with the multiple-choice score into the 200–800 range.

Naturally, it will be difficult for you to score your own essay here. Ask someone whose opinion you respect to read it and assign it a value from 1 to 6, based on the following criteria:

6. **Outstanding essay**—Though it may have a few small errors, it is well organized and fully developed with supporting examples. Displays consistent language facility, varied sentence structure, and range of vocabulary.

5. **Solid essay**—Though it has occasional errors or lapses in quality, it is generally organized and well developed with appropriate examples. Displays language facility with syntactic variety and a range of vocabulary.

4. **Adequate essay**—Though it has some flaws, it is organized and developed adequately with some examples. Displays adequate but inconsistent language facility.

3. **Limited essay**—Does not adequately fulfill the writing assignment and has many flaws. Has inadequate organization and development, along with many errors in grammar and/or diction. Has little variety.

2. **Flawed essay**—Demonstrates some incompetence with one or more weaknesses. Ideas are vague and thinly developed. Has frequent errors in grammar and diction and has no variety.

1. **Deficient essay**—Demonstrates incompetence, with serious flaws. Has no organization, no development, and severe grammar and diction errors. Is so seriously flawed that basic meaning is obscured.

STEP 2: FIGURE OUT YOUR RAW SCORE FOR EACH PRACTICE TEST

First, check your answers to the multiple-choice questions against the answer keys on the previous pages. Count up the number of answers you got right and the number you got wrong for each section. Remember, do not count questions left blank as wrong. Round up to the nearest whole number. Next, plug them in to the scoring tables provided for each Practice Test.

Note: Grid-in questions do not have a wrong-answer penalty. So do not deduct anything for wrong answers.

DIAGNOSTIC TEST

CRITICAL READING

	Number Right	Number Wrong	Raw Score
Section 2:	☐	− (.25 × ☐) =	☐
Section 4:	☐	− (.25 × ☐) =	☐
Section 7:	☐	− (.25 × ☐) =	☐

Critical Reading Raw Score = ☐
(rounded up)

WRITING

Section 1: ☐
(Essay Grade)

	Number Right	Number Wrong	Raw Score
Section 6:	☐	− (.25 × ☐) =	☐
Section 9:	☐	− (.25 × ☐) =	☐

Writing Raw Score = ☐
(rounded up)

MATH

	Number Right	Number Wrong	Raw Score
Section 3:	☐	− (.25 × ☐) =	☐
Section 5A: (QUESTIONS 1–8)	☐	− (.25 × ☐) =	☐
Section 5B: (QUESTIONS 9–18)	☐	(no wrong answer penalty) =	☐
Section 8:	☐	− (.25 × ☐) =	☐

Math Raw Score = ☐
(rounded up)

PRACTICE TEST ONE

CRITICAL READING

	Number Right	Number Wrong	Raw Score
Section 3:	☐	− (.25 × ☐) =	☐
Section 6:	☐	− (.25 × ☐) =	☐
Section 8:	☐	− (.25 × ☐) =	☐

Critical Reading Raw Score = ☐
(rounded up)

WRITING

Section 1: ☐
(Essay Grade)

	Number Right	Number Wrong	Raw Score
Section 5:	☐	− (.25 × ☐) =	☐
Section 9:	☐	− (.25 × ☐) =	☐

Writing Raw Score = ☐
(rounded up)

MATH

	Number Right	Number Wrong	Raw Score
Section 2:	☐	− (25 × ☐) =	☐
Section 4A: (QUESTIONS 1–8)	☐	− (.25 × ☐) =	☐
Section 4B: (QUESTIONS 9–18)	☐	(no wrong answer penalty) =	☐
Section 7:	☐	− (.25 × ☐) =	☐

Math Raw Score = ☐
(rounded up)

PRACTICE TEST TWO

CRITICAL READING

	Number Right	Number Wrong	Raw Score
Section 2:	☐	− (.25 × ☐) =	☐
Section 4:	☐	− (.25 × ☐) =	☐
Section 7:	☐	− (.25 × ☐) =	☐

Critical Reading Raw Score = ☐
(rounded up)

WRITING

Section 1: ☐
(Essay Grade)

	Number Right	Number Wrong	Raw Score
Section 6:	☐	− (.25 × ☐) =	☐
Section 9:	☐	− (.25 × ☐) =	☐

Writing Raw Score = ☐
(rounded up)

MATH

	Number Right	Number Wrong	Raw Score
Section 3:	☐	− (.25 × ☐) =	☐
Section 5A: (QUESTIONS 1–8)	☐	− (.25 × ☐) =	☐
Section 5B: (QUESTIONS 9–18)	☐	(no wrong answer penalty) =	☐
Section 8:	☐	− (.25 × ☐) =	☐

Math Raw Score = ☐
(rounded up)

PRACTICE TEST THREE

CRITICAL READING

	Number Right	Number Wrong	Raw Score
Section 3:	☐	$- \left(.25 \times \square\right) =$	☐
Section 6:	☐	$- \left(.25 \times \square\right) =$	☐
Section 8:	☐	$- \left(.25 \times \square\right) =$	☐

Critical Reading Raw Score = ☐
(rounded up)

WRITING

Section 1: ☐
(Essay Grade)

	Number Right	Number Wrong	Raw Score
Section 4:	☐	$- \left(.25 \times \square\right) =$	☐
Section 9:	☐	$- \left(.25 \times \square\right) =$	☐

Writing Raw Score = ☐
(rounded up)

MATH

	Number Right	Number Wrong	Raw Score
Section 2:	☐	$- \left(.25 \times \square\right) =$	☐
Section 5A: (QUESTIONS 1–8)	☐	$- \left(.25 \times \square\right) =$	☐
Section 5B: (QUESTIONS 9–18)	☐	$\left(\begin{array}{c}\text{no wrong answer} \\ \text{penalty}\end{array}\right) =$	☐
Section 7:	☐	$- \left(.25 \times \square\right) =$	☐

Math Raw Score = ☐
(rounded up)

STEP 3: CONVERT YOUR RAW SCORE TO A SCALED SCORE

For each subject area in the tests, convert your raw score to a scaled score using the table below.

RAW	Critical Reading	Math	SCALED* Writing (with Essay score of 0)	Writing (with Essay score of 1)	Writing (with Essay score of 2)	Writing (with Essay score of 3)	Writing (with Essay score of 4)	Writing (with Essay score of 5)	Writing (with Essay score of 6)
67	800								
66	800								
65	790								
64	770								
63	750								
62	740								
61	730								
60	720								
59	700								
58	690								
57	690								
56	680								
55	670								
54	660	800							
53	650	790							
52	650	760							
51	640	740							
50	630	720							
49	620	710	670	700	720	740	780	790	800
48	620	700	660	680	700	730	760	780	790
47	610	680	650	670	690	720	750	770	780
46	600	670	640	660	680	710	740	750	770
45	600	660	630	650	670	700	740	750	770
44	590	650	620	640	660	690	730	750	760
43	590	640	600	630	650	680	710	740	750
42	580	630	600	620	640	670	700	730	750
41	570	620	590	610	630	660	690	730	740
40	570	620	580	600	620	650	690	720	740

*These are not official College Board scores. They are rough estimates to help you get an idea of your performance.

(continued on next page)

RAW	Critical Reading	Math	SCALED* Writing (with Essay score of 0)	Writing (with Essay score of 1)	Writing (with Essay score of 2)	Writing (with Essay score of 3)	Writing (with Essay score of 4)	Writing (with Essay score of 5)	Writing (with Essay score of 6)
39	560	610	570	590	610	640	680	710	740
38	550	600	560	590	610	630	670	700	730
37	550	590	550	580	600	630	660	690	720
36	540	580	540	570	590	620	650	680	710
35	540	580	540	560	580	610	640	680	710
34	530	570	530	550	570	600	640	670	700
33	520	560	520	540	560	590	630	660	690
32	520	550	510	540	560	580	620	650	680
31	520	550	500	530	550	580	610	640	670
30	510	550	490	520	540	570	600	630	660
29	510	540	490	510	530	560	590	630	650
28	500	540	480	500	520	550	590	620	640
27	490	530	470	490	510	540	580	610	640
26	480	520	460	490	500	530	570	600	630
25	470	510	450	480	500	520	560	590	620
24	460	500	440	470	490	510	550	580	610
23	460	500	430	460	480	510	540	570	600
22	450	490	430	450	470	500	530	570	590
21	450	490	430	450	470	500	530	570	590
20	440	480	420	440	460	490	520	560	580
19	430	470	410	430	450	480	520	550	570
18	420	460	400	420	440	470	510	540	570
17	410	460	390	420	430	460	500	530	560
16	400	450	380	410	430	450	490	520	550
15	390	440	370	400	420	450	480	510	540
14	380	430	360	390	410	440	470	500	530
13	360	420	360	380	400	430	460	500	520
12	340	400	340	370	390	420	450	490	510
11	330	390	340	360	380	410	450	480	510
10	320	380	330	350	370	400	440	470	500
9	310	370	320	350	360	390	430	460	490
8	300	360	310	340	360	390	420	450	480
7	290	350	300	330	350	380	410	440	470

(continued on next page)

			SCALED*						
RAW	Critical Reading	Math	Writing (with Essay score of 0)	Writing (with Essay score of 1)	Writing (with Essay score of 2)	Writing (with Essay score of 3)	Writing (with Essay score of 4)	Writing (with Essay score of 5)	Writing (with Essay score of 6)
6	270	340	290	320	340	370	400	430	460
5	270	330	290	310	330	360	390	430	450
4	260	300	280	300	320	350	390	420	450
3	240	280	270	290	310	340	380	410	440
2	230	260	260	280	300	330	370	400	430
1	210	240	250	270	290	320	340	380	410
0	200	220	250	260	280	310	340	370	400
neg 1	200	200	240	260	270	290	320	360	380
neg 2	200	200	230	250	260	270	310	340	370
neg 3	200	200	220	240	250	260	300	330	360
neg 4	200	200	220	230	240	250	290	320	350
neg 5	200	200	200	220	230	240	280	310	340
neg 6	200	200	200	210	220	240	280	310	340
neg 7	200	200	200	210	220	230	270	300	330
neg 8	200	200	200	210	220	230	270	300	330
neg 9	200	200	200	210	220	230	270	300	330
neg 10	200	200	200	210	220	230	270	300	330

CD COMPANION COPYRIGHT AND PERMISSION NOTICES

System Requirements

WINDOWS®:

- Windows® 98SE, NT 4.0 (with Service Pack 6), 2000, ME, XP, Vista, 7
- Pentium® II 300 MHz or faster, 15 MB free hard disk space, 640 × 480–thousands of colors (millions recommended), SoundBlaster-compatible sound card, 4× CD-ROM or higher.

    Note: An Internet connection is required for the Web features of the program.

MACINTOSH®:

- Macintosh® OS 8.6, OS 9.1, 9.2.2, OS 10.1.3, 10.1.5, 10.2.4, 10.2.8, 10.3, 10.3.7, 10.3.8, 10.4
- 400 MHz Power PC®, G3, G4 or faster, 15 MB free hard disk space, 640 × 480–thousands of colors (millions recommended), 4x CD-ROM or higher.

    Note: An Internet connection is required for the Web features of the program.

Installation

WINDOWS®:

1. Exit all open applications; make sure you have no applications running.

2. Insert the Higher Score CD into your CD-ROM drive. The installation window opens automatically if Autorun is enabled on your system.

3. If you have Autorun disabled, from the Start Menu choose Run and type (or browse for) d:\setup.exe (where d: is your CD-ROM drive). Press OK and follow the prompts.

4. To launch the program, go to the Start Menu, choose Programs, then Kaplan, or double-click the SAT icon on your desktop.

MACINTOSH®:

1. Exit all open applications; make sure you have no applications running.

2. Insert the Higher Score CD into your CD-ROM drive.

3. Double-click the Kaplan install icon. Follow the prompts.

4. To launch the program, double-click the Higher Score on the SAT icon.

If you are experiencing any problems installing this program, please visit our website, kaptest.com/support.